The
AMERICAN
MORALIST

Also by George Anastaplo

Books
The Constitutionalist: Notes on the First Amendment
Human Being and Citizen: Essays on Virtue, Freedom and the Common
   Good
The Artist as Thinker: From Shakespeare to Joyce
The Constitution of 1787:   A Commentary
Plato's *Meno:*   Translation and Commentary (in course of preparation)

Book-length Law Review Collections
Human Nature and the First Amendment
What Is Still Wrong with George Anastaplo? A Sequel to 366 U.S. 82
Church and State: Explorations
Slavery and the Constitution: Explorations
Freedom of Speech and the First Amendment: Explorations
The Constitution at Two Hundred: Explorations
On Trial: Explorations (in course of preparation)
The Amendments to the Constitution: A Commentary (in course of prepa-
   ration)
On Freedom: Explorations (in course of preparation)

The
AMERICAN
MORALIST

On Law, Ethics, and Government

George Anastaplo

OHIO UNIVERSITY PRESS
Athens, Ohio

This book has been brought to publication with the generous assistance of Loyola University of Chicago.

George Anastaplo is
Professor of Law
at Loyola University of Chicago,
Lecturer in the Liberal Arts
at the University of Chicago,
and Professor Emeritus of Political Science and of Philosophy
at Rosary College.

Library of Congress Cataloging-in-Publication Data

Anastaplo, George, 1925–
    The American moralist : on law, ethics, and government / George Anastaplo.
    p.   cm.
    Includes bibliographical references and index.
    ISBN 0-8214-1001-6   ISBN 0-8214-1079-2 (pbk.)
    1. Law—United States—Philosophy.   2. Law and ethics.   3. Law and politics.
4. Political science—Philosophy.   5. United States—Moral conditions.   I. Title.
KF 380.A57   1992
349.73—dc20   91-35715
[347.3]   CIP

99   98   97   96   95   94   5   4   3   2   1 (pbk.)

To
THE SACRED MEMORY
of
SEVEN VERY YOUNG MEN
we grew up with in Carterville, Illinois
and who went off to war with us a half-century ago
but
WHO NEVER RETURNED

I never think a mouse is up to much
That only has one hole in all the house;
If that should fail, well, it's good-bye the mouse.

The Wife of Bath

Since the modern world began in the Sixteenth Century, nobody's system
of philosophy has really corresponded to everybody's sense of reality; to
what, if left to themselves, common men would call common sense. Each
started with a paradox; a peculiar point of view demanding the sacrifice
of what they would call a sane point of view. That is the one thing common to Hobbes and Hegel, to Kant and Bergson, to Berkeley and William
James. A man had to believe something that no normal man would believe, if it were suddenly propounded to his simplicity; as that law is
above right, or right is outside reason, or things are only as we think them,
or everything is relative to a reality that is not there. The modern philosopher claims, like a sort of confidence man, that if once we will grant him
this, the rest will be easy; he will straighten out the world, if once he is allowed to give this one twist to the mind.

G. K. Chesterton

One feels of [Mohandas Gandhi] that there was much that he did not understand, but not that there was anything that he was frightened of saying
or thinking.

George Orwell

Of course, the affairs of human beings are not worthy of great seriousness;
yet it is necessary to be serious about them.

The Athenian Stranger

In the evening of October 11 [1944] Stalin came to dine at the British Embassy [in Moscow]. . . . Among other topics, we discussed the next General Election in England. Stalin said that he had no doubt about the result:
the Conservatives would win. It is even harder to understand the politics
of other countries than those of your own.

Winston S. Churchill

There is no longer in existence a philosophic position apart from neo-
Thomism and Marxism, crude or refined. All rationalistic liberal, philosophic positions have lost their significance and power [in the Twentieth
Century]. One may deplore this, but I for one cannot bring myself to cling
to philosophic positions that have been shown to be inadequate. I'm afraid

we shall have to make a very great effort in order to find a solid basis for rational liberalism. Only a great thinker could help us in our intellectual plight. But here is the great trouble: the only great thinker in our time is Heidegger.

Leo Strauss

It is very difficult to make an accurate prediction, especially about the future.

Niels Bohr

CONTENTS

ISSUES OF THE DAY

A. Catalogues of "Cases"

B. The Use and Abuse of the First Amendment

C. Public Opinion and Majority Rule

D. Nature and Revelation

E. Sovereignty of the Law

F. Politics and Government

G. Lessons From Abroad

EPILOGUE

PREFACE

*All who have ambitions to literary excellence in democratic nations should
ever refresh themselves at classical springs; that is the most wholesome
medicine for the mind.*

ALEXIS DE TOCQUEVILLE

I attempt in these essays to encourage principled moderation in the consideration of our public affairs, suggesting for each of the many issues of
the day examined here what kind of questions have to be addressed if the
subject under consideration is to be taken seriously. One is repeatedly
reminded in these essays of the uses to which our considerable freedom of
speech should be put. One is reminded as well of what a prudential approach grounded in nature calls for, an approach which looks to what Leo
Strauss has called "a solid basis for rational liberalism." These reminders
are appropriate as we celebrate this year the Bicentennial of the Bill of
Rights.

The reader who is interested primarily in contemporary issues can proceed directly to the second part of this book, which begins with Essay No.
14. The essays in the first part of this book are of a more general character,
indicating how one might begin to think about the principles which should

---

The epigraph for the Preface is taken from Alexis de Tocqueville, *Democracy in America*,
vol. II, pt. I, chap. 15 (George Lawrence translation).

The epigraphs at the front of this book are taken from (1) Geoffrey Chaucer, *The Canter-
bury Tales* (Harmondsworth: Penguin Books, 1951), pp. 291–92; (2) G. K. Chesterton, *Saint
Thomas Aquinas* (New York: Sheed & Ward, 1933), pp. 176–77; (3) *The Orwell Reader*
(New York: Harcourt, Brace & World, 1956), p. 334; (4) Plato, *Laws* 803B (Thomas L. Pangle
translation); (5) Winston S. Churchill, *The Second World War* (Boston: Houghton Mifflin
Co., 1951), VI, 229–30; (6) Leo Strauss, "An Introduction to Existentialism" (typescript), p. 3;
(7) Robert G. Sachs, Department of Physics, The University of Chicago (oral tradition).

The very young men from Carterville, Illinois (population 2,900) referred to in the Dedi-
cation include John L. Boren, Joseph S. Boren, William Lee Craig, James Fozzard, Ralph G.
Halstead, Dennis Jones, and George R. Priddy. There were nineteen other older casualties
from the town whom I did not happen to know personally: Robert Adams, Otis Chambers,
William J. Chronister, Smith Edwards, Raymond Frost, Charles C. Ghent, Jr., Ray J. Grimes,
William Hall, George Harris, Robert V. Jeter, Guy E. Lauder, Gather Phillips, Paul Smith,
Albert Stephenson, Wilbern Tottleben, Ivan W. Williams, Milton R. Williams, Frank J. Win-
ters, and James Woolerton. Another very young man from Carterville whom I knew well,
Bobby Burton, was killed in the Korean War (along with four others from the town).

The Dedication for Anastaplo, *The Artist as Thinker* (Athens: Ohio University Press,
1983), should have its last line corrected to read (in parentheses),
(He is a god, and handsomer than him.)

guide us. It will be evident to those familiar with the authors drawn upon in
this first part, and elsewhere in the book, that I do not pretend to comprehensiveness in my sketches of such challenging thinkers. (It should also be
evident that I assumed that the audiences I have addressed on various occasions were already somewhat acquainted each time with the text, author or problem then being dealt with.) In these essays I again and again
presume to draw upon my betters even at the risk of oversimplifying their
thought. Samples of much more extended, and hence perhaps less superficial, analyses by me of important texts may be found in the introduction
to Plato's *Apology of Socrates* (in my *Human Being and Citizen*) and in
my recent commentary, *The Constitution of 1787*. In addition, others
should find as instructive as I have the work of many gifted associates of
mine over the years, such as the essays about serious books by some three
dozen scholars provided by Joseph Cropsey in *Ancients and Moderns* and
in *History of Political Philosophy*, Larry Arnhart's *Political Questions: Political Philosophy from Plato to Rawls*, the materials available in the St.
John's College review and in the *Political Science Reviewer*, the collection
by Allan Bloom of his essays in *Giants and Dwarfs* and by Harry V. Jaffa
in several volumes of his own, and the articles that Hilail Gildin has published for two decades in his remarkable journal, *Interpretation*. If American grade and high school teachers could be somehow returned, in the
tens of thousands, to the reading of serious books, we would not have to
be as concerned as we now are to figure out programs and methods for
educating our children.

My opening essays in this book suggest what it is that any moralist must
take into account, what the foundations and limitations are of sound morality. The later essays suggest what is "American" about the American
moralist. An overriding concern throughout this book is to show how one
can be moral without being cranky, sentimental, or moralistic. Critical
elements in my work over the years, as well as in this book, are suggested
by Laurence Berns in his essay in the useful Deutsch-Soffer collection,
The Crisis of Liberal Democracy. His observations there can help serve as
an introduction to this book (pp. 156–57):

> The most impressive attempt known to me to combine classical thought with
> the principles of the American polity is to be found in the work of Harry V.
> Jaffa. I will for the most part confine myself here to his discussion of the Dec-
> laration of Independence in the essay, "What is Equality? The Declaration of
> Independence Revisited" [in *The Conditions of Freedom*]. Jaffa builds on
> George Anastaplo's observation that the references to God in the Declaration
> of Independence portray him in terms of the three powers of constitutional
> government. [See *The Constitution of 1787*, pp. 21–22.] . . .

An interesting contrast to the classicism of Harry Jaffa is to be found in the classicism of George Anastaplo. While Jaffa emphasizes the natural equalities of superiority and defect upon which the moral principles governing the American polity are based, the central consideration for Anastaplo's "Constitutionalist" are the blessings of liberty. He reviews [in *Human Being and Citizen*] Jaffa's *Equality and Liberty* in an article entitled "Liberty and Equality." Civil liberties, in contrast to civil rights, make for popular influence over, as well as protection against, government. But most importantly during "a time of effective popular rule," they provide for the protection within democratic government for natural aristocracy. While Jaffa's rhetoric emphasizes the transformation of self-evident truth into "living faith," the sacramental character of our moral and political principles, Anastaplo recurs to the distinctions between human being and citizen, politician and scholar, thoughtful man and partisan, and nature and circumstance. The inevitable partiality and relativity of any effective political statement point to prudence and moderation as indispensable political virtues—even in the pursuit of justice. [See *The Artist as Thinker*, pp. 279–83; Leo Strauss, *Natural Right and History*, chap. 4.]

Professor Berns's helpful observations continue (p. 157):

The most useful way of beginning to account for these differences [between Jaffa and Anastaplo] may well be in terms of different judgments about the needs of our situation, about "the crisis of liberal democracy," about the political conditions for philosophizing, on the one hand, and the reliability of nature, on the other. The moral fervor of the political savior is not usually associated with the cool deliberation of the man of prudence. And yet both Jaffa and Anastaplo find their paradigms in Abraham Lincoln. After a careful line-by-line analysis of the Emancipation Proclamation, "recreating" the complex of problems Lincoln had to deal with, Anastaplo reflects on prudence in general . . .

I do not repeat here reflections by me on prudence, quoted at length by Mr. Berns, which are developed further in this book. (Nor do I repeat here most of the citations that Mr. Berns provides, which the reader can secure by consulting the instructive essay from which I have just quoted, "Aristotle and the Moderns on Freedom and Equality.") My old friend and teacher continues, reminding me thereby of conversations about liberal education and politics that we have had since our heady days together in the Hutchins College some forty years ago (p. 158):

[T]he classical emphasis on the ethical implications of all political arrangements reminds us conversely that every political arrangement presupposes certain qualities in the populace that is to live under that arrangement. Free government based on enlightened consent is not going to survive if its citizens are regarded as unworthy of such government and if they are incapable of making it work. The cultivation of excellence, or, more euphemistically, liberal education for leadership, may be indispensable for the survival of such government. If it should be that capacities for liberal education are not created equal in all men, religious education for all the people must supplement liberal education. Did the Founding Fathers rely on the virtues of a religiously trained populace without making provision for the continuance of that training? However that may be, although they did concentrate more on the structure of government, they did not forget the character of the people. . . . Classical and American thought seem to come together most in their reliance on "moral principles grounded in thoughtfulness," political prudence, that is, the avoidance of unreasonable expectations and the concern for enlightenment, for liberal education.

However much political prudence is studied, it should be recognized that prudence itself cannot have rules. But it *can* have illustrations: one can be instructed, as well as encouraged, upon seeing how prudent men and women have acted and spoken in various circumstances. Prudence means that one can defend virtually unlimited public discussion of some matters (see, e.g., Essays No. 17 and No. 18) and counsel restricted public discussion of other matters (see, e.g., Essays No. 19 and No. 20). The forty-nine essays collected in this book, which are somewhat autobiographical as well as self-examining (and hence somewhat therapeutic?) in effect, range across four decades. They are bracketed, that is, by a 1966 discussion of the despair of the Cold War in Vietnam and a 1990 discussion of the euphoria at the apparent end of the Cold War in Eastern Europe.

This preface is prepared at a time when we have somehow ended up with one in every five hundred Americans assigned to the Persian Gulf, a highly questionable venture indeed. My difficulties with what we have been up to in the Middle East are hinted at in a letter of August 17, 1990 to a United States Senator, a liberal Democrat, who had written to me about another matter:

> I have noticed in the papers that you are said to have suggested that Iraqi oil pipelines be bombed, etc. Permit me to suggest that such a use of force in this situation should be backed away from. (I recall my presuming to caution Paul Douglas in the same way about Vietnam, in our last conversation, which was during his last campaign for the Senate. Liberal Democrats do have to be urged not to "overreact" in order to assure their constituents of their patriotism when the passions of war are aroused.)
>
> Much more should be made of the United Nations connection in the Iraq

matter. Also, it would be salutary for Senators to say, loud and clear, that we should not plan or try to starve the Iraqi people into submission.

In short, I am somewhat dubious about what is being done by us in the Persian Gulf. My reservations go back to observations I made in 1973, when I wondered why oil should be treated differently from other important commodities produced all over the world.

The Iraq intervention seems closer to Korea (which I favored in 1950) than to Vietnam (which I disapproved of from the beginning). Our critical error in Korea, which we show signs of repeating this time in Iraq, is that we did not recognize when we had done enough to serve our legitimate objectives.

This letter, written within a fortnight of our original response to the brutal occupation of Kuwait by Iraq, includes this postscript:

I should add, lest I be misunderstood, that my reservations about the Iraq intervention do *not* question our general support of Israel. Much is to be said for supporting Israel even more than we have in recent years. Certainly, it is understandable, perhaps even natural, for the Israelis to try to secure firm control of their country, the only place *they* have. It is going to be difficult for them not to squeeze many of the Arabs known as Palestinians out of Greater Israel, perhaps mostly into what is known as Jordan. Some of the billions that will be spent on Iraq could well be used to ease this salutary transition.

In any event, we should be alert to what can happen if Jordan should be torn apart by our encounter with Iraq: Israeli leaders will find it difficult to pass up the opportunity to finish turning *that* place into the Palestinian homeland that so many current Arab residents of Israel make so much of. What can we do to make that transition, if it should come about, as humane, as just and hence as stabilizing as possible? In the long run, it seems to me, Israel should show the way in the Middle East to a productive order.

One profound consequence of what has been happening in the Persian Gulf is that Saudi and other Arabian men will be reminded by their women in the decades ahead that they had to rely for defense of their own country upon Americans, including armed American women in uniform. (This can be comparable, in long-term effects, to the instructive spectacle of having United States marshals and troops protect grade-school children from unruly segregationists who thereby forfeited any claim they may have had to moral ascendancy in the South.) Consider, also, the reservations expressed by a former Secretary of the Navy in the Reagan Administration (James H. Webb, Jr., *Wall Street Journal*, January 31, 1991, p. A14):

The Bush administration . . . has relentlessly maneuvered our nation into a war. One must reach back to William Randolph Hearst's urging us into the Spanish-American War to find a parallel to the editorial pressure [as in the *Wall Street Journal*] that preceded our present conflict. One must go even further back, perhaps to the Mexican War, to find a president so avidly desirous of putting the nation at risk when it has not been attacked.

I had occasion to comment on the Gulf War during a North Carolina talk on American constitutionalism. That talk of March 1, 1991, the day after the cease-fire took hold, included these observations:

The presumptuousness of Presidents, especially during the past half century, has been disturbing. This has been seen most recently in how the current Administration so manipulated matters (with United Nations Security Council resolutions, with the shipment of more and more troops to Saudi Arabia after the original emergency consignment, and with the issuance of one ultimatum after another)—so manipulated matters (including American public opinion) as to make it very difficult for Congress to do anything but authorize an immediate use of massive force, on the scale of a major war, against a country of less than twenty million people. (This should be contrasted with the deference toward Congressional authority displayed repeatedly by George Washington and Dwight Eisenhower.) We see in this recent development a remarkable failure in imagination, including moral imagination.

I concluded my talk of March 1, 1991 with these remarks:

Presidential presumptuousness had been dramatically exposed during the Iran arms-Contra aid scandal. The prerogatives of the Congress had been usurped by that Administration in what it did in selling arms and "appropriating" money in a clandestine fashion. A decade earlier there had been the Watergate scandal, which had seen clumsy attempts by another Administration to usurp the prerogatives of the electorate during a Presidential election campaign.

Despite the chastening effects of these two dubious episodes, the Presidency has once again exhibited in recent months a spirit foreign to that expected by the Framers of the Constitution, but this time in a form that is, at least so far, less obviously dubious. The people at large do not yet appreciate the enormity and implications of the damage done by us in our Gulf War. We are still too captivated both by the brilliance of our efforts and by the evils of our principal adversary on that occasion.

It should be evident from these developments both what the Framers were fearful of at the hands of anyone who happens to wield the powers of the Commander in Chief and how profound transformations (including an incipient Caesarism) can take place in a constitutional regime without any authorization by formal amendments of its constitution.

I am afraid that we saw, among the major participants in the Gulf War, still more episodes of what Malcolm Sharp used to call "governmental insanity." The classic example for him was the First World War. (See, on true patriotism, Essay No. 8. See, on the Middle East generally, my articles on the Gilgamesh Epic and on the Koran in the 1986 and 1989 volumes of *Great Ideas Today*.) In any event, just as the Russians must, as one result of the Gulf War, assess the efficacy of their military weapons and training (and not only as employed by the Iraqis), so we should assess the inordinate fear of the Russians that has cost us dearly in blood and treasure for decades. It would not be healthy for either the United States or the Soviet Union if the Russians should now become as unreasonably apprehensive about us as we have long been about them. The sad, even dangerous, consequences of the ill-conceived Gulf War remain to be discovered by the American people. First, however, we must have our parades. (See Plato, *Gorgias* 521D–522A, *Theaetetus* 176A–B, 179A, 210C–D.)

Some of the essays collected here address matters that have been resolved in one fashion or another over the years. An assessment *now* of how I thought and talked *then* about issues that are today considered "settled" can help the reader determine how my more recent analyses, as well as my general approach, should be regarded. The role of chance in determining what could (and could not) be known and what did in fact happen should be evident—and chastening.

The circumstances of each presentation, indicated in the headnotes for each essay and often referred to in the essay itself, need to be taken into account in considering what I have had to say. My personal circumstances bear upon how I have proceeded in various of the essays: I took my J.D. degree from the Law School of the University of Chicago in 1951 and my Ph.D. degree (with a dissertation on the First Amendment) from the Committee on Social Thought of the University of Chicago in 1964, having served as a flying officer with the United States Army Air Corps during the Second World War. I have been teaching since 1956 in the Basic Program of Liberal Education for Adults at the University of Chicago, and since 1981 in the School of Law at Loyola University of Chicago as well. Between 1964 and 1984 I also taught at Rosary College in River Forest, Illinois, where I am now Professor Emeritus of Political Science and of Philosophy.

All of the essays in this collection are published in their entirety even though an occasional overlapping results thereby. I have, in preparing these essays for this publication, kept in mind the sensible prescription laid down by John Kenneth Galbraith upon publishing his Indian diaries (*Ambassador's Journal*, p. xvi):

> I have made many cosmetic changes in the original—tightening sentences, rectifying number and tense, eliminating redundant words, improving syntax. . . . No historical merit attaches to bad English. . . . On matters of major historical interest, the Vietnam record for example, I have avoided changes and certainly any which reflect either hindsight or a desire to improve on my own performance.

The notes originally prepared for these essays, some of which have been previously published in journals, are *not* included here. (Previous publications are recorded in the headnotes, permitting the reader to consult what are in some instances quite extensive notes. The index serves as a source of extensive cross-references among the essays. Consider, for example, the entries for *chance, constitutionalism, death, equality, justice, liberty, nature, philosophy, prudence, pursuit of happiness, race relations, religion,* and *right of revolution.*) I have been relieved of the duty to provide a guide on this occasion to more than a few of my other publications by the inclusion of a detailed bibliography of my work in the volumes soon to be issued by Ohio University Press, *Law and Philosophy: The Practice of Theory* (edited by William T. Braithwaite, John A. Murley, and Robert L. Stone). The good will exhibited by the Press in publishing both that *Festschrift* and this collection of essays is heartening. I have been most fortunate in my scholarly associations over the year, not least in the publishers I have been privileged to work with.

I have been very much helped in preparing these essays by generous readers of the manuscript for this book. Particularly exacting as readers have been Mervin Block of Chicago and New York, William T. Braithwaite of Loyola University of Chicago, Keith S. Cleveland of Columbia College of Chicago, Christopher A. Colmo of Rosary College, Thomas S. Schrock of the University of California at Santa Barbara, Stanley D. McKenzie of the Rochester Institute of Technology, and Stephen J. Vanderslice of Louisiana State University at Alexandria. (Professor McKenzie must be one of the best editors in this Country today. The helpful copy editor supplied by Ohio University Press for this book has been Anne Wenner.)

Extensive suggestions have been provided as well by John Alvis of the University of Dallas, Larry Arnhart of Northern Illinois University, Laurence Berns of St. John's College, Wendy Ann Braithwaite of the Illinois bar, Helen C. de Alvarez of the University of Dallas, Leo Paul S. de Alvarez of the University of Dallas, J. Harvey Lomax of Memphis State University, Gregory Fried, a University of Chicago graduate student, William R. Marty of Memphis State University, David Murdoch of the Rochester Institute of Technology, John A. Murley of the Rochester Institute of Technology, Andrew Patner of Chicago, and John Van Doren of the Institute of Philosophical Research in Chicago. (Mr. Van Doren's annual *Great Ideas Today* volumes, in which I have been privileged to publish a series of introductory essays on non-Western thought, are noteworthy accomplishments.) My discussions of Jewish things have been informed by conversations over the years with Mordechai Goodman of Rosary College, Monford Harris of the Spertus College of Judaica, and Raymond L. Weiss of the University of Wisconsin at Milwaukee. My readers have registered both enthusiastic endorsements of and vigorous dissents from what I have offered them. Fortunately, the essays that some readers roundly criticized did find sympathetic champions in other readers.

I hope to continue to be at least as helpful to my fellow citizens as my readers have been to me. I learned a few years ago that the oldest essay in this volume, No. 13 on the Vietnam War, happened to be circulated, in its mimeographed form and without my knowledge, in an American army barracks in South Vietnam a quarter of a century ago. I have been told by a soldier in that barracks, whom I had not known before, how reassuring it had been for him and his comrades to realize, even though by chance on that occasion, that they had not been simply forgotten, that the war *was* being openly and responsibly discussed back home.

However important the role of chance may be in these matters, it is important to sense the degree of control one might still exercise over one's life, at least one's private life (including how one responds personally to public challenges). The range of situations and issues dealt with in these essays should suggest the spirit as well as the details of the ethical and political approach relied upon here. The scope of these essays encourages the reader to put things together that people do not ordinarily put together. One key question for the prudential citizen should be apparent throughout: "How much does one need to know in order to be reasonably confident about one's judgment and conclusions in this particular situation?" It is essential, in dealing with serious matters, to have a reliable sense of what can go wrong, of how much can be known, and of what provision should be made for unforeseeable consequences.

The apparent resolution, or at least transformation, of the Cold War may now complicate matters for us in this Country. A powerful foreign challenge, which countries such as Iraq cannot supply for long, may help a people organize or at least occupy itself. Now we all have to face up to what has long seemed to me to be true, that our most serious problems are not how we should conduct ourselves abroad but rather how we should live at home—that is, what kind of people we should be. The devastating effects of such innovations as broadcast television, aggravated by that growing commercialization of our everyday life which is corrupting our tastes and cheapening our language (which in turn subverts our thought), have yet to be generally appreciated, along with the limitations in what we can now do about such things. I confess to being, to *this* extent, a Heideggerian. (Compare, e.g., Essay No. 12.)

A December 27, 1990 column in the *Washington Post* by the chairman of the political science department at Howard University, reminds us of how one chronic national problem, that of race relations, can be seen by men of color who continue to be desperate despite the professional success they personally happen to enjoy:

> Blind loyalty of blacks to the President is prevented by the knowledge that the expenditure of billions of dollars in Saudi Arabia gives the lie to the frequent protestations of the lack of resources available for domestic urban priorities. This duplicity has contributed fundamentally to our own domestic "gulf" policy, creating the generally different attitudes of blacks and whites toward the current crisis in the Middle East. A stubborn segment of the American public wants to pretend that racial disadvantages do not exist, that social policy must be operated on an individually "objective" basis. As a result, ameliorative policies are held hostage and the racial divide is widening in a country that holds out the promise of multiracial democracy. . . .
>
> To put it bluntly, the Bush administration is playing race politics in a manner that would continue to deny national resources to blacks, while black lives are disproportionately at stake as a result of his foreign policy [in the Persian Gulf]. If no one will respect the nature of their sacrifice, then why should blacks especially be motivated to demand that their sons and daughters give it?

The future of African-Americans is critical to the fate of constitutionalism in the United States. Any imaginative affirmative-action programs dealing with them should be guided even more by what the Country needs than by what they as a still-submerged class of citizens among us may be entitled to. The *Washington Post* column I have drawn upon includes the observation that "it is arguable that, considering the number of high-ranking black officers there [including the Chairman of the Joint Chiefs of Staff!], the military is the truest meritocratic system we have, far more so than the society as a whole."

I have argued in my 1983 Orwell essay and elsewhere (e.g., Section V of Essay No. 26, originally published in 1979) that there is something in nature which undermines tyranny in the long run. But, it is only prudent to notice, there is something in nature that eventually undermines good, perhaps even the very best, regimes as well. Much is to be said, then, for doing and being the best one can without an overriding concern for the ultimate outcome. It is not practical in these matters to try to be merely practical. Nor is it practical to subscribe to an apocalyptic view of things, something which I have thus far been fortunate enough to be shielded from by my temperament.

A reviewer of *The Artist as Thinker* reports: "Anastaplo writes for an audience that believes 'are moral and political standards rooted in nature and discernible by reason.' His audience died on July 14, 1789." (23 *Victorian Poetry* 290 [1985]). This book is still another contribution to the attempt to resurrect among us the vital teaching that there are indeed moral and political standards rooted in nature and discernible by reason. Is there not, in the respect still accorded generally in the modern world to common sense, a reflection of the hold upon human beings of the sound practical judgment traditionally associated with natural law or, perhaps better still, natural right?

GEORGE ANASTAPLO

Hyde Park
Chicago, Illinois
March 15, 1991

PROLOGUE

1

"WHO AM I?"

I shall try in this way, men, to praise Socrates, through likenesses. Now he perhaps will suppose it is for raising a laugh; but the likenesses will be for the sake of the truth, not for the sake of the laughable. I declare he is most strictly like those silenuses that sit in the shops of herm sculptors, the ones that craftsmen make holding reed pipes or flutes; and if they are split in two and opened up, they show that they have images of gods within. And I declare, in turn, that he bears a likeness to the satyr Marsyas. Now, that you are like them at least in looks, Socrates, surely not even you would dispute; and as for your likeness to them in other respects, just listen to what I have to say.

ALCIBIADES

INTRODUCTION

I am intrigued by the looks of people as I try to *see* the child in the adult (to see what this celebrated or miserable or pompous adult must have looked like as a child) and as I try to *see* the adult in the child (to see what this child will eventually look like). Such physical correspondence over decades is perhaps a clue to a much more important correspondence, the correspondence in psyche or character early and late, to say nothing of the correspondence between character and looks. In short, what is there in one's past that accounts for one's present, what is there in one's present that accounts for one's future?

We naturally move in these matters between belief in *free will* and belief in *determinism* (or what might once have been called *fate*). We sense that there is something to each side of the perennial argument here, and so

---

This talk was given at the Annual Convention, National Association of Social Workers, Chicago, Illinois, November 7, 1985. (Original title: "What Does It Mean To Say That Someone Has Nobody But Himself To Blame?")

The epigraph is taken from Plato, Symposium 215B (Seth Benardete translation).

we wonder whether there can be a science of human action, whether people should be held accountable for what they are and do.

All of you are familiar with the great old stories which turn around the place in human life of fate and free will, such stories as those about Oedipus, Jonah, and even Judas Iscariot. I will use a dozen or so less familiar stories, since they are most apt in their freshness to be accounts we can approach directly: you are more likely to be intrigued, if only because of their novelty.

But, one might wonder, why resort to stories at all on this occasion? Perhaps partly because you are social workers and hence people quite adept in dealing with "cases." One often hears of "case histories," but "case stories" may be even more instructive. What is the difference between histories and stories? It has been said that in history only the dates may be correct, while in stories or art everything but the dates may be correct. Stories draw upon or reflect experiences that induce in us a sense of considerable self-conscious freedom tempered by an awareness of limitations to which we are subject and over which we have little or no control.

Stories may more readily express the common way of looking at things, even as they engage the passions aroused by any inquiry into the nature of human destiny. Do we not consider ourselves fairly responsible for what has happened to us? And yet we can discern the profound workings of fate or chance in our own lives, reflected in the people we have or have not married, in the careers we do and do not have, in the health and the happiness we do or do not enjoy. However free we consider ourselves to be, we can easily recognize that others may be largely shaped and bound by their circumstances.

Each story I draw upon here will attempt to illuminate one facet of a complicated problem. This means, among other things, that quite different, even contradictory, things can be held together by the use of stories. A few of my stories have humorous aspects, which may help to relieve what may otherwise seem a dreary subject or a grim, if not hopeless, human situation.

I

You will now see that not all of my illustrations are, strictly speaking, stories. I may have told you a story in having promised you stories.

I begin with the concluding passage in Alexis de Tocqueville's *Democracy in America* (from the George Lawrence translation). He sums up what he sees in the democratic future of mankind with these observations:

For myself, looking back now from the extreme end of my task and seeing at a distance, but collected together, all the various things which had attracted my close attention upon my way, I am full of fears and of hopes. I see great dangers which may be warded off and mighty evils which may be avoided or kept in check; and I am ever increasingly confirmed in my belief that for democratic nations to be virtuous and prosperous, it is enough if they will to be so.

He then says something that very much bears upon our paramount question today, "Who am I?":

I am aware that many of my contemporaries think that nations on earth are never their own masters and that they are bound to obey some insuperable and unthinking power, the product of pre-existing facts, of race, or soil, or climate.

These are false and cowardly doctrines which can only produce feeble men and pusillanimous nations. Providence did not make mankind entirely free or completely enslaved. Providence has, in truth, drawn a predestined circle around each man beyond which he cannot pass; but within those vast limits man is strong and free, and so are peoples.

Tocqueville concludes his book,

The nations of our day cannot prevent conditions of equality from spreading in their midst. But it depends upon themselves whether equality is to lead to servitude or freedom, knowledge or barbarism, prosperity or wretchedness.

We have begun this investigation with a reminder of what a French observer has said about Americans and hence perhaps about all mankind. He has brought to bear upon these matters opinions and experiences very much influenced by, however much they challenge, the Old World. One gathers from what he says that one is, at least to some extent, responsible for what one is and does. Tocqueville seems to say that one can have something to say and do about whether one will be happy or wretched.

II

Another Old World approach, an even older one perhaps, may seem to call into question the Tocquevillian optimism so uncharacteristic of the Old World. Just as Tocqueville's reflections may shine better in French, so the story I am now about to share with you may sound better in Yiddish.

Two Jews were reviewing all the terrible things that have happened to their people: wars and epidemics, persecutions and pogroms. One of them lamented, "With all these troubles, it would be better not to be born at all." "Ah yes," replied the other, "but such luck not one in a hundred has."

We are reminded by this story that there *are* fundamental things about oneself that one cannot affect or control. These may be related to the very nature of the universe and the biological makeup of the human species. Some of you will look to the laws of physics which have determined the formation of the galaxies and the circumstances of the earth; others of you will consider all this to be "God's fault"; still others will want to make much of evolution and psychology in an effort to explain why human beings are the way they are. This story about two Jews raises questions about existence itself and its goodness. Even so, we should be reminded of the Jewish injunction, "Choose life," as well as of the Aristotelian insistence that, by and large, existence (and particularly human life) is sweet.

III

Our third story draws upon one of the great stories I mentioned at the beginning, the story of Oedipus. But it is not the part of the story that you are most familiar with to which I now look, but to the very end of Oedipus' life, as described in Sophocles' *Oedipus at Colonus*. The blind and battered old man, in confronting Creon (the brother of Jocasta, Oedipus' mother-wife), is taunted about his having killed his father and married his mother. Oedipus says in his defense (this is after much suffering, and reflection by Oedipus on that suffering, many years after the outburst which had led to his self-mutilation upon learning what he had done to and with his father and mother) (lines 960–99, in the Robert Fitzgerald translation):

> O arrogance unashamed! Whose age do you
> Think you are insulting, mine or yours?
> The bloody deaths, the incest, the calamities
> You speak so glibly of: I suffered them,
> By fate, against my will! It was God's pleasure,
> And perhaps our race had angered him long ago.
> In me myself you could not find such evil
> As would have made me sin against my own.
> And tell me this: if there were prophecies
> Repeated by the oracles of the gods,
> That father's death should come through his own son,
> How could you justly blame it upon me?
> On me, who was yet unborn, yet unconceived,
> Not yet existent for my father and mother?

If then I came into the world—as I did come—
In wretchedness, and met my father in fight,
And [killed him,] not knowing [what I had done]
Nor whom I killed—again, how could you find
Guilt in that unmeditated act?
As for my mother—damn you, you have no shame,
Though you are her own brother, in forcing me
To speak of that unspeakable marriage;
But I shall speak, I'll not be silent now
After you've let your foul talk go so far!
Yes, she gave me birth—incredible fate!—
But neither of us knew the truth; and she
Bore my children also—and then her shame.
But one thing I do know: you are content
To slander her as well as me for that;
While I would not have married her willingly
Nor willingly would I ever speak of it.

No: I shall not be judged an evil man,
Neither in that marriage nor in that death
Which you forever charge me with so bitterly.—
Just answer me one thing:
If someone tried to kill you here and now,
You righteous gentleman, what would you do,
Inquire first if the stranger was your father?
Or would you not first try to defend yourself?
I think that since you like to be alive
You'd treat him as the threat required, not
Look around for assurance that you were right.
Well, that was the sort of danger I was in,
Forced into it by the gods. My father's soul,
Were it on earth, I know would bear me out.

We need not try to decide here whether, or in what way or to what degree, Oedipus himself may have been responsible for the dreadful things that happened. Certainly, he vigorously calls his blameworthiness into question: "I suffered [these things] by fate, against my will!" he insists. Even so, he recognizes that perhaps "our race" (that is, the family of which he is a part) had done something to anger the gods "long ago." And he insists that he tried to avoid the fate assigned to him. We notice that, unlike the two Jews in our earlier story, Oedipus takes for granted the primacy of the desire to preserve oneself.

What makes the Oedipus story particularly gripping is that Oedipus' very efforts to escape his fate contribute to his doom: had he stayed in

Corinth, instead of fleeing his supposed mother and father who lived
there, he would not (in the ordinary course of things) have had to deal
with his natural father and natural mother (who lived in distant Thebes).
Are we not all familiar with conscientious efforts by us which have made
matters far worse than they would otherwise have been? And yet we do
not consider an Oedipus completely determined: if we did, we would not
see in his career a truly interesting *human* story. But we do recognize that
things happen to him that are not completely within his control, whatever
their origins may have been.

IV

Socrates, a contemporary of the playwright who gave us the Oedipus play
I have been quoting from, suggests another way of looking at what accounts for the things, and especially the dreadful things, that do happen to
human beings. It is neither the gods nor one's ancestors who are responsible, he argues. We ourselves choose the lives we will have. This may be
seen in the tale, relayed by a messenger, with which Socrates concludes
the account found in Plato's *Republic,* a tale about how souls, which have
been through a thousand years of reward or purgation after their preceding life on earth, select the lives (the fates) they will have their next time
around on earth (I draw on Allan Bloom's useful translation) (617D–620A):

> Now, when they arrived, they had to go straight to Lachesis. A certain spokes-
> man first marshaled them at regular distances from each other; then, he took
> lots and patterns of lives from Lachesis' lap, and went up to a high platform
> and said, "This is the speech of Necessity's maiden daughter, Lachesis. Souls
> that live a day, this is the beginning of another death-bringing cycle for the
> mortal race. A demon will not select you, but you will choose a demon. Let
> him who gets the first lot make the first choice of a life to which he will be
> bound by necessity. Virtue is without a master; as he honors or dishonors her,
> each will have more or less of her. The blame belongs to him who chooses;
> god is blameless."
>
> When he had said this, he cast lots among them all, and each picked up the
> one that fell next to him—except for Er [the messenger] who wasn't permit-
> ted to do so. To [each] man who picked it up it was plain what number he
> had drawn. After this, in turn, [their guide] set the patterns of the lives on the
> ground before them; there were far more than there were souls present.
> There were all sorts, lives of all animals, and, in particular, all the varieties of

human lives. There were tyrannies among them, some lasting to the end, others ruined midway, ending both in poverty and exile and in beggary. And there were lives of men of repute—some for their forms and beauty and for strength in general as well as [for] capacity in contests; others for their birth and the virtues of their ancestors—and there were some [lives] for men without repute in these things; and the same was the case for women, too. An ordering of the soul was not in them, due to the necessity that a soul become different according to the life it chooses. But all other things were mixed with each other and with wealth and poverty and with sickness and health, and also with the states intermediate to these.

. . . And the messenger from that place then also reported that the spokesman said the following: "Even for the man who comes forward last, if he chooses intelligently and lives earnestly, a life to content him is laid up, not a bad one. Let the one who begins not be careless about his choice. Let not the one who is last be disheartened." . . .

He said that this was a sight surely worth seeing: how each of the several souls chose a life. For it was pitiable, laughable, and wonderful to see. For the most part the choice was made according to the habituation of their former life.

The messenger from the other world reports that it had been announced that "the blame belongs to him who chooses; god is blameless." We are assured that one can "choose intelligently and live earnestly," leading to a contented life and not a miserable one. Such sentiments, I have suggested, do conform to the sense we often, perhaps usually, have that we have indeed chosen much of what has happened to us. Still, there is something in Oedipus' protest that rings true also. Even in Socrates' account it is said, "For the most part the choice was made according to the habituation of their former life." We put aside the problems suggested by "For the most part," as we wonder about how one had gotten to be habituated the way one was in one's former life (or former lives, since a series of earthly lives, every thousand years or so, seems to be assumed).

We also wonder how far back we should go in assessing who is responsible for what. I need not remind an audience of social workers about the correlation between, on the one hand, economic and other deprivation and, on the other hand, the incidence of violent crimes, at least among us. Compare the Hindu approach to these matters. Although both the typical Hindu account and the Socratic account in the *Republic* assume reincarnation, are they not radically different in spirit? Is not the tendency of the Socratic account to induce us to take more seriously than we otherwise might the opportunities before us, the things that we ourselves can do?

V

It is not only someone as ancient as Oedipus who can consider himself the prisoner of his circumstances, as we can see in my next story, which I have by courtesy of William Clohesy of the Rochester Institute of Technology. We have moved from two anonymous Jews wondering about the inexorability of human existence to two named Irishmen wondering about how we get to be the way we are. Professor Clohesy had a few years ago this exchange with William O'Donnell, proprietor of the Anchor Pub, in Bantry (on the south coast of Ireland):

O'DONNELL: Where are the Clohesy's from?

CLOHESY: Originally from Clare, but since Cromwell most of us have lived in Limerick City.

O'DONNELL: Cromwell was a bad one, altogether. I suppose you wonder why I, with a grand northern name such as O'Donnell, why I am here on the southwest coast of Ireland?

CLOHESY: No, but—

O'DONNELL: My family fought in the great war of the Earls against the first Elizabeth [in 1602]. We fought all the way south to these shores. The English routed us though [when they were reinforced through Bantry port]. So we retreated north into County Limerick. When we tried to cross the Shannon, a villain named O'Rourke brought out a force that beat us back. He was looking for a reward from the English. We scattered back South. *That's* why I'm here today.

What do we make of thus laying the blame on the villain O'Rourke and his perfidy three and a half centuries ago? Of course, there *is* something to it—one can feel trapped by one's "history" (even if, as in the case of the O'Donnell of Bantry, the narrator happens to be someone who has himself travelled the world as a sailor). And yet, do we not sense that one may choose to be affected this way rather than that by one's past?

VI

Although there may be critical aspects of one's past which are beyond one's control, would any of us go so far (in assessing his "fate") as the Arab in my next story? This story, told by a Syrian author, Zaharia Tamer, has the narrator reporting this episode:

[There] stands a small cafe opposite the factory from which I was discharged a month ago for accidentally damaging a machine. The customers are factory workers, peasants, peddlers, drivers of cabs, tractors and carriages, and unemployed people like me. These men sit, relaxed, sipping tea leisurely, and chit-chatting without knowing one another.

Abu Ahmad, the owner of the cafe, is a tall, old man with wide shoulders and a moustache that lends a touch of cruelty to his fully-wrinkled face. He is very proud of his cafe. A few days ago, he told me: "My father was poor. He died, leaving me nothing. I sweated, starved and lived in exile to buy this cafe. For man to be happy, he must have something—his own property. I hated my grandfather. If he had married my mother off to a rich man, I wouldn't have known the taste of misery."

I find this a particularly intriguing story, in part because of what it presupposes about one's individual soul. Does it not assume that someone remains the same through various manifestations? (Is this indicated, as well, in my third and fourth stories, taken from Sophocles and from Plato?) Where we would speak of genetics and of environment, and perhaps of fate, this Arab cafe owner speaks of the decisive doings of his parents and grandparents, doings which he has had to work hard to counteract. He evidently sees his "self" as somehow independent of his particular circumstances and his physical make-up: his self had come to life through his mother's womb into the material circumstances determined by his father's situation. According to him, it seems, one's fortune comes through one's father, while one's mother is primarily a conduit for one's soul. It is also significant that he could, by great efforts and sacrifices, remedy somewhat his grandfather's unforgivable error. The cafe owner could conclude this conversation by asking the narrator, "Do you hate your grandfather?"

VII

I have suggested that the stories we have drawn upon appeal to us (if they do) because they, in their variety (and sometimes in their absurdity), play with the somewhat contradictory thoughts and feelings we do have about whether we should in fact be considered responsible for our lives, characters, and actions.

Several of our stories have reminded us of what one can do in desperate circumstances—of how well one may play the poor hand one has been dealt. This is pointed up by a speech by Shakespeare's Henry V as his army confronted what seemed overwhelming odds before the battle of Agincourt (*Henry V*, IV, i, 1–12):

> Gloucester, 'tis true that we are in great danger;
> The greater therefore should our courage be.
> Good morrow, brother Bedford. God Almighty!
> There is some soul of goodness in things evil,
> Would men observingly distill it out.
> For our bad neighbor makes us early strivers,
> Which is both healthful, and good husbandry.
> Besides, they are our outward consciences,
> And preachers to us all, admonishing
> That we should dress us fairly for our end.
> Thus may we gather honey from the weed
> And make a moral of the devil himself.

There are always opportunities available, if one but sees them—even, we have occasionally seen, in slums and in severe deprivation. Or, as Theodore Roosevelt (like his contemporary, Booker T. Washington) urged his fellow-citizens, "Do what you can with what you have where you are." With this quotation we move from the foreign approach to these matters to a more or less American approach. *Is* there a different spirit among Americans, reflected in and determined in part by our considerable mobility and the increased opportunity that that mobility makes possible?

We have been concerned both with what shapes an entire people and with what shapes this man or that; hence we have been concerned with matters both public and private. Do we Americans not have, more than most peoples of the world, a sense that our destiny is in our hands to a considerable degree? Does not the American approach (a noble illusion, of sorts?) take it for granted that one can make a difference, both personally and in the community?

VIII

Our series of a half-dozen American "stories" can well begin with the opening paragraph of the *Federalist Papers* addressed to "the People of the State of New York":

After an unequivocal experience of the inefficacy of the subsisting Federal Government, you are called upon to deliberate on a new Constitution for the

United States of America. The subject speaks for its own importance; comprehending in its consequences, nothing less than the existence of the UNION, the safety and welfare of the parts of which it is composed, the fate of an empire, in many respects, the most interesting in the world. It has been frequently remarked, that it seems to have been reserved to the people of this country, by their conduct and example, to decide the important question, whether societies of men are really capable or not, of establishing good government from reflection and choice, or whether they are forever destined to depend, for their political constitutions, on accident and force. If there be any truth in the remark, the crisis, at which we are arrived, may with propriety be regarded as the era in which that decision is to be made; and a wrong election of the part we shall act, may, in this view, deserve to be considered as the general misfortune of mankind.

Publius sees here a unique opportunity (not for Americans alone, but for all mankind) to show that men can so reason as to control their lives, liberating themselves from the tyranny of "accident and force." (We need not consider today either the question of what *is* better and worse or the sense in which sound reasoning curtails one's freedom.) It is easier to see that men can sometimes control their separate lives than to see that societies (or a people) control their collective lives: it does seem easier for individual human beings than for peoples to do the right thing, to be varied and flexible. And yet much of what one is and does depends on the community that has shaped one. The high hopes and the sense of opportunity reflected in the *Federalist Papers* were anticipated by the Declaration of Independence, with its insistence upon the right, the duty *and* the capacity of a people to control its destiny.

IX

The American belief that public life can and should be deliberately controlled may extend to an effort by some of us to control the past, an effort which testifies in effect to the grip that the past may have upon us, perhaps even paralyzing us with the oppressive sense of opportunities which have been missed, opportunities as magnificent (it can seem to those devoted to a lost cause) as the opportunity that the Founding Fathers had been able to do so much with. For our next story we go south, to an American version of the rascal O'Rourke and the fate of the O'Donnell—but here we have the fate of a people as determined by the outcome of the American Civil War. Here is how this effort to come to terms with one's past can look in the art of William Faulkner (*Intruder in the Dust*, chap. 9):

[A young man is thinking:] . . . [H]is uncle for this too, anticipating this too
two or three or four years ago as his uncle had everything else which as he
himself became more and more a man he had found to be true: 'It's all *now*
you see. Yester-day wont be over until tomorrow and tomorrow began ten
thousand years ago. For every Southern boy fourteen years old, not once but
whenever he wants it, there is the instant when it's still not yet two oclock on
that July afternoon [at Gettysburg] in 1863, the brigades are in position behind the rail fence, the guns are laid and ready in the woods and the furled
flags are already loosened to break out and Pickett himself with his long oiled
ringlets and his hat in one hand probably and his sword in the other looking
up the hill waiting for Longstreet to give the word and it's all in the balance, it
hasn't happened yet, it hasn't even begun yet, it not only hasn't begun yet but
there is still time for it not to begin against that position and those circumstances which made more men than Garnett and Kemper and Armstead and
Wilcox look grave yet it's going to begin, we all know that, we have come too
far with too much at stake and that moment doesn't need even a fourteen-
year-old boy to think *This time. Maybe this time* with all this much to lose and
all this much to gain: Pennsylvania, Maryland, the world, the golden dome of
Washington itself to crown with desperate and unbelievable victory the desperate gamble, the cast made two years ago . . .

Is not the character of a regime, of the Southern regime perhaps down
to our day, reflected in this daydream? We can see that it is not only the
Irish, but enterprising Americans as well, who can feel trapped by their
past. Is it not suggested in the Faulkner passage that mistakes by Southern
leaders at Gettysburg had contributed to the debacle? But one must wonder, If not these mistakes, should there not have been others? Was there
not something at the very root of the Cause which made defeat not only
highly likely but also ultimately desirable (and hence, in a sense, inevitable)? With such a question we wonder, with Socrates, about the moral
order of the universe and about the ultimate cause of things.

We can see here the dependence each of us may have on the community, on the political. This is a collective opportunity missed, by which all
may be affected altogether as well as one by one. The way one's community shapes one can make the passions one has seem instinctive, so habituated one may be as to develop "a second nature" about the ancestral
things.

X

We, Northerners as well as Southerners, can also see that vital things not
done have helped make all the difference for us. Sometimes the workings

of chance have been all too apparent, but so have been the workings of bad judgment, which bad judgment can often be reduced to ignorance. The nature of the American regime, with its remarkable opportunities and the consequent stories of great and not-so-great successes (if not even of failures)—the nature of the American regime is such that virtually every family must have such a story as the one my family treasures:

My father, when he was a young immigrant in St. Louis, was approached by the Skouras brothers to join them (fellow-immigrants from the same locality in Greece) in a new nickelodeon venture. He declined and advised them, "Boys, there's no future in the entertainment business." He preferred to take his chances instead with the restaurant business. The Skouras brothers went on to fame and fortune in the movie industry. (Whether they really avoided thereby "the taste of misery" that our Arab cafe owner spoke of is another story.)

In addition, I married someone from a family with a similar experience in the Southwest, with another newly developed art. My wife's father, Jack Prince, would recall from time to time his advice to "old man Braniff" when Mr. Braniff suggested that they fly passengers between Oklahoma City and Tulsa, "Tom, there's no money in flying people around." Or, as I believe Louis Pasteur put this sort of thing, "Chance favors the prepared mind."

Thus, the Skouras and Braniff stories should remind us of the American dream—and of the American nightmare as well? It is significant that there are so many such opportunities among us, which most cannot help but lose out on when they experiment and gamble—or when they fail to gamble and to experiment. Cannot all of us recall critical opportunities in our youth which would have made our lives different, usually better, if we had had the sense and the character to take advantage of them? Perhaps even our high divorce and remarriage rates reflect a sense of missed opportunities, the yearning for that which might have been.

XI

Still, one must wonder how much knowledge of or control over one's actions one may truly have. The bombardier in our air crew (when we were stationed at our overseas training base in New Mexico during the Second World War) pointed out to me a small, unremarkable-looking youngster, observing, "That's the best bombardier in the Air Corps." It turned out that this newly minted officer could do wonders with the Norden bombsight, breaking all records in the bombardier school they had attended.

He was so remarkable that the word got back to the War Department in Washington—and so one day the youngster found himself flying in a trainer, with several generals hovering over him, eager to learn the secret of his phenomenal success. The plane moved into its bombing run with a general pleading, "Now, kid, show us how you do it"—no doubt, they had visions of a markedly increased bombing proficiency, perhaps even in effect a secret weapon that would hasten the end of the war. "Well, sir," the kid replied as he watched intently through the bombsight, "I just wait and wait until it feels ju-u-u-st *right*"—and with this he pressed the bomb-release button for still another bull's eye.

The generals had to return to Washington not much wiser than they had left the city: they had been told everything the wizard knew, and yet they had been told nothing. Does not this story remind us that much of what we do does depend on attributes which may be natural to us, attributes which seem instinctive, if not even God-given, neither acquired by instruction nor capable of being transmitted to others?

XII

But lest we believe, and believe to our detriment, that the most important things we do personally are really beyond our control, I have for you still another story, one that suggests how "instruction" can sometimes overcome "instinct" (or temperament or nature).

This story, like the one about the lost opportunity in commercial aviation, also comes from my father-in-law, who remembered a vigorous fellow in Point, Texas who was a good provider for his family, except in one critical respect. This man, when he got roaring drunk, would beat his wife. Then he would pass out and sleep it off. When he sobered up, he would realize what he had done and would apologize profusely to his battered wife. But this did not keep him from mauling her the next time he got drunk, which would not be too long after.

One night, after he had again beaten his wife in his drunken rage and then passed out, she took off all his clothes, rolled him up tightly in a sheet, and sewed it up with strong twine. He was immobilized as in a straitjacket. She waited for him to regain consciousness—and to sober up. Then she took a buggy whip and lashed her husband with it long past the time when he began pleading for mercy.

It is said that he spent several weeks in the hospital, recuperating. It is also said that he never beat his wife again thereafter, drunk or sober. It seems, that is, that he was taught a lesson that reached to the very depths of his psyche, overcoming whatever subconscious or "natural" inclination he may have had to enjoy himself roughing up his wife.

This story suggests that the passions we have, or inherit, are more susceptible to reason, and to the lessons addressed to our reason through our bodies, than may be generally appreciated. Should we not recognize that there was something in the drunken wife-beater that could be blamed for what he did? That something could be reached and instructed by a mercilessly applied buggy whip, so much so that he lost all effective desire to batter his wife again.

Of course, this buggy-whip instruction (which addressed the man's instinct for self-preservation, thereby countering one instinct by another) was not the most refined. But then, the conduct to be corrected was hardly refined either. In any event, did not this resourceful wife, who simply could not afford to abandon even so hazardous a marriage as hers was, understand things about free will and determinism, about the relation of reason to the passions, that we can all take to heart?

XIII

My final story reminds us that the lessons that are taught by experience can be remarkably durable—but as Mark Twain once put it, a cat that sits on a hot stove-lid will never sit on a hot stove-lid again, or on a cold one either.

Some thirty-five years ago we rented an apartment in Paris. In the course of things—one is tempted to say, "in the natural course of things"—we came to need a plumber. Our landlord, a successful businessman who had recently purchased and remodeled our building, instructed me to make the necessary arrangements with the plumbing shop in our neighborhood, which I did. I reported to my wife, after leaving the shop, that the proprietor—a short, fat man in his seventies—had positively glowered at me when I gave him my address, "12, rue Pierre Mille." She blamed the man's reaction on my poor French.

A plumber did come from the shop but, unfortunately, he was not sober enough to be entrusted with the serious operation that he wanted us to take the responsibility for. (Our consent was sought and denied as he poised a sledgehammer over the offending porcelain fixture.) A second plumber had to be sent a day or two later. Thereafter, the plumbing shop charged for two calls. Our landlord and the proprietor had to settle accounts between them—out of which heated negotiations came the proprietor's angry declaration, "When I heard '12, rue Pierre Mille,' I knew there would be trouble." Only then did we learn that the last time that that proprietor had sent a plumber to our address there had also been an argument about the bill. That previous occasion had been a few years before the *First* World War, more than a decade before I was even born— and here *I* was, in my middle twenties, several years after the Second World War. This proved for us a most useful lesson in the French, perhaps the European, way of life.

I opened this series of a dozen stories with the reflection of a Frenchman upon American circumstances and prospects. I conclude this series with the reflection of an American upon French circumstances. It is well to be reminded, as we are by the Paris story, that there may be seen in the Old World a stability—or, if you will, an inflexibility—that obviously reduces around one the Tocquevillian circle within which one can freely maneuver. In other places, no doubt, the circle may be even tighter, the spiritual counterpart perhaps of the circle in which the brutal wife-beater was confined by his long-suffering wife. But without some inflexible limits, there may be nothing by which one can take one's bearings in the ordinary course of things. This means, if one is completely unrestrained, that one can be trapped, if not even appalled and paralyzed, by one's freedom.

CONCLUSION

I offer you these stories, drawing upon our own experiences and our receptivity to the experiences of others, as suggestions bearing upon the fascinating complexity of our subject. You are entitled—indeed, you are encouraged—to wonder what my organization of stories, to say nothing of the stories themselves, may presuppose about the nature of things. How much were my stories dependent, for what happens in them, on chance? Several of the stories were about things I have myself witnessed or have gotten first-hand. (These were mostly in the latter half of my collection.) No doubt, this selection has reflected to some extent my temperament and my own career.

No doubt, also, these stories—or, at least, the way I recall and think about them—reflect a Western perspective. This suggests how liberal education, as we in the West know it, bears upon this subject. Is there any basis for choosing between the East and the West with respect to these matters? Does not a proper answer to this question depend on the nature and status of nature in human life? But this inquiry, too, may have to be reserved for another occasion. For a serious study of this subject, one should begin by looking into Aristotle on the voluntary and the involuntary and into Thomas Aquinas on freedom of the will.

The element of control—the ability to choose and to change—may be central to the work of the social worker. For if there is no self-control, and hence no moral responsibility, in what people do, then the social work profession is likely to be less attractive to its practitioners than it would otherwise be. Whether one is client or guide, it can be depressing to regard human beings as foreclosed from any genuine choice between meaningful alternatives. Is it not much more salutary to believe oneself free to act? Is it not healthier for human beings to regard each other as pretty much responsible most of the time? One's self-respect and hence one's energy may be enhanced thereby.

Even so, there *is* something mysterious about this question of free will. Somehow or other, we are in charge of our lives, or at least seem to be—and all kinds of institutions, sanctions, and everyday expressions reflect a general understanding that we *are* in charge, that we are "responsible." And yet we also sense that we are shaped in ways we are barely aware of—shaped by our genetic makeup, by our family and personal circumstances, by political, historical, and religious developments, by chance influences of all kinds. The stories I have shared with you suggest the various ways we are pushed and pulled on this issue. We are back to where we started, but perhaps with a clarification, or at least a question, here or there which enlivens and informs the subject for us as we try to figure out where we have come from, where we are, and where we are going —and what such questions mean.

It may be in large part a matter of chance, or of fate, what happens to us. How we respond to what happens to us—which may mean, ultimately, how we understand things—may be less a matter of chance. Do we not sense that a soul can liberate itself more from chance in the realm of thought than it can in the realm of action? May not one reach a level of understanding—no doubt, chance can be somewhat important here, too— may not one reach a level of understanding where one is thereafter more or less in control of one's life, the life of the mind (at least so long as one's body happens to hold up)? Does not such liberation—here and there, now and then, if only among a few—remind us, if only by comparison, of the many limitations to which we are all subject in the everyday world, which may not be a simply bad thing?

2

ANCIENTS AND MODERNS

2-A. Aristotle on Law and Morality

I believe that what is said by many is very true, namely, that those Athenians who are good are good in a different way. They alone are good by their own nature without compulsion, by a divine dispensation: they are truly, and not artificially, good.

MEGILLUS, a Spartan

I

The dependence of morality on law is insisted upon in the closing pages of Aristotle's *Nicomachean Ethics*, perhaps the most detailed treatise on the moral virtues in antiquity. It is recognized there that law is needed if the moral virtues described in the *Ethics* are to be nurtured. (The law can contribute as well to the development of the intellectual virtues by promoting the conditions that they require.)

This is true in the United States as well, and not only in how our legally mandated school systems and our criminal laws contribute to the shaping, including the moral training, of citizens. Yet the typical opinions in a contemporary liberal democracy are likely to be (1) that morality cannot be legislated; and (2) that even if morality could be legislated, it should not be—that to do so is somehow improper, even tyrannical, either because

---

This talk was given at the Annual Convention, American Political Science Association, Denver, Colorado, September 4, 1982. (Sponsor: Claremont Institute for the Study of Statesmanship and Political Philosophy.) It has been published in 3 *Windsor [Ontario] Yearbook of Access to Justice* 458–64 (1983). See, also, the headnote for Essay No. 24, below.

The epigraph is taken from Plato, *Laws* 642C-D (Thomas L. Pangle translation).

there is no morality objective enough to justify legal enforcement or because one's autonomy and individuality would be violated by attempts to legislate morality or perhaps even because one really has no autonomy that can respond to any external directive.

Such concerns are not evident in the *Ethics:* law is needed both to help habituate citizens to virtuous actions and to help maintain the salutary habits they acquire. These needs can be recognized even by those who are aware that the virtues generally fostered by law are not the highest. The opinions one may have about the good, the true, and the beautiful are a secondary concern of most laws. Still, it is well to keep in mind Aristotle's counsel that one who is "to listen intelligently to lectures about what is noble and just must have been brought up in good habits." For proper habituation, laws can be most useful, if not indispensable.

Although intellectuals of liberal democratic sympathies may not believe that morality depends on law, it is almost impossible for any regime that takes itself, and is to be taken, seriously not to shape its citizens with respect to morality. To deny that legislation of morality can or should take place does not eliminate such legislation; it merely conceals it, perhaps distorts it, and otherwise confuses and misleads rulers and ruled alike. (Here, as in physics, much that Aristotle noticed and relied upon is tacitly relied upon by us as well, but relied upon haphazardly because it is not properly noticed.)

It would be useful, therefore, to indicate how pervasive Aristotle understands the law to be with respect to morality in a community. When we see what *law* can mean, and how it works, we may better appreciate what the law does in the service of morality, even in such a liberal democracy as ours. To speak of the influence of the law is, we shall see, to speak of the many ways that the community forms the citizen and guides the human being. For us, however, the term *law* does tend to be limited to what "government" does, to the statutes and decrees that governments issue.

II

We have noticed the most conspicuous way, drawn upon at the end of the *Ethics,* in which morality is dependent on law. The dependence of morals on law may also be seen in Book V of the *Ethics,* where justice is discussed at length. It is evident in the discussion there of justice as a particular virtue, the virtue that is intimately related to what is called fairness. Not only is law needed to secure justice among men, but law helps define or establish what precisely is fair in various circumstances. A concern for fairness and trust is reflected, for example, in a community's provision for a currency.

Justice is also presented in Book V as somehow encompassing all the virtues, at least insofar as those virtues bear upon one's relations with one's neighbors. The just in this sense is the lawful. Justice may be seen in the courage (or, at least, lack of cowardice) one is obliged by conscription and military laws to display on specified occasions or in the intemperance one is sometimes obliged by the law of crimes, of torts, and of marital relations to avoid. This role of the law anticipates what is said in the closing pages of the *Ethics*.

It should be added here that not only is morality somewhat dependent on law, but also that the law itself is to a considerable extent dependent on morality. A properly trained, morally alert citizen-body tends to be appalled by the lawbreaker. But does not this response (which can help keep many would-be lawbreakers in line) rest, in turn, upon the presumption that the law is likely to be, and in fact usually appears to be, itself moral and in the service of the common good? There is a critical reciprocity between law and morality. Reciprocity, we recall from the *Ethics*, can be vital to justice as a particular virtue.

III

We have been looking primarily at the direct dependence of morality on law. This dependence may be seen to be indirect as well.

Various of the virtues—liberality is among the more obvious—require equipment, if one is to be able either to acquire or to exercise them. But to speak of equipment, and of the opportunity to use it properly in one's training and in one's career, is to take for granted the laws of property that determine the conditions and privileges of ownership.

Of course, more equipment is needed for some virtues than for others. But even for those virtues which require little equipment for their exercise, such as the intellectual virtues, considerable equipment (in the form of available leisure time as well as of books and other intellectual supplies) may be needed to prepare one for the kind of life in which a continuing reliance upon equipment becomes relatively minor.

The exercise of most virtues requires a stable community, one in which one's body and life as well as property are fairly secure—and, of course, the law is essential here. To become or to remain a civilized human being usually requires a sound community—that is, one in which the law plays a considerable part. Is there not an intimate relation, at home and abroad, between justice and peace? To recognize this is not to deny that friendship also seems to hold communities together nor that legislators may care more for it than for justice. Even so, is not proper habituation needed for reliable friendships, as well as for justice? Who but the legislator, who must always be distinguished from the tyrant, can insure such habituation?

IV

Leo Strauss suggested, "The quarrel between the ancients and the moderns concerns eventually, and perhaps even from the beginning, the status of 'individuality.' " (*Natural Right and History*, p. 323) The problem here of modernity and free will may be seen in a most dramatic form when we notice how far the law could go among the ancients in regulating activities we would regard as essentially private. Consider, for example, the casual observation by Plutarch at the end of his life of Coriolanus:

> When the Romans heard tidings of [Coriolanus's] death, they gave no other signification either of honor or of anger towards him, but simply granted the request of the women, that they might put themselves into mourning and bewail him for ten months, as the usage was upon the loss of a father or a son or a brother; that being the period fixed for the longest lamentation by the laws of Numa Pompilius . . .

Community control of mourning is assumed among the Greeks as well, as is evident throughout Pericles' funeral address.

The city was evidently guided by its sense of propriety, its sense of what was fitting and useful. How seriously such concerns were regarded may be gathered upon considering the execution of the victorious Athenian generals who failed to recover, at Arginusae, the bodies of the Athenian dead.

When we recall the extent to which ancient law would go in regulating what we regard as the most private affairs, we can see how plausible is the Aristotelian contention that what the law does not require, it forbids. This is said, by the way, in the context of a comment on suicide: one's body, to say nothing of one's life, is not something one is entitled to do with as one happens to please.

All this is tacitly qualified by what is said in Book V of the *Ethics* about that which is by nature just. Mere legality is thereby called into question. Even so, Aristotle would hardly be inclined to believe, as we sometimes seem to believe, that the most serious moral virtue is expressed in resistance to government. Rather, he would suggest that the highest moral virtue may be seen in the man able to rule well. Whatever reservations

Aristotle has about legality and even tyranny are presented tacitly, not explicitly, lest he be irresponsible in his teachings. Our own circumstances may be in critical respects different, especially since our age does tend toward an aggressive relativism. It is as a reminder of enduring standards, and indeed of the nature of man, that the Declaration of Independence, with its affirmation of the right of revolution, remains our founding instrument.

V

We have been considering, by and large, the approach taken by the ancients to these matters. Still, the law, in its broadest sense, very much affects what even we regard as virtuous. Consider again the example of whom or how one may mourn or the example of how parents are to be treated, matters that we seem to prefer to leave to everyone to decide as he sees fit. But even among us, how one treats one's parents or how one buries one's dead—what expenditures should be made, what practices are to be respected, what ceremonies are to be followed—still very much depends, for most people, on the prevailing opinions of that part of the community they are governed by.

Customs can be decisive here. Such customs are a sort of law. That is, it may be a mistake in these matters to distinguish an authoritative public opinion from "the law." After all, the unwritten law, as an expression of the community will, was a vital, perhaps even the major, part of the law among the ancients.

In the broadest sense, then, the rules discovered and set forth in the *Ethics* are laws, at least to the extent that community opinion adopts and insists upon them. Some necessary sanctions, as well as systematic programs for habituation and supervision, do depend on statutes and decrees for their full effectiveness.

For us, as for Aristotle, the laws most broadly conceived very much define what is virtuous or vicious. Consider again the virtue of courage. Precisely what is courageous can depend in large part on whether one is called up for military service, where one happens to be sent, and what one is expected to do. Thus for us, as for Aristotle, both the law and that public opinion which is shaped, directly or indirectly, by the law help determine how the citizen should act, what one should be moved to do, and what one should be ashamed to do.

That the law usually has more, directly, to say about what constitutes cowardice or adultery or theft than about what constitutes gluttony does not mean that it does not express an opinion about gluttony as well. One may have a duty to keep oneself in good shape, and a self-confident community would make known to citizens that it takes such a duty seriously. Even among us, there is much that dictates how we should look, what shape we should be in physically (to say nothing of how we should feel and act). Social and other sanctions await anyone bold enough, or careless enough, to disregard the models provided by employment guidelines, personal tips in the mass media, advertisements, all kinds of fiction, and the protocols of the many "voluntary organizations" we are obliged to join. In addition, could not a conscription act, for example, provide among us youthful physical and moral training for those who may someday be needed for military service?

VI

We believe we dispense with Aristotle's reliance on the legislation of morality by relying instead on what we consider private shapers of morality. That is, we look for moral instruction to the family, to society and to religion, not to the state or government. But in thus distinguishing these sources of morality, we fail to appreciate the extent to which the ancient *polis* encompassed what moderns know as society, religion, and the state. We also fail to appreciate the dependence, even among us, of society and of religion, as well as of the family, on the law. The dependence that Aristotle saw of morality on law remains in effect, however concealed (and hence obstructed and distorted) it may be by our understanding both of morality and of law.

That the family is not only defined by the law, but also is empowered and in many ways supported and reinforced by law, should be evident to us. Laws of property, marriage, child care, inheritance, and taxation readily come to mind as very much affecting how families, constituted and privileged as they are by law, conduct themselves.

How these laws work reflects long-established opinions about what a family is, what relations among its members should be, and what kind of conduct by people as family members is anticipated and desired. Similar observations can be made about the place of religion in the community, the privileges it has, and the effects among us of the activities of religious associations. The community endorses and supports both families and religions in large part because of what it believes it gets from them in the form of productive, law-abiding, and otherwise virtuous citizens.

VII

The considerable talk in this Country about "the separation of church and state" can be misleading. It tends to conceal the fact that religion has always been among us a particularly effective way for the community to manifest itself, to shape opinions and hence souls, and to guide actions. Which religious sects prosper and are influential among us still depends, to a considerable extent, on the opinions and standards of the community. Although little is said about these matters in the statutes of this Country, that does not mean that religious sentiments do not exist among us as powerful community influences.

Besides, it should be noted, curiously little is said explicitly about religion and its bearing upon morality even in the *Nicomachean Ethics*. Aristotle seems to be primarily concerned to discover and refine the moral standards by which human beings should be governed. What laws are to be used to establish and maintain those standards depends on the good sense of the community and the prudence of its leaders, including its poets and other educators. The institutions to be used, and how they are to be used, depend also on circumstances and hence should be adjusted from time to time. Such institutions comprehend the formal religious practices of the community. But Aristotle tends to see these as secondary, reasoning perhaps that what is decisive in a community is its generally accepted sense of morality. Religious and other institutions, especially if they are promoted and regulated if not even subsidized by law, can be expected to strive for morality to the extent possible in an imperfect community.

2-B. Kant on Metaphysics and Morality

You would have thought that this practical dreaming must have soon brought Carrigaholt to a bad end, but he was in much less danger than might be supposed: for besides that the new visions of happiness almost always came in time to counteract the fatal completion of the preceding scheme, his high breeding and his delicately sensitive taste almost always befriended him at times when he was left without any other protection; and the efficacy of these qualities in keeping a man out of harm's way is really immense. In all baseness and imposture there is a coarse, vulgar spirit, which, however artfully concealed for a time, must sooner or later show itself in some little circumstance sufficiently plain to occasion an instant jar upon the minds of those whose taste is lively and true: to such men a shock of this kind, disclosing the ugliness of a cheat, is more effectively convincing than any mere proofs could be.

Thus guarded from isle to isle, and through Greece and through Albania, this practical Plato, with a purse in his hand, carried on his mad chase after the Good and the Beautiful, and yet returned in safety to his home.

ALEXANDER W. KINGLAKE

I

Lying seems to be the primary example given by Immanuel Kant, in his *Fundamental Principles of the Metaphysics of Morals,* of what one ought not to do. He places particular emphasis upon the deliberate making of a promise one knows will not be kept. A determination to tell the truth, no matter what the cost, is critical both to the spirit of morality and to the desire for certainty that permeate Kant's ethical approach. Such an approach can lead to a remarkable steadfastness in the face of great challenges: temptations and rationalizations are rigorously disposed of. (See Section II of Essay No. 12, below.)

That so much is made of keeping one's promises is intriguing, considering that an inquiry into promise-keeping provides the primary example

---

This talk was given at a Staff Seminar of the Basic Program of Liberal Education for Adults, The University of Chicago, Chicago, Illinois, March 2, 1985.

The citations in this essay are to Immanuel Kant, *Fundamental Principles of the Metaphysics of Morals,* Thomas K. Abbott translation (Indianapolis: Library of Liberal Arts, Bobbs-Merrill Company, 1949).

The epigraph is taken from Alexander W. Kinglake, *Eothen* (London: John Lehmann, 1944), p. 59.

exploited by Socrates in the opening pages of Plato's *Republic* in dealing with Cephalus' unexamined notions about justice. Also intriguing is that there should be for Kant no proper place for even the noblest of lies. Does not this in turn mean, among other things, that Kant legitimizes only utopian politics, something that the author of the *Republic* (who is the author as well of *The Laws*) does not do? Indeed, Kant, as an impolitic moralist, challenges us to reconsider what we have been taught about politics as well as about morality. For our immediate purpose, a much-simplified account of Kant's complicated teaching suffices.

II

"The truth, the whole truth, and nothing but the truth" is what Kant seems to insist upon from the ethical man. And yet Kant is identified as the philosopher who has made much of the difficulty of our knowing anything in itself.

This insistence upon the limits of our knowledge seems to be compensated for by what is said by Kant against lying. One is to offer as the truth only what one believes oneself to know to be true. Radical skepticism is thereby countered by a remarkable purity, and hence a kind of knowing, in morality.

Ethical purity becomes possible, it seems, only if one need not take consequences into account in determining what one is to do on any particular occasion. Prudence is set aside: reason, Kant tells us, "is not competent to guide the will with certainty in regard to its objects." (p. 14. See, also, p. 20.)

III

However useful the reason may be in helping one determine which general rule applies to one's particular situation, the most critical use of the reason is evidently to be devoted to the development of general rules, not to their particular applications. Such disregard, or at least radical subordination, of particulars (and especially consequences) reflects the Kantian determination to seek, through moral action, the supreme and unconditioned good. (See pp. 14–15.) Compare Socrates, who seems to find the greatest good only in philosophy, not in action.

The unconditioned good can be attained, it would seem, only if moral decisions are "perfectly cleared of anything which is only empirical" or anthropological. (p. 5) Even (if not especially) human nature is to be disregarded, and hence the deep connection between morality and mortality. After all, the rules laid down, or discovered, by Kant apply to all rational beings, immortal as well as mortal. Critical to the Kantian calculation is the question one should always put to oneself, "Can you also will that your maxim should be a universal law?" (See p. 21.)

Although much is made by the Kantian of the disregard of the consequences of one's actions, the typical consequences expected to follow from acting upon a universal law may be reflected in the rule itself. (See pp. 5, 17–18, 21.) When the test of what may awkwardly be called *universalizability* is relied upon, does that not look to or at least implicitly rely upon probable consequences?

We can wonder: what if the exercise of one's pure will, acting pursuant to the universalizability criterion, should result again and again in obvious disasters? Should not the rule be suspended when its evident purpose, or at least its anticipated result, is denied? Or does one still insist in such circumstances upon the satisfaction, and the justification, of having maintained the purity of one's will?

IV

The universalizability criterion may be another way of insisting upon the importance of truthfulness. It perhaps points up why there is such an emphasis by Kant upon deception as perhaps the cardinal vice.

Few would counsel deception merely to avoid inconveniences. But it is not only when one is personally in distress that one might want to lie. (See p. 20.) Should we not be willing to concede that one can resort to lying when it is fairly clear that serious injustice to others may thus be avoided? Cannot that be made an acceptable general rule?

Such a determination would require the use of prudence. One does have to exercise judgment. Differences of opinion might result, or at least more differences of opinion than under the Kantian approach. Prudential considerations threaten the certainty and purity that Kant associates with genuine morality.

Such purity cannot be secured if self-interest affects one's judgment, something that is more apt to happen if circumstances and consequences are taken into consideration in determining what one is to do. Certainty as to one's own moral worth sometimes seems more important for Kant than good effects or even moral action itself. (See pp. 16, 24.) This means, in turn, that one cannot *know* (and it is important that one should know?)— one cannot know that one is morally worthy unless one is gaining nothing personally from one's act and enjoying no personal pleasure therefrom.

This understanding of moral things seems to lead to far less of an emphasis upon habituation than one would find in, say, Aristotle. In addition, less would be made of the simple pleasure of doing the right thing. (See, e.g., p. 16.) One consequence of Kant's approach may be that one finds one's moral worth in effect declining (from Kant's, but not from Aristotle's, perspective) as one repeatedly does the right thing, because one's initial effort in doing the right thing may thereby be steadily reduced or one's pleasure in doing it may even increase.

In any event, the Kantian aloofness with respect to consequences, inclinations, and pleasures in moral matters can lead to a stance that is either godlike or monstrous or both.

V

Depreciation of habituation, of proper pleasure, and of concern for consequences is further indicated in the emphasis by Kant upon the unique goodness of the good will. This is said to be the only good without qualification, suggesting thereby a metaphysical transformation of something as homely as a moral decision.

But however metaphysical one's morality is taken to be, it does not imply that virtue for Kant is knowledge: that identification also would run the risk of placing too much reliance upon prudence. Rather, metaphysics seems to be used by him to keep people of common sense from having recourse, as they naturally would, to prudence. (See pp. 22-23.) In this way he renders the practical "theoretical."

To place an emphasis upon the will is to make much of a certain probity or rigidity. The good will is not, despite its name, to be confused with benevolence: benevolence can involve deriving pleasure from helping others. Although deriving pleasure from doing something does not make such action immoral for Kant, it does deny one the assurance, evidently much to be treasured, that one is indeed acting morally.

VI

Accompanying this emphasis upon the will is the Kantian insistence that the moral decision consists in making oneself conform to a law. Here, too, one can see that a depreciation of prudential judgment follows whenever law-abidingness becomes critical.

Do not an insistence upon universalizability and an emphasis upon law go together for Kant? What is done is to be done not for the sake of the end or result, even though law itself might ordinarily seem to be keyed to some end or result. The much desired purity seems to depend on a certain abstractness—and so Kant can insist that the proper moral act is done *for the sake of* the law, rather than for any end beyond the law.

Does not all this reflect the opinion that words, or one's descriptions of things, can be better known than the things themselves? The words one uses and hears used by others can be better or more reliably known than other things, and especially the things which one might try to assess in making prudential judgments.

The Kantian respect for law-abidingness raises questions about the right of revolution. (This is aside from the difficulty one has in preparing adequately to exercise that right if one must never deceive one's government.) Does not the traditional right of revolution presuppose that one can know and judge the world, that there are objective standards to which one may have recourse, independent of what the law may happen to be? Is not the Kantian reliance upon law-abidingness, on the other hand, a somewhat positivistic approach to human affairs, so much so as to legitimate in effect the very subjectivity that Kant strives to avoid?

VII

Kant seems to suggest that all we can reliably know (aside from logic, mathematics, and the words of others and of ourselves [including those words that take the form of laws laid down?]) are the movements of the "will." This line of thought leads, especially when certainty is made so much of in the development and exercise of a pure morality, to an emphasis upon one's intentions as vital. This approach somehow abstracts radically (if not unnaturally) from morality as a whole, reducing it virtually to a sense of "duty" alone, or to one's sense of obligation.

This kind of integrity may look remarkably noble; it may also be very useful in some extreme cases, however crippling it may be in other extreme cases. It may also be, all too often, no more than misleading rhetoric, if not even a kind of self-indulgence. It does reflect what many people consider "moral." (See p. 21.) Yet it can also be recognized as too "moral." Thus, for example, it is significant that most of one's decent-minded students simply cannot talk themselves into agreeing that one should never lie, however intriguing and otherwise challenging they may find Kant's argument.

In a sense, Kant makes more of morality than did the ancient moral philosophers from whom he deliberately departs in several respects. (See, e.g., pp. 3, 11.) He is more apt to look to the Scriptures than to the Classical writers for guidance (but not as authority) in eliciting the pure moral impulse. (See, e.g., p. 17.) He tends, that is, to depreciate reliance upon nature as a guide, that nature on which prudence very much depends. (See p. 11.)

It is prudence that reminds us of the limitations (if not the immorality) of "morality" in its purest form even as it helps us enjoy both the good intrinsic to a moral decision and the good secured in the everyday world as that decision's likely consequence.

PRINCIPLES
and
QUESTIONS

A.

The
Old Way

3.

PLATO AND THE SOURCES OF TYRANNY

For who would bear the whips and scorns of time,
Th' oppressor's wrong, the proud man's contumely,
The pangs of despised love, the law's delay,
The insolence of office, and the spurns
That patient merit of th' unworthy takes,
When he himself might his quietus make
With a bare bodkin?

PRINCE HAMLET

I

Aristotle's approach to political things is often distinguished from Plato's. Plato is considered to be "idealistic," Aristotle to be "realistic." Aristotle, however, was Plato's greatest student, someone who is said to have studied with the master for two decades. Should it not be assumed that he understood what Plato was saying? If we recognize that Plato has much to teach us about political things, why should not Aristotle have believed this as well? Should not what Aristotle learned from Plato be evident in Aristotle's work?

Still, Aristotle's work does seem different from Plato's, as may be seen when one compares his *Politics* with Plato's *Republic*. (For one thing, the role of *eros* may seem somewhat diminished in Aristotle's work.) That there should be some differences is to be expected; there would be no point simply repeating what had been said before. The evident differences between the works of Plato and Aristotle for the most part reflect

---

This talk was given at the Annual Meeting, Midwest Political Science Association, Chicago, Illinois, April 23, 1983. (Original title: "Plato's *Laws* and the Aristotelian Succession.")

The citations in this essay are, unless otherwise indicated, to Plato, *Laws*, Thomas L. Pangle translation (New York: Basic Books, 1980).

The epigraph is taken from William Shakespeare, *Hamlet*, III, i, 70–76.

differences in subject-matter and circumstances rather than in the fundamental understanding by each of political things. The radical differences between Aristotle and Plato that so much is made of depend on a failure to appreciate what Plato says about many of the things that Aristotle addresses in his own way.

II

A particularly illuminating passage for our immediate purposes may be found in Book III of Plato's *Laws*. I reproduce this passage as it appears in the useful translation of the *Laws* by Thomas L. Pangle. The conversation here is between the Athenian Stranger and Kleinias (689E–690D):

ATH. Now I suppose there must necessarily be rulers and ruled in cities.

KL. But of course.

ATH. Well then, which and how many are the worthy titles to rule and to be ruled, in large and small cities and in households as well? Wouldn't one be that of the father and mother, and in general, wouldn't it be everywhere correct for parents to have title to rule over their descendants?

KL. Emphatically so.

ATH. And, following upon this, for the wellborn to rule over those who are not wellborn. Thirdly, following these, the elderly ought to rule and the younger ought to be ruled.

KL. But of course.

ATH. Fourthly, then, that slaves be ruled and masters rule.

KL. How could it be otherwise?

ATH. Fifth at any rate, I think, that the stronger rule and the weaker be ruled.

KL. Now you've mentioned a kind of rule that is compellingly necessary.

ATH. And the one most widely spread among all living things, and according to nature, as the Theban Pindar once asserted. But it's likely that the greatest title would be the sixth, the one bidding the ignorant to follow and the prudent to lead and rule. Indeed it is this title, O most wise Pindar, that I at least would hardly assert is against nature, but rather according to nature: the natural rule exercised by the law over willing subjects, without violence.

KL. What you say is very correct.

ATH. "Dear to the gods" at any rate, and "lucky," is what we call the seventh sort of rule—where we bring forward someone for a drawing of lots and assert that it is very just for the one who draws a winning lot to rule and for the one who draws a losing lot to give way and be ruled.

KL. What you say is very true.

ATH. "Do you see then," we would say, "O lawgiver," (joking with one of those who undertakes lightly the task of laying down laws) "how many worthy titles to rule there are, and that they are by nature opposed to one another? Here, indeed, we have discovered a source of civil strife, which you must treat. . . ."

Leo Strauss, in a seminar he gave on the Laws at the University of Chicago in 1959, called this passage one of the most important in Plato's writing. He spoke a few minutes later, at the conclusion of his discussion of the passage, of "this strange enumeration of the seven titles to rule."

What can be said about this passage? A few hints are given by Mr. Strauss himself both in his seminar and in his instructive book on the *Laws*. I will try to keep in mind what I have learned from him on this subject, even as I venture several observations of my own.

III

"Seven titles to rule" are touched upon by the unnamed Athenian Stranger in his discussion with a Cretan (Kleinias) and a Spartan (Megillus). It is useful to notice at the outset of this discussion something that is quite obvious but yet is likely to be overlooked: whatever the basis of one's rule over others, it does not seem to be complete without some effort to justify it. It is not enough that one does rule, or that one wants to. It is not enough to seize power without at least an effort to explain why the strong are entitled to special consideration. This may be in part because there are few who can rest easy as rulers, especially if there is a natural desire in most men for assurances of their own justice, if they do not have some plausible justification for their exercise of the powers of a ruler.

Among the "seven titles to rule," it seems, an eighth is touched upon. This is in the course of the description of the sixth title, that which is called "the greatest title," "the one bidding the ignorant to follow and the prudent to lead and rule." This, it is suggested, is "according to nature." Had the Athenian Stranger stopped here, with an emphasis upon the natural right of the prudent to lead and rule the ignorant, we would be back in Plato's *Republic* with its culmination of the development of the political order in the philosopher-king. But the Socrates-like Athenian Stranger goes on to speak of this sixth title as something seen in "the natural rule exercised by the law over willing subjects, without violence." The rule of law is not simply rule by the wise, even though the wise may prudently provide that the rule of law should be relied upon in most circumstances.

That the rule of the prudent is *not* central to this array in the *Laws* of the seven titles to rule reminds us of the differences between this dialogue and the *Republic*, as does the transformation of the rule of the wise into the rule of law. (Reference can be made in the *Laws*, but only in passing, to "arguments that come close to philosophizing." [857D] Neither Kleinias nor Megillus is as open to philosophy as are, say, even Glaucon and Adeimantus in the *Republic*.)

IV

To notice what is and is not central to this array in the *Laws* is to recognize that there may be something instructive about the principle of order relied upon here. Consider what can be said about various connections in this array:

The first three titles to rule (those titles rooted in parentage, in good birth, and in age) are connected by the use of the term, *following*, whereas the last four titles to rule (those titles rooted in slavery, in strength, in prudence, and in good fortune) are not thus connected. In this way, then, the first three are linked and the last four are not linked. On the other hand, the first four titles to rule are associated in a way differently from the way that the last three titles to rule are associated. The interlocutor says in the course of the presentation of the first four titles such things as, "Emphatically so," "But of course," and "How could it be otherwise?", whereas he says in the course of the presentation of the last three titles such things as, "Now you've mentioned a kind of rule that is compellingly necessary," "What you say is very correct," and "What you say is very true."

In one way the first three titles are connected by the use of *following* (but not the last four titles); in another way, the first four titles are connected by the character of the interlocutor's response, and so are the last three titles. It is evident here that Title #4, the one keyed to slavery, is connected according to one method of linking to the first three titles and according to another method of linking to the last three titles. (Is it not fitting that the response by the interlocutor to the fourth title to rule

["How could it be otherwise?"] is the most equivocal of the responses made by him here?)

Much more has to be said about slavery, which is, after all, that to which the central title to rule is keyed in the entire array of seven titles to rule. But before we turn to slavery itself, guided in part by what we have just seen, let us consider the principle of order in the entire array of seven titles to rule.

V

Although large cities, small cities and households are spoken of together by the Stranger—an amalgamation that Aristotle suggests, in the *Politics*, is not useful for the more discriminating political analysis—, it is evident that distinctions *are* made in the *Laws* between cities and households.

Thus, it can be said, the opening three titles to rule (claimed by parents, by the wellborn, and by the elderly) tend to be family-oriented, the closing three titles to rule (claimed on behalf of the strong, of the prudent [or the law], and of the fortunate) tend to be city-oriented (or at least not predetermined by birth, but rather adapted to circumstances). Central to each set of three titles is one which, in each set, is the most respectful of what we can conveniently call *quality*: in the opening set of three, the title keyed to the wellborn (#2) is central; in the closing set of three, the title keyed to prudence (#6) is central. These two titles to rule (#2 and #6) are similar in that each is tied to what is next to it toward the overall center: Title #2 is tied to Title #3 in that there is no opportunity given to the interlocutor to say anything between #2 and #3; Title #6 is tied to Title #5 in that a comment about Pindar and nature used with respect to Title #5 is drawn upon with respect to Title #6.

To notice these things about what is central to the opening set of three titles and about what is central to the closing set of three titles points up once again the incongruity of that which is dramatically central to the entire array of seven titles, the title claimed by the master over the slave. The relation of master and slave can be seen as a transition from relations rooted in the family or household to relations rooted in the city or the political: slaves can be determined by birth or by law (or other extrinsic factors); slaves are used in households, for the most part, but they come, usually, from outside the household as a result of the city's doings (either with the stronger seizing the weaker, or as the law prescribes, or as fortune dictates). The centrality here of slavery institutions may reflect a troublesome ambiguity with respect to slavery, something that Aristotle too is very much aware of. (See 762E, 966B.)

No doubt, one can see throughout the *Laws* practices and institutions that reflect one or another of these seven titles to rule. Thus, at one point Megillus claims the prerogatives of the elder in speaking before Kleinias does. (712C) Thus, also, strength matters again and again—as it does to this day in, for example, considerations of appropriate male-female relations. (See 944D sq.)

VI

We have already noticed ways in which the parts of the second half of this array of titles to rule are linked. But an even more important way, which has been already referred to, is with respect to the use of *nature* in the second half of the array. Nature is referred to explicitly in connection with Title #5 and Title #6 (having to do, respectively, with titles rooted in strength and with titles rooted in prudence). And the gods are referred to in connection with Title #7, which may be seen as one way of talking about nature (as, for example, in the American Declaration of Independence, with its invocation of "the Laws of Nature and of Nature's God"). (See 682A, 683C, 715E–716A, 875C, 899B.)

A different aspect of nature, in a cruder, more physical sense, may be seen as well in the first three titles to rule keyed to birth (having to do, respectively, with parentage, with family connections, and with age); but nature is not mentioned there, nor is the divine. Once again, we can see that slavery, as the basis of the fourth, or central, title to rule, straddles the two modes of reliance upon nature: for slavery, as we have noticed, may be due to mere birth, or it may be due to an inferiority of some sort, be it with respect to strength or to prudence or to fortune.

The significance of the centrality of slavery to this array, to which we will turn directly, does depend on the integrity of the array as a whole. Testifying to that integrity is the symmetry which we have noticed, to which can be added this observation: the first and last titles to rule (that which is keyed to parenthood and that which is keyed to the fortuitous) are the only ones of the seven titles to rule that make use of pairs, mother and father in the first instance, the divine and fortune in the last instance. We see in the juxtaposition of these extremes a movement from an emphasis upon the family (or the private) to an emphasis upon the city (or the public), a movement that is reflected in the concern expressed at various places in the *Laws* to impose restraints upon such things as private worship, private shrines, and attempts by fathers to disinherit sons. (See 708C, 717B, 908D, 909D sq., 928D sq., 948C–D.)

We have noticed the integrity of the array of titles. If there is something plausible about the principles of order we have observed in this arrangement, what more should be said about that item around which everything appears to turn in this array of titles to rule, that title keyed to the rule of the master over the slave?

VII

We have already observed that the place of honor in this array of seven titles to rule, a place taken here by the rule of master over slave (Title #4), should be reserved, in the best of arrangements, for the rule of the prudent over the ignorant (Title #6). Mr. Strauss noticed some curious correspondences between Title #4 and Title #6: only with respect to these two are the ruled (the slaves and the ignorant, respectively) mentioned before the ruler (the masters and the prudent, respectively); and, it can be said, the true slaves, those most in need of guidance, are the ignorant. It can further be said that Title #4 and Title #6 are in some ways interchangeable, reminding us once again of the extent to which the arrangements made in the *Laws* are indeed compromises with the very best. (Should it also be said that putting the ruled first suggests that at least in these two cases the respective rulers may not be absolutely necessary, that their very existence as rulers depends on the existence of the ruled? That is, if there are no ignorant or slavish people, there is no need for the prudent to rule but only a need for laws or rules by which traffic-regulations-like directions are to be provided, something which *would* be needed even if everyone were prudent.)

Are we not shown, in this placement of the rule of master over slave as central to this array, what rule looks like in its most elementary form? Are we not at least reminded that a reliance upon force with respect to ruling cannot be dispensed with? This is something that Aristotle could very well have learned from the opening pages of the *Republic* itself and made use of in his own intricate discussions of the institution of slavery in the *Politics*, discussions that are often misunderstood by readers today. (See "Slavery and the Constitution: Explorations," 20 *Texas Tech Law Review*, at 691–96 [1989].)

In short, is there not something tending to the tyrannical or despotic about all rule, no matter what form it takes? (See *Laws* 709E, 710D, 712E–713A, 735D–E. See, also, Aristotle, *Nicomachean Ethics* 1177b12–15.) Despotic rule is seen in the rule of men over cattle, sheep, etc.; the same is provided by a god in having daemons rule men. (See 694E–695A. 713C–D.) The best rule, we are told (which is rule by a god, directly or indirectly), is in a way despotic. (See 713E–714A.) But we are told, in the same context, that we give the name *law* to the distribution ordained by intelligence. Thus the despotic, the prudent, and the lawful are tied together. (Consider the use of *despoti*, or bishop, in modern Greek. Consider, also the Athenian Stranger's observation "that no human being would ever become a praiseworthy master unless he has been a slave [of sorts]." [762E])

To recognize that there may be something despotic about all or almost all rule, no matter what form it takes, is not to say that there cannot be more or less despotism, more or less reliance upon genuine consent by those who are ruled. Still, having acknowledged this, it is instructive also to notice—and the Athenian Stranger's arrangement of the titles to rule may point to this—that there is always, or almost always, some compulsion associated with ruling: everyone, or almost everyone, is made, at one time or another, to conduct himself other than he would if left completely to his own devices. Even so, no one is ultimately under compulsion, in that everyone does have the means, by putting an end to life itself, to fend off any force brought to bear against him. (This essay's epigraph with its array of seven causes of misery, taken from Hamlet's most famous soliloquy, is instructive here. Consider, moreover, the compulsion associated with divine law which, for the moment at least, restrained Hamlet from suicide. Compare Shakespeare, *Hamlet*, V, ii, 336: "Absent thee from felicity awhile.")

The centrality of slavery in the Stranger's array of titles to rule reminds us of another enduring political problem, the determination of who are "the people" who are subject to a particular regime. Is not the master-slave relation, more than any of the other six ruler-ruled relations noticed by the Stranger, the one which assumes, in effect, that rulers constitute one people and the ruled another people, if not even another race of beings? What indeed constitutes the people of any particular regime? May there not be something arbitrary, or the workings of chance, at the root of any determination of just who "the people" are, an arbitrariness made most apparent by the institution of slavery?

VIII

The rule of law is apt to moderate the kind of arbitrariness usually found in slavery. For if there is a rule of law, there should be a deference to standards by which all should be bound, standards that can even mean that the children of today's slaves could be tomorrow's masters. If the law should provide for that possibility, then the institution of slavery becomes far less attractive than it might otherwise be for some people. Aristotle's distinctions between natural slavery and conventional slavery should remind people of these difficulties.

In any event, the rule of law that, in practice, is the critical alternative to the rule of the slave-master (an alternative reflected, as we have noticed, in the way Title #4 and Title #6 point to each other), is presented by the Stranger as a kind of embodied reason. Aristotle finds this suggestion congenial in both his *Nicomachean Ethics* and his *Politics;* so does Thomas Aquinas with the inclusion, in his definition of law, of the element, "an ordinance of reason."

That a law is not simply reason ruling is evident when one considers that the law cannot always provide for what would be sensible exceptions. That it is not simply reason ruling is evident also in that the law must, in its very formulation, conform to what may be unfortunate circumstances. Thus, the Athenian Stranger laments upon learning that the site available for the colony to be founded "has the best possible harbor," making a salutary isolation more difficult to secure. (See 704B–C, 949E sq.) Various other provisions made in the course of the discussion reflect an awareness of limitations posed by circumstances, including the fact that the people to be colonized *are* mostly Cretans with definite expectations with respect to property and family relations. (708A sq.) Again and again we are implicitly reminded that this is not the *Republic,* where the constraints of circumstances are assumed to be minimal as the truly wise rule. But even there, one can notice, circumstances are not without their effects, so much so as to lead the Socrates of the *Republic* to anticipate the inevitable deterioration of his city.

IX

Deterioration of the Athenian Stranger's city is also anticipated: "Where the law is itself ruled over and lacks sovereign authority, I see destruction at hand for such a place. But where it is despot over the rulers and the rulers are slaves of the law, then I foresee safety and all the good things which the gods have given to cities." (715D)

We again see here the relation between the central title to rule, that of master (or *despot,* in the Greek) over slave, and the sixth title to rule, that which is embodied in law. The rule of the strong provides a link between these two: the master may tend to see strength in terms of the body, the thoughtful may tend to see strength in terms of understanding and virtue (that is to say, prudence). (See 630B.)

The Athenian Stranger, as he prepares here in Book IV to apply the principles that have been laid down, reminds his companions of the Book

III passage we have been discussing, that in which there are collected the worthy titles to rule. (See 689E sq., 714E sq.) But not everything said earlier is repeated: parents should rule over offspring; the wellborn should rule over those not wellborn. These are the first and second titles to rule. Thereupon the Stranger says, "[T]here were several others, if we remember, and they were obstacles to one another." He skips the third and fourth titles to rule (having to do with age and slavery) and mentions thereafter only the fifth: "One of them was this very thing," rule of the strong, which by this time has been transformed into rule of the most violent. (The earlier use of Pindar is drawn upon: "We asserted, I suppose, that, according to nature' Pindar pushes through and makes just what is most violent,' as he asserts." (714E–715A) This reference, and the one in connection with Title #5 earlier, are the only two uses of Pindar's name in the entire dialogue.)

What, then, has become of the array by this time in Book IV? The prerogatives of parents and the wellborn *are* recalled. The prerogatives of the strong are challenged; that kind of rule easily degenerates, it seems, into rule by the most violent, and this leads to an unsteady regime, which is always on the watch, lest those pushed aside revolt. (In such circumstances, "the laws exist for the sake of some." [715B])

What becomes also of the prerogatives of the elderly and of the fortunate? (We have seen how, in this context, the rule of the slave-master is transformed into the rule of law, with rulers becoming subservient to law-as-embodied-prudence.) That is, only the rule of the elderly and the rule of the fortunate remain to be accounted for in the Stranger's return to his array of titles to rule.

The wise founder would know how to make use of all claims for rule; the Stranger would have this city depend on councils of elders. But is not this with a view to making use of the elders' prudence, rather than with a view to enthroning age as age (which *would* be a kind of piety)? (See 634D–E, 752A, 879C, 950D sq.) In any event, we learn in this context that the law directs how parents should be treated. (717B–D) This reminds us that the elderly, and after awhile parents, do tend to be weak and that they become weaker and weaker. (We notice that the elderly Kleinias seemed to forget, by Book IV, the titles-to-rule passage in Book III. [714D–E] Is this, in part, because he rejected most of those titles? A good memory is vital to the philosopher, as well as a certain openmindedness.) Also, we are obliged to notice that the law has, in practice, a good deal to say about the relations of parents and children, even prescribing who may become, and who are to be considered to be, parents. All this obliges us to notice as well that the law has a good deal to say about the wellborn, especially to the extent that the status and power of good birth depend on recognized familial identifications and on property allocations.

There remain for our consideration here, in this return in Book IV to the worthy titles to rule originally set forth in Book III, the prerogatives of the fortunate or blessed. It is in this context that the Stranger refers to an ancient saying to the effect that the god is the beginning and the end and the middle of all the beings. (We also see that nature is invoked here. See, as well, 624A sq., 642D.) Would not the Stranger have us notice that the divine, insofar as it influences political activity, may be seen in the ordering of things, including such ordering as the Stranger's array of titles to rule? He would have us notice that there are, among these various titles, connections that point both to the need of a founder to take advantage of all these titles and to the need to invest the rule of properly fashioned laws with an almost despotic power. That the prudent have an opportunity to do this may depend on the divine, or chance, or on an ability to point out what is divine about what chance has offered up. (See 709B–C, 757E, 759C, 856E. See, also, 702B–E, 709A–B. See, as well, Plato, *Euthydemus* 272E.)

Much of this dialogue can be seen as a series of inquiries into what each of the titles to rule supplies the prudent founder. The reference in Book IV to "the beginning and the end and the middle of all the beings" (716A), in the context of the recollection of the titles-to-rule passage in Book III, encourages us to believe that it should be fruitful to reflect further upon the array about which we have been privileged on this occasion to make some tentative suggestions. These suggestions might well be made use of and reassessed as one once again reads this dialogue. (Such a reading should include a consideration, especially with respect to the titles-to-rule passage, of the context in which each passage is found. For this Mr. Strauss is, as usual, most helpful.)

X

A few more suggestions, briefly stated, are collected here for future development. We have noticed a certain symmetry to the array of titles to rule: this array can be seen to turn around the central item, with the first and last titles exhibiting various similarities, as do the second and the next-to-last. We have not made explicit the relation of the remaining pair of titles, #3 and #5, rule rooted in age and rule rooted in strength. Cannot these two be seen as mirror images of each other, with each very much in need of the other if there is to be a ruler who is both prudent and vigorous?

The relation of the first and last titles to rule, those of parents and those of the blessed, can here be usefully touched upon as an indication of how this array bears upon the dialogue as a whole. Much is made in the *Laws* of the two mothers of all regimes, monarchy and democracy. (693D sq.) The regimes we still encounter every day exhibit various combinations of these fundamental kinds of regimes. Do we not see, in these two regimes, reflections of the first and last titles to rule in the Stranger's array? Monarchic rule, as could then be seen on the grandest scale in Persia, is rooted in the claims of parents over their children; democratic rule, as could be seen in Athens with its remarkable reliance upon selection of some officers by lot, is dependent on the workings of chance or of divine guidance. (Americans proclaim, on their money and elsewhere, "In God we trust.") That the two fundamental regimes are called "mothers" reminds us of the enduring appeal (as in Aeschylus' *Oresteia*) of the first title to rule. (Compare *Laws* 754A–B.)

Should slavery, the central item in the array of seven titles to rule, be seen, in practice, as an unhappy exemplar of the extreme of monarchic (that is, despotic) rule over those who chance to have been taken captive?

XI

We have noticed that there are two senses of nature evident in the two halves of the Stranger's array: that sense of nature manifested in matters of birth and family relations, and that sense drawn upon in the proper ordering of a city. The former sense identifies nature as original or prepolitical power, the latter sense identifies nature as rational or political power.

Perhaps, also, there is something natural in the movement from the family to the city. This movement is so natural that it may be seen not only in Aristotle's *Politics*, but also in works as diverse as the *Oresteia* and modern anthropology.

Nature may be seen as well in the fact that the various titles to rule do conflict with one another. It is said in our principal passage for this occasion that these "worthy titles to rule . . . are by nature opposed to one another." (690D) Later, they are reported to be "obstacles to one another." (714E) Are they naturally opposed to one another, at least in that sense of *nature* which makes much of what does happen normally? I have suggested that someone who knows what he is doing makes use of all of the titles to rule in founding a regime that adapts itself sensibly to circumstances of time and place.

Similar ambiguities with respect to the significance of nature may be seen in the fifth book of Aristotle's *Nicomachean Ethics,* in the course of the discussion there of what is by nature just.

XII

It is natural to believe that such things as strength or wealth give one a natural title to rule. But we can see, in the uses of *nature* in the Stranger's account of the array of titles to rule, that the more thoughtful recognize that it is natural for the prudent to rule, while the less thoughtful, or "realistic," make more of physical strength.

Physical strength may be seen among citizens in the claims of the many—in the claims, that is, of democrats. A kind of strength may be seen as well in the claims of the few, who make much of wealth. (See 710E, 831C sq., 870 sq., 938B.) The Stranger brings these together, as well as the claim of the wellborn, when he says, "We will not apportion the offices in your city on the basis of someone's wealth or any such possession, be it physical strength or size or descent." (715B–C)

The Stranger recognizes that there *will* be differences in strength, be they with respect to physical prowess or to property or to family ties. He must, as we have noticed, work with people already shaped by the Cretan and other regimes. His efforts are directed at moderating and transforming somewhat the material he is provided. (Compare, in the *Republic,* the requirement that anyone over ten years old be cleared out of the newly constituted city. [540D sq.]) Thus restrictions have to be placed in the *Laws* on property transfers and on accumulations and expenditures of wealth, as may be seen, for example, in the provision that the lavishness of burials must be regulated by lawgivers. (See 632C, 717D–E, 869A sq., 931E, 947B sq., 958D sq.)

Still another way of expressing the need to place restraints upon the claims of families, of the propertied, and of the many, is the insistence that one should never regard one's life as completely one's own. (942A) (Compare Hobbes's permitting, if not even encouraging, cowardice in battle. See *Laws* 707D, 727C–D.)

XIII

Again and again one sees in Plato's *Laws* anticipations of points that Aristotle develops at greater length in his perhaps more systematic investigations of political things. The differences between Plato and Aristotle, as should be evident upon considering the principal passage we have examined on this occasion, may be far less significant than is generally believed. Mr. Strauss observed in his 1959 *Laws* seminar, as he did on other occasions, that Aristotle can always be trusted to get to the heart of Plato's arguments, although he does not necessarily quote literally the Platonic passages he discusses.

In any event, this essay suggests the "Aristotelian" aspects of the Platonic approach to political matters. It attempts to unearth the treasures to be discovered by delving into what Plato does say, working from the literal surface of his argument and noticing how its parts can plausibly be ordered.

4

XENOPHON AND THE NEEDS OF TYRANTS

O reason not the need! Our basest beggars
Are in the poorest thing superfluous.
Allow not nature more than nature needs,
Man's life is cheap as beast's. Thou art a lady:
If only to go warm were gorgeous,
Why, nature needs not what thou gorgeous wear'st,
Which scarcely keeps thee warm. But, for true need—
You heavens, give me that patience, patience I need.
You see me here, you gods, a poor old man,
As full of grief as age, wretched in both.
If it be you that stirs these daughters' hearts
Against their father, fool me not so much
To bear it tamely; touch me with noble anger . . .

KING LEAR to REGAN

I

If both Xenophon and Simonides know what they are doing, then the final speech of Xenophon's *Hiero*, which is Simonides', is something that Simonides has been aiming at all along. We have here perhaps the best dialogue from antiquity after Plato's Socratic dialogues, best in the craft of correlating depiction of character with development of thought.

To suggest that this final speech is something that Simonides has been aiming at all along is not only to suggest that Simonides wanted to say

---

This talk was given at a Staff Seminar of the Basic Program of Liberal Education for Adults, The University of Chicago, Chicago, Illinois, June 1, 1985. (Original title: "On Xenophon's *Hiero*.")

The citations in this essay are to Xenophon, *Hiero*, Marvin Kendrick translation, in Leo Strauss, *On Tyranny* (New York: Free Press of Glencoe, 1963).

The epigraph is taken from Shakespeare, *King Lear*, II, iv, 259–71.

what he does say here, but also that he wanted to say it in the circumstances and in the way he did; that is, he wanted to speak as he did in response to a particular kind of question from Hiero. Otherwise, he could have said much earlier what he says at the end, but that would have been far less effective. In short, he manages things so as to be invited to say what he does.

II

The immediate context of Simonides' final speech is Simonides' advice and Hiero's response to that advice about how a tyrant (that is, a usurper of sovereignty) can avoid being hated, with special attention being paid here to the proper uses of prizes by the ruler, even as he allows others to do his dirty work for him. (One can see why it was that Machiavelli found Xenophon particularly interesting, perhaps the most instructive of the ancient *writers*. Leo Strauss, in turn, has been very instructive with respect to both Xenophon and Machiavelli. Does Xenophon assume that his reader knows that Hiero was very much a patron of the arts?)

Before we consider Hiero's response (10.1) to Simonides' advice about rewarding and punishing, we must go back a little further to see how things arrived at this pass. Simonides, after extended deprecations by Hiero of the life of the tyrant, is moved (indeed, practically obliged) to ask, "But why, Hiero, if being a tyrant is so wretched, and you realize this, do you not rid yourself of so great an evil, and why did no one else ever willingly let a tyranny go, who once acquired it?" (7.11) Hiero explains that the tyrant is unable, at least not without grave risk to his life and property, to relinquish power, especially because he has made so many enemies in seizing power and thereafter in maintaining it.

This in turn leads to Simonides' observing, ". . . I think myself able to teach you that ruling does not at all prevent your being loved . . ." (8.1) It is particularly important for Hiero that this offer be put in terms of being loved, for the love of others (of certain others) seems to be something he particularly cherishes. But the tyrant's circumstances are such that it is far easier for him to know who his enemies are than who his friends are, so much so that the only safe thing for him to do is to regard all, or almost all, of his associates as his enemies. Hiero, it seems, is where he is because of his prowess and success in military campaigns, and so even the city he holds is for him a battleground. Does Hiero mean what he says, about finding the life of a tyrant miserable and yet being unable to give it up? He at least finds it politic to take this approach, considering it safer to proceed thus.

In any event, Hiero hears Simonides out. Simonides' advice *is* hard-headed enough, with respect to how to distribute pleasures and pains, to lead Hiero to ask the question Simonides has been priming him for (10.1), "Well, Simonides, you seem to me to speak well as far as these matters go; but have you anything to say regarding the mercenaries, so that I may not incur hatred because of them? Or do you mean that once a ruler wins friendship he will no longer need a bodyguard at all?" More needs to be said about this, Hiero's last, question, but let us consider first what Simonides says in the speech that ends the dialogue.

III

No, Simonides advises, Hiero should not give up his bodyguard; he will continue to need help (and not only because of his past misconduct, it is indicated, but also because of the possible future misconduct of others). Rather, Hiero's mercenaries should be transformed: they should be turned into what we know as a police force, serving thereby as the bodyguard of all law-abiding citizens in the city. Thus the mercenaries should become agents of justice.

This means, among other things, that Hiero must himself be transformed as well. In effect, he is to become Minister of Justice, using his personal bodyguard for the good of all. I believe that it is only in this context that the term "common good" or its equivalent is used in this dialogue. (11.1) It is here also that there is a repeated use of *rule* and *ruling*, thereby reflecting a shift from the mastering or domination that the tyrant normally resorts to. But a considerable distance (if not even generations) must be traversed along the royal road before a usurper such as Hiero can become a proper king. (See, for example, the last long speech by the King in Shakespeare, *2 Henry IV*, IV, v.)

All this points up the inevitable vulnerability of tyranny, if not because of the danger the tyrant himself is always in "externally" from his subjects as well as from foreigners, then because of the danger he is in "internally" in his inability either to relax or to be satisfied.

IV

This dialogue instructs readers about, or at least reminds them of, the problem of dealing with a tyrant: the tyrant is the epitome of self-aggrandizement so much so that there is something fundamentally self-contradictory what he most wants, real affection or love, along with whatever love provides or serves as an assurance of.

We have been working thus far primarily from the final speeches of this dialogue, speeches that suggest the measures to be taken for the salvaging of the tyrant. But useful as they may be, these measures are, in a sense, mere trappings. The heart of the problem is, of course, in the tyrant's soul—and for a clue to this we turn to the central speech of the dialogue, the speech made by Simonides in response to Hiero's question, on the sated appetites of tyrants, "For why . . . do you see so many contrived dishes served to tyrants: sharp, bitter, sour, and the like?" Simonides says that "they seem to me very unnatural for human beings." (1.22)

This is the first of seven uses in the dialogue of some form of *nature*. Is there not something unnatural in Hiero's way of life—that is, in the use to which he puts the governance of other human beings? One consequence of such unnaturalness is that self-contradictions can be expected to abound. Hiero indicates early in the dialogue that a tyrant wants to be able to thwart "those who [might commit] the injustice" of depriving him of his rule; yet later, he laments he cannot give up such rule. (1.12, 7.12–13) Real unnaturalness or perversity may be seen in that the tyrant must view various virtues as threats. (5.1)

So unnatural is the tyrannical approach, the dialogue seems to suggest, that even the word *natural* can be applied to what would generally be regarded as more or less unnatural relations. Thus, the next two uses of nature are in connection with Hiero's love for the boy Dialochus. (1.31, 1.33) How far the life of the tyrant is from that preferred by nature may be seen in the fourth, or central, use of *nature*, in Hiero's lament that tyrants must be wary of parents, children, and the like. Tyrants must be wary, that is, even of those who "are inclined by nature and compelled by law to love them." (3.9)

Thereafter, there is a resurrection, so to speak, of *nature*. This comes at the hands of Simonides. It begins with his observation that "ambition does not arise naturally either in animals without reason or in all human beings." (7.3) This passage, which has two uses of *nature*, points up the differences between brutes and human beings, differences that are ignored by Hiero's emphasis throughout upon a calculus of pleasures and pains. The final use of *nature* is seen in Simonides' observation that evil doings "arise less naturally in those who are busy." (9.8) (Compare, at the very beginning, the need for leisure for these two men to talk properly. To the extent that Simonides occupies Hiero's leisure time, to that extent he may help keep him out of mischief. The untroubled sleep that Hiero longs for would also serve that end. [See 6.3, 6.9–11.])

Why can Simonides proceed as he does? How is it that he can get

Hiero's ear at all? Hiero, in his first speech, refers to Simonides as "wise." But Hiero had been preceded by Xenophon himself, who refer to Simonides simply as "the poet." We may have here, then, an apparently wise man who appears in the form of a poet. As such he can cater, as he seems to do from the outset, to that balancing of pleasures and pains on which Hiero so much depends. Furthermore, Hiero expects from Simonides "a finer view of most matters" than he expects from the multitude (2.5). This may acknowledge Simonides' poetic gifts.

V

Simonides, it seems, would prefer not to appear to be moved ultimately by honor. (7.1) That is, he does not depend on another's opinion of his goodness, which is what a dependence on honor, in its best sense, connotes. Still, he was known in antiquity for having carried off more than fifty prizes in his poetical career.

However useful and even encouraging of virtue honor may be in a well-ordered city, Hiero's circumstances are such that he cannot trust what others say to him: even genuine acclaim, or genuine affection, must always be suspect for him. Hiero may not "believe" everything he says; he considers his circumstances to be such that he can rarely if ever reveal his true sentiments. We again see that the life of the tyrant is that of the beleaguered soldier who must make certain of friends as well as of enemies, if only by regarding just about everyone as hostile or at least as a threat.

Consider here one implication of the suggestion, made early in the dialogue, that every lover is a potential tyrant. (1.26) Does not the true lover really desire the best, whereas the tyrant is driven by his circumstances to destroy or at least suspect the best and to rely upon the worst? (5.1–2)

This is still another reminder of the inevitable vulnerability of tyrants, even so self-confident and evidently cosmopolitan a man as Hiero.

VI

One has to proceed carefully in dealing with a man such as Hiero. First, as we have seen, there is the need to catch him at leisure. Simonides can more easily divert himself by going to see "the spectacles" than can Hiero. (1.11–13) Perhaps Hiero is for Simonides one of the sights, especially since Hiero had evidently made something of a name for himself in the Greek world.

Then there is the problem of not seeming foolish to Hiero and thereby losing his respect and attention. Here we must return to the key question, a test question of sorts, put by Hiero to Simonides in the next-to-last speech of the dialogue: the question about whether Hiero should give up his mercenaries. How Simonides answers this question determines whether Hiero regards him as usefully sensible or as hopelessly naive. Simonides is sensible enough to know that he must disguise whatever "idealism" he may have in talking with this man; he in effect tells him to give up his mercenaries, but he does so, as we have seen, by speaking of transformation rather than of abolition.

He had to proceed carefully for still another reason: one does not lightly offend a tyrant while one is still within his reach, or if one wants to continue to enjoy his patronage. Hiero himself recognizes that no one is sure of anything given him by a tyrant until he is beyond the tyrant's control. (6.13)

Simonides must lead Hiero into the subject by stages, even beginning with a suggestion of Hiero's superiority with respect to wisdom. Hence Simonides does not "attack" Hiero, but allows Hiero to "attack" himself while Simonides "defends" him. That is, Simonides does not permit Hiero to get into an open adversary relation with *him*.

VII

The dialogue opens on the theme that some know certain important things better than others. Hiero is "big enough" to question the proposition that he should know anything better than does Simonides, even though (it soon becomes evident) he all along believes he does know many things better, indeed the most important things.

It is evident as well that Hiero does not intend to share all that he does know, especially about those things which might strengthen a political rival. But, one suspects, Hiero reveals more than he is aware of. For example, he reveals that he does not understand the things he believes he does understand.

Again and again, Hiero exposes himself as a creature of desires, including a desire for a recognition, in the form of "love," that would make him seem, and perhaps even permit him to believe he is, better (or at least other) than he is. The desiring element in him seems to be thrust forward in Simonides' opening question, "Would you be willing to tell me something, Hiero, which you probably know better than I?" The *will* of Hiero seems to be repeatedly addressed by Simonides in this dialogue.

Is not willing particularly vivid in battle and in other contests? One such contest is that of the chariot race at the great games of the Greeks, something that Simonides in his final speech can take up and can discourage Hiero from entering with teams of his own. I find it startling that Simonides can say, "[I]t is not fitting for a man who is a tyrant even to compete against private men." (11.6) I say *startling* because we do have odes from Pindar and from Bracchylides celebrating victories of Hiero's chariots in various Greek games. (Bracchylides is Simonides' nephew.) But we do not have any ode for Hiero from the great Simonides himself, even though we do have Simonidean victory odes for others. (See, also, Plato, *Protagoras* 346B.)

Did Hiero put up with all this and even resort to self-deprecation in order to obtain from Simonides a highly prized ode in the event of victory in the games to which Hiero planned to send chariots? Had Simonides learned of Hiero's plans? Would the promise of an ode from Simonides have helped legitimate for Hiero what he proposed to do? Had Simonides himself *not* been at leisure to talk with Hiero until he had learned what he needed to know about Hiero? Simonides teaches Hiero and us how prizes should be distributed, perhaps even showing that one skillful and sometimes safe way of punishing and of instructing is to withhold certain prizes while seeming to give others (in the form of praise). One way or another, Simonides does manage to suggest a radical critique of Hiero's way of life. Perhaps we are to understand that the true victory ode that Hiero needs would follow upon reform of his life. (Perhaps, also, we should read this dialogue as Xenophon's commentary upon the famous victory odes [subsequently?] commissioned by Hiero, odes that may themselves quietly indicate reservations about the much-ballyhooed career of Hiero.)

No assent from Hiero is recorded at the end of this dialogue, nor is there a dissent. But Hiero *is* silenced, perhaps because he knows he has been rebuked by Simonides for what he had his heart set upon doing with both his chariots and his city. Conversion of Hiero would probably take much more soul-searching than is recorded here. Longstanding unnatural desires are not easily ministered to or transformed. (In this sense, perhaps, the *Hiero* is a prelude to Xenophon's *Cyropaedia*.)

One can well wonder whether the eminently practical Simonides is liberally rewarded by Hiero for displaying his wares before him. One way to answer this question is to determine not whether Hiero "appreciates" what Simonides has and has not said, but rather how the ambitious Hiero would appear here and elsewhere if Simonides should not be given a reward befitting true royalty. Simonides, we are told elsewhere, lived the last decade of his very long life (556–468 B.C.) in the court of Hiero at Syracuse, dying the year before his notorious host did. Do we have in this dialogue still another attempt by Xenophon to illuminate the "impractical" career of his stay-at-home master, Socrates?

5

MAIMONIDES ON REVELATION AND REASON

Since we see that every polis *is some kind of association and that every association is constituted for the sake of some good (for all men do everything they do for the sake of what seems to be good), it is clear that while all associations aim at some good, it is the one which is most authoritative of all and comprehends all the others that does so in the highest degree and aims at the good which is most authoritative of all: and this is the one called* polis, *the political association.*

ARISTOTLE

I

Aristotle, as he prepares to bring his *Nicomachean Ethics* to its close, takes up the following question (1179a33–1179b4, in the Rackham translation):

If then we have sufficiently discussed in their outlines the subjects of Happiness and Virtue in its various forms, and also Friendship and Pleasure, may we assume that the investigation we proposed is now complete? Perhaps however, as we maintain, in the practical sciences the end is not to attain a theoretic knowledge of the various subjects, but rather to carry out our theories in action. If so, to know what virtue is not enough; we must endeavor to

---

This talk was given at the Annual Meeting, Midwest Political Science Association, Chicago, Illinois, April 20, 1979. (Original title: "The Bearing of Principles and Ends on Political Action: Maimonides's 'Politics' as a Case in Point.") It was dedicated to the memory of Simon Kaplan (1893–1979), Tutor Emeritus, St. John's College, Annapolis, Maryland. See, also, the headnote for Essay No. 19, below.

The principal citations in this essay are to Maimonides, *The Guide of the Perplexed*, Shlomo Pines translation (Chicago: University of Chicago Press, 1963), and to Maimonides, *Ethical Writings*, Raymond L. Weiss and Charles E. Butterworth translations (New York: New York University Press, 1975).

The epigraph is taken from Aristotle, *Politics* 1252a1–8 (Laurence Berns translation).

possess and to practise it, or in some other manner actually ourselves to become good.

"Now," he goes on to say (1179b4–18),

> if discourses on ethics were sufficient in themselves to make men virtuous, "large fees and many" (as Theognis says) "would they win," quite rightly, and to provide such discourses would be all that is wanted. But as it is, we see that although theories have power to stimulate and encourage generous youths, and, given an inborn nobility of character and a genuine love of what is noble, can make them susceptible to the influence of virtue, yet they are powerless to stimulate [the many to perfect gentlemanship]. For it is the nature of the many to be amenable to fear but not to a sense of honor, and to abstain from evil not because of its baseness but because of the penalties it entails. . . . To dislodge by argument habits long firmly rooted in their characters is difficult if not impossible.

He then argues that the law is needed to help make men virtuous, summing up the next stage in his argument in this way (1180a15–29):

> If, as has been said, in order to be good a man must have been properly educated and trained, and must subsequently continue to follow virtuous habits of life, and to do nothing base whether voluntarily or involuntarily, then this will be secured if men's lives are regulated by a certain intelligence, and by a right system, invested with [strength]. Now paternal authority has not the power to compel obedience, nor indeed, speaking generally, has the authority of any individual unless he be a king or the like; but law on the other hand is a rule, emanating from a certain wisdom and intelligence, that has compulsory force. Men are hated when they thwart people's inclinations, even though they do so rightly, whereas law can enjoin virtuous conduct without being invidious. But Sparta appears to be the only or almost the only [*polis*] in which the lawgiver has paid attention to the nurture and exercises of the citizens; in most [*poleis*] such matters have been entirely neglected, and every man lives as he likes, in Cyclops fashion "laying down the law for children and for spouse."

The conclusion of Aristotle's *Ethics* serves for him as the introduction to his *Politics*.

Aristotle would have us examine regimes with a view to the kinds of people they produce and preserve. Every decent regime makes civilization possible. What civilization is may be universal, including a respect for and a promotion of various moral virtues. Civilization also takes for granted and promotes, one way or another, the development and use of human reason and hence the intellectual virtues. Regimes do vary, of course, depending in part on circumstances; some come closer than others to attainment of a fully civilized way of life.

II

Sparta was particularly remarkable for Aristotle in its attention to "the nurture and exercises" of its citizens. What such attention means and how it bears upon an understanding of our own regime can perhaps be usefully seen by examining still another regime, that of Israel.

There, political action was manifested in an elaborate set of laws and obviously promoted a definite ethical development. What *ethics* means, and aims at, remains to be seen. Moses Maimonides's *Ethical Writings,* conveniently collected in a New York University Press edition, can be instructive for our purposes, as can a University of Chicago Press edition of his *The Guide of the Perplexed.* I mention now something to which I will return, that the ethical-political development of Judaism can be plausibly said to culminate in the greatest "political action," the emergence of the Messianic age. (This age reminds one, at least in Maimonides's presentation, of Plato's philosopher-king.)

An examination of the Mosaic code can be particularly instructive, since it seems to be rooted less in nature and more in revelation than the regimes elaborated by Aristotle, Plato, and Xenophon. Even so, Maimonides argues, the rationale for many, if not most, of the laws can be worked out by the unassisted reason; the laws are certainly not arbitrary or irrational. By considering them, one can notice the bearing that principles and ends have upon the political actions that these laws represent.

Consider, therefore, how Maimonides addresses himself to the question of the sense to be made of or discovered in the hundreds of commandments facing the Jew (*Ethical Writings,* p. 138; *Guide,* III, 26):

> Just as there is disagreement among the men of speculation among the adherents of Law whether [God's] works, may He be exalted, are consequent upon wisdom or upon the will alone without being intended toward any end at all, there is also the same disagreement among them regarding our laws, which He has given to us. Thus there are people who do not seek for them any cause at all, saying that all the laws are consequent upon the will alone. There are also people who say that every commandment and prohibition in these laws is consequent upon wisdom and aims at some end, and that all the laws have causes and were given in view of some utility. It is, however, the doctrine of all of us—both of the multitude and of the elite—that all the laws have a cause, though we are ignorant of the causes for some of them and we do not know the manner in which they conform to wisdom.

Maimonides goes on here to say the following about various of the commandments, such as those concerning the wearing of certain "mixed fabrics," the cooking of "meat in milk," or the "sending of the goat" (see *Deuteronomy* 22: 11, *Exodus* 23: 19, *Leviticus* 16: 10, 21) *(Ethical Writings,* pp. 138–39):

> They are not believed by the multitude of the sages to be things for which there is no cause at all and for which one must not seek an end. For this would lead, according to what we have explained, to their being considered as frivolous actions. On the contrary, the multitude of the sages believe that there indubitably is a cause for them—I mean to say a useful end—but that it is hidden from us either because of the incapacity of our intellects or the deficiency of our knowledge. Consequently there is, in their opinion, a cause for all the commandments; I mean to say that any particular commandment or prohibition has a useful end. In the case of some of them, it is clear to us in what way they are useful—as in the case of the prohibition of killing and stealing. In the case of others, their utility is not clear—as in the case of the interdiction of the first products [of trees] and of [sowing] the vineyard with diverse seeds.

Maimonides devotes two dozen chapters (see *Guide*, p. xv) to a discussion of the various commandments, of which he says *(Guide*, III, 26; p. 508),

> What everyone endowed with a sound intellect ought to believe on this subject is what I shall set forth to you: The generalities of the commandments necessarily have a cause and have been given because of a certain utility; their details are that in regard to which it was said of the commandments that they were given merely for the sake of commanding something.

He concedes with respect to whether the causes of certain particulars are knowable *(Guide*, III, 26; p. 509),

> [A]ll those who occupy themselves with finding causes for something of these particulars are stricken with a prolonged madness in the course of which they do not put an end to an incongruity, but rather increase the number of incongruities. Those who imagine that a cause may be found for suchlike things are as far from truth as those who imagine that the generalities of a commandment are not designed with a view to some real utility.

He goes on *(Guide*, III, 26; pp. 509–10):

> The constant statements of [the Sages] to the effect that there are causes for all the commandments, as well as the opinion that the causes were known to

Solomon, have in view the utility of a given commandment in a general way, not an examination of its particulars.

This being so, I have seen fit to divide the six hundred and thirteen commandments into a number of classes, every one of which comprises a number of commandments belonging to one kind or akin in meaning. I shall inform you of the cause of every one of these classes, and I shall show their utility about which there can be no doubt and to which there can be no objection. Then I shall return to each of the commandments comprised in the class in question and I shall explain to you the cause of it, so that only very few commandments will remain whose cause has not been clear to me up to now. Some of the particulars of, and conditions for, some of the commandments have also become clear to me, and it is possible to give their causes.

Some of the commandments, for example, were designed to eliminate practices connected with idolatry. This, Maimonides explains, is the reason for the prohibition of the wearing of certain "mingled stuff" (*Guide,* III, 37; p. 544):

> [F]or this too was a usage of these [idolatrous] priests, as they put together in their garments vegetal and animal substances bearing at the same time a seal made out of some mineral . . .

(See, on the prohibition against eating "meat [boiled] in milk," *Guide,* III, 48; p. 599.) Often, it seems, those who were subjected to these prohibitions did not understand their purposes. Nevertheless, Maimonides explains (*Guide,* III, 32; p. 527):

> Through this divine ruse it came about that the memory of idolatry was effaced and that the grandest and true foundation of our belief— namely, the existence and oneness of the deity—-was firmly established, while at the same time the souls had no feeling of repugnance and were not repelled because of the abolition of modes of worship to which they were accustomed and than which no other mode of worship was known at that time.

But he immediately recognizes difficulties *(Guide,* III, 32; pp. 527-28):

> I know that on thinking about this at first your soul will necessarily have a feeling of repugnance toward this notion and will feel aggrieved because of it; and you will ask me in your heart and say to me: How is it possible that none of the commandments, prohibitions, and great actions—which are very precisely set forth and prescribed for fixed seasons—should be intended for its own sake, but for the sake of something else, as if this were a ruse invented for our benefit by God in order to achieve His first intention? What was there

to prevent Him, may He be exalted, from giving us a Law in accordance with His first intention and from procuring us the capacity to accept this? In this way there would have been no need for the things that you consider to be due to a second intention. Hear then the reply to your question that will put an end to this sickness in your heart and reveal to you the true reality of that to which I have drawn your attention. It is to the effect that the text of the Torah tells a quite similar story, namely, in its dictum: "God led them not by the way of the land of the Philistines, although it was near, and so on. But God led the people about, by way of the wilderness of the Red Sea." [*Exodus* 13: 17–18] Just as God perplexed them in anticipation of what their bodies were naturally incapable of bearing—turning them away from the high road toward which they had been going, toward another road so that the first intention should be achieved—so did He in anticipation of what the soul is naturally incapable of receiving, prescribe the laws that we have mentioned so that the first intention should be achieved, namely, the apprehension of Him, may He be exalted, and the rejection of idolatry. For just as it is not in the nature of man that, after having been brought up in slavish service occupied with clay, bricks, and similar things, he should all of a sudden wash off from his hands the dirt deriving from them and proceed immediately to fight against "the children of Anak," [see *Numbers* 13: 28] so is it also not in his nature that, after having been brought up upon very many modes of worship and of customary practices, which the souls find so agreeable that they become as it were a primary notion [or, intelligible], he should abandon them all of a sudden. And just as the deity used a gracious ruse in causing them to wander perplexedly in the desert until their souls became courageous—it being well known that life in the desert and lack of comforts for the body necessarily develop courage whereas the opposite circumstances necessarily develop cowardice—and until, moreover, people were born who were not accustomed to humiliation and servitude—all this having been brought about by [or, through the instrumentality of] Moses our Master by means of divine commandments . . .—so did this group of laws derive from a divine grace, so that they should be left with the kind of practices to which they were accustomed and so that consequently the belief, which constitutes the first intention, should be validated in them.

One is reminded, upon considering this extended explanation by Maimonides, of the recourse in Plato's *Republic* to certain stories about the causes of the natural differences among men. (*Republic* 414B sq.) One notices also, in what Maimonides says here and elsewhere about the way the commandments are devised, an assumption about "the nature of man" (and hence about the nature of law-making). That is, he looks to nature in accounting for the "political action" that the Law is in the service of. (See, for example, *Guide*, pp. 382, 571.) Maimonides leads us to believe that Moses was aware of the limitations and possibilities inherent in the nature of things. (See, for an account of Moses consistent with this view of him, Machiavelli, *The Prince*, chap. 6.) This approach to Revelation puts the miraculous in its proper ("natural"?) place, the place to which the thoughtfully reverent man believes God to have assigned it (*Guide*, III, 32; pp. 528–29):

> As for your question: What was there to prevent God from giving us a Law in accordance with His first intention and from procuring us the capacity to accept the capacity to accept this?—you lay yourself open to an inference from this second question. For one may say to you: What was there to prevent God from making them march "by the way of the land of the Philistines" and procuring them the capacity to engage in wars so that there should be no need for this roundabout way with "the pillar of cloud by day and the pillar of fire by night?" [*Exodus* 13: 22] Also you lay yourself open to a third question as an inference, a question regarding the reason for the detailing of promises and threats with regard to the whole Law. One may say to you: Inasmuch as God's first intention and His will are that we should believe in this Law and that we should perform the actions prescribed by it, why did He not procure us the capacity always to accept this intention and to act in accordance with it, instead of using a ruse with regard to us, declaring that He will procure us benefits if we obey Him and will take vengeance on us if we disobey Him and performing in deed all these acts of vengeance? For this too is a ruse used by Him with regard to us in order to achieve His first intention with respect to us. What was there to prevent Him from causing the inclination to accomplish the acts of obedience willed by Him and to avoid the acts of disobedience abhorred by Him, to be a natural disposition fixed in us?

> There is one and the same general answer to all these three questions and to all the others that belong to the same class: Though all miracles change the nature of some individual being, God does not change at all the nature of human individuals by means of miracles. Because of this great principle it says: "O that they had such an heart as this, and so on." [*Deuteronomy* 5: 26] It is because of this that there are commandments and prohibitions, rewards and punishments. We have already explained this fundamental principle by giving its proofs in a number of passages in our compilations. We do not say this because we believe that the changing of the nature of any human individual is difficult for Him, may He be exalted. Rather is it possible and fully within [the capacity of God]. But according to the foundations of the Law, of the Torah, He has never willed to do it, nor shall He ever will it. For if it were His will that the nature of any human individual should be changed because of what He wills, may He be exalted, wills from that individual, sending of prophets and all giving of a Law would have been useless.

Maimonides can reduce the Biblical commandments to the following purposes (*Guide*, III, 51; p. 524):

[E]very commandment from among these six hundred and thirteen commandments exists either with a view to communicating a correct opinion, or to putting an end to an unhealthy opinion, or to communicating a rule of justice, or to warding off an injustice, or to endowing men with a noble moral quality, or to warning them against an evil moral quality. Thus all [the commandments] are bound up with three things: opinions, moral qualities, and political civic actions.

He later elaborates upon this summary in this fashion (*Guide*, III, 49; p. 612):

In the case of most of the statutes whose reason is hidden from us, everything serves to keep people away from idolatry. The fact that there are particulars the reason for which is hidden from me and the utility of which I do not understand, is due to the circumstance that things known by hearsay are not like things that one has seen. Hence the extent of my knowledge of the ways of the Sabians [pagans] drawn from books is not comparable to the knowledge of one who saw their practices with his eyes; this is even more the case since these opinions have disappeared two thousand years ago or even before that. If we knew the particulars of those practices and heard details concerning those opinions, we would become clear regarding the wisdom manifested in the details of the practices prescribed in the commandments concerning the sacrifices and the forms of uncleanness and other matters whose reason cannot, to my mind, be easily grasped. For I for one do not doubt that all this was intended to efface those untrue opinions from the mind and to abolish those useless practices, which brought about a waste of lives "in vain and futile things." [See *Isaiah* 49: 4.] Those opinions turned away human thought from concern with the conception of an intelligible and from useful actions, as our prophets have explained to us, and have said: "They walked after vain things that do not profit." [*Jeremiah* 2: 8. See also I *Samuel* 12: 21.] Jeremiah says: "Surely our fathers have inherited lies, vanity, and things wherein there is no profit." [*Jeremiah* 16: 19.] Consider how great was the extent of this corruption and whether or not it was fitting to spend one's efforts on putting an end to this. Most of the commandments serve, therefore, as we have made clear, to put an end to these opinions and to lighten the great and oppressive burdens, the toil and the fatigue, that those people imposed upon themselves in their cult. Accordingly every commandment or prohibition of the Law whose reason is hidden from you constitutes a cure for one of those diseases, which today—thank God—we do not know any more. This is what should be believed by one who is endowed with perfection and knows the true meaning of His dictum, may He be exalted: "I said not unto the seed of Jacob, Seek ye Me for nothing." [*Isaiah* 45: 19.]

It seems that it "should be believed by one who is endowed with perfection" that all the commandments are useful. Indeed, it seems from the be-

ginning of the long passage I have just quoted that it serves to keep people
away from idolatry if they are taught *not* to disregard commandments
"whose reason is hidden from [them]." Is there not a kind of idolatry in an
insistence upon private judgment, in the determination not to adhere to
any regimen that one does not know the precise reason for?

Even so, we are informed by the prophet, "[God] said not unto the seed
of Jacob, Seek ye Me for nothing." Inquiry, it seems, is encouraged, provided it is in the right spirit. We are assured by Maimonides that we can
think about what is aimed at by the Law. This is to be contrasted with the
fashionable opinion today that only the means to our ends, not the ends
themselves, can truly be thought about. We are further assured by Maimonides, even when it is the Bible which provides him the material with
which he works, that *nature* is critical in any thinking we may do about
our ends. (See, for example, *Guide*, pp. 201, 213–14, 226, 230–31, 329,
345f, 382.)

III

Nature, it seems, directs us to the conception of "an intelligible" and to
useful actions. These two major ends, in the light of which so many of the
commandments make sense, should themselves be examined with a view
to seeing what, if anything, makes sense of them in turn. To try to "make
sense of them" means, at the least, to try to understand what "useful actions" and "the conception of an intelligible" mean.

First, the "useful actions." There are actions prescribed by the Law
which are, it seems, desired for themselves as well as for their consequences. Other actions seem to be prescribed primarily, if not exclusively,
for their consequences, including the consequence of the effect on opinion.
Consider, for example, Maimonides's discussion of continence and temperance. He recognizes that, according to the philosophers (*Ethical Writings*, pp. 78–79),

> the virtuous man is better and more perfect than the continent man. How-
> ever, they [the philosophers] said that the continent man can take the place of
> the virtuous man in most things, even though he is necessarily lower in rank
> due to his desire to do something bad. Even though he does not do it, his
> strong desire for it is a bad state of the soul.

But, according to Maimonides, his investigation of the Jewish sages disclosed that, according to them (*Ethical Writings*, p. 79),

someone who craves and strongly desires transgressions is more virtuous and perfect than someone who does not crave them and suffers no pain in abstaining from them. They even said that the more virtuous and perfect an individual is, the stronger is both his craving for transgressions and his pain in abstaining from them.

He must reconcile the two approaches, that of the Jewish sages with that of the philosophers. It is critical to Maimonides's understanding of things that the two approaches can and should be reconciled. One does not arrive at Maimonides's insistence upon an attempt at reconciliation unless one, as an observant adherent to the faith of one's fathers, appreciates the demands that philosophy makes on the mind of man. (See *Guide,* pp. xiv–xx, xliv; also, p. xlvi.)

Consider how Maimonides's reconciliation of the teachings of the philosophers and of the Jewish sages is presented (*Ethical Writings,* pp. 79–80):

If the external meaning of the two accounts [about continence and temperance] is understood superficially, the two views contradict one another. However, that is not the case; rather, both of them are true, and there is no conflict between them at all. For the bad things to which the philosophers referred when they said that someone who does not desire them is more virtuous than someone who does desire them and restrains himself—these are the things generally accepted by all the people as bad, such as murder, theft, robbery, fraud, harming an innocent man, repaying a benefactor with evil, degrading parents, and things like these. They are the laws about which the [Jewish] sages, peace be upon them, said, "If they were not written down, they would deserve to be written down." . . . There is no doubt that the soul which craves and strongly desires any of them is defective and that the virtuous soul neither longs for any of these bad things at all nor suffers pain from the prohibition against them.

When the [Jewish] sages said that the continent man is more virtuous and his reward is greater, they had in mind the traditional laws. This is correct because if it were not for the Law, they would not be bad at all. Therefore they said that a man needs to let his soul remain attracted to them and not place any obstacle before them other than the Law. Consider their wisdom, peace be upon them, and the examples they used. For [Rabban Shimon ben Gamliel] did not say, "Let a man not say: 'I do not want to kill, I do not want to steal, I do not want to lie, but I want to—but what shall I do?'" On the contrary, he mentioned only traditional matters: "meat with milk, mixed fabric, and illicit sexual unions." . . .

Thus, from everything we have said it has become clear what the transgressions are for which, if a man has no desire, he is more virtuous than someone who desires them but restrains himself, and which [transgressions] are the opposite.

To deny oneself something which is not in itself bad—and which may even be inherently good—can be, it seems, good for one. (Even when the Messianic age comes, we are told, the dietary laws will not be changed. [*Ethical Writings*, p. 181]) We have all observed this kind of useful restraint on an *ad hoc* basis. But what is to be made of systematic self-deprivation? Is it to be seen as a form of sacrifice or at least as an indication of submissiveness and of allegiance with respect to the faith (and hence to the memory) of one's fathers? Certainly it can provide a certain discipline, inducing one to put first things first.

The "useful actions" prescribed by the Law can be said to have diverse uses. The moral virtues, of the kind Aristotle describes, are promoted; the health of the body, and probably long life, are served; and social relations are advanced. Critical to Maimonides's understanding of things, and to our understanding of his understanding, is the connection between the moral virtues and social relations. It sometimes seems that the moral virtues do not have the independent status for him that they sometimes seem to have for someone such as Aristotle. (Is Maimonides more like Plato or perhaps Xenophon in this respect?) Consider also that a commendable piety can consist in some instances of an *extreme*, whereas for Aristotle the mean is to be systematically sought for. (Piety itself warrants no special discussion in the *Nicomachean Ethics*.)

The character and status of piety point to still another "use" for the "useful actions" prescribed by the Law. The traditionally pious man could well regard this use as decisive, worth far more than all the others to which one, including Maimonides, might look. I refer to the *holiness* that the Law contemplates: useful actions shape not only one's conduct, but also, and perhaps even more, one's opinions and attitudes.

The root of the Hebrew word for *holy* refers, I am told, to separateness. The Law in its many particulars induces, in the observant Jew, separation from various bodily things, from many everyday concerns, and from other peoples. (Must a holy people be, at the least, a separate people?) The primary purpose of the Mosaic regimen seems to be to develop and maintain holiness, a special relation with God independent of worldly consequences, whatever the earthly rewards may tend to be for the disciplined submissiveness that is urged. Thus holiness seems to be intimately related to obedience to God's commandments, without any ulterior purpose in view. The attempted sacrifice of Isaac provides the model for such obedience. To obey thus is to worship God with all one's heart and might. An obligation to preserve the Jewish people can often be seen as a limitation upon compliance with the Law. But the length to which Abraham was evidently prepared to go suggests that holiness does not necessarily draw a line this side even of the effective removal from this earth of the very people that seemed to depend on Isaac and his seed. (See *Guide*, III, 24; p. 500: "the most extraordinary thing that could happen in the world"; p. 501: "he holds this beloved son as little, gives up all his hopes regarding him".) Consider how different the story would appear, at least to the Jews, if (as the Muslims say) Ishmael had been designated for sacrifice rather than Isaac.

If holiness, as traditionally understood, is to be decisive, it can have a profound effect on all "political action." If it is not decisive, but rather instrumental and a contribution to a still higher purpose, then is not its character changed in a vital respect? It is here that Maimonides may separate himself from traditional Judaism. By briefly examining that separation we can consider further the bearing of principles and ends on political action.

IV

Maimonides tells us, in Chapter 27 of Part III of *The Guide of the Perplexed* (*Guide*, p. 510),

> The Law as a whole aims at two things: the welfare of the soul and the welfare of the body. As for the welfare of the soul, it consists in the multitude's acquiring correct opinions corresponding to their respective capacity. Therefore some of them [namely, the opinions] are set forth explicitly and some of them are set forth in parables. For it is not within the nature of the common multitude that its capacity should suffice for apprehending that subject matter as it is. As for the welfare of the body, it comes about by the improvement of their ways of living one with another. This is achieved through two things. One of them is the abolition of their wronging each other. This is tantamount to every individual among the people not being permitted to act according to his will and up to the limits of his power, but being forced to do that which is useful to the whole. The second thing consists in the acquisition by every human individual of moral qualities that are useful for life in society so that the affairs of the city may be ordered.

Much of what I have said here may be summed up in this passage from Maimonides. Illustrative of how the moral qualities of individuals can be affected by commandments with respect to rituals is an earlier passage (in Chapter 26, at pages 508–9, of the *Guide*):

> The generalities of the commandments necessarily have a cause and have

been given because of a certain utility; their details are that in regard to which it was said of the commandments that they were given merely for the sake of commanding something. For instance the killing of animals because of the necessity of having good food is manifestly useful, as we shall make clear. . . . As necessity occasions the eating of animals, the commandment [on how they are to be killed] was intended to bring about the easiest death in an easy manner. For beheading would only be possible with the help of a sword or something similar, whereas a throat can be cut with anything. In order that death should come about more easily, the condition was imposed that the knife should be sharp.

I return now to Chapter 27 of Part III of the *Guide*, where Maimonides discusses the two aims of the Law, the welfare of the soul and the welfare of the body (pp. 510–11):

Know that as between these two aims, one is indubitably greater in nobility, namely, the welfare of the soul—I mean the procuring of correct opinions— while the second aim—I mean the welfare of the body—is prior in nature and time. The latter aim consists in the governance of the city and the well-being of the states of all its people according to their capacity. This second aim is the more certain one, and it is the one regarding which every effort has been made precisely to expound it and all its particulars. For the first aim can only be achieved after achieving this second one. For it has already been demon- strated that man has two perfections: a first perfection, which is the perfec- tion of the body, and an ultimate perfection, which is the perfection of the soul. The first perfection consists in being healthy and in the very best bodily state, and this is only possible through his finding the things necessary for him whenever he seeks them. These are his food and all the other things needed for the governance of his body, such as a shelter, bathing, and so forth. This cannot be achieved in any way by one isolated individual For an individual can only attain all this through a political association, it being already known that man is political by nature.

It is this repeated movement between the most mundane and the most elevated which sometimes seems to characterize Maimonidean as well as Biblical thought. This is seen, for example, in Maimonides's "Laws Con- cerning Character Traits" (*Ethical Writings*, p. 41):

A disciple of wise men is not permitted to live in any city that does not have these ten things: a physician, a surgeon, a bathhouse, a bathroom, a fixed source of water such as a river or spring, a synagogue, a teacher of children, a scribe, a collector of charity, and a court that can punish with lashes and imprisonment.

(See, also, *Guide*, pp. 598–99.) Maimonides evidently altered the order of the items, as well as some of the items themselves, from the source he drew upon here. By so doing, did he not choose to make central the low and the high (the fixed source of water and the synagogue), one contributing directly to the perfection of the body, the other contributing directly to the perfection of the soul?

I again draw upon the passage from which I have been quoting, in which Maimonides now discusses the perfection of the soul (*Guide*, III, 27; p. 511):

> His ultimate perfection is to become rational in actu, I mean to have an intellect in actu; this would consist in his knowing everything concerning all the beings that it is within the capacity of man to know in accordance with his ultimate perfection. It is clear that to this ultimate perfection there do not belong either actions or moral qualities and that it consists only of opinions toward which speculation has led and that investigation has rendered compulsory. It is also clear that this noble and ultimate perfection can only be achieved after the first perfection has been achieved. For a man cannot represent to himself an intelligible even when taught to understand it and all the more cannot become aware of it of his own accord, if he is in pain or is very hungry or is thirsty or is hot or is very cold. But once the first perfection has been achieved it is possible to achieve the ultimate, which is indubitably more noble and is the only cause of permanent preservation.

But, as we have seen at the outset of this passage, the extent to which one can achieve the ultimate perfection, the welfare of one's soul, depends on one's capacity. It seems to be indicated that something of that ultimate perfection is available to a man of ordinary capacity if he adheres in his everyday life to the commandments of the Torah. Is such worship a kind of "knowing" of that which can be known? Such observances should be helpful in many ways. Maimonides's comments on the Messianic age emphasize that the leisure then available would be devoted "to learn wisdom and to perform the commandments," "to become wise in the Torah and to be occupied with it." (*Ethical Writings*, p. 170) Both right action and wisdom follow upon faithfulness to the Torah (*Ethical Writings*, p. 169):

> The Holy One, blessed be He, gave us the Torah; this is the tree of life. Everyone who does everything prescribed therein and knows it completely and correctly, merits the life of the world-to-come. His merit depends upon how great his actions and his wisdom are. [God] promised us in the Torah that if we follow it with joy and a glad soul and we continually meditate on its wisdom, He will remove from us everything preventing us from following it—such as sickness, war, hunger, and so forth—and He will cause an over-

flow toward us of all the good things that strengthen us in following the entire Torah—such as satiety, peace, and an abundance of silver and gold.

In such a passage Maimonides seems to come closer to the traditional Jewish concern with health, holiness, and the righteous community, something to which all can contribute and in which all can participate as "citizens." But he does not leave it at that, for it is again and again evident that he sees the resulting long life, serenity, and leisure to be ultimately desirable as means to the "ultimate perfection," that of becoming "rational in action, [which] consist[s] in [a man's] knowing everything concerning all the beings that it is within the capacity of man to know . . ." The Messianic age, which is like the ordinary age in its reliance on nature, is best for providing the necessary leisure and so forth. (See *Ethical Writings*, pp. 23, 165f.) An ultimate preference for intellectual perfection—for what the philosophers call the contemplative life—may be seen in what Maimonides says about harnessing all one's activities, *including one's transgressions of the Law,* to the service of the pursuit of knowledge of the most important things (*Ethical Writings*, pp. 77–78):

If a man sets this notion [i.e., knowledge of God] as his goal, he will discontinue many of his actions and greatly diminish his conversation. For someone who adheres to this goal will not be moved to decorate walls with gold or to put a gold border on his garment—unless he intends thereby to give delight to his soul for the sake of its health and to drive sickness from it, so that it will be clear and pure to receive the sciences. . . . For the soul becomes weary and the mind dull by continuous reflection upon difficult matters, just as the body becomes exhausted from undertaking toilsome occupations until it relaxes and rests and returns to equilibrium. . . .

Know that this level is very lofty and is difficult to reach. Only a few perceive it and then, only after very great discipline. So if a man happens to exist in this condition, I would not say that he is inferior to the prophets. I refer to a man who directs all the powers of his soul solely toward God, may He be exalted; who does not perform an important or trivial action nor utter a word unless that action or that word leads to virtue or to something leading to virtue; and who reflects and deliberates upon every action and motion, sees whether it leads to that goal or not, and then does it. This is what the Exalted requires that we make as our purpose when He says: "And you shall love the Lord your God with all your heart and with all your soul." [*Deuteronomy* 6: 5] He means, set the same goal for all the parts of your soul, namely, "to love the Lord your God." The prophets, peace be upon them, have also urged this purpose. [Solomon] said: "In all your ways know Him." [*Proverbs* 3: 6] The sages explained this and said: "Even with a transgression;" i.e., you should make your goal the truth when doing such a thing, even if from a certain point of view you commit a transgression. The sages, peace be upon them, summarized this whole notion in the briefest possible words and encompassed the meaning with utmost perfection, so that if you were to consider the brevity of those words—how they express the greatness and magnificence of this notion in its entirety, about which so many works have been composed without being able to grasp it—then you would know it was undoubtedly spoken by divine power. This is what they say in one of their commands in this tractate: "Let all your deeds be for the sake of Heaven."

"Even with a transgression"? A wise man happens to be in a city for a rare visit at the very time that an annual celebration honors one's parents' marriage. What should the scholarly son do, honor his parents or take advantage of a fleeting opportunity to learn from the wise man? (Consider, for example, *Matthew* 4:21–22.) Or is Maimonides thinking of even more serious questions, such as the need to consider whether certain prohibitions of the Law would, if adhered to, permanently keep one from learning what could be learned, and not just about the taste of pork? One is reminded of the discussion of equity in the *Nicomachean Ethics*. (See *Ethical Writings*, p. 15.)

There is more than a reminder of Aristotle in what Maimonides says of the contemplative life as the ultimate perfection of the human being. Notice in the passage just drawn upon the suggestion, "[I]f a man happens to exist in this condition [that of the fully rational man], I would not say that he is inferior to the prophets." This can make one wonder what Maimonides takes revelation to mean. (See, for example, *Guide*, pp. xxxvii, 360f, 620; *Ethical Writings*, pp. 14, 60, 73–74, 620.) Notice also that a particularly sage remark could be regarded by him as having been "undoubtedly spoken by divine power." The Aristotelian position in these matters is set forth in a passage from the *Nicomachean Ethics* before the one drawn upon at the beginning of this essay. We have heard, in what I have already taken from Maimonides, several echoes from the following passage (*Nicomachean Ethics* 1178b8–1179a31):

The following considerations also will show that perfect happiness is some form of contemplative activity. The gods, as we conceive them, enjoy supreme felicity and happiness. But what sort of actions can we attribute to them? Just actions? But will it not seem ridiculous to think of them as making contracts, restoring deposits and the like? Then brave actions—enduring terrors and running risks for the nobility of so doing? Or liberal actions? But to whom will they give? Besides, it would be absurd to suppose that they actually have a coinage or currency of some sort! And temperate actions—what will these mean in their case? Surely it would be derogatory to praise them for not having evil desires! If we go through the list we shall find that all forms of virtuous conduct seem trifling and unworthy of the gods. Yet nevertheless they have always been conceived as, at all events, living, and therefore living actively, for we cannot suppose they are always asleep like Endymion. But for a living being, if we eliminate action, and a *fortiori* creative action, what remains save contemplation? It follows that the activity of God, which is transcendent in blessedness, is the activity of contemplation; and therefore among human activities that which is most akin to the divine activity of contemplation will be the greatest source of happiness. . . .

But the philosopher being a man will also need external well-being, since man's nature is not self-sufficient for the activity of contemplation, but he must also have bodily health and a supply of food and other requirements. Yet if supreme blessedness is not possible without external goods, it must not be supposed that happiness will demand many or great possessions; for or great possessions; for self-sufficiency does not depend on excessive abundance, nor does moral conduct, and it is possible to perform noble deeds even without being ruler of land and sea: one can do virtuous acts with quite moderate resources. . . .

And it seems likely that the man who pursues intellectual activity, and who cultivates his intellect and keeps that in the best condition, is also the man most beloved of the gods. For if, as is generally believed, the gods exercise some superintendence over human affairs, then it will be reasonable to suppose that they take pleasure in that part of man which is best and most akin to themselves, namely the intellect, and that they recompense with their favours those men who esteem and honor this most, because these care for the things dear to themselves, and act rightly and nobly. Now it is clear that all these attributes belong most of all to the wise man. He therefore is most beloved by the gods; and if so, he is naturally most happy.

Evidently Maimonides, like Aristotle before him, believes the worth of the contemplative life to be considerable. In emphasizing the contemplative life as he does, however, he seems to transform the Biblical and rabbinic traditions, and to do so especially in the light of what he has learned from the Greek philosophical teaching. Before Maimonides, it seems, Jewish thinkers would have tended to say that the primary end of man is to lead a holy life in accordance with God's will as manifested in the Law. That is, he should be righteous, should be observant, and should study the Torah. But to "study the Torah" cannot be equated, we are told, with the contemplative life. (See, for example, *Guide*, p. xliv.) Maimonides, confronted by the claims of philosophy and evidently alert to the threat it poses to traditional piety, and himself profoundly respectful of that rational element which seems to distinguish man from the animals (see, for example, *Guide*, pp. 23–24), can be understood to have searched the tradition out of which he came, and to which he owed a considerable debt, for what it indicated about the contemplative life. The traditional emphasis upon "knowing God" seemed to provide support for the proposition that serious inquiry and contemplation were called for. (See, for example, *Guide*, pp. 111f, 122, 124f, 138–39, 144–45, 154, 157; *Ethical Writings*, pp. 7, 14, 35, 75, 80f, 83, 94, 109, 177.) Support seemed to be provided as well by *Deuteronomy* 4: 6, which Maimonides, and Leo Strauss after him, was fond of quoting:

> Observe therefore and do them [the commandments]; for this is your wisdom and your understanding in the sight of the peoples, that, when they hear all these statutes, they shall say, "Surely this great nation is a wise and understanding people."

(See, for example, *Guide*, p. 276.)

The question remains, of course, whether what Maimonides found to have always been "meant" and "intended" by the prophets, especially by Moses, is indeed so. This is the kind of question with which students of American constitutional law are familiar. For Maimonides, just as for the American constitutionalist, the principles and ends settled upon very much affect the "political action" one advances. They can also affect the enduring vitality of a regime. Does not every regime depend more on generally accepted opinions than on any understanding available to the few, those few whose obvious skepticism about generally accepted opinions can undermine a regime's sometimes fragile sense of legitimacy and of purpose? (See, for example, *Ethical Writings*, p. 129.)

V

However much Maimonides identifies the ultimate perfection aimed at by the Law with the philosophic way of life, he does separate himself from philosophers in two key respects: he says that the world had a beginning in time; he is dedicated to the preservation of his people. Is the latter position one that honor obliges him to take? Or should Judaism be regarded as a unique benefactor of all mankind? (See, for example, *Ethical Writings*, pp. 116, 180.) It has been suggested that the secrets of the Torah are "the fountainhead of ancient Greek and, consequently, also of Arabian wisdom." (Leo Strauss, *Persecution and the Art of Writing* [1952], p. 50, quoting from Salo W. Baron's "The Historical Outlook of Maimonides", [*Proceedings of the American Academy for Jewish Research*, VI (1934–35)], with a further reference to Chapter 71 of Part III of the *Guide*.)

As for the former position, that the world had a beginning in time, Maimonides insists that the philosophers have not demonstrated that the world has no beginning. This is, he argues, no more than a belief on their part—albeit a belief that does seem in the spirit of a dependence on a comprehensive system of nature?—and so there can be no philosophic objection to believing that the world had a beginning in time. (See, for example, *Guide*, pp. 180, 265, 282f, 294, 298, 308, 314f, 320–22, 327f, 333, 359–60, 460, 515–16, 565; also, pp. liv, 166–71.) To believe thus is to retain one's access, *as a Jew*, to one's people. But such a belief can be held with a minimum of beliefs in subsequent miracles. (The Messiah, for instance, does not depend on miracles.) This approach to miracles and to the beginning of the world prompts one to wonder what Maimonides considers to be the status of revelation, what he considers to be the nature of prophecy, and what he suggests the answer to be to that all-embracing question, "What is God?"

All, or almost all, opinions can be questioned in the Maimonidean scheme of things. That is, all can be usefully investigated. Thus, as we have seen, he suggests it is sickness to assume that there are no reasons for the various commandments laid down by God, that they are due only to His will, not to His wisdom. He further suggests (*Guide*, III, 25; p. 504),

> As for those who say that no end is intended in any of the acts of God, they were led to this by necessity, namely, by considering the totality of what exists in accordance with their opinion. For they say: What is the end of the existence of the world as a whole? Hence they assert of necessity what everyone asserts who maintains that the world] was created in time: He willed it so, there being no other cause. Thereupon they proceed to apply this assertion to all the particular things in the world.

But, he also indicates, it may be madness to seek an explanation for all the details of the various commandments. (See *Guide*, pp. 65–86.)

As for why the world exists as a whole, Maimonides has this to say (*Guide*, III, 25; pp. 505–6):

> Know that the majority of the false imaginings that call forth perplexity in the quest for the end of the existence of the world as a whole or the end of every part of it have as their root an error of man about himself and his imagining that all that exists because of himself alone, as well as ignorance of the nature of inferior matter and ignorance of what is primarily intended—namely the bringing into being of everything whose existence is possible, existence being indubitably a good. It is because of this error and of the ignorance of these two notions that the doubts and the perplexity arise, so that some of God's actions are imagined to be frivolous, others futile, and other vain.

The obvious goodness of existence is something affirmed by Aristotle as well. Is it not implicitly affirmed also by the pious man's total submission to the will of God? Furthermore, is not a concern for the nature of existence at the heart of the general philosophical inquiry, which can be seen by some as turning around the question, "What is being?" (See *Guide*, pp. 440, 448f.)

In this and other ways, then, Maimonides can be said to reconcile reason and revelation. (Compare *Guide*, p. xiv.) The prophet, he indicates, has the intellectual virtues and most of the moral virtues. And is not philosophy a kind of "worship"? Still, philosophic wisdom cannot simply be equated with religion-based righteousness, which makes more of both ritual and the moral virtues than can philosophy. The preeminent place given by Maimonides to the development of human reason is reflected in his judgment that it is far better for a man to commit in public what men generally would regard as the most shameful actions than to allow himself to become drunk and hence, among other consequences, to deprive himself of the use of his reason, if only temporarily. (See *Guide*, p. 434. See, also, *Ethical Writings*, p. 42.) This curious ranking suggests the limits of Maimonides's attempt to reconcile single-minded philosophy and conventions-minded religion.

VI

Still another reconciliation of natural "opponents" may be found in Maimonides's bringing together of philosophy and the city. This reconciliation is seen in his teachings about the Messianic age. (There is no conflict, in principle, between religion and the city, at least if religion is seen as primarily ethical-political in its interest. Not all can do, or understand, everything. But all, or almost all, can contribute to the well-being of this world; a community needs all kinds of people.)

Plato's *Apology* reminds us of the threat philosophy and the city can seem to pose to one another. We have seen Maimonides argue, in effecting his reconciliation, that the city can be understood to be ultimately in the service of philosophy. Is to see political life this way, just as to see moral virtue as ultimately in the service of intellectual virtue, to deprive it of some of its dignity, to see it not as it is seen by those most devoted to it?

The Messiah is presented as the peak of political judgment to be found in a mortal being. Maimonides's doctrine of the Messiah points to the ultimate in earthly ends. (See *Ethical Writings*, p. 165f.) The Messiah is prudence incarnate, enjoying an opportunity to use his skills in the right circumstances. (There is nothing automatic or miraculous about such prudence taking over or sustaining itself. Xenophon can be instructive here.) To concern oneself with wisdom and justice is to be concerned with that which makes the Messiah possible, with that which the Messiah represents or is the ultimate practitioner of. Maimonides can be considered to have done for the diverse prophetic doctrines about the Messiah what Shakespeare does, from the perspective of classical thought, for the otherworldly Christian message: Maimonides invests those doctrines with an immediate practical significance keyed to life here and now. To place the emphasis upon the Messiah, rather than upon the state (as Hobbes does, for example), is to avoid the kind of idolatry seen in the *Leviathan's* designation of the state as a "mortal god."

The Messiah has no "supernatural" powers. (His *use*, however, of the Holy Spirit invites investigation.) What the Messiah does is the result of superlative human wisdom. (See *Ethical Writings*, p. 24.) Nor is his regime necessarily eternal. (See *Guide*, p. xlii.) But it can be inferred from what Maimonides says that the Messianic age can appear again and again once it has run its course. (For example, David can be referred to as "the first messiah," whatever that may mean. See *Ethical Writings*, pp. 172–73.) Is not the Messianic implied by the nature of human aspirations and of prudence? Does Maimonides use Plato's *Republic*, or its equivalent, in interpreting and using the Messianic teaching and possibilities? That is, does Maimonides do what Plato, Aristotle, or Xenophon would have advised thoughtful men to do in circumstances such as those in which Maimonides finds himself as a Jew, circumstances that have his scattered yet still gifted people threatened, even more than they had been, by the combined influence of Islam, Christianity, and resurgent philosophy?

The reconciliation suggested by Maimonides between philosophy and the city by recourse to the Messianic age—an age in which men will truly be liberated from everyday concerns to pursue (to the limits of their capacities) the contemplative life—this reconciliation points up the continuing tension between philosophy and the city in almost all circumstances. The Jew of philosophical inclinations, who retains his identification and hence allegiance to his fathers' way, recognizes that that tension (reinforced by the widespread and deep disabilities of the Jews at the hands of those who always hate them) can periodically take the form of ruthless violence directed against Jews, which he must use all his prudence to anticipate and avoid. Here too it can be seen that a clear sense of one's principles and ends can very much bear on the political action upon which one relies.

VII

The bearing of all this on a study of our own regime should be evident. We have considered how principles and ends shape political action and how tradition can be interpreted, and reinterpreted, to serve ever-changing necessities.

It should also be evident how such shaping and such interpretation can distort key principles. One must take care, that is, not to discard what is vital to a way of life. Vitality may depend on certain widely held opinions of the community, not on the highest understanding of a few members of the community. Certainly the few must take care not to exhibit gratuitous disbelief in that which the community as a whole cherishes.

The few and the many share an interest in civilization and in the conditions for the full development of that reason which all human beings share, one way or another. (Thus, philosophy depends to some extent on a general respect for various of the moral virtues.) *Civilization* is to be distinguished, however, from dedication to unlimited progress or to any other kind of hedonism. It depends on a respect both for works of the mind and for that multitude who make it possible for a few to develop and preserve the best that human minds are capable of as they examine what nature teaches. (Does the curious Maimonidean term *multitude of the sages* bring the few and the many together in one critical respect? See, for example, the passages I have quoted from *Ethical Writings*, pp. 138–39, *Guide*, III, 26, and *Guide*, III, 27.)

Among the useful works of the mind are those bodies of plausible opinions on which decent regimes depend. One of those opinions is that it is possible for men both to know what is and to know what is good. Without the possibility of such knowing at the core of human life, not only as a guide but also as an end, an abyss opens up before mankind. Life then seems to have no meaning and the goodness of existence is lost sight of. Here too principles very much bear upon political action. The conviction that life is meaningless can do much to rob life of its vitality, that vitality reflected in the opening lines of Aristotle's *Nicomachean Ethics* (1094a1–3):

Every art and every investigation, and likewise every practical pursuit or undertaking, seems to aim at some good: hence it has been well said that the good is that at which all things aim.

B.

The
American Way

6.

SCIENCE AND POLITICS, OLD AND NEW

For know well, men of Athens, if I had long ago attempted to be politically active, I would long ago have perished, and I would have benefited neither you nor myself.

SOCRATES

I

I consider here republican government, its precedents and presuppositions, and how it, along with the rule of law, looks today. I will be drawing for my discussion primarily upon two authors, one ancient and one modern. The ancient, Marcus Tullius Cicero, can serve as the spokesman of Rome and ancient republicanism. The modern, René Descartes, can serve as a spokesman of a worldwide republic dedicated to the welfare of mankind and rooted in the science of recent centuries. My discussion probes the relations between politics and science.

Cicero and Descartes are from the First Century B.C. and the Seventeenth Century A.D., respectively. I will be referring to two other authors

---

This talk was given at Memphis State University, Memphis, Tennessee, November 29, 1979. (Sponsor: Political Science Department. Original title: "Cicero and Descartes: Politics and Science.")

The principal citations in this essay are to Cicero, *Republic*, as published in *On the Commonwealth*, George Holland Sabine and Stanley Barney Smith translation (Indianapolis: Library of Liberal Arts, Bobbs-Merrill Company, 1976); to Cicero, *On Moral Duties*, as published in *The Basic Works of Cicero*, George B. Gardner translation (New York: Modern Library, 1957); to Rene Descartes, *Discourse on Method*, Laurence J. Lafleur translation (Indianapolis: Library of Liberal Arts, Bobbs-Merrill Company, 1950); to Alfred North Whitehead, *Science and the Modern World* (New York: The Free Press, 1967); and to Whitehead, *The Aims of Education* (New York: The Free Press, 1967). See, on *truly knowing oneself* as the condition for all other knowing, Plato, *Phaedrus* 229D–230A, *Theaetetus* 158B sq., 160B–161E, 170C–171D, 173C–174B, 185D–E, 191C sq.

The epigraph is taken from Plato, *The Apology of Socrates* 31D (Thomas G. West and Grace Starry West translation).

as well, Plato of the Fourth Century B.C. and Alfred North Whitehead, the distinguished mathematician and historian of science in our century. These latter references supplement what I will have to say about Cicero and Descartes and about how our understanding of science or cosmology, as well as our understanding of how and what we know, affects our political and legal discourse and our sense of life itself and its meaning. My remarks are in large part about ancients and moderns, about the relation of science to politics, and about the relation of public life to private.

What I say here about Cicero and Descartes does not present the most refined view of either. Rather, it suffices for my immediate purposes to settle for a rough, even popular, version of what these two men said. I especially want to emphasize the patriotism of one and the self-consciousness of the other as the starting places for what they did. It is not decisive here whether these men meant precisely what I attribute to them. The names may not matter but they are convenient and, I have indicated, it is not implausible to attribute the positions I will be discussing to these particular men. The appearance of things is of significance in these matters, whatever the true positions of such men might be.

Modern thought, very much influenced as it is by modern scientific discoveries, can be usefully approached by us through Whitehead. He reminds us in an "anatomy of some scientific ideas" that Occam's Razor is critical for scientific progress. William Occam announced, *Entia non multiplicanda praeter necessitatem*. That is to say, assumptions should be kept to the minimum in any attempt to explain any phenomena. Or, as Whitehead develops Occam's rule, "[E]very use of hypothetical entities diminishes the claim of scientific reasoning to be the necessary outcome of a harmony between thought and sense-presentation." Thus, Whitehead concludes, "As hypothesis increases, necessity diminishes." (*The Aims of Education*, p. 145)

The implications of Occam's rule have long been appreciated; Occam can be considered to have enunciated in his Fourteenth-Century formulation what had been known since antiquity. But what may be characteristic of modern thought is the extent to which what is hypothesized is reduced in the interest of enlarging necessity—that is, in the interest of expanding the realm of certainty. The origins of this tendency I will be touching upon shortly. But first, consider the form the tendency takes in Whitehead, who reports, "The material universe is largely a concept of the imagination which rests on a slender basis of direct sense-presentation." He adds, "But none the less it [presumably, the material universe] is a fact; for it is a fact that actually we imagine it. Thus it is actual in our consciousness just as sense-presentation is actual there." (*The Aims of Education*, p. 133)

One Whitehead sentence here is critical to our purposes: "The material universe is largely a concept of the imagination which rests on a slender basis of direct sense-presentation." Minute sense-presentations, of which we can become almost as certain as we can of anything, suffice to serve as the basis of the most elaborate concepts of the imagination. Two illustrations of this should suffice here: one is taken from the starry heavens above, the other from what happens within each of us.

Take what happens within us: the slightest scrapings of bodily tissue or minute traces of blood can be used as the basis for extensive descriptions ("concept[s] of the imagination"?) about the body as a whole, about its vital characteristics, about its present condition, and about its likely future. Diagnoses, upon which life-and-death decisions rest, routinely proceed from "a slender basis of direct sense-presentation." There can be something uncanny in the obvious ability of the competent pathologist to say so much based on what seems, at least to the layman, so little.

Or take what happens as we look into the heavens: the slightest glimmer of light (or, in recent years, the minutest particles of dust or the faintest radiation or sound) can be used as the basis for extensive speculations about vast galaxies—about what they have been doing for immense ages past, about their present condition, and about the cataclysmic changes that they will undergo in the ages ahead. It is not generally appreciated how little in the way of direct sense-presentation is available as the foundation of the accounts we accept of gigantic stars and of tremendous movements that are incredibly far away in time and in space. These particles of dust, signs of radioactivity, levels of background sound, and glimmers of light, which permit observation of minute gravitational aberrations, are part of the foundation of such accounts. That foundation also includes what has been done for decades, if not centuries, with other such observations—what has been done, for example, by measuring the intensity of light and by analyzing spectra of light. That foundation includes as well the principles and methods that are brought to bear upon whatever observations we can make with our senses: principles and methods which others, who have reported their own observations and made their own conjectures on the basis of them, are believed to have relied upon in their time.

It has long been recognized not only that there is but a slender basis of direct sense-presentation upon which our opinions about the observable world rest and that assumptions or hypotheses should be minimized if there is to be rigorous investigation, but also that a very little can lead to everything. For this last reminder we have such authority as that of Socrates in Plato's *Meno* (81D):

For since the whole of nature is of common origin and the soul has learned all things, there is nothing to prevent one who recollects (which mankind calls learning) one thing only, from finding out all other things, if he is courageous and does not tire of seeking.

But the understanding in antiquity of such propositions differs significantly from the modern opinion with respect to these matters, especially in that more seems to have been made by the ancients of the natural apprehension of things as the basis of inquiry and understanding. The soul seems to have been conceived of (or, better still, observed?) *not* as a blank page upon which experience manifests itself but rather as something which by its very nature apprehends, or at least is equipped if not even disposed to apprehend, many enduring things, especially those things known as ideas. But we can put aside for the moment these distinctions between ancients and moderns while we consider other distinctions of more immediate use to our inquiry here.

What may be distinctive to modern science are (1) the use of mathematics and of the method generated by mathematics and mathematized physics, and (2) the self-centeredness of the inquirer as somehow the basis of certainty. The use of mathematics and of methods somehow modeled on mathematics we can disregard here, partly because it can be considered secondary if not even derivative from the other feature of modern science I have just mentioned. Besides, there have been significant developments in modern science—for example, with respect to evolution—which did not directly depend for their emergence on any considerable use of mathematics. It is the self-centeredness of the modern inquiry with which we shall principally be concerned here, all with a view to what can usefully be said in this context by way of contrast about Cicero, the Roman republic, and their successors.

II

The slender basis in direct sense-presentation of much of modern thought consists ultimately not of observations of the kind I have touched upon, such as pieces of tissue or traces of light, but consists rather of the determined if not obsessive observation of one's self, of one's own consciousness. That is, the entrance to reality is quite narrow, consisting of the psyche's self-awareness. It is on this deliberate self-awareness that certainty depends and from which alone, it has been argued, that great scientific and technological achievements can proceed with confidence.

With these comments we return to Descartes, one of the founders of the modern scientific development (at least, of one approach in that development). He can be usefully compared to Cicero. Each thinker has something solid and enduring upon which to build. Cicero's point of departure seems to be Rome: its traditions, laws, and forms. Rome is an enduring community, encompassing the dead, the living, and those yet to be born. His approach is emphatically civic-minded in its tone and interests.

Descartes's point of departure, on the other hand, is the self: the sense one has of one's consciousness, the assurance one has that however uncertain all one's sense perceptions may be, at least one's awareness of one's own existence is decisively reliable. That bare minimum provides not only something upon which to build, but also a standard of what it means that something is known. Everything else is questionable, among the things men believe themselves to observe, but this certitude about one's own being opens a reliable way to extensive, if not unprecedented, investigations and constructions.

True, the Cartesian approach may have seemed in its beginning to sacrifice the scope and grandeur of that ground upon which Cicero and his predecessors had built their edifices. But even greater things can be built up, once quite humble but secure foundations grounded in individual self-awareness are laid down. One might wonder whether this decisive awareness of one's self, of one's own existence, does not itself depend on an extensive and deep shaping of the soul by some community. One can even argue that Descartes's wide-ranging doubt and his consequent recourse to a consciousness of self as the basis of certainty themselves presuppose ideas and methods that rest upon assumptions and even certitudes somehow or other generally available to man, as if by intuition. Still, the stress placed by Descartes is not upon either intuition or institutions, both of which can be understood to draw upon nature. Rather, stress is placed upon the individual as the point of departure, and this initial orientation (anticipated perhaps by St. Augustine) continues to influence inquiries and projects since Descartes.

Much is made by Descartes of the isolation to which he had had recourse in order to work out his understanding of things. Not only was he physically alone during the period of his original insights, but he was ignored by other people both before and during those productive days. That is, he was out of his native country and hence mostly on his own. A virtual abandonment of the political community was necessary before he could search out and exploit that which he could know and do. The contrast here with Cicero is striking, insofar as Cicero believed that the best in a man depends for its proper development on immersion in serious political life and a response to it. Even Socrates, who avoided an active political career, evidently believed he needed a city such as Athens in order to become what he became. He argues in Plato's *Republic* that philosophers would be routinely produced by the best city and would thereafter be obliged to be in its service.

Insofar as Descartes relies explicitly upon some community, it is not primarily the political community, an association usually defined by blood and history, to which he looks, but rather, it seems, an intellectual community, an association defined by professional and technological interests. National boundaries are in principle irrelevant as men work upon common projects, publishing their results and pooling their discoveries to advance the power of mankind to vanquish ignorance, disease, and poverty. The science and related technology generated by such organized self-centeredness permit us to grasp, or at least to manipulate, the world for the benefit of mankind. It should at once be acknowledged that modern science *has* been most productive; its accomplishments have obviously been spectacular. Although the technology made possible by modern science has been put in the service of the political order (for example, in strengthening rule at home and in waging war abroad), science nevertheless tends to undermine the pre-scientific opinions and attachments on which the political order usually depends. (Francis Bacon, another modern founder, is in several critical respects different from Descartes, not least in his much greater respect for the political life of a country. See, for example, his *New Atlantis*.)

The deepest loyalty of intellectuals (and here we are talking *not* about the rare philosopher but about a significant number, albeit a minority, in each country) tends to reach beyond national borders. This can be seen in Descartes's own career: his wanderings are important to what he thought. He is a modern Odysseus, but with neither the Ithaca nor the Penelope by which Odysseus can be said always to have taken his bearings. Descartes prefers to be left alone, in order to be able to build from the most personal (and hence most reliable?) grasp of things. And so he can settle in Holland— he makes a point of this—where one is left pretty much to oneself. Whitehead can speak of "the wide tolerance of the Dutch Republic." He can also speak of "a Dutch Republic which would not ask questions."[*Adventures of Ideas*, pp. 50, 59])

This displacement of the citizen by the private man (the man who, not altogether unlike Socrates, looks primarily to his personal gratification and to associations of his own choosing) is a radical departure from that dedicated dependence on Rome celebrated in Cicero's *Republic*. Perhaps even more radical a departure from the orientation of the citizen is the insistence by Descartes that things, including institutions, built pursuant to the design of one mind are superior to things built by many hands over time. (See *Discourse on Method*, pp. 7–8.) In principle, that which a single mind would design should be like that which another equally adept mind would design. It does not matter whether the truly thinking mind, possible only if the foundations have been laid as Descartes has discovered, is Roman, French, or Dutch: that which happens to be one's own, by birth or by residence, should not matter when people come to discover and to do that which reason dictates.

III

This is Descartes's—or, we can say, the moderns'—rationalistic approach. The Roman, on the other hand, makes much more of his own country. But it is argued in Cicero's *Republic* that Rome would not be as good as it is if it had been built in a day. Thus it is said (II, 33; p. 185):

> In the very nature of things . . . it was inevitable that the people, once they were freed from the kings, should demand for themselves a greater degree of authority. This enlargement of their power they attained, after a brief interval of about sixteen years . . . There was perhaps no element of design in this change, but there is a principle of growth inherent in public affairs which often overrides design.

Not that anything goes. To say that there was no fixed design in the development of Roman institutions is not to say that there are no principles by which adaptations in those institutions were made or can be judged. To consider Rome the best, as do various of Cicero's characters, is to invoke standards in accordance with which such a judgment can be made. This passage about the enlargement of the power of the people continues in these words by Cicero's Scipio (II, 35; p. 185):

> For you should master the principle which I laid down at the beginning: Unless there is in the state such an equal distribution of legal rights, functions, and duties that the magistrates possess an adequate power, the council of the chief men an adequate influence, and the people an adequate measure of liberty, the balance of the commonwealth cannot be preserved unchanged.

We can see here that Rome, not the self, is in the center of things. It rests upon big assumptions and sweeping opinions. We also notice that opinions about the gods and the cosmos are intimately linked to Rome. The gods as well as the family are to a considerable extent determined by the city and are in its service. This is another way of saying that politics is the master art: it dictates and relies upon, among other things, proper respect by citizens for the gods of the city.

I say *politics* rather than *political philosophy* since it seems to be insisted upon in this dialogue and elsewhere in Cicero that statesmanship is ultimately preferable to philosophy as a way of life even for the most gifted. Political philosophy (as it may be seen in Plato, Aristotle, and even Xenophon) looks at political life from a perspective that sees statesmanship as ultimately secondary, however important it is both for life and for philosophy itself.

Cicero is, in a way, a man with one foot in the ancient world, one in the modern, at least to this extent: he is somewhat divergent from Descartes and closer to Plato's Socrates in that he makes a good deal of political life as vital to the conditions for the contemplative life. Whatever the status of the contemplative life, Cicero agrees with Plato that the political life is better than the ordinary (that is, non-philosophical) private life.

On the other hand, Cicero can be considered allied with Descartes, as against Plato's Socrates, in his emphasis upon the importance of the practical life over the contemplative life. They are allied as well in the assumption that the best is available to men if they should be properly instructed as to what it is and if they should be determined to have it.

But Cicero differs from Descartes (and perhaps from Socrates) as to the true starting place for the enterprises that men should be drawn to. Cicero builds not from the self and the small, but from the public and the grand. *The* public and the grand is Rome: not only is it *our* city, but it is the best regime. It is argued by Scipio that not monarchy, as some of the Greeks believed, but rather a mixed regime of the kind found in Rome is truly the best. (See Cicero, *Republic*, I, 34; pp. 139–40.) Dedicated statesmen, who somehow knew what they were doing, have been in large part responsible for the emergence in Rome of the best (or at least a very good) regime. (The emergence of the best has not depended, as the Socrates of Plato's *Republic* thought, upon the philosopher-king; nor has the emergence of the best been as much affected by chance as Socrates thought in the *Republic*. Whether the Roman understanding of what the best is depends, as much as does Socrates' understanding, on nature is a question we must set aside for the moment.)

The Roman republic of Scipio and his companions is eminently self-confident, as well as self-centered. One *can* expect, when such a city is at the heart of things for the more intelligent men in the community, that the emphasis will be placed on statesmanship rather than on the contemplative life. Platonic philosophy can be criticized as neglectful of duties:

those who, in the philosophical tradition, mind their own business can even be regarded as "traitors to society." (Cicero, *On Moral Duties*, I, 9; p. 14) One sees here the kind of civic resentment of philosophic aloofness that helped to get Socrates killed in Athens. The human end emphasized is moral and political virtue, not truth-seeking. Insofar as man does desire to learn the truth about things, the city provides sufficient matter for serious thought, or so it seems as one listens to Cicero's characters discussing the wonderful things Rome has done and is.

Their respect for Rome is reinforced by the opinion that God is pleased most of all by well-ruled states. (Cicero, *Republic*, VI, 13; p. 259) Their opinions about what the divine is and how it manifests itself seem to be in large part generated by the city. It is under the auspices of the city that the most authoritative opinions about the divine develop—under the auspices of a city that is favored by the gods (as can be seen in its remarkable accomplishments?) and that somehow or other senses what is called for in the conduct of men with respect to both the gods and other men.

IV

Let us return to the self-confidence so critical to Rome. Vital to that self-confidence was the publicly held opinion that a city *can* conduct itself without injustice. Scipio insists that a community is not a true commonwealth unless it conducts itself justly. (Cicero, *Republic*, pp. 195–96) He and his colleagues are shown to believe that Rome is such a community. This is consistent, it seems, with the frequent wars in which Rome was engaged; it is also insisted by patriotic Romans that such wars were either defensive in character or in fulfillment of sworn duties toward allies. In this way, Rome conquered the world—almost against her will, one might say.

Is such faith in the justice of Rome warranted? Was it a self-deception, and if so, was it a salutary one? What did Cicero himself believe the truth to be about these matters? It is difficult to say, especially since Cicero's personal character is curious in several respects. He was, from the perspective of a Socrates, to say nothing of a Kant, unduly concerned about death and about his circumstances. This can be seen again and again in Plutarch's account of Cicero's life. It could even be suggested about him that his desire for glory washed out the tinctures of philosophy in his soul.

The status of glory among the Romans seems to have been such as to have promoted what we now know as Caesarism. Ambition is stressed, and a few could be depended on now and then to try to go "all the way."

Even so, much was made of the sense of honor and of respect for oaths. (Cicero, *On Moral Duties*, p. 9f.) But did the very success of Rome, exposing her best citizens to varied customs all over the world, feed ambition even as it undermined the provincialism which made for that old-fashioned piety and patriotism on which the sense of honor and the respect for oaths depended? Did not Sparta have a similar experience, but more slowly?

Still, Rome can claim a considerable achievement. Whitehead said, "The Middle Ages were always haunted by the ghost of the old Roman Empire, with its message of vast success in the imposition of order upon men." (*Adventures of Ideas*, p. 31) Elsewhere he speaks thus of Rome (*The Aims of Education*, pp. 74–75):

> The marvelous position of Rome in relation to Europe comes from the fact that it has transmitted to us a double inheritance. It received the Hebrew religious thought, and has passed on to Europe its fusion with Greek civilization. Rome itself stands for the impress of organization and unity upon diverse fermenting elements. Roman Law embodies the secret of Roman greatness in its Stoic respect for intimate rights of human nature within an iron framework of empire. Europe is always flying apart because of the diverse explosive character of its inheritance, and coming together because it can never shake off that impress of unity it has received from Rome. The history of Europe is the history of Rome curbing the Hebrew and the Greek, with their various impulses of religion, and of science, and of art, and of quest for material comfort, and of lust for domination, which are all at daggers drawn with each other. The vision of Rome is the vision of the unity of civilization.

The Rome made so much of in the passage I have just quoted *is* the Empire which succeeded the Republic. But that Empire remained itself rooted in the Republic, which it always remembered and could never entirely repudiate. Much of what the Empire did was with institutions that continued to bear the impress of the Republic. One characteristic of the Republic, carried over into the Empire, should be noted here. It is indicated in what Whitehead says of Roman literature: "There is very little aloofness about [Roman] authors, they express their race and very little which is beyond all differences of race." (*The Aims of Education*, p. 67) He goes on to say, "It is not a literature in the sense that Greece and England have produced literatures, expressions of universal human feeling. Latin has one theme and that is Rome—Rome, the mother of Europe, and the great Babylon . . ." (*The Aims of Education*, p. 68) We need not try to determine here whether such assessments of Rome are sound, but they certainly reflect the appearances of things, as evident in the way the Romans presented themselves.

V

Cicero purports to take the city seriously, whatever he truly believed. Modern thought, of which Descartes is one founder, tends to liberate us from Roman-style dependence on the city, including the gods of the city. Something of this tension between moderns and ancients may be seen today in Iran, as is evident in the following comment on what the old-fashioned mullahs, or religious leaders, of that much-troubled country stand for (*American Spectator*, December 1979, p. 13):

> As for the attitude of the Shia religious establishment toward modernization, the matter has often been obfuscated by trivia. Naturally, even a poorly educated, simple mullah enjoys having a telephone, running water, electricity, or—as occurs more and more frequently since the revolution—his own automobile. But while he appreciates the *products* of Western techniques, he neither understands nor accepts the intricate *process* by which they are produced. This process calls for an emphasis on secular education, science, freedom of inquiry, work habits, and a hierarchical social structure which does not square with the mullahs' concept of the right social and moral order and threatens to whittle down their authority among the populace. The Pahlavis were reformers, modernizers, and, in certain ways, Westernizers—and invariably their first major clashes were with the Islamic establishment. Indeed, Khomeini's violent opposition had been triggered back in the early 1960s by the Shah's land reform, which greatly reduced the power of the feudalists and their religious allies.

The modernity for which thinkers such as Descartes prepared the way does threaten regimes like the Roman republic of Scipio's day or like the Iranian republic of Khomeini's day. Such modernity means, among other things:

1) Cosmopolitanism. This is in place of what I have called provincialism.

2) Skepticism, for example with respect to revelation. The relation between religion and politics is not appreciated by the modernist; rather, they are to be kept separate.

3) Relativism. This is related to the skepticism I have just mentioned, but goes even further in that science (which is used by some to undermine received opinion about such things as the divine) can itself be undermined.

4) Privacy. We have moved in this inventory of what modernity means from cosmopolitanism, which considers the entire world its city, through skepticism and relativism to an emphasis upon the private self. All opinions, whether theoretical or practical, are keyed to one's own judgment; one is left free to select what one wishes from the infinite variety that is

available. The self thereby becomes the ground for all that one chooses or comes to believe.

5) Hedonism. When one is left free to choose for oneself, the dominant tendency is to try to make oneself comfortable, to enjoy oneself, to "do one's own thing." Commerce and consumption tend to replace citizenship as the guide to life. One can even hear in such circumstances the self-satisfied observation, "Now this is really living!"

6) Small people. All are considered equal by the modernist, and much is done to keep or make everyone equal, even if some must be cut down to a generally attainable size. These mediocrities are in contrast with the giants, the "characters," celebrated by Plutarch.

7) Tyranny. Small people are more apt to permit, and even to encourage, tyrants, if only out of desperation as relativism and hedonism take their toll of public-spiritedness and sound government. It can even be said that modern tyranny, which rarely has the benevolent aspects that ancient tyrants sometimes exhibited, is a symptom of nature rebelling against her neglect. I say *symptom* because tyranny is in modern circumstances a sign of infection, of something that has gone wrong in the health of the body politic.

One must wonder, of course, how the American republic is affected by these modern developments. For example, commerce is worked into the very fabric of our constitutional system. Is it thereby recruited for public purposes? Or is it left free to serve self-indulgence, a sovereign sense of privacy, and anything but citizenship among us?

VI

I return to the last of the things associated with modernity: tyranny. Tyranny itself is nothing new; certainly it is not an exclusively modern phenomenon.

But modern tyranny does tend to be particularly dreadful, and not only because of the technology available to it. The doctrinaire character of modern movements reinforces the extent and durability of modern tyrannies: they can be comprehensive in a way that ancient tyrannies could not be. The ancient pre-Christian world (including pre-Christian tyrants) was by and large tolerant of divergent creeds if one's public actions conformed to the decree of the community. (*Adventures of Ideas*, p. 52) We, on the other hand, have become accustomed to massive, even continent-wide, programs in "thought control."

Such developments are possible in large part because man is seen as the maker of all that he does and thinks, rather than as the discoverer. All is rooted in his self-awareness and his will. Truths are not believed to have an existence independent of man; they are not grounded in nature, there for all to search out and to know. Rather, they are to be made and chosen, or chosen and made, and if so, why not chosen and made by the tyrant? In principle, what the tyrant chooses and makes is as good as that which other men happen to choose and make. If there is no natural basis for the truth, is there any reason to prefer one thought over another? Why should not the tyrant be humored? Although this is not what Descartes argues, such conclusions do seem to be generated either by the new way he helped develop or by the demise of the old way he helped to undermine.

What doctrinaire tyranny means can most graphically be seen in what has happened recently in Cambodia. The Pol Pot faction which took over in 1975, in part because of conditions contributed to by the way the Vietnam war was conducted, "proceeded to establish one of the most ferocious totalitarian regimes ever known." (*New Yorker*, November 5, 1979, p. 39) That regime was overthrown by the Vietnamese invasion in January 1979. Western relief workers reported on what the Pol Pot regime had been like (*New Yorker*, November 5, 1979, pp. 39–40):

> There are many modern buildings in Phnom Penh [the capital city], but almost all were empty. Long grass grew up around them, and in the streets. The few people who *were* in the buildings didn't really seem to be living there; they seemed more to be sort of camping out. The streets were filled with trash and broken things . . . Our guides told us that the entire city, of two million people, had been evacuated in twenty-four hours by the Pol Pot forces shortly after they took over [in 1975]. . . . [The people driven out into the country] lived in compound[s] and were given two meals of rice per day. They worked in the fields, . . . for fourteen to sixteen hours, and then had to go to political-indoctrination classes at night. No one was allowed to cook his or her own meals. If you were caught with a pot of your own, you could be shot. . . . You could be killed for wearing glasses . . . Glasses meant that you spent your time reading and were an intellectual. Intellectuals and professionals had to hide all sign of their identities. . . . No religious practices were permitted. I was told by one of our guides that among the Cham people—a Muslim sect—about ninety per cent of the men had been killed. . . . When we asked people, "Why did Pol Pot do this? How could it have happened," they would only say, "He's a madman." But later, when I arrived in Thailand, Thai friends told me that Pol Pot had believed that he was following an ideology. He wanted to build the New Socialist Man and the New Socialist Woman. All Western technology was to be rooted out. Cambodia would be self-reliant. At first, everyone would work in agriculture, and be pure. They would create a surplus of rice, and export it. Then they would build up their own Cambodian-style industry. You see, they had this *whole plan*. But it didn't work.

One can be reminded here of what Descartes said earlier about the superiority of a design worked out by one mind compared to designs that have developed over time and at the hands of many. (One must wonder, however, whether a design which develops over time might not be more apt to be respectful of what nature prefers.) I end this reminder of what has happened in Cambodia, which had happened in related forms and on a grander scale in countries such as Russia, Germany, and China earlier in this century, by quoting still another relief worker's observation (*New Yorker*, November 5, 1979, p. 41):

> Even while I was there, it was hard for me to grasp how enormously the country had been reduced. One thing that drove it home was to see how important a simple kitchen pot had become. I had never stopped to think just how important a pot is—especially to a population that subsists on rice, which cannot be eaten until it is cooked. A pot is a sort of irreducible rudiment of human civilization. In Cambodia, because pots are extremely rare, owing to the previous government's confiscation of all cooking utensils, each pot that you see being carried on the road has a small community of people moving along with it. It is their link to survival. Wherever their pot goes people have to follow.

All this also reminds one of Dante's *Inferno,* however with this qualification: in the *Inferno* the dreadful things that are portrayed reflect natural or at least plausible consequences of the various sins dealt with. That is, the *Inferno* appears to make sense.

We should at once add, lest we lose sight of the pervasive effects of the modern addiction to ideology, that Americans, too, have sacrificed good sense to doctrinaire irresponsibility from time to time. Consider, for example, how Woodrow Wilson (in his War Message to Congress on April 2, 1917) justified American participation in the First World War, often lamented as one of the most senseless wars of all times and a major cause of the conditions for the devastating tyrannies we have seen in Europe and elsewhere the past sixty years:

> It is a fearful thing to lead this great peaceful people into war, into the most terrible and disastrous of all wars, civilization itself seeming to be in the balance. But the right is more precious than peace, and we shall fight for the things which we have always carried nearest our hearts—for democracy, for the right of those who submit to authority to have a voice in their own governments, for the rights and liberties of small nations, for a universal dominion of right by such a concert of free peoples as shall bring peace and safety to all nations and make the world itself at last free. To such a task we can dedicate our lives and our fortunes, everything that we are and everything that

we have, with the pride of those who know that the day has come when America is privileged to spend her blood and her might for the principles that gave her birth and happiness and the peace which she has treasured. God helping her, she can do no other.

(*The Annals of America*, vol. 14, p. 82. Compare pp. 101–110.) In thus invoking "the principles that gave [America] her birth and happiness," President Wilson called to mind the Founding Fathers. But one thing which characterized the Founding Fathers is strikingly absent from such ideological statements as we have been routinely subjected to in the Twentieth Century, and that is prudence. This prudence is evident in the cautious invocation of the right of revolution by the Declaration of Independence: that right reminds us of nature and of that which is right by nature, even against the claims of constituted authority.

Ancient political thought is also very much concerned with prudence; it accepted the limits of beneficent human action, the limits of the ability of men to eradicate evil from the world. It understood that civilization depends on compromises, including compromises with the truth in the interest of social peace. Modern political thought, insofar as it is influenced by doctrinaire approaches, abandons prudential restraints in the formulation and execution of public policy. This can lead—indeed it is almost bound to lead—to monstrous things.

VII

I have suggested that prudence is keyed to a recognition of what it is that nature ordains for both men and communities. The prudent man has ends in view by which immediate actions are to be judged and in the light of which choices are to be made. Critical here are the ends given by nature, not the choices of means that men make, nor the fact that men are choosing and making. This is to recognize prudence as "teleological"—that is, as guided by a standard of excellence, however dimly perceived. This recognition does not depend on, and may even be wary of a belief in, the possibility of steady and indefinite progress. The prudent man recognizes that there *is* a perfection to be aspired to which will be achieved or manifested only now and then and only here and there, not everywhere, not always somewhere.

Modern science, with its marvelous achievements and with its implicit depreciation of old-fashioned ways of thinking and feeling, has tended to undermine reliance by the more advanced men among us upon prudence in the formulation and execution of public policy. But science itself, I have suggested, has been undermined by the radical skepticism it is grounded in and by the relativism it promotes. Science is certainly far from confident about that which it purports to know: it may not truly know *that* it knows, except perhaps in terms of the remarkable applications it may happen to have.

The uncertainty intrinsic to modern science is suggested by the announcement a few years ago by three astronomers who said "that because a mistake [had been] made in the way distances in space are measured, the universe is only about half as old and half as big as [was] previously thought." (*Chicago Sun-Times,* November 14, 1979, p. 44) They explained that "astronomers believe that the stars and planets have been rushing outward since the 'big bang,' the primordial explosion that most scientists believe started the universe." (I assume that what they meant when they spoke of something which "started the universe" is that event which rearranged all available, or at least considerable, matter for the cycle that the universe is *now* in.) Thus those three astronomers could then say that "the universe is only 9 billion years old, not 15 billion to 18 billion, the usually accepted age." The scaling down of the universe follows, they reported, because of "a major error [they had found] in Hubble's Constant, a yardstick used to determine the distance between objects in space." They found that the Constant, "which is the ratio of speed to distance, should be almost twice as large as previously thought." This meant that "everything determined with the Constant should be scaled down by a factor of two."

Consider two implications of this illustration drawn from contemporary astronomy. One is that scientists *are* prepared to have fundamental and far-reaching discoveries of recent decades as well as of earlier centuries radically revised periodically. This testifies not only to their sincere respect for the truth, but also to their sense of the unavoidable tentativeness of everything they do "discover." The other implication is that errors of the magnitude reported by these three astronomers (we need not assume, in this case, that they are *now* correct) do not seem to have kept the predictions or the technologies keyed to astronomy from being effective (for example, with respect to the occurrences of eclipses or with respect to the uses of space ships). Of course, it can be said, the errors now detected manifest themselves only on the grandest scale (in billions of years) and need not make any practical difference "up close" (for example, in our solar system or even in our galaxy). Fair enough, but perhaps this should at least remind us that the truth of modern scientific doctrines is not necessarily established by those marvelous technological applications that draw upon modern science.

I have provided, by looking to accounts of the starry heavens above, an illustration of the uncertainty intrinsic to modern science. Another fundamental question about modern science can be raised by considering not its inquiry into the heavens above, but rather its repeated efforts to find its way (indeed, to blast its way) to the tiniest particles out of which the universe, including man himself, is fashioned. I had occasion to argue in this fashion in 1974 (reprinted in *The Artist as Thinker*, pp. 252953):

> What seems to be missing in the current scientific enterprise is a systematic inquiry into its presuppositions and purposes. That is, the limits of modern science do not seem to be properly recognized. Bertrand Russell has been quoted as saying, "Physics is mathematical not because we know so much about the physical world, but because we know so little: it is only its mathematical properties that we can discover." But the significance of this observation is not generally appreciated—as one learns upon trying to persuade competent physicists to join one in presenting a course devoted to a careful reading of Aristotle's *Physics* [where, among other things, an extended examination of the meaning of *cause* is to be found].

> Is there any reason to doubt that physicists will, if they continue as they have in the Twentieth Century, achieve again and again "decisive breakthroughs" in dividing subatomic "particles"? But what future, or genuine understanding, is there in *that?* I believe it would be fruitful for physicists—that is, for a few of the more imaginative among them—to consider seriously the nature of what we can call the "ultron." What must this ultimate particle be like (if, indeed, it is a particle and not an idea or a principle)? For is not an "ultron" implied by the endeavors of our physicists, by their recourse to more and more ingenious (and expensive) equipment and experiments? Or are we to assume an infinite regress (sometimes called progress) and no standing place or starting point? Or, to put this question still another way, what is it that permits the universe to be and *to be* (if it is) intelligible?

I should add that modern science may be bound to fail in its determined pursuit of the fundamental nature of matter because matter may be, intrinsically and permanently, elusive: it may not be, beyond a certain point, subject to analysis. (There is some indication of this in, say, Plato's *Timaeus*. Or, as Aristotle put it, "Matter is unknowable in itself." *Metaphysics* 1036a9.) That may simply be the way things are. What, then, can truly be thought about? Only the reasonable, if not only the reasoning?

I return now to political things proper. Consider one implication of the scientific view of a universe that is constantly changing, repeatedly (that is to say, every eighteen billion years or so, if not every nine billion years or every thirty-six billion years)—repeatedly going in and out of "existence" (that is to say, in and out of its "present form"; we may now be halfway through the current run). Thus, Whitehead can speak of this planet as "temporary." (*Adventures of Ideas*, p. 46) The temporariness of the planet, as well as of ways of thinking about things, is stressed throughout Whitehead's work as it is in modern science itself. What happens to the tone of political life when people come truly to believe that even the earth upon which they stand is temporary? Compare the Aristotelian assumption of the eternity of the visible universe. What Aristotle meant by this and why, and whether it can be translated into familiar modern assumptions about the eternity of always-observable energy/matter, cannot be examined here. But it suffices to notice that there is indeed something unsettling about modern relativism, about the questioning of everything men have "always" taken for granted. Both the beginnings and the end of man are called into question: the sense of purpose, of meaning, is undermined.

A critical step in this development may be seen in the thought of Friedrich Nietzsche, about which Leo Strauss has said, "Nature has ceased [in Nietzsche's view] to appear as lawful and merciful. The fundamental experience of existence is therefore the experience, not of bliss, but of suffering, of emptiness, of an abyss." (*What Is Political Philosophy?* p. 54. See *Modern Age*, Winter 1978, p. 43.) Another critical step, perhaps preparing the way for Kant and hence for Nietzsche, may have been the work of Thomas Aquinas and his associates, about which Mr. Strauss has said, "The Thomistic doctrine of natural right or, more generally expressed, of natural law is free from the hesitations and ambiguities which are characteristic of the teachings, not only of Plato and Cicero, but of Aristotle as well." (*Natural Right and History*, p. 163) Be that as it may, modern man finds himself suspended over an abyss or—in some ways worse, in some ways better—already falling into it (which means, among other things, that at least the suspense is over). To what extent are modern science and its doctrinal implications responsible for this state of affairs? Did the ancients sense that a healthy life depends on a confident political order, which depends in turn on salutary opinions about the meaning and meaningfulness of human communities and other human things?

This is not to say that the better thinkers of antiquity did not recognize the fragility of human life on earth along with the fragility of the earth itself. Consider how Scipio, toward the end of Cicero's *Republic*, speaks of these matters as he relates the dream he had had in which his glorious ancestor, the great Scipio Africanus, appeared to him.

Scipio is shown by Africanus how small Rome, even with its empire, appears to someone who sees the earth as but a speck in the universe as a whole. Scipio reports on this famous dream episode between himself and his ancestor (Cicero, *Republic*, VI, 19; p. 263):

Though I was filled with awe at the celestial harmonies, I kept turning my eyes constantly towards the earth. "I see," said Africanus, "that you still contemplate the abode and home of man. If the earth appears insignificant to you—as indeed it is—ever lift up your eyes to these heavenly realms and despise the concerns of men. For what fame can you win among men or what renown worthy of your striving?"

Africanus deprecates further the fame that men strive for, stressing the limitations in time and in space that such fame is subject to. (Cicero, *Republic*, VI, 19–22; pp. 264–65) It is, I suspect, Cicero's purpose to place a curb upon the considerable Roman ambition, a curb that is shown to issue from one of the illustrious ancestors whom the more spirited Romans strive to emulate if not even to surpass.

Not that Africanus does not care for Rome; he certainly does, and for his descendant as well. But he also cares that both Rome and Scipio be aware of and dedicate themselves to the best: *that* is the source of true distinction. Scipio is instructed (Cicero, *Republic*, VI, 23; p. 266):

[H]ow puerile is the renown conferred by man, lasting as it does for only a small portion of a single year! But if you wish to look on high and to contemplate this abode and eternal home [where Africanus is], you will not yield to the flattery of the rabble or set your hopes upon the rewards that men may give. Excellence itself, by its own inherent charm, must draw you towards true glory.

(Is the "single year" referred to here something like "the Great Year" of the Pythagoreans, that period of thousands of years necessary for sun, moon, and planets to reach again the same position in relation to each other as they occupied at any given moment?) Africanus shortly after this ends his instruction of Scipio (Cicero, *Republic*, VI, 26; pp. 267–68):

Now the noblest concerns of the soul have to do with the security of your country, and the soul which is employed and disciplined in such pursuits will fly more speedily to this [heavenly] abode, its natural home. This journey it will make the swifter, if it looks abroad, while still imprisoned in the flesh, and if, by meditating upon that which lies beyond it, it divorces itself as far as may be from the body. For the souls of men who have surrendered themselves to carnal delights, who have made themselves as it were slaves of the passions, and who have been prompted by lust to violate the laws of gods and men, wander about near the earth itself, after their escape from the body [that is, after their deaths], and do not return hither until they have been driven about for many ages.

The reference, in these closing lines of Africanus' speech to Scipio, to "the laws of gods and men" reminds us of the critical difference, already alluded to, between the modern project and the ancient way. The ancients, by and large, considered lively opinions about gods who are somehow interested in the affairs of men to be vital to a healthy political life. The moderns, by and large, have subjected such opinions to a ruthless and generally devastating critique. But must not such a critique, in order to be responsible, understand the nature and hence limitations of political life as well as the ancients did? In any event, Cicero assigns to Africanus the following assurance for Scipio (Cicero, *Republic*, VI, 10; pp. 258–59):

> All men who have saved or benefited their native land, or have enhanced its power, are assigned an especial place in heaven where they may enjoy a life of eternal bliss. For the supreme god who rules the entire universe finds nothing, at least among earthly objects, more pleasing than the societies and groups of men, united by law and right, which are called states. The rulers and saviors of states set forth from that place and to that place return.

Notice here that the commendation is put in general terms: "All men who have saved or benefited their native land . . ." It seems to be suggested that not only are Roman patriots favored by the gods but all true patriots, wherever they hail from. Those men are favored who do well by their country, men who presumably do all they can to promote and sustain in their separate countries the excellences they are capable of. One wonders here what is to be made of Scipio's insistence earlier in the dialogue that Rome is the best regime. Perhaps it is the inclination and sometimes even the duty of the patriot to speak of and act toward his country as if it is indeed the best, or at least capable of the best that is thereby testified to. This is to take political life seriously, even as one prudently points to something that goes beyond political life and for the sake of which political life is ordained and established among human beings.

7

ARISTOCRATIC IMPERATIVES
IN A DEMOCRATIC AGE

*Four score and seven years ago our fathers brought forth on this conti-
nent a new nation, conceived in Liberty, and dedicated to the proposition that all men are created equal.*

ABRAHAM LINCOLN

I

Thomas Jefferson's First Inaugural Address as President of the United
States is a distillation of his position as a partisan politician, but a politician
who was nevertheless able, because of his eloquent advocacy of toleration
for opposition opinions, to appeal to the enduring good sense of his countrymen of all parties.

An examination of one critical aspect of that 1801 address should help
us understand how Americans have managed to moderate their democratic impulses, drawing thereby upon the classical heritage of the West.
For Jefferson himself, the classical heritage is sounder in Cicero than in
Plato. (See, e.g., his letter of July 5, 1814 to John Adams.)

This essay was prepared for *The Jeffersonian Heritage* program, The Chicago Public Library Cultural Center (with the support of the Illinois Humanities Council), Chicago, Illinois, December 7, 1977. It has been published in Anastaplo, "Mr. Justice Black, His Generous
Common Sense, and the Bar Admission Cases," 9 *Southwestern University Law Review* 977,
at 1042–46 (1977).

All quotations in this essay from Thomas Jefferson are, unless otherwise indicated, from
his *First Inaugural Address*, March 4, 1801. See, also, the epigraph for Essay No. 8, below.

The epigraph is taken from Abraham Lincoln, *Gettysburg Address*, November 19, 1863.

II

At the heart of Jefferson's First Inaugural is an emphasis on equality. This emphasis is found in the central lines of the address. In those lines, Jefferson sees us "entertaining a due sense of our equal right to the use of our own faculties, to the acquisitions of our own industry, to honor and confidence from our fellow-citizens, resulting not from birth, but from our actions and their sense of them." (Jefferson's statement of "the essential principles of our Government," in his First Inaugural Address, affirms "equal and exact justice to all men, of whatever state or persuasion, religious or political.")

Political distinctions resting upon birth—that is, upon family connections or origins—are repudiated. It seems to be recognized that natural faculties may differ. But each is entitled to the use of the faculties he happens to have. Each is entitled as well to the acquisitions secured by his industry—acquisitions made in accordance with the rules established for economic activities.

Also important, it seems, are the opinions one's fellow citizens have of one, opinions that should correspond to the deeds one has performed.

III

There is for Jefferson, we have noticed, no legitimate hereditary aristocracy in the American regime. It would seem as well to follow from his assumptions here, although he is prudently reserved about the matter on this occasion, that hereditary slavery is also questionable in this regime. (Consider, for example, Jefferson's observation that one is entitled "to the acquisitions of [one's] own industry"—an observation which was critical to Abraham Lincoln's condemnation of slavery as fundamentally unjust.)

Since all are somehow equal, majority rule seems to follow as the only legitimate means of deciding public issues. Jefferson insists that such rule, including deference by outvoted minorities to the expressed will of the majority, is fundamental to republican government.

It should at once be added, however, that this deference is to majority rule which is expressed in accordance with the established electoral forms and which is itself properly respectful of minority rights. It is, at least to this extent, a disciplined and fairly stable but yet not permanent majority. It is not a majority tossed by the random shiftings of passions or licensed to do whatever it pleases: "All, too, will bear in mind this sacred principle, that though the will of the majority is in all cases to prevail, that will, to be rightful, must be reasonable . . ."

Nothing is said about how the decisive minority rights and electoral forms have been recognized or established. Do they too depend on majority rule, on a prior majority judgment? How is that authoritative majority determined? By what rules does *it* define and express itself in devising constitutional provisions?

Are there not better and worse forms, forms which are better or worse in bringing out and reflecting the good sense of a people? Are there not more and less important rights to be preserved against majority usurpation?

IV

To ask such questions is to remind ourselves of a perennial problem: is an aristocracy of some sort required for reliable government in a republican regime?

Jefferson himself, in his First Inaugural, ridicules the notion that there are "angels in the forms of kings" by whom men can be ruled. Still, everyone knows that this great democrat did speak, in a letter (of October 28, 1813) to John Adams, about those whom he called "natural *aristoi*"—those whom he considered members of a "natural aristocracy" of "virtue and talents" as distinguished from those whom he considered members of an "artificial aristocracy founded on wealth and birth, without either virtue or talents." He asked Adams, "May we not even say that that form of government is best which provides the most effectually for a pure selection of these natural *aristoi* into the offices of government?"

To ask whether there is an intellectual or moral aristocracy is to ask by whom or by what the "sovereign public" in a republican regime should be guided. It is also to ask how such an aristocracy establishes itself, or how it is that a republican people becomes responsive to one set of opinions rather than to another.

It is to ask as well what the relation is between intellectual superiority and moral superiority. Does one depend on the other? Or is the dependence reciprocal? Certainly, it is difficult to act properly if one does not know how things are.

It may also be difficult to learn how things truly are if one cannot control oneself. (See Section III of Essay No. 31–C, below.)

V

The best republican institutions would seem to be those that routinely permit a people to draw upon its ever-changing moral-intellectual aristocracy in a reliable manner. (The partnership of moral virtue and intellectual virtue may be seen in Jefferson's references to "the wisdom of our Sages and blood of our Heroes" and to "resources of wisdom, of virtue, and of zeal.") Does chance play a role in the establishment of relevant institutions, if only in the opportunity somehow made available to exceptional men to lay down the original ground rules for a regime dedicated to the proposition that all men are created equal?

Whatever Jefferson might have said in his private correspondence about natural aristoi (or, years earlier, about the "assembly of demi-gods" who wrote the Constitution in 1787), he does not in his public statements talk as if there is any kind of aristocracy recognized or utilized by American republicanism. Instead he wonders, upon his assumption of the Presidency, whether anyone can be adequate to the great task before him.

Jefferson admits that he depends on others to help him in the performance of his duties as President. The collective experience of many is relied upon to make this constitutional regime work. Can chance be depended on to have distributed among those found in the various offices of government the diverse experiences needed for effective government?

How *did* it happen that the experiences and opportunities of Eighteenth-Century Americans combined to form the institutions that permit republican government to work here as well as it has? Must there always be something of a mystery about this, so much so as to have led earlier generations here to speak confidently of the influence of Divine Providence in the founding of the American regime?

VI

Jefferson understood, we have seen, that the equality for which he stood did not deny that men might have unequal faculties. But an essential sameness among men entitles them to equal rights to use their diverse natural talents.

Diversity in talents among men means that there will often be a diversity in their opinions as well. Men may be in certain respects equal, but that cannot be said about the opinions that they happen to hold, opinions that may be shaped by their circumstances and training as well as by their talents.

Jefferson does recognize that there *is* such a thing as wisdom (or the reasonable), that there *are* standards by which opinions may be judged, that there are better and worse opinions, better and worse solutions to the problems the Country faces. He speaks of some radical sentiments in opposition to his as "error of opinion."

He would grant, no doubt, that he might be mistaken in considering his own opinions to be truths or in considering others' opinions to be errors. But he would not grant that he might be mistaken in believing that there *is* such a thing as truth or such a thing as error, however difficult it may be in some circumstances to distinguish one from the other.

VII

Republican wisdom recognizes that there are standards ascertainable by men, that there are limitations to what any particular man may discover about those standards and their applications, and that those standards can be dramatized in public discourse by invocations of an "Infinite Power," the instinctive deference to which in the governance of the universe reflects and reinforces in most men an awareness of intellectual and moral virtue. (Jefferson, in his First Inaugural Address, considers Americans to be "enlightened by a benign religion, professed, indeed, and practiced in various forms, yet all of them inculcating honesty, truth, temperance, gratitude, and the love of man; acknowledging and adoring an overruling Providence, which by all its dispensations proves that it delights in the happiness of men here and his greater happiness hereafter . . .")

Wisdom recognizes as well that the temper of a people must be taken into account and that a genuine aristocratic element, if it is to serve republican purposes, must avoid both the relativism which denies the possibility of its superiority and the ostentation which undermines republican authority.

However dedicated the thoughtful republican might be to the principle of equality, that principle does not require him to deny profound differences between Inferior and Superior, between Mortal and Immortal, between the Human and the Divine.

8

ON PATRIOTISM

Every difference of opinion is not a difference of principle. We have called by different names brethren of the same principle. We are all Republicans, we are all Federalists. If there be any among us who would wish to dissolve this Union or to change its republican form, let them stand undisturbed as monuments of the safety with which error of opinion may be tolerated where reason is left free to combat it. I know, indeed, that some honest men fear that a republican government can not be strong, that this Government is not strong enough; but would the honest patriot, in the full tide of successful experiment, abandon a government which has so far kept us free and firm on the theoretic and visionary fear that this Government, the world's best hope, may by possibility want energy to preserve itself? I trust not. I believe this, on the contrary, the strongest Government on earth. I believe it the only one where every man, at the call of the law, would fly to the standard of the law, and would meet invasions of the public order as his own personal concern.

THOMAS JEFFERSON

I

My point of departure for this discourse on patriotism is a classroom observation made in 1965 by one of my teachers, Leo Strauss, a "conservative" of note, who said that "the conscientious objector, however wrong he may be, is a much more respectable human being than the mere coward." What, we may well wonder, is the relation between the "respectable" and the "patriotic"?

I have long associated a firm dedication to patriotism with the University of Dallas. I have also long considered its political science department,

This talk was given at the University of Dallas, Irving, Texas, October 19, 1988. (Sponsor: Politics Department.)

The epigraph is taken from Thomas Jefferson, *First Inaugural Address*, March 4, 1801.

shaped as it has been by Willmoore Kendall and thereafter by Leo Paul de Alvarez, to be one of the finest in the Country. Competence in political science and soundness in patriotism may well go together: the patriot takes political life seriously and hence the common good; such seriousness is essential for meaningful political science. I shall try on this occasion fully to give patriotism its due by putting my remarks about it in the form of a patriotic address, something difficult to do in the closing weeks of a Presidential Election campaign without making a political speech. What is unpolitical, but rather pedagogical, about this talk is that I do not bother to say to you conservatives some of the things I would say to a liberal audience criticizing various of *its* follies. Some here will recall the reservations I expressed before liberal audiences in 1974 about the impeachment campaign against President Nixon.

I have always found it a challenge to visit this campus. For two years during the Vietnam War, when I was flown down here fortnightly to conduct weekend seminars in political philosophy, I could expect one of the half-dozen sessions in the course of each visit to turn into an intensive dispute between the students and me about the war. The students knew that I regarded our part in that war as foolish and destructive of American interests. They never wanted me to leave town without being challenged by them on that score. In those days, also, I repeatedly had to question the assumption, then so prevalent here, that liberal Democrats were somehow unpatriotic.

I depend this evening on your good will as I begin to examine the patriotism issue, an issue which the Republican candidate for President has made so much of this year. I remind you that my last talk here (in November 1986) anticipated Chief Justice Rehnquist's remarkable First Amendment opinions during the last Term of Court. (That talk was published in the Spring 1987 issue of the *Intercollegiate Review*.) The Chief Justice, I suggested at that time, is more liberal than it was believed—and that is cause for celebration. Conservatives, I must now suggest, are less patriotic than it was believed—and that is cause for alarm.

II

Consider this example. Two decades ago an ambitious man, born to wealth and privilege, found himself in circumstances where his self-interest was threatened if he simply did his obvious duty. He chose to look out primarily for himself, even if that should exact a dreadful toll of others.

What should be done about such conduct when exposed to public view? Should not such a man be denied elevation to the highest office in the land, especially an office which sometimes requires one to sacrifice one's own interest to the common good? That is, can such a man be entrusted with the power to put others' lives at risk as Commander-in-Chief?

My conservative friends, as well as many of my liberal friends, have agreed that such a man should be considered to have disqualified himself for high executive office—they have thus agreed when the man in question is Ted Kennedy of Chappaquiddick. But my conservative friends have, by and large, backed away from such a conclusion when the man in question is Dan Quayle of the Indiana National Guard.

III

Before we examine the Quayle problem, we should notice that we need not assume that Mr. Kennedy did not himself make valiant efforts to save his companion at Chappaquiddick. The question need not be that of his personal courage. But the serious charge is that nothing further was done on her behalf that very night, evidently because of the efforts made to find means of avoiding the political repercussions of immediately going public with the accident. Mr. Kennedy has been properly repudiated since Chappaquidick—that is, since an episode which saw him leave a young woman overnight in a submerged automobile despite the outside possibility of her rescue if the authorities had been alerted at once. Even if she were dead, as almost certainly she was, he conducted himself without exhibiting what would generally be considered proper respect for her remains.

My conservative friends do not seem to have any difficulty with the Kennedy problem and the questions it raises about moral and political issues. But their eagerness to explain away the facts, when the Quayle problem with the questions it raises about patriotism is before them, is distressing. If they of all people do not stand firmly for genuine patriotism, then the Country is indeed in trouble.

It teaches the wrong lessons to permit mere political calculations to stand in the way of an honest response to the Quayle nomination, a response which would recognize that it is hardly evidence of good judgment to choose, or to stand by, someone so unqualified for the Vice-Presidency as Dan Quayle seems to be. I mention in passing that I do not question Mr. Quayle's personal courage or his private life. The failings of the Quayle clan in their private lives, it should become evident, are not the failings of the Kennedy clan.

This is not an isolated example of questionable compromises by conservatives. The allure of power, and the intense partisanship that that can spawn, may be seen in how all too many conservatives have endorsed not only the Quayle candidacy but also both unprecedented deficits and the Iran-Contra shenanigans. It should be instructive, with a view to throwing light on what patriotism means, to consider how these three delusions are justified.

IV

One of the surprises, at least for me, of the Reagan Administration has been its willingness to put up with the deficits we have seen the past decade. Congress is pointed to as the real culprit, but that does not take due account either of the massive tax reductions vigorously promoted by the Administration seven years ago or of the insistence by the Administration upon undisciplined military expenditures. The Administration justifies itself by criticizing repeatedly the expenditures by Congress upon domestic programs. This is related to the perceived lack of sympathy in the Reagan Administration toward minorities, the homeless, and the poor. The Administration makes much instead of a need for a balanced-budget amendment, a naively conceived remedy which would have little if any salutary effect in our circumstances.

I do not pretend to know what the effects will be on the economy, during the next decade, of the tremendous national debt that is evidently piling up. A number of things can happen, and few of them are likely to be good. I do recall the inflation that followed upon Lyndon Johnson's attempt to conduct a war in Vietnam without paying for it, an inflation (fueled also, it seems, by the OPEC conspiracy) to which the Carter Administration finally fell victim.

What is intriguing now is that conservatives who at last came to power after years of unrelenting campaigns against deficit financing are now heard arguing that deficits do not matter as much as was once thought. It is also said, not without some plausibility, that the current deficits are less than they seem when viewed in proportion to an increased Gross National Product. They may well be correct on both counts.

Particularly troublesome, however, is the impression we get that those who are thus papering over the difficulties here do not know what they are really saying. We can get the impression as well that they believe that the American people can be gulled into acquiescence so long as the more articulate and influential among them are prospering.

V

A similar repudiation by conservatives of their long-espoused principles may be seen in their response to the Iran arms-Contra aid debacle. The Reagan Administration came to power in 1981 in part because of the dissatisfaction that various conservatives promoted with the Carter Administration policy toward Iran and the Embassy hostages held there. Then we learned in 1986 of our disgraceful dealings with the Ayatollah's regime, evidently with the very people who had been implicated in the murder of scores of sleeping Marines in their Beirut barracks.

I must say that the only missiles I would have provided *those* people, if any were to be provided at all, would have been launched from a firing range, not delivered by cargo planes. If Mr. Carter in office had himself done what was later done by Mr. Reagan, evidently with the approval of Mr. Bush, his impeachment would have been demanded by conservatives. Even more serious has been the willingness of the current administration to circumvent Congress in its clandestine "appropriation" of money for the Contras. In that direction lies Caesarism.

Related to this is what all too many conservatives have done in making a hero of someone as immature and unreliable as Oliver North. (One can be reminded here of the uncritical conservative response in some quarters, a generation before, to the dramatic Whittaker Chambers.) Although it can be said of Colonel North that he at least is no shirker, his judgment and that of his superiors are most questionable. Adulation of him is silly business as is the insistence (another expression of conservative *machismo*) that Americans are entitled to stock private arsenals. The Second Amendment is looked to in justification—but the people who invoke it are usually far from willing to serve in the militias to which the "right to bear Arms" is keyed in that amendment, especially if combat duty seems likely. (I remind you that the Second Amendment reads, "A well regulated Militia, being necessary for the security of a free State, the right of the people to keep and bear Arms, shall not be infringed.")

VI

I have touched on how conservatives have compromised themselves with respect to both the deficit and the Iran-Contra matter. Let us return now to Mr. Quayle. What can "they" be thinking of in the efforts being made to promote him?

There would be only one thing worse for conservatives than to try to persuade the American people to take Mr. Quayle seriously—and that would be to succeed in doing so. For that would contribute further to the repudiation of the noble principles and useful sentiments that conservatives properly espouse and that we must depend on them to espouse.

However well-advised, or "handled," Mr. Quayle would be as Vice-President or even as President, he would long, perhaps permanently, remain a politician who could not be respected by the true patriot. It is anomalous, even a travesty, that so much is now made, considering Mr. Quayle's personal military record, of his service on the Senate Armed Services Committee. Also anomalous is that such a man should be permitted by public opinion to question the patriotism, including the reliability in military judgment, of a Democratic candidate for President who has had a long and clearly honorable career in public service.

There is something disturbing in the state of public opinion that permits Mr. Bush to make as much as he does, with ominous echoes of the McCarthy Period, of the flag and of the pledge of allegiance even as he considers himself obliged to extol as his running mate a man who showed what his allegiance to his Country meant when the chips were down.

VII

Then there are the rationalizations I have heard from conservative friends to justify putting Mr. Quayle in line for the Presidency, several of which rationalizations I will now touch upon in turn.

Dan Quayle's tenure in Congress is compared favorably with John Kennedy's. But one cannot help but remember, even without Lloyd Bentsen's dramatic put-down during their recent joint appearance, that the Congressional Kennedy, whatever his limitations, did have proper military service behind him.

The mediocre academic record of Dan Quayle is compared favorably by his apologists with Winston Churchill's. How serious can they be? Any half-hour's conversation with the young Churchill would, I suspect, have revealed the makings of a first-class mind. In addition, we can read with profit Churchill's account of his successful efforts as a youth to get into combat again and again. It is not insignificant that the systematic survey of the moral virtues in the *Nicomachean Ethics* should begin with courage.

Then we have Mr. Bush's defense, upon learning that Mr. Quayle had been given shelter in the National Guard, that he had not resisted the draft, or burned the flag, or run off to Canada. Can we take seriously the suggestion that the failure to do those things is to be considered a prime recommendation for the Vice-Presidency? Besides, the men who resisted the draft, or fled to Canada, or otherwise opposed the Vietnam War often showed a public-spirited courage—and they at least usually exposed themselves to disabilities that impaired their careers. Public efforts in opposition to a particular war can be judged on their merits, as could be Lincoln's opposition as a Congressman to the Mexican War. I am reminded here of a revealing joke now going the rounds: "Question: What is the difference between Dan Quayle and Jane Fonda? Answer: Jane Fonda went to Vietnam."

Finally, there is the rationalization which explains that Mr. Bush could not drop Mr. Quayle, once he learned the truth about him, because that would have jeopardized his own chances for election. But is not this still another instance of sacrificing the Country's interest to one's own ambition and self-interest? The liberal George McGovern, we remember, was man enough to drop a running mate who came to be widely regarded, whether or not fairly, as unfit for the Presidency.

Does the resort to such rationalizations on behalf of the Quayle candidacy as I have just touched upon assume that the American people need not be talked sense to? Does all this warn us about how Mr. Bush would conduct himself as President?

VIII

Let us return to the Vietnam War. It *was* a dubious war. That now seems to be widely accepted. What, then, was the patriotic response to it? That can be debated: there may have been a range of proper responses available to the genuine patriot.

But, I have argued, there should not have been available the response resorted to by Mr. Quayle. That is, it simply will not do for a man to promote a war, which he did as a campus conservative, and then deliberately, if not even cynically, avoid risks when the respectable student deferment he shared with hundreds of thousands of others ran out.

His family and its newspapers, as was well known, were enthusiastic about the war. What could he and his family have been thinking of in using their considerable influence to make sure that another man would be sent to fight and perhaps die in place of one of their own? The gross impropriety of this approach is made even worse when it is noticed that the Quayle family had gotten many more material benefits from our Country and had much more to defend than the typical family.

I am reminded of Lincoln's devastating criticism of slavery as a system which he understood to be built on the principle, "You work, I eat."

IX

Systematic avoidance of service in the Vietnam War by the sons of most of the comfortable families in this Country that supported the war led to its being fought in perhaps the worst possible way. Would Congress and the President's men have run that war the way they did if their own sons and those of their most influential constituents had been routinely involved in it, risking life and limb?

This points up the problem even with the student-deferment program—but that, at least, was open and available to large numbers of young men all over the Country, in modest community colleges as well as in the elite universities. I find it passing strange that the Reagan Administration, which likes to think of the Vietnam War as having been a worthy American enterprise, should be as unresponsive as it now is to that part of the population that eventually supplied far more than their proper share of the soldiers who died in Vietnam.

It should not do, in defending any risk-avoiding candidate, to inform the electorate that the media personnel who expose the failings of others as soldiers are not themselves distinguished for their military careers. *Those* people are not in the running for Commander-in-Chief. Besides, the same media have helped expose, and dispose of, Gary Hart and Joseph Biden for less serious offenses, even though no one believes that the media people are generally models of marital or literary fidelity either.

X

We must now consider the prudence of making as much as I have on this occasion of a satisfactory response in one's youth to a military challenge, whatever natural antipathy one might have toward the shirker. How far should one go with my approach?

For example, are not both Bill Bradley, an attractive young Democratic politician, and Jack Kemp, an attractive young Republican politician, also suspect? They were All-Americans who managed, while still impressive competitors as professional athletes, to avoid serious military service during the Vietnam War. In order to assess fairly what they did and did not do, one should consider, among other things, both whether they supported the war then and what they say about it now. In any event, the model for celebrities in a just war should be Joe Louis who put himself completely at the service of his Country throughout the Second World War and Ted Wil-

liams who, I believe, returned to aerial combat during the Korean War after honorable service during the Second World War.

Then, of course, there is the problem of Mr. Reagan himself, who sat
out the Second World War in Hollywood—and then occasionally pretended afterwards to have done considerably more than that. Is it not odd
that he and people such as John Wayne, another tough *hombre* who
avoided serious military service when *his* opportunity came, should now
be regarded as *the* images of patriotism, walking tall and talking big? I
cannot help but recall that the much-maligned George McGovern risked
his life as a bomber pilot during the same war and that Jimmy Carter undertook dangerous submarine missions in the Navy.

I am also reminded that the Roman Senate did exile to Sicily, for the duration of the Second Punic War, the survivors of a large contingent of their
soldiers who had been ingloriously routed by Hannibal. Were not the
Romans particularly prudent about such matters? At least they seemed to
know what republican virtue is capable of and what it requires for its
perpetuation.

XI

The patriotism issue I have been examining cuts even deeper than I have
already suggested. It bears upon what we have permitted to happen to
public discourse in this Country. That Mr. Reagan, who is anything but a
thoughtful speaker, should be regarded as a Great Communicator is itself
a disturbing symptom of our decline. His use of "L-word" talk in disparaging liberals is the most recent testimony to the superficiality of the approach he exploits.

We are not hearing coherent arguments from politicians these days but
mostly pat one-liners and cute rejoinders. Mr. Reagan is not the only culprit here, of course. This is related to the status and effects of television in
this Country, for which much of the national campaigning is designed.
The way the so-called Presidential debates were organized testifies to the
sorry condition of what now passes for serious discussion among us. The
media people who are selected to put one combative question after
another to the four candidates exhibit themselves as probably more superficial, and certainly as more irresponsible, than the politicians they
badger.

How all of us, including the media people and the politicians, get
trapped by the debased rhetoric of the day may be seen in how we have

allowed ourselves to be crippled in recent years by the sad plights of hostages. We have to be more toughminded about such things, but that in turn requires clear thinking guided by genuine patriotism.

The steady deterioration in public discourse may be seen in the arguments being made to us at this time, and not only by Mr. Quayle and his defenders. The deeper malaise in public discourse is reflected in the fact that no one else, so far as I can tell, is still making in public the old-fashioned arguments I have made here tonight. It is also reflected in the fact that such arguments have to be made at all. A self-confident republican people would have made it impossible to select for the Vice-Presidency or to keep, if inadvertently selected, someone with Mr. Quayle's unfortunate record. The public loss of confidence has been induced in part by supposedly conservative jurists on the United States Supreme Court who proclaim that "there are no absolutes" and that "one man's vulgarity is another's lyric." (*Dennis* v. *United States* [1951]; *Cohen* v. *California* [1971])

XII

What, then, do conservatives really care about now? What are they truly moved by?

They, by and large, are no longer primarily anti-communists. "Evil empire" talk is not in vogue these days. That is not altogether a bad thing, considering how much damage has been done in this Country and in our foreign policy by "Red scares." But if the Russians are to be permanently improved, it will be partly by their recognizing the civil liberties that the unjustly derided American Civil Liberties Union can be relied upon to defend.

How do conservatives stand on abortion? I have long had the impression that neither Mr. Bush nor Mr. Reagan fully believes what he is saying about it. Certainly they could not permit the exceptions they do (such as for rape, incest, and a threat to the life of the mother) if they believed that abortion was murder. My own position is that there is no constitutional issue here for the judiciary to concern itself with, that these are matters for the political process to dispose of. I suspect that the political process, if left to itself by the courts, will have to rely more and more on the moral judgment of the pregnant woman, especially as safe abortion-inducing medication becomes readily available.

How, then, do conservatives stand generally on family values and on issues of piety? It has always seemed to me ludicrous to prefer Mr. Reagan to Mr. Carter on either score. Certainly, Mr. Carter's exemplary conduct here should have spoken louder than Mr. Reagan's opportunistic words.

As for the patriotism issue I need only add here, to what I have already said tonight, an observation I have made in my review of Allan Bloom's best-seller: "It is hardly fitting to hear those without military experience of their own berating the young for their reluctance [during the Vietnam era] to fight in what seemed to them, and may very well have been for us, an unjust war." (*Essays on The Closing of the American Mind*, R. L. Stone, ed., p. 272. See, also, pp. 229–30, 233.) An overriding problem with Mr. Quayle was that he considered Vietnam a just war for others to have to fight.

The critical thing we are obliged to assess is what Dan Quayle personally did, and had others do for him, in response to that war, not what his family did. Families do have a natural inclination to protect their own, something which a young man of spirit sometimes has to resist. The determined insensitivity here of conservative partisans is not heartening.

What, then, do conservatives believe in now? The passion that seems most to move them is connected with money-making and money-keeping. Particularly stirring for them seems to be the cutting, or at least the not-raising, of taxes. Drawing upon this sentiment, which evoked the fiercest approval at the Republican National Convention, is a Bush-Quayle advertisement I heard a few nights ago on a San Antonio radio station. Listeners were warned that when Mr. Dukakis talks about cutting military expenditures, he is not just talking about letting American "lower its guard." Even more important, it was indicated, he is talking about the loss of jobs for Texans. Indeed, listeners were told, sixty thousand jobs in the San Antonio area were in jeopardy. Listening to that ad was for me like Old Home Week, since this warning was accompanied by an inventory of all the military bases I had served at in that area four decades ago while I was earning my wings.

To be this blatant about local interests, without much regard either for national security or for the healthy economy upon which an enduring security depends, is hardly the approach of the dedicated patriot but rather that of the mean-spirited and otherwise suicidal hedonist. It can be sobering to recall the observation by Livy as he looked back on the decline of the Roman republic, "Of late years wealth has made us greedy, and self-indulgence has brought us, through every form of sensual excess, to be, if I may so put it, in love with death both individual and collective." (Livy, *The War With Hannibal* [Penguin Books], p. 15)

XIII

Perhaps the controversy about Mr. Quayle will at least serve to remind us, eventually if not immediately, of how limited the Presidency should be under the Constitution. Now that national elections are conducted as they are and now that national political discourse is at the level it is, perhaps the Presidency should be even more limited than it was originally intended to be.

Furthermore, much is to be said for using the Twenty-fifth Amendment approach routinely in choosing the Vice-President. That is, we should not continue to leave the choice substantially to one man. The risks of that should now be evident. A more sensible decision is apt to be made if the duly elected President has to submit a nomination for deliberate consideration by Congress, as was done in the cases of Gerald Ford and Nelson Rockefeller.

If Mr. Quayle is installed as Vice-President, it should be an early concern for the Congress, in cooperation with his President, to ease Mr. Quayle out of office and to replace him with a much more suitable conservative. Out of fairness to Mr. Quayle, this possibility should be pointed out to him before he relinquishes his seat in the Senate where, so far as I know, he represents adequately his Indiana constituents. I myself would not lose any sleep with Mr. Bush, or Mr. Dukakis, or Mr. Bentsen in the White House, however troubling it may be that Mr. Bush may never be able to acknowledge publicly his grave error in the choice of Mr. Quayle. No doubt, some in this audience would be apprehensive about Mr. Dukakis—but that misjudges the man, who is temperamentally conservative as well as fundamentally decent, as was seen in the forthright manner he defended Mr. Bush's Second World War record from attack two months ago. (See, e.g., *Wall Street Journal,* August 18, 1988, sec. 1, p. 21.) What Mr. Dukakis has not yet dared to do, no doubt because it is likely to be misunderstood as unpatriotic, is to observe that it is on principle questionable to choose for the Presidency a man who once headed up the Central Intelligence Agency. Shades of Comrade Andropov!

Whatever reservations one may have about one or more of the other three candidates, Mr. Quayle in the White House, or immediately in line for it, would be an affront to national sensibilities. I am reminded here of the unfortunate choice of Richard Nixon by Mr. Eisenhower in 1952. The character of such men can be expected to trip them up again and again. I expect that even more things will be exposed adverse to Mr. Quayle, considering the temperament, the desires, and the limitations of the man.

It is difficult to imagine Dan Quayle, no matter how the Presidency falls into his lap, as ever being invested with the moral as distinguished from the legal authority to send men into combat. An anonymous letter to the editor in the September 15th issue of the European edition of *Stars and Stripes,* the military newspaper, expresses class-conflict-engendering sentiments that will fester and corrupt if they are not properly ministered to:

> With regard to this new fuss and fury over J. Danforth Quayle.
>
> I don't believe anyone condemns someone for asking his parents' help in obtaining a spot in the National Guard. However, Sen. Quayle states he really did this because he wanted to join the National Guard and serve his country proudly. It seems that he must think the average citizen of America is a bit thick.
>
> Oh, wouldn't it have been great if we all could have used our parents' influence in getting a coveted National Guard position!
>
> Sen. Quayle supported the conflict but did not want to fight in it, no disrespect to the National Guard. However, I imagine that he told his parents: "Get me into the Guard and I will have done my national service with no chance of dying." I believe that many would have loved to have been able to give their sons that opportunity. However, not everyone had the contacts the Quayles had.
>
> Sen. Quayle is just plain and simply a hypocrite; he supported a war but wanted others to die for his ideals. So I guess that really does point out how much of a people's candidate he really is. The only people the *Quayle people* think about is *their* type of people—the *money people.*
>
> So Sen. Quayle didn't go to Canada or tear up his draft card. That's because he believed in *The War* and also because he didn't have to run—he had enough contacts through his family to avoid combat and still appear honorable.
>
> Well, all I can say is that if in all wars American boys had been able to do what Dan Quayle did, we never would have won World War I and World War II and Vietnam would have never begun.
>
> Sen. Quayle, you deliberately sought to avoid a war you and your family supported but it didn't matter to you about all the others, not so rich and fortunate, who had to go. I guess they were not your *type* of people. Why don't you just admit that, Sen. Quayle?

I return to conservatives and the Presidency. I call your attention to Willmoore Kendall's justly famous article on "The Two Majorities." He came down in 1960 on the side of the prosaic Congress as against the glamorous Presidency; he believed that the proper arena for conservatism was the legislature. But many conservatives now tend to ridicule the Congress and to celebrate the Presidency, if only because they can hope to control the one branch but not the other. Other conservatives have learned over the centuries, however, that plebiscitary government, which an exalted presidency promotes, is a far greater threat to the security of property than is a republic dominated by a duly elected legislature.

There are, I have argued here, developments among conservatives that bode ill for the Republic, and not only when men are again called upon to go to war. Conservatives are abandoning their principles, not least with respect to the true meaning of patriotism and the common good. The nation is lost sight of as special interests are catered to and served. Conservatives are settling for a Hollywood version of patriotism, as could be seen in the contrived and otherwise dubious passions associated in this Country with the 1984 Summer Olympic Games.

This abandonment of the finer conservative principles is related to the general problem of education. When self-interest becomes truly sovereign, people are not apt to know and to take seriously the constitutional principles and the demands of natural right that should help shape their passions and inform their understanding.

Permit me to acknowledge in closing that I appreciate your respect for that old conservative principle of freedom of speech that has obliged you, in the name of the common good, to hear me out on this occasion. This, too, testifies to the significance for the citizen of duty.

C.

The New Ways

9

SOME QUESTIONS ABOUT NIETZSCHE

To me this pretty tale no news can tell;
Some hundred thousand years I've known it well.
. . . .
Past and pure nothingness are one at last!
Whatboots this evermore creating, when
Things all sweep into nothingness again?
"There! Now 'tis past!" From this what can we glean?
'Tis all the same as though it ne'er had been;
Yet round and round it goes, as though it were.
I, for my part, Etrnal Void prefer.

Mephistopheles

I

The opening words of the first section of Friedrich Nietzsche's *Beyond Good and Evil* are these:

> The will to truth which will still tempt us to many a venture, that famous truthfulness of which all philosophers so far have spoken with respect—what questions has this will to truth not laid before us! What strange, wicked, questionable questions!

Philosophers so far have spoken a certain way about truth and its pursuit.

This talk was given at a Staff Seminar of the Basic Program of Liberal Education for Adults, The University of Chicago, Chicago, Illinois, May 24, 1980. (Original title: "Nietzsche's *Beyond Good and Evil*.") Leo Strauss said that this "always seemed to [him] the most beautiful of Nietzsche's books." 3 *Interpretation* 97 (Winter 1973).

The citations in this essay are, unless otherwise indicated, to Friedrich Nietzsche, *Beyond Good and Evil*, Walter Kaufmann translation (New York: Vintage Books, 1966).

The epigraph is taken from Johann W. von Goethe, *Faust*, II, iv, 10210–11, and II, v, 11597–603 (Theodore Martin translation).

125

Nietzsche, we learn, will speak otherwise: he will investigate what this "will to truth" amounts to, with an emphasis in his account upon the will rather than upon the truth. He will venture much in his investigation, for he will call into question, with his "strange, wicked, questionable questions," much that had been taken for granted. Among the things he ventures is a transformation of what previously was assumed to be good and of what was assumed to be evil, with special affection entertained by him for the "wicked."

Will is critical not only in the opening lines of this book; it is critical throughout. This emphasis is to be contrasted with classical writers on morality, such as Aristotle, who dwell much less on what Nietzsche calls the will. Will and willing are referred to in more than forty of the 296 sections of Nietzsche's book. In one section (19), they are referred to more than two dozen times; in another section (208), almost twenty times; in still another section (36), more than a dozen times. Altogether, there are some 140 references to will and willing. But these quite varied references are not evenly distributed. I have, working with the Walter Kaufman translation, noticed about fifty references in Part I, twenty in Part II, six in Part III, three in Part IV, six in Part V, thirty in Part VI, eleven in Part VII, four in Part VIII, and nine in Part IX. (Sometimes the will referred to *is* disparaged.)

The massive recourse to will and willing may be found in Parts I and II, which hold about one-half of the book's total. It is almost as if Nietzsche exerted his own will in those opening parts to establish himself: to define the terms, set the tone and indicate the presuppositions and scope of his project. Having established in Parts I and II the priority of the will, he can turn to other matters in Parts III, IV, and V which include the central sections of this book and where there are, altogether, only about one-tenth of the book's total references to will and willing. In the latter half of the book (with the possible exception of Part VIII), he reasserts and perhaps refines the opening emphasis upon the will, especially in Part VI.

The will, he seems to say, is a fundamental fact, whereas the "truth" is an arbitrary projection and perhaps best kept within quotation marks. He can speak of "*my* truths," as in Section 231, suggesting that what is designated as the truth varies from person to person. There may even be an intimation in Section 2 that the will comes closer to participating in Being than does the truth.

II

An emphasis upon the will and what such an emphasis presupposes may be noticed in various other things in Nietzsche's book. I touch on a few of these.

Consider first the central part of the work, Part V, "Natural History of Morals." Nietzsche reviews various schools of thought respecting morality. If the will is to be regarded as critical to human endeavor, including thinking itself, then motivation or whatever happens to shape one's will is likely to be decisive. This relation is anticipated in Section 6, where he observes,

> Indeed, if one would explain how the abstrusest metaphysical claims of a philosopher really came about, it is always well (and wise) to ask first: at what morality does all this (does *he*) aim? Accordingly, I do not believe that a "drive to knowledge" is the father of philosophy; but rather that another drive has, here as elsewhere, employed understanding (and misunderstanding) as a mere instrument.

We are provided in Section 187 the motivations for various moralities: ten sets of commandments, or ways of commanding, are enumerated here, with the underlying motivation determining each of the sets suggested. Perhaps this is related to what Nietzsche observes in Section 204, that moralizing is showing one's wounds.

Moralities are to be seen in terms of motivation or what the moralist really wants (in spite of his image of himself)—in terms of what he is really driving at, no matter what he says. It has long been evident (consider, for example, the "realism" of Plato's Thrasymachus) that the role of reason in human affairs is limited, that most men implicitly justify what they want on the basis of considerations they dare not make explicit. But Nietzsche argues, in effect, that the role of reason is far more limited than has ever been suspected. He denies that it has more than a subordinate role even among the philosophers regarded, or at least who regard themselves, as metaphysical and dispassionate.

III

Not only does Nietzsche expose what he considers to be (and no doubt all too often are) the hidden motivations of the various moralities men espouse, he also proposes a morality of his own. We should not be surprised to learn that this morality is moved by the desire for self-assertion. It tends to be ruthless and determined in its willful application, and is in a sense noble in its boldness. Nietzsche invites his readers to notice the discipline necessary for the flowering of an aristocracy, a discipline that can even be cruel in its dedication.

The instincts of the most talented should be permitted to manifest themselves. There is something natural in such willfulness. Ordinary morality, on the other hand—the prevailing morality, not only of Nietzsche's day but for centuries, if not for millennia—is herd morality. It is soft, undemanding, addicted to pity. (See Sections 61, 201, 203.) This morality suppresses both the instincts that the strong, or would-be strong, have and a people's efforts to test and thereby to shape and prove the best among them. It is observed in Section 126, "A people is a detour of nature to get to six or seven great men.—Yes, and then to get around them."

Herd morality, seen today in the democratic ethos, is highly suspect in that it discourages assertiveness and encourages permissiveness. Assertiveness seems critical to Nietzsche's emphasis on the will. Domination is made much of. We shall see that the philosopher, particularly, is one who dominates. (See Section 13. See, also, Sections 204, 206, 207.) Is not this in contrast to the emphasis placed upon gentleness in Plato and Shakespeare (to mention two representatives, early and late, of the classical tradition)?

IV

Assertiveness extends (does it not?) to the desire to conquer "history." (See Section 203.)

A conquest of history includes, among other things, the elimination of chance in human affairs. Is not this conquest crucial to the doctrine of "the eternal return" alluded to in Section 56? That doctrine means, among other things, that one passionately accepts (that is, one wills, one creates, as it were) all.

Even so, does not Nietzsche himself want to be remembered, perhaps even treasured, as the one who first formulated this doctrine of the infinite cyclical character of all that human beings endure? (See, also, Section 2.) In some sense, he may want to be godlike. (See Sections 9, 23, 43.) One is reminded of God's answer to Moses, upon being asked His name: "I will be what I will be."

Does Nietzsche prefer not to make much of what it is that happens to shape the will of the individual? He does recognize the vulnerability of those best fitted by nature for the most exalted willing. (See Section 205. Compare Section 274.)

V

An emphasis upon willing may be seen in the way moral judgments are talked about. Much is made of *values* and *valuations*—in some twenty sections. (See Sections 1, 2, 4, 43, 61, 191, 195, 200, 201, 203, 210, 211, 212, 224, 260, 261, 293.) Does not the term *values* suggest making and hence willing more than it does finding or discovering? (See Sections 11, 12.) To value, at least in the sense Nietzsche seems to use, is to allocate praise and blame, approval and disapproval, according to some standard beyond good and evil. One does not submit to something higher, to a standard of perfection; rather, one chooses (that is, constructs) one's own standards.

Philosophy seems to be a willing on a grand scale: "the greatest thoughts are the greatest events," we are told. (Section 285) But, it should at once be added, philosophers are rare: scientists and scholars are not philosophers, not even those scholars who staff philosophy departments and call themselves philosophers. (See Sections 56, 206, 210, 211.) Philosophers harbor an exceptional desire of the heart. (See Sections 5, 8.) How (according to Nietzsche) they manifest the willing we have been examining is indicated in Section 211:

> *Genuine philosophers* . . . *are commanders and legislators:* they say *"thus* it *shall* be!" They first determine the Whither and the For What of man, and in so doing have at their disposal the preliminary labor of all philosophical laborers, all who have overcome the past. With a creative hand they reach for the future, and all that is and has been becomes a means for them, an instrument, a hammer. Their "knowing" is *creating*, their creating is a legislation, their will to truth is—*will to power.*

There is something bold about this formulation, just as there is in what Nietzsche suggests about the Anti-Christ. (Section 256) His translator tries to soften the effects of Nietzsche's radical formulations by saying in a note to Section 213:

> The element of snobbery and the infatuation with "dominating" and "looking down" are perhaps more obvious than Nietzsche's perpetual sublimation and spiritualization of these and other similar qualities.

Is not such an excuse for Nietzsche an instance of the flight from tough-mindedness that he deplored?

One must also wonder what the "will to power" comes down to. May it not be little more than a "will to will"? I shall return to this point.

VI

Willing and valuation require Nietzsche to go beyond good and evil. The truly remarkable man is not bound as others are. To will—to be in charge of what one does, independent of standards—is to go beyond good and evil.

What *is* beyond good and evil? Is there something to be aimed at beyond? (See Sections 4, 23, 44, 116, 153, 201, 207, 212, 255, 260, 295.) But, then, why is not that something itself a good? Or does Nietzsche merely disavow good as conventionally understood?

Is it the assertion of the will that is vital here? Does it come down to personal self-assertion, to an insistence upon differentness? Is there not something radically unpolitical about this approach?

Is it the *going* beyond that matters, not what one is going to? That is, is it the process that is decisive here, or does the direction one moves matter? How does one know that one is going "beyond" rather than falling "back"? One's reading of "history" may have something to do with determining the direction that is to be insisted upon. But is this not to take one's bearings, in one's willfulness, by what has chanced to be dominant in one's time? Is this not like the child who resists without rhyme or reason whatever happens to be put before him, asserting thereby his independence, an oppressive or otherwise threatening independence that his instincts may want him to be saved from?

A playful image of an emphasis upon the will, a willfulness that abjures goals that may confine one, may be seen in Tristram Shandy's account of the choices before the traveller (Laurence Sterne, *Tristram Shandy*, VII, iii):

> It is a great inconvenience to a man in a haste, that there are three distinct roads between *Calais* and *Paris*, in behalf of which there is so much to be said by the several deputies from the towns which lie along them, that half a day is easily lost in settling which you'll take.
>
> First, the road by *Lisle* and *Arras*, which is the most [round]about—but most interesting, and instructing.
>
> The second that by *Amiens*, which you may go, if you would see *Chantilly*——
>
> And that by *Beauvais*, which you may go, if you will.
>
> For this reason a great many chuse to go by *Beauvais*.

Only if one goes by way of *Beauvais* (is the meaning of the name played upon here?) may one *assert* oneself. Is this what Nietzsche's will to power almost comes down to? If Tristram Shandy is to be believed, "a great many" (a herd?) have chosen as Nietzsche advocates. One is reminded of the Kantian suggestion that we should suspect any moral alternative that is pleasurable.

Do I exaggerate in making as much as I do of the will in Nietzsche and in playing up as much as I do his repudiation of ends or goals, at least as these are commonly understood? He, with his poetic genius, exaggerates much more than I can safely do. My exaggerations are offered in the spirit of his, if only to point up the implications and risks of his doctrines as they come to view among the uninitiated. I appreciate that I run the risk, in proceeding as I do here and elsewhere in what I hope are salutary political reflections—I run the risk of trivializing the challenging arguments of truly great thinkers, thinkers superior to me in both heart and mind.

VII

The nobility Nietzsche yearns for is found beyond good and evil. We are familiar with this juxtaposition from Greek tragedy in which, for instance, a hero may be somewhat unjust and yet obviously noble.

The willfulness of the noble permits a certain greatness. It is said in Section 212:

> And the philosopher will betray something of his own ideal when he posits: "He shall be greatest who can be loneliest, the most concealed, the most deviant, the human being beyond good and evil, the master of his virtues, he that is overrich in will. Precisely this shall be called *greatness:* being capable of being as manifold as whole, as ample as full." And to ask it once more: today—is greatness *possible?*

Such greatness, he asserts, depends on retaining the distinction between slave morality and master morality, on recognizing thereby the immeasurable value for genuine aristocracy of the "pathos of distance." (Sections 260, 257)

Greatness appears first in "monstrous and frightening masks." We can be reminded of what Niccolò Machiavelli says about foundings: Rome, for example, was grounded in a fratricide. The greatness Nietzsche advocates takes the place of the just, as conventionally understood. Justice is redefined: it is said of certain aristocrats that "they consider intolerance itself a virtue, calling it 'justice.'" (Section 262) What men call the "common good" and the "general welfare" are called into question. (Sections 43, 228) Indeed, all of the cardinal virtues are transformed. It is instructive to consider, in Section 284, what form each of the cardinal virtues as understood by the ancients takes for Nietzsche. (See, also, Section 295.) He is not simply irresponsible, but rather indicates that the human species would eventually be healthier under his dispensation, whatever the immediate trauma of making the necessary changes.

Much of this argument was anticipated in Nietzsche's Preface by his repudiation of Plato's "pure spirit and the good as such." The end is not critical, we are told, but rather the origins of things for a people and its great men; those origins can be troubling because of the toughness needed to break the fetters by which mankind binds itself from time to time. For this liberation a "new species of philosophers" is needed, for whom this book is to be a guide, if only as an escape plan. (See Section 2.)

I have suggested that much is made of process, especially when goals are repudiated as the primary concern. This is put most pithily by Nietzsche: "In the end one loves one's desire and not what is desired." (Section 175) Does not this lend support to the proposition that the will to power, of which so much is made in this book, comes down to little more than the will to will?

VIII

Still another consequence or reflection of the emphasis upon willing may be seen in the indication that the decisive science is to be, at least for the time being, psychology, not philosophy as traditionally understood. Nietzsche reviews in the opening part of this book the competing schools of philosophy, laying bare the often-concealed prejudices on which each school depends. If one emphasizes the will, study of how the psyche moves and especially how it wills becomes critical.

References to psychology may be found in at least a dozen sections of this book. (See Sections 12, 23, 45, 56, 58, 61, 196, 218, 222, 229, 230, 254, 269.) Even more striking is the exhibition of Nietzsche as a psychologist, which may be seen throughout the book. Psychology is critical also if much is to be made, as is done by Nietzsche, of instinct. The references to this too are numerous. (See, for example, Sections 3, 4, 10, 13, 26, 145, 158, 191, 233, 238, 239, 251, 256, 258, 260, 261, 263.) Bearing upon this is what is said about laying bare the motivation for the various moralities. (Section 187)

Perhaps it is also the emphasis upon willing which makes Nietzsche's references to conscience so plentiful, again in marked contrast to the classical writers on ethics. More than thirty sections in the book deal explicitly with conscience. (See Sections 5, 10, 25, 29, 31, 32, 33, 45, 46(?), 58, 61, 98,

134, 188, 191, 199, 201, 203, 204, 205, 208, 211, 212, 214, 216, 228, 230, 247, 251, 258, 264, 265, 291.) Is it not the conscience to which one must look to guide one's willing when traditional standards of good and evil, some of them rooted in nature, have been disavowed? Even so, does not *conscience* tend to suggest, and not only etymologically, something intrinsic to the soul, something innate that provides guidance, even though it can be informed and instructed and otherwise shaped? (Something like this can also be said of the traditional *natural right*.) Furthermore, does not conscience somehow reinforce the importance of the self and its choices, its shaping (not its finding?) of the course to be followed? I am reminded of Nikos Kazantzakis's characterization of Nietzsche, in the early years of this century, as a prophet of the deification of self. (Kazantzakis, *Serpent and Lily*, p. 97.)

Psychology is also critical because of the importance for Nietzsche of the male-female relationship. In his formulations here he finds himself opposed to that Goethean elevation of the Eternal Feminine which had had by Nietzsche's time considerable influence in Germany. (See, for example, Section 236.) The importance of the male-female relationship is evident throughout Nietzsche's book.

Perhaps this fascination with the male-female relationship and especially with the mystery of the female is a Nietzschean way of dealing with nature and her conquest. This is related to what he suggests about instinct. (See Section 9.)

IX

Can psychology suffice? Or is philosophy necessary if the psychologist is to know what he is doing—that is, if he is to know what he does and does not know? Does not philosophy in the classical sense address better the problems of nature? Does not Nietzsche sense this as an alternative, which may be seen in his repeated efforts both to come to terms with the meaning of Socrates and to separate Plato from Socrates? That Nietzsche has a lively awareness of what philosophy once meant may be seen in his comments on and recourse to esotericism. (See Section 30. See, also, Sections 26, 40. See, as well, Sections 33, 188, 260.)

Psychology may be useful in any effort to understand Nietzsche himself. He knows what we do, that his work very much depends on many others. Yet he seems at times to resent that he is in any way subordinated to the past, however radical his proposed departures from it. He conjures up the eternal return, which means among other things that *he* is "before" as well as "after" "the others."

Again and again one gets the impression that Nietzsche strives for effect, that his primary concern may be not with the truth, but rather with changes in the souls of his readers without which the truth does tend to be trivialized. Does such an effort by him express a kind of willfulness? (Socrates is a problem for him here also in that Socrates does less, if any, of this kind of posturing.) Much of Nietzsche's effect depends on "shock value," on his spectacular departures from what has been said and long accepted by his predecessors. But in a peculiar sense, this too is to *be* dependent on others, upon what *they* have happened to say.

Nietzsche ends the final section of his book with an affectionate farewell to his "old beloved—*wicked* thoughts!" (Section 296) The "wicked" here echoes the opening lines of the first section, where he speaks of "strange, wicked, questionable questions." Why is so much made of "wickedness"? How does this bear upon his effort to plunge beyond good and evil? Perhaps the following suggestions can contribute to that deeper reading which Nietzsche requires. To be wicked is to assert oneself; to be good is to be bound by rules, to be essentially like others who are good. Or, put another way: there may be only one way to go right in a particular set of circumstances, but there are many ways to go wrong. There are many ways to be wicked or to think wicked thoughts. To act or at least to think wickedly is to be an individual, to be somewhat in control of one's life. Or is it? (With this we return to the problem of Gyges' ring put by Glaucon to Socrates in Book II of Plato's *Republic.*)

Perhaps it suffices to close this somewhat tentative essay on *Beyond Good and Evil* with a reminder, drawn from Leo Strauss, of the old saying that wisdom cannot be separated from moderation, however venturesome and hence attractive a thinker may be. (See *The Constitutionalist,* pp. 494, 694, 738, 763.)

10

SOME QUESTIONS ABOUT THE FREUDIAN PERSUASION

It is safer to try to understand the low in the light of the high than the high in the light of the low. In doing the latter one necessarily distorts the high, whereas in doing the former one does not deprive the low of the freedom to reveal itself fully as what it is.

LEO STRAUSS

I

Some of my audience may be tempted to wonder about the dubious psychic forces that impel me to adopt the position I do in venturing to sketch an Aristotelian assessment of what Freudian psychiatry offers us. But I know they will try to resist that temptation, especially if they should recall that others, some with obviously different temperaments, have espoused positions similar to mine. A position such as the one I now suggest should be considered on its merits, and no doubt will be by everyone able to escape both the prejudices of his times and the promptings of his own psyche.

I will try to indicate, both through an illustration and in more general terms, what the ancients knew about the proper way of looking at and shaping the human soul. I should note that *our* most useful bridge between the ancients and the moderns may be Shakespeare, even though he seems to have far more concern than do the ancients for what we call con-

This talk was given at the Brent House Ecumenical Center, The University of Chicago, Chicago, Illinois, October 21, 1973. (Original title: "An Aristotelian Assessment of What Modern Psychiatry Offers Us.") The other participants on the panel were Malcolm P. Sharp and Lawrence Z. Freedman. See the headnote for Essay No. 28, below.

The epigraph is taken from Leo Strauss, *Spinoza's Critique of Religion* (New York: Schocken Books, 1965), p. 2.

science and guilt. In this respect the moderns, and especially the psychiatrically oriented, seem to be very much affected by Christian influences.

II

First, there is my illustration of what the ancients knew. The truly temperate man, as described in Aristotle's *Nicomachean Ethics,* simply does not have illicit desires in any serious or significant way. That is, men may be so trained and instructed that they do not have any improper desires that distort in a sustained way their thought or their actions. (I am not talking about fleeting apprehensions of passing beauties, which tend to be much more theoretical or inquisitive than practical or acquisitive in their implications and their effects.) Such temperance, it should be added, does not seem to be regarded by Aristotle as rare.

Modern psychiatry must challenge this ancient teaching on at least two grounds. It must question whether any desires should be labelled *improper*. In addition, it suspects that the deliberate disparagement of any particular kind of desire as improper reveals an unhealthy repression that is potentially destructive. Psychiatry at times denies, in effect, the authoritative role of reason either in assessing or in regulating the desires that men are heir to. So much for my illustration.

I shall now try to put the differences between the ancients and the moderns in more general terms. A critical question, upon comparing antiquity and modernity, is where the emphasis is to be put, whether the higher is to be understood in terms of the lower or the lower in terms of the higher. Put another way, the question may be whether movements of matter are ultimately fundamental to any effort to understand both our humanity and the ideas.

I should add that there were in ancient times serious materialists, materialists who were perhaps more sophisticated than most of their modern counterparts. Heraclitus, for example, could observe, "It is hard to fight desire; what it wants it buys with the soul." It suffices for our immediate purposes, however, for me to suggest that the ancient materialists were "moderns" before their time.

All this is not to deny that both the ancients and the moderns have something to be said for their respective positions. The ancients would grant that the material conditions for human existence seem evident. The moderns would concede that mind is critical for human life, if only to permit one to respond intelligently to the sovereignty of matter.

Nor do I intend to deny that modern psychiatry has much to offer. Indeed, whom else is one likely to rely upon today for the treatment of common psychic disturbances? Whom else is it prudent to turn to but the medical man who has had considerable experience with such suffering and who controls the appropriate drugs and hospital facilities? But it is also prudent to remember that someone who can be depended on to be helpful still may not really know what he is doing. That is, the psychiatrist, however useful he often is, simply may not understand what the human soul is truly like. He does depend on certain theoretical opinions about the nature of the soul that remain essentially unexamined. These opinions may even be so formulated as to be unexaminable and hence difficult to distinguish from articles of faith.

Does not modern psychiatry have to deny that there is any normality rooted in nature, that there can be such a thing as perversions of the psyche? In a sense, modern psychiatry is necessarily much more concerned with ministering to individuals who happen to consider themselves (and may well be) ill or at least maladjusted than it is with serving the community. A healthy community naturally tends to direct its attention primarily to discovering and securing enduring standards for the citizen-body, less to treating troubled patients. The limits of modern psychiatry are suggested by its origins in and preoccupation with the study of dramatic aberrations of the human soul. On the other hand, the thoughtfulness of psychiatry is suggested by its insistence that even the most bizarre aberrations are never senseless: such aberrations have an explanation in terms of the experiences of an individual who may have had certain genetic predispositions; they are not simply wild and meaningless.

III.

The critical difference between the ancients and the moderns may be stated in still another way. The ancients believed, or at least believed it salutary to affirm, something that the moderns tend to deny: a judgment of whether a human activity is natural or unnatural, good or bad, is an essential, perhaps even the most important part, of any description of it. It is partly in reliance upon this opinion that Plato and Aristotle always had in view *the best* in all their efforts to describe what is and what may be, and hence in their efforts to guide both the human being and the community to achieve what they could in their circumstances.

One must, the ancients seem to say, be at least aware of the highest if one is to make a serious attempt to understand anything, even the lowest things. A critical feature of the lowest is that it is clearly low. Common sense, reflected in everyday language, does depend on a grasp of things that distinguishes the high from the low, the noble from the base. Intellectuals tend to suppress what men have "always known" about such things, including about the distinction between human and inhuman. But modern intellectuals do share the general awareness, however much they sometimes insist upon the importance of the animal element in man, that when the reason goes, the decisively human element is gone. Does not psychoanalysis itself depend on the assumption that the most disturbed of men can usually be talked to, that reason is somehow vital to man?

It should be remembered, on the other hand, that Socrates seems also to have recognized the erotic element as a vital part, however transformed, of the psyche of the philosophical man, of the human being who is truly and fully reasoning. Perhaps it would provide an appropriate starting-point for any discussion of the differences between the ancients and the moderns to examine how the transformed *eros* in Socrates is to be compared with the phenomenon of sublimation in Freud.

Does not one of these approaches suggest that a man can know what he is doing and thinking and that he can at least begin to know what it is to know, while the other approach reflects the opinion that knowing, whether about one's self or about the nature of things, is an illusion without a respectable future?

11

SOME QUESTIONS ABOUT "EXISTENTIALISM"

Because justice is a kind of "rightness" as Anselm teaches (On Truth, 12) or "equality," as the Philosopher teaches (Nicomachean Ethics, V, 1), justice in its essential nature will depend primarily upon whatever has that measure by which the equality and rightness of justice are established among things. Now the will cannot be characterized as the first rule but rather as ruled, inasmuch as it is directed by reason and intellect. This is not only true for us but for God as well, although the will in us is really distinct from the intellect. This is why the will and its rightness are not the same thing. But in God the will is really identified with the intellect, so that the rightness of his will is really the same as the will itself. So the primary thing upon which the essential nature of all justice depends is the wisdom of the divine intellect, which establishes things perfectly, in proportion to one another and to their cause. The essential nature of created justice consists in this proportion. In asserting that justice depends only on the will, one is declaring that the divine will does not act according to the order of wisdom, a blasphemous assertion.

THOMAS AQUINAS

This talk was given at the Annual Convention, American Political Science Association, Denver, Colorado, September 4, 1982. (Sponsor: Claremont Institute for the Study of Statesmanship and Political Philosophy.) It was in response to papers by Christopher A. Colmo (on Soren Kierkegaard), Gregory B. Smith (on Martin Heidegger), and Jules Gleicher (on Jean-Paul Sartre). See, e.g., Colmo, "Reason and Revelation in the Thought of Leo Strauss," 18 *Interpretation* 145, 313 (1990); Jules Gleicher, *The Accidental Revolutionary: Essay on the Political Teaching of Jean-Paul Sartre* (Lanham, Maryland: University Press of America, 1983); Gregory B. Smith, *Between Eternities: Existentialism and Political Philosophy: A Study of Nietzsche and Heidegger* (University of Chicago doctoral dissertation, 1987).

The epigraph is taken from Thomas Aquinas, *On Truth*, Q. 23, A. 6, c. See Mary T. Clark, ed., *An Aquinas Reader* (Garden City, N.Y.: Image Books, Doubleday & Co., 1972), pp. 337, 356–57. "[A]ll directing is necessarily achieved through the wisdom of someone gifted with intelligence. Thus in the world of mechanical arts, architects are called the wise men of their craft. Now, there is a mutual order in the things produced by God, because this order is always or nearly always uniform. It is clear then that God brought things into existence through ordering them. And so God brought things into existence through his wisdom." *Ibid.*, p. 337.

I

Much is made by some "existentialists" (or should we simply say, "moderns"?) of the *absurd*. This seems to be a term used to disparage unrealistic attempts to act well, attempts based on an all-too-human longing to do the right thing. Thus both ancient philosophy and ancient revelation, if not philosophy and revelation simply, are shown to burden mankind with aspirations that are, when properly understood, beyond realization, perhaps even beyond comprehension. This is what Soren Kierkegaard and Jean-Paul Sartre, as well as perhaps Friedrich Nietzsche and Martin Heidegger, can be taken to say.

There is no objectively determinable way out for the desperate human being of conscience. This can be said despite the life-guiding claims made not only by revelation, but also by philosophy with its reliance on nature. Things are so much beyond objective comprehension (or prudent control, with a view to a knowable or obvious end) that the only source of certainty and guidance resides in the actor himself. Subjectivity, as we call it, is made much of.

II

Decisive, then, is one's will. One must act, even though one can have no reason to prefer one action to another.

The refusal to act in accordance with what one has had prescribed to oneself, whether by one's own completely free choice or by one's completely ungrounded faith, is due not to ignorance (as, say, Socrates indicates), but rather is due to insubordination (as Kierkegaard puts it), or to a loss of nerve (as Heidegger perhaps puts it), or to bad faith (as Sartre puts it).

III

Related to this emphasis upon the will is the insistence sometimes heard today that philosophy is at its most fruitful in the context of, albeit in opposition to, the closed society. (For some this becomes an argument against liberal democracy.) This opinion about the relation of philosophy to the closed society seems to go hand in hand with the opinion that the will is vital to human accomplishments, especially since accomplishment is measured primarily in terms of the resistance one encounters and overcomes.

Does this too reflect the radical subjectivity of leading modern thinkers? Is it not to see the high too much in terms of the low? (See the epigraph for Essay No. 10, above.)

IV

One must wonder upon encountering gifted moderns of an existentialist turn of mind what it is they know that the ancients did not and vice versa. The influences upon intellectuals, whatever their presuppositions and creeds, of Christianity and of modern science with its technology are virtually impossible to exaggerate, however difficult it may be to be precise about them. These influences seem to contribute to a disposition in modernity to make even more of human ignorance than Socrates ever did. Easily overlooked are the vital things that Socrates seemed to know about knowledge itself.

The critical problem here may be how well authors such as Kierkegaard and Sartre (to say nothing of Nietzsche or Heidegger) read the Greeks and the Bible. One can appear to be perverse and the other shallow, however brilliant both may be. Certainly, there is a problem when someone does not seem to understand that pleasure is generally better than pain.

V

What is there that attracts the young of this century to authors such as Kierkegaard, Nietzsche, and Sartre? One's talent is seen to be serious and worthy of emulation only when it is "original," not when it is "derivative" (that is, when it is dedicated to understanding and reviving the best that has already been learned and taught). And yet the thoughtful student can be attracted to Kierkegaard by his perceptive concern with the problem of "the same and the other."

The status both of nature and of the community is called into question by modern intellectuals. It seems to be believed that each of us is somehow on his own; nature is limited to one's temperament (with a low view of human nature taken for granted here?). We are reminded once again of the status of "individuality" in modernity.

To notice such things is to return to the significance, especially among existentialists, of an emphasis upon the will. It is believed that one's "personality," or uniqueness, is most obviously manifested in one's will. It can be said with some plausibility, even though perhaps unfairly, that no matter what the subject, both Kierkegaard and Sartre talk primarily about themselves.

A further indication of the importance of the personality and hence of the will may be seen in certain distinctively modern terms made so much of by the authors under consideration: *abyss, anxiety, authenticity, fear and trembling, self*. *Authenticity*, for example, may exhibit more concern for the feelings and circumstances of the self, including the roots one sprang from or the abyss over which one finds oneself suspended, than simply for the truth.

Anything but the serenity of the classics may be discerned in such terms, or rather in the cast of mind and in the way of life they reflect and encourage. To dwell upon *fear and trembling* or upon *anxiety* is hardly edifying. Compare such sentiments as those of the Athenian Stranger in Plato's *Laws* (707D):

[I]n our consideration of the nature of the land and the order of the laws, we're looking now to the virtue of the regime. We do not hold, as the many do, that preservation and mere existence are what is most honorable for human beings; what is most honorable is for them to become as excellent as possible and to remain so for as long a time as they may exist.

It would be curious indeed if modern intellectuals, the contemporary imitations of Plato's rare philosophers, should resemble in critical respects "the many" of antiquity.

VI

I return to two questions I have raised about existentialism and politics.

First, there is a question about the relation of philosophy to the closed society. Cannot philosophy be usefully described as that intellectual activity which strives for a godlike contemplation of unchanging things? Certainly any divine grasp of eternal things must ultimately be independent of any political order. Certainly, also, something vital to philosophy is lost sight of if philosophy should be seen substantially if not even primarily in terms of what it is in opposition to, however much the closed society might have influenced the mode of the best philosophical discourse that happens to be available to us.

VII

The second question to which I return has to do with the role of the will or resoluteness, if not faith, in these matters. What *is* the character of the will? It does not seem to be reasoning. Can it truly be distinguished from desire? May it not be little more than a spirited or otherwise respectable way of making much of personal ambition and of mere pleasure as one's guide to life? Desire tends to be more individualistic or self-centered than even spiritedness: for the desires are infinite, and each man can have his unique combination of desires, whereas the spirited does naturally try to "identify," if not to ally, itself with the highest or the best.

One suspects that any emphasis by a talented man on the will as sovereign is likely to be self-deceptive, permitting him to insist that genuine understanding, whether for its own sake or as the basis for prudent action, is not possible. Does not such an insistence, however fashionable it may now be in some quarters, ignore the promptings of the natural inclinations of most reasonable men?

12

HEIDEGGER AND THE NEED FOR TYRANNY

*As to those philosophical gentlemen, those Citizens of the World as they
call themselves, he owed he did not wish to see any of them in our public
Councils. He would not trust them. The men who can shake off their attachments to their own Country can never love any other. These attachments are the wholesome prejudices which uphold all Governments.*

GOUVERNEUR MORRIS

I

Even more remarkable than the many other wondrous things that technology, which is grounded in the modern natural sciences, has brought us
are the habits and expectations that technology has promoted. Not only
have wonders become routine, but the anticipation and assimilation of
ever more remarkable wonders are taken for granted.

For example, I have been told by an expert that a few seconds delay at
one's computer terminal because of heavy traffic is rather annoying; a ten-
second delay is well-nigh intolerable, even though it encompasses compu-
tations that would once have taken a mathematician months to do
manually. It is, my expert also tells me, like playing a piano: one wants an
immediate response from one's instrument.

A godlike power is thus assumed by man. Is there not posed here the
problem of piety, in that old relations are seriously distorted as unprece-

---

This talk was given at the Basic Program Weekend, The University of Chicago, East Troy,
Wisconsin, November 8, 1981. (Original title: "Martin Heidegger—On the Perils of Technology and Nazism.")

Martin Heidegger's 1966 *Der Spiegel* Interview, published May 31, 1976, is available in
English translation in *Philosophy Today*, Winter 1976, pp. 267–84.

The epigraph is taken from a statement in the Constitutional Convention of 1787 by Gouverneur Morris, August 9, 1787. See *Notes of Debates in the Federal Convention of 1787 Reported by James Madison* (Athens: Ohio University Press, 1960), p. 421.

dented human control of "the world around us" is acquired? Consider the significance of being able, by manipulating a modest-looking device in one's house, to make a bell ring almost instantly in any one of hundreds of millions of places across vast oceans and in distant lands. This reminds us of how extensive our power has become. It should remind us as well of how vulnerable we have become: for a bell in one's own home, in one's most private refuge, can similarly be activated by anyone elsewhere. This is a quite benevolent version of what others, tens of thousands of miles away, can quickly do to us here by pressing buttons there.

It is amazing how intricate and ingenious so many of the devices are to which we have become accustomed. But, as I have noticed, perhaps even more amazing is how easily we adapt to new technological marvels. This means for all too many of us the dulling of a sense of wonder and of curiosity. An effort must be made to see these things with fresh eyes, even as we recall that many wonders have already been developed and that many more can be expected.

II

What, in these circumstances, is the status of the miraculous insofar as it can be distinguished from the wondrous? Does not something happen to the status of the miraculous when we can not only perform wonders on demand, but also casually discard the wondrous things of another day? One is struck by the signs of outmoded or used-up technology all around us, from small portable radios and ingenious devices used in the operating room of a hospital to obsolete buildings along miles of abandoned railroad track.

Consider what "instant replay" does to our sports. Does it empower us to see better what we are watching or does it distort games that depend a lot for their appeal on immediate judgments by which one has to stand? Consider also the finely manicured lawns of some fancy homes: one can see machines at work sucking up the leaves that are shed, robbing the earth of nourishment it might have acquired in the age-old cycle of death and life.

These illustrations suggest problems with the wondrous technology to which we have become accustomed and which, we should acknowledge, few of us would be willing to do completely without. For example, what are we likely to do if the useful life of someone we care for can be prolonged only by an operation that depends on quite sophisticated technology that has just been perfected?

One useful way of assessing technology, of examining the problems it does bring with it, is to look at some responses to it. The desperation of the cure resorted to can point up the seriousness of the disease. The seriousness of the disease can be usefully illustrated for us by glancing at the experience of Martin Heidegger with the Nazis. It would be difficult to exaggerate the reputation of this thinker in Twentieth-Century philosophical circles. His notorious public collaboration with the Nazis in the early days of Hitler's power is instructive, especially if we take him at his word in his postwar ratification of his prewar suggestion that "the inner truth and greatness" of the Nazi movement was directed to "the encounter between global technology and man." (See Heidegger, *An Introduction to Metaphysics,* p. 166; *Spiegel* Interview, p. 275.)

The disease accompanying technology may be seen not only in what it was that Heidegger was responding to, but also in the form of his response. His response was peculiarly infected by the disease itself. It was a response by perhaps the greatest European thinker of his time, but it was a response that was not in the best tradition of European thought.

This is illustrated by the report in 1968 by Hans Jonas, a scholar (now living in the United States) who had fled from Germany to Great Britain in the 1930s. His report contrasts the conduct of Heidegger with that of an undistinguished practitioner of an old school in German philosophy (*Journal of Central Conference of American Rabbis,* January 1968, p. 27):

To illustrate the plight of ethics in contemporary philosophy, let me open this paper with a personal reminiscence. When in 1945 I re-entered vanquished Germany as a member of the Jewish Brigade in the British army, I had to decide on whom of my former teachers in philosophy I could in good conscience visit, and whom not. It turned out that the "no" fell on my main teacher [he refers here to Heidegger, without naming him], perhaps the most original and profound, certainly one of the most influential among the philosophers of this century, who by the criteria which then had to govern my choice had failed the human test of the time; whereas the "yes" included the much lesser figure of a rather narrow traditionalist of Kantian persuasion, who meant little to me philosophically but of whose record in those dark years I heard admirable things. When I did visit him and congratulated him on the courage of his principled stand, he said a memorable thing: "Jonas," he said, "I tell you this: Without Kant's teaching I couldn't have done it." Here was a limited man, but sustained in an honorable course of action by the moral force of an outmoded philosophy; and there was the giant of contemporary thought—not hindered, some even say helped, by his philosophy in joining the cause of evil. The point is that this was more than a private failing, just as the other's better bearing was, by his own avowal, more than a private virtue. The tragedy was that the truly twentieth-century thinker of the two, he whose word had stirred the youth of a whole generation after the first World

War, had not offered in his philosophy a reason for setting conduct in the noble tradition stemming from Socrates and Plato and ending, perhaps, in Kant.

"Thus, there is in this personal experience," Professor Jonas continued,

an indication of the plight of modern philosophy when it comes to ethical norms, which are conspicuously absent from its universe of truth. How are we to explain this vacuum? What, with so different a past, has caused the great Nothing with which philosophy today responds to one of the oldest questions—the question of how we ought to live?

Mr. Jonas then suggested an answer to the question of how this had come to be:

Three interrelated determinants of modern thought have a share in the nihilistic situation, or less dramatically put, in the contemporary impasse of ethical theory—two of them theoretical and the third practical: the modern concept of nature, the modern concept of man, and the fact of modern technology supported by both. All three imply the negation of certain fundamental tenets of the philosophical as well as the religious tradition.

We notice that Mr. Jonas observed that "ethical norms" are "conspicuously absent" from "modern philosophy." To what extent did technology, or the modern natural science on which it depends, replace old-fashioned "ethical norms"?Did Heidegger's radical approach to philosophical questions help undermine the best of German idealism (seen, perhaps, in thinkers such as Kant)? Or was it that Kant and those immediately influenced by him were themselves decisively affected by modern natural science and other developments and hence contributed to the subversion of the natural basis for "ethical norms"?

Mr. Jonas could himself speak of the principled German professor who resisted the Nazis as having been sustained by "the moral force of an outmoded philosophy." Such a man might have been one of thousands. I suspect that not enough credit is given to many, albeit a minority of, Germans who had to make very difficult decisions and who did stand for humanity. It should be remembered that the Nazis had to conceal from the German people at large the worst atrocities they committed, which suggests that the Nazis were obliged to recognize that there remained among the German people a residual sense of humanity that it would have been dangerous to offend too much, even in the name of national security in time of war.

This residual sense of humanity, I might add, goes far deeper than even whatever Kant provided. Modern philosophical thought has all too often weakened the effectiveness of this sense, thereby permitting mere technological considerations and the economic and other so-called practical considerations closely allied to technology to dominate communal developments. One consequence of this is the subversion of the status of the natural. I will return to this later. For the moment it suffices to notice further that for Mr. Jonas not only would Kantianism be outmoded, but also perhaps Platonic thought, which does provide the life of Socrates as a model of how the thoughtful man should live, especially in dark times.

Let us return directly to Heidegger, whose scholarly thought, as Mr. Jonas noticed, some say even helped Heidegger to ally himself with the cause of evil. That thought, to which some contemporary intellectuals subscribe "in theory" however much they may abhor its practical alliance with Nazism, may be in decisive respects too abstract and metaphysical, with insufficient concern for the ethical and the political. This may be a critical Twentieth-Century failing: ethical questions tend to be regarded as beyond the realm of philosophy or science; rather, the things truly knowable are "questions of fact."

Technology as well as modern metaphysics can be seen as peculiarly well-qualified to deal with questions of fact. But people cannot help noticing that when technology is in the saddle something vital is missing from human life, and so a political remedy is sought. It is all too often sought by men who have themselves contributed to the problem or who are, in any event, ill-equipped to think politically (that is to say, with prudence, which must be distinguished from the cunning and opportunism to which Heidegger himself all too often resorted).

With these preliminary observations behind us, we can turn to the 1966 Heidegger interview that was published in the May 31, 1976 issue of *Der Spiegel*, which was shortly after Heidegger's death. It should be evident not only that my own study of Heidegger's major works is quite limited, but also that even the *Spiegel* interview is used by me only for the light it throws upon our immediate inquiry.

III

The aspects of the *Spiegel* interview of interest to us here, in our investigation of the place of technology in modern life, include Heidegger's explanation of his collaboration with the Nazis and his treatment of certain Jews, especially his teacher Edmund Husserl (who died in 1938). There are evident here the ramifications of his understanding of the Nazis as a response to modern technology, which leads to his conclusion as a patriotic thinker very much concerned for the future of his country if not of mankind: "Only a god can save us." (*Spiegel* Interview, p. 277) Thus the problem of his Nazi collaboration is intimately linked by Heidegger himself to the problem of modern technology.

Mrs. Husserl, a mere woman, did not see things the way Heidegger did. She exhibited what one might call a genuinely human response when she announced to Heidegger the breaking of all relations between the Heidegger and Husserl families.

It is apparent from all this and how it is explained (indeed by Heidegger's need to explain, decades after the event) that his Nazi collaboration was not a mere episode nor a stray moment in his career. This support of the Nazis in the early 1930s by a forty-four-year-old professor who was eminent enough to have been able to go anywhere in the world was never publicly repudiated by him. Exculpatory letters and essays may someday turn up among Heidegger's posthumously published works, but in these matters a contemporary public examination of the facts and issues is almost indispensable. The failure to subject oneself to such scrutiny in one's lifetime while informed critics are still around is highly suspect.

The most interesting question here may be, as has been suggested, what the relation is between the doctrines of perhaps the most influential Twentieth-Century thinker and his political career, the career of a man who collaborated with the Nazis and never decisively repudiated what he had done. This question, I have suggested, may throw useful light on our inquiry into the relation between technology and society.

IV

How questionable Heidegger's Nazi collaboration was may be inferred from the evasiveness and quibbling he resorts to when he tries to explain himself three decades later. Here as elsewhere on this occasion I characterize rather than attempt to summarize the *Spiegel* interview. Anyone who wants to assess, and indeed understand, what I am saying must read that interview for himself.

Fairness also requires that we notice the dangers that Heidegger was trying to avoid. One can get some idea of how desperate the social and psychic effects of modern life had become for Heidegger from the extreme measures to which he was willing to resort in order to straighten things out. How bad things were is suggested by the very fact that someone such as Heidegger should have seen the Nazis as the only way out, at least for the Germany he cared for.

It should be noticed as well that patriots such as Heidegger consider national disintegration to be at least as threatening and as much a cause for anxiety as others consider persecutions, concentration camps, and wholesale extermination. Such patriots see in their country the grounding of everything worthwhile and the very possibility of Being itself, either Being as something knowable or Being as something livable. This is what can come of an apocalyptic view of things.

Technology and the relations undermined, as well as the relations promoted, by technology are serious concerns. Years after his Nazi experiment Heidegger could still be disturbed by large-scale movements and their social implications. The fates of individual human beings, even millions of them, evidently did not trouble him, but only his misjudgment.

Critical to the threat posed by technology is the cosmopolitanism which technology both depends on and promotes. Gypsies, foreign capitalists, Jews, international socialists and many Christians were condemned by the Nazis as subverting the ultimate sanctity of Germanness. The German patriot could be moved in the 1930s by the plight of the many Germans, part of *the people*, who were not within the German state. The effort to reassert the authority of the nation is presented as an effort by a people to resume control of its glorious destiny. It may even reflect an effort to reassert old virtues related to honor, sacrifice, and dedication to one's own. It is, in short, an effort to confront the technology that seduces mankind with its offers of unprecedented comfort and universal brotherhood. Socialists, we have been reminded by Winston Churchill, boasted before the First World War that "they had no country and that their first act in power would be to make short work of [long-established] thrones." (*Great Contemporaries*, p. 22)

Heidegger, when he assumed under the aegis of the Nazis the post of rector of his university in 1933, proclaimed a need to discipline scholarship. This was an intellectual concern and, as such, legitimate. The concern of Hitler and his followers, however, was more primitive. Churchill found it prudent to say of Hitler's efforts before 1935, "He, and the ever-increasing legions who worked with him, certainly showed at this time, in their patriotic ardour and love of country, that there was nothing they would not do or dare, no sacrifice of life, limb or liberty that they would not make themselves or inflict upon their opponents." (*Great Contemporaries*, p. 207)

The sentiments of the Nazis in those days drew upon nationalist passions of which Germans hold no monopoly. Thus it could be said recently of certain English conservatives that "they are enraged by the decline of their country and inclined to put the blame on unions, blacks and foreigners." (*Guardian Weekly*, October 25, 1981, p. 5) But in Germany such passions, in the service of a demonic leader, were not restrained by established institutions. Churchill pointed out in the mid-1930s, "The victorious democracies in driving out hereditary sovereigns [at the end of the First World War] supposed they were moving on the path of progress. They have in fact gone further and fared worse. A royal dynasty looking back upon the traditions of the past, and looking forward to a continuity in the future, offers an element of security to the liberty and happiness of nations that can never come from the rule of dictators, however capable they may be." (*Great Contemporaries*, p. 29)

Heidegger, it seems, thought otherwise, if only because he might have seen no plausible royal dynasty to be available in Germany. Perhaps he also thought he could provide the doctrinal guidance of which the politically successful Nazis were very much in need in 1933. In any event he gambled and many years later he found himself trying to explain what his single extended public venture into politics had been all about.

V

Two concerns are expressed most dramatically by Heidegger in the *Spiegel* interview. The first is that he has been slandered: that is, *he* is the true victim, not those who were mistreated by the Nazis to whom he had lent his prestige. I know of no public statement by Heidegger in which he explicitly expressed sympathy for the millions of victims of the Nazis. The most he has said, as in this 1966 interview, is that he was not responsible for any of the terrible things that happened. But even here he does not *call* them "terrible."

His second dramatically expressed concern in the *Spiegel* interview may be seen in his observation that he had found American travel to the moon "frightening." He saw this (especially the "pictures coming from the moon to the earth") as confirming and reinforcing the radical uprooting of man from the earth on which he so much depends. (*Spiegel* Interview, p. 277) Was not this concern about roots related to the earlier attraction for him of Nazism as a radical rootedness? Certainly, Heidegger did not share the opinion of those who saw space trips as exuberant testimony to man's dedication to adventures in exploration and to the most daring inquiries. In any event, many of us would consider what the Nazis did as far more frightening and sobering than what space programs have meant. Does this merely expose *our* limitations?

It is important to notice that Heidegger, in making the defense he does, tacitly concedes that there are old-fashioned principles with respect to human decency and political propriety by which even he is obliged to be judged. Whether the facts are as he states them is another matter. For example, he does give the impression in the *Spiegel* interview that his association with the Nazis ended when he resigned his rectorship in early 1934. But there is evidence that that association lasted at least another two years, with Heidegger making speeches to academic groups extolling the virtues of National Socialism. (I have recently [in the Fall of 1981] talked with a Greek academician from Thessaloniki who said he heard, as a graduate student in Germany, such speeches by Heidegger well after he resigned his rectorship.) The greater Heidegger's deception now as to what he did and for how long, the more he tacitly recognizes that his position and actions then were indefensible. He concedes, furthermore, that his authority in philosophy does not suffice to justify him. In short, he condemns, by the distortions and misstatements he resorts to, the man he had been, if not also the man he was to remain to the end of his life.

VI

I recapitulate some of the things I have noticed about Heidegger's assessment of the effects of technology, that technology which has seen as one of its most dramatic achievements the flight of men to the moon and, perhaps even more impressive, their safe return to the earth: We can see in our time the marvels of science and its technological implementations. We can see the worldwide consequences of these manifestations, in which "everyone" is interested. We can see the tendency of these developments to tear men loose from the earth, not only from their particular part of the earth but even from the earth itself. Man has now fallen into a physical abyss, of all of space, to match the spiritual abyss with which he has long had to contend.

We have become rootless or, perhaps worse still, uprooted. Uprootedness leads to desperate measures to reassert ourselves, with that strong emphasis on the will of which German thinkers from Martin Luther to Immanuel Kant have made much. This emphasis is particularly important for someone such as Heidegger who depends so much on *country,* which is the visible and enduring expression of the collective will, especially through a people's language.

We must wonder, of course, whether his way, including the tradition in which he worked, contributed to the state of affairs that made sensible politics virtually impossible in Germany in the 1920s. Before we try to deal with this question, however, we should say more about the technology of which Heidegger speaks.

VII

A series of questions suggests something about what technology means, or at least what it means to someone who is driven, as Heidegger seems to be, to proclaim (perhaps not without irony) that only a god can save us. Thus the critical question here may be, "What is God?" This question is perhaps led up to by the following series of questions:

1) What does technology do to our understanding of God and hence to our idea of man? (Is to speak of God usually to recognize an eternal ordering of things both physical and moral? In circumstances somewhat reminiscent of Heidegger's "Only a god" situation, Leo Strauss has suggested, "Only a great thinker could help us in our intellectual plight.")

2) What does technology do to and with nature?

3) What guides or drives technology? Does it have a rhythm or momentum of its own, with one thing "naturally" leading to another?

4) What is the meaning of *country?* Technology, as we have seen, disregards the traditional and seemingly natural distinctions among peoples of the world.

5) What is the meaning of *history? Is* there meaning to all that mankind or at least particular peoples have done and said? Does what has happened make sense? This bears upon the question of what guides or drives technology. Some see economics, not history, as the only human science that matters here.

6) What, indeed, is the meaning of life? Are there any ruling principles for the universe, for nature, for mankind, for human communities, or for individual human beings?

7) What does technology do to our ability to understand things? Is this related to the status of nature? If there is no comprehensible nature, there is no philosophy, or metaphysics, but merely "thinking"; process becomes far more important than goals; and in political science, we are told, value-free techniques become all that the scholar can offer his fellow-citizens.

These questions, and the answers one might offer to them, suggest what technology is like and the effects it has had. Still, we should not ignore the fascinating aspects of technology, which unfortunately are not unrelated to its pervasive and trivializing aspects. Technology does reflect, after all, something of man's capacity to discover and to innovate, as well as to persevere.

Does technology mean that chance tends to take over in human affairs, perhaps more than ever before in some respects? (Compare, however, the control of chance epidemics today.) Who knows what unanticipated gimmick will next sweep a people and affect longstanding relations? It can lead—indeed, we can now say from our considerable experience, it is likely to lead—more and more to the promotion and service of desires, desires that are not limited to one people.

At the root of the difficulty with technology, I have suggested, is the suppression of nature as a guide. Nature is there, if it is there at all, only as something to be exploited, not something for man to be restrained by. To proclaim that "only a god can save us" is to point up the absence of the transcendental in contemporary human affairs.

What lies behind Heidegger's notion that technology is now on its own? Would the intervention of a "god" mean that technology is no longer sovereign? Do not we all have, at least on occasion, the sense that technological developments do have a rationale or at least an impetus of their own? Morality, country, and tradition no longer matter as much as before.

Some are more sensitive than others to these developments. Or, at least, they see them in gloomier terms and hence are open to more desperate measures. Is invoking a god here to look to something deeply rational and truly caring, something with an effective will to back up its concerns? Would a certain zest be thereby added to life? Or is the god that Heidegger invokes here little more than a spiritualized version of the political leadership he looked to in 1933?

VIII

Perhaps fundamental to the political appeal of the Nazis was the promise they held out to serve the desire of their country and its people for self-preservation. This included the need for self-assertion, the assertion of a collective self that can be not only glorified but can be preserved indefinitely, perhaps even for a millennium.

That the appeal of self-preservation is a strong one we all know. We can all remember threats to our own personal existence that we have made desperate efforts to counter. Many are responsive to the insistence not only of authorities such as Thomas Hobbes but also of authorities closer to home, such as the United States Supreme Court, that the right of self-preservation is "the ultimate value any society." (360 U.S. 128 [1959]; 341 U.S. 509 [1951]) Thus one's very existence is made one's greatest good; it is not merely a condition for one's good.

But the right of self-preservation cannot truly be the "ultimate value of any society." Few of us would deny if pressed that there are things worth dying for, or at least that there are things one would rather die than do. There are some things, then, of even greater "value" than one's own life, however difficult we may usually find it to live up to our true "ultimate value."

If self-preservation is made too much of we are bound to be deeply frustrated in our lives. After all, we are mortal. Overemphasis upon survival is likely to lead either to desperation, including mad adventures, or to apathy. It is also likely to lead to an undue emphasis upon the community and upon that which the community can do so much better than individuals: preserve people from death, at least for awhile. The community of which we are a part *can* try to live forever.

The proclamation by Heidegger that only a god can save us seems to have been adapted from the sixth book of Plato's *Republic*. (492–93) Socrates uses this kind of talk to explain how someone who is philosophically inclined by nature can be saved *for* philosophy. He has to be saved from, among other things, the voracious demands upon him of his city. Heidegger would use the rescuing god not to save the would-be philosopher from the community, but rather to save the community from the ravages of the technology that modern science (itself derivative from philosophy) makes possible. The community takes the place for him of philosophy, reflecting perhaps the replacement of nature by history. But then, does he not consider old-fashioned philosophy to be no longer possible in the modern world?

This substitution by Heidegger of the community for philosophy seems consistent with what he did in 1933 when he put his great talents at the service of the Nazis.

IX

Do both ambition and resentment move men such as Heidegger? One does see both grandiosity and baseness in his actions and perhaps even more in his recent efforts to explain them away. One cannot help comparing his approach to the Socratic, of which one is reminded by various (perhaps not altogether conscious) allusions in the *Spiegel* interview. The Socrates of Plato is intrigued by novelty, but he can easily keep his curiosity within limits. He is not ambitious, as ambition is commonly understood, nor does he make much of his personal salvation. Heidegger complains about having had to work on border fortifications toward the end of the war. This shows, he suggests, how much he had fallen from grace. But Karl Barth had had to do the same kind of work in Switzerland. Such service can become routine in extreme situations for even the most eminent. There is, by way of contrast, the military and other civic service by Socrates, service that put his life in jeopardy on more than one occasion.

Whatever moves men such as Heidegger and his sometime master Nietzsche, much is made by them of will. This may be seen in the emphasis upon the will and history of the German people in Heidegger's rector's speech in 1933. If will is made so much of, rather than nature or philosophy simply, then one is "naturally" inclined (if of a secular bent) to defer to the most authoritative will, that of the State. Indeed, the State can be considered to be that aspect or version of Country or People which is peculiarly devoted to *expressing* a will. The concept of "State" almost seems, at times, to emphasize ruling for its own sake.

What came first for Heidegger, the devotion to country or the devotion to willfulness? Both country and willfulness make much of one's own. It is will, much more than reasoning with its dependence on a truth independent of one's self, that may be treasured as most one's own.

Is not the very technology that Heidegger attempts to counteract itself built upon or in the service of willfulness or desire, rather than being in the service of nature and understanding or thoughtfulness? Technology empowers the will and perhaps reinforces it, licensing and inducing it to assert itself more and more. We have returned to the question of the extent of ambition or self-assertion in men like Heidegger.

X

Critical to Heidegger's troubles, I suspect, is *amour propre*. This suspicion is reflected in my characterization of him a decade ago as the Macbeth of philosophy. (See *The Constitutionalist,* pp. 738–39.)

Heidegger could never face up publicly to the fact that he had misjudged "those people," having allowed himself to be used by gangsters, and that he, by doing so, had compromised himself in the eyes of those whom he had once cared most for.

The kind of defense he made, with its quibbles, evasions and half-truths, exposes him as a curiously small man, whatever his intellectual prowess. He was always explaining away what could only be repented. Do his spiritual limitations instinctively guide him to dependence on a country or a people? It is only thus that he can assert or "find" himself.

One is reminded of Critias' refusal in Plato's *Charmides* to face up to difficulties in the opinion he had been defending. This refusal, Socrates observes, leads Critias into unintelligibility. (169C) In some respects, Heidegger's account in the *Spiegel* interview resembles Critias' in the *Charmides:* it is on a very high, even abstract, level and thus avoids having to face up to whatever defect there may be in the soul.

All this raises serious questions about the relation of knowledge to virtue.

Or, rather, all this compels us to wonder about not only what virtue is, but also what knowledge is, at least for the purpose of virtue. It would seem that the knowledge of knowledge for which Heidegger is celebrated does not require knowledge of justice as well.

XI

Is knowledge of justice, which necessarily includes a *respect for* justice, required in some measure even for those who devote themselves primarily to the knowledge of knowledge?

Heidegger told us many times during his long career that he was concerned to grasp Being itself. Did this concern serve to conceal from him the limits both of politics and of "one's own"? Socrates often asked the "What is" question, such as, "What is virtue?" "What is justice?" "What is man?" But Heidegger asked, "What is it, to be?" He asked, that is, "What is Being itself?" Should not what Being is be apparent to us for most important practical purposes? (I am told that Heidegger addresses this point in *Being and Time*.) To probe Being the way Heidegger evidently does may be to risk undermining common sense, promoting an undue abstractness. Perhaps it also serves to disparage nature, or at least to expose all inquiry to an infinite regress and hence no starting point, thereby leaving human thought to cope with an unsettling nothingness at its foundations. Does not this in turn incline men by way of compensation to an emphasis upon will as an expression of Being, as an effort to assert the self that threatens to be cut loose from its moorings by the radical pursuit of Being itself?

To emphasize the will (an emphasis especially to be found in the tradition that Heidegger immediately comes out of but which he perhaps pushed to its "logical" extreme) is almost naturally, in the circumstances of the early 1930s, to expose a politically naive man to the attractions of the Nazi movement. The urbane Socrates, also interested of course in Being, provides a salutary contrast, as do the Socratics Xenophon, Plato, and Aristotle. Nietzsche, too, would have recognized the Nazi movement for what it was, an abomination in the sight of the Lord. (For this purpose God would have been, to Nietzsche, still as much alive as He had ever been.)

The devastations of technology (that is, of all that modernity has meant) might well have seemed to Heidegger to require extraordinary political efforts. But that those efforts should have taken the form they did for him may testify to a poverty of soul. This may be seen, I have suggested, in the shallowness of his 1966 defense for *Spiegel* of his Nazi years, a defense that is in its mechanical character itself a product of the technological age.

An even more serious question awaits us, which we can do little more than notice here. What do Heidegger's conduct of the 1930s and his evasions of the 1960s reveal about his conception of Being itself or about the character of the Being he does grasp? Is not one moved to suspect that that grasp is indeed compromised, that it is not reliable? His approach may tend to undermine general reliance upon that grasp of Being that men have "always," or innately, had by nature. (Does not the "What is" question itself presuppose an intuitive grasp of "is," or Being? Do I, in these remarks, mistakenly treat Being more as a *thing* than Heidegger does? See, on Being, Plato, *Republic* 509B sq.)

Technology does have a reliable grasp of Being, to a degree. But it seems to grasp only so much of Being as can be transformed into a certain kind of power. This approach to knowledge provides considerable leverage for certain purposes. But Heidegger and others before him have warned us that this approach is not ultimately conducive to genuine, wide-ranging understanding, however useful it may be for making our lives comfortable. Certainly if power (that is, harnessable Being) and self-preservation become dominant, then not the *good* or the *truth*, but rather *will* (or self-assertion) will become authoritative in our lives. If that should happen, we would have cheapened our lives immeasurably and gained in the bargain neither genuine power nor any life truly worth preserving.

XII

The Faustian bargain that Heidegger can be said to have made should put us on our guard, especially against presumptuous apocalyptic visions that call into question old-fashioned morality and long-established institutions.

Heidegger never seemed to appreciate the merits of constitutional government, especially when it is compared with the alternatives available in the world today, and so he repeatedly disparages "negative liberty." (See, e.g., *Spiegel* Interview, p. 269.) It is liberal democracy, with its defense of property and liberty, that helps make unsupervised technological innovations routine matters. But it is also liberal democracy that makes it possible for us to diagnose the ills of technology and, if we are prudent, to take command of our lives and to do so long before we are left only with desperate measures to resort to.

Socrates, we should remember, did seem to have *some* respect for the democracy of his day, as seen in the Athens that he found so congenial for so much of his life. But along with Socrates' patriotism, there was his disdain for an undue emphasis upon self-preservation and prosperity. This is a healthy corrective among any self-governing people that is tempted to make too much of its own.

No doubt Socrates would have had much to say about modern technology and the many blessings it offers us. Perhaps he would have been tempted to add along with Henry Thoreau that "a man is rich in proportion to the number of things he can live without." (See Roy Larson's column, *Chicago Sun-Times*, October 24, 1981, p. 14. See, also, Plato, *Laws* 736E.)

XIII

In whatever Socrates would have said and done in assessing our technology, our political life and our knowledge of Being, would he not have insisted upon the sovereignty of nature, that very nature which modern philosophical thought, modern science and its technology have seriously called into question? We saw at the outset of this essay that Kant provided to a German disciple the moral stamina needed for proper conduct in the face of the Nazis. But even Kant can be understood to have undermined that traditional understanding of nature which contributes to a reliable sense of what is prudent and right by nature. Certainly he called into question the necessary illusions or "wholesome prejudices" by which communities must often take their bearings if they are to act decently in times of adversity or, better still, if they are to head off the worst adversities.

If we do not retain a lively awareness of nature, vital distinctions are apt to be lost sight of, not only those between life and death and between male and female, but also those in ethical and political matters between right and wrong and between the healthy and the unhealthy. In short, without a sound awareness of nature, philosophy (including political philosophy) becomes impossible.

This is not the occasion for an extended inquiry into the nature of nature. It suffices for our immediate purposes to say that if one's thought, or the tradition one draws upon, is properly grounded in nature, one is more apt to exhibit sound judgment in the affairs of one's day. Martin Heidegger, one remembers from the *Spiegel* interview, saw in the Nazi movement a "new dawn." (See *Spiegel* Interview, pp. 269, 270, 275.) What did he mistakenly believe that led him astray? Or was it something he did not believe, which he should have believed, that left him susceptible to the demands of his will?

Caution about what is and what is not a new dawn is one mark of the political man who is sensible about the nature of things and about the limits of political action. One such politician, who was himself a great scientist very much interested in technology, was Benjamin Franklin. While the just-drafted Constitution was being signed on September 17 by members of the Constitutional Convention of 1787 in Philadelphia, James Madison tells us,

Doctor Franklin looking towards the President's Chair, at the back of which a rising sun happened to be painted, observed to a few members near him, that Painters had found it difficult to distinguish in their art a rising from a setting sun. I have, said he, often and often in the course of [this convention, with] the vicissitudes of my hopes and fears as to its issue, looked at [the sun] behind the President without being able to tell whether it was rising or setting. But now at length I have the happiness to know that it is a rising and not a setting Sun.

This should serve to remind us at a time when technology can be so intimidating, when its misuse can evidently destroy all life on this planet, that some who are careless believers in technology can be quite sensible as political leaders, even while others who are remarkably sensitive to the perils of technology can be in their political judgment monumentally foolish. (See, for further discussion of Martin Heidegger and the Nazis, my examination of the 1945–1946 Nuremberg Trial in my collection, "On Trial: Explorations," prepared in 1991 for the *Loyola University of Chicago Law Journal*.)

13

ORWELL AND THE LIMITS OF TYRANNY

To the man who announced to Socrates that the Thirty Tyrants had condemned him to death, he replied, "And Nature, them."

MICHEL de Montaigne

I

I must confess that I did not "like" George Orwell's *1984* when I first read it in Southern Illinois shortly after its original publication in 1949. (I "liked" much more Arthur Koestler's *Darkness at Noon,* published the year before.) Not only did I find *1984* painful and oppressive, but it also struck me as somehow seriously flawed in what it undertook to describe. Orwell has said, in his 1949 "Reflections on Gandhi," that "there is reason to think that [Mohandas] Gandhi, who after all was born in 1869, did not understand the nature of totalitarianism and saw everything in terms of his own struggle against the British government." (*Orwell Reader,* p. 333) It is as *the* student of "the nature of totalitarianism" that Orwell is best known to us today. It is what he has to say about this subject that I discuss here, saluting at the outset the informed nobility of his unrelenting resistance to the dreadful tyrannies of both Hitler and Stalin.

I have found upon returning to *1984* more than three decades after my first reading of it that I still do not like it, however better equipped I may now be to appreciate the merits of Orwell both as a stylist and as a com-

---

This talk was given at the Basic Program Weekend, The University of Chicago, East Troy, Wisconsin, November 6, 1983. (Original title: "George Orwell's *1984* and the Limits of Tyranny.")

The citations in this essay to *1984* are to Irving Howe, ed., *Orwell's Nineteen Eighty-Four: Text, Sources, Criticism* (New York: Harcourt, Brace & World, 1963). The other principal citations are to *The Orwell Reader* (New York: Harcourt, Brace & World, 1956).

The epigraph is taken from Michel de Montaigne, "That To Philosophize Is To Learn To Die," *Essays,* I, 20 (E. J. Trechmann translation).

passionate human being of talent and experience. Indeed, I find it somewhat curious that the book should continue to have upon me much the effect that it had in its and my youth, even though I have myself gotten into trouble since then with tyrannies of both "the Right" and "the Left" in other lands. It does seem about time, then, that I should try to say what there is that I find deeply questionable about this book.

There is another sense of *about time* that is appropriate here: for is not *1984* in critical respects about *time*, about the consequences of time or history and what can be done about managing time, not only the time yet to come, but even more the time that has come and gone? At the heart of Orwell's profound dissatisfaction, which took the form of this dramatization of tyranny, may be one's despair upon confronting human mortality at a time when all too many honest men of talent cannot help believing that *this* is all there is to human life. What makes this belief a deadly affront to modern men is that there is so much in their upbringing, including the language in which they see everything, which had disparaged everyday life and extolled the world to come, at least in the form of "the new Jerusalem" on earth if not paradise elsewhere. It is important in any effort to understand Orwell's spiritual malaise to notice the component in it of disillusionment and disenchantment, which depends of course on a people's once having entertained and relied upon considerable illusion and enchantment.

It is instructive to notice how much different *1984* is from still another book with a remarkable "instant" appeal, Charles Dickens's *A Christmas Carol*. That book, written a century earlier by an author Orwell admired, lifts the human spirit and leaves one hopeful about the more generous elements in the community. It, like *1984*, is a short novel, almost a long short story; and it, again like 1984, is quite English, catering to and reinforcing (if not even creating in an authoritative manner) a certain mood.

The typical response to Orwell's masterpiece today is to lament that "1984" is upon us even in the West. We are reminded of insidious intrusions into our personal lives, of all-knowing computers, of unrelenting propaganda, and of devious Cold War manipulations. Or is it that we tend to the other extreme from "1984"—that is, to a considerable privatization of our lives? One might wonder to what extent such privatization, as an attempt to head off "1984," is itself a major contributor, however inadvertent, to the very evil that *1984* represents.

Orwell would have us recognize that with respect to totalitarianism, the *prevention* is much easier than the *cure*. He would also have us recognize that proper prevention depends on taking a good look at what totalitarianism is and inclines toward. But we should recognize as well that the very state of mind that Orwell induces may lead decent but fearful people to acquiesce in, and even to seek relief through, strong government of a totalitarian bent.

Thus, I am suggesting, *1984* must be taken seriously, even though it is tempting to dismiss it as one would science fiction of a peculiarly dismal cast. (In science fiction, technique and the bizarre, reflecting a certain kind of imagination, often take the place both of sound thought and of serious character development.) If *1984* is not to be regarded as mere fantasy, its author's presuppositions, politics, and opinions about human nature must be examined with some care.

Perhaps Orwell's most critical presupposition is that such a regime as that described in *1984* can "work," that it can both impose itself upon a politically mature people, such as the English were just after the Second World War, and perpetuate itself indefinitely. Even more instructive than examining this presupposition is the informed insistence upon our part that such presuppositions can indeed be examined, that it is possible to look beyond one's temperament and circumstances to the truth about such matters.

II

Part of the appeal of Orwell is that he can be recognized as a painfully honest man. He is particularly authoritative because he is known to have been a socialist who hated the monstrous collectivism he described so well. What can be said of that description? Is it accurate and useful?

As to its usefulness, one can wonder whether Orwell does not both subvert the spirit and dull the sensibilities that make sustained tyranny difficult to achieve. He may, by engendering a sense of hopelessness about a tyranny once established, induce a depressing, self-perpetuating fatalism.

Consider, for example, his account of Winston Smith's response to torture. How seriously should Smith's compelled submission be taken not only by us but, even more importantly, by Smith himself? It should be obvious that one may be so tortured as to be forced to do, deny, or say things otherwise than a good man would ordinarily do or say. Sensible men know that torture, both physical and psychic, can have such an effect. They also know that such forced acquiescence does not change the truth of the matter under consideration. What is there to be ashamed of, or to be bound by, in such circumstances? Yet Orwell has Winston Smith believe that he betrayed Julia. Is not this a verbal trick? Once Julia is arrested, why not "betray" her in the way Smith did even earlier than he did and spare himself and perhaps her, considerable unnecessary torment? (Compare *1984*, p. 58.)

Is it useful, therefore, to make as much as Smith and Orwell do of the submission seen here? Is there not something perverse in considering it significant and in dwelling upon it as Orwell does? One can imagine a Socrates saying, as Joan of Arc in effect did say to her captors, "It is quite possible that you can make my body give in to your fiendish power, but what can you prove by that which people have not always known about the limitations of the body and any extended reliance upon it, limitations that may be seen in fevers, in severe pain or in one's last hours?"

Thus Orwell's assessment of how one is likely to respond under torture may not be truly useful. It may even be irresponsible of Orwell to make as much of such things as he evidently does.

In addition to the question of usefulness, there is the question of accuracy: not so much accuracy about the likely human response to this or that practice or institution, but rather accuracy about what tyranny is like and how communities get to where none of us wants to be.

1984 is not primarily a study in character. The kind of hapless hero and the urban squalor described here are better rendered by authors such as Graham Greene. Orwell's claim to our appreciation of his book is for what he has to say about politics and history. Is he sound in what he depicts? In particular, is he correct in so presenting totalitarianism that a decent man is left only with futile, even silly, opposition and an inevitable, if not even welcomed, capitulation? Is this, indeed, the way things are in such circumstances.

III

Orwell's depiction of tyranny makes totalitarian government appear both stronger and weaker than it is. In both ways, then, he does public-spirited citizens a disservice.

I have suggested that the illusions promoted by uses of torture can make tyranny appear stronger than it is. It is ultimately force, not the principles or ideas held by the Inner Party, that is presented as the basis of comprehensive rule in *1984*. But for the force it happens to command, the Party could not control the past to the extent it does, changing the historical record as it pleases. Nor could it manipulate, as it must, the passions of people. It has no genuine authority, only a forced submission. Macbeth, for one, long ago recognized the limited attraction and unreliable strength in that kind of allegiance. We will see again and again how the Shakespearean understanding of things differs from the Orwellian.

It is revealing that even a regime with the overwhelming power depicted here must make public claims of justice against both domestic opposition and foreign enemies. This should not be surprising, considering what we know about what even Stalinist and Nazi rulers *had* to be silent about, not only in public but also among themselves. It does make a difference, it seems, whether certain terrible things, of which "everyone knows," are spoken of openly. (Consider the changed circumstance of the woman who is explicitly *told* about her husband's marital misconduct, even though she had long before figured out what was going on. Consider, also, the effect of having to confess one's sins to another man, albeit a priest.) One must wonder what there is in the typical human community that naturally respects justice and goodness, however defined.

The ruling class in *1984* is presented as utterly ruthless, selfish, and cynical. But how long can that state of affairs last? If all of the ruling class truly believed as O'Brien believed (O'Brien being the only member of the Inner Party that Smith ever has much to do with), would not the regime be in serious trouble? Must not even O'Brien believe at least that it is good for the strong to rule? If so, one can begin to consider, as in the first book of Plato's *Republic*, who the truly strong are.

All men, we have been taught by Aristotle, aim at the good in all that they do. (There may even be *something* good in mere perseverance, in the perpetuation of even a bad regime. Existence itself is thus celebrated, however much that existence is outweighed in some instances by the evil of the regime.) One must wonder about the morale of leaders such as O'Brien. Do they not need some sincere belief, aside from mere self-interest, if they are to consider their own lives meaningful and worthwhile? Otherwise, would there not be a void that they or their successors, the youth of the following generation, will fall into and be engulfed by? (This is, it has long seemed to me, one of the serious problems faced by Russian leaders since at least the Second World War.)

The Inner Party is vulnerable in another way. The rulers indulge themselves in choice food and wine, comfortable housing and nice clothing, to say nothing of their sexuality. That is, they are uninhibited and not altogether secret lovers of pleasure. Does not their hedonism make them peculiarly susceptible to pain? And yet there is little talk in *1984* of assassinations of rulers. Would not the constant threat of death disturb such rulers, whatever O'Brien may preach about the Party members' supposed conquest of death? Perhaps even more important for the hedonist in the circumstances of these rulers is the lack of true respect, to say nothing of genuine love, from the people: whatever *is* respected and feared by the people is an image of something other than their rulers. Are not such rulers seriously deprived people, and would not their deprivation eventually demoralize and hence cripple them? Do we not all know the emptiness of mere physical pleasures when the soul is starved?

These rulers are vulnerable in still another way. O'Brien insists on selfishness as the ruling principle of the regime, a self-conscious, thoroughgoing, and deliberate selfishness on the part of power-hungry men. But any regime that permits and ratifies its "best" people in their devotion to personal selfishness alone is a regime that is likely to be considerably weaker than others of comparable size and resources. It can hardly stand up to another regime in which "the best" will sacrifice themselves for something higher or greater than personal gratifications. The selfish can always be "bought" when it is evident that they might otherwise be destroyed. And why not? They have been taught that it is "smart" for a man to look out only for himself.

I have thus far compared the relative strengths of regimes that rest upon different attitudes toward self-sacrifice as they compete in the world at large. But at home, also, the regime built on selfishness is likely to be vulnerable to the resistance of those open to self-sacrifice—not just any form of resistance, of course, but that which is sensible and appropriate to the circumstances. The resistance of someone such as Winston Smith is hardly what has to be worried about. He is shown from early on in the novel as weak and self-centered, whatever justified resentments and plausible reservations he might have. (See, e.g., *1984*, pp. 72–73.) His name combines the family name of the common man with the first name of the great wartime leader of the British about the time he was born. But both the sensible common man and the uncommon Churchill would be far more effective in opposition to this kind of regime than is Mr. Orwell's "hero."

There is no recognition in *1984* of what an effective form of resistance would be, aside from vague reliance upon the "proles." In fact, the reader is left (and is meant to be left?) with the impression that there really is no hope. The Anti-Party book, of which so much is made, turns out to have been produced at least in large part by the Inner Party itself. But we do know that even in both Nazi Germany and Stalinist Russia significant resistance took place, even though not on a large scale. Significant independence of thought has certainly been evident for some time in intellectual circles in the Soviet Union, which can be seen in someone such as Aleksandr Solzhenitsyn. Had the Nazi regime lasted long enough, would not the finer elements in the German community have asserted themselves more and more, especially as conditions obviously worsened even in peacetime for everyone?

Effective resistance to a tyrannical regime, however useful some physical actions in opposition may be, must rest ultimately upon appeals to common sense and to elevated passions. One who does not recognize this fails to appreciate how to respond to and deal with such regimes, whether in one's own country or abroad. Critical to any enduring opposition is the avoidance of attributing a sense of inevitability and invulnerability to such a regime, a sense that *is* hard to avoid when any ruthless regime *is* established.

Particularly revealing here is an observation Orwell makes in his "Reflections on Gandhi": "It is difficult to see how Gandhi's methods could be applied in a country where opponents of the regime disappear in the middle of the night and are never heard of again." (*Orwell Reader*, pp. 333–34) But does no one "keep count" even in such circumstances? Can the suppression of information be total? What does Orwell assume about the comprehensiveness of control? Is he truly being "realistic" about that? One can and perhaps should have reservations about Gandhi's understanding of things. But is not his approach in opposition to an oppressive regime substantially more effective than what Orwell can offer us and is not this so because the spirit is preserved and ministered to in Gandhi's approach? Orwell asked, "Is there a Gandhi in Russia at this moment? And if there is, what is he accomplishing?" (*Orwell Reader*, p. 334) An answer has been suggested in what I have said about the emergence in recent decades of various dissidents, including those who *have* been keeping records of, and writing extensive accounts about, what had happened even in the most repressive circumstances.

In short, Orwell underestimated what the spirit is capable of and how adaptable it can be to changing circumstances, as a Gandhi could be. Hence he overestimated the strength of the regime portrayed in *1984*. This kind of response contributes to the sense of hopelessness in the face of such a regime when it is once established, however much one may be moved by Orwell to head it off *if one sees it coming.*

IV

Unfortunately, our assessment of *1984* cannot be left at this. For however weak the regime in this novel may in fact be, totalitarian regimes can be far stronger than Orwell depicts them.

For one thing, tyranny can draw upon claims of justice and it can appeal both to the patriotic instincts and to the deep fears of a people. (See, e.g., *1984*, p. 66.) Orwell is obviously aware of the Grand Inquisitor episode in *The Brothers Karamazov*, yet he has O'Brien ridicule the notion that the Party really does all that it does for the sake of the people. Rather, it is insisted, power is sought by rulers entirely for its own sake: the interests of the people, or of the community, have nothing to do with their efforts. (The Grand Inquisitor makes more sense than this, however questionable *his* approach may also be.)

We know from experience, however, that the tyrannies of our time derive much of their strength from their "ideologies." Are these doctrines devised merely for the people, not for the rulers themselves to believe? Must not the ruling class also believe there is something truly good about what they are doing? Is it likely that the simply cynical regime described in *1984* could escape both massive rebellion from its people and the demoralized collapse of its ruling class?

Granted that few rulers are without selfish interests, must not even the most venal of them somehow believe that what they do aims at more than mere self-gratification? The supporters these rulers have to depend on must believe in something more than that if they are to be willing to run risks for the regime.

It should be remembered that any military power that is simply cruel and brutal is apt in the long run to be inferior to military power that is disciplined and principled. Sensible generals have always known that there are significant differences between a sadist and a soldier. Cannot the same distinction be drawn between a thief and a ruler? Is it not unrealistic to be completely "realistic" in these matters? Again I must wonder whether a ruling class that "understands" itself as Orwell presents the one in *1984* is as powerful as another that somehow believes itself to be serving the common good along with its own selfish ends. Must not *some* considerations of the common good come to bear, for example, upon determinations by rulers of who their successors are to be? Otherwise, on what basis can they choose among those who will rule after their deaths? Is a regime apt to prosper for long if the succession is always the result of little more than a bloody battle? (The history of the Roman Empire invites careful examination here.)

To insist that even tyrannies must rely upon some notion of justice and the common good is not to deny that tyrannies do tend to depend on dubious opinions. I was struck, while attending in Chicago in 1983 the sentencing hearings in Judge Prentice Marshall's federal district court in a Teamsters Racketeering case, with how mobsters were reported to have talked among themselves about the wicked things they do. It was evident that they speak not insincerely of "territory," "rights," "chiselers," "honor," and the like. That is, they have a sense of justice and of community that they invoke in explaining themselves *to themselves*. It can all be dismissed as rationalization, of course, and they are certainly mistaken as to the rights and wrongs in the situations they talk about. But more significant seems to me both the fact that they must rationalize and the fact that they are able to do so. I suspect that they would be even weaker than they in fact are if they did not account for themselves as they try to do. (It is not insignificant that mobsters look to society for guidance as to how to conduct themselves. For example, movies about them seem to be influential among them.)

All this questions the common opinion that rulers such as O'Brien really "get away" with what they are doing. Is not their punishment "built in"? Does not Orwell as artist "instinctively" show this, even though his "argument" is otherwise? What does it mean to deceive oneself deliberately, as Orwell would have us believe O'Brien does, about what is truly good? What does it mean to have to keep watching everyone, as the authorities must in *1984?* After all, that *is* a lot of trouble! What does it mean to be constantly on the alert, if not at war, both at home and abroad? What does it mean to be trapped with so much ugliness around one? What does it mean to have an ugly soul, which the reader can surely recognize in O'Brien, even if O'Brien himself cannot?

We can see that O'Brien's life is not truly good, however he may delude himself. Orwell, of course, would agree. But does he recognize how vulnerable O'Brien truly is and how much stronger O'Brien would be if he believed in what he was doing as something other than mere self-interest? It could be argued that Orwell subverts the would-be tyrant by encouraging him to be altogether selfish and self-centered, but I suspect this is overly subtle. In any event, an enduring tyranny "knows better" and hence is stronger than Orwell depicts it in *1984.*

Even the worst regime, if it is to endure, must *respect* the truth. Not that the leadership of such a regime will always be truthful, even to itself. But it must be enough aware of the truth to be able both to maneuver itself around it and to provide the public some semblance of it. It must be rare for a regime to continually present lies as truth without coming to believe such lies, thereby crippling itself.

For a variety of reasons, then, even the worst regimes are deluded into believing that they know the truth and pursue the good, not merely a selfish interest. In this way, therefore, genuine tyrannies tend to be stronger than the contrived regime with which Orwell threatens us.

V

Another way of putting all this is to say that the regime Orwell describes has madness at the very core of it. Madmen, however diabolically clever they can be at times, are simply unable to cope indefinitely with the challenges with which life confronts them. O'Brien, for one, is mad.

Orwell can speak of "a lunatic intensity" in connection with O'Brien, who is presented by Orwell as critically "unhinged." (*1984*, p. 112) Orwell as artist seems to be aware of this, but Orwell as thinker does not draw the proper lesson from what the artist has sensed and depicted.

O'Brien's madness may be detected in more than the opinions he holds about the good and the bad, which the traditional criminal law relies upon. Consider the episode of the incriminating photograph depicting an event that the Party is determined to erase from public memory. Winston Smith has happened upon that photograph; he must be made to forget he ever saw it. O'Brien, we are told, succeeds in persuading Smith that he (Smith) had never seen it. Does this episode make sense? (See *1984*, p. 109.)

It does not make sense if O'Brien means what he says. O'Brien produces and then destroys the photograph and argues (and, we are asked to believe, means) that it no longer exists or ever existed, either for Smith *or for O'Brien himself*. It seems to be vital for the regime, as Orwell presents it, that the photograph not be remembered at all by anyone.

But what happens when O'Brien confronts (or creates) another Winston Smith? Must he not produce such a photograph again in order to destroy it and thereupon to persuade still another victim that it never existed, etc.? Is not this necessary in order to effectively counter future resistance? But if so, O'Brien or someone like him must know that such a photograph exists. He must know enough about its significance to be able to bring it forward and to use it as he does. But he must not in the meantime be moved himself by that significance. Is this plausible?

O'Brien as ruler cannot function effectively without remembering the photograph. One is again reminded of the adage that one must know the truth in order to be a really good liar. But is it not madness both to remember and not to remember, as seems to be required of O'Brien? If O'Brien and his colleagues are truly mad, they surely can be circumvented by sensible resistance. If so, the "double-think" technique that Orwell conjures up is mere verbal legerdemain, a *tour de force* on the author's part. Is it not merely a metaphysical trick, and bad metaphysics at that? (What, for example, does O'Brien mean by "perfect" at *1984*, p. 108?)

It is recognized in the novel that Winston Smith is weak in metaphysics. (*1984*, p. 117) What, then, is the point of forcing *him* to submit. What are his coerced assent and his passivity worth, especially since he is, we are told, "tortured . . . to the edge of lunacy." (*1984*, p. 111)

There is throughout the book a running argument between "objectivism" and "subjectivism" (or solipsism?). O'Brien, who prevails, stands for subjectivism. Is not Smith presented as naive in "believing in" objective truth? But then Smith's (and Orwell's?) objectivism is deeply flawed, as may be seen in the disparagement of chastity in the rebellion against the Party (to which I will return). People have always known that evidence can be manufactured and manipulated, but this does not affect the character of truth. Nor does it make traditional moral standards merely the emanations of the regime, to be flouted at will as a form of resistance. Does not Orwell himself, as artist, purport to present the truth about human things and about totalitarian government, including the truth about the enduring character of moral standards?

Is there not something wrong with Orwell in that he can see the kind of distortions evident in O'Brien as plausible? Does not the rhetorical effectiveness of Orwell's presentation depend on certain impossibilities? Somehow, both human nature and art are distorted by Orwell himself. It is as if Shakespeare were to leave an Edmund or Iago or Macbeth triumphant at the end. It would also be as if we were to believe that such regimes as the hideously suicidal Pol Pot regime in Cambodia could, without foreign support, endure for a long time.

Orwell, we suspect, could not make Winston Smith too solid, lest O'Brien's authority and plausibility suffer. Yet, one must wonder, what is Smith guilty of that O'Brien himself is not? Presumably O'Brien knows all that Smith does. If the subversive book is at all sound, why would not O'Brien and his colleagues be corrupted by it also? But, it can be said, O'Brien, too, has been broken. If so, can he and his like be said truly to rule? How can anyone be said to rule who has become as heartless and ruthless and hence possessed as the Inner Party people are shown to be?

A serious problem with Orwell's depiction here is that the leaders of this regime know the better and choose the worse, deliberately so. (See, e.g., *1984*, p. 61, on privacy and courtesy.) Big Brother is presented as knowing all, as understanding what is happening and what will happen, as expert in psychology, etc. But, we must wonder, if one knows what the good man knows, why would not one act as the good man does? Because of some passion? But are not the passions themselves keyed to, if not dependent on, reasons? If one's reasoning is sound, should not passions be brought into line, except in someone crippled by a pathological condition that subverts the natural sovereignty of reason?

We return to the problem of torture. Sensible men have always known that acquiescence secured by torture is simply not reliable, even if the victim himself is permanently broken. Must not O'Brien, for example, face up to the "untortured" truth? Does he not know that certain propositions he relies upon are elicited and maintained only by compulsion, and hence are intrinsically unreliable? Not only that, but does not the truth that such propositions are designed to conceal remain a stumbling block to the tyrant?

Consider again Orwell on Gandhi: "Moreover the assumption, which served Gandhi well in dealing with individuals, that all human beings are more or less approachable and will respond to a generous gesture, needs to be seriously questioned. It is not necessarily true, for example, when you are dealing with lunatics." (*Orwell Reader*, p. 334) True enough, perhaps, at least up to a point. But if lunacy immunizes one from a humane appeal, it also cripples one, as we have seen, in getting one's way when one confronts someone who knows how to deal with lunatics.

Orwell endorses Gandhi's proposition that "in the end deceivers deceive only themselves." (*Orwell Reader*, p. 329) But does he apply this to O'Brien's Inner Party, and to the consequences of such self-deception for the would-be ruler? We are obliged to consider *1984* in the light of the Platonic-Aristotelian teaching that the greatest pleasures come from doing what one thinks is good, especially if it is indeed good. We are reminded as well of a vital teaching of Plato's dialogues, that no one truly desires evil.

Of course there have always been people who have desired evil things, but is not this because they have mistaken them for the good? No doubt such people have to be resisted; but even more importantly, they should be reasoned with when opportunities present themselves. They should be shown their limitations. That is good not only for them and the community they afflict. It is good also for the man who reasons with them, for he is reconsidering and strengthening his own reasonableness and adapting it to changing circumstances. But he does have to know what he is doing and whom he is dealing with.

Proper reasoning depends on a sound understanding of natural right and of prudence, not the facile relativism, the crippled sensual gratification, and the pervasive subjectivity with which Orwell burdens rebelliousness against the Inner Party. Proper reasoning must be at the core of any sensible hope for justice and peace, both at home and abroad. This means, in the context of this novel, that Orwell's opinions about such things as history, politics, and religion must be examined, for it is these opinions that make it possible for Orwell to dramatize the enduring triumph of evil as he does.

VI

We are asking how it was that Orwell went wrong in his opinions about man and community. The way Orwell went wrong is by and large the way of the modern intellectual, a way that exhibits the influence of a spotty education. Much of what can be said about the causes of Orwell's errors is not distinctive to him and so it can be presented in outline only.

The modern intellectual is very much the product of the Enlightenment. That movement sought to liberate mankind from the shackles on both mind and body forged by religion, patriotism, and the propertied classes.

A new science of history has been developed in an effort to explain what has happened among men. Arguments made and opinions held in the past are not addressed on their own terms; rather, they are explained away as rationalizations of the exploitation which has always characterized social relations. Ideas are seen as subordinated to, if not derived from, material interests and relations: *forces* and *masses* can be regarded as fundamental; materialism rules the intellectual world. (Does "Perpetual Peace" mean perpetual war? See *1984*, p. 88.)

The new science of history is decisively new to the extent that history is regarded, for the first time, as scientific. Critical to this science is the study of economics. One must wonder, however, how sound Orwell's economic principles are. Much seems to be made by him of a labor theory of value, with truly productive labor conceived of quite narrowly. This can perhaps be seen more clearly in his *Animal Farm*. He does not seem to appreciate how much of a people's prosperity and standard of living depends on the work of those who organize the resources of the community.

Orwell seems to believe that poverty is not at all either the result of the failings, including the ill fortune, of the poor or the result of faulty organization of production and distribution, but rather primarily the result of the greedy self-interest of those on top, of those rulers who routinely use wars, monopolies, the law, and the police to keep "the masses" in subjugation and deliberately to impoverish them. What has always been true of the ruling classes everywhere is particularly vivid on the part of the rulers in *1984*. But now at least, it would seem that the utter selfishness of the ruling class is no longer concealed from the more perceptive students of society: an O'Brien can acknowledge to someone such as Smith what his predecessors in earlier centuries had not dared admit even to themselves.

So powerful are the rulers in *1984* that they need not rely, as ruling classes have heretofore, upon religion to support them. Rather, the techniques and practices of traditional religion have been adapted by the new ruling class to its own purposes. These rulers are able to support themselves in power by using directly what ruling classes, by allowing priests and believers to have a semblance of independence, had once used indirectly.

Orwell himself is very much in the intellectual tradition that regards religion with suspicion, perhaps even as "the opiate of the masses." He observes in his Gandhi essay, "One must choose between God and Man, and all 'radicals' and 'progressives,' from the mildest liberal to the most extreme anarchist, have in effect chosen Man." (*Orwell Reader*, p. 332) In his *Animal Farm*, Orwell has religion, in the form of the ravens, deliberately employed by the usurpers to help keep their miserable subjects under control.

One must wonder whether the supposed necessity to "choose between God and man" is soundly perceived by Orwell. May not certain religious faiths—just like networks of love and friendship and just like widely distributed private property, a free market economy and the rule of law on which such an economy depends—tend to throw up barriers to totalitarianism? Orwell avoids this issue in *1984* by having Winston Smith concede that he does not believe in God. (*1984*, p. 119) This seems to make Smith even more vulnerable than he otherwise would be. We are reminded of still another observation by Orwell, that Gandhi's teachings "make sense only on the assumption that God exists and that the world of solid objects is an illusion to be escaped from." (*Orwell Reader*, p. 331)

The humanizing and salutary political effects of certain religious sentiments may be recognized by Orwell in the use made in *1984* of the ancient rhymes associated with the chimes of London churches. Does not Orwell thereby reveal instincts surviving, however weakly, from an earlier day? Such trappings of civilization as the rule of law, a humane religion, and a respect for private property can all too easily be explained away by the modern intellectual as instruments of exploitation.

This intellectual attitude, it seems to me, is evident in the revolutionary book of which so much is made in *1984*. Winston Smith regards it as "the product of a mind similar to his own, but enormously more powerful, more systematic, less fear-ridden." (*1984*, p. 88) By and large, the sentiments of the revolutionary book in *1984* do seem to be Orwell's as well. (This is despite the fact that the Inner Party may have had a hand in shaping the book. Even so, the Party would have had to say certain things adverse to itself in order to make the book plausible.)

Yet the account, in that Anti-Party book, of human nature and history could be regarded by some opponents of a *1984*-type regime as rubbish. Such opponents could say that it has been opinions of the kind long held by intellectuals such as Orwell that have helped make modern totalitarianism possible, if not even likely. For example, is not the state control of the means of production advocated by many intellectuals around the world likely to make the subversion of liberty by tyranny more thorough? Orwell also seems to make much of the "proles," at least in *1984*, whatever reservations he had about them there and in other books of his. (See *1984*, p. 96f.) Does not faith in the "proles" subvert a reliance upon serious thinking and make much of the passions, the very passions that certain kinds of tyranny are so adept at manipulating?

One must wonder, in short, how thoughtful Orwell truly is. He may not consider it useful for men to believe in God. But he does seem himself to believe in, even to have a lively sense of, the Devil: the all-knowing and all-powerful State he describes is, in effect, a malevolent deity. Here, as elsewhere in Orwell's work, one must raise the question whether one can truly understand what is really going on without being good.

VII

The great predecessor to George Orwell is someone whom he admired, Jonathan Swift. But Swift's *Gulliver's Travels* seems to me more solidly grounded than is *1984* both in philosophy and in human nature.

The questions Swift raises are more serious, questions that would challenge not only the totalitarianism of *1984*, but also the modern intellectual opinions that so subvert natural right and community as to make totalitarianism both more likely and more enduring. To be reminded of Swift, the great observer of the battle between the ancients and the moderns, is once again to be reminded of the inadequacies of the modern intellectual's education.

One must wonder, however, whether the shortcomings in Orwell's understanding of things are due in any way to causes distinctive to him personally, in addition to the manifestations in him of the modern intellectual.

Some have made much of the fact that Orwell was a dying man while he was writing *1984*. But Orwell's *Animal Farm*, written several years before his fatal illness took hold of him, is very much like *1984*. Although the tone of *1984* may have been affected by Orwell's awareness of his impending death, his general opinion about things must have been due to other causes.

Among those other causes, perhaps, were his searing experiences fighting in Spain for the Republican cause. These contributed to his political disillusionment in a way that was rare among English intellectuals of his time. (See *Orwell Reader*, pp. 211–12.) Orwell's bitter repudiation of Stalinists matched the abhorrence he already had of the Nazi regime.

Of course, Orwell had to have been a certain type of man to go to Spain as he did. The same may be said of the other major and also somewhat chance experience in his career, that he should have been a journalist. Much of what he says, especially about history and the doings of governments, is seen from the perspective of the journalist. (See *1984*, pp. 86–89. Karl Marx, too, was in decisive respects a journalist.) Does not the modern journalist-intellectual tend to be a professional skeptic? Thus, as we have seen, Orwell was tempted to question Gandhi's credentials as a student of totalitarianism in part because he was "after all born in 1869," neglecting the fact that Winston Churchill, perhaps the greatest Twentieth-Century adversary of totalitarianism, was born only five years later. (See *Orwell Reader*, p. 333.)

We have to keep the indispensable reports of journalists in proper perspective. Journalists, or at least their editors, tend to magnify a certain aspect of things; they are more adept with the low, the sensational, the quick-changing. They are not likely to grasp the whole and the enduring. Would they remain journalists if they did? They must report *something* and that "something" as *happening*, thereby promoting and catering to a special appetite for the catastrophic. Certainly there *are* problems with what one is "taught" by experience.

One who is taught primarily by experience tends to believe in the primacy of forces over ideas. This reinforces the presuppositions of the modern intellectual, presuppositions that make much of individuality and that implicitly suspect nobility. Individuality is discouraged by the Inner Party as "own life." (*1984*, p. 37) There is something to this criticism of individuality, as there is to that regime's reservations about the integrity of history as a science, but in these as in other cases the regime may be right for the wrong reasons. (See, on the status of the self, *1984*, pp. 87, 88–89.)

The modern intellectual's suspicion of nobility brings us to what may be the most critical defect in Orwell's practical understanding, his opinions about the nature of politics and of rulers, past, present, and future.

VIII

Cynicism and an insistence upon "realism" in viewing the ways of governments and countries may mean, among other things, that the highest things are beyond one's ken. Does not *1984* tend to encourage individuality at the expense of traditional civic-mindedness, particularly since it considers selfishness to be at the root of most government action, no matter what the regime?

Furthermore, selfishness itself is left in the novel as an ambiguous flaw. Betrayal does seem to be regarded as questionable, but on what basis? Winston Smith is presented as hating virtue, especially if it happens to be a virtue endorsed by the regime. This is seen most vividly in his disparagement of chastity, as he endorses and possibly relishes Julia's many affairs in defiance of Party policy. (See *1984*, pp. 55–59.) He talks as if the only source of various virtues or rules of conduct is the regime. Does not such an attitude make the regime stronger, partly because it denies objective goodness? Genuine virtue, I have argued, is needed in order to resist *this* regime effectively.

Certainly one cannot take one's guidance simply by doing the opposite of what the Party ordains. Since the Party is fundamentally irrational, it can sometimes be correct by chance. But to speak of correctness in these matters is to draw upon a natural basis for determining the good and the bad.

It will not do to rely either upon one's rebelliousness or upon one's feelings to chart one's course of conduct. Such an approach tends to become nihilistic. It is an approach that is reflected in what Orwell, along with O'Brien, believes about the malleability both of character and of language. The flaws in Smith's character from the beginning, including his tyrannical self-indulgence as an unlovely child, should warn us that he is not truly to be relied upon. Even before he is arrested, he is willing in the "testing" of him by O'Brien to *say* that he would do *anything* to further the revolution. One recalls by way of contrast Socrates' report in Plato's *Apology* of his refusal to cooperate in the crimes of the Thirty Tyrants, and one suspects he would have considered many deeds routinely resorted to today to be actions that should be shunned, no matter what cause they were said to be in the service of.

We are obliged then to look, for our standards, to nature and to that which is by nature right. But nature does not seem to serve Orwell well. It is nature, he seems to indicate, that accounts for man's overwhelming selfishness, for his willingness under the cover of pious sentiments and patriotic slogans to exploit his fellow man. Perhaps as much as anything else, Orwell's generally poor treatment of women throughout his writings suggests his inability to take nature seriously. (See, on nature, *1984*, pp. 54, 56, 60. Does Orwell draw, perhaps unconsciously, upon some notion of original sin? Does he see a hollowness naturally at the core of the human being? Consider Bertrand Russell's appreciation of him at pages 237–38 of *1984*.)

Another way of putting this is to say that what is needed in Orwell's own thought is far more political philosophy and far less ideology. It is political philosophy, rooted in nature, which recognizes that a critical and perhaps primary purpose of the political order is to help establish and perpetuate the virtues that nature reveals to sensible men. So instructive is nature in this respect that a considerable goodness guides men most of the time. Thus people are rarely cruel or perverse when there is nothing substantial to be gained by it. By and large, the people we associate with, even most casually as when driving on the highway, conduct themselves decently, although there may be no one around threatening to punish them for misconduct.

But compare how politics is regarded by Orwell. He can say in his Gandhi essay that politics are, "of their nature," "inseparable from coercion and fraud." (*Orwell Reader*, p. 328) It can be said by a theoretician in *1984*, "All rulers in all ages have tried to impose a false view of the world upon their followers . . ." (*1984*, p. 87) If one considers all governments up to now as illegitimate, as "Goldstein," Smith, and evidently Orwell seem to do, then there may be only one realistic thing (short of utopia) for the political man to do, and that is to struggle for power for its own sake.

It is a curious effect of Orwell's work that one comes away from it with a greater respect for such quite different political men as Gandhi *and* Machiavelli and of course for that politician after whom Winston Smith (born in 1944 or 1945) was evidently named. Whatever flaws these three politicians had, they did not share Orwell's opinion that government was mere exploitation and otherwise illegitimate. (Orwell did respect Gandhi, as he did Dickens, without fully appreciating why. See, e.g., *Orwell Reader*, p. 335, for a compliment to Gandhi which is a backhanded slap at politicians generally: "how clean a smell he has managed to leave behind!")

To say that Orwell's disparagement of politics tends to justify the pursuit of power for its own sake is not to say that O'Brien is on sound ground in proclaiming the decisive selfishness of rulers. O'Brien makes much of things that are rather ugly: the intoxication with power and with the pleasure of crushing others. Why should such sadism be taken seriously as anything but pathological? Why should one be taken seriously who does not understand that power makes no sense if it is not directed toward a proper end? For O'Brien, a means is transformed into an end, further revealing that he does not truly rule. After all, as we have noticed, a man does not rule if he does not know what he is doing, however much he has to be reckoned with in his irrationality by the people he is hurting.

People such as O'Brien lose by "winning." For someone to rule ultimately by torture in the service of deception, which seems to be critical to the regime in *1984*, means that he is not truly in charge. Not he but at best a false replica of himself "rules." That the wicked are vulnerable as well as deprived is a lesson that has been taught us again and again. I do not believe that Orwell recognizes that *1984*, in spite of him, teaches us that lesson once again, as well as two other lessons: that virtue, knowledge, and genuine happiness go together and that civilization depends on law-abiding governments confident of their authority and prudent in their administration.

Insofar as Orwell's novel reveals these lessons to us, it is because he is a better artist than he is a political thinker. (The same may be said of other gifted but scarred men, such as Solzhenitsyn.)

IX

Much is made in discussions of *1984* of the fact that Winston Smith can finally be moved to love Big Brother. What does it mean to "love" another? Great respect for the other may be exhibited; or one may be overwhelmed by the other; or one may be completely subordinated to, dependent on, and in need of the other. In these senses of "love," therefore, it can be said that Orwell himself also loves Big Brother, and this *he* does without the compulsion necessary to make Smith submit. For Orwell does see Big Brother as omnipotent, as mysterious, as someone he (Orwell) himself very much relies upon to develop his masterpiece.

Consider, by way of comparison, Shakespeare's *The Tempest*, where reason and humanity are carried out to their "logical" conclusion, a conclusion which reflects the fact that good *is* more powerful and more enduring than evil. We also see in *The Tempest* that rulers *can* be moved to promote the good, that civilization and humanity can be consistent with and reinforced by enlightened self-interest.

What is needed when these subjects are discussed, and what the great artist or prophet perhaps alone can provide for most people, is a reaffirmation of the human spirit. This is something that *1984* does not provide, indeed just the opposite, however useful the novel may be as a grim warning against certain innovations.

Men need to be taught that one can resist tyranny and often survive in decent shape. That is, the limits of tyranny need to be recognized, even a tyranny which makes considerable use of technology. Also in need of recognition is what is truly dangerous *for us* in our time: not the highly contrived tyranny described in *1984*, but rather those opinions that make totalitarianism possible. Such opinions, so fashionable for intellectuals, make too much both of utopian solutions and of demonic regimes and too little of natural right and prudential politics.

The modern intellectual tends to say with Friedrich Nietzsche, "For me—how could there be anything outside of me? There is no outside!" (*Independent Journal of Philosophy*, III, iii) This is hardly an elevating sentiment, however liberating it may have once seemed to be. I prefer to conclude my respectful dissent from the authority of George Orwell by drawing upon *The Pilgrim's Progress* of John Bunyan. We can see there what an affirmation of the human spirit can mean at the hands of authors who may, for one reason or another, seem questionable to us today. Here is the great speech by Valiant-for-truth as he contemplates his death:

> I am going to my Fathers, and tho with great Difficulty I am got hither, yet now I do not repent me of all the Trouble I have been at to arrive where I am. My Sword I give to him that shall succeed me in my Pilgrimage, and my Courage and Skill to him that can get it. My Marks and Scarrs I carry with me, to be a witness for me, that I have fought his Battels, who now will be my Rewarder.

"The heart," we can agree with one critic even as we recall the suppressed church chimes faintly remembered in *1984*, "vibrates like a bell to such utterances as this." (See *The Artist as Thinker*, p. 76.)

ISSUES
of the
DAY

===

A.

Catalogues of "Cases"

14

THE MORAL FOUNDATION OF THE LAW

Sir: The command of the Department of the West having devolved upon you, I propose to offer you a few suggestions, knowing how hazardous it is to bind down a distant commander in the field to specific lines and operations, as so much always depends on a knowledge of localities & passing events. It is intended, therefore, to leave a considerable margin for the exercise of your judgment & discretion.

ABRAHAM LINCOLN TO DAVID HUNTER

I

One of my University of Chicago Law School classmates, who went on to become Attorney General of the United States, recalled recently that I had a way of perplexing our law faculty. "George always approached issues from what I called a moral foundation," he said, "which was distressing to some professors who felt this was essentially irrelevant to the practitioner." The primary concern of this discussion is to consider whether what has been called "a moral foundation" is indeed "essentially irrelevant to the practitioner." Much of what I will say here consists of suggestions about what "a moral foundation," or the moral judgments on which we depend, must look like in a variety of circumstances. Although considerable interest has been expressed by some of you in the Illinois bar admis-

This talk was given at The College of Law, DePaul University, Chicago, Illinois, November 7, 1979. (Sponsor: Phi Alpha Delta Law Fraternity.)

The United States Attorney General quoted is Ramsey Clark. See *Chicago Tribune*, March 18, 1979, sec. 3, p. 10. The Chicago Council of Lawyers talk of October 12, 1979 quoted from several times in this essay is published in my collection of documents, "What Is Still Wrong With George Anastaplo? A Sequel to 366 U.S. 82 (1961)," 35 *DePaul Law Review* 551, at 624–28 (1986).

The epigraph is taken from *The Collected Works of Abraham Lincoln*, ed. Roy P. Basler (New Brunswick, N.J.: Rutgers University Press, 1953), V, 1 (October 24, 1861).

185

sion matter that began for me in 1950, I can do no more than glance at it at the end of my prepared remarks, leaving it to you to pursue the matter further in our discussion period.

It should become evident, in considering various "cases," that it is difficult to distinguish between the private and the public in what lawyers do. Even lawyers in private practice, where I take it most of you are destined to be, are to some degree public servants, and not only because they are "officers of the court." It is well to remind the typical lawyer of what was said about a famous Roman in Cicero's *Republic:* "Though [Junius] Brutus held no public office, he upheld the whole common weal. Thus he was the first man in our commonwealth to teach the lesson that, when it is a question of preserving the liberty of the citizens, there is no such thing as a private station." (II, 35; p. 178) But, I presume to add, it is not only the liberty of citizens that should be the concern of men of influence in the commonwealth, but also those things for the sake of which liberty is cherished.

II

In these matters generally acknowledged principles and standards are critical. What these principles mean can usefully be examined by considering various instances in which they are brought to bear. Especially critical here is the virtue of prudence. But prudence, I should immediately add, is not mere cautiousness or an excuse to avoid inconveniences.

Prudence depends on reliable information, including information about the likely consequences of alternative actions. It also depends on a reliable sense of what is higher and lower, of what is better and best, since one's choices are apt to be among contending goods. It is here that principles are critical: one needs to be able to judge matters while they are still vital, sometimes well before the community has had time to settle into a reliable opinion about them. Thus, it has been noticed, there is a need to train students how to pass the simpler types of judgments on men and policies. This training, I submit, is particularly important among those who are, or who are about to become, lawyers.

III

I ventured, on October 12th, to make some remarks to a Palmer House gathering of lawyers and judges which, in the few minutes then available, barely touched upon the matters I should like to examine with you today at leisure. Those remarks were in response to an award from the Chicago Council of Lawyers. Among the things I said on that occasion relevant to our subject today was the observation that the most crippling punishment that misguided men suffer is that they remain precisely themselves. That is, those men and women are worst off who "get away" with their misconduct. It is important that this be emphasized, since the most effective and reliable policing of what is done among us is carried on by each of us with respect to his own conduct. In these matters, the sense of shame is not without its uses.

Much of what I said to the bar association on Columbus Day was anticipated by a talk I heard that very day on the way down to the Palmer House to receive my award. It was, in effect, a talk on nature, civility, and justice and was delivered on a crowded bus to two young men (one White, the other Negro) who remained seated while several elderly women were left standing. This talk was given by a Black Muslim who had himself given up a seat earlier in the run to a frail white woman of years. I do not recall ever hearing a better sermon. It was instructive both as to content and as to style. Ethical arguments were developed which took into account personal passions and reminded the selfish youngsters of mutual dependence. It was low-keyed but firm, wide-ranging and yet always relevant, as it invoked elementary notions of right and wrong. Much of what was said, and the way it was said, very much needs to be said again and again and again in large, anonymous cities where the sense of community (and hence the sense of shame, as well as of duty) is likely to be weak. That the young man who said these things looked big enough to be able to take care of himself in case of trouble and that he said what he did with an evident good will and not without humor meant that these things *could* be said and that they would provide salutary lessons to everyone who heard them or who heard about them thereafter.

The principles invoked that day on the bus are old-fashioned and generally known. They are principles on which all decent communities depend and which need only to be stated properly for them to inspire respect among those who have not become thoroughly demoralized. I note in passing that I offered my bus seat to an older woman on the way down here today—to a woman who turned out to be rather fierce, as exhibited in how she fought her way to my seat in order to thwart a younger woman heading for it who did not realize what I had intended. I was caught in the middle of a vigorous shoving match. Well, so much for civility and the good life!

IV

But we must get on to the Palmer House and to the three issues I thought it useful to comment upon there to a liberal bar association that is sympathetic to judicial activism. I will consider each in turn, elaborating a little upon each before going on to the dozen or so instances that I believe it salutary to add for your further consideration. Our concern, you will recall, is to uncover that moral foundation upon which the life and work of the legal practitioner should rest.

1) I presumed on that occasion last month "to draw upon my reputation as a constitutional scholar as I indicate[d] reservations about three opinions that the 'better' lawyers and judges among us hold these days." "My first dissenting opinion," I went on to say, "is that we now face here in Chicago, in the prospect of mandatory busing of public school children, a tiresome ritual which promises to do little in this city for education and the invaluable neighborhood school, for racial justice, or for ordinary people's faith in the Constitution, bureaucrats and federal judges. It would make far more sense, and hence be a far better use of the passions and resources which forced busing will waste, to do something (if only in the form of an urban equivalent of the Civilian Conservation Corps) about the scandalous unemployment rate, especially among the young, in the remarkably patient Negro community." To notice, as I did, the high unemployment rate in the Negro community is not to deny that considerable progress in race relations and in racial justice has been made in this Country since the Second World War. To recognize that progress *has* been made means that we are aware of the relevant standards here. It also means that we do have standards by which to call for, work for, and judge further progress in this respect. That the Negro minority in our community is, despite considerable progress in recent decades, still sorely deprived was brought home to me once again last week at Orchestra Hall. An excellent Negro soloist appeared with the Chicago Symphony: this singer was well received, but by an audience that was almost entirely white, and this in a city in which her race constitutes well over one-third of the population. I was reminded on that occasion of what I have noticed again and again at Wrigley Field in recent years, that a good half of the baseball players on the field might be Negro while very few in the crowd are. This disparity is, I suspect, in large part due to the economic depression that Negroes continue to suffer. This does not seem to me a healthy state of affairs. The prudent community cannot help but be disturbed by such chronic disparities.

V

2) I return, after this elaboration upon my "first dissenting opinion," to what I then said to the Chicago Council of Lawyers: "My second dissenting opinion is that the virtually unlimited access to abortion now available in this country is an unconscionable state of affairs. The Roman Catholics among us are substantially correct in their deep opposition to what we now have, even though they (because of a misunderstanding of the dictates of natural law) have long been misled by their leaders with respect to birth control. Particularly serious here is the unwarranted reading of the Constitution by the United States Supreme Court, which has left local governments paralyzed in any attempt to deal compassionately but firmly with our dreadful abortion epidemic (which represents, among other things, a callous exploitation of women and an endorsement of mindless gratification)." I will return to the question of natural law. But I do notice immediately here, following up my reference to the exploitation of women, that there is something unnatural about our widespread war on the fetus. What does that war say about love and sexuality among us? I should also call to your attention something that it may be more useful to recognize here today than it would have been at that Palmer House gathering of liberals last month, and that is that there may be good reasons for countenancing abortion in some instances. Legitimate questions come up here, for instance, with respect to the consequences of rape and of incest, with respect to danger to the very life of the mother, and with respect to the prospect of crushing physical or mental defects in the child. Legitimate questions may also be raised about whether the concern we may have about resorting to abortion should apply to routine measures taken during the first forty-eight hours after conception or among those of advanced age. But however difficult it may be to answer such questions, it does seem to me dubious to hold, as a conscientious federal judge evidently did this past week in entering a temporary restraining order blocking enforcement of Illinois's new abortion law, "[T]he threatened injury to [women seeking abortions] outweighs the threatened harm to the State." (*Chicago Tribune*, November 1, 1979, sec. 1, p. 8) Critical to any determination here should be the recognition that the State has a proper concern and often a duty to help people do the right thing. Everyone may be harmed, including the State, when private parties choose and are permitted to do terrible things that supposedly hurt only themselves. To this too I will return. In any event, the continuing paralysis of local governments in abortion matters (a paralysis induced by questionable readings of the

Constitution) remains a serious problem for all who are dedicated to self-government.

VI

3) The principle of self-government and a due appreciation of what constitutes a legitimate community interest are reflected in the final instance I shared on Columbus Day with the Chicago Council of Lawyers, when I said, "My third dissenting opinion is rooted in the argument, which I have made again and again in my publications, that the primary purpose of the First Amendment is to protect our right and duty to discuss fully, as a sovereign people, the political questions that come before us from time to time. (The 'clear and present danger' test is, in these matters, simply without support in the Constitution.) Among the questions always open for discussion is that of what the community should do to train itself and its citizens for self-government and for a decent life together. Certainly, no community is obliged in the name of liberty and self-expression to allow itself to be corrupted by the demented, the vulgar, the selfish, the thoughtless or the doctrinaire." Critical here is the question whether we are able and justified in any attempt to control influences that shape us as a people. This can be seen in what we permit to be done to us by such entrepreneurs as are found in television, professional sports, and real estate development. Thus shopping centers, which are destroying the integrity of our towns and small cities, should probably be strictly regulated if not virtually eliminated by county governments. Thus also, to carry my First Amendment point further, I believe it dubious to consider obscenity issues to be freedom-of-the-press questions, whatever good reasons there may be on due process and other grounds for restraining government attempts at regulation in this area.

These three sets of opinions—about racial justice, about abortion, and about the dominant political concerns of the First Amendment—that I touched upon before the Chicago Council of Lawyers need considerable research and elaboration. The same should be said as well about the opinions that I have collected for this occasion. It is important to notice that all these opinions are somehow related to one another, and that decent, intelligent people should be able to raise these questions without calling into question either their competence or their good will. Be that as it may, here are a dozen or so additional opinions or issues that I consider appropriate for people being trained in the law to be reminded of:

VII

4) My first additional opinion for your consideration has also to do with the First Amendment. I do not believe it useful to consider the *Progressive Magazine*-type case a serious threat to freedom of the press in this Country. Certainly we can do without panic with respect to the First Amendment. The simple fact is that the *Progressive* could and probably should have published without consulting the government any material it truly believed in the public interest to be published about the information generally available on how to make a hydrogen bomb. If it had not consulted the government, there would have been no opportunity for the government to attempt to block publication, and this is what usually happens in this Country. It should be remembered that there would not have even been a *Pentagon Papers* case in 1971 if the *New York Times* had published everything it had in one issue, as it could have done, rather than in installments. Thus the *Progressive* either should have published whatever it considered fit to publish or, if it believed it had the duty to secure a government opinion, it should have been more respectful than it evidently was of the government's concern. On the other hand, the government, by conducting itself as it did, discouraged future consultations by publishers sitting on a "hot story."

5) Nor do I believe it useful to consider public marches essentially like speech, publications, or assembly. This is so whether the march is by Martin Luther King and other Negroes in Cicero or by Frank Collin and his "Nazis" in Skokie. Marches are opportunities for people to do much more than talk or exchange ideas, and that *more* is what we are not *obliged* by the First Amendment to tolerate, whatever we may *choose* to permit to be done from time to time according to general rules and as circumstances change.

6) Also a problem today is a reading of the First Amendment that on the one hand cripples government regulation of the misconduct of various "religious" cults, and on the other hand keeps governments from purchasing from church-sponsored schools the educational services and benefits that the community very much needs and often wants. Again and again, we see political and often partisan judgments disguised as constitutional necessities.

VIII

7) We continue to indulge those among us who irresponsibly encourage belief in conspiracy theories—those who believe these days not in such

things as the 1968 Democratic National Convention conspiracy, but rather
in such things as Assassination conspiracies. Such conspiracy advocates
are using their First Amendment rights, but we should also use ours in calling them to account. Related to this is our continued reliance upon those
who in the form of extended anti-trust prosecutions testify to the still un-
substantiated faith that conspiracy really makes much difference in the
economic life of this Country. Perhaps at the root of our indulgence in
conspiracy theories is the sense that our lives otherwise seem to be subject
far too much to chance.

8) Reliance upon conspiracy theories may be seen as well in much of
what one hears these days about the consequences of corporate mergers
and of multinational companies. My own impression is that bloated con-
glomerates tend to be easy pickings for smaller, efficient firms. Fantasies
about corporate manipulations are particularly vivid in our responses to
the "energy crisis." We continue to make much of this crisis without explaining why substantial price increases for oil, with appropriate subsidies
for the poor, would not take care of this so-called crisis, as it would for
any other critical commodity we import. Instead, we hear of a professional investigator (in this case, on behalf of the States of California,
Oregon, Washington, Arizona, Florida, and Connecticut) testifying before a Congressional committee last June "that the western part of the
country was 'an arena for very tightly controlled markets through collusion and conspiracy' and that [the major oil companies] were engaged in a
'very carefully organized conspiracy to end . . . competitive price wars.' "
(*National Law Journal*, September 24, 1979, p. 5) The truth of the matter
may be that the "gas shortages" experienced in the Western States and elsewhere last Spring have been largely due to the scope, and hence the inef-
ficiencies, of government regulation in this field. In any event, I had
occasion back in 1973 to warn, "The most serious threat likely to impress
itself upon the American public in the years immediately ahead has to do
with the so-called energy crisis and the resulting concern about our vulnerable 'jugular vein' in the Middle East oil countries. Thus, doubling
the cost of our gasoline at home makes much more sense than desperate
adventures abroad." (See 40 *University of Pittsburgh Law Review* 778, n.
104 [1979].)

IX

9) The ultimate desperate adventure in our time, it sometimes seems,
would be recourse to nuclear war, something that economic crises, parti-

san maneuvering, and a careless scattering of tactical nuclear weapons can prepare the way for. To be discouraged by us with an almost religious fervor is any use in battle of any nuclear arms or radical biological weapons by anybody in the foreseeable future. Such recourse should be regarded much as we do the cannibalism to which people have been driven to resort in the most desperate circumstances.

10) Partisan maneuvering has particularly to be guarded against in considering such revelations as the recent news about a Russian brigade in Cuba. The *hiding* there of three thousand combat troops for some years now can hardly be considered a challenge to American prestige or security. An effort has been made in some quarters to link this matter with the SALT ratification issue now before the Senate. There is perhaps something to this. But would it not be even better for our security and that of Europe if we could oblige the Russians as a condition for our ratification of SALT to station not three thousand but rather three million fully equipped troops in Cuba? I can think of few places on earth where such troops could be so useless to the Russians. On the other hand, if we had wanted to confront the Russians on a *serious* issue, we had opportunity enough to do so some weeks ago when a ballerina was held by them on an airplane in New York for a couple of days. There was something disgraceful, especially for someone of a legal turn of mind, in the way we conducted ourselves there, if the press reports of the episode are reliable. We do have to do some of the Russians' thinking for them, if only because we alone can publicly discuss and thoroughly explore the issues between us. Even so, the Russians and the Americans have learned to depend on each other to some extent: each side counts on the other to remain somewhat sensible, as could be seen during the foolish Cuban Missile Crisis of 1962. My ballerina reference reminds me of a related problem, that of airplane hijacking. Is it not prudent to be known to have an ironclad rule that no hijacked plane will be permitted to take off from any airport in this Country?

11) All this is to say that we should keep our heads on straight and retain a sense of proportion. Consider, however, the forty-year sentence meted out for espionage last year to an evidently disturbed young man in Hammond, Indiana. It is far from clear what the Russians got from him or what, of even greater importance, they have gotten legally from official American sources. I have not yet seen a transcript of the Hammond trial, but both the newspaper accounts of that trial and the appellate briefs I have seen suggest that this matter is in need of both further investigation and sensible reassessment. I am reminded, by the rather excited way the trial judge is reported to have justified his sentence in the Hammond case, of the dreadful *Rosenberg* case of 1951–53.

X

12) Various of these observations presuppose critical differences among the regimes available in the world today. It is vital, if we are to think clearly about moral as well as political matters, that our judgment about these matters remain unimpaired. Our profound affinity with an Israel deeply scarred by holocausts must continue to be recognized, however we may differ from time to time about what contributes to that country's security. When we recall the aberrations that we despite our enormous strength have been subject to in the name of national security since the Second World War, we should be respectful of the Israeli sense of vulnerability and its consequences. Thus, also, the need for sensible working relations with the Russians should not blind us to the fact that there continues to exist in the Soviet Union a formidable tyranny. It is important, if we are to understand how things are, that we do retain a lively awareness of the better and the worse. This means, for example, that as questionable as the regime in South Africa is, far worse is that regime in mainland China which many critics of South Africa regard so highly.

13) Even more critical than the differences among regimes presupposed by my observations on this occasion is the understanding of human nature upon which reliable moral and political judgments rest. It is nature, I presume to suggest, that calls into question much of what is being said by the more "emancipated" among us these days about homosexual relations, about the relations of male and female, about the relations of the old and the young, even about what is a better and worse life—and about the uses of law in helping the human being achieve the very best. We need, in these matters, to be toughminded without being cruel.

XI

14) One effect of our distortion of the promptings of nature and of the fashionable insistence that the community has little if any legitimate power to regulate our "private lives" is what is said and done these days about "victimless crimes." It has led to such scandals as the recourse we have had to government-promoted gambling in this State. Our lottery is a blatant effort to exploit the weaknesses of some among us in order to save the rest of us the taxes that would otherwise have to be raised to pay for what we believe ourselves to need. Or consider the increasing tolerance being shown to the doing of things that supposedly hurt only oneself, whether they be indulgence in drugs, corrupting film and print, or dangerous stunts. All this culminates in the supposed right to commit suicide, about

which one hears more and more these days. A bizarre form of this "right" may be seen in our inability to prevent executions whenever the condemned man refuses to prosecute an appeal. (A recent instance of this was called by two members of the United States Supreme Court "State-assisted suicide.") But, I submit, the state should not be bound by what the condemned man wants, either in the decision to execute him or in the decision to reprieve him. After all, nature prefers that the strong should rule the weak, that the wise should rule the ignorant, that the good should rule the bad. In any event, it should be evident upon examination not only that there are few private actions which do not affect others (a suicide, for example, can have devastating effects on a wide circle of survivors), but also that the supposedly private person very much depends on his community as well as on his family to become what he is. For both sets of reasons, and for other reasons as well, his duty to the community is considerable. It is not solely up to him to decide how long he should "serve" (that is, live) or in what form.

15) Related to the enthronement of the principle of private choice, of "doing one's own thing," is a corresponding depreciation of political life and of politicians. One form this depreciation takes is the willingness to disregard the chronic moral deficiencies of various men who offer themselves as candidates for public office from time to time. Consider, on the other hand, how the greatest republic of antiquity thought about the relation of the private to the public. Plutarch writes, in his *Life of Marcus Cato*,

> For the Romans thought that no marriage, or rearing of children, nay, no feast or drinking-bout, ought to be permitted according to every one's appetite or fancy, without being examined and inquired into; being indeed of opinion that a man's character was much sooner perceived in things of this sort than in what is done publicly and in open day. They chose, therefore, two persons, one out of the patricians, the other out of the commons, who were to watch, correct, and punish, if anyone ran too much into voluptuousness, or transgressed the usual manner of life of his country; and these they called Censors.

XII

16) Related to the depreciation of political life is the failure to appreciate properly the purposes and benefits of established political and constitutional procedures. This may be seen in the doctrinaire attacks from time to time on such institutions as the Electoral College or on such constitutional requirements as the need for Senate ratification of treaties negotiated by the President. Foreigners, we are told, are dismayed that carefully

prepared treaties can be wrecked by a branch of the American legislature. But does not the expectation of Senate review have, by and large, a salutary effect? Have we not suffered more in the Twentieth Century from Presidential misjudgment than from Senatorial recalcitrance? Certainly foreigners should recognize by now that this *is* the way things are going to be and should conduct themselves accordingly.

17) The magnification among us of private life, on the other hand, may be seen in the repeated exploitation of procedures by lawyers and others to avoid the immediate demands of justice. All too often this is done in such a way as to give the law a bad name. Consider, for example, the case here in Cook County of a man who was found to have killed several dozen boys in recent years. From all indications, considerable public resources are to be expended over months if not years upon the disposition of a matter that should have been settled within a few weeks after this man was detected. There are limits, it should be remembered by lawyers, to the interests of their clients. Thus one sees again and again the willingness of respectable corporate counsel to exploit every technical advantage that the law provides. It is bad enough when this happens in civil litigation. But when it appears in criminal proceedings, whether on the part of government counsel or on the part of defense counsel, it can be most disturbing. Consider, on the other hand, my concluding remarks in an article I published this past summer in *The Chicago Lawyer* on the *Rosenberg* atomic-espionage case (see, also, "On Trial: Explorations," pt. 12):

> Why, then, was there such unlawyerlike haste [as seen in the closing days of the case, in June 1953, when a stay of execution was vacated at noon by the U.S. Supreme Court and the Rosenbergs were executed by sunset]? In order, it would seem, to attempt to stop the agitation, in this country and abroad, of the question of what should be done with the Rosenbergs. I have yet to hear of any other explanation that makes any sense at all. That is, the executions were rushed, in the spirit of impassioned partisanship, in order to deprive us of the opportunity, sorely needed, to think about what was being done in our name.
>
> It is difficult for me to escape the conclusion that what the authorities did here was, however sincere, far worse than anything that we know to have happened in connection with Watergate. This kind of misconduct by the authorities is hardly likely to produce or to maintain a sensible and humane people dedicated to the rule of law.
>
> In such desperate circumstances, lawyers (who are, after all, a privileged class, trained to be "above the battle") should have the good sense and the fortitude to say to a client, even if that client should happen to be the Government of the United States: "What you propose to do is simply wrong, and I for one am not going to help you do it."

No doubt you have noticed that I began this last point with my reservations about a criminal proceeding that had not been disposed of within a few weeks after the mass killer had been discovered, and I concluded it with my reservations about a criminal proceeding that was disposed of far too quickly in its closing days. (The Rosenbergs were convicted in March 1951 and executed in June 1953.) If I have been correct in my assessments throughout this talk, it should be evident that there is no mechanical formula that can be applied in such matters, however useful "ironclad rules" may be for certain purposes. Rather, there is in all such matters a need for prudential judgment. Indeed, it is prudence that must be brought to bear in all of the situations I have collected for you on this occasion.

To rely upon prudence is *not* to depend on an ability to foresee the future. That is too much to expect. Rather, it is to depend on the use of common sense to see the present: to see what is before us and to see it properly. This means that one must be able to recognize things that are bad in themselves, as well as things that ordinary human experience indicates are highly likely in some circumstances to have terrible consequences. Various of the opinions I have suggested today *are* somewhat impolitic for anyone in public life to stand by. No doubt the prudent man who hopes to serve the community in a political capacity should be sensible in how many such opinions he endorses and in what way. Lawyers, who are in that in-between world straddling private life and public life, can be equipped, and can afford, to be both more thoughtful and more outspoken than practicing politicians in this respect. Even so, an experienced civil liberties lawyer in this city said to me a few months ago, "Academics may be asking the wrong questions, but lawyers are not asking any questions at all."

XIII

I have attempted to suggest some of the questions that you as lawyers should ask. Much of what I have said depends on an awareness of what the best by nature would be: the best in a community, the best in a human being. I should not have to argue in this university for the teachings of natural right upon which I have been drawing throughout my talk today. After all, the Roman Catholic Church *has* been, despite its shortcomings in such matters as its birth-control teachings, a determined guardian of the natural-law tradition in modern times. The effectiveness of natural-right teachings in a community depends on sensible guidance by men of practical wisdom, and this is where properly trained lawyers come in.

Certain questions are especially critical today if the community is to be guided by practical wisdom. It is generally asked among intellectuals, "Are there any standards for personal conduct which are not mere matters of taste or of chance?" It is also asked, "Even if there are standards that are more or less rooted in nature and hence objective and knowable, is the community able to do anything to advance or protect these standards for the sake of individuals?" It is further asked, "Even if the community is able to do something, is it *proper* that it should do so?" What these and similar questions usually reveal is the current lack of self-confidence on the part of communities with respect to making judgments and exercising moral authority. The restoration of a justified self-confidence, restrained in part by a sense of shame (if not even enhanced by a proper pride), remains a vital task for the law and hence for lawyers in the years ahead.

I say "*restoration* of a justified self-confidence" since there *was* such self-confidence during at least the first century of the life of this country. A sense of rightness, grounded in nature, is to be seen for example in the right of revolution set forth in the Declaration of Independence. Evident there is the "moral foundation" upon which the political institutions of this Country do rest. The Declaration of Independence invoked both nature and an obligation to judge, and it made it clear that these standards and duties could be properly invoked by the community as a whole as well as by citizens on behalf of the community.

The key difference of opinion between the Illinois bar authorities and me throughout my bar admission controversy turned upon the significance of the right of revolution as affirmed by the Declaration of Independence. Critical to such an affirmation is the importance of sound judgment. The right of revolution is not primarily an assertion of any liberty of self-expression, or of mere rebelliousness, or even of "the individual against the state."

The Declaration of Independence recognizes that tyranny may be resisted and that liberties may be insisted upon. But even more is made by the Declaration of the recognition that a people should be able to control its life, including the shaping of the character of its citizens, all with a view to the promotion of prosperity, of true happiness, and of an enduring peace rooted in justice. Vital to this communal enterprise is the right and duty of citizens to explain themselves, to account for what they have been doing, and to examine with others what should be done in their lives, both public and private.

15

THE OCCASIONS OF FREEDOM OF SPEECH

But no rules need to be given about what is done in accordance with the established customs and conventions of a community; for these are in themselves rules; and no one ought to make the mistake of supposing that, because Socrates or Aristippus did or said something contrary to the manners and established customs of the city, he has the right to do the same. It was only by reason of their great and divine virtue that they had such license.

CICERO

I

It is a curious fact that an occasional reader of my 1971 book, *The Constitutionalist,* somehow concludes that I believe "principles must be given priority over consequences." Perhaps this is because I once did find it salutary to insist upon standing on a principle which cost me my career at the bar.

It is partly to correct careless misconceptions about my opinions on controversial issues that I have been obliged again and again to quote from and cite to various of my publications. Something more can usefully be said here, if only in outline form, about my opinions, supplementing thereby the generous introduction to *The Constitutionalist* recently provided for readers of the *Political Science Reviewer.*

No sensible man (unless his name is Immanuel Kant?) can knowingly insist upon abstract principles without regard to preconditions or circum-

---

This essay was published, with extensive notes, in 5 *Political Science Reviewer* 383–402 (1975). It was in response to a review by Raleigh Smith of my book, *The Constitutionalist: Notes on the First Amendment* (Dallas: Southern Methodist University Press, 1971), in 4 *Political Science Reviewer* 169 (1974). See, for additional discussions of noteworthy trials, Anastaplo, "On Trial: Explorations," *Loyola University of Chicago Law Journal* (forthcoming). See, also, the headnote for Essay No. 21, below.

The epigraph is taken from Cicero, *On Moral Duties,* I, 41 (Walter Miller translation).

stances. I have several times suggested that our extensive "freedom of speech [and] of the press" makes sense only for a people of a certain character, a character that our current openness to obscenity and our growing dependence on television are likely to undermine. This is not to say, however, that it can *never* be politically useful and hence rhetorically sound to set forth everyday rules couched in "absolutist" terms.

Considerations both of justice and the common good should be applied to the political issues that we happen upon. As an aid to such application (an aid, that is, to the study of prudence) the work of the greatest minds is invaluable. I had occasion to observe in the last bar admission petition I filed in the United States Supreme Court (June 19, 1961),

> Petitioner, exercising the prerogative of one retiring from a profession, would advise the new lawyer that he learn well not only the tools of his craft but also the texts that have come to us from the ancient world. It is in those texts that one may find the best models, both in word and in deed, for the conduct of oneself in public as well as in private affairs. It is there that the better natures are most likely to be exposed to the accents and majesty of human excellence.

(See *The Constitutionalist,* p. 382.) The massive notes I append to many of my publications are intended to provide introductions to the work of the greatest minds, ancient and modern, for readers who ordinarily rely only on legal documents and scholarly commentary.

There are, I have indicated, places where American-style freedom of speech would do little good. It might even do considerable harm. There may even come a time when our national freedom of speech would be a disservice to good government on this continent as well. What that freedom of speech means, in our constitutional system, I summed up in this way in *The Constitutionalist* (pp. 15–16):

> The First Amendment to the Constitution prohibits Congress, in its lawmaking capacity, from cutting down in any way or for any reason freedom of speech and of the press. The extent of this freedom is to be measured not merely by the common law treatises and cases available on December 15, 1791—the date of the ratification of the First Amendment—but also by the general understanding and practice of the people of the United States who insisted upon, had written for them, and ratified (through their State legislatures) the First Amendment. An important indication of the extent of this freedom is to be seen in the teachings of the Declaration of Independence and in the events leading up to the Revolution.
>
> Although the prohibition in the First Amendment is absolute—we see here a restraint upon Congress that is unqualified, among restraints that *are* quali-

fied—the absolute prohibition does not relate to all forms of expression but only to that which the terms *freedom of speech, or of the press* were then taken to encompass, political speech, speech having to do with the duties and concerns of self-governing citizens. Thus, for example, this constitutional provision is not primarily or directly concerned with what we now call artistic expression or with the problems of obscenity. Rather, the First Amendment acknowledges that members of the sovereign citizen-body have the right freely to discuss the public business, a privilege theretofore claimed only for members of legislative bodies.

Absolute as the constitutional prohibition may be with respect to Congress, it does not touch directly the great State power to affect freedom of speech and of the press. In fact, I shall argue, one condition for effective negation of Congressional power over this subject (which negation is important for the political freedom of the American people) is that the States should retain some power to regulate political expression. It seems to me, however, that the General Government has the duty to police or restrain the power of the States in this respect, a duty dictated by such commands in the Constitution of 1787 as that which provides that the "United States shall guarantee to every State in this Union a Republican Form of Government."

What my understanding of "freedom of speech" and of "political speech" does and, perhaps more important for our immediate purposes, does not mean in practice may now be illustrated by my commenting upon a few notorious controversies of this century, a couple of which I have discussed at much greater length elsewhere.

One conservative student of freedom of speech has "selected" the illustrations I might usefully address myself to here. That is, he spoke recently of "episodes or issues of the past which still today arouse the passions— *e.g.,* Sacco-Vanzetti, Alger Hiss, the Rosenbergs, and McCarthyism." He referred to these controversies as having "involved alleged persecution of individuals for the exercise of freedoms intimately related to free speech," adding that "[t]hose who have lived through one or more of these episodes know full well that they evoked a degree of bitterness, hatred, and vindictiveness far surpassing that normally associated with intense partisan controversy."

I consider below these four passion-arousing controversies. I hope to display thereby my approach to political problems, an approach that very much bears upon my understanding of freedom of speech and its proper use. My approach assumes that the community which a healthy freedom of speech depends on and serves is likely to be subverted by enduring "bitterness, hatred and vindictiveness." We should take to heart the February 1861 lament by a Maryland Congressman, on the eve of the Civil

War: "We are at the end of the insane revel of partisan license which, for thirty years, has, in the United States, worn the mask of Government. We are about to close the masquerade by the dance of death."

II

First of all for our purposes, there is the Hiss Case. For all I know, Mr. Hiss was guilty of the perjury of which he was convicted in 1950. The more serious question for the community, however, was not with respect to Mr. Hiss's guilt, but with respect to whether he should have been pursued in the late 1940s for acts alleged to have been performed by him a decade before. That decade had included a great war, leading to radical changes in the relations among the countries of the world. (I know nothing about Mr. Hiss's conduct in connection with the 1945 Yalta Conference, nor did his case turn on any evidence about that conduct.)

I had occasion in February 1974 to make the following remarks to liberals in a university community:

> A candid examination of the current drive for impeachment—the standards employed, the passions aroused, the arguments used—permits liberals to see the "McCarthy period" from the other side of the pursuit. That is, all this permits sensitive liberals to realize what it feels like to be on the hunters' side of a witch-hunt for a change.

> Far be it from me to suggest that liberals today (such as the American Civil Liberties Union, which is pushing impeachment) are really behaving like Senator Joseph McCarthy or like Representative Nixon in his heyday. Of course, there are differences: there is now, for example, more of a conscious effort to be fair than there was then. Still, there are disturbing resemblances, including the extent to which the unleashing of certain passions has led to a cavalier attitude with respect to evidence. That is, the parallels are remarkable, including the reliance in each of the pioneering cases of the two periods—the Hiss case in the 1940s and the Watergate case in the 1970s—upon bizarre recordings to dramatize the matter for the public. (I refer to the "pumpkin papers" microfilms and to the "Watergate tapes.") Perhaps liberals can, if they look into their own souls, come away from all this with a more sympathetic appreciation of what moved Senator McCarthy, his predecessors and his allies of a quarter of a century ago.

> Liberals should remind themselves, for instance, that their counterparts of the 1940s saw the threat to the country to be at least as critical as that now seen to be represented by Mr. Nixon. After all, Joseph Stalin and those who supported him (in this country or abroad) were not angels: there was a good deal

of evil, both in deeds and in intention, let loose in the world at that time. Certainly, some of the Stalinists then were far worse than any of the crowd around Mr. Nixon today.

Even so, what should have been done about Alger Hiss, who was (by the late 1940s) no more (if that) than an ex-Stalinist, an ex-Communist of a decade or so before? Should not that case have been regarded as "ancient history" and had the books closed on it? Would not that have been the mature thing to do? Did not the good of the country require such a tacit amnesty, lest unhealthy passions be aroused and orderly self-government be threatened? May it not be obvious to us *now* that that is how that matter should have been handled *then?* But what about Mr. Nixon's recent misdeeds and those of his lieutenants? Could we not live with them? Has the turmoil stirred up by their investigation and prosecution been justified by the satisfaction of exposure? Or, put another way, are not anti-Nixonites at least as unrealistic about seeing danger to the country at this time as anti-Communists were in seeing it back in the late 1940s?

Or, to put my challenge still another way, is not John Dean the liberals' Whittaker Chambers? Mr. Dean is not as interesting (or as imaginative) as Mr. Chambers. But does he not serve the same function, that of the persuasive reformed co-conspirator who brings down the mighty? Is it politically healthy that those in exalted positions—whether Mr. Hiss or President Nixon—should depend, for their security, on the likes of Mr. Chambers and Mr. Dean? Should the standing of an administration—whether Mr. Truman's (or Mr. Roosevelt's), on the one hand, or Mr. Nixon's, on the other—depend on such patently self-serving, if not unreliable, witnesses?

I grant you that there would be a kind of poetic justice if Mr. Nixon, the unrelenting Congressional inquisitor, should be brought to bay by methods similar to those by which he rose to prominence. But we need not concern ourselves for the moment with what he "deserves" but rather with what the country needs. Furthermore, as I have said, liberals can learn what it means to be in hot pursuit "in a good cause": when pursuit is hot, the quality of evidence does not really matter; the sense of an ominous threat, and of the bad character of one's quarry, suffices. At the core of such pursuit is, I am afraid, a dominating self-righteousness. . . .

. . . I do not mean to suggest that Mr. Nixon and his subordinates have not misbehaved—but I do wonder whether their misbehavior is of a magnitude to warrant the extraordinary remedy we are now considering. . . .

In addition, it should be acknowledged that we *are* seeing the Presidency being cut down somewhat closer to constitutional size. But we should also realize that Mr. Nixon is paying now for the sins of every Democratic President since Franklin Roosevelt. Just as Alger Hiss and others were the scapegoats for the Cold War (and perhaps somewhat for the Second World War),

so Richard Nixon may be the scapegoat for the steady Presidential usurpation
of Congressional power since the 1930s [and perhaps somewhat for the Vietnam War].

(See *Human Being and Citizen*, pp. 162–64, 165, 170–71. See, also, Essay
No. 30, below.)

My remarks on that occasion, questioning the determined drive to impeach the President, depended on no illusions either about Mr. Nixon's
character or about his conduct. Rather, they depended on a judgment as
to what the good of the Country called for. What good *did* it do us to
hound Mr. Nixon out of office? For that matter, what good did it do to
put Mr. Hiss in prison? Thus, my February 1974 talk included these suggestions (pp. 172–73):

> It would be most useful if liberals, at the height of the power at which they
> now find themselves, would provide the country a model of deliberate self-
> restraint and magnanimity which could help us all to control our self-righteous
> saviors in the years to come. Magnanimity and self-restraint would dictate, at
> the very least, an offer from Congress, on the eve of impeachment, of com-
> plete immunity for Mr. Nixon from any future prosecution for any past con-
> duct in the event he should resign. Also salutary, it seems to me, would be an
> arrangement whereby everyone else involved in the offenses thus far alleged
> as abuses of Presidential power would be granted pardons. Indeed, I tend to
> believe it would be ungracious of Mr. Nixon to resign his post without par-
> doning prospectively (as I believe can be done) those of his associates who
> have misbehaved out of dedication to what they mistakenly took to be the
> Presidency and the common good. All this could be accompanied by a general
> amnesty for those who illegally opposed American participation in the Viet-
> nam War.
>
> In short, American involvement in that war, of which "Watergate" and its
> ramifications are really a part, should be brought to a merciful end.

To speak in this manner in an effort to restrain what one's fellow citizens say and do seems to me a sober, sobering and hence responsible use
of one's freedom of speech.

III

There is, next, the Rosenberg Case.

Julius and Ethel Rosenberg were, for all I know, guilty of the espionage
of which they were convicted in 1951. The more serious question, how-

ever, was not with respect to their guilt, but with respect to whether they should have been executed upon conviction.

I had occasion, in May 1975, to engage in the following televised exchange (on the Lee Phillip Show in Chicago) about the Rosenberg Case with Michael Meeropol, the elder of the two sons of Mr. and Mrs. Rosenberg:

PHILLIP: I know you are both interested in whether it was a fair trial. I wonder if you could each give us your opinion.

ANASTAPLO: It certainly was not fair in the sentence that was meted out on that occasion. It was a barbaric sentence and people today who were alive then should really ask themselves how it was they could sit still for such a sentence as that.

PHILLIP: Why *did* they sit still?

ANASTAPLO: They thought something terrible had happened, and they thought this was a way both of punishing those who had contributed to the terrible things which had happened and of deterring others who might do such terrible things in the future.

MEEROPOL: And let's put what the terrible thing was that they thought had happened. The judge in his sentencing speech said that they had stolen the secret of the atom bomb, and that armed with the secret of the atom bomb, the Russians had developed the bomb and therefore were confident to launch the aggression in Korea. He blamed them, therefore, for the Korean War; he blamed them for all the civil defense preparations that we had to have; and he blamed them for the death of untold millions in a future nuclear war. Now with that kind of rap, it is no wonder that the average citizen thought of them as horrible traitors who deserved to die.

P: Did anybody find out whether the Russians *were* given the information? Was that proved?

M: I don't believe there was any—

A: Well, the Russians have never confessed. There *were* people being convicted here and abroad for atomic espionage, in England as well as in the United States; and in Canada there were things going on also. There were evidently people who were thought to be involved in atomic espionage. One of the questions was whether or not this particular couple, the Rosenberg couple, had been part of that "gigantic, world-wide conspiracy." Now I understand, of course, that you would argue that there was no atomic espionage at all.

M: In fact, I would urge all listeners to have a look at the recent *New Times* magazine where there is an article which is entitled, "Were the Rosenbergs Framed?" And one of the conclusions the author has come to, for instance, after taking the sketches which were supposedly representative of secrets and which were introduced as trial evidence— and they are available right now in the federal district court in New York—taking these sketches and showing them to top scientists, one of whom, George Kistiakowsky, was on the government's witness list and was never called by the government, was never even contacted by the government—it was a way of scaring the defense into believing that the government had the scientific goods when in fact they didn't.

A: On the other hand, it should be noticed that there were at the same time competent scientists who did believe that there were—

M: I don't know of—

A: Harold Urey, for instance, of the University of Chicago, was not prepared to say—and he was very strong in the defense—

M: Yes, he was—

A: —he was not prepared to say that the crude information that Mr. Greenglass had available could not have been of use to people working on atomic research abroad, as to the directions the Americans were going—

M: Yes, but unfortunately, when Dr. Urey made that statement, he did not have access to the diagrams. The scientists, like Morrison, who was one of the people who built the atom bomb, who saw the diagram, said that it was a caricature, that it was full of errors, and was a secret of nothing. And Kistiakowsky looked at the same material and said that it's uselessly crude. In fact, the scientific principle, the principle of the shaping of high explosive lenses—I don't know if you want to get into that—the Russians were just as up on the theoretical issues as we were. In fact, many people have argued that the only real secret was, Would the theoretical critical mass set off a massive explosion? And that was given away at Hiroshima. I think we *do* disagree on this.

A: I don't think it would be prudent, in the long run, to insist that there was no secret. That is to say, that would be going against at least the conventional opinion on both sides of the Atlantic, among the Americans and their allies and among the Russians. It would be saying, in effect, that both sides, in making efforts both to steal and to protect secrets, didn't realize there was no secret at all. I think that might be a very hard bow to draw.

P: Gentlemen, we will let you continue this at a later date, because I imagine this could go on for hours.

This "*could* go on for hours," and for years, if not even for decades.

We are beginning to have now the informed discussion of the case we should have had then. Whether such discussion is helpful will depend, in part, on how it is responded to by sober citizens who realize that times are apt to change again—and again and again! It *is*, in any event, the kind of case that can lead the more talented young to question "the system."

One need not assume there was no espionage committed by the Rosenbergs (on behalf of a wartime ally, it should be remembered) in order to recognize the sentences imposed and executed as barbaric. It is highly unlikely that there were any secrets involved in the Rosenberg case of the significance implied by the unnatural, even monstrous, retribution exacted by the trial judge on that occasion.

On the other hand, it is salutary to notice that "the system" *is* evidently such as to permit and perhaps even to require a thorough airing of these issues. It can also be noticed that the Rosenberg children do seem, from what I have seen of both of them, to have turned out much better than one had a right to expect a quarter century ago. This is due in part to the devotion and good sense of their adoptive parents. It is also due in part to the fundamental good nature of the American people: there was no sustained vindictiveness directed against the children or, as it turned out, against those entrusted with their upbringing.

The Rosenberg children *were* permitted to "hide" for two decades. Our political and social diversity, made much easier by an economy grounded in private property, provides nooks and crannies for the unorthodox, including for those who would dare to do away with most private property in this Country.

IV

Next, there is the Sacco-Vanzetti Case.

I have with respect to this case, which looks in many ways like the Rosenberg Case, no informed opinion entitled to publication.

V

There is, finally, "McCarthyism."

The personal and social costs of what is generally known as "McCarthyism" were considerable. This *national* vendetta meant in effect that there should not be within the United States any nooks or crannies.

Of the four notorious controversies I am reviewing, this is the one that clearly included systematic efforts to penalize people for the political opinions they held. The principals in the other three controversies can be said to have been condemned for criminal acts. Whether their suspected opinions made their convictions more likely and their punishments more severe than they should have been are subject to debate. Not subject to debate, however, is the proposition that the ways they were treated did tend to silence thereafter certain unorthodox opinions.

Decent men and women had their careers blighted by the sort of thing Joseph McCarthy was permitted to get away with. Perhaps even more importantly, we let ourselves in for a dubious war in Indochina and for a badly shaken community at home. But what else can one expect when a people blinds itself to the facts of life? The forays of Senator McCarthy and others like him, reinforced and indeed made possible by Mr. Truman's loyalty program for government employees, kept the American people from informing itself as it should have, from being able to discuss what needed discussing, and therefore from being able to govern itself as it can and should.

Of course, "McCarthyism," which continued in its effects into the 1960s, can be explained, even if it cannot be justified, if one remembers "the sense of an ominous threat" to the country to which I have referred. In addition, the passions aroused by the Second World War had not been tempered for Americans by devastation at home or by great loss of life abroad. It is unfortunate that in 1961 we did not get another pacific Republican to follow Mr. Eisenhower in the Presidency instead of crusading Democrats still capable of being stirred by the passions of the Cold War.

To say all this is not to assume, of course, that Joseph Stalin conducted himself as he should have. But there was no good reason why Americans should have crippled themselves because the Russians insisted on atrocities both at home and abroad. It is we, not they, who need an effective freedom of speech to govern ourselves properly as a national community.

The American sense of fair play as well as perhaps an instinct for self-preservation finally asserted itself with respect to "McCarthyism." We have now moved almost naturally to a state of affairs that finds us enjoying under the First Amendment a more extensive national freedom of speech than at any time since before the First World War.

VI

One distinctive feature of the understanding of the First Amendment I have developed in *The Constitutionalist* is the recognition of a considerable State power to regulate the local abuses of freedom of speech that one can anticipate. This recognition should reassure those who suspect that my suggested restraints upon Congress are too sweeping. Is it not the prospect of local abuses that made the unfortunate and still dangerous "clear and present danger" test so plausible to many jurists and scholars?

I believe it salutary to argue for States' Rights, for that protective as well as innovative diversity which the States provide us—that is, for the preservation among us of handy nooks and crannies, if only because the States are not likely to be uniform in any repressive measures they resort to. Even so, it is useful to recognize, as I have indicated, that there *are* limitations imposed by the Constitution (aside from what has been done with the Fourteenth Amendment) upon what the States may do here. The Republican Form of Government guarantee is one such limitation. This neglected safeguard serves as well to remind us of the very nature of our regime.

Another safeguard, which also reflects the nature of our regime, depends on the people of each State and what that people requires of its local government independent of the federal constitution. Consider in this connection the remarks I prepared in April 1975 for use before the House Judiciary Committee of the General Assembly for the State of Illinois in Springfield, remarks in support of a proposed "Public Records Access Act" that I had helped draft as research director for the Governor's Commission on Individual Liberty and Personal Privacy:

It seems to me fitting and proper that this legislative committee, on the day of the final collapse of American policy in Indochina, should be considering a Public Records Access Act for the State of Illinois. Can we not learn and thus take heart from this unprecedented national debacle? Permit me to make the following suggestions:

Perhaps the most decisive criticism one can make of American policy in Vietnam is that it was never really an *American* policy. That is to say, it was never a policy faced up to and deliberately endorsed by the American people.

Thus, only last week, the Chicago *Tribune* observed (in its lead editorial of April 22), "For more than a decade, our policy in Indochina has been conceived thru rose-colored glasses and marked by deceptive statements which led to secrecy which in turn led to worse lies."

Is it not likely that if Presidential policy in Indochina had been properly discussed in public, the American people either would have refused to go along with that policy or would have prosecuted the war in a radically different manner? And would not either result have been much better than what did happen? What *can* be said for opening up to public view the workings of government? A self-governing people needs to know, and to believe itself to know, what its governments are doing. This requires that there routinely be made available to a people the information generally available to public servants.

Both so-called hawks and so-called doves, it seems to me, should be able to agree that inadequate public discussion and a persistent lack of candor on the part of "the White House" led in the case of Indochina to disastrous policies. Inadequate public discussion also meant that an effort could be made to fight that war without paying for it—and for this shortsighted economic calculation we have paid with a demoralizing inflation and with chronic unemployment.

You will have noticed, I trust, that I have put an emphasis in what I have said thus far upon the failures of the Executive Branch of government in Washington, rather than upon the shortcomings of a passive Congress. In these matters, it is important to take due account of the critical differences between, and the distinctive failings of, legislatures and executive officers. The doings of legislatures have always been intrinsically more public than those of governors, presidents and other administrators. There are a number of reasons for this difference, not all to the credit of legislators, of course.

A recognition of this natural difference may be seen in the bill before you. It explicitly provides at the outset that the public bodies regulated therein do not include the judicial or legislative branches of government. Indeed, one could say that the purpose of this act is to permit the people of this State to learn as much about what administrators are doing as it already knows about the doings of legislators. All this is provided for in such a manner as not to impede unnecessarily the ability of administrators to act with vigor, with dispatch, and (where essential) with secrecy.

The doings of the legislature that I have observed down here thus far have been far more sensible than I had been led from reports over the years to expect. That is to say, I have found remarkable the ability of legislative committees to make quick, often not unreasonable, judgments on the multitude of bills before them. You realize even better than I do, of course, that those judgments are not invariably correct and that the motives of legislators are not always irreproachable. I am sure you also realize that the calendar to which you subject yourselves may not always be a sensible one.

Be that as it may, legislatures do depend, by and large, upon arguments which are more or less public—and a monument to that fact is the two-foot-high pile of bills one can see upon each legislator's desk, a pile surrounded by stacks of memoranda, newspapers and amendments. To the extent that there have been shortcomings here in Springfield this week, they have been by and large because of your failure to get to one another the information and documents needed for sensible consideration of the issues you deal with. The complaint which you yourselves voice again and again—that you do not know what is going on—is precisely the complaint which citizens all too often make in trying to pass judgment upon the workings of their governments.

I have suggested that you, as legislators, know what discussion is like and how critical it is if you are truly to act in the public interest. You also know, I suggest, how critical informed discussion is if the people of this State are to be able to make responsible judgments about the laws you enact and about the public servants who administer those laws.

The bill now before your committee attempts to help citizens learn what they are entitled to know about the workings of their government. In preparing this bill, the Privacy Commission and its staff have had the benefit of considerable discussion of this subject by other legislatures as well as the benefit of numerous articles in the press, both scholarly and popular.

The version of the bill before you is different in several decisive respects from comparable legislation elsewhere. There is in this bill careful provision for the personal privacy of citizens; this provision governs except where there is "a compelling, demonstrable and overriding public interest in disclosure." Further respect for privacy may be seen in the protection of personal working papers provided to public servants, papers which are developed solely for their own use. Thus, there is respected the integrity of the research stage and deliberative process in the day-to-day workings of government. What is important is that there be made clear to the public what *has* been decided and done, rather than all the speculations and deliberations which may have led up to the final decision, except to the extent that such preliminary work is evident in, or is used to justify, the final product.

In addition, this bill is simpler and clearer than what is available elsewhere with respect to the procedures to be followed by agencies in dealing with requests for information. An effort has been made to help everyone involved to learn where they stand: the agency is both allowed to avoid unreasonable burdens and required to explain why it does not supply what is requested. All in all, it is a moderate bill you are considering: it recognizes that openness is necessary for informed deliberation and responsible decision, an openness guided by practical rules and aware of obvious risks. This kind of realistic openness can contribute to a useful faith in one another—and head off, it should be noted in passing, other legislation which is not apt to be as carefully drawn or as mild-mannered as is this bill.

Permit me to observe, as I prepare to close this personal statement, that this bill provides what Illinois citizens have, for a long time now, understood to be available from their governments. For many public bodies in this State, this bill may do no more than ratify what is already everyday practice. But everyday practice all too often does give citizens the impression that what they get from bureaucrats they get as a privilege, not as a matter of right which public servants have a duty to respect.

Thoughtful public servants should welcome legislation which confirms their proper relation to the citizens they serve. After all, public servants, in exercising the powers and in performing the duties entrusted to them, do depend upon the confidence of the community. They cannot be sure of such confidence if the people at large remain uninformed, or believe themselves to be uninformed, about what is being done in government and why. The known availability for public inspection of most public records can help remove many causes of suspicion and cynicism in a community, allowing public servants to perform their duties as well as—it is only prudent to assume—they really want to do.

Once again one can see, this time upon examining remarks I prepared for members of a State legislature, how principles might well take account of consequences, how one might speak responsibly in the circumstances in which one happens to find oneself. (The House Committee I addressed, chaired by Harold Washington who was later elected Mayor in Chicago, endorsed the mearure I had argued for. See Appendix to Essay No. 31-D, below.)

VII

I conclude these comments on the limits of freedom of speech by drawing upon my preface to the collection of essays in *Human Being and Citizen:*

I have, as circumstances have changed, shifted my positions on men and issues when I have thought it salutary to do so. (A case in point is what I have been obliged to say *and to whom* during the past quarter century about the elusive Mr. Nixon.) In considering whether and how to speak on various affairs of state, I have again and again been reminded of Abraham Lincoln's prudent observation in 1862, "I am very little inclined on any occasion to say anything unless I hope to produce some good by it." . . .

Intellectuals are today in particular need of prudent counsel, of a defensible common sense. Their unphilosophical partisanship and optimistic recklessness need to be moderated. Intellectuals all too often conduct themselves as if there should be no past from which to learn and no future to take account of. . . .

It is often difficult today to stand for prudence without seeming vacillating and even unprincipled. It is always difficult to be independent without seeming simply rebellious and truculent, to stand for the proprieties without seeming simply rigid if not even obsessed. One must somehow be courteous and yet firm, steadfast and yet restrained. It is useful to respect old-fashioned civilities and pieties, even as one recognizes their limits. . . .

I trust that the essays in this collection can serve to guide the open-minded reader to reflections of his own upon the questions and problems touched upon in them, reflections which may help him determine what he should think and how he should live. Perhaps most important, these essays may contribute to the development in the reader of a useful understanding of "should" with respect to things both of the city and of the mind. It is well, in these troubled times, to be reminded of the "shouldness" of things, of the roots of the *should* in nature, and of the sense in which it can be said that to think and to act as one should is the fullest realization of one's freedom.

How one should speak determines both what one says and what one remains silent about. Among the ideas a prudent man learns to respect is that ideas do have consequences.

16

THE OCCASIONS OF RELIGIOUS LIBERTY

Therefore he who does not recognize evils when they are being born in a principate is not truly wise; and this is given to few . . . .

. . . It is therefore to be concluded that good counsels, from whomever they may come, need must arise from the prudence of the prince, and not the prudence of the prince from good counsels.

NICCOLÒ MACHIAVELLI

I

In constitutional law, as in political life generally, much is to be said for the adage, "It's not what you don't know that can hurt you; it's what you know that ain't so!"

This adage particularly applies, it can be added, to the things we so take for granted that we never examine them. The study and teaching of politics, including the study and teaching of constitutional law, provide instructive illustrations here.

II

Consider the current concern with the so-called energy crisis. People line up for hours in California for supplies. I have talked to someone who was

---

This talk was given to the Public Law Seminar, Political Science Department, The University of Chicago, Chicago, Illinois, May 16, 1979. (Original title: "The Limitations of Experts.") It has been published, with some notes, in Anastaplo, "Church and State: Explorations," 19 *Loyola University of Chicago Law Journal* 61, at 100–109 (1987).

The epigraph is taken from Niccolò Machiavelli, *The Prince*, Chaps. 13 and 23 (Leo Paul S. de Alvarez translation).

obliged this past week to get in line at 5 A.M. at a gas station in the Los Angeles area in order to have a chance to get gas when the station opened at 7 A.M. The Governor of that State is exercised about what has happened. So is the President of the United States. And so, of course, are many, many citizens, not least those who rush to "fill'er up" before the hoarders get all the gas.

One California skeptic, who suspects an "oil company conspiracy," observed, "Once gasoline hits $1.00 and $1.25 a gallon around the country, we'll be able to get all we want." (*Chicago Tribune*, May 12, 1979, sec. 1, p. 2.) One hopes so! That is, is there not a price at which the available gas (whatever "available" means in this context) can be easily gotten? Or, put another way, why is oil different from any other useful commodity that we regularly consume? Precisely what does "energy crisis" mean?

It is a crisis, I suppose, when people are obliged to pay more for something than they are used to paying, or more than they would like to pay, especially if it means that they must forego pleasures or conveniences or even "necessities." But what is wrong here is not the market or its operations, but rather how people think about their expectations and entitlements.

Is there a conspiracy at work, at least in the sense that oil companies are holding back oil in anticipation of higher prices? Again, one hopes so! That is, one hopes that there are, here and there, producers and suppliers who are doing what they should be doing: using and not using, reserving and producing, when and how they think it most profitable for them to do so. I assume that these producers and suppliers are proceeding independently of each other, however much they know and take account of what is happening elsewhere and of what is likely to happen. Illegal collusion on their part would be folly, considering the present climate of opinion.

To put all this still another way, it is in our long-run interest to have fuel prices go up to "where they should be," namely the prices that make it possible for a motorist to purchase gas without more than a few minutes' delay. Of course, it is likely to be a price level that would discourage some driving. It could also become a price that requires, in the interest of social justice and domestic tranquillity, that gasoline stamps join food stamps as welfare measures on behalf of the poor.

To say all this is not to suggest that politicians can ignore the present "energy crisis." They, unlike us, cannot afford to identify foolishness as foolishness, especially if their actions, such as various forms of price controls, have contributed to our difficulties. But it is one thing for the political man to accommodate himself to the foolishness of the moment; it is quite another for him to be swept along by the uninformed passions of others, thereby making the prevailing foolishness more damaging than it need be. The risks of damage to the national interest, both at home and abroad, should be evident.

III

So much for the energy crisis and what it can remind us of about the limits of political understanding.

Consider another illustration of these limits. I recall a conspiracy of another day: not that of the oil companies but rather that of the American Communist Party. That too has had unfortunate consequences due not to the activities of a few thousand so-called conspirators, but rather to the activities of the millions who were mobilized against the conspiracy.

It is generally evident now (some of us thought it evident enough then) that the efforts of the Communist Party of the United States were, so far as they affected the military security or the political stability of this Country, quite trivial. The period I refer to is one I observed close up, that of the late 1940s and the 1950s. No foreign agent in his right mind would have used members of the American Communist Party, an organization under extensive surveillance, for purposes of espionage or sabotage or anything of that sort. As for their revolutionary effort in this Country, that should have been the least of anyone's legitimate concerns.

But trivial as the effort of American Communists may have been, they had dire consequences in that the responses to them, or to what they were supposed to be, hurt this Country badly. These responses, by well-meaning patriots of limited understanding, not only led to numerous injustices, to numerous personnel dislocations in government and elsewhere, and even (in 1953) to a pair of dreadful executions, but they also led to a befuddlement of public opinion and a misdirection of the national will. One result of this, I suspect, was the fierce toll exacted of us at home as well as abroad by our unnecessary involvement in the Vietnamese War. But then, this is the sort of thing one can expect when one does not think.

We are somewhat over that now. Even so, we need to be reminded from time to time that the Russians have massive problems of their own that are more or less independent of our existence, just as we have problems (not as intractable, we can hope) that do not depend on their existence. I hardly think, therefore, that any advantage one side gains over the other as a result of the acceptance or rejection of the current SALT proposals will change these facts of life.

But here too the political man must accommodate himself to the foolishness of the moment, whether the foolishness takes the form of a Red scare in the 1950s, of energy crises in the 1970s, or of the fear of a Soviet first-strike capability in the 1980s.

IV

We are primarily concerned here, however, not with "Red scares" or "energy crises" or "nuclear vulnerability," but with constitutional law.

Still, what I have said about these other matters does bear upon how one can begin to think about constitutional law. Each of these concerns—concerns with Communist intrigues, fuel shortages, and surprise attacks—can induce us to play fast and loose with constitutional restraints, especially restraints that are designed to protect broadly conceived property rights. We need to be reminded repeatedly that much of what passes for the wisdom of the moment in political life can neither bear much examination nor be simply ignored.

It is important to be sensible. This includes a recognition of the limits of sensibleness in much of political discourse. Much of what the learned commentators say about the Constitution, to say nothing of what the courts say and upon which the commentators comment, seems to me to border on foolishness. The most that can be said for much of what one reads about constitutional law is that it is conscientious elaboration keyed to unexamined and usually unrecognized hypotheses of a dubious character.

Yet the recognized experts in constitutional law are sober citizens, respected and made much of. I am somehow reminded of an observation I associate with Cicero: "It is held to be a matter of amazement that one soothsayer can happen upon another soothsayer in the street without laughing." (See Cicero, *On the Nature of the Gods,* I, 26; *On Divination,* II, 24.)

Unfortunately, the consequences of constitutional adjudication can be serious or at least can ratify serious developments. I have already referred to what the courts did with the Red scare a generation ago. Constitutional doctrines were manipulated to cater to public fears. In more recent years they have been manipulated to cater to public desires, as can be seen in what we have come to tell ourselves about our *constitutional* rights to abortions, to obscenities of all kinds, and even to immunity from justly deserved sentences of death and from conscription for community service.

In this way, we have broken down the longstanding and still useful distinction between policy judgments and constitutional determinations.

V

Perhaps in no field of constitutional law is so much foolishness accepted as gospel by so many as what the courts (guided and reinforced by the commentators) have said about the Religion Clauses of the First Amendment.

The aberrations with respect to the Speech and Press Clauses of the First Amendment have been intermittent. One can see in what the United States Supreme Court now says about *those* clauses some relation to what the First Amendment provides. What those clauses are principally concerned with is the right of citizens to learn what they need to know in order to be able to govern themselves. This right *is* usually respected by the courts, however far they sometimes extend the scope of protected discourse and despite the unwarranted restrictions that have been placed on genuine political discourse from time to time.

The aberrations with respect to the Religion Clauses, however, have been longstanding and continuous. I sometimes think that the United States Supreme Court has said very little that is sensible on this subject since the 1878 Mormon bigamy case of *Reynolds* v. *United States*. What, then, does it mean that Congress shall make no law "respecting an establishment of religion or prohibiting the free exercise thereof"? It means something like this (setting aside for the moment the effects here of the Fourteenth Amendment):

Congress cannot itself establish any religion or do anything either in support of or in opposition to an establishment of religion in any State. What establishment means, primarily, is official action designed to promote one or a few religious sects at the expense of all of the others. Nor can Congress interfere with the free exercise of religion, which means, primarily, the holding and expressing of presumably sincere opinions about divine matters and gathering together (or refusing to gather together) to share and to express those opinions.

Conduct which is said to be based upon religious doctrines is to be treated like any other conduct except for that religion-based conduct that consists either of professing the beliefs one has or of *attending* religious services. (*Attending* does not necessarily include everything that might happen at such services.) A legislature's exception of any conduct from regulation, because it is deemed to be religious, is hardly likely to contribute to an establishment of religion unless there is also a more direct and obvious attempt to do so.

What *religion* is for the purposes of these two clauses of the First Amendment was once fairly evident and, I suspect, still is to the community at large. Certainly Americans generally agree that people should not be compelled to witness, or even to seem to witness, to what they do or do not believe in with respect to religious matters. Even so, the legitimate political and social interest in religion has something to do with a general concern for morality. This concern, which is worthy of support by public funds, has even found expression in such Congressional enactments of constitutional stature as the Northwest Ordinance of 1787, where it is said, "Religion, morality, and knowledge, being necessary to good government and the happiness of mankind, schools and the means of education shall forever be encouraged."

VI

What the "free exercise of religion" does *not* mean can be seen by considering the judicially sanctioned activities of a sect with which we are all familiar. I say we are all familiar with this sect because we confront it whenever we travel, and I do not mean the Salvation Army! (Other sects could have served as illustrations at other times. What the Peoples Temple was permitted to do in the San Francisco area, in the name of religious freedom, could also serve as an illustration. But its subsequent Guyana atrocities make it too bizarre an illustration to serve our purposes.)

I have several times stepped aside from the stream of traffic at airports to watch members of our sample sect accost travellers. Their dubious operations are conducted in broad view, day in and day out, but sensible people, such as airport authorities, are said to be prohibited by the Constitution from stopping them. For some four decades now the United States Supreme Court has considered itself obliged to rule in effect that prosecutors and judges should not notice what all other sensible men in the community can see, that the gullible, weak, and lonely are being cheated by religious frauds. (See, for example, the 1944 case of *United States* v. *Ballard*.) It is instructive to watch who is now being "taken" by aggressive missionaries at airports: it is difficult for decent, naive people to go about their business without paying what amounts to a toll.

Of course, it does not stop with this. Now one can see men and women in downtown Chicago pretending to be confined to wheelchairs as they accost passersby to sell them things or to solicit contributions. There is something shameless, sometimes amusingly shameless, about these persistent efforts. It remains to be seen whether even this particular kind of extortion, to say nothing of more serious forms of fraud and sources of harm, should be immunized from governmental interference because it is said to be dictated by religious doctrine.

Those hurt most of all, however, are the calloused and often exploited participants in such activities, not their fleeting victims. This is suggested by the recent announcement of a mass wedding for dozens of members more or less dictated by the leader of this association. Does not the community at large have a legitimate interest in, if only because it will have to deal with the social consequences of, such a cavalier approach to marriage? But then, it will be asked, does the community have the right to keep adults from harming themselves? The old-fashioned answer would have been, "Yes, both a right and sometimes a duty," an answer accompanied by the reminder that it is virtually impossible for the self-destructive human being to hurt *only* himself.

The distortion to which we have become accustomed of the right to the free exercise of religion is based, I suggest, not upon religious sentiments, but upon an inordinate desire to be permitted to do with oneself whatever one happens to want. The proper concerns and authority of the community are brushed aside; the autonomy of the "self" and the sanctity of privacy are asserted. Perhaps at the root of this aberration is the assumption that there are no standards of right and wrong, of good and bad, of the beautiful and the ugly, which can be generally known and by which human beings are bound either individually or as communities. So much, then, for what the "free exercise of religion" does not mean.

VII

What the prohibition of an "establishment of religion" does not mean can be seen by noticing what has happened to repeated efforts since the Second World War to use public funds to support the educational activities of church-sponsored schools. These schools are said to provide services that the community wants and at a cost that is significantly less than what the community would have to pay if it provided the services itself. Why should not a community be permitted, when and so long as it should want to, to support such schools, especially if the alternative is that these schools are likely to have to close their doors because of escalating financial difficulties?

On the other hand, why should not the community be permitted, if it should determine that separate school systems are divisive or are otherwise harmful to the community or to some part of it, to prohibit all such schools? Whether a State chooses to support such schools or to suppress them, it is obliged to do so in conformity with its duty to provide equal protection of the laws and due process of law for all persons. Is it not sensible, and anything but an "establishment of religion" problem, for a community to be able to decide in its circumstances what it wants to support or to forbid, in what way, and how much?

The fashionable constitutional doctrines of our day stand in the way of such sensibleness. One result of those doctrines is that the efforts to circumvent them have meant that we have been obliged to allocate massive Federal funds for education in ways we might not otherwise have chosen to do. In order to pass constitutional muster, we have had to place the emphasis here upon welfare rather than upon education.

VIII

What I should like to emphasize is not my analysis of the Religion Clauses, but rather my opinion that what the courts have said on this subject has little if anything to do with the First Amendment. Yet again and again the Founding Fathers are invoked in support of sweeping declarations by the courts.

If anything is certain in the American constitutional system, it is that the Founding Fathers had no intention of applying against the States, with their varied religious establishments and with their then generally acknowledged power to "establish" churches, the prohibition placed in the First Amendment upon Congress. What the Fourteenth Amendment did to the States here remains a much-vexed question; that is another story. But even with respect to Congress, the Establishment Clause surely did not mean what the courts now say it has always meant.

How does one determine what the Constitution means? One cannot rely simply upon judicial pronouncements. Those statements, especially in situations where the law has not been long settled, are no more than opinions deserving respectful consideration, however much we are obliged to conform to and take account of them in practice. Rather, one must look to the language of the Constitution, guided in one's seeing by an understanding of the regime which is reflected in that language and elsewhere. History, properly used and preferably in small doses, may be helpful. But perhaps even more helpful is an awareness of the enduring teachings of political philosophy, especially if one is to be alert to what various regimes presuppose, require, and promote.

The recognized constitutional experts *are* obliged to take the courts seriously. One is reminded of the contests among the shackled residents in the Cave in Book VII of Plato's *Republic*, contests as to who is most adroit in interpreting the distorted shadows on the wall. No doubt such adroitness on the part of constitutional experts serves a purpose: clients do have to be advised as to tendencies; the public needs a rationale, or at least a likely story, for the constitutional developments issuing from its courts.

Passions, and the errors as well as the right opinions resulting from passions, have to be taken into account. It is only politic to do so.

But the true statesman knows what he is doing and why. This permits him to lead his community through if not around morasses, away from self-destruction, and toward justice. Only someone who is not swept along by current movements in constitutional law can truly see what is going on, what is sound and what is questionable in the fashionable opinions of his day. Only he is apt to avoid both the impassioned partisanship and the cynical apathy to which those not satisfied with mere scholarship and the rewards of ordinary ambition are subject. Precisely what he should say and how will depend somewhat on the circumstances of those whom he would rescue.

IX

The American statesman does recognize that the people of his Country, if they are to be truly self-governing, have to be of a proper character. That recognition, which can be said to be reflected both in the Religion Clauses and in the Speech and Press Clauses of the First Amendment, is suggested in *Federalist* No. 49. There Publius observes, "[I]t is the reason of the public alone that ought to controul and regulate the government. The passions ought to be controuled and regulated by the government."

B.

The Use and Abuse of the First Amendment

17

VIETNAM AND THE PRESUMPTION
OF CITIZENSHIP

*When [Abraham Lincoln] got into the House [of Representatives], being
opposed to the [Mexican] war, and not being able to stop the supplies,
because they had all gone forward, all he could do was to follow the lead
of [Thomas] Corwin [of Ohio], and prove that the war was not begun on
the right spot, and that it was unconstitutional, unnecessary, and wrong.
Remember, too, that this [Lincoln] did after the war had been begun. It
is one thing to be opposed to the declaration of a war, another and very
different thing to take sides with the enemy against your own country
after the war has been commenced. Our army was in Mexico at the time,
many battles had been fought; our citizens, who were defending the
honor of their country's flag, were surrounded by the daggers, the guns
and the poison of the enemy. Then it was that Corwin made his speech
[in the Senate] in which he declared that the American soldiers ought to
be welcomed by the Mexicans with bloody hands and hospitable graves;
then it was that [George] Ashmun [of Massachusetts] and Lincoln voted
in the House of Representatives that the war was unconstitutional and
unjust; and Ashmun's resolution, Corwin's speech, and Lincoln's vote
were sent to Mexico and read at the head of the Mexican army, to prove
to them that there was a Mexican party in the Congress of the United
States who were doing all in their power to aid them. [Shouts from the
audience: "That's the truth," "Lincoln's a traitor," etc.]*

STEPHEN A. DOUGLAS

This talk was given at the Hillel Foundation Jewish Student Center, The University of
Chicago, Chicago, Illinois, April 29, 1966. (Original title: "Vietnam and the First Amend-
ment: The Presumption of Citizenship.") It has been published, with extensive notes, in
Anastaplo, "Freedom of Speech and the First Amendment: Explorations," 21 *Texas Tech
Law Review* 1941, at 1979-2007 (1990). A "follow-up" talk by me at the same Hillel House
was arranged twenty-five years later (April 26, 1991): "Overwhelming Power and a Sense of
Proportion: From The Melian Dialogue to Desert Storm, by way of Vietnam." See, on the
1990-1991 Gulf War, the Preface to this book.

The epigraph is taken from *The Collected Works of Abraham Lincoln*, ed. Roy P. Basler,
V, 319-20 (October 18, 1858; seventh of the 1858 Lincoln-Douglas Debates).

I

To entitle this talk as I have is to assume, in a discussion of Vietnam, the approach to our subject of the American citizen.

There *are* other approaches. There is, for instance, that of the man who considers himself a citizen of the world—that is, the man, whether artist, scientist, or anthropologist, who regards as more important in determining his actions the things that make him like every other man than the things that distinguish him and his neighbors from associations of men elsewhere. Although there is about this approach something humane and highminded, the ordinary citizen remains suspicious of it. It is, in a sense, too good for this world. The citizen may even regard it, with some justice, as unwittingly destructive of the good society.

Another approach is that of the pious man. He too is a citizen of the world, but of another world. His standards ultimately are not those of his political community, even when that community is a good community. He hears a distant drummer or rather, for drums may sound too military, the music of the spheres: he has a divine calling or at least a divine injunction against militant actions called for by the community. He may not recognize any salvation for the soul of man in the salvation of states. Of this too the ordinary citizen remains suspicious, but his suspicion may be lulled by the sacrifices the pious man seems prepared to make in the name of a faith that the citizen also pays homage to.

Still another approach is that of the philosopher. The world of which he is a citizen can be said to be within him; he has no need, as philosopher, for the impermanent and even fortuitous institutions all around him. This is the most harmless and yet the most dangerous of men: he poses no threat to anyone, and yet his way of life, his questioning of everything if only for the sake of his own understanding, and his turning away from the things other men cherish threaten everything that other men (whether citizens, cosmopolites, or the pious) hold dear. (See the discussion, in my *Human Being and Citizen* volume, of Plato's *Apology of Socrates*.)

Let us put these three men to one side, at least for the moment. It is as American citizens that I propose we discuss this matter with one another. We must remind ourselves of the scope and purpose of the First Amendment: it provides for the unlimited discussion of public matters, protecting this discussion by the sovereign American citizen-body from any interference by the Government of the United States. Only if such a discussion is available, and is generally known to be available, can we begin to rule ourselves.

II

The remarkable thing about current discussions of the Vietnam War is the extent to which the constitutional protection of freedom of speech is being respected. It is my impression that practically everything is being said in public about the war that anyone should want to say. Governmental sanctions are not being imposed. Even social sanctions have had little effect. The war is being questioned on all fronts.

This is particularly remarkable for anyone who remembers the circumstances of the Korean War. There was then far less significant dissent than we have today; there were then prosecutions, both of Communist Party leaders and of alleged spies, that we do not have today. A number of factors account for this healthy difference. This war has come on slowly for Americans, not overnight as did the Korean War. The press has been able to watch closely as the conflict developed. Perhaps too there are men in responsible positions, both in government and out, who do not want to be trapped again in the kind of destructive repression to which we were subjected last time. Related to this is the attitude of the young, for they have been in large part responsible for bringing the issue to a head in this country: youngsters are dubious, and I believe rightly so, about the conduct of their elders during "the McCarthy period." It is important as well that the dissenters this time are able to use persuasive denunciations of the war made not too long ago by prominent members of the American government. Nor does the current Administration position have the sanction of the United Nations that our Korean police action did. For a number of reasons, therefore, there does not happen to be an authoritative American pro-war position against which it is unpatriotic to speak out.

This freedom of speech, I have suggested, conforms to American constitutional principles. How are we to choose among our candidates for public office, and by implication among policies to be followed, if we cannot discuss fully the broad issues on which public officials have to pass judgment? How can we assess a candidate, except on the basis of an illusory "personality" or "public image," if we cannot address ourselves to the very issues that that man will have to consider once in office? To rule ourselves must mean this if it means anything. But is it merely a pretense that we rule ourselves? It is this question I should like to consider here. I have no objection to the scope of discussion available to us about this war, however much I may differ about the judgment and style of some of those who exercise this freedom.

Anyone seriously interested in freedom of speech must wonder whether it can withstand the most serious threat it faces: not the threat of government interference nor the occasional misuse of that freedom, but rather the threat that is posed to any institution whenever it does not do what it is intended to do. Further questions suggest themselves: Are citizens able to speak and listen to one another in a manner likely to elicit sensible decisions about war and peace? To what extent do men in office in Washington or elsewhere possess information, abilities, and experience that make it likely that their judgment is clearly superior to the judgment of other citizens? That is, is it prudent for us to exercise our freedom of speech by addressing such matters?

A consideration of the discussion by Americans of the Vietnam War provides us an opportunity to assess, at a time when many feel they are powerless to control their lives, the possibilities of self-government.

III

The most obvious limitation to which the citizen is subject is that of lack of access to information that is routinely made available to government officials. Reports come in daily to the State Department and the Pentagon that are not available to the general public. One can wonder, however, whether anything essential not itself originated by the press is included in such reports with respect to politics and international relations which does not find its way into the press within a few weeks, if not within a few days. Sometimes, of course, an alert press discerns long-run developments before members of our government do. Nor does the government always exploit whatever advantage there may be in learning before the citizen does what is daily happening abroad. Consider, for instance, the implications of this exchange at the Presidential press conference reported earlier this month (*New York Times*, April 1, 1966, p. 18):

Q. I wonder, sir, if you can give us your views and comment on the current domestic political trouble in South Viet-Nam, and specifically, if there should be a change in government? What effect might this have on the war?

A. [by President Johnson] I would answer all your questions in one sentence, that there is not any information that I could give you that would add to what you have read in the papers. I think that there is very adequate free flow of information out there, and everything that is reported to this Government in that field is pretty well known to you either simultaneously, by the time I get it, or maybe sometimes a little ahead of me.

It is when we turn to military matters that we may expect to find significant gaps in the public's knowledge. But consider the situation as it existed in 1961, only five years ago (New *York Times,* January 26, 1961, p. 11):

> Mr. Salinger [President Kennedy's press secretary] said that, as a test, a committee recently had been assigned the task of developing estimates of the nation's military strength, policy and capability, using only materials available to the public. "Their estimate was almost totally accurate," Mr. Salinger said. "And I believe this indicates we have been going too far in discussing matters affecting the national security."

Such official misapprehensions as the 1960 "missile gap" also should make us wonder how much conjecture there is on the part of men whose official analyses are popularly respected as factual reports rather than as the guesses they sometimes have to be.

I have had occasion to advise students, in an effort to induce them to look beyond the ever-engaging present, that if they really want to understand what is happening around them, they should read relatively little of anything written after 1900. I believe there is enough truth in this to permit the properly concerned American citizen today to become as well-informed as the highest officeholder on the principal issues confronting the Country. Someone has to make decisions from day to day, and from this a familiarity with problems does develop. But it seems to me unlikely that men in office are necessarily better informed than we citizens can be about the long-run problems and opportunities confronting the Country.

This may be confirmed by reading both Presidential memoirs and the accounts of men close to the powerful. Rarely does one come upon revelations of significance. After all, our politicians, when hardpressed, usually reveal the facts and make public the arguments that they believe might support their decisions. One is often surprised upon reading memoirs to learn how frivolous and distorted were the "facts" and the opinions about alternatives on which Presidential deliberations depended. This is as true of descriptions of events a decade ago as of those a century ago. One does pick up in such accounts interesting anecdotes, but usually not much else that could not have been known to a thoughtful observer on the "outside." Thus, the best of Lincoln's thought and why he acted as he did are to be found in his public speeches, not in gossip from the White House.

The most obvious, and sometimes the most significant, facts frequently escape the notice of the busy, practical politician. In preparing this talk, I have read a number of things about Vietnam. Perhaps the most revealing item I have come across, an item that I had not seen mentioned or taken into account by public officials or for that matter by the press, is the abdication proclamation of August 1945 by the Emperor Bao Dai. I find particularly significant in this statement by a man generally dismissed as a "playboy" the first of "three wishes" he expressed to "the democratic Republican Government" of Ho Chi Minh: "We request that the new Government take care of the dynastic temples and royal tombs." (*Vietnam: History, Documents and Opinions*, p. 60) To speak thus of the tombs of one's ancestors reveals, among those to whom he addressed himself and perhaps even in this man of the world, old-fashioned concerns that are concealed but not obliterated by either modern materialism or decadent sophistication. I am reminded of Rabbi Maurice Pekarsky's characterization of one of the students he encountered here at Hillel House as "an atheist with a good Jewish heart." One must look to what is deep within the soul of a man or of a people if one is to understand what is truly going on there. I am also reminded of what one reads in accounts of the ancient Greek city about the opinions among those people about the ancestral, about the city, and about one's own. From such people one can expect deep-rooted resentment of any domination by foreigners: for better or for worse, blood will mean more to them than ideology. The recent anti-American agitations in South Vietnam should not surprise us. We can expect them to get worse until those people come to believe that they really run their own affairs. This they will not believe until they have ordered the Westerner out so as to be able thereafter to invite him back at will.

IV

The concerned citizen need not suffer from a lack of information about the enduring problems that confront the Country. He may even be in a better position than the public servant to face up to such problems. This depends in part on the relative capacity of citizen and public servant. This in turn depends on the native ability and the daily life of each.

The life of the public servant gives him ready access to information and makes it his duty to be interested in the problems of the community. But he cannot pick and choose his problems: they are chosen by circumstances, and the higher up he is the more dependent on circumstance is his schedule likely to be. We all know this is true of the President: he literally does not have time to think for himself. This is what comes from having to make decisions about all kinds of problems. If one issue should engage a "disproportionate" part of his attention, other issues must be let slide. Can he know then as much about a critical issue as the public-minded citizen who devotes himself to the subject he is most concerned with?

Take the case of the Secretary of State, the man officially charged with doing the President's thinking, or at least with keeping track of developments, in international relations. President Eisenhower's Secretary of State, Mr. Dulles, evidently spent most of his official career travelling all over the world. If he knew much about world affairs (the basis on which such men presumably are chosen), he had to learn about them before he entered government service. On the other hand, President Johnson's Secretary of State, Mr. Rusk, travels much less, but if his weary estimate is to be trusted he spends most of his time reading the cables and reports that pour into the State Department.

The life of the public servant inhibits his intellectual development in still another way: he cannot think for himself because he is obliged to spend so much of his time saying what he is supposed to say. Disappointed admirers fault Mr. Johnson's Vice-President on this count. It is a rare man who, day in and day out, year in and year out, can continue to think his own thoughts even as he says only what is expected of him. He comes to believe what he says. It often becomes impossible for him to talk as if he is not in public: the more intelligent and conscientious he is, the more apt he is to mold everything, including even his dinner-party conversation, to his political life.

This is obvious with respect to style. It is likely as well with respect to ideas; few politicians in America have been able during the past two decades to think sensibly about Communism, and Vietnam merely reflects this inability. The distinctions among Communist regimes and their capacity for change, for instance, are too often lost upon them. Few of our politicians seem to be considering seriously the tendency our attacks upon North Vietnam may have to drive the Vietnamese into the arms of their traditional Chinese enemies. Nor can any respectable American politician acknowledge that for some peoples in the world a Communist regime may be better than the alternatives immediately available to them. It is even more difficult for a politician either to perceive or to acknowledge that the fundamental problem facing our Country and indeed the world may not be that of Communism, but rather that to which both Communism and Nazism have tried to address themselves, the emptiness of a life that is dominated by a worldwide technology dedicated to consumption, a life that is alienated from nature and from meaningful participation in the life of one's community. What one cannot suggest, or hear suggested, one does not think about.

I have been talking about the life of the public servant as it bears on his capacity. But that life bears upon his native ability as well. The best of men will not submit, except in the most extreme or the most favorable circumstance, to the confinement of the human soul that I have been describing. The better the man, the more he wants to be free and is equipped to be free. This freedom is best found in the full development and use of his mind. It is *not* found "where the action is," as President Kennedy thought. I have no doubt that the intelligent, hard-working men who serve as corporation executives earn everything they make; indeed, they do not seem to me to earn enough. They are where the action is, but they are devoting to such action—action which is generously rewarded by the rest of us because it contributes so much to our material well-being—the only life they will ever have, at least here on earth.

High public office is much the same. It is truly a sacrifice, although the men who devote themselves to it do not usually see it as that, whatever they may say. It is a better life than most men do lead, but it is not the best that a man can lead. This is especially true in an age when the public man is confined as much as he is by the schedule I have described. Consider the modern institution of the ghostwriter. The Sorensen book on John F. Kennedy provides an intimate portrait of the relations between speech-writer and speech-giver: both are prisoners, neither is master. The writer tries to give his employer a speech that the writer believes expresses the speaker's sentiments. We are told that Mr. Kennedy always went carefully over the text of important speeches. But this is quite different from writing a speech oneself: as one writes, and rewrites, one discovers what the problems really are; one learns—as one works through one's ideas, discarding some, revising others—what can and cannot be said about a subject. The thoughtful man undergoes priceless education in the very process of developing and clarifying his thoughts on a question, whether in preparing a speech or in making a decision.

But, Mr. Sorensen explains, it is impossible today for any President, or for that matter any Presidential candidate, to write even his most important speeches. That may well be true in the United States. But that only means that we can expect to have from now on only second-rate men in the Presidency. They will be second-rate not because of any native incapacity, but because they will have, once in office, neither the time for nor the experience of working through their thoughts on the vital issues of their administrations. In such circumstances, it becomes even more important to allow and depend on men outside everyday politics to do the thinking that the public servant is no longer capable of doing for himself.

The man of capacity who recognizes all this becomes reluctant to enter political life; he knows he cannot do his best in such circumstances, even if he should be assured that he will notbe punished for doing as well as he can.

V

Whatever the information and native abilities of our public servants, do not they have access to something the public does not have, the benefits of experience dealing with affairs of state? The doctor and the shoemaker have experiences that no doubt make them superior with respect to their arts. Why not the politician as well? There is, however, one critical difference that should be noticed: we too are political men, since we as citizens are in a sense and to some degree the sovereign body in our regime. We are habituated to thinking about and making choices respecting political questions. The nature of our regime is such that this activity becomes second nature to us. The arts of medicine and of shoemaking are constantly subject to modification that only the technician can keep up with. That does not seem to be the case with the political art. Rather, a people may take its bearings by old teachings that define its way of life.

The exceptional man makes his mark on political affairs whether in office or out; he does not depend merely on experience in office, which is often no more than gradual addiction to day- to-day drudgery, to guide his understanding of the most important affairs of his era. It is well to remember that for every "triumph" scored by a man in public office, there is usually a "defeat" suffered by another man in public office, either in the same country or abroad. Many more horses gain experience losing races than winning them.

When one looks at five American crises in recent years, one sees judgments by experienced men that seem dubious in retrospect, various of which judgments seemed dubious to some of us at the time. I confine myself to recent years so as to be able to refer to what has been experienced by all of us here tonight.

First, I call to mind the Bay of Pigs invasion of 1961, the account of which Mr. Sorensen concludes by reporting President Kennedy asking himself out loud (*Kennedy*, p. 309): "How could I have been so far off base? All my life I've known better than to depend on the experts. How could I have been so stupid, to let them go ahead?" The explanation usually given for this unfortunate episode is that the President, in his first few months in office, was inexperienced. But what he had already experienced, and hence was so painfully reminded of, with respect to experienced experts itself raises doubts about the value of mere experience.

We move then to what is considered a triumph of that President, his handling of the Cuban Missile Crisis of 1962. The Sorensen account makes exciting reading. I confess that I was surprised by the emphasis placed in this and other accounts on the nearness to world war that the men close to the President regarded this crisis to have taken us. If things were as dangerous as they subsequently reported them to have been, then their attitude during the crisis was most imprudent. My own impression at the time was, and still is, that there was no serious danger we could not control. There was exhibited in the crisis even a taste for dramatics, not without predictable effect on the then-impending Congressional elections. In any event, we confidently counted on a return to prudence by the presumptuous Russians. The peculiar unreality of the Cuban Missile Crisis is suggested by the fact that the Russians now have Polaris-type submarines, some of them evidently parked off our coasts, with much more destructive missile power than was ever in Cuba. Such submarines, we were promised when money was being requested for the development of our own, are far less subject to hostile destruction than land-based missile sites. The missiles are back, perhaps no further away and far more difficult to deal with than those in Cuba were, and yet we somehow live with them. I do not suggest that we should not have made serious efforts to see nuclear weapons removed from Cuba; but I do suggest that if we, by insisting on an immediate capitulation by the Russians, did risk a world war to get the missiles out of Cuba, we acted neither in our interest nor in accordance with the dictates of that humanity of which our enormous power obliges us to be the principal guardians. Our self-righteousness was apparent even at that time: we had long insisted that our intercontinental missiles and aircraft, whether here or on the edge of the Russian empire, were essentially defensive in character; but when a country recently invaded under our auspices has similar equipment installed, we fail to appreciate that that may be because they feel as we do about self-defense. Even the inexperienced observer can, without becoming unpatriotic, see the difficulty in such recourse to a double standard by his Country's leaders.

My central illustrative crisis I touch upon only briefly, leaving you to develop its implications: that is the assassination of President Kennedy. This illustrates among other things the limits of experience and the role of chance in political affairs. What is the significance, furthermore, of the fact that so much energy and money have to be expended upon the protection of our Presidents? What does it suggest about the nature and problems of a community such as ours? To what extent is the United States truly a community?

Last year's Dominican crisis has been too well exposed to require much discussion at this time. One can wonder whether public servants who can become so confused about the nature of the Communist threat only a few miles from us can be relied upon to understand it on the other side of the world. To what extent is our inability to think clearly about Communism abroad shaped by our naiveté since the Second World War about the danger of Communism in this Country?

Finally in this catalogue of five crises that permit us to raise doubts about the necessary superiority of the judgment of experienced men, we have our current engagement in Vietnam. We would feel more confident about the understanding, to say nothing of the purposes, of the officials involved if their publicly expressed expectations of the past five years had been more often borne out by subsequent events. Defense Secretary McNamara's unfortunate predictions most readily come to mind. Even more telling is the recognition that we have in the past year alone done much more to North Vietnam than was called for by Senator Goldwater during his 1964 Presidential campaign. Indeed, we have already done much more than we were ever led to expect would be necessary to get "the enemy" to surrender, let alone to the conference table. True, we do not yet bomb population centers, but this seems to be because we believe that that would lose us much more in the eyes of world opinion than it would gain us as a military measure in Vietnam. It would deprive us, as well, of the feeling that there is still something more we could do to gain a relatively cheap victory in Vietnam. I venture to make a prediction based on little more than that prudence which is derived from watching one hopeful prediction after another fail: if we insist upon the objectives we now pursue, modest as they seem, we will have on our hands not a world war but a war comparable to Korea; we can then hope we have a moderate Republican President elected in 1972 to deal with the immoderate Stalinist succession to Mao Tse-tung firmly entrenched in Peking, to say nothing of Hanoi; we will also remember nostalgically how freely we talked about these matters back in 1966.

I do not mean to dismiss experience, but merely to put it in its proper place. The fact of the matter is that mere experience does not suffice: choices still have to be made among the positions contended for by various men of experience. We must not forget that however unanimous our public men of experience sometimes seem with respect to a particular issue, there are many men of experience elsewhere who are skeptical. I refer not only to experienced men out of office in this Country, but also to experienced men in office abroad. Thus in this instance of Vietnam, there are the French, with their bitter experience in Southeast Asia, who insist that we are pursuing the wrong course in Indochina; there are the British who have just gone through a national election in which Vietnam seemed so insignificant to their interests as to play hardly any part; and there are our non-Vietnamese "allies" in Southeast Asia who do no more than offer token forces in support of a war that we proclaim to be essential to the defense of freedom in their part of the world. There is also what the Chinese and the Russians are saying, to say nothing of the North Vietnamese, but we evidently do not regard what they say with any more seriousness than we expect them to regard what we say.

It is when he looks at what is said and done throughout the world, at what is known by all to be said and done, that the reasonably well-informed citizen with common sense can ask questions that do not require special talents or secret information to answer sensibly:

Why were General MacArthur and his experienced colleagues mistaken, if they were, in their insistence that it would be folly for the United States to commit troops to another land war on the mainland of Asia?

Why, if the President knows more than the intelligent and thoughtful citizen about such matters, was a dramatic change in Vietnam policy required in 1965, a change that repudiated the conclusions announced the year before on essentially the same facts?

Is French prestige higher or lower since France had to leave Indochina and Algeria?

I have suggested that the "inexperienced" citizen is not as inadequately prepared to think about public affairs as might be thought. Indeed, there is one way in which he might be decidedly superior to the public servant, and that is in the moral sense which he is in a position to express. There is about a moral sense something naive, a naiveté that the community as a whole, as distinguished from the more successful and hence more sophisticated, tends to preserve. The healthy community may become impassioned and hence foolish, but it is apt to remain good-intentioned. I suspect that it is the general ethical assessment of this perhaps unconstitutional and certainly unnecessary war that is at the bottom of a national discontent that will not go away. Consider the moral judgments to be made. The Secretary of State observed that the North Vietnamese

> have discovered that they are not going to be permitted to send tens of thousands of people into the south to attack South Viet Nam and live in safety and comfort there in the north. The idea of a sanctuary is dead as far as this situation is concerned, and that is something that all of the others who may be supporting Hanoi must take fully into account.

(*Chicago Tribune*, April 27, 1966, p. 1) This observation needs revision: "The idea of a sanctuary" is dead only for our adversaries, "as far as this situation is concerned," since it remains quite a lively idea for us. We send out air strikes from sanctuaries on aircraft carriers and troops from that sanctuary of sanctuaries, the Great Society where "safety and comfort" abound. Obviously, Mr. Rusk does not recognize what he is saying. But if one does not recognize what one is saying, that suggests that one does not recognize what one is doing either.

One difficulty with the moral sense of many public men (and the President is, to say the least, typical in this respect) is that it may be blunted by their craving for success, for public approval, for honor. The very desire for honor reflects a need for reassurance of one's virtue, a reassurance that is vital for one who cannot rely upon his own standards for self-appraisal. Men with such appetites are apt to make the sacrifices they regard as useful to secure public approval. The President is, indeed, a case in point. (I can say this with a certain proprietary interest, since I may be the only one in this hall tonight who is recorded to have thought before 1960 that Lyndon Johnson could make a good President. I still think so, especially if he can be restricted to, and checked by, the domestic politics he knows so well.) His concern with public opinion polls; his lack of inhibitions where publicity is available; his inability to allow others a share of the limelight, except where it serves his purposes; his temper tantrums, which make one wonder about the caliber of the men who can stay close to him—all this reveals a childishness that is a serious flaw in a man of great talents. I suspect that this may have been the flaw that induced him to gamble away the opportunity to settle the Vietnam War without further American intervention, the opportunity provided him by the overwhelming election mandate for which he had asked in 1964. He tried, that is, to exercise even more control over the situation than he could have had easily for the taking. He tried, in an effort to win even more public approval ("consensus") than circumstances permitted, to satisfy doves and hawks alike—the hawks by a sudden display of force, the doves by securing peace—with the result that he has gotten into trouble with both flocks and has lost the fleeting opportunity with which he had been entrusted by the electorate. I am reminded of an old lady in my Southern Illinois hometown: she would not go to Hell for a dime, but she would fish around the edge for it until she fell in.

It is such matters and such men about which moral judgments can be made and which we the people are equipped to review. We may not have that special inhibition of public men, that pride of self, which prevents one from seeing the truth if it should contradict the public stand in which one may be trapped. The typical public man needs our curbs and guidance to protect him and his Country, as well as any other people unfortunate enough to suffer from his miscalculations.

I do not need to recapitulate here the accounts we have had in print and on film of what has been happening to the people of Vietnam. One must wonder what right we have to sacrifice them to our purposes. Much of what I have read about the Vietnam War is usefully summed up in the moral and political judgment found in the opening paragraph of the Quaker publication, *Peace in Vietnam:*

> The scene was a small square in the city of Hue, South Vietnam, on a summer day in 1965. The place was known as a rendezvous for American GI's and Vietnamese girls. A couple of military police were on duty to keep order. On this day one of them had supplied himself with some candy for the children who played in the square and crowded around the Americans. As he started his distribution in a friendly mood, a swarm of youngsters, jumping and reaching, pressed about him. With a laugh, he tossed the candy out on the cobblestones. Immediately the children descended like locusts, each intent on grabbing a piece. A young Vietnamese school teacher happened by at this moment, and seeing the scrambling children, he spoke to them in stern and emphatic tones. He told them to pick up the candy and give it back to the Americans. After some hesitation they sheepishly complied. Then, facing the soldier and speaking in measured English with a tone of suppressed anger and scorn, he said, "You Americans don't understand. You are making beggars of our children, prostitutes of our women, and Communists of our men!"

The American citizen must be concerned for the effect of this war—I do not presume to speak against all war—upon our own children also, to say nothing of our men and women as well. The institution of the "Green Berets" is illustrative. The only prior reference to them I have come across is in Henri Alleg's *The Question,* a book describing the tortures inflicted by the French special forces (also known as the Green Berets) upon their enemies in Algeria. Anyone who visited a passion-torn France during that period would like to spare his Country the domestic consequences of similar foreign travails. We already hear too much talk of torture and terror by our forces. Our children are exposed to such sentiments as are seen in this exchange in last Sunday's "comic strip," "Tales of the Green Beret" (April 24, 1966):

> Chris [sic]—you came down right into the middle of Operation Falling Rain! We're a Special Forces Ex-Filtration and Counter-Subversion Action! We kidnap—we burn—we execute.
>
> Execution of the Communist political big-wigs?
>
> Affirmative! We clobber the Viet Cong from the inside—where they live! It's cruel—ruthless—the type of war they invented! They use terrorism, assassination. We're giving it back to them—in spades!

It is in spiritual as well as political self-defense, then, that the citizen insists upon both the right and the duty to exercise that freedom of speech guaranteed him by the First Amendment.

VI

I have overstated the neglected case for the citizen's exercise of freedom of speech. It would be irresponsible to leave my argument where it now is. For the citizen must take care not to fall into the error of the public servant and consider his opposite number essentially inferior to him. One must, in order to discuss Vietnam properly, remind oneself of the case our political leaders present. Great disasters, we are warned, may have small beginnings and can be more easily dealt with at their inception than later. We are reminded of Munich as we are urged to make the effort required to secure and protect freedom in the world for years to come. I think the position of those who defend the Administration is best stated in what Pericles had to say about the Athenian policy he recommended toward the city of Megara (Thucydides, *History of the Peloponnesian War*, I, 140):

> Now let none of you conceive that we shall go to war for a trifle by not abrogating the act concerning Megara [by which act the Megarians were forbidden access to both the fairs of Attica and all ports within the Athenian dominion] (yet this by them is pretended most, and that for the abrogation of it war shall stay), nor retain a scruple in your minds as if a small matter moved you to the war. For even this small matter containeth the trial and constancy of your resolution. Wherein if you give them way, you shall hereafter be commanded a greater matter as men that for fear will obey them likewise in that. But by a stiff denial you shall teach them plainly to come to you hereafter on terms of more equality.

Pericles' policy required limited warfare. But we should remember that he and his successors were not able to contain the forces and passions let loose by that limited war, with the result that their city went on to its ruin.

Ghana and Indonesia have been pointed to as desirable results of our Vietnam policies. I suspect that this is another exaggeration of our power to shape the lives of others. Our experts may be surprised some day to learn how little of the time of Chinese leaders in recent years has been devoted to considering Vietnam. Why should we assume that people in Ghana and Indonesia or anywhere else are still impressed with our punitive power, when the people against whom we are using so much of it in North Vietnam continue to defy us? Besides, the United States should not want to claim credit for the incredible slaughter the Indonesians let loose among themselves last year. But whatever happened there, it happened without any American soldier or aid and evidently without any awareness by the United States that it was about to happen. Nor must we rule out the role there both of chance and of gross miscalculation by the Indonesian Communists.

I return to Munich. What does it teach us about Vietnam? If Vietnam is like Munich, then perhaps one course would be better than another. But is it like Munich, and like Korea? Or is it more like the Spanish Civil War or perhaps even more like the Italian war against the helpless Ethiopians? It is curious in any event that the two heroes of Munich, Winston Churchill and Anthony Eden, did not in 1954 see the crisis in Vietnam as Munich-like. As the British Prime Minister and Foreign Minister at that time, they refused to intervene with air strikes to help the French at Dien Bien Phu. Mr. Eden's explanation in the House of Commons a decade ago continues to be timely (June 23, 1954):

> Her Majesty's Government have also been reproached in some unofficial quarters for their failure to support armed intervention to try to save Dien Bien Phu. It is quite true that we were at no time willing to support such action, for three reasons which seemed to us to be good, and still do. First, we were advised that air action alone could not have been effective. Secondly, any such military intervention could have destroyed the chances of a settlement at Geneva. And thirdly, it might well have led to a general war in Asia. I should add that we have at no time been reproached by our French allies for our decision, in spite of the fact that the burden of it fell upon them.

When we recall that we first intervened in Vietnam by aiding the French colonial effort to maintain control of that country, we can appreciate the difficulties in the argument that it is the cause of freedom we have been supporting there for more than a decade.

If Mr. Churchill and Mr. Eden did not see Vietnam as another Munich—and Mr. Eden confronted the charge that his role in the Geneva Conference turned him into a "Municheer"—why should we? Developments since the 1954 Geneva Conference are described in this manner by Quincy Wright, a student of international affairs (*Vietnam Reader*, pp. 11–12):

> The United States has contended that South Viet-Nam is the victim of armed attack by North Viet-Nam, and that the United States is therefore justified under Article 51 of the U.N. Charter to engage in "collective self-defense" at the invitation of the government of South Viet-Nam. This argument assumes that the two Viet-Nams are independent states and they have actually functioned as such since 1954. The Geneva Conference of that date, however, rec-

ognized Viet-Nam as one state, referred to the two zones into which it was temporarily divided by the cease-fire line, and provided for an election in 1956 to effect the union. North Viet-Nam sought to arrange for this election for three years, but was frustrated by the refusal of the government of South Viet-Nam to concur, and finally sought to effect union by supporting the Viet-Cong, which included migrants from North Viet-Nam and which in 1960 began to oppose the government in Saigon by guerrilla operations. The Diem government of South Viet-Nam in Saigon took this obstructive attitude toward the election because under United States advice it had not ratified the Geneva Accord. The United States had given this advice because, as President Eisenhower said in his memoirs, it was clear that in an election, 80 per cent of the people of Viet- Nam would vote to unite under Ho Chi Minh, the President of North Viet-Nam and for years the leader of Vietnamese nationalism, although he was a Communist. Other states in the Geneva Conference— France and Great Britain—had urged, along with India, that the elections be held, and the United States, while not ratifying the Geneva Agreements, had made a unilateral statement that it favored the principle of self-determination. In view of this history, it would appear that the hostilities against the South Viet-Nam government, whether by the Viet-Cong or by North Viet-Nam, constitute civil strife, and that outside intervention is forbidden. Furthermore, the United States' contention that it has a legal commitment to defend the independence of South Viet-Nam appears to have no basis. No commitment was made except to the Diem government, which ceased to exist in 1963, and in any case the Geneva Agreements contemplated a union of the two Viet-Nams.

This description, which is supported by the materials I have studied, certainly does not remind an American of Munich, but rather more of the Mexican War.

The fact of the matter remains, however, that these historical analogies are not of much use: for every one of them, a plausible counter-analogy can usually be suggested. One is left where one was, with the need to look at the facts of the case at hand and to think about them. The discipline to be brought to bear upon the issue is not that of history, but that of politics in the service of ethics. Historical material is of a subordinate character: it can be useful if properly handled; it can help remind us not to lose sight of the opportunities provided by even our mistakes. My impression has long been that the dreadful execution of Julius and Ethel Rosenberg, parents of two young children, at the beginning of President Eisenhower's administration in 1953 confirmed his "anti-Communism" and perhaps contributed to the efforts to improve relations with Russia that Americans entrusted to him. Similarly, the dramatics, and hence the alarm, of the Cuban Missile Crisis in 1962 may have contributed to the development of the Test Ban Treaty. Now, perhaps, the long-standing and serious problems of our relations with China can be settled in a reasonable manner. That is, one result of our unreasonable and conscience-stirring policy in Vietnam may be a more reasonable policy on our part toward China, if we can manage to settle our affairs in Vietnam without provoking open Chinese intervention. (The best proof that China is not today really a threat to us may be found in the fact that we are behaving the way we are only a few miles from her borders: if she were a serious threat, we would not be acting or be permitted to act so cavalierly out there.)

We, with our concern about Communist aggression, should derive some comfort from what we have learned in Vietnam about the limits of the use of force: even small countries can hold out against great powers if properly motivated and supported. Are not the North Vietnamese holding as firm in the face of threats and destruction as we would want our people and our friends to do in similar circumstances? This suggests the limits both of war and of material impositions upon the human spirit, even as we are reminded of the terrible uses to which technology may be put.

You will notice that I have not made any suggestion about what we should do now in Vietnam. Few of the respectable critics of the war have yet advocated immediate withdrawal of American armed forces. Richard N. Goodwin, formerly of the White House Staff, gave last week an insider's view of "the bedrock vital interest of the United States" (*New Yorker,* April 16, 1966, p. 90):

> That interest is to establish that American military power, once committed to defend another nation, cannot be driven from the field. It is not to guarantee South Vietnam forever against the possibility of a Communist takeover.

What is ruled out by Mr. Goodwin's formulation is all talk of Communist threats to our immediate security, or of the cause of freedom, or of falling dominoes. It is clear that he is skeptical about our decision to get into Vietnam in the first place. I do not see, however, that our Government is entitled to risk the life of a single American soldier simply to prove that we can stay where we neither want nor need to be. Such dramatics would indeed be childish, if not criminal.

I take my own cue from Maxwell Taylor. General Taylor has said explicitly what the President and the Secretary of State had already indicated, that if we were asked by the Vietnamese to leave their country, we would do so. He added, in his talk here in Chicago Wednesday night, that if a legitimately elected government in South Vietnam were to ask Americans to leave, "it would be good news for us." If the President's advisor can say this, why shouldn't we? I add this further observation: the only "legitimately elected government" to determine what we should do in Vietnam or anywhere else is our own, not whatever may happen to be thrown together from time to time in Saigon. So, with General Taylor, I can say that it would be good for the United States to get out of Vietnam. But I add the suggestion that we should *not* do so without offering to take with us everyone who would be thereafter endangered because of their association heretofore with us. If we disengage ourselves with grace, we can still expect whatever government settles down in Vietnam to invite us to return with our money and our technical assistance. I believe the American people would then want to respond to the great work of reconstruction with that generosity in which they surpass all other peoples on earth.

VII

The public servant is obliged by circumstances to use his opportunities; he cannot be irresponsible; he must make an effort. Whether we citizens make use of our opportunities is another matter. Our attention shifts easily: those interested in civil rights yesterday are interested in Vietnam today and will be interested in poverty tomorrow and perhaps even religion the day after tomorrow.

One problem we have, as we use our opportunities as citizens with respect to the war in Vietnam, is to do so in such a way as to prevent or at least to restrain the emergence of bitterness. There are citizens defending the war who are as patriotic, as sensitive, and as well-intentioned as any critic of the war. One must be reminded of and thus moderated by the broader issue to which the artist, the pious man and even the philosopher would direct our attention. All three aspire for eternal things, as the citizen does in his own way as well. Consider the terms in which a twenty-year-old soldier in Vietnam wrote his family in North Carolina shortly before his death in battle (*Chicago Sun-Times*, March 9, 1966, p. 8):

> I'm writing this letter as my last one. You've probably already received word that I'm dead and that the government wished to express its deepest regret. Believe me, I didn't want to die, but I know it was part of my job. I want my country to live for billions and billions of years to come.
>
> I want it to stand as a light to all people oppressed, and guide them to the same freedom we know. If we can stand and fight for freedom, then I think we have done the job God sent down for us. It's up to every American to fight for the freedom we hold so dear. If we don't the smells of free air could become dark and damp as in a prison cell.

We won't be able to look at ourselves in a mirror, much less at our sons and daughters, because we know we have failed our God, country and our future generations. . . .

Don't mourn me, Mother, for I'm happy I died fighting my country's enemies, and I will live forever in people's minds. I've done what I've always dreamed of. Don't mourn me, for I died a soldier of the United States of America.

Immediately below the newspaper article reporting this letter there was, almost as a footnote, a two-sentence news item that displays how futile and even absurd a death can be:

Kampala, Uganda (AP). Sheik Mohammedi Mayanyanja, Masaka town councilman, was killed when a buffalo he shot recovered as he was sitting on it to pose for a picture. The wounded beast sprang up and attacked.

This providential juxtaposition of newspaper reports serves to warn us: we must take care that the families which have made sacrifices not feel betrayed by whatever we now do in Vietnam. We see here the ultimate test both of the Administration's position and of public criticism of that position: we do not want to disparage sacrifices already made—we *have* learned something important because of the sacrifices made in Vietnam as well as in Korea; we do not want to see additional sacrifices made without purpose and effect; we do not want so to conduct ourselves now that our people will not respond properly hereafter when the Country faces genuine dangers that require great sacrifices. (See Section VIII of Essay No. 32, below.)

Our primary concern as citizens should be with what we do to, with, and for ourselves. I was recently told by two Swiss visitors that our public discussion of the war disturbed America's friends abroad. Once the President and his experts decide on a policy, they argued, the people should simply obey. I have elaborated this evening the response I made on that occasion: "In America there are no experts in political matters, but only sovereign citizens." Besides, I asked our visitors in the spirit of the First Amendment, should not foreigners be reassured rather than disturbed to see the most powerful country in the history of the earth subject its governmental policies and decisions to public discussion and, it is to be hoped, to rational correction? Is this not the measure of the superiority of life under this kind of regime to any other available elsewhere today?

18

THE PENTAGON PAPERS AND
THE ABOLITION OF TELEVISION

Delenda est Carthago.

CATO the Elder

I

It should be instructive, in assessing the significance among us of the mass media, to consider how we deal today with the press and the television industry.

Our ways of handling television and the press remain quite different, both for historical reasons and for reasons bearing on what is distinctive, if not even natural, to each. There is considerable effort made by some theorists to have us treat these two means of communication the same way. To treat them the same way, however, not only would overlook vital differences between them, but would also threaten the integrity of our regime even more than it may already be. We must, above all, be practical about these matters.

We should take care, whatever we may say or do, not to undermine the privileges and hence the usefulness of a press that has traditionally had a

---

This talk was given at the Colloquium on the Mass Media, Public Affairs Conference Center, Kenyon College, Gambier, Ohio, Fall 1972. It has been published, with extensive notes, in Harry M. Clor, ed., *The Mass Media and Modern Democracy* (Chicago: Rand McNally, 1974), pp. 161–232. Margaret Clor was most helpful in preparing the notes for publication in 1974. (Original title: "Self-Government and the Mass Media: A Practical Man's Guide.") This essay has been reprinted, in part, in several editions of Mary Pollingue Nichols, ed., *Readings in American Government.*

On the *Pentagon Papers Case*, 403 U.S. 713 (1971), see Anastaplo, "Preliminary Reflections on the Pentagon Papers," 118 *Congressional Record* 24990–99 (July 24, 1972).

See, on the epigraph, the conclusion of Plutarch, *Life of Marcus Cato.*

vital part to play in our constitutional system, a part that is ratified by the
First Amendment to the Constitution of the United States. The First
Amendment, I have argued, prohibits Congress in its lawmaking capacity
from cutting down in any way or for any reason "freedom of speech, or of
the press." The extent of this freedom is to be measured not merely by the
common-law treatises and cases available on December 15, 1791, the date
of the ratification of the First Amendment, but also by the general understanding and practice of the people of the United States, who insisted
upon, had written for them, and ratified through their State legislatures
the First Amendment.

I have further argued (as in Section I of Essay No. 15, above) that although the prohibition in the First Amendment is absolute (we see here a
restraint upon Congress that is unqualified, among other Bill of Rights restraints that *are* qualified) the absolute prohibition does not relate to all
forms of expression, but only to that which the term *freedom of speech,
or of the press* was then taken to encompass: political speech, that is,
speech having to do with the duties and concerns of self-governing citizens. Thus, for example, this constitutional provision is not primarily or
directly concerned with what we now call artistic expression or with the
problem of obscenity. Rather, the First Amendment acknowledges that
the sovereign citizen-body has the right freely to discuss the public business, a privilege theretofore claimed only for members of legislative
bodies.

II

This can be said to be the "theory" of a constitutional privilege that we all
sense to be at the heart of American republicanism. It is a theory that does
conform fairly well to current practice in the United States with respect to
the press. How does it bear on regulatory practices with respect to the
television industry?

The rules governing the press and television *are,* at this time, quite different. For example, the press is barely regulated as such; the television
industry as such is quite extensively regulated. I will try to show that there
are vital differences in the nature and effects of these two means of communication, differences that are somewhat reflected in current regulatory
practices and in immunities from regulation. These differences with respect to regulations may reflect, among other things, some awareness of
what each means of communication is likely to do to people.

A discussion of the centuries-old problem of "previous restraints" can
provide us, on this occasion, an instructive way of seeing not only what

the mass media are like, but also what the character and requirements of our way of life are. The press has long been, among us, virtually free of previous restraints. These are restraints, imposed on a publisher prior to publication, by government acting in the public interest. Such restraints have traditionally been distinguished from, for example, curbs placed by judges upon public comment by participating lawyers and witnesses on pending court cases for the purpose of ensuring justice in a particular trial. The television industry, on the other hand, has always had many previous restraints to contend with in the broadest sense of the language, which can extend to the licensing of transmitters, the determination and supervision of program content, and the allocation of broadcast power, frequencies, and hours.

I propose to examine, with a view to the common good, the sense there is in the extensive freedom we traditionally accord the press. That is, I propose to examine such things as the risks run and the safeguards provided as well as the advantages offered by our traditional way of regarding what the press may do. I also propose to consider the rationale for the extensive regulation of the television industry to which we are accustomed.

A somewhat detailed discussion of the June 1971 Pentagon Papers litigation should remind us of what the press means to us. I will consider, first, how we live with an absolute prohibition, in practice, of previous restraints upon the press, what that means, and why it should be that way. I will thereafter consider what television is like and what should be done about it.

I am prepared to defend two propositions: first, for the sake of our way of life there cannot be in ordinary constitutional circumstances any previous restraints of publications; second, there should be much more "previous restraint" than we now have of the television industry.

III

i

The publication of excerpts from the Pentagon Papers archives began in the *New York Times* on June 13, 1971, and continued for two more daily installments before being enjoined in the federal courts until June 30, at which time it resumed again for seven more installments. In the meantime, publication started in the *Washington Post*, the *Boston Globe*, and the *St. Louis Post-Dispatch*, all of which evidently drew extensively on copies of the top-secret archives of some seven thousand pages originally made available to the *New York Times*. Each newspaper was similarly enjoined in turn as it appeared in print with the story. The United States Supreme Court decision of June 30 permitted all newspapers with access to the archives to publish what they chose. (403 U.S. 713 [1971]) These archives dealt with the history of American involvement in the Vietnam war.

ii

Had there been more that was truly new in the Pentagon Papers than there was, the adverse effect of publication upon security might have been more of a problem for the courts than it was. But it would be rash to insist that no possible harm resulted from the massive publication on that occasion. The *New York Times* did insist in its editorials that it would not have made its decision to publish "if there had been any reason to believe that publication would have endangered the life of a single American soldier or in any way threatened the security of our country or the peace of the world." (June 16, 1971) I do not believe this to be a prudent test: any course of action, ranging from rigorous censorship to uninhibited publication, runs risks and endangers lives. What must be determined is which course is most likely in the circumstances to serve the common good: an episode-by-episode "body count" does not suffice.

It should be noticed that the government was obliged to concede during the Pentagon Papers litigation that it is irrelevant, strictly speaking, to consider as a cause of harm and hence as a basis for suppression by injunction the fact that the documents in question might have been stolen. Indeed, American newspapers frequently publish, and are even expected to publish, purloined documents. The government would have been foolish to make much in court of the theft of the documents; to have done so would have misled the judges relying upon guidance from the attorneys appearing before them. The traditional American opinion about the publication of documents concealed by the government from public view is such that even so "antiliberal" a journal as the *National Review* began its June 29, 1971 report on the publication of the Pentagon Papers with the concession, "We regretfully conclude we cannot fault the *New York Times . . ."*

The government was also obliged to concede during the litigation that designation of a document as a state secret does not settle the question of whether publication of it may be enjoined, not even if the designation seems to be both authorized and reasonable. After all, our form of government is such that periodicals are obviously left free in ordinary constitutional circumstances to publish materials that may harm the national interest. Yet the government's case and the concessions made by the newspapers during the Pentagon Papers litigation would tend to permit Congress to provide for suppression by injunction of any publication that is likely to cause serious damage to the Country. The orthodox opinion with respect to these matters does not seem to me to recognize that it permits, in principle, press censorship in the national interest, irrespective of whether the materials involved have been classified. We see here the fundamental First Amendment questions touched upon by this litigation, questions that should indicate why the current general prejudice against absolutes conceals genuine dangers to our form of government.

It seems to me constitutionally improper for the government, in its effort to suppress by injunction the intended publication of secret documents, to rely upon any standards or reasons that would justify as well the suppression of publications based not upon secret or classified materials but upon what anyone may figure out from unclassified materials to be happening in the United States or abroad. The latter kind of publication, despite its lack of reliance upon any classified materials, may be in a particular instance much more damaging to the national interest than the former. Would not "everyone" agree that informative publications based on unclassified materials should be beyond the reach of the law both before and after publication? Still, if the test is that which was evidently agreed to by the government and the newspapers in the Pentagon Papers litigation, why should not Congress be able to act against such publications even though they are not based on classified materials? This is one reason I suggest that the current orthodox approach with respect to these matters does not appreciate what it opens the door to.

What, one might then ask, *is* the purpose of classifying documents if newspapers cannot be prevented by injunction, at the option of the government, from publishing whatever should come into their possession? Classification is justified, as I have already indicated and as I shall develop further, with a view to the way the national government, pursuant to law, tries to control the information it considers important to the national interest to keep secret, not with a view to what the government may do to recapture information of which it has lost control. In other words, if the government is permitted to recapture or immobilize by injunction information of which it has lost control, at the same time that it concedes that some classified documents may be published by the newspapers without judicial interference, it can do so only on the basis of legal principles and standards that would undermine and endanger that general freedom of the press on which our regime so much depends to keep the sovereign public informed about what its governments are or should be doing.

Thus I submit, in the face of the current orthodox opinion on this subject, that government can have no authority in ordinary constitutional circumstances to secure, even "in the national interest," a previous restraint upon publication of any materials, classified or unclassified, that happen to be in the possession of the press. This submission seems to me not only to be doctrinally sound, echoing as it does the traditional and sounder orthodoxy of Milton's *Areopagitica*, but also to be in accord with contemporary journalistic practices.

iii

We need not assume in making these observations about the legal merits of the newspapers' position in the Pentagon Papers controversy that American journalistic practices today are necessarily the best way of ordering things. We need only assume that they are what we have come to expect and to depend on, partly because of the character of our regime, and that any realistic effort to justify suppression must take those practices as well as the character of that regime into account. Lest too much be made of the harm that may be caused by publication of classified material (it *is* obvious that harm can result from such publication as well as from the publication of unclassified material), it should be kept in mind that leaks of classified documents and of high-level military decisions were expected and experienced throughout the Vietnam War. Such leaks are frequently promoted and exploited by our government, especially by high officials in the Pentagon, for political as well as for military and propaganda purposes.

There have been, it should be remembered, revelations about the conduct of the war published in newspapers in recent years more important than anything found in the Pentagon Papers, revelations that did not have their news value dramatized either by massive publication or by the Attorney General's repressive efforts. There was probably little in the Pentagon Papers that the Viet Cong and the North Vietnamese did not already long know. It is evident in these papers that all too often the primary "security" concern of our Executive was not to keep information (say, about air strikes or about other military operations) away from the enemy, for the enemy had already experienced them and may have sometimes known of them in advance, but away from the American public and even from Congress.

It seems common knowledge in Washington that most government documents (some experts have testified to as many as 95 percent of those that are restricted) should not be classified. It seems that the use of the "secret" classification is often exploited either to prevent political embarrassment or to make a document or the official classifying it seem worthy of serious attention. For good as well as for bad motives on the part of suppliers, publishers *will* be provided classified documents from time to time. Is it not obvious that the best way to improve security, and to enlist the necessary cooperation of publishers in such an effort, is scrupulously to reserve the "secret" classification for appropriate documents?

I continue this review of arguments about the possible adverse effect on national security as a result of the publication of the Pentagon Papers. It is also said that the prospect of more such revelations inhibits our private negotiations with foreign governments. Once again, one has to examine cases and circumstances. Curiously enough, the Pentagon Papers suggest that it was secrecy rather than exposure that often inhibited negotiations during the past decade. One sees again and again that our government pretended in public during the course of the Vietnam War that it was open to negotiations even while it worked in private to prevent them.

The relative lack of conversations with foreign governments in the documents published by the *New York Times* is, we are told, in part due to the fact that the supplier of the material to the newspaper retained the four volumes of the Pentagon Papers archives dealing with negotiations. That is to say, *he* also evidently tried to take the interests of the United States into account, as did the publishers who drew upon the materials they received. This should point up the fact that the primary concern of the government should not be improper publication, but rather keeping truly sensitive materials from coming in the first instance into the possession of anyone inimical to the interests of the Country. Such a possessor of sensitive materials is not likely to send them to American newspapers for publication, but rather to foreign governments. This he is likely to do in secret, not giving the American government an opportunity either to intervene before he or his recipient acts or to apprehend someone afterwards.

I go one step further concerning our dealings hereafter with foreign governments. Did not the publication of the Pentagon Papers improve rather than damage our standing abroad? That is, did not publication help the American people begin to repair the damage done by our government, because of Vietnam, to our standing and hence our interests among civilized people everywhere? Was there any serious criticism of the 1971 publication from communities with a form of government similar to ours? I suspect that many governments were relieved to learn that a country as powerful as ours had begun to pay greater respect than theretofore to what an informed world opinion thinks about the way we use our power.

It is said as well by critics of the press that publication of operational documents inhibits discussion among the President's advisers. One is tempted to reply, "Well and good, let's have more such inhibitions. That is, let's have it understood that it *can* become known (within a short time, if political in-fighting among such advisers gets serious) what considerations are taken into account in the making of public policy. Perhaps this will make our public servants take old-fashioned morality more seriously and 'realistic' power politics less seriously than they have heretofore." But even this reply may not appreciate how brutal the maneuvering and hence the disclosures around the President can be, so brutal (or so altruistic) that it often does not matter to the disclosing agent that the government might try either to secure an injunction to halt an impending publication or to punish after publication the parties involved.

In any event, we the people simply cannot tolerate a dispensation under which vital public information about what goes on in government councils is limited to what the dominant faction in government chooses to disclose, as would be the case with a tame press. Here too the character of our regime virtually requires the practices to which we are accustomed, practices that offer important advantages along with the occasional risks they pose.

iv

What, then, should the press not be "legally" entitled to print? That is, what should be subject to previous restraint upon application by the government? Most orthodox students of this subject would agree that tactical information and decisions should, if the government wishes, be kept secret *through the use of injunctions* until the immediate military advantage of keeping them secret passes. (I believe it is an illusion that injunctions can, except on rare occasions, be usefully employed even in this limited fashion.) Such a rule, these orthodox students might concede, should not preclude public debate on national policy, certainly not when there is no state of war declared or in effect. Should there not be a presumption against keeping secret either what the enemy already knows or discussions of the overall purpose of what our government is doing?

There does remain the problem of morale, but suppression of publications with a view to morale (which recalls the Eighteenth-Century offense of "seditious libel") presupposes that there cannot be any substantial question legitimately open to the community about the purpose of what the government is doing and for which maintenance of morale is needed. The responsible public servant should be taught not to try to conceal from the community either that which is safely subject to public debate or that which is so decisive in determining public policy as to require public examination and ratification. The responsible servant of the public, whether in the government or in the press, knows that attempts to keep the wrong things secret, or the appearance of having tried to do so, can corrode public opinion, corrupt the Country's leadership, and permanently damage the political morale of the people. The responsible servant of the public, whether in office or out, should also know how to talk about delicate matters when they do need to be aired publicly.

Thus our concern for security and for breaches in security brings us back to the question of the kind of regime ours is or should be. What is the effect on the competence and morality of our people and its Congress if the public does not have and believe itself to have a pretty good idea of what is going on? Lord Halifax included, as No. 26 of his "Maxims of State" (in 1692), the observation, "That the People will ever suspect the remedies for the diseases of the state where they are wholly excluded from seeing how they are prepared." The President of the United States said (in 1972), in ordering more liberal procedures to be used in classifying information, "Fundamental to our way of life is the belief that when information which properly belongs to the public is systematically withheld by those in power, the people soon become ignorant of their own affairs, distrustful of those who manage them, and—eventually—incapable of determining their own destinies." (*Chicago Sun-Times*, March 11, 1972, p. 23)

The more complicated or diseased any community becomes, the less the kind of secrecy sought by our government with respect to Vietnam is likely to be useful. Secrecy is more apt to hurt us than disclosure is apt to help any potential enemy. Even our economic difficulties of the 1970s, for example, can be traced back to the unwillingness of the Johnson Administration in the middle 1960s to tell Congress what it planned to do about the war. The refusal of the administration to face up publicly to what it was doing and what it was likely to do meant that our vast expenditures for Vietnam could not be financed properly. Such secrecy is also apt to hurt us when it raises fundamental doubts for a generation, especially among the more articulate young, about the good faith of any government in the United States.

Still, it is realistic to recognize explicitly and to help the young recognize, even as we attempt to confine legitimate government secrecy to the narrowest possible extent, that any regime in which public opinion is as critical as it is in ours does have serious limitations. It is no doubt better to be ruled by wise men than it is to be dependent upon what the public may happen to believe from time to time. Wise men can safely determine, for example, what it is salutary to reveal to the public. Unfortunately, there are far fewer wise men among us than there are men who believe them-

selves, or are believed by others, to be wise. It must be recognized as well
that it is rare when the genuinely wise man, who must be distinguished
from the ideologue, is permitted to rule, even if he should be willing to do
so. It is a mark of practical wisdom for us to recognize that we must often
settle for far less than the best possible regime. Considering the dreadful
alternatives we have been offered this century, constitutional government,
especially when tempered by a sense of its own limitations, by a people's
sense of natural justice, and by tradition, may be the best kind of regime
available in our time.

Justice Hugo L. Black, in his concurring opinion in the Pentagon Papers
litigation, observed that "paramount among the responsibilities of a free
press is the duty to prevent any part of the Government from deceiving
the people and sending them off to distant lands to die of foreign fevers
and foreign shot and shell." (403 U.S. 717 [1971]) There is something archaic about his "foreign fevers and foreign shot and shell." It was appropriate, in the course of unprecedented litigation that touched upon questions about the very nature of our regime, that one of the oldest justices
ever to sit on the United States Supreme Court should have in his last official pronouncement before resigning instinctively reached back in language as well as in thought to the very foundations of this republic.

v

I believe it salutary that it be generally believed that both the Supreme
Court and the press have begun in recent years to redeem American honor and to restore the faith of Americans in their institutions, especially at
a time when many have become resigned to mindless violence. It is important for our civic health that the United States diligently expose its
own misdeeds and that it be generally understood that it will continue to
do so. It is important to notice that although the three dozen analysts who
originally prepared the Pentagon Papers were selected by Department of
Defense officials, they were nevertheless willing and able to *begin* a serious assessment of the mistakes of our government in Vietnam. It is also
important to notice that the district court judge in New York who ruled
for the *New York Times* had just been appointed to his post by the administration which was bringing before him its unsuccessful suit for injunctive
relief.

One can see both in the press and in the courts, when its members are
served by and drawn from a high-minded bar, the institutionalization of a
respect for reason and for ethical judgment in public affairs. In this case
the Supreme Court in effect ratified what the press had done, and it did so
at a time when the public was prepared to be assured that its mounting

ethical concerns about the war were in fact justified. I suspect that the fact that the Court did not forbid the *New York Times* and the *Washington Post* to continue publishing the Pentagon Papers may be far more important in this case than what the Court said in acting as it did. Much of what the Court said, after a hurried argument and on the basis of an inadequate record, seems to me dubious, as was its refusal to repudiate categorically the use of temporary restraining orders in such circumstances.

What the Supreme Court did hold depended on two propositions: first, there has always been a presumption in American constitutional law against any restraint upon a publisher prior to publication except in the case of immediately impending irreparable harm to the security of the United States; second, the government did not show on this occasion that there *was* "irreparable harm" threatening the Country as a result of the intended publication of the Pentagon Papers. (The analysis that follows accepts for the moment what I have already questioned, that there are circumstances in which the government may properly suppress by injunction a publication that is likely to cause serious damage to the Country.)

It should be evident in light of the comments I have made about the security aspects of this matter why the government could not measure up to the "heavy burden of showing justification for the imposition of such a restraint" as it had asked for. (See 403 U.S. 714 [1971].) The sort of evidence that might have been persuasive to the Supreme Court, but which the government could not provide, would have described an impending publication in time of war of information about troop movements, weapons developments, and strategic planning or perhaps an impending publication of materials that would seriously interfere with negotiations vital to the very survival of the Country.

The three justices who dissented in the Pentagon Papers case did *not* claim that the government had made the required showing, but argued instead that the government should have been given a further opportunity to show what it could in the federal district courts. In fact, the Supreme Court was unanimous on certain fundamental issues.

Complaints were registered in the dissenting opinions about the lack of sufficient time to make the kind of record needed for proper consideration of the issues in the case. There is something to the complaints of undue haste. It was pointed out in a dissenting opinion that the *New York Times* was pressing for an immediate disposition of the case in the name of its readers' "right to know," when it had itself held back the documents and its story for months. On the other hand, is it relevant how long a publisher has been contemplating publication? When he moves, he is constitutionally entitled to be able to publish immediately unless there is a clear legal prohibition.

Still, it should be said that if the government's argument is accepted to the extent that it was accepted by the newspapers (to the effect that injunctions may indeed be secured to prevent "irreparable harm" to the Country), then the government should have been given more time to make its case at the trial-court level, even to change if necessary its original allegations and to introduce new evidence as it itself became more familiar with the voluminous record. In such circumstance it is unrealistic to expect everyday rules of civil procedure and of evidence to be scrupulously observed.

But there would have been no case at all if the *New York Times* had published in one issue everything it had, foregoing thereby the considerable commercial advantages of serial publication. Nor would there have been a case requiring immediate appeal to the Supreme Court, after accelerated hearing in the trial and intermediate appellate courts, if the government had limited itself to what it clearly had a legal right to try at leisure (assuming the existence of a relevant statute): a criminal prosecution of those persons improperly possessing or communicating classified documents.

That is to say, the government has in such circumstances a remedy, even if there should be as I have argued an absolute prohibition upon previous restraints of the kind sought in the courts on this occasion. In fact, it has several remedies, including recourse to the power in the event of certain truly critical emergencies, to say nothing of an impending nuclear holocaust, of declaring martial law or of suspending the writ of *habeas corpus*. Such emergency measures would permit, for example, effective control for the moment of any publisher regarded as likely to attempt to publish anything, classified or not classified, that the government believes should not be published under the circumstances. Extraordinary remedies are available that permit our people and its government to set aside temporarily our traditional constitutional privileges and practices. Such remedies are of so obvious a magnitude, however, that no sensible people will permit them to be invoked except in the most extraordinary circumstances.

Nor does an absolute prohibition upon previous restraints mean that the government cannot take, in circumstances far less serious than the most critical emergencies, vigorous measures to try to prevent newspapers from acquiring government documents that, once they have them, they cannot be prevented at law from publishing. To illustrate, the government can make it evident that it will, *pursuant to legislation*, discipline all who transmit documents they are not supposed to transmit; the government can from time to time discipline those responsible for such unauthorized transmission to the press and others, without being obliged to show "irreparable harm"; the government can guard carefully the documents it is most concerned about; the government can be careful also about the people to whom it entrusts such documents. In addition, the government can attempt to "persuade" newspapers not to publish certain documents that do happen to come into their possession. Such persuasion (which can take various forms, some of which it may be better to leave veiled) depends in part on the government's being able to show publishers that it is serious and knows what it is doing, that its classification system is reasonable, and that it is dealing in good faith with both the press and the public.

When the state of affairs becomes such that one respectable publisher after another refuses to respect the requests and decrees of government that there be no publication, is not that in itself a good reason for getting to the root of the apparent loss of confidence in the government? We should be reminded by these observations of the most important measure available to a besieged government, and that is to redress the long-standing grievances that in a healthy community usually lie at the heart of such open defiance of government and such generally endorsed repudiation of the Vietnam War as we saw in the Pentagon Papers episode.

vi

It can be argued that the *New York Times* did "freedom of the press" a disservice by not publishing in one issue all that it intended to publish from the Pentagon Papers archives, thereby preventing the Attorney General from even attempting to secure an injunction and from establishing the dubious precedents that may survive the litigation. True, the Supreme Court ruled that the injunctions in this case could not be continued, but no majority of the Court said that they should never have been issued even on a temporary basis. I believe it would have been healthier as well as a sounder reading of the Constitution if the Court had lifted the remaining restraining orders immediately upon reading the lower courts' opinions after each case had been placed on its docket. It would have been sufficient, under the circumstances, simply to have affirmed the final substantive rulings of the district court in each case. It would have been even better to have singled out for approval the initial ruling by he district court in Washington.

Instead, it may seem to have been established by what the Court did and did not do that a temporary injunction may properly be secured merely upon an allegation by the government of grave danger to national security. In a sense, such a remedy can be said to have always been available for the government, for it did secure it the first time it was moved to seek it. But it may have been better for us not to have had such a "first time." It took a massive and even unprecedented stimulus to prod the government into an attempt this first time. Far less may suffice next time, now that the wall has been breached. It remains to be seen whether we will remember this litigation primarily for what it confirmed about the extent of freedom of the press, or primarily for what it suggested about previously unsuspected powers in the government to abridge, if only temporarily on this occasion, that freedom. To suggest that the government has powers from which, in practice, it cannot really benefit makes it likely that we will lose sight of the rationale for the powers the government does have and from which it can benefit.

The relevant constitutional doctrine, concerned as it is primarily with the ability of citizens to discuss freely and fully all matters necessary for making political judgments, is itself reflected in the everyday practice that is so revealing about the character of our regime. Suppose, for example, that the government had succeeded in preserving its injunctions, if only until extended hearings had been conducted in the district courts. Precisely what would such hearings, or even the entering of permanent injunctions thereafter, have meant both in these circumstances and as precedents? It appears that nothing could have prevented publication of the Pentagon Papers by *some* newspapers in the United States.

That is, the permanent injunctions sought by the government against the *New York Times* and the *Washington Post* would not have applied to other newspapers even in this Country until the government had moved specifically against them as well, as it had already moved against the *Boston Globe* and the *St. Louis Post-Dispatch*. The government would have had no legal basis for thus moving until such other newspapers had published, or had indicated they were about to publish, articles based upon the same or similar top-secret archives. A "victory" by the government in the *Times* and the *Post* cases would have meant that the enterprising editor on another newspaper with access to the same material, if *he* desired to publish without government interference, should have brought out in one issue everything he intended to publish. This he could have done, it should be noticed, without the special liability, psychological as well as legal, that would follow upon deliberate defiance of an injunction.

It should also be noticed in this connection that no sensible judge wants to issue an impotent decree. The Supreme Court obviously realized that it would not do much if any good to maintain restraints upon the *Times* and the *Post* in order to give the government time to make whatever case it could, when newspapers all over the Country were appearing almost daily with their own gleanings from the "secret" documents under review. There is something to be said for having court orders reflect an awareness of what people are going to do anyway.

vii

One result of all this litigation may be to induce dedicated, as well as irresponsible, publishers hereafter to print immediately all that they have which they believe the government might be disposed to challenge in court, unless they decide that they or the community might benefit from the publicity attendant upon an attempted suppression. By printing immediately everything that they intend to publish and taking their chances on criminal prosecution thereafter, publishers avoid the inconvenience and sometimes considerable expense attendant upon even a temporary injunction, contingencies that they will be advised to assess in the future.

It should now be apparent why it is that everyday practice, as well as the constitutional doctrine that reflects and ratifies such practice, makes previous restraint an illusory remedy for the government to rely upon. When a newspaper has unauthorized possession of any material, the first the government usually knows of it is when it is published, and then no injunction is useful. *This does not mean, of course, that the conscientious publisher should not, in certain instances, consult with reasonable government officials before he uses the material that comes to hand.* He is not bound to publish whatever he cannot be legally prevented from publishing. Will the memory of government efforts with respect to the Pentagon Papers tend, however, to discourage publishers from consulting government officials before publication (as, it seems to me, it would be sometimes patriotic for publishers to do)? Should not the government now counter such a tendency by disavowing recourse to injunctions when consulted voluntarily by publishers? That is, should we not try to restore that traditional relation between the press and the government which the Pentagon Papers litigation has to some extent disturbed?

It also should be apparent from what I have said that whatever the illusions and dangers of certain precedents, there cannot be among us an effective system of previous restraints upon publication through the use of specific injunctions. Previous restraint requires, except in rare circumstances calling for suspension of some constitutional processes, a comprehensive system of censorship which ensures that all prospective publication must be reviewed by the government. That seems hardly likely in the foreseeable future.

What should the press do with the virtually unlimited right it has been shown to have, at least in everyday practice, to publish what it chooses to publish without previous restraint? Perhaps all one can say here is that the press should try to act responsibly, and that we the people should speak up when we believe it has not done so. Certainly it is delusive and hence self-defeating, considering our traditions and constitutional circumstances, to expect either injunctions or criminal sanctions to compel the press to conduct itself other than it always has.

But the education, as distinguished from the intimidation, of the press is always in order.

IV

I have referred to "the character of our regime" and to the necessary "ability of citizens to discuss freely and fully all matters necessary for making political judgments." What is required to create and preserve a public that is fit for the conduct of a republican form of government?

Some means of general communication among us is, of course, required. The size of the Country has never permitted exclusive reliance upon speeches promulgated only by natural means. Artificial means of communication are indispensable, and this the press has traditionally provided the American people.

The right of the people to know, of which we hear much today, includes the duty to think. This has as a precondition the opportunity to learn as well as the ability to discern what it is necessary to learn. Information and opinions about vital matters of public concern are needed among us on a day-to-day basis.

Even more important than day-to-day concerns, however, and indeed central to this essay, are several perennial questions: What kind of people is presupposed by institutions that include the absolute prohibition, at least in practice, of previous restraints on the press? What produces and preserves such a people? Is not a people of a certain character, rather than merely a people with certain information, political opinions, and morale, presupposed by our institutions? Of course there could be the prior question of whether we want the institutions we do happen to have. Are there better ones available? On this occasion we must set aside this somewhat theoretical question, however engaging it might be, and proceed on the patriotic assumption that our traditional institutions are to be preserved and utilized.

Serving our traditional institutions, and indeed shaped by and shaping them, has been the press. Whatever its faults (and they have always been serious), the press has been something to which we have accommodated ourselves and upon which we have relied for generations. It is essentially old-fashioned, having developed in this Country along with our other institutions and with the character of our people. For the most part, the possible mistakes in editorial judgment to which I have referred in this essay affect national security interests; they do not threaten directly the character of the regime itself. I now propose to argue that in considering what we should do about the mass media, our primary concern should not be with the unauthorized revelation of secrets (that is, information about military weapons or strategic policy or diplomatic negotiations), but rather with the promulgation among us of images and other influences that shape and reshape the character of our people.

I have argued that for most practical purposes there has been since at least 1791 no effective legal limitation upon the information made available to the public about the performance of its governments, once the press has managed to secure such information. It seems to me too late in the constitutional day to change this dispensation: too much depends upon it; we are accustomed to it; well-intentioned men, both in the press and in the government, have learned how to deal with this considerable freedom from previous restraint of the press.

Vital to a people's self-governance are its experience and ability in forming, choosing, and assessing its leaders and policies. This means that the character of our people cannot be left only to chance, private influences, or the vagaries of a "free trade in ideas." We should be concerned to preserve in our people a character that permits it to use responsibly the extensive freedom of speech and of the press traditionally and constitutionally available to it.

Before we turn to a consideration of what the mass media do to the character of a people such as ours, we should note one immediate effect that television has on our political institutions. The modern mass media tend more toward centralization of power, while the old-fashioned press tended to be more localizing in its efforts and effects. The local is apt to be both more provincial and healthier; certainly, it is to be encouraged in this day and age. When we "go national" today, whether in the media or in politics, everything tends to become somewhat more gross and less discriminating. A facile simplification is rewarded and hence promoted. Is there then a tendency toward homogeneity of tastes and opinions as well as a general lowering of effective moral, political, and intellectual standards?

Industrialization with its marvels-laden technology can be said to be in large part responsible for such developments. With these developments comes also that sense of helplessness and rootlessness to which modern man is peculiarly subject: one has less the impression of being "one's own man," of being able to do things for oneself. One is forced into a passive role: not the role of the alert observer, but that of the pampered slave.

Since television is distinctively dependent on the technology of modern industrialization, it is so new that there has not yet developed, and one must wonder whether there *can* develop, the carefully-thought-out system of checks and balances there is among us in practice with respect to the press. Do we not all recognize that television has had profound effects upon our way of life? Should we not ask, then: What are the effects of television? Have those effects been good? What *is* the nature of the medium? What is there about television that is different from everything previously relied upon or accounted for by our institutions? What, if anything, can now be done about television?

V

i

I have suggested that the press, despite its efforts to imitate television and to modernize itself, is still essentially old-fashioned. Partly because of things intrinsic to it, it is still moved somewhat by a sense of natural justice, as is the public opinion that it serves.

The press continues to provide us with the serious searching out and recording of the news of the day, whereas television is in this respect for the most part parasitic. I believe it significant that the newscaster on television is rarely the man who has investigated the story being broadcast. Rather, he is usually part of a "show" that draws primarily upon what newspapermen have gathered and put on the wire. Thus there is no necessary connection between the influence or "image" of television "personalities" and their competence. These television personalities wield tremendous influence, but such influence is both ephemeral and beyond their comprehension and hence their control.

Television may help keep the press "honest" by presenting events that will be subsequently described on the printed page. But, one must wonder, at what level is such honesty promoted? What level suffices to satisfy the television viewer? What can be adequately described by television?

ii

To speak as I have of "public opinion" is to recognize in *public* a body that acts and is somehow keyed to political concerns; it is also to recognize in *opinion* something that does depend ultimately on notions of right and wrong and hence on reason. This is quite different from the passive audiences on which television depends and which it creates.

The television industry, in its distinctive modernity, is representative of the *mass media* and their infatuation with appearances. The term mass media aptly records what happens when modern electronic technology is applied to communications. The decisive factor becomes the necessarily "mass" character of passive and pacified audiences made up of countless private or isolated parties. The emphasis in the term *media* is upon the industry as little more than a conduit. Does not a people lose its moral and hence political sense when it becomes the "masses"? One may even be obliged to consider whether some previous restraint of the press might not become necessary if the people should, because of the debilitating effects of the mass media, remain or become so childish as to be unable to govern itself.

Both the massive character of the audience and the conduit character of the media very much affect the content and the effect of broadcasts, even though the principal concern of broadcasters may not be with either content or effect, but with the constant compulsion upon them to attract large audiences and with the pressing need to keep supplying something to ever-changing (and yet "always there") audiences. To regard a people as a "mass" is to say and perhaps make likely that it will become something that is moved primarily by what *Federalist* No. 1 called "force and accident," by arousals of passion rather than by appeals to reason.

We should not be surprised to hear the effect of television upon audiences spoken of as an "impact" that can be "surveyed" and "marketed." The intrinsic quality of particular programs becomes irrelevant if the surveys do not "measure up," as television executives will sometimes admit and their conduct almost always exhibits.

iii

The effects of television are pervasive and felt both directly and indirectly: directly through what almost six hours a day of *exposure* (not necessarily of viewing) do to the souls of our people; indirectly through the adjustments the press and others consider themselves obliged to make to compete with the television industry in capturing people's attention and thus being able to stay in business. It should be noticed that much of the time devoted to television must be taken from other activities, such as reading, writing, conversation, courting, or playing. What had been the effect heretofore of such activities? What is the effect of their radical curtailment? It is unrealistic to assume that such revolutionary changes as we have undergone have no significant effect on the souls of people.

Commercial considerations are obviously much more important for television than for the press, whatever may be said about the influence of advertisers upon publishers. Television was invented during a more commercial age than was printing; the press developed more naturally as an extension of thinking and writing rather than as a tool for advertising and selling. The commercial aspects of the press simply cannot assert themselves as much as the commercial aspects of television do. For example, one can easily ignore the advertisements in a newspaper. No one doubts the considerable effect that sponsors have in the United States upon the content of television programs and upon audiences.

The commercial aspects of television, however important they may be in so many critiques of the industry, are not our primary concern. (Commercial considerations do lead producers to try to provide what they believe audiences want. This can have the effect of accentuating the bad tendencies intrinsic to television. Thus, since television thrives on "action," there is frequent recourse to the coarsening violence about which we hear more and more complaints.) Nor need the specific content of television broadcasting concern us here, insofar as this can be corrected by a people determined to do so, but rather the very form of it and the consequent effects of the displacement by television of the other means by which souls have been engaged heretofore. The remarkable success of television since the Second World War in sweeping all before it should make us wonder what there is that makes it so attractive. What is the effect of having such a window to the world? What comes through and what is held back by the filter of the television camera?

It need not be denied that there are good programs from time to time on television, genuinely good things in addition to the many apparently good things to which large audiences are attracted. Nor need it be denied that television can seem a blessing to old people, the ill, and harassed mothers with young children. Other salutary effects can be catalogued: the promotion of an acceptance among us of racial justice because of the displays before national television audiences of attractive athletes, politicians, and actors who happen to be Negroes; the sometimes cathartic dramatization of national ceremonies, such as the inauguration or funeral of a President; the presentation of intelligent men and women attempting to discuss serious problems of national concern. It has also been noticed that television does reveal the personalities of public figures, that it "takes the clothes off a man." The audience may well get an impression it might not otherwise have been able to get of what some public figures are like.

And yet, are not the good things on television always an incidental part of the whole? Are not even the good uses to which television has been put due in large part to chance? The issues that capture public attention and get considerable "play" are all too often contrived or accidental. However adept television may be at exposing some public figures, the professional television personalities are themselves little more than animated masks so far as the viewing audience is concerned. Why this should be so depends on the very nature of the medium.

Distortion and superficiality are among the inevitable effects of television, including effects of the technology itself that are accentuated by the expense of television and its consequent need for huge audiences. Television cannot help but cater to the worst in us, even when it is trying to do its best. Certain things are made to appear easier than they really are. Shallow illusions are promoted, including the illusion that the viewer can learn enough from capsule presentations (a kind of discourse by headline) to get a serious notion of what is going on in the world and to be able to make sensible judgments and responsible choices. Television seems to liberate even while it really cripples, and it does this in so enticing a manner as to drive its competitors either out of the "market" or into suicidal imitation.

Thus television helps create the illusion that it has informed us and that we have "participated" in something we have witnessed "close up." It emphasizes that one must "get it" at once; one can't tarry to look at what has been broadcast, to take one's time studying what one may not understand. One must get it all *now*, for something else is coming soon. One is discouraged from looking back: everything is before us; recollection and reflection are discouraged or at least made difficult. Is not all this more appropriate for entertainment than for serious discourse?

With an emphasis upon the immediate, appearance becomes crucial; it is hard to pin things down. Is not almost everything about television ephemeral? If so, are not ephemeral qualities in the soul appealed to and legitimated? The unreality of it all is intensified by television's reduction of the visible world to a box that is smaller than the size of the human being; this can be both immediately enticing and eventually unpersuasive, if not even psychologically disturbing. The illusion of immediacy is fostered (an illusion that the press finds it more difficult to sustain), and then with the click of a switch the "real world" is gone. Reality is thus distorted, as it is as well with the unnaturalness in the amount and variety of things shown on television, and with the apparent intimate access to things that human beings are used to having and keeping at a distance.

The electronic media are voracious and insatiable. Consequently, they promote novelty, which seems to fit in better with youthfulness, with those who are by nature always changing and experimenting. A "culture" keyed to or shaped by the mass media is bound to be youth-oriented, an unnatural state of affairs for a community. There is constant change, with a consequent profound dissatisfaction and rootlessness. Fashions become more important and character less. Since the visual is necessarily emphasized, the length of discourse that can be presented on television is much shorter than serious issues require, much less than what would be possible in a meeting hall. Yet most viewers are given the impression that television presents enough.

The addictive effect of television is revealing; one turns it on and it stays on for hours. It is much less likely that this sort of thing can happen routinely with reading. Even if one moves through a prosperous American suburb—that is, among those who have the material resources and the education to be able to do whatever they choose—one can see through almost every living room window the dominating television set turned on all evening as well as much of the day. Are our lives so empty as to be in need of such narcotics? Television reinforces, even as it tries to minister to, whatever sense of emptiness there may be in modern life.

We also can see the effects of television upon the faces of our children. Observe them watching even the commercials with vacuous avidity. It is no wonder that many teenagers become jaded and even psychically disturbed with nothing to challenge them, nothing to excite them but the most bizarre and the most violent things. Broadcasters hardly do all this deliberately; in fact, just as they are really unknown to their audiences, so their audiences are unknown to them. Contact between broadcaster and audience is not human, but rather mechanical, artificial, and fleeting. It is remarkable that broadcasters can stand the life they lead. Are they sustained by what is said about them face-to-face or now and then on the printed page?

It is sometimes said that the young, and some of the old, know today much more about the world—how big and diverse it is, for example—than people did a generation ago. The mass media no doubt contribute to this sense of liberation: they do "open up" the world. But because of the inefficiency of television (consider the amount of material that can be spoken as against what can be read in a given time) one simply cannot get much detail beyond the immediately visible. Even the "educated" young probably know less than any generation heretofore about what has gone before or about the serious questions to which human beings have always addressed themselves. The young spread themselves over much more than did their predecessors, but much more thinly. Hence they cannot begin to know themselves. Yet they readily believe themselves to be more enlightened than their predecessors.

iv

Television means that it is even more difficult than heretofore for reason to contribute to assimilating and ordering the information that comes to people every day. The pictures and sounds that dominate contemporary "culture" are not speeches; the stimuli of television may go from the passions of the televiser to the passions of the audience without lingering in the reason of either.

Once the need to speak well is reduced by a general addiction to moving pictures, the common language is likely to degenerate. The politician who once made weekly radio reports to his constituents finds, upon being obliged to switch to television because of what is happening around him, that he cannot continue to be as idea-oriented as he had been on radio: he must move from dealing *somewhat* in ideas to "plugging" almost exclusively his name and picture (that is, his "image"). The practical politician conforms to the demands and limits of the dominant communications medium of the moment, and the next generation is trained (or should we say "conditioned"?) accordingly.

Children, as well as adults, are discouraged by television from becoming practiced in reading. Once television becomes available, reading appears to most people laborious and less attractive; the attention span is likely to be shortened for activities requiring deliberate effort; discipline is not encouraged for serious work, and this suggests that everyday passions are even more likely to make themselves felt than they have always been. The general deterioration of serious reading ability will eventually lead to deterioration of the ability to write. Does not this entail for us the impairment of the ability to think seriously?

Despite what is said about television's ability to "take the clothes off a man," his television "image" is likely to be quite different from what he is truly like. In fact, it may be virtually impossible for anyone to be more than an image before the camera. But one's written statements may be very much what one is. In fact, they may be essentially what one is, insofar as one is a thinking being. (I question in passing whether it is desirable for television, or anything else, "to take the clothes off a man." What kind of public man would permit himself to be routinely stripped? Is it not natural for human beings to attempt to conceal their nakedness?)

It can be said of the mass media that they promote an "education at once universal and superficial." We inexorably move, as Winston Churchill noticed, "toward goals which are ill-defined and yet magnetic." We sometimes seem oblivious of "the enormous processes of collectivization which are at work among us."

v

It should immediately be added, however, that collectivization is not the same as community, just as ill-defined goals may not truly be goals at all. I turn now from considering primarily the effects of television on human beings to saying something more about the effects of television on a community and on the possibility of community.

Serious association with one another, whether for purposes of entertainment, education, worship, politics, or sports, is undermined by television, especially since viewers and performers (or, as they once were, people and leaders) can make no serious contact with one another. For example, politicians tailor what they say and eventually believe to what can be "put across" on the television screen. The screen depends on and encourages the wrong kind of simplification. No matter how complicated the subject presented may be, it is all too often pretended if not sincerely believed that it can be adequately dealt with, as if magically, in a few minutes.

May not the frequent public protests in this Country against the partisanship of the mass media be crude reflections of a deeper and perhaps instinctive concern among us about what is being done to the human soul by the mass media? Yet it is also felt that something like television is needed for an aggregate as large as the United States has become. It is, some might even say, a necessary evil to cure an even worse one, the divisiveness of bigness.

Television does bring us all together, in a way, but too many at a time and at too low a level. In the process it breaks down smaller communities that until its coming had still been viable despite the onslaughts of the automobile and of the Second World War. The isolation of people, whether the elderly or the infirm or the housewife, that is intensified if not induced by the disruption of our towns and urban neighborhoods, seems to lead to a "need" for television.

Some, however, see the American people, in tens of millions, elevated politically and culturally by the mass media. Such elevation, others reply, is not good for these millions: they cannot become truly enlightened; they are much more likely to become frustrated. Most people, it seems to me, have not been elevated; rather, their cultural life, as well as their politics, has become inferior to what it had been, and their thinking less disciplined and more sentimental than it need be. If people are frustrated, it is perhaps because they have acquired a sophistication that their circumstances cannot permit them to enjoy; the old loyalties and consequent simple pleasures have been undermined. All the while their precious linguistic inheritance is being cheapened.

It is my impression that television fits better with an emphasis upon Presidential rather than Congressional or State politics. Rule by television plebiscite seems to be developing among us, a kind of rule that is peculiarly responsive to the volatile mass tastes that television promotes and serves. The constitutional tendency of television—of the way of life that permits and is in turn shaped by television—is to unleash desires and arouse expectations that undermine among us the moderation of tradition, the restraints both of a healthy diversity and of a genuine respect for quality, and the requirements and advantages of federalism.

This social indictment of television can be summed up thus: Each of us is constantly addressed by television apart from the others, and yet none of us is ever really spoken to. The ability to read, and hence to think and to join in serious common discourse, suffers. Every kind of association is filtered through the camera and stripped of its humanity. The community is depreciated while a hollow privacy is emphasized; communal tastes are reduced to the lowest common denominator and then shamelessly catered to. Spectacle replaces theater; feeling replaces thought; image replaces character. The world shaped by television is an empty one, starved and frenetic, dreamlike and debilitating. It can be expected to culminate eventually in a crippling mediocrity and perhaps even in tyranny.

vi

It is curious that such innovations should be permitted among us without serious authoritative consideration of what they may do to our way of life. But then, we are all too often inclined to take our way of life for granted, as if there should be no conditions for its existence or, for that matter, any transcendent standards and purposes to which it is dedicated. Perhaps we see the only thing necessary to our way of life to be an openness to constant change and hence experimentation.

Human beings may, by their nature, seek newfangledness. We do seem to have an "unbounded passion for variety." Is there not in such openness to novelty a constant challenge to piety, to what should be worthy of reverence? Certainly there is a challenge to the established way with respect to both opinions and conduct. When a feverish taste for novelty is legitimated among a people, even a good community can become suspect merely because it has been so well-conditioned as to survive and become old.

I do not believe that most of the harmful effects of television can be avoided so long as we have it. Some of television's more obvious abuses can perhaps be ameliorated from time to time, but the intrinsic character of this electronic possession is such as to have profound effects on fundamental relations among us: between man and man, between community and human being, between lover and beloved. The easy intrusion of television into our lives undermines what friendship and influence should mean. Appearance becomes even more important than it had been. In short, television in both its means and its inevitable consequences is simply unnatural and remarkably corrupting.

It has long seemed obvious to me that the television industry should be abolished completely in this Country and that nothing short of this can purge its crippling influence from American life. If this is indeed a society open to experimentation, then let us deliberately experiment for at least a decade with the remedy of complete suppression of television.

If television should be abolished, we should be obliged to go out again into our streets, if only to attend movies. Local entertainment, local gatherings (religious as well as secular), and even genuine popular culture might become important again. Even more importantly, the intrinsically harmful influences of television would no longer have to be contended with.

Is it not revealing that something so harmful as television should have become so entrenched so soon? It is like noxious weeds that happen to be blown in by the wind. Its abolition today is, of course, virtually unthinkable; yet we did not have it a generation ago, however natural it may now seem to most of us.

If we move against television, we reassert ourselves as a community even as we act together on behalf of communal interests. We would show we care about what affects us, thereby again becoming a community. We would show as well that we recognize that mere desires should not govern our lives, that temperance is vital to enduring happiness. But, it may be objected, if we should abolish television, that would open the door to further infringements of our liberty: there might be attempted public interference thereafter with other activities among us which also aim at self-expression and self-gratification. This objection is not groundless. Would we not be obliged, upon the abolition of television, to consider what else needs to be remedied? After all, modern industrial society was far from perfect before television took root among us.

vii

I believe it salutary to argue that there should be in ordinary constitutional circumstances both an absolute prohibition against previous legal restraints of the press and an absolute previous restraint (that is, total abolition) of the television industry. We want the press a certain way because of the nature of our regime. The considerations that lead to an advocacy of extensive guarantees for the press may lead as well to an advocacy of complete suppression of television.

I see in the abolition of television no serious First Amendment problem. Rather than abridge the "freedom of speech" guaranteed by the First Amendment, the abolition of television, and hence a radical reform of the mass media, would enlarge freedom of speech among us. Television interferes, I have argued, with serious general education in a country such as ours; it affects adversely the ability to read and hence the ability to think and the very status of thought among us, playing up to the passions as it does. The abolition of television would probably contribute *among us* to the preservation of self-government and hence genuine freedom. (I stress "among us" since it would be doctrinaire to insist that television may not have a salutary, even civilizing, effect on certain peoples.)

Such abolition, it should be noticed, need not bring with it the problems of widespread attempted evasions, with all their attendant evils, that we have known from time to time with respect to prohibitions upon alcohol, narcotics, and obscenity. Abolition should be fairly easy to effect *if the community should ever decide to do it.* Nor must we accommodate to television as we must to the existence of nuclear weapons. We may be obliged to develop various weapons as part of our effort to neutralize the possession of them by others, for we can be critically affected by their behavior. But this is not the case with television: if people in other countries are corrupted by television, that is no reason why we should be also.

It should be noticed that the major economic cost of the abolition of television would be borne not by the broadcaster, but by those who would benefit most of all from such abolition, the millions of owners of private television receivers. The aggregate cost of private receivers is far larger than that of all the capital invested by broadcasters. If cigarette advertising, previously the largest single source of television revenue, can properly be eliminated in what is thought to be the public interest, there is no reason in principle why all television advertising cannot be eliminated in the public interest or, to go one step further, television itself. Or are we to assume that there is such a thing as physical health, but no such thing as moral character and social health, for the community to protect and to promote?

VI

We are no more likely to abolish television and to purge the public and the press of its corrupting influences than we are to curtail radically the private use of the automobile. I recognize that I have been talking in effect about the constant need to review the consequences of our technological development. Is television an essentially derivative manifestation of this overall development? Do I attack merely a symptom? Perhaps such an attack can be so put as to illuminate the underlying problems, thereby provoking serious discussion of what we are and are not doing, and why. To ask, as I have, for the abolition of television may do no more than to remind ourselves, in a pedagogically useful manner, that the common good should take precedence over private gratification.

One can see in the role of television among us a powerful industry enlisted in the thoughtless and virtually inevitable service of the passions. Mutual exploitation as well as unthinking toleration becomes the order of the day. It is not incidental that spectacular rewards and influence seem to some to be available through television. This makes it even more difficult for us as a people both to do what is necessary to conserve what we can of the old way and to resume humane, local, and deliberate control of what instructs and entertains us and hence forms our character and our institutions.

All this may be no more than to say that the way of life brought forth on this continent two centuries ago is in the course of profound alteration, that we have become unable to understand and control what is happening to us. All this should remind us of the vulnerability of reason in the conduct of human affairs, of how difficult it is for any people truly to govern itself.

To govern oneself does mean that one must accommodate oneself to circumstances, that one must make do with what happens to be available, and that one must be prepared to settle for less than the very best. What can be done about television, short of the total abolition I have advocated? Various reforms which reflect some of the criticisms I have made in this essay can be attempted. I collect here, as illustrative of how one may begin to think about reforms, a half-dozen suggestions:

1) There should be a curtailment in the amount of television available daily. It would be good not to have continuous television, but only a couple of hours of transmission at a time, followed by extended intermissions during which there is no local transmission at all. It would also be good to have certain evenings of the week, and perhaps most, if not all, of Sunday, completely free from television as well as from most other commercial activity. In any event, the total number of hours of transmission each week should be markedly reduced.

2) The commercial influence upon television in this Country should be reduced. It would be good to experiment with the means by which British commercial television has insured that there be no identification of advertisers with particular programs.

3) What is the relation between television's pervasive commercialism and its national programming? Whatever it may be, there is much to be said for encouraging local programming, thereby emphasizing the importance of the local community. We should expect with more local programming a decline in the professional quality of programs, at least until local talent began to assert itself.

4) The immediate effect of television upon our political life should be

eliminated if we are to be left free and equipped to assess such things as television upon that way of life. Should not television be explicitly reserved for entertainment, leaving the discussion of politics to more appropriate forums? It would probably be good to permit no political activity at all on television. Perhaps, indeed, all news broadcasts, except for emergency announcements, should be eliminated or should be confined to extended readings from newspaper accounts.

5) If there is to be politics on television, the emphasis should be on lengthy talks and extended civic proceedings. It would probably be prudent to reconsider the "fairness doctrine," for that may provide an overly zealous administration in Washington too great an opportunity to control the political discourse of the country. Insofar as television *is* permitted to provide a forum for political discourse, it is good for us that it should be able to rely on First Amendment privileges.

6) The nonpolitical content of television, with a view to the effects on viewers of such things as portrayals of violence and legitimation of greed, should be periodically assessed by civic-minded people who recognize that the virtues, vices, and accomplishments of human beings are not without causes. In addition, there should be on television considerable instruction in reading and a number of hours each week during which the pictures are accompanied only by well-written subtitles and good music, not by talk. It should be routinely emphasized on the screen that the viewer must supplement, by extended reading and discussion, what he sees on television if he is to understand the matters under consideration.

7) It should go without saying that any family or neighborhood that "deprives" itself of television is likely to be better off than those families or neighborhoods addicted to it. It may become generally apparent someday, perhaps even in time to make a difference, that the many who are saddled with television are being exploited by the few who profit from it, and that the exploited are so deluded as to "choose" this form of self-enslavement. This is like the relationship between cigarette manufacturers and their victims. It may then become generally apparent that any community respectful of its integrity or concerned about the underprivileged should abolish television root and branch.

VII

How long will our present decline take to reach bottom? In the United States it could take generations, since we do have considerable political capital to draw upon. But the present generation of Americans may be the last one with a genuine opportunity to return the Country to "the old way":

there are still many among us who have been raised without the influence of television. Thus it can truly be said, quoting again from *Federalist* No. 1, that "the crisis, at which we are arrived, may with propriety be regarded as the era in which that decision is to be made," the decision whether "accident and force," rather than "reflection and choice," are to shape our lives. People shaped by television—by that most influential of the mass media, are (I have argued) destined thereafter "to depend for their political constitutions on accident and force."

It is instructive that we do not (perhaps, by now, cannot) see various of the risks we are running. It is also instructive that we will not do anything serious about the risks we do notice, partly because of immediate pleasures and profits, partly because of profound confusion about causes and effects, and about the nature itself of cause and effect, in moral and political matters. An attempt to return ourselves to a more austere and healthier way of life, a life more conducive to a republican form of government and to the full development of the human soul, is virtually unthinkable. It would also be instructive if the reader, in attempting to assess the argument I have presented here, should be induced to investigate and to make explicit what we take for granted as to how a particular way of life is established and perpetuated.

It should be evident from what I have said about the curtailment of television that the case I have made in this essay for an absolute prohibition upon previous restraints of the press cannot rest simply upon a sentimental desire to see freedom "maximized." If we are truly to govern ourselves, we are obliged to consider what among us promotes and serves human perfection, the common good, and hence a rational liberty. Such considerations can lead citizens to the reasoned conclusion that some activities in a community such as ours should be given free rein while others should be vigorously held in check.

Unless we are prepared to curtail the mass media and to restore the local press to its rightful place as the principal forum for general discourse among our citizens, we should expect to have hereafter only the masses rather than a community of citizens to reckon with. Indeed, there would then not even be any "we" to make judgments and to act. For "we," as in "We the People," presupposes a public, not mere spectators, as fundamental to community and to the body politic.

19

LEGAL REALISM AND THE NEW JOURNALISM

Welcome, dear Rosencrantz and Guildenstern. / Moreover that we much did long to see you, / The need we have to use you did provoke / Our hasty sending. . . . I entreat you both / That, being of so young days brought up with [Hamlet], / And sith so neighbored to his youth and havior, / That you vouchsafe your rest here in our court / Some little time, so by your companies / To draw him on to pleasures, and to gather / So much as from occasion you may glean, / Whether aught to us unknown afflicts him thus, / That opened lies within our remedy.

KING CLAUDIUS

I

Bob Woodward and Scott Armstrong report in *The Brethren* some of the things that happened among members of the United States Supreme Court from 1969 to 1976, "the first seven years of Warren E. Burger's tenure as Chief Justice of the United States." (p. 2)

The authors indicate the scope of and justification for *The Brethren* in these terms (p. 1):

> Virtually every issue of significance in American society eventually arrives at the Supreme Court. . . . [For] nearly two hundred years, the Court has made its decisions in absolute secrecy, handing down its judgments in formal written opinions. Only these opinions, final and unreviewable, are published.

This essay was published, with extensive notes, in 1983 *Duke Law Journal* 1045–74 (1983). (Original title: "Legal Realism, the New Journalism, and *The Brethren*.")

The citations in this essay are, unless otherwise indicated, to Bob Woodward and Scott Armstrong, *The Brethren: Inside the Supreme Court* (New York: Simon and Schuster, 1975). The final quotation in this essay is taken from Laurence Berns's talk at the Memorial Service for Simon Kaplan at St. John's College. See the headnote for Essay No. 5, above. See, for related comments by Mr. Berns, the Preface, above.

The epigraph is taken from William Shakespeare, *Hamlet*, II, ii, 1–18.

No American institution has so completely controlled the way it is viewed by the public. The Court's deliberative process—its internal debates, the tentative positions taken by the Justices, the preliminary votes, the various drafts of written opinions, the negotiations, confrontations, and compromises—is hidden from public view.

The Court has developed certain traditions and rules, largely unwritten, that are designed to preserve the secrecy of its deliberations. The few previous attempts to describe the Court's internal workings—biographies of particular Justices or histories of individual cases—have been published years, often decades, after the events, or have reflected the viewpoints of only a few Justices.

Much of recent history, notably the period that included the Vietnam war and the multiple scandals known as Watergate, suggests that the detailed steps of decision making, the often hidden motives of the decision makers, can be as important as the eventual decisions themselves. Yet the Court, unlike the Congress and the Presidency, has by and large escaped public scrutiny.

The authors make much of the fact that the Supreme Court's "deliberative process is . . . hidden from view." This can be said as well of all, or almost all, of the hundreds of State and Federal appellate courts in the United States as well as of the deliberative processes of trial judges and of juries. But the final products that appellate courts produce—the reasoned opinions upon which their influence ultimately depends—*are* subject to considerable "public scrutiny," much more so perhaps than is true of the final products of any other branch of our governments. Be that as it may, *The Brethren* undertakes to subject "the inner workings of the Supreme Court" to the public scrutiny which, it is argued, the Country is both in need of and entitled to.

This unprecedented exposure of the Supreme Court depends, we are informed, on unprecedented sources. Thus, we are told by the authors (pp. 3–4),

> Most of the information in this book is based on interviews with more than two hundred people, including several Justices, more than 170 former law clerks, and several dozen former employees of the Court. Chief Justice E. Burger declined to assist us in any way. Virtually all the interviews were conducted "on background," meaning that the identity of the source will be kept confidential. This assurance of confidentiality to our sources was necessary to secure their cooperation.

Without such cooperation *The Brethren* could not have been written. The authors scrupulously refrain from revealing the names of the many sources upon whom they relied. But they do characterize the sources and what they got from them in this way (p. 4):

> The sources who helped us were persons of remarkable intelligence. They had unusually precise recall about the handling of cases that came before the Court, particularly the important ones. However, the core documentation for this book came from unpublished material that was made available to us by dozens of sources who had access to the documents. We obtained internal memoranda between Justices, letters, notes taken at conference, case assignment sheets, diaries, unpublished drafts of opinions and, in several instances, drafts that were never circulated even to the other Justices. By the time we had concluded our research, we had filled eight file drawers with thousands of pages of documents from the chambers of eleven of the twelve Justices who served during the period 1969 to 1976.

I anticipate much of what I have to say here by observing that the "Authors' Note" at the front of their book includes an acknowledgement to a named colleague of the authors on the *Washington Post*, of whom it is said, "A devoted and resourceful assistant, no one could have been more loyal and trusted." No doubt the authors would condemn the people they rely upon to preserve the confidentiality they insist that they require for their work if they were to learn that another investigative reporter had managed to secure access to their "eight file drawers" or to what their associates know about their more than two hundred sources. Yet are these authors entitled to any more fidelity from their employees and associates than the Justices of the Supreme Court expected from theirs? As Macbeth put it, contemplating the betrayal of his king in order to secure the throne for himself, "[W]e but teach bloody instructions, which, being taught, return to plague th' inventor." (I, vii, 8–10) Or, as Justice Holmes once said of wiretapping, this is "dirty business." (277 U.S. 470 [1928]) But then even wiretapping can be justified on some occasions. If wiretapping can be justified, why should we not condone what these and other journalists do in the interest of helping us become as well informed as a sovereign citizen-body should be?

We are obliged to consider what it means to be "well informed" and how one goes about becoming so. Consider, for example, the New Hampshire "debate" among Republican candidates for President that was broadcast February 20, 1980. A half-dozen men spent an hour and a half broadcasting to the electorate a series of one-minute answers to the great questions of the day! How seriously should we take problems that are dealt with thus? How seriously should we take men, or the system of producing and presenting them, that can approach important issues thus? That such encounters can be regarded as "debates" reflects the poverty both of our imagination and of our recollections. It should not take much imagination for us to appreciate that much more than this, and something much different from this, is required for serious thinking. We should recall what we know about genuine debates, such as those between Abraham Lincoln and Stephen A. Douglas in Illinois more than a century ago. Those debates were organized by the participants, who were quite capable of putting searching questions to each other without the aid of journalists.

Some people would say that we can no longer have extended, searching public examinations of the issues of the day. But this is only to say that we are trapped by our technology and by the techniques and way of life generated by that technology. It is also to say that we can no longer appreciate what we are missing. If we did recognize how superficial our public discourse has become, we would surely try to do something about it or, at least, we would be put on notice that whatever is produced by such discourse is probably inadequate.

We should constantly remind ourselves that our cherished freedom of speech is primarily for the purpose of permitting civic-minded citizens to discuss the issues of the day at length and without fear of governmental reprisal. Human nature being what it is, it is inevitable that this freedom will be abused from time to time. We are obliged to put up with such abuses in order to preserve vigorous public discourse. We should also recognize that much depends on the good sense and the self-restraint of those who use freedom of speech to bring to our attention things we should know.

The failings of Mr. Woodward and Mr. Armstrong are in large part the failings of many intellectuals today, among whom journalists must be numbered. What they have done not only reflects what they have been taught by their peers, but also caters to what the people who read books have come to expect as their due. Consider, for example, how politics, including the acts of judges, are regarded by these authors. They tend to believe that "reality" is most likely that which has been hidden from view and that which *is* hidden from view is likely to have something wrong with it. In a sense, they seem to say, only the conspiratorial is real; at the least, it is an exposure of the conspiratorial that is most revealing.

A secret is considered significant because it *is* secret. It is not recognized that certain things may be kept secret precisely because that which is *not* secret (but rather is published for all to see) could not be as good as it should be if all deliberations leading to it were known to be subject to periodic and inevitably selective exposure. Thus, as one constitutional scholar has observed, judges, if they are to do their work responsibly, must have the "freedom to wrangle with each other." To make such wrangling public, or to make it uncertain whether or not it will be made public, would tend to discourage frankness and flexibility. It is far from clear that there is anything improper or sinister in conducting judicial deliberations in private, which is, after all, the way that has been generally accepted among us for centuries. Anyone who has served on a jury, or who has confided in his parent, his spouse, or his child, or who has consulted a priest, a doctor, or a lawyer can appreciate how critical an assurance of enduring confidentiality can be.

The tendency of journalists, when they become more interested in hidden motives than in public arguments (which, in the form of opinions, appellate judges are primarily engaged in developing), is to make a great deal of gossip, if only because that is something they can add to what is routinely provided to the public by courts and legal commentators. This journalistic version of "legal realism" tends to lead to an undue regard for the seamy side of life, to an eager exposure to public view of the things that sensitive people have always been reluctant to publicize. Not only are quirks of personalities made a good deal of, with the implication that one learns something significant about a man when one learns about his peculiarities, but also the afflictions we are all subject to are feasted upon. The most shocking instance of this in *The Brethren* is the extended account of the effects, both physical and psychic, of a debilitating stroke upon a respected Justice who had served long and honorably. The details were not necessary in order to make the legitimate point that the Court, as it had had to do before on several occasions, adjusted its mode of operation in the expectation that this Justice would soon be replaced. But much more than this is said, probably because it had become available and could be counted upon to appeal to an insensitive curiosity among readers. What is particularly significant here is not that ambitious journalists should want to exploit such material, but that respectable publishers and editors encourage and permit them to do so.

The emphasis that these authors place on the things they relish exposing distorts what they purport to describe: the doings of the Supreme Court between 1969 and 1976. What is novel and accurate in their revelations is not likely to be important, and what is important is not likely, by and large, to be accurate. One can see in their accounts the sorts of things that people who do not understand what is important look for or are titillated by. That is, one can see reflected in *The Brethren* the limitations of those who are devoted to legal realism. The term *legal realism*, we are told by the *Encyclopedia of the American Constitution* (III, 1134),

signifies the basic thrust of the movement [that emerged within American jurisprudence during the 1920s and 1930s], which was to uncover and to explain legal realities. This effort reflects the allegation that some of the most cherished beliefs of lawyers are myths or fictions. The major purpose of the realists' provocative criticisms of these beliefs was not, however, to undermine the American legal system. Rather, it was to facilitate development of an accurate understanding of the nature, interpretation, operation, and effects of law. The realists insisted that achievement of this goal was essential for intelligent reform of legal rules, doctrines, and practices.

I have suggested that there is something deeply irresponsible in the way the authors of *The Brethren* have proceeded. I am afraid that some of my readers, perhaps many of them, do not share the opinions about the failings of intellectuals among us upon which my criticisms rest. That those opinions are not shared is indicated by the considerable rewards, even fortunes, authors such as these can earn. Who but intellectuals are their market? Certainly not the man in the street.

Before I turn to further examination of what is "deeply irresponsible," I should mention an instance of irresponsible reporting in the book which does *not* require that one share my assessment of the authors' basic approach. They charge that Justice Brennan, in order to stay in the good graces of another Justice whose support he wanted in other cases, withheld the critical fifth vote to overturn the murder conviction of a petitioner. That Justices may occasionally trade votes should not surprise us: they do have to work, and virtually live, together. But only the flimsiest evidence indicates that Justice Brennan did trade votes on this occasion. The charge is considered a serious one by the authors. They report that the "clerks were shocked that such considerations would keep a man in prison." (p. 225) No sources are identified, of course, in support of what is reported. Fortunately, Anthony Lewis, a longtime student of the Court who has both a reputation to risk and reliable contacts, has shown us in print, as well as anyone can who does not have all of the authors' sources to examine, that the charge against Justice Brennan in this instance is without ascertainable foundation. (See *New York Review of Books*, February 7, 1980, p. 3; June 12, 1980, p. 48.) One is reminded here and elsewhere in the book of the kind of character assassination indulged in by Senator Joseph McCarthy, justified, as the authors of *The Brethren* have tried to justify their work, by invocations of the people's right to know.

We do not need exposés to show us that judges are "human," especially since such exposés are apt to capitalize upon the highly questionable. To right the balance and to confirm that judges *are* human, I share with my readers still another "inside" story about what judges can be like. This story too is about Justice Brennan. A law school teacher of mine, the late Harry Kalven, told me about a lawyers' meeting he was to address. When he got to the reception held before he was to speak, he found to his dismay that all of the lawyers there were in formal wear; he alone was in an ordinary business suit. His discomfort grew as he mingled with his audience, for they were indeed dressed most elegantly. As he circulated about the hall he came upon a group that was obviously gathered around someone of importance; he figured that it must be the other guest speaker, who was, on that occasion, Justice Brennan. Sure enough, when Mr. Kalven penetrated that crowd he did find Justice Brennan in the middle—dressed also in an ordinary suit. When the Justice saw the similarly dressed Professor, his face lit up as he said, "Boy, am I glad to see you!" I have, since the original publication of this essay, received a letter from Justice Brennan further describing the Kalven episode about which I had asked him. He has given me permission to use here his original letter (of March 26, 1984), the text of which I now reproduce in its entirety:

> Thank you so much for sending me your very fine piece. Your story about Professor Kalven and me is completely accurate. It was the occasion of the annual meeting of the American College of Trial Lawyers at one of the fancy Virginia resort hotels. Not only was I in civilian clothes but, because it was hot, I had a seersucker suit on. There I was scheduled to be the main speaker! But for Harry it would have been a horribly embarrassing evening. Thank you so much for mentioning it.

II

The reservations one can develop about *The Brethren* and contemporary journalism are perhaps even more important for what they suggest about the quite influential "legal realism" movement among us. Certainly, the courts and the Country often need rigorous criticism of what judges say and do. (Consider, for example, Abraham Lincoln's criticisms of the Supreme Court for its *Dred Scott* decision and Franklin D. Roosevelt's criticism of the Court for its early New Deal decisions.) Unfortunately, journalists writing on judicial matters frequently misconceive their subject. For one thing, it is naive to regard closed deliberations as virtual conspiracies. There must be frankness and confidentiality if certain kinds of deliberations are to be effective. Important issues are at stake in such deliberations, and conscientious men will make all kinds of efforts to persuade one another. They can and do say all kinds of things, especially "in the heat of battle," which they and their more mature associates are aware they do not mean and which they certainly do not mean to have recorded for posterity. Any good novel on this subject can remind us at least as well as *The Brethren* does that judges can and should act like human beings. Perhaps one balanced behind-the-scenes account of how the Supreme Court operates can be useful every quarter-century or so, but a balanced account would be one that recognizes that judges usually have more good things than bad to say about their colleagues. It is the cutting remark about a colleague, however, that the journalist tends to treasure: *that* is "news." Virtually nothing is said in *The Brethren* about the social relations outside the Court building among the Justices or between the Justices and their friends. Remarks uttered in the midst of struggle are not balanced by thoughtful assessments made at leisure by the Justices.

Personal relationships aside, one would have to know much more than these authors do about the final products of the Court's deliberations to be able to describe and assess sensibly how and why the Justices developed their public positions. Reliance upon stray quotations and an occasional early draft of an opinion is likely to be misleading unless one knows a good deal about the context. Similarly, it is often difficult, if not impossible, to determine a good teacher's position on a serious question from the things a student may happen to remember about what is said in a lively class discussion. But this is, in effect, what the authors have attempted to do by questioning former law clerks about their conversations with Justices. Certainly it is difficult to understand a continuing give-and-take process from the outside, as anyone who has tried to counsel others about their family relations knows.

The Court's published opinions are what matter. Most opinions are critical more for what the Court said in them than for who lined up behind them and how the lineup was achieved. A quite different situation often faces someone who attempts to assess Executive actions and explanations, as may be seen in the Pentagon Papers exposures. Often the writer of a Supreme Court opinion does not matter, whatever pride of authorship particular judges may have. The opinions themselves, rather than the reconstructions journalists may happen to piece together about how those opinions came to be, are more important for permitting us to understand what has happened and for giving everyone, including the Justices themselves, an indication of what to expect. Journalistic reconstructions do not make us more secure in our grasp of what has happened, but rather less secure. They not only promote second-guessing about what the Court intends by the opinions it does issue, but they also encourage others to dig up still more gossip and drafts which "oblige" us to revise further the public position we would otherwise rely upon. A kind of anarchy is thereby invited.

Such undocumented revelations as chance to be in this not uninteresting book are difficult to rely upon as authority for the serious investigator or analyst, if only because the revelations are so fragmentary and intermittent. Those things which *are* useful, such as the observations by the Justices as to the dubiousness of the position taken by counsel for the *New York Times* in the *Pentagon Papers* case (pp. 144–45), are usually already known by students of the Supreme Court independent of such revelations. Even the transcripts of records and the briefs filed with the Court are of limited interest and use to students of what the Court does. Consider by way of illustration a recent telephone conversation I had with a Federal Trade Commission regional director (a lawyer) who called from another city with various questions about matters he was working on. We talked for almost an hour, mostly about the implications of a dozen Supreme Court opinions in recent decades—opinions which bear upon the nature and extent of the Congress's commerce power and hence upon the Commission's regulatory power. Not once in the conversation did we consider it useful to mention the name of a single Justice (not that it would *not* be useful to consider the sources of opinions in some instances). I am sure both of us would have regarded it as a waste of time to draw upon any revelations, of the sort found in *The Brethren*, about how the cases we discussed happened to be decided. Such revelations, however realistic they may seem, do not address the serious questions one might have; indeed they are likely to distract one from them. They are like television news broadcasts that give people the illusion, much more so than do newspaper accounts, that they now know enough to understand what is going on, when in fact viewers might know far less than they did when "all" they did was read books and journals or simply relied for their opinions upon those who did read.

III

No doubt some critics have overreacted to *The Brethren*, but then they tend to be scholars who have invested a great deal in a respectful study of the Supreme Court. An old-fashioned response, but not an overreaction, was that of a law school teacher of mine, Malcolm P. Sharp, who recently died in his eighty-third year. He considered "dreadful" what the law clerks did in revealing to journalists what had gone on less than a decade before, in most cases, in the chambers of the Justices they had served. Other lawyers I have talked with have by and large agreed that the book is inaccurate and unfair and that it should not have been written. They are disturbed by the breach of confidentiality, especially on the part of the Justices' law clerks—the bright youngsters from the best law schools who are chosen to serve, three or four to a Justice, for a year or two at a time. These lawyers recognize that their own professional obligations would be seriously compromised if young lawyers in their offices should conduct themselves as did the clerks who served as informants to these journalists. I have already indicated the difficulties that journalists and editors would have if their associates and employees should routinely prove to be as unreliable as these law clerks have evidently been.

There should have been no serious question what the generally accepted standard of confidentiality is for Supreme Court clerks. The insistence upon anonymity by the law clerks who served as informants suggests that they knew they should not reveal what they did. It is clear throughout the book that the law clerks were aware of the standards to which they were being held. The Court had made clear to all the clerks that candor in judicial deliberation depends on confidentiality. The authors portray the clerks as sometimes dismayed by the Justices' concern about confidentiality and about the prying press. Yet, as we have seen, such confidentiality does not seem significantly different from that which journalists themselves use and rely upon. Any doubts these authors might have had about the importance, at least to the Court, of confidentiality should have been dispelled by their own touching account of Justice Black's insistence on his deathbed that certain of his papers be burned immediately (p. 157):

> Black's major concern, from the moment he entered the hospital, was to make sure that his most private papers, memos and conference notes were burned. Publication would inhibit the free exchange of ideas in the future. He felt that he had been treated unfairly in the late Justice Harold H. Burton's diary, in which Burton had written that Black at first resisted desegregation. Black had also been shattered by the biography of former [Chief] Justice Harlan Fiske Stone, written by Alpheus Thomas Mason. Black had told Burger that when he read Stone's biography [which had drawn upon papers left by Chief Justice Stone, who died unexpectedly, in office], he had discovered for the first time that Stone couldn't stand him. Black didn't want that kind of use made of his private papers.

The authors were aware of such sentiments, sentiments which argue that a law clerk should respect confidentiality at the very least during the tenure of his Justice's colleagues. Yet they went ahead with their exposés. Did they think about what they had written? What did these clerks know that judges like Hugo L. Black and generations of lawyers did not know? Or, should we ask, what had they forgotten about the conditions and consequences of civility that their predecessors had respected?

Critical to an understanding of *The Brethren* is a recognition of the authors' animus toward Chief Justice Burger. The book is largely about him and the way he handles, or tries to handle, the Court. I do not believe that the authors appreciate the extent to which the book is subordinated to their attack upon the Chief Justice. He is, no doubt, an easy target. One does not need *The Brethren* and its methods to become aware of the impression he all too often makes on his associates. All one needs is to talk to lawyers who have had dealings with him at bar association meetings. The book is more a critique of the Burger personality than it is a study of the work of the Court. We see the issues and controversies as they develop around a Chief Justice who has, besides his own perhaps insecure personality, two other things working against him: he was appointed by Mr. Nixon, whose doings have all become suspect, and he followed a Chief Justice who had the magic political touch. Consider the report on Chief Justice Warren written by Laurence Berns, a thoughtful observer of a 1960 oral argument in the Supreme Court (Anastaplo, *The Constitutionalist*, p. 364):

> Despite Justice Frankfurter's occasional displays of bad temper, I was impressed by the great dignity of the Court. The manly bearing of the Chief Justice contributed to this impression. His large size, handsomeness and apparent strength, combined with his kindly, pleasant and almost gentle in addition to his quite plain diction, would seem to have the effect of putting those facing the Bench at their ease and at the same time impressing them with the dignity of the Court. I thought him a kind of living argument for democracy.

The Brethren makes too much of Chief Justice Burger's interests and desires when, after all, he has but one vote. This misplaced emphasis comes from an attempt to simplify and dramatize. The problem is aggravated by the fact that the authors' more sensational revelations are limited by and large to the materials that malcontents of bad faith have chanced to make available to them. This is not to suggest that a Chief Justice is not important. But he too has to count votes and all too often it seems that this Chief Justice is not very good at counting.

In any event, it is far from clear why, if the Chief Justice is as bad as the authors regard him to be, the other Justices do not strip him of various critical powers as presiding officer in the Conference. No doubt, custom inhibits them to some extent, although there are indications that the Justices effectively control him when they have to. I suspect that the principal reason the Justices have not done more about the Chief Justice is that he is more an annoyance than he is a threat. Besides, he seems to me to come through, despite the vanity and befuddlement that the authors perhaps correctly report, as a rather decent, good-intentioned man and not without redeeming social value. For instance, he seems to sense how to treat colleagues who suffer afflictions. In this he is kinder, as well as more sensible, than the authors of *The Brethren*. Again and again, I have the impression that the authors do not truly appreciate critical implications of some of the things they report. Nor do they appreciate that their own highhanded way with confidential materials is far more questionable than anything they report the Chief Justice to have done.

IV

Anyone with access to lawyers who have been law clerks in any court can easily learn that it is a clear breach of trust to provide outsiders the texts of memoranda and draft opinions, especially relating to recent cases. So, one must ask, how reliable are the informants who betrayed their trust? Clerks who act as these clerks did cannot be relied upon for the moral sensibilities that are needed if one is to understand what went on among the Justices. Much the same should be said about any *Justice* who might have surreptitiously supplied these authors information that he should not have. Would not much of what such informants choose to report be tainted by a defective ethical sense? Furthermore, how reliable are researchers who develop and exploit such betrayals of trust? After all, many of the critical revelations and interpretations found in this book do depend on moral judgments, especially when the authors assess the Justices. But does it not require someone of sound moral judgment to assess serious matters adequately?

I have suggested as have others before me that *The Brethren* is largely about Chief Justice Burger. It is also obvious to many that the book is primarily from the perspective of law clerks. What is said is presented from a clerk's-eye view, on the part both of the informants and of the authors themselves. The authors are impressed by the bright, self-important young men and (now) women who receive these coveted appointments. But, it should be remembered, these are inexperienced youngsters, usually in their late twenties, and what do they really know anyhow? How can such youngsters properly assess the moral and political, as well as the strictly legal and constitutional, issues confronting the Justices? What such youngsters know is, for the most part, what they have just learned in law school. This all too often means that they are imbued with the prevailing prejudices of their peers. Journalists do tend to be impressed by such "stars," but, then, journalists in this Country do not tend to be well-educated.

The clerks, as presented in *The Brethren*—in other words, the clerks as they allowed themselves to be quoted and described, come across as presumptuous and arrogant. Such people are hardly likely to be able to see or report serious matters properly. Much of one's interest in this investigation collapses if one is not very much concerned with or impressed by the opinions, dismay and anger of inexperienced youth. The most vigorous moral judgments reported to have been expressed in the Supreme Court Building are, it seems, primarily those of the clerks. When the Justices express moral judgments, it also seems, they do so primarily upon the prodding of their clerks. One must wonder how Justices get to where they are without their clerks to show them the way.

But then one must not make too much of law clerks. That should be left to the likes of Mr. Woodward and Mr. Armstrong. The decisive comment here may be that of Justice Rehnquist, who had himself been a law clerk in his youth: he called the "bad mouthing" of the Chief Justice that he heard in his own chambers "sport for law clerks." (p. 413) Several reviewers have been reminded of the observation that no man is a hero to his valet, not because the master may not be a hero, but because the other *is* a valet.

V

I have suggested that a certain moral stature is needed if one is to deal properly with moral questions. A certain intellectual competence is similarly needed if one is to deal properly with legal and constitutional questions.

The Brethren tells us more that is significant about journalism (its interests, standards, and limitations) than about the Supreme Court. It is often instructive to see how someone understands what and how other people understand.

The limitations of journalists should be evident to the careful reader of the press. They are notoriously inadequate when they report what courts do. This is partly because they usually do not or cannot do the homework required, and partly because they deal only with the occasional controversial case, and then only at the last minute when a decision is announced. Journalists do not have a reliable sense of what is routine in the law; nor do they study opinions carefully. Even when they do read the current opinion being reported, they usually do not know much about the critical opinions that preceded the one immediately under consideration. (It might help train journalists to be sensible about judicial matters if newspapers would devote a full page to court news every day—if, that is, political journalists were obliged to become as familiar with what does, and does not, happen in and around courts as sports writers are with what does, and does not, happen on and around a baseball field.)

Journalists today appeal to an all-too-human interest in what is curious and unusual. They tend to be unreliable: a lawyer or a politician is, I am afraid, more apt to keep a promise than an editor. This is perhaps in part because the journalist is so much surer than a lawyer or a politician is apt to be that he is on the side of the angels. Journalists tend to be unaware of their inadequacies. Thus, a patronizing tone is evident throughout *The Brethren*. One consequence of these authors' limitations is that they can inadvertently hurt those whom they want to help: in some ways, the Justices who come off worst in this book are (besides Chief Justice Burger) Justices Douglas, Brennan, and Marshall, those whom the authors evidently hold (along with Chief Justice Warren and Justice Black) in the highest esteem. Truly, it can be said of these authors that they know not what they do.

One of the things they *do* is jeopardize future relations among the Justices. The authors indicate in their introduction that they do not consider current cases, lest they affect their outcome. But they are not as careful about current Justices as they claim to be about current cases. The consequences of public revelations about what the Justices think of each other are evident from the book itself. We should be reminded of the effect upon Justice Black when he learned what Chief Justice Stone had "really" thought of him. Yet the authors publish cruel, or at least callous, comments supposedly made by the Justices about one another. Are the authors not aware of what they are doing? Or is it that they have done a lot of work digging up these barbs, filtered for the most part through the psyches *and vocabularies* of unprincipled law clerks, and they want to profit from their work?

One can be sure that the Justices soon located the references to themselves in *The Brethren*. Many of the comments by their colleagues were no doubt laughed off. But some of them will rankle. In a few cases, personal and professional relations may be permanently affected. The authors recognize that there is a tradition among the Court of "complimenting the 'learned Judge' before ripping him to shreds." They also recognize the purpose of this practice: "The tradition help[s] keep disputes on an impersonal plane, or at least maintain[s] the facade that battles [are] legal and not to be taken personally." (p. 215) Nevertheless, the authors can report that on one occasion a Justice hurriedly left the scene, lest he burst out laughing at the foolishness of a colleague. (p. 269) Both Justices, whose names are given, are still on the Court. Does it serve a useful purpose to have one Justice learn that another found him laughable? This is a mild illustration. Much harsher instances could be cited. Mr. Armstrong has been reported as saying, "It's not going to change the Justices' relationships. These guys already know what they think about each other." (*Time*, December 17, 1979, p. 79) This assumes that it does not matter whether another's private opinion about oneself is published or not.

One need not believe that the Court is entitled to extraordinary consideration in order to recognize that there is something dubious about this sort of thing. One does not see *published* such contemporary assessments of members of Congress or of members of the press by their colleagues, even though comparable information *is* available, and even though members of Congress or members of the press do not depend as much as the Justices do on being able to work together intimately and for years at a time.

All this bears upon a question that is vital to our republican regime, and that is whether we can control through social, not legal, institutions the passions we are subject to. Developing such control is a special problem for intellectuals, especially since they have been led by the Enlightenment to believe that the truth cannot do any harm, that exposure of everything public figures say and do is almost a public duty.

We are told in *The Brethren* of a Justice who withdrew his name from consideration for the position of Chief Justice. Why had he done so? Because, it is reported by the authors, he "had a private matter that might be embarrassing"—not a scandal or anything improper, but a difficulty in his family. His wife had a drinking problem. Would that come out if he were nominated? Was it fair to his family? Would he have to wonder whether his private business might appear in the newspapers, if only in a gossip column? (p. 16) He did not have to worry; it would not appear in a gossip column. Instead, it was put by supposedly conscientious authors and publishers in a best seller for the whole country to read! (President Nixon, when he talked with this Justice about the Chief Justiceship, did not seek or receive such information. Must not this Justice be the ultimate source of this revelation in the book [if it is accurate]? And if so, of what else in addition? That is, one *must* wonder about the sensibleness of various of the Justices in this affair.)

How does one understand such obtuseness on the part of these authors? How does one assess a profession that can nurture, reward and cherish such professionals? After all, these men *have* long been associated with one of the finest newspapers in the Country. What understanding of things legal, moral and political do these journalists have that they can risk sowing devastation as they do? Is not something wrong with their training, with the tastes of their respectable readers, and with the education of the eminently successful young lawyers whom they draw upon as their principal sources? Perhaps we should be grateful that we are again reminded so dramatically of some of the things that are questionable about the brightest and best among us. We are reminded as well, and this may be far more important, of the intellectual limitations and moral pitfalls of legal realism.

VI

A thorough review of *The Brethren* should include an assessment of what is said about some of the Supreme Court cases described at some length by the authors. Such an assessment would throw further light on the intellectual equipment and the moral standards of legal scholars and journalists such as these authors.

The book describes cases dealing with busing orders in segregation matters, with abortion, and with the death penalty. The authors' positions here are the conventional liberal ones. They do not truly appreciate that a reasonable man can find busing destructive of neighborhood schools, that a reasonable man can regard our widespread recourse to abortion as a moral catastrophe, and that a reasonable man can find merit in a community's conscientious use of the death penalty.

Similarly, the authors are always clear about what the correct answer is in obscenity cases. The danger to freedom of speech and to discussion of political issues, posed at this time by direct suppression, is magnified by them. They do not see that freedom of speech may be undermined if character is corrupted and if permissiveness and lack of discipline should prevail. They are quite self-righteous here, seemingly unaware that citizens may sincerely believe that constitutional government requires a healthy moral community if it is to endure and prosper.

Particularly revealing is the authors' assumption that of course freedom of speech should permit an entrepreneur to display on an outdoor movie screen, for an entire neighborhood to see, what he chooses to show "inside" to consenting customers, even though the material thus displayed was not so long ago reserved for the most intimate privacy. I say that this is "particularly revealing" because the aggressively intrusive outdoor movie screen is a fitting symbol of what the authors themselves do in this book.

Finally, it would be useful to examine at length the authors' treatment of the Watergate tapes controversy. The authors are so intent on showing how Chief Justice Burger had to be corralled by his colleagues in the disposition of that controversy that they do not properly notice how well the Justices did work together. Their account of the Watergate tapes case should remind us that early drafts and passing comments often mean little with respect to the final product. The authors, in their effort to show Mr. Nixon's privilege fittingly curtailed, fail to notice what there was that was dubious about the insistence upon making public what would once have been considered confidential conversations in the Oval Office. It remains to be seen whether the cause of liberty and constitutional government gained more than it lost by the determined effort to topple Mr. Nixon.

Space does not permit further discussion here of the busing, abortion, death penalty, and obscenity cases dealt with in *The Brethren*. Such cases are more complicated than these authors believe and their superficial grasp of the issues makes it difficult for them to see and report properly what the Court did in these cases. The technical legal issues dealt with in the cases commented upon in *The Brethren* are often beyond the competence of the authors. Reviewers have pointed out numerous errors.

VII

Nor does space permit an extended discussion of still another problem raised in the book, and that is how the *entire* Watergate controversy (not just the question of tapes) is to be regarded. Was the political trauma we were subjected to for several years good for us? Was it not a nonviolent equivalent of the Kennedy Assassination, from which we have yet to recover fully? Would a more responsible press have allowed the Watergate burglary issue to be dealt with by the Justice Department and by Congress in their own ways, which probably would have meant allowing a chastened Richard Nixon to serve out his second term? If Mr. Woodward brought to his Watergate investigation the limited moral sensitivity and dubious intellectual standards he exhibits in *The Brethren*, then the fashionable case against Mr. Nixon may be in need of some revision.

Some of my sentiments in this book review were anticipated in a memorandum I prepared upon the publication in the press, in 1976, of the more sensational passages in the Bob Woodward and Carl Bernstein book, *The Final Days*. The full text of my 1976 *Final Days* memorandum, entitled "More Bad News from Mr. Nixon," follows (it was published in an abridged version in the *Chicago Sun-Times*, April 12, 1976, p. 38, with an editorial comment on p. 39):

> The recent publication in the press of substantial excerpts from a dramatic book on "the final days" of the Nixon Administration should remind us how much Richard M. Nixon has contributed to the corruption of the American people, so much so that it has become virtually impossible for us to deal fairly with him. The passions he shamelessly exploited and aroused have evidently made it impossible for us to maintain a sense of proportion with respect to him. There is something about the man which does bring out the worst in us.

We should have been, for his good as well as ours, far more critical of Mr. Nixon on his way up—and far more compassionate toward him on his way down. I myself particularly regret that some of those who have enjoyed their hot pursuit of Mr. Nixon in recent years were not available to help us "contain" him and his allies a generation ago—at a time when constitutional government in the United States was truly threatened.

The measure of our corruption may be seen not only in the extent and brutality of the public probing into the psyches and intimate relations of Mr. Nixon and those around him but also in the general assumption that the press is entitled (if not even obliged) to expose to immediate view the various episodes we have had thrust upon us. Conscientious publishers and editors now seem trapped by practices and expectations which permit, if they do not even demand, more and more uninhibited delving into what would once have been thought to be strictly private matters. At the same time, the harassment of Daniel Schorr for his handling (as a reporter) of classified documents is inadequately challenged by the press.

There has been for me personally, in the recent sensationalized exposures of Mr. Nixon and his associates, something of the shock I experienced in 1969 as a spectator during those grim days of the Chicago Conspiracy Trial when a self-righteous judge was permitted to bind and gag a defendant before our very eyes. In such matters, the aberrations of a particular man (whether a judge or an author or an editor) are not as significant as the fact that he is allowed by a careless community to behave as he does.

A self-governing community grounded in decency and a sense of fair play is one which lets it be known, in an authoritative manner, "We cannot have *that*." The principal safeguard to be relied upon in keeping the press in line is not official censorship or prosecution but rather the guidance of an informed and firm public opinion, that vigilant guidance which in turn depends upon the sensitivity and prudence of those who shape and monitor public opinion.

It would, on the other hand, be foolish to insist that there is nothing useful to be learned from "inside" accounts of the last days of the Nixon Administration, even when those accounts have been distorted for commercial exploitation. One can confirm, for example, that the power of a President is severely limited by the men upon whom he necessarily depends, so much so that things are seldom as bad (or, for that matter, as good) as they may seem from the outside.

But, the problem remains, what price have we had to pay for whatever useful information we have received? For one thing, we have had ratified for us by the recent revelations still another set of unprecedented infringements upon personal privacy, and in such a way as to whet the public appetite for much more of the same. The vindictive probings and destructive Red-baiting of the House UnAmerican Activities Committee, which Mr. Nixon encouraged and profited from a generation ago, *sometimes* seem rather tame by comparison with that which has been done to him and his associates in recent years. Certainly, the domestic Communist conspiracy seemed to me as exaggerated then as the threat to constitutional government and civil liberties now said to have been posed by the Nixon Administration.

However that may be, human anguish and a sense of helplessness, as well as a pervasive vulgarity, all too often result from the kind of callous journalism to which we have become accustomed. We will, unless we make deliberate efforts to reconsider our principles and to retrain our appetites, deteriorate even further in these respects—and we run the risk as well of an eventual unthinking reaction which takes the form of a dangerous suppression of freedom of the press.

No doubt, the common good may occasionally call for such painful exposures as we have recently seen. But does not our current addiction to the political gossip which we reward so lavishly deprive us of serious political discourse? Such gossip—an indulgence in political pornography—is an unhealthy diversion from that vital discussion of public issues for which our freedom of the press is primarily intended.

This diversion has meant, among other things, that the genuine accomplishments, as well as the inevitable failures, of the Nixon Administration are not likely to be properly appreciated for another generation. Thus, our growing concern with trivia, including the trivia of Mr. Nixon's complex psyche and of the mechanics of the ouster of a President, has prevented us from making the sensible assessment we require and are entitled to make if we are to understand and (if need be) to correct what really happened during that unfortunate Presidency.

I have discussed elsewhere the reservations I have had about the way the ruthless campaign for Mr. Nixon's impeachment was conducted. The genuine impeachable offenses of the past decade or so have had to do with our involvement in and the conduct of the Indo-Chinese War. Whether it would have been prudent for Congress to pursue *those* offenses by impeachment is, of course, another question. (Would such a pursuit have torn the country apart, and perhaps too late to affect the conduct of *that* war? The War Powers Resolution may be a sensible compromise between such an impeachment and doing nothing.)

I believe, if only because *we* do know better, that our ungenerous treatment of President Nixon has been shabbier than his actual treatment of his domestic "enemies." I also believe that there is considerable merit in the observation reportedly made by young David Eisenhower to his desperate father-in-law (on the eve of his resignation), "It's been my feeling that we're not as innocent as we said, or as guilty as they said."

It has been heartening to notice in recent weeks that many people who never liked Richard Nixon at all are nevertheless deeply troubled by the presumptuous liberties now being taken with him and hence with our sense of fair play. It is salutary, it seems to me, to assure such people that their instincts are sound and their sentiments healthy.

I return in closing to a theme I have already touched upon both in this review of *The Brethren* and in my 1976 memorandum on *The Final Days*. The exploitation of the private and confidential has as one of its consequences the subversion of the public—that very public in whose interest such unprecedented exposures are justified. The worst tastes of the community are thereby catered to. I am reminded of the Athenian multitude which shouted, whenever deprived of anything by customs and laws, that it would be terrible if the people should not be permitted to do whatever they wished.

It is salutary in this connection to be reminded as well of what was said in 1979 at a St. John's College memorial service for a prudent refugee to this Country:

> [H]e was concerned for the land of his refuge. What troubled him has been called many things: pseudo-sophistication, permissiveness, moral decline. His own way of putting it was much simpler, barbarism and, most dangerous of all for America, hedonism. What seemed to bother him was the fact that when people cease to observe and impose limits on themselves, it becomes natural to think more about having limits imposed by others from above.

We can be grateful to our not uninteresting authors that they have reminded us of the constant need we Americans have to impose limits upon ourselves, and especially to curb *by the moral force of an informed public opinion* those who would cater to our baser desires. We should take care in our responses to the opinion-makers of our day that we not permit a cheap realism to be substituted for a noble awareness.

20

SPEECH AND LAW IN A FREE COUNTRY

The quarrel between the ancients and the moderns concerns eventually, and perhaps even from the beginning, the status of "individuality." [Edmund] Burke himself was still too deeply imbued with the spirit of "sound antiquity" to allow the concern with individuality to overpower the concern with virtue.

LEO STRAUSS

I

The hero of Franklyn S. Haiman's book on the First Amendment is the Chief Justice of the United States, Warren E. Burger. To be sure, the Chief Justice is used in this book, perhaps more than any other member of the United States Supreme Court in recent decades, to represent an unenlightened and even reactionary point of view. But if one should have fundamental objections to Professor Haiman's freewheeling interpretations of the First Amendment, then one can come to respect the Chief Justice as a champion of common sense and of the American constitutional tradition.

Upon assessing Mr. Haiman's notions about the First Amendment, one may even be moved to question not only what is said by him against the Chief Justice, but also what is said by him on behalf of the American Civil Liberties Union (of which Mr. Haiman has been national secretary and by which he has obviously been influenced in the development of his own opinions). Just as the Chief Justice can usefully be considered the hero of this book, so can the A.C.L.U. be considered its sinister spirit, despite that

---

This essay was published, with extensive notes, in 3 *Windsor [Ontario] Yearbook of Access to Justice* 436–64 (1983). Appended to it was Essay No. 2–A, above.

The citations in this essay are, unless otherwise indicated, to Franklyn S. Haiman, *Speech and Law in a Free Society* (Chicago: University of Chicago Press, 1981).

The epigraph is taken from Leo Strauss, *Natural Right and History* (Chicago: University of Chicago Press, 1953), p. 323.

organization's tacit reliance upon Divine Providence in the affairs of the American people.

We need not dwell on the Chief Justice's opinions. Issue can reasonably be taken with some of them, as with the opinions of any judge. What the Chief Justice has had to say about loyalty oaths seems to me dubious. (pp. 344–45) But there does seem to be something sensible in what he suggests about the prerogatives claimed by the press (which should be no more than those of any citizen) (pp. 12, 386), about his concern lest "absurd and immature antic[s]" be mistaken for principled stands (p. 16), about his resistance to the liberation of obscene impulses (pp. 97–99, 171), about his "sermon on etiquette" and his argument for civility (which Mr. Haiman puts down) (pp. 125–26), about his suggestion that people should be protected from the development among them of debasing attitudes (p. 165), and about his reliance upon "unprovable assumptions" (which *are* often the dictates of common sense) (p. 176).

Mr. Haiman does have a good word to say about the Chief Justice here and there, particularly with respect to his endorsement of open trials (pp. 112, 375–76) and with respect to his reservations about the statutory requirement that even quite small contributions to political causes be disclosed (pp. 357, 361). But, by and large, Mr. Haiman's usual approach to these matters reflects the tendency of liberals, at least in the United States, to give up the cause of old-fashioned morality to the Right.

One must wonder whether there is much of a future for liberalism in the Twenty-first Century, not because of what conservatives are doing to liberalism, but because of what it is doing to itself. I have nothing really new to say on this occasion about all this; rather, I presume to remind readers of what many others before me have said and to apply what has already been said to some of the immediate problems in constitutional law suggested by Mr. Haiman's often doctrinaire extrapolation from contemporary liberal opinions about the proper relation between the individual and his community.

II

There is to be found in Mr. Haiman's book a detailed and hence useful survey of First Amendment issues, both as they have arisen in litigation and as they appear in other government action. This survey is provided us by a non-lawyer long prominent in A.C.L.U. activities. His interests as a Professor of Communications at Northwestern University are reflected in how he approaches problems of language and meaning: he is much more concerned with communication and individual self-expression than with political discourse and the common good. Since Mr. Haiman's book, which has been well received, does represent a significant aspect of contemporary liberalism, it should be instructive to consider at length what he has to say.

Indications of both the argument and the tenor of this book may be conveniently given my reader by drawing upon passages in which Mr. Haiman sums up what he says. I attempt in this essay to allow Mr. Haiman to speak for himself, but in such a way as to reveal, with a minimum of commentary by me on the long passages reproduced from his book, what is dubious about the all-too-fashionable liberal position he represents so well. He announces at the outset (p. 6),

> It is the purpose of this book to explore some of the most troublesome problems involving freedom of speech, attempting to bring to bear upon them a more careful analysis than has commonly been applied in the past, and to evolve more consistent, predictable, and principled criteria for dealing with particular cases. Greater clarity, coherence, and service to our ultimate goals, as we confront free speech controversies, will be the aim of this endeavor.

Mr. Haiman concludes the introductory part of his book with this statement of his intention (p. 40):

> In all of these cases, whether the Supreme Court placed reliance on a clear-and-present-danger test, a categorization of speech into protected and unprotected classes, an integral-part-of-illegal-conduct criterion, a balancing doctrine, a time and place regulation, or an incitement-to-lawless-action formulation, the determination was made that certain kinds of competing interests can justify restrictions on communication. It shall be the purpose of the remainder of this book to examine each of the claims that are put forth as potential competitors to freedom of expression and to assess the validity of those claims in light of the long-range goals of the First Amendment and the basic values of an open society.

The following two parts of the book are described in this fashion by Mr. Haiman (p. 131):

> Part 2 of this book has dealt with possible harms to people that may result from unrestrained communication about them to others. Part 3 is concerned with modes of expression that are said to be injurious to those who are on the receiving end of the communication. It explores the kinds of harms that are thought to occur and assesses the justifications that are offered for restraints.

By and large, both the kinds of harms and the justifications for restraints are minimized by Mr. Haiman, just as he had concluded Part 2 with the observation (p. 127),

> We run the risk that journalists may sometimes act in grossly irresponsible ways and that serious criminal offenses may go unpunished as a result. But these costs must be regarded as necessary and tolerable if we are to be serious about the First Amendment.

A fair indication of Mr. Haiman's general approach to these matters may be gotten from his chapter, "Lies and Misrepresentations" (pp. 206–7):

> It bears repeating, as we conclude this chapter, that the arguments which have been presented on behalf of a narrowly limited role for the law with respect to deceptive communication do not spring from any feelings of moral acceptance toward calculated falsehoods nor from any innocence about the harm that they can do to other people. If uncontradicted and believed, they are a serious infringement on the freedom of choice of the listener, and it is that very freedom which the First Amendment was designed to preserve. Yet, as we have seen, there are good reasons for moving cautiously in imposing legal restraints. We must not invest our government with the power to declare what is "true" and "false" in the realm of political, social and religious *beliefs*, and we must diligently segregate the utterance of beliefs from empirically falsifiable statements of fact. Where there is "time to expose through discussion the falsehood and fallacies"—in other words, where there has been a call to think bad thoughts rather than a direct inducement to engage in financially or physically harmful acts—and where there are people with the motivation and channels of communication to respond, we should opt for that remedy rather than for reliance on the law.

At the heart of this approach may be the assumption that what is *true* and *false* "in the realm of political, social, and religious beliefs" is something arbitrary, something to be declared (and kept within quotation marks) rather than to be *discovered*.

Further implications of this approach may be seen in the following passage (pp. 232–33):

> Just as the law, in my opinion, has been properly invoked to prohibit genuine threats against life and limb, so it has been appropriately wary of intervention when it comes to psychological pressures. Reprehensible as it may be from an ethical point of view for human beings to subject one another to the kind of emotional exploitation and social pressures that are so widespread in our so-

ciety, there is simply no way to draw an unwavering line between legally acceptable and unacceptable "coercive persuasion." . . . There are simply too many imponderables of the human psyche in the delicate balance between voluntary acceptance and involuntary compliance for the heavy hand of the law to be a useful instrument of adjudication. Better that these things be left to exposure, analysis, condemnation, counterpropaganda, psychotherapy, and education than to government censorship.

It would seem that the community, through its government, simply has "too many imponderables of the human psyche" to contend with if it should attempt to adjudicate among contending claims in these matters, no matter how widespread "emotional exploitation and social pressures" may be or become "in our society."

Whatever the imponderables in these matters may be, Mr. Haiman evidently does not consider *himself* to be as unknowing as he believes the community is obliged to be. He can present the argument of his book in this forthright manner (pp. 425–26):

> The central purpose of this book has been to seek a coherent set of guiding principles for the resolution of conflicts between freedom of expression and the competing interests with which it may clash—principles rooted in a keener understanding of the communication process and a more vigorous commit ent to the values of a free society than have characterized the adjudication of these issues in the past. It was not expected that a perfect philosophy could be found which would provide ready answers to the closest questions that might arise. It was hoped, however, that a careful review and critical analysis of each of the areas in which serious controversy has occurred would uncover common threads that might be woven into a sturdier fabric of First Amendment doctrine than has yet been fashioned by our legal system. What follows is a summary of that quest.

> We began with the proposition that one must look at the particular context in which acts of communication occur in order to assess the appropriateness of limitations on expression, thus rejecting the view that there are certain categories of speech which, by definition, are always out of bounds. We also assumed that the First Amendment applies to a broad range of symbolic conduct, whether oral or written, rational or emotive, verbal or nonverbal. Even behaviors which are not normally engaged in for communicative purposes were nominated as potential candidates for First Amendment protection when functioning symbolically.

> Four basic principles have emerged from this study:

>   I. Unless the harm done by an act of communication is direct, immediate,

irreparable, and of a serious material nature, the remedy in a free society should be more speech. The law is an inappropriate tool for dealing with expression which produces mental distress or whose targets are the beliefs and values of an audience.

II. Unless deprived of free choice by deception, physical coercion, or an impairment of normal capacities, individuals in a free society are responsible for their own behavior. They are not objects which can be *triggered* into action by symbolic stimuli but human beings who *decide* how they will respond to the communication they see and hear.

III. So long as there is a free marketplace of ideas, where the widest possible range of information and alternatives is available, individuals will be the best judges of their own interests. The law is properly used to enrich and expand that communications marketplace and to insure that it remains an open system.

IV. Government in a free society is the servant of the people and its powers should not be used to inhibit, distort, or dominate public discourse. There must be compelling justification whenever the government requires unwilling communication of its people or withholds information in its possession from them.

Mr. Haiman's "four basic principles," which are grounded in the physical (or in an implicit materialism), are further explained by him (pp. 426–28):

The first principle, as we have seen, necessitates abandonment of the law of defamation except for those circumstances in which a communicator of allegedly defamatory material refuses to disseminate a reply or, in those rare instances, like the eve of an election, where calculated falsehoods about a candidate may do damage before there is time to refute them. Otherwise we should operate on the assumption that the right to reply to alleged defamations will be a sufficient remedy in a society whose members have learned to listen critically and with suspended judgment to personal attacks.

. . . The second principle calls for a substantial departure from our current understandings of the respective responsibilities of communicators and their audiences. It holds only the members of an audience liable for any violence or other illegal behavior to which they may be provoked or solicited, except in those circumstances where the inciting communicator coerces or deceives them into taking the action in question. In such cases, the speaker, having presumed to take control over the lives of others, must accept the responsibility which goes with that power. . . .

In a modern mass media-oriented society such as ours there are powerful tendencies in the direction of homogenization of the marketplace of ideas and the presentation of a monochromatic view of the world. In order for there to be the diversity of communication which is necessary for people to make free and informed choices, the third principle contemplates affirmative action to counterbalance these pressures toward uniformity. To begin with, the law must be uncompromising in its protection of the right of nonconformists, as well as others, to disseminate their views in public places so long as the primary function of those places is not substantially impaired. Inconvenience, annoyance, or offense to aesthetic sensibilities should not be sufficient justifications to prohibit expression in the public forum. . . . Diversity must be a guiding principle for the operation of public schools and public libraries as well as for the allocation of public moneys to the support of quasi-private cultural, informational, and scholarly enterprises. . . .

The fourth principle recognizes that the government of a large and technologically advanced nation, although perhaps originally designed to facilitate the self-fulfillment of its citizens, develops inclinations to subvert the free marketplace of communication which is essential to that purpose. The "servant of the people" acquires an appetite for power which, if unchecked, transforms the servant into master.

A challenging note is struck by Mr. Haiman as he concludes the argument of his book (p. 429):

All of these [four] principles require a strong and vigilant citizenry for their faithful implementation. The regime which they envision is not one for the squeamish or apathetic. It is not for those who lack the courage of their convictions. It is not for those, described long ago by Thomas Jefferson, as "timid men who prefer the calm of despotism to the boisterous sea of liberty."

Vital to a proper examination of the Haiman argument, which *is* that of the aggressively permissive liberal today, must be a consideration of what is truly "a strong and vigilant citizenry" and how such a citizenry is to be developed, employed, and preserved. One must wonder as well whether the licensing of virtually all irresponsible talk and the sometimes unnatural restraint upon vigorous social responses to such talk are not likely to lead to a general debasement of the language by which a competent citizenry is shaped and sometimes inspired.

III

What Mr. Haiman's principles mean in practice may be gathered from a half-dozen passages drawn upon in this section of my essay which fairly illustrate his approach to these matters. What is significant in various of these instances is that there should even be any First Amendment question at all with respect to highly questionable *conduct*. Mr. Haiman tends to be remarkably open to the "symbolic speech" justifications that are sometimes advanced here, if only because his concern is ultimately more with liberation of individual expression than with pursuit of the common good (insofar as these two ends are to be distinguished).

Consider, for example, the array of activities collected in the following paragraph (p. 26):

> The problem in dealing with nonverbal communication from a legal perspective lies not in the question of *whether* the First Amendment applies to such behavior, but *when*. Clearly a march or a silent vigil, either in honor of the war dead or in anger against racial discrimination, is a symbolic event entitled to First Amendment protection, but what about a lunch counter sit-in or lying down in front of a troop train? No one would question that a lone picketer, walking up and down on the sidewalk in front of the White House, is engaged in the exercise of freedom of speech, but what about a union picket line that effectively seals off entry to a store or factory? The U. S. Supreme Court has had little trouble recognizing a black armband or the refusal to salute an American flag as First Amendment behavior, but it has had a great deal more difficulty extending the concept of speech to protect the public burning of a draft card or alleged misuses and "desecrations" of the flag. Federal and state courts all over the country have been trying to figure out for several years whether wearing a beard or long hair to a public school or a public job is a constitutional right, and whether topless dancing in a night club or scenes of sexual intercourse in a movie are a part of our system of freedom of expression.

I dare say that the framers of the Bill of Rights would have had to spend far less time than Mr. Haiman has spent in trying to figure out whether most of these activities qualify for First Amendment protection as "symbolic speech." For them, only the silent vigil, the black armband, and the lone picketer might have *raised* freedom of speech questions. This is not to deny, of course, that it may be *just* to do many things which the First Amendment itself should not be expected to protect.

The same considerations apply to still another array, evidently of hard cases, provided us by Mr. Haiman (p. 33):

> Almost any activity that is ordinarily engaged in for its own sake can be converted . . . into a "message to the world." The length or style of one's hair, or one's state of dress or undress, can be designed for personal pleasure and comfort, or they can advertise an attitude or a culture. One can sit at a lunch counter just to eat, or to make a point, or perhaps both. One can urinate, defecate, or spit in order to eliminate substances from the body, or one can perform any of those acts as a sign of anger and contempt for their

target. One can refuse to pay taxes just to cheat the government, or because one does not wish to support government policies that are alien to one's point of view.

> Ordinarily digging a grave is for the purpose of burying someone. But when [protesters] dug a grave in the front yard of [the Chevy Chase home of the] Secretary of Defense . . . in September 1976 and mounted signs beside it reading "The Future of our Children" and "Life on Earth," they were trying to communicate a political message . . . Most arson and murder spring from some private impulse and serve some private end. However, the burning of a school that is about to be desegregated or the assassination of a Martin Luther King, Jr., may be an attempt, tragically misguided as it is, to make a statement on a public matter.

One must wonder to what extent people may be misled into believing, because of the tendency of some liberals to regard all too many deeds as forms of expression, that such acts as are referred to here are indeed "statement[s] on a public matter."

Mr. Haiman's principles lead him to argue "that absolute bans on all demonstrations at courthouses are unjustifiably overbroad and that a distinction should be made between those that, in the particular circumstances, pose a real danger of intimidation and those that do not. Such a standard would provide adequate protection of the judicial system against mob rule and, at the same time, preserve the legitimate First Amendment interests that may be implicated in a courthouse demonstration." (p. 103) But here too there is the risk of misleading people into believing that since some courthouse demonstrations are permissible, why then their own must surely be, since *their* cause is just, etc.

If, as Mr. Haiman suggests, people would be "more enlightened" (or is it more callous?), then various of our traditional restrictions on both words and deeds could be relaxed. Consider, for example, how Mr. Haiman discusses whether newspapers should be permitted to publish "truthful information contained in official court records open to public inspection" (pp. 70–71):

> A judgment that the victim's name is not a necessary element of a news story about a rape seems plausible on its face, yet it must be recognized as a proposition that depends on one's perspective and on the circumstances of particular cases. . . . How can we be certain in almost any case that knowledge of the name of a rape victim might not be of critical value to somebody? That possibility must be weighed in the balance against the alleged values of nondisclosure. [It has been pointed out] that a primary motive for suppression of rape victims' names is what [is called] the "gallantry justification"—presumably resulting from an attitude in our culture that a woman who has been

raped has been disgraced. . . . The notion that it is a disgrace to have been raped provides the basis, also, for what [is called] the "law enforcement justification" for non-disclosure of rape victims' names. The theory here is that women who have been the victims of rape will not come forward to lodge a complaint with law enforcement officials unless they feel assured that their names will not be revealed publicly.

Mr. Haiman then adds (p. 71),

Neither the "gallantry justification" nor the "law enforcement justification" would carry any weight, of course, if our culture had a more enlightened attitude toward the victims of rape. We certainly do not regard it as shameful to be the target of any other kind of physical assault, and personally knowing people who have been attacked may produce a livelier concern about the problems of crime. It is also quite possible that the hush-hush sentiment which now prevails about the names of rape victims is itself a large contributor to the stigma attached to those victims, and that less secretive treatment of the topic would help to bring about a more understanding cultural norm.

To argue as Mr. Haiman does here may be to assume that the deep hurt that rape victims now feel is due primarily to how they are regarded by others, that a woman's sense of a profound violation of personality is not intrinsic to what has been done to her, independent of who knows about it or how it is described. His approach here may be very much affected by what he has to say generally about the relation between words and deeds. He seems to regard language as far more malleable than have traditional students of the subject. However that may be, the rape victim usually does not want to find her name bandied about in the mass media, either before multitudes whom she does not know or before those few who already know of her affliction. In either case, she is likely to feel sullied, further demeaned, and otherwise exploited. Fancy talk about "a more enlightened attitude" and "a more understanding cultural norm" is not likely to ease the pain of still another violation, this time by the community at large in the name of freedom of expression. (Had it not been a perverse "freedom of expression" that the rapist had resorted to?) The few cases in which the victim's name might be "of critical value to somebody" are to be compared with the many cases in which that name should not truly matter to the public.

Are we indeed unable as a community to identify and thereupon to reduce, if not altogether to eliminate, obvious assaults upon one another's sensibilities in sensitive circumstances? Still another illustration from Mr. Haiman's book indicates what permissiveness with respect to these matters comes down to (p. 138):

As with so many other aspects of our system of free expression, there is a painful price that must be paid. This can best be illustrated by an incident that occurred in connection with the funeral of Eleanor Roosevelt at Hyde Park, New York, in 1962. Two men, who were arrested after telling a policeman they intended to picket that funeral carrying signs hostile to Mrs. Roosevelt, pled guilty and were sentenced to ninety days in jail for violation of a New York penal statute prohibiting any act that outrages public decency. Here was a situation where speech that would indisputably have been protected by the First Amendment at any other time or place was put outside the umbrella of that protection because the site chosen for the expression would have made it deeply offensive to the sensibilities of the mourners on the scene. No other harm was alleged. It was solely the context of the communication, interacting with the particular occasion, that placed it beyond the pale of our societal mores.

As tasteless and repulsive as the proposed picketing in that situation would have been to most of those present—and one recoils emotionally at the thought of it—we must ask ourselves whether ninety days in jail is the appropriate response for a free society to make. Can we not rely instead on the faith that the common sense of most people and the informal workings of social pressure will make such occurrences rare? And when they do happen, can we not wince and take them in our stride rather than using the law to shield our sensibilities from what we perceive as the world's ugliness? For what is ugly to one may not be ugly to another, and we run too great a risk of suppressing ideas and feelings of which we should be made aware when we allow conformist impulses to place certain kinds of communication "out of sight and out of mind."

We should notice the use here of *perceive* and the suggestion as well that ugliness is merely in the eye of the beholder. Is not this too an instance of misapplied sophistication? Should not the impassioned protester be aware, or be made to become aware, that there are sensibilities entitled to respect? What need is there to permit vituperative expressions and to exact "a painful price" on such occasions as funerals, whether the person being buried is a widely-respected humanitarian or a much-detested scoundrel? What need, indeed, when it is obvious that the expressions in question "would indisputably have been protected by the First Amendment at any other time or place"? The Roosevelt protesters had had and would continue to have ample opportunity to put their sentiments before the community. Should not a self-confident community be able to recognize, and to do something vigorous to check, blatant activity "that outrages public decency"? Why does obvious ugliness, especially in situations when everyone should know better, *have* to be put up with? Why should decent people be obliged to "wince" and bear it, while the indecent or perverted or seriously misguided are insulated from any sanctions which affect *them?* Why should a natural taste for propriety be condemned as "conformist"? One is again obliged to wonder what the First Amendment means and aims at.

Mr. Haiman's aggressive permissiveness is further indicated by his comments on how the community should deal with "the so-called How To Do It publications—those which describe in detail the techniques for committing antisocial acts." (p. 278) Among the publications referred to here are a guide for the "construction of . . . instruments with which one can cheat the telephone company out of charges for long-distance calls," a manual "listing ten ways to kill a person, with illustrations of decapitation and hatchet murders," and an underground newspaper, "distributed free of charge to high school students," "suggesting that readers take care of their Christmas chores by shoplifting from major department stores." (p. 278) The First Amendment is then applied in this manner by Mr. Haiman (pp. 278–79):

> How, for instance, could it be shown that a generally circulated newspaper, magazine, or book posed a threat of *imminent* lawless action where such action was *likely* to occur? Where, in these instances, is the absence of time for reflection on the part of the reader, or the lack of capacity to understand that what is described or proposed in the publication is illegal and to decide not to do it? Where is the deception, coercion, or control of will that could legitimately be characterized as a "trigger"? If restraints were to be allowed for such communication, we would have to purge our libraries of all mystery tales about the "perfect crime" and all technical treatises providing information on how to manufacture explosives or produce chemical poisons. Better that we rely on the people into whose hands such material falls to use it responsibly. If they do not, let them, not the publisher or writer, be punished.

Of course, punishing those who use instructions irresponsibly need not preclude punishing or otherwise restraining those who provide such materials. The question remains: Why should it be considered a First Amendment issue whether destructive "How To Do It" publications are permitted to circulate freely? (Consider as well my discussion of the *Progressive Magazine*-type case in Section VII of Essay No. 14 of this *American Moralist* volume and my discussion of gun control in Essay No. 25.)

What is and is not a First Amendment issue is also suggested by what Mr. Haiman has to say about "the peculiar problems raised by still or moving pictures that show the commission of presumptively illegal acts of violence or sexual abuse of children—so-called snuff films and child pornography" (p. 165):

To the extent that the law seeks to prevent or punish any injurious and illegal *conduct* that is portrayed *in* these pictures, or that may be involved in their preparation, there is no First Amendment issue present.

This is well and good, but then Mr. Haiman adds (p. 165):

Once such material has been produced, however, and is being sold or distributed by persons who have not been party to its creation, restraints designed to interrupt its passage into the hands of consumers raise the same First Amendment questions as do restraints on pictures of simulated violence, of legally permissible sexual activity, or of gory news events.

Why should the First Amendment be taken to mean that we cannot keep out of commercial circulation, if we should decide to do so, the deliberate depiction of vile acts which we *are* entitled to prohibit and punish? Does not immunity for the commercialization of the depiction of such acts encourage their commission? Besides, do we really want to live in a community in which this kind of thing goes on and in which known exploitation of this kind of thing is possible? Is it not enough of a disgrace for us that a few should consider us so pliable that they dare try to hide their sleazy operations behind our constitutional principles?

IV

What are the relevant constitutional principles here? Due process standards are of course critical: legal sanctions should not be applied except in accordance with established procedures, and it should be made clear to the typical citizen what activity *is* proscribed. In short, even known rascals (including the worst exploiters) are, except in the most dire emergency situations, entitled to the safeguards of the rule of law before they are condemned as criminals.

Much more than this is needed, however, to establish the "system of freedom of expression" Mr. Haiman advocates. It is obvious that he, in attempting to persuade the public at large, cannot yet rely primarily upon his own predisposition in favor of completely unfettered expression. His position remains a minority position, whatever some judges and other intellectuals may believe. It must be buttressed by invocations of the First Amendment itself. But the First Amendment as understood by whom?

Mr. Haiman recognizes he must claim that his preference for virtually unrestricted expression follows from the original understanding of the First Amendment. Otherwise his position is bound to be dismissed by the sober majority as merely an irresponsible proposal. Thus we encounter talk here and there in his book about "the original understanding of the Founders" (p. 12), about how the First Amendment "was intended to be treated" (p. 176), about "the public dialogue the First Amendment was designed to secure" (p. 234), about "a vigorous system of freedom of speech" (p. 288), and about "a robust interpretation of the First Amendment" (p. 347). Yet one also encounters again and again in his book disparagements of reliance "on the naive premise . . . that words may have an 'intrinsic meaning' apart from that which is in the eye of the beholder." (p. 200) (This is very much in line both with modern analytic theories in linguistics and with that debasement of language that I have wondered about.)

Does Mr. Haiman ever sense that he is somehow out of step with the framers of the First Amendment? He does concede that "if there is any category of expression that historians might agree upon as not intended to be protected by the authors of the First Amendment it would be that of personal defamation—in other words, libel and slander." (p. 43) Yet he argues, as we have seen, that laws against defamation are generally ruled out by the First Amendment. (pp. 43f, 426) Consider, also, his suggestion that Articles II and VI of the Constitution "are archaic in their oath requirements, reflective of an era in which there was considerably more ritual and deference to authority than today, and a less expansive understanding of freedom of expression." (p. 348) Again and again Mr. Haiman sees himself as offering a broader reading of the First Amendment than its framers intended. On what authority does he do this—and why should he be followed? Why should we respect his language and formulations more than he respects the language, and the possibility of enduring meanings in the formulations, left in the First Amendment and elsewhere by his distinguished predecessors? Their achievements, and the conditions for their achievements, are almost impossible to be understood by anyone who approaches political things as Mr. Haiman does.

Perhaps critical to Mr. Haiman's reading of the First Amendment is the opinion he endorses to the effect that "it is the rebel and the heretic for whom, to a large degree, the First Amendment protections were forged." (p. 360) This can be doubted. Is not the First Amendment best understood as primarily an assurance that the people at large would be able to discuss, virtually without limitation, the doings of their government and of their community and would thereby be equipped truly to govern themselves? Also to be doubted is still another opinion Mr. Haiman seems to endorse, this one from Justice Holmes who announced (268 U.S. 673 [1925]), "If, in the long run, the beliefs expressed in proletarian dictatorship are destined to be accepted by the dominant forces of the community, the only meaning of free speech is that they should be given their chance and have their way." (p. 272) On the other hand, prudent statesmen (and the Founders were certainly prudent) would advise us, "If adherence to your routine constitutional principles and procedures is about to get your people subjected to a tyranny, then you had better set aside your constitution until it is generally in the public interest to rely upon it once again."

I have long believed that a salutary way to approach the freedom of speech and press provisions of the First Amendment is by recalling the risks, purpose, and effects of the freedom of speech provided in the Constitution for members of Congress while transacting the public business. Mr. Haiman's observation on that Constitutional privilege is appropriate here (pp. 418–19):

> [I]nsofar as statements made by congressmen and senators are concerned, the Constitution explicitly provides that "for any Speech or Debate in either House, they shall not be questioned in any other place." This congressional immunity was created to insure that government policymakers could engage in frank and uninhibited discussion of the public's business. But, like any privilege, it can be abused. What is needed, in the interest of fairness, is self-restraint on the part of legislators when what they say may inflict injury on the target of their remarks.

Thus, it can be argued, the public at large, as the ultimate authority in this Country, should have substantially the same kind of privilege that members of Congress have to "engage in frank and uninhibited discussion of the public's business." (It should be immediately noticed, however, that it is not only personal self-restraint that controls legislators here: the Constitution provides each House of Congress the power to discipline members who do not conduct themselves as they should. I developed this argument more than a decade ago in a treatise on the First Amendment, *The Constitutionalist*, which was very much influenced by Laurence Berns, Hugo L. Black, William W. Crosskey, Alexander Meiklejohn, Harry Kalven, Jr., Malcolm P. Sharp, and Leo Strauss. (I have had to depart from various of my guides on such critical questions as the status of States' Rights in the American constitutional scheme. My summary in that treatise is incorporated in Section I of Essay No. 15 and is drawn upon in Section I of Essay No. 18 of this *American Moralist* volume. We need not concern ourselves on this occasion about the precise effect of the Fourteenth Amendment in extending against the States various provisions of the Bill of Rights.)

An A.C.L.U. brief in the *Progressive Magazine* case, which Mr. Haiman quotes with evident approval, does point up what I believe to be the originally intended purpose of the First Amendment (p. 401):

> The article written by Howard Morland, to be published by *The Progressive*, discusses the important political issues of proliferation of nuclear weapons and the dangers of government secrecy. The article is not a blueprint for the manufacture of a hydrogen bomb. Rather, it is political speech designed to foster and encourage public debate about important public issues. As such, it is precisely the kind of speech protected by the First Amendment.

V

Whatever the originally intended meaning and purpose of the First Amendment, it should be evident from Mr. Haiman's account of the status today of First Amendment law that "almost anything goes." Mr. Haiman is inclined to applaud this expansion of meaning. He goes so far as to suggest that "none of the values of free expression which have been identified here or elsewhere need be, or should be, excluded as foundation stones of our First Amendment edifice." (p. 433) We, however, might well wonder just what has gone wrong, especially since some supposed "values of free expression" do seem to conflict with others.

Two particularly troublesome cases in recent years should remind us of problems with the approach Mr. Haiman endorses: *Cohen* v. *California,* 403 U.S. 15 (1971), and *Erznoznik* v. *Jacksonville,* 422 U.S. 205 (1975). *Cohen* considered the right of a young man publicly to display on his jacket an indecent epithet expressing his contempt for the Selective Service Act; *Erznoznik* considered the right of a drive-in theater manager to include nude and related scenes on a movie screen visible to the public passing by outside his theatre. In both cases a divided Supreme Court upheld the right of the alleged offender, and in both cases much was made of the ability of offended passersby "effectively [to] avoid further bombardment of their sensibilities simply by averting their eyes." (pp. 92, 142) Mr. Haiman stands with the Supreme Court majority in both cases. (See pp. 16–17, 92, 95, 133, 137, 142f, 254, 465. See, also, pp. 136f, 142, 144–45, 161–62.)

In *Cohen,* one still sees the primary emphasis upon a concern for protecting the right of citizens to engage in discussion of public issues. The questionable language is not treated as an end in itself, but rather as a means of effectively expressing one's political sentiments. But, as Justice Stevens has noticed elsewhere, "There are few, if any, thoughts that cannot be expressed by the use of less offensive language." (p. 133) Mr. Haiman's rejoinder to this kind of remonstrance makes more of passion than of thought in one's "expression": "Clearly something is lost in the translation." (p. 17) Still, it can plausibly be argued by some "that our Founding Fathers were, above all, rationalists, who intended by the First Amendment to protect serious and 'decent' discourse about public affairs and not the kind of 'vulgar' emoting [and consequent cheapening of language?] that characterized so much of the countercultural protest of the 1960s which Cohen's jacket so vividly exemplified." (pp. 16–17) But not Mr. Haiman, who insists (p. 133),

> [M]ost people have a preferred way of expressing themselves in particular situations, and they may not be as articulate, effective, or as true to themselves in other modes. Despite Justice Stevens's assertion . . . that a "requirement that indecent language be avoided will have its primary effect on the form, rather than the content, of serious communication," the First Amendment ought not to be regarded as giving our government the power to prescribe the style in which people communicate their beliefs.

That is, we should be as concerned to allow the passions full expression as to ensure reason full statement. Mr. Haiman's insistence upon the impropriety of governmental concern for public decorum would no doubt have astonished the framers of the First Amendment who expected rules of order, including the avoidance of unseemly language, to prevail during the most heated debates. No doubt also some of the framers would have pointed out that it does a disservice both to the public and to the enduring cogency of any speaker's thought to permit ready recourse to vulgar and otherwise undisciplined language. (One thing that can be said on behalf of *Cohen* is that so sensitive a student of the First Amendment as Jamie Kalven does insist that it can be read more sympathetically then I read it. But here, as so often elsewhere, I prefer Justice Black's response.)

Be all this as it may, by the time of the *Erznoznik* case there was no need for libertarians arguing before the Supreme Court to rely upon any concern for protecting the right to engage in discussion of public issues. One sees instead the right to self-expression becoming an end in itself. By that time many if not most of the longstanding obscenity restraints in the United States had been set aside by the Court. So Mr. Haiman now has judicial authority for arguing, "If the local drive-in theater showing 'sexually-oriented' films is required to build a fence high enough to block viewing of the screen from outside, that same requirement must be imposed on all drive-in theaters within the same jurisdiction." (pp. 161–62) Of course, as we are repeatedly reminded, we *can* avert our eyes, which means in effect that decent men and women are obliged to march (or is it to stumble?) to the drums played for them by the lowest element in the community.

This unnatural state of affairs is not likely to last. One can dread as long-term consequences of this approach, if persisted in, general demoralization and then tyranny. Certainly there is nothing in the First Amendment that permits a corrupt few to make prisoners of and to exploit the decent majority of a community.

VI

Less dramatic than *Cohen* and *Erznoznik*, but perhaps even more instructive, has been the expansion of First Amendment protection to include commercial speech. This expansion, which Mr. Haiman heartily endorses, moves us even closer to the gratification of self-indulgence and away from the implementation of self-government as the primary purpose of freedom of speech and of the press. Mr. Haiman insists on "the recognition that there is sometimes a self-expression value for the communicator in commercial speech that goes beyond the interests of just the listener." (p. 201)

Such considerations oblige Mr. Haiman to go so far as to challenge any limitations, including with respect to advertising, on behalf of children (pp. 178–79):

> Even assuming it were feasible—which I cannot imagine it to be—to devise a system that would screen out of the audience only those incapable of making discriminating judgments, whether because of their age or other reasons, would that then be a course we should take? I think not.
>
> First, we ought to be aware that for many of those we would be trying to protect, our solicitude would be unnecessary. In order to be harmfully influenced by some of the communication we are discussing, the message must first be understood, and then there must be the capability of acting on that understanding. With very young children, or persons with severe mental retardation, both of those conditions may well be absent. Regarding sexually oriented material or "indecent" language, they may neither comprehend it nor will they endow it with the heavy emotional freight it might carry for a more aware adult. . . .
>
> With regard to the advertising of unhealthful products directed to young children, even if understanding is achieved and wants are aroused, unless there are adults around who are willing to put up the money for the purchase of these items, harmful action cannot be taken. Youths who are mature enough

to make their own money to buy candy and cigarettes also ought to be capable of learning the hazards involved.

One hardly knows whether to laugh or to cry upon confronting such arguments. But there are more arguments of a similar tenor as Mr. Haiman continues (p. 179):

> Second, we must raise the questions as to how people develop the capacity to discriminate and make better choices in their tastes, attitudes, and values. Are they suddenly and magically endowed with that ability at the age of ten, or twelve, or sixteen, or when they pass the STEP examination for high school freshmen? Does insulating them from debasing stimuli during their "tender" years help to achieve it? Or should they, on the contrary, be exposed to whatever they may encounter in the real world and given the guidance that will aid them in learning how to respond wisely and healthfully?

The question remains, What *should* "the real world" include? Should it not include a recognition of the traditional role of the community in providing the guidance once thought vital for the development and perpetuation of civilized modes of thought and action? Is it prudent to disregard what has been learned by countless generations about what contributes to wise and healthy responses by young people to the temptations and challenges they are likely to encounter?

Those who now insist that commercial speech should be afforded First Amendment protection nevertheless recognize that limitations (with respect, say, to "false and misleading commercial speech") can properly be placed by government upon advertising. (p. 199) Mr. Haiman concedes that "restrictions are acceptable on statements which are factually false and are made in the selling of goods and services." (p. 360) But if such statements are truly covered by the First Amendment, what justification is there for restricting them because of their falsity? We surely would not permit such routine testing with respect to political discourse. Which way, then, will we move in the years ahead? Should we provide commercial speech the virtually absolute protection traditionally accorded among us to political discourse? Or should we begin to restrict political discourse under the First Amendment the way common sense still tells us we should restrict commercial speech, even though it too is supposedly under the First Amendment?

Of course, some will say, common sense will also dictate that what is done to commercial speech need not be done to political discourse. But then one would once have thought that common sense should oblige us to understand why commercial speech was never contemplated by the framers of the Bill of Rights as falling within the purview of the First Amendment. Rather, they would have said, commercial speech is fully subject to such powers as those found in the Commerce Clause of the Constitution. But Mr. Haiman would remind us that speech is speech, and who is to say that there is less significant self-expression (and hence self-gratification) in commercial speech than in political discourse? Who also is to say that the political life of the community should take precedence over its commercial life or, indeed, over any other private endeavor of individuals?

Mr. Haiman asks us to recognize that the government of our "large and technologically advanced nation" may be inclined to subvert its original intention to "facilitate the self-fulfillment of its citizens." (p. 428) Does this mean that the language provided in the First Amendment should no longer be considered authoritative? Of course, it is hardly likely that the Founders would have put the emphasis where Mr. Haiman does, upon "self-fulfillment" and the perhaps related "freedom of expression." Compare the use, in the Preamble to the Constitution of such terms as *Justice, domestic Tranquility, common defence, general Welfare, the Blessings of Liberty,* and *our Posterity.* The nearest the Founders came to "self-fulfillment" as a goal may have been their recognition, in the Declaration of Independence, of "the Pursuit of Happiness." But what is critical there, the pursuit itself (the "process") or the happiness pursued? And if the latter, must one not consider what truly makes for the enduring happiness of self-respecting citizens?

VII

We thus face the prospect of reducing the "absoluteness" of First Amendment protection even as (and because?) we expand the coverage of that protection. At the core of Mr. Haiman's approach to First Amendment matters is a radical depreciation of the political as well as a related emphasis upon *process* at the expense of *ends.* (Such an emphasis upon process, almost for its own sake, can be traced back to such founders of modernity as Machiavelli and Hobbes.) Consider, for example, the passage found where the central chapters of the Haiman book meet (p. 181):

> The positions asserted in this chapter may seem to some readers to reflect too great an optimism about human capabilities and too little a concern about the quality of our lives. I think that both perceptions would be inaccurate.

It is true that considerable emphasis has been given to the *capacity* of people, even of children, to protect themselves from presumptively harmful communicative stimuli. But that does not mean that this capacity is ordinarily as well developed or as fully utilized as it needs to be. Whatever optimism is reflected in the arguments that have been made here is based on future potential in this area rather than on past performance. Moreover, it is profoundly influenced by my conviction that there is no better alternative. For while reliance on government to act as the arbiter of tastes and values provides no assurance that the decision it makes for us will be the best ones, it guarantees that whatever capacity people have to make healthy choices for themselves will remain underdeveloped.

As for the concern about the quality of our lives, it should be clear from what has been said throughout this chapter that my disagreement with critics of the debasing communication that bombards us is not with their lamentations about the problem but with the paternalistic solution some of them propose. [It has been suggested] that there are essentially two views of democracy— one that sees it as a process of decision making above all, and the other that regards those processes only as means to the greater end of achieving a good life. Or, to put it another way, the first sees human freedom as an end in itself and the second as a means to other ends. . . . I am in the former [camp]—not because I am uninterested in the good life but because I am more interested in how we go about the quest for it. I do not want somebody else deciding for me or my children what it is and handing it over to us. Unless we seek it for ourselves, it is not, in my view, worth finding.

To speak thus is to fail to appreciate just how much has already been "handed over" to one, how much many communities and generations have had to be "paternalistic" (that is, political) in discovering, establishing, and preserving the good things we take for granted. Nor is it appreciated that the "somebody else" Mr. Haiman resents are governments that "we" do effectively control in this Country.

To speak thus is also to cripple statesmen: anyone who is converted to the highfalutin' sentiments Mr. Haiman is captivated by will be unable to mobilize the community to do what may be necessary to defend itself from the "debasing communication" of enterprising corruptors who do not share the Haiman scruples against imposing *their* opinions upon the community. Is not Mr. Haiman's invocation of considerable "optimism about human capabilities" a tacit reliance upon Divine Providence? And yet we have been taught that "God helps those who help themselves."

This central passage from Mr. Haiman's book does permit the alerted reader to examine both the idealistic hopefulness, if not even piety, and the remarkable ingenuousness about political and social realities evident in the conventional liberal approach today to the First Amendment, an approach that is so well represented by Mr. Haiman as to have made it most instructive to quote at length from what he has to say. It is characteristic of this approach to make much of *expression* and *communication* rather than of the far more disciplined and far less self-centered *freedom of speech and of the press*, to shun traditional "paternalism" as virtual tyranny, to make much of material and physical harms and relatively little of psychic and moral harms as legitimate community concerns, to talk more about *self-fulfillment, commitment,* and *values* than about *virtue, duty,* and *the good*, to make much of free will even as fewer and fewer people are held responsible for the despicable things they say or do, and to be so concerned about the possibility of being oppressed by government that the significance of nature and of any such authoritative guidance in human affairs is neglected if not even denied.

Each of these half-dozen points is worth an extended discussion in any thorough assessment of Mr. Haiman's position. I trust, however, that enough has already been indicated by me to suggest what should be said about these topics, all of which may ultimately depend for reliable treatment in this context on a sound opinion about the proper relation between law and morality in genuine communities. Even so, American *freedom of speech* still means both that someone such as Mr. Haiman is entitled to make the most outlandish proposals about public policy without any reasonable fear of official retaliation and that a competent people, in providing for the common good, is entitled in turn to accept, experiment with or reject his proposals.

I have in this essay, with a minimum of commentary, allowed Professor Haiman to speak for himself at some length. His theory of freedom of speech has been given enough space to reveal itself fully. Perhaps no single sentence in his instructive book is in its charming presumptuousness so characteristic of his approach to constitutional integrity and so little in need of commentary here as the following (p. 26):

> Indeed, it is surprising that it has taken so long for lawyers and judges to recognize the greater accuracy in substituting for the word "speech" in the First Amendment more contemporary terms like "expression" or "communication."

C.

Public Opinion and Majority Rule

21

ON THE HUNTING OF WITCHES TODAY

Every art and every inquiry, and similarly every action and pursuit, is thought to aim at some good; and for this reason the good has rightly been declared to be that at which all things aim.

ARISTOTLE

I

It is good to be back in St. Louis, the first time for me since the Second World War.

This is a particularly appropriate time to return to the city of my birth, since today is the Greek Orthodox Easter. We would come up every year, from the town of Carterville a hundred miles away in Southern Illinois where I grew up, to attend Easter services at St. Nicholas on Forest Park Boulevard. It was most instructive last night once again to attend after so many years the Resurrection Service in that church.

My wife accompanied me last night to the very church in which I was reared, just as I accompany her this morning to a church of the denomination in which she was reared and to which she still owes allegiance. In fact her grandfather—a Davidson in Texas, by way of Mississippi and North Carolina—was a minister in the Presbyterian Church.

I presume then upon old associations as I attempt to challenge you this morning with some opinions I have about the hunting of witches, a subject I recently looked into for a lecture I gave at the University of Texas

---

This sermon was given at the Des Peres Presbyterian Church, St. Louis, Missouri, April 26, 1981. See, on witch trials generally, Anastaplo, "Church and State: Explorations," 19 *Loyola University of Chicago Law Journal* 61, at 65–86 (1987). See, also, the headnote for Essay No. 15, above, and the headnote for Essay No. 22, below.

The epigraph is taken from Aristotle, *Nicomachean Ethics* 1094a1–3 (W. D. Ross translation).

Law School. The traditional text for any discourse on witchcraft in the Western world is the injunction in the 22nd chapter of *Exodus*, "Thou shall not suffer a witch to live." But my own text, if I may be permitted to deviate this morning from reliance upon Scripture as my point of departure, is taken from the opening lines of Aristotle's *Nicomachean Ethics*, where it is recognized that everything human beings do aims at some good.

II

It can be reassuring to notice at the outset of our inquiry that the Salem witch trials, about which we hear so much, almost did not happen. They came at the very end of the witch-hunting craze which swept Europe from the Fifteenth Century into the Eighteenth Century. North America was barely touched by that craze.

Among the many notable and even hideously fascinating facts about the witch-hunting mania that occupied Europe for some four centuries are the following: It has been estimated that perhaps as many as eight million people were executed as witches during those centuries. No less than one hundred thousand women and children are said to have been killed in Germany alone during the Sixteenth Century. The witch-hunts which accounted for such wholesale executions occurred *not* during the so-called Dark Ages, but rather during the Renaissance and into the Age of Enlightenment. It could well be that the progress represented by the development of the printing press made systematic witch-hunts more likely and more efficient.

Relatively few people in the West today believe that human beings are able, because of their association with the Devil, to exercise supernatural powers or to be responsible for the dreadful afflictions to which mankind is subject. We look to more or less natural causes for the ills of the world. We may even deny that there are in the world any genuine evils of a diabolical character to be accounted for or to be dealt with.

Still, one must wonder whether it is more dangerous to ignore or deny genuine evil among us than it is to indulge in bloody witch-hunts: to be blissfully unaware of the existence of evil—to deny that there is any objective difference, rooted in nature, between good and bad—may expose us to even more deadly perils than those posed by old-fashioned witch-hunts.

III

Witch-hunts are very much determined by fear, pain, ignorance, anger, and hate. Such hunts and their underlying belief in witches were ways of coming to terms with "the world" and with one's sense of vulnerability in the face of worldly afflictions.

Yet by and large those accused and condemned as witches were power-less people, usually miserable old women. Some of the accused may well have imagined themselves in league with the Devil, partly because of their misery or because of their resentment. But they must usually, if not always, have been sad cases, whatever their desires or intentions. No doubt something *was* wrong with many of them, if *wrong* refers to senil-ity, physical handicaps, pathological conditions, bad temper, malevolence, ugliness, and decrepitude.

Much *was* attributed to witches, and under form of law much was done to them. What was done to them was obviously bad. But what was done at the same time to the witch-hunters was in some ways even worse, and that is something of particular interest for us: people in our circumstances in those days would more likely have been numbered among the witch-hunters rather than among the witches.

The witch-hunters and the communities that supported them were, it can be argued, the most serious victims of the witch-hunts. Everyone must believe this who holds that it is far worse to do evil than to have evil done to one.

IV

What was needed in the face of the witch-hunting craze were calmness and common sense. It should have been noticed that witch-hunts "pro-mote" witchcraft: the more witches there are exposed, the more there will remain to be exposed. An effective witch-hunt, partly because of the re-sort to torture and to confessions that implicated still more witches, was (once triggered) something like a self-sustaining chain reaction.

It should have been remembered during the witch-hunting craze that we *are* mortal, which means that if it is not one thing, it is another that will "get" us. One need not conjure up witchcraft to account for the afflictions of mankind. A natural view of things is to be preferred in these matters to an apocalyptic view, but by *natural* I do not mean the all-too-common modern view which denies that there is any objective right or wrong, any ascertainable good or bad.

It should have been known, as some did know during the witch-hunting centuries, that an exaggerated fear of witches and of what they could do had come to be generally accepted. No doubt there *were* desperate or wicked people who tried incantations, pacts with diabolical potentates, and the like. If their impotence had been recognized, they would have been more pitied than feared. There was about such people something childish.

What was needed, in short, was a more informed and hence relaxed response to perversions, malevolence, and afflictions.

V

Of course, it is often easy to second-guess the judgment of bygone ages. What about the witch-hunts, if any, of our own time?

Perhaps it is inevitable that there be "witches" from time to time: a belief in and campaigns against witches may be related to man's "need" to fear and to hate, which in turn may be rooted in man's sense of vulnerability. Do all too many of us have a desire to hurt or to punish ourselves, or to punish others, as a substitute for facing up to our own shortcomings?

Who are the people mistakenly treated as witches today? If this congregation and its enlightened minister were different from what I take them to be, I might presume to caution them against the prejudices and fears that find expression in any one of the following ways:

1) the development of ever larger and ever more efficient nuclear-weapons systems which are designed to protect us from threats from abroad, but which may make us ever more vulnerable to unprecedented destruction;

2) the intermittent campaigns we are subject to against subversives on the home front, campaigns which have the tendency to silence much-needed dissent;

3) the suspicions we entertain about the undeserving poor, who seem one way or another to rebuke our ever-rising standard of living;

4) the even deeper suspicions we resort to about conspicuous minorities among us, particularly Negroes and Jews, especially as troubles at home get worse from time to time;

5) the callousness we can exhibit toward the afflicted, the eccentric, and the immature among us, such as homosexuals and the unruly, people who all too often cannot help or enjoy being different or otherwise troublesome.

6) the intermittent suppression, even more by social sanctions than by prosecutions, of the heretical challenges we depend on to shake us out of our dogmatic slumbers; and

7) the determined resistance to obvious restraints which would reduce our ability to kill one another with guns and automobiles, and with various foods, drinks, and drugs.

But, I take it, there are among you many who are better equipped than am I to make the arguments that can be made against the various attitudes and campaigns I have just collected. Calmness and firmness are needed if one is to deal properly with the prejudices and fears I have been glancing at.

VI

What cautions, then, does an enlightened congregation such as this one need with respect to witch-hunts since it is not likely to succumb to the prejudices and fears enumerated just now? Permit me to remind you of one critical feature of the old-fashioned witch-hunts: the witches who were very much feared—and, in the campaign against whom the community crippled itself—were by and large impotent.

Who then are the witches that we liberals have to be most concerned about hunting mistakenly or in the wrong way? Perhaps for *us* the principal candidates as witches are those *we* regard as our contemporary witch-hunters. They may be our witches in the sense that they are considered by us to be malevolent and destructive, even though they are by and large not likely to be very effective for long.

VII

Permit me to presume upon your hospitality by suggesting various of the witch-hunters that people like us are apt to identify as our enemies, enemies who serve as our witches:

1) There are, of course, the creationists about whom we have heard so much recently. But it should be evident that whatever the merits of their cause (and it is not without some merit, I should add), creationists are not apt to get very far; the overriding opinion of the time is against them. Consider the sort of problem they are going to confront: wherever they are successful, for a limited time in a limited locality, their children will begin to fall behind others seeking admission to medical schools and similar institutions, thereby leading disappointed parents to withdraw the support they had given to creationists meddling with school curricula.

2) Then there are the library vigilantes. They are not likely to be effective either, even if they should "seize control" of our public libraries. There is something nostalgic about our concern here, referring as it does to a danger which assumes that libraries are still the virtually exclusive

source for information and books they once were. *Would* that it were true that libraries *were* still the primary source of "culture" and education for our people!

3) Then there are the "church and state" problems we get exercised about from time to time, even though we live in an era when there is no practical interference with the free exercise of religion among us and no foreseeable risk of the establishment of religion in any part of this Country. Our unrealistic concerns here mean that we now have this dubious state of affairs: some church-sponsored schools are willing and able to provide what the public wants but cannot always get from its public schools, and yet a willing public cannot find a "constitutional" way to help pay for what it now gets and will stop getting as these private schools close for lack of funds.

4) There is what is known as McCarthyism: political purges and character assassination. What we do not notice is that "McCarthyism" is suspect everywhere today in this Country. Even those of our fellow citizens who are regarded as the most reactionary can be heard condemning "McCarthyism." I believe we should take them at their word and thereby reinforce the general determination in this Country to avoid a return to that aberration. No one wants to be accused today of McCarthyism, just as no one wants to burn witches.

5) *Our* witches also include capitalists whom we regard as exploiters, especially as the economy continues to baffle us. *Do* capitalists exploit us? Are they not buffeted as much as we are? In fact, are they not by and large our benefactors, assuming that a steadily rising standard of living *is* good for us? If life is too precious to be devoted primarily to making money, then it is difficult to escape the conclusion that the gifted and hardworking men and women caught up in the management of productive enterprises are, no matter what they are paid, the servants that we exploit.

6) *Our* witches include as well those in authority generally, including the police, the military and the government. But by and large, do they not do well by us? It stands to reason that they are likely to be about as decent as the community out of which they come and which they serve. In our heart of hearts, we know they are needed, however wrongheaded they may be at times.

7) Finally, our witches include the determined moralists of an evangelical persuasion who have concerned themselves with our political life in recent years. I will be talking at length this afternoon before the Elijah Lovejoy Society about one such organization, the Moral Majority. Whatever the shortcomings of those people, which include their reliance upon

self-contradictory positions and upon a distorted view of politics, do they not serve a useful function in reminding us that there *are* standards of patriotism and morality that the community depends on and that many people do take seriously?

I have suggested that those whom we regard as witch-hunters, of whom I have provided a sampling, have become for all too many of us witches. This is not to suggest that there is nothing wrong with any of those men and women we condemn as witch-hunters today. But by and large they do stand for things—irrational things, in some respects, to be sure—which make family and community possible. It is far easier to ridicule such people as bigoted, puritanical, and oppressive and to demolish them than it is to replace them, and replace them we would have to do, with the risks of innovation we would thereby run.

It may be that those whom we consider the most dangerous witch-hunters are the men and women among us who take moral principles seriously. However mistaken and harmful they can be, even more dangerous would be the denial (all too common among the more enlightened members of our community) of objective standards of right and wrong, even as we experiment dangerously with new modes and orders to gratify our desires. Our greatest danger in the years ahead may not be that moralists will become ever more demanding, but that most moralists among us will become even more defensive and even more unsure of themselves than they already are and thus less effective and less useful.

VIII

I therefore suggest a tolerant, relaxed response to the witch-hunters we detect among us. We need to acknowledge the legitimacy of some of their concerns, even as we stand firm, as stand firm we must, against their excesses.

The people and movements most to be feared among us are not the witch-hunters we usually identify as our targets, but rather various respectable institutions that corrupt us daily such as the mass media and especially television. These institutions not only play up the witch-hunters and dramatize them, but they also distort our political life and cheapen our culture. That is a long story, however, appropriate for another occasion.

It is well in any event to remember that the lethal antics of the unruly girls at Salem, which came to be regarded as "Satanic" in origin, could have been interpreted by an astute leadership as "divine" or could have been otherwise deflected from the destructive effects.

IX

Permit me to close by returning to my opening remarks. Some things, like the great river running by this city, which is all I have recognized thus far (beside St. Nicholas Church) in the place I knew as a child, keep right on rolling along: old communities, old churches, old families, and associations of all kinds.

Much is to be said for them all, however different they may be from one another: the long-established does have a good deal to be said for it, whether it is a religion, a newspaper, a political regime, a business, or a military academy. The dictates of natural right and of an enduring sensibleness have thereby had time to make themselves felt and to moderate whatever original passion there was. Thus, it can be said, the Kaiser's regime was more civilized than Hitler's, and the Czar's more civilized than Lenin's. Or, as one of our children once observed, surprises tend toward the unpleasant. Perhaps this can be said generally of innovations as well, even though we do need adaptations and change to stay alive.

I mentioned at the outset that I have not visited St. Louis since the Second World War. I am reminded by this recollection that it *has* been more than four decades since that great war started—four decades during which, however many mistakes we have made, there has not been another great world war. On the other hand, only two decades separated the second world war from the first.

Whatever the shortcomings of the major powers, and there *are* many, they must have been doing something right to make possible the decades of fitful peace among them that now approach the half-century mark. A sensible combination of calmness and firmness continues to be needed if civilization is to endure. Certainly we should take care not to become unduly concerned with either witches or witch-hunters. In any event, curiosity and good humor are likely to be more useful and safer in these matters than dogmatism and indignation.

22

THE MORAL MAJORITY:
THE NEW ABOLITIONISTS?

And every man that striveth for mastery is temperate in all things.

St. Paul

I

I had looked forward to being here with Irving Dilliard, my predecessor in this lecture series on human rights, but he has been obliged to return to Harvard University for a special reunion of Nieman Fellows. I have enjoyed for more than a quarter of a century now his support and encouragement in my instructive encounter with the Illinois bar, about which so much has been said in the generous introduction of me this afternoon. Mr. Dilliard is in many respects a classic American type, not the least in his ability as a journalist to figure out ways to be helpful to those whose causes he considers himself obliged to champion. He is, in short, a man with old-fashioned morality who takes his civic duties seriously. (See, e.g., 9 *Southwestern University Law Review* 953 [1977].)

Another classic American type is Elijah Lovejoy, whose memory is honored by this society and this lecture series. This talk is about the movement from Lovejoy to Lincoln as seen in contemporary terms, that movement which began with a Jefferson who saw his people saddled

---

This talk was given to the Elijah Lovejoy Society, Des Peres Presbyterian Church, St. Louis, Missouri, April 26, 1981. (The meeting was chaired by Robert W. Tabscott, Minister of the Des Peres Presbyterian Church.) It has been published, with notes, in Anastaplo, "Church and State: Explorations," 19 *Loyola University of Chicago Law Journal* 61, at 163–75 (1987). See, on the recent dismantling of the Moral Majority organization, *Wall Street Journal*, September 25, 1989, p. 1.

The epigraph is taken from *1 Corinthians* 9: 25.

with the institution of slavery, a great evil which it seemed dreadful either to perpetuate indefinitely or to abolish immediately.

The abolitionists of Lincoln's day and the Moral Majority of our day share various attributes that I should like to examine with you. For one thing, each group has been dubious about various orthodox constitutional interpretations of its day and about the political "establishment."

II

I need not dwell, before this society, upon the obvious merits of the old abolitionists. They were deeply troubled by the evil of African slavery in this Country. They did not see slavery withering away. It seemed to them rather to be growing, and the repeal of the Missouri Compromise, the resort to "Popular Sovereignty," and the *Dred Scott* decision all seemed to confirm their fears of an ever more vigorous expansion of the slave power on the North American continent.

The abolitionists invoked something deep in the human soul and in the American regime, a regime with roots in the "created equal" language of the Declaration of Independence. They struck out against slavery and even against the Constitution, laws and compromises or deals which, it seemed to them, made slavery possible if not even permanent.

Yet the abolitionist position could be seen by a Lincoln as in some ways making matters worse. For one thing, it threatened to abandon the Southern States to slavery and to a revived slave trade, unimpeded by the Government of the United States.

III

The new abolitionists—the Moral Majority and many Christian fundamentalists, whatever they may call themselves—also have obvious merits. They stand for old-fashioned moral standards and for the fact that there *are* standards, not just chance opinions or tastes, by which we should take our bearings.

Their standards, or the way they understand old-fashioned standards, have led them (in a recent handout) to take such stands on moral and religious issues as the following: They endorse (1) voluntary prayer in public schools, (2) the right to life, which means legal opposition to any unrestricted right to abortion, (3) something called a family protection act, (4) support of Christian education, (5) new tax deductions for church and charitable giving, and (6) parental supervision of sex education for elementary students. They oppose what they consider to be (7) promotion of homosexuality, (8) federal control of church youth camps and conference grounds, (9) support for the religion of secular humanism, and (10) any constitutional amendment, such as the Equal Rights Amendment, to eliminate all legal differences between men and women.

A further indication of the tone and terms of the Moral Majority appeal may be gotten from a full-page advertisement they ran in the *Wall Street Journal* on March 25, 1981 (p. 23). The headline for this recent advertisement is a statement by the president of the organization, "They have labeled Moral Majority the Extreme Right because we speak out against Extreme Wrong!" The concluding section of the advertisement reads:

Now is the time for all Americans to stand up for what is right in our nation and attempt to change that which is harmful and injurious.

Millions of Americans have already joined Moral Majority, Inc. and have pledged their time, talent, and treasure to the rebuilding of this Republic.

The pornographers are angry. The amoral humanists are livid. The abortionists are furious. Full-page ads, employing McCarthy-like fear tactics, are appearing in major newspapers. The sponsors of these ads, of course, are attempting by these means to raise funds for themselves.

The opposition has every right to legally promote their goals and attack ours. But, certainly, we have that same right.

Therefore, we invite you to join our ranks. Moral Majority, Inc. is a non-profit organization and does not give tax-deductible receipts for contributions. It is supported by Americans who are willing to invest in their country. We are spending millions of dollars at this time to return this nation to the values and principles on which it was built.

The positions taken by the Moral Majority may be seen by many as efforts to resist change of any kind. But each of their positions can be put in such a way as to have a considerable appeal. I have suggested that these new abolitionists, like the old abolitionists before them, do invoke something deep in the human soul and in the American regime. Consider, for example, the blatant sexuality all around us, which is anything but a celebration of healthy sexual desire and activity. Thus our neighborhood grocer in Chicago can casually put on display magazine covers that would have been available a decade or two ago only in the sleaziest establishments. The significant thing is not that an obtuse merchant operates thus, but that he is permitted to do so by a rather staid neighborhood, no longer confident enough of its moral judgment to resort to protest or to boycott. This means that a minority is making choices for us all, since that minority's tastes and purchases as "liberated" people taint us all and lead to an obvious lowering of standards all around us, if not even to a kind of self-loathing.

There are various ways in which the new abolitionists resemble the old abolitionists: they tend toward "single issue" politics; they are led, in large part, by clergy; they see political issues in Biblical terms; they are susceptible to what may be called an Armageddon complex, with a great war considered feasible, if not even desirable; and yet they are, in a sense, self-centered. What these similarities mean bears thinking about, but first I should say more about the Moral Majority itself.

IV

I do not need to dwell before this society upon the more obvious defects of the Moral Majority, not the least of which is that they, like the old abolitionists before them, run the risk of making matters worse if only by giving morality a bad name, making it seem hopelessly puritanical in tone and far too limited in scope.

But just as Lincoln made good use of the abolitionists, for he needed them and did make use of them, so can the Moral Majority be made use of by astute leaders among us, but only by those who, like Lincoln, know what they are doing.

I have suggested that these elements are needed in the community. They are easy to ridicule, to fear, and eventually to discredit, but they do speak, however crudely at times, to vital issues. It is no surprise, I have also suggested, that they do emerge from time to time. Something would be wrong with us if they did not emerge, just as something would have been wrong in pre-Civil War America if there had been no abolitionist passion at all, however misdirected it might have been at times.

In any event, we can be grateful that our abolitionists have appeared in the form they have, if only because they can be usefully dealt with in their contemporary form.

V

What is at the heart of the limitations of these people—that is, of both the old abolitionists of the Nineteenth Century and the new abolitionists of our time?

At the heart of their limitations, I suggest, is the dubious status of prudence among them. Prudence tends to be seen by them as an unworthy and even immoral surrender of principle. This attitude makes effective compromise difficult; it makes it hard for them to grasp that enduring wholeness in the light of which much of one's conduct should be regulated. (Is there not something Wilsonian and hence dangerous about this approach when it is applied to foreign relations?)

Related to this limitation is the suspicion among the abolitionists, new as well as old, of old-fashioned (or, some would say, genuine) political life. Sloganeering and crusades, however much an impact they can have for a while on political life, are not politics, and such an approach cannot endure. Rather, it invites uninformed counteraction and unthinking recrimination.

I should at once add, however, that it is not a valid argument against the Moral Majority that it sometimes does seem to be a single-issue cause: some issues are big enough to matter on their own, issues such as the status of slavery in America in the 1830s or the status of Jews in Germany in the 1930s. But how best to deal with such an issue may be much more complicated than the ardent moralist can discipline himself to work out.

The limitations of the abolitionists, old and new, are made worse in the community because of their perceptions of their most extreme opponents. Each side is largely ignorant of the other side in such controversies. Just as the abolitionists and the slaveowners did not really know each other, so the Moral Majority and sophisticated liberals do not really know each other. This has been evident to me as I have talked at length with leading figures on both sides of this controversy. The Moral Majority sees liberals as "Big Brother," intruding upon private lives and trying to impose offensive moral standards upon ordinary people, and so they can tell me that "the people who work, who hold society together, have a stomachful." Liberals, on the other hand, can see the Moral Majority as "mindless barbarians," as aggressive, intolerant, and dangerous.

If the abolitionists, new as well as old, do not know their opponents, this means that they do not know the community as a whole. Hence they cannot truly know themselves. Compare Lincoln's approach: he did know what was behind each extreme of his day and had some sympathy for each, however much he differed from each either as to objective or as to method. He also knew, once war began, that he needed to keep both conservative legalists and radical abolitionists together if the effort to preserve the Union was to be successful, that Union which alone could keep slavery from having its way in the Western Hemisphere. Prudence meant that Lincoln could not, without jeopardizing the common cause, give either the legalists or the abolitionists all that they wanted. His master stroke in this endeavor may have been the way the Emancipation Proclamation was developed.

VI

The Moral Majority cannot be both given their due and made salutary use of if one notices merely their defects and their merits. The astute leader among us must also be aware of what accounts for their strengths and weaknesses. He must, for instance, be aware of what is solid rock as well as of what is quicksand in their foundations, and why.

I have already referred to the attitude about prudence and politics that is at the heart of the limitations of the Moral Majority. But there are additional factors which help account for their attitude toward prudence, and it is to these that I now turn.

The Moral Majority do stand against hedonism and for the family in their espousal of moral standards. These sentiments can contribute to a sound foundation in moral discourse. But it has not been generally noticed that at bottom the Moral Majority also stand for a radical individualism, especially if the "individual" is extended, as it is in the traditional perception, to include one's own family. Personal liberty is made much of by them, at least so long as offensive uses of that liberty are not flaunted in public. Insofar as the Moral Majority is a majority, it is a majority made up of individuals who make much of their personal autonomy.

This means that they stand for the individual as against the community with respect to such matters as education and morality. Put another way, they do not seem to appreciate the extent to which the individual, his family, or his church depends on the political community.

That is, they seem to believe that it is enough if government is not used against their moral standards. What they do not see in their considerable reliance upon exhortation is the extent to which a viable morality depends on a sound public opinion, and how that in turn depends on law, written or unwritten. For many people, what the law says is perhaps the most important indication of and guide to what is right and wrong. True, the law cannot prescribe or ensure the very best, but it can prevent the worst and prepare the way for the best, even as it routinely provides for the good and decent.

One consequence of the emphasis of the Moral Majority upon individuality is that they do not face up to the extent that the very definition or determination of one's property and one's family, and hence even the legitimacy of one's children, usually depends on some community with its laws. This means that each person is for them somehow on his own, that all taxes except for national defense and internal security are suspect, and that all welfare services are dubious. Callousness, if not meanness of spirit and vindictiveness, is all too often the result of this approach, and truly political men know better.

The approach of the Moral Majority to everyday problems tends to be piecemeal. They do recognize certain things on television as corrupting, but they cannot appreciate the extent to which the entire television industry, even on its best behavior, is a calamity and should be shut down. (Perhaps the only sustained good from television in this country is the contribution it has made to racial justice.) A thoughtful fundamentalist I know is amazed at the amount of television that members of his sect watch: "When they have nothing to do, they sit in front of the TV." It certainly does not occur to *them* to call for the abolition of broadcast television. But such advocacy, at least in our circumstances, takes seriously the duty of government in shaping the language, moral standards, and objectives of the community.

VII

However disturbed the Moral Majority people may be by specific programs on television, they do not attack television as such. After all, are not various of their leaders themselves largely "media creations"? They certainly make considerable use of television, and they may be permanently tainted by its hucksterism, its superficiality, and its hit-and-run tactics.

To the extent that the Moral Majority are dependent on the media, as the New Left were in the 1960s, they are superficial and hence probably ephemeral: slogans and catch phrases, not thoughtful, extended statements, set forth their positions. Both speakers and audiences are thereby limited, and the character of politics is affected.

In any event, one would expect that any influence grounded upon such flimsy stuff is bound to be exaggerated, or at least that it cannot be sustained.

However all this may be, the Moral Majority will have their troubles. They will have troubles partly because they do not make enough allowances for people's passions and foibles and for the need for considerable good-natured hypocrisy in any healthy community. They are and are not a majority: they are a majority, perhaps, with respect to some of the aspirations they voice; they are not a majority with respect to performance. Most of us do not do all of the time the various commendable things the Moral Majority espouse.

The Moral Majority will also have their troubles because, as their ambivalence about television indicates, they accept most of the modern technological development. As moderns and capitalists, they accept for the most part a way of life that promotes an ever-higher standard of living, considerable liberty, innovation, and mobility. The free enterprise on which we so much depend means, for all its advantages, that unpredictable change is virtually guaranteed.

When we look at comparable moral and political conservatives in other lands, we can perhaps better appreciate the dilemmas and plight of the Moral Majority in this Country:

1) Consider first what is happening in South Africa where the whites who want a higher and higher standard of living must make more and more use of native African labor, labor that must be trained at ever-higher levels, thereby making it increasingly difficult to keep them in political subjection or even to keep them socially separated from the whites.

2) Consider next the Muslims of the Middle East and North Africa, who also want a high standard of living. This requires them to redefine the old prohibitions, especially with respect to paying or collecting interest, prohibitions that stand in the way of full-scale economic development along Western lines. Such redefinition, as well as other ever more farreaching changes in the way of life which are permitted, seem to be undermining long-established customs of the Islamic peoples.

3) Consider finally the Russians who can no longer maintain, at least in their cities, the comprehensive repression upon which Stalin relied. For them too industrialization and modernization have meant that the ways of the West, bad as well as good, have had to be imported. In addition, minimum efficiency in any economic system operating on a large scale requires more respect for due process and the rule of law, and hence for a free market, than Russian autocracy is accustomed to.

The Moral Majority and people like them face similar dilemmas, the troublesome dilemmas faced by anyone who wants to eat his cake and have it too. Their moral attitudes remind one of communities such as the Amish, but they are not willing to make the genuine sacrifices with respect to "life style" that some Amish have been noted for. In this sense, then, the Moral Majority are doing little more than fighting a rearguard action. An enduring moral revitalization among us would have to probe deeper than they are prepared to go, looking to such matters as the status of individualism, the proper function of the community in legislating morality, and the significance in moral matters of technological, economic, and other innovations. Whether their considerable reliance upon Biblical language and authority can suffice is itself a major question. If our community is to be soundly constituted and prudently governed, must not some among us look to nature, to natural right, and to that informed judgment which knows how to make use of religious sensibility and of traditional guides?

Sloganeering, television, and advertising campaigns are no substitute for thinking things through and for educating some to assess sensibly the many glittering prospects held out before us. One illustration reminds us of what "progress" can mean. Each time I visit the small town in Southern Illinois where I grew up after my earliest years in St. Louis, I am struck by the abandoned look of the downtown area in that town and in many neighboring towns. People have been enticed to spend their money at fancy shopping centers. Because merchants have been permitted to open such shopping centers and to exploit the American infatuation with the automobile, the vital centers of the towns have been destroyed, centers to which youngsters could walk in the evening and where they could easily mingle with each other and with the adults of the community. Instead, everyone is on the road, out of sight of neighbors and beyond the practical control of families. In such circumstances, it is no wonder that the old moral rules are subverted. Does it make much sense to concern oneself with the rules themselves if one is not also prepared to deal with the social and economic developments, as well as the institutionalized greed, that make those rules so vulnerable? But the Moral Majority, who are often businessmen at heart, will tell us that it is not the job of government to tell us how to live or how to use "our" property. This is only to admit that they do not appreciate the conditions of the morality which they have inherited and which they, properly enough, are concerned to preserve and to pass on to their children.

VIII

I do not mean to suggest that the Moral Majority people have no notion of what is happening. I do mean to suggest that their unexamined principles stand in the way of the serious reforms they yearn for.

Such people, no matter how confident and belligerent they sometimes sound, are very much on the defensive. I sense when listening to them that they are aware of their vulnerability.

For one thing, they do not want to appear ridiculous. They do not want to be the William Jennings Bryans of their generation, completely out of step with the modern age. Thus they do not support official censorship, but settle instead for economic boycotts. In addition, they again and again repudiate anything that might be condemned as "McCarthyism." They recognize that their credibility depends on their ability to show that they are respectful of differing opinions.

Nor do they want to seem racist, however dead set they may be against court-ordered busing. (I note in passing that the case for the neighborhood school, and against busing of school children, is far stronger than all too many liberals admit.) Particularly significant, it seems to me, is the

Moral Majority's repeated insistence that they are not anti-Semitic; this is often coupled with their strong support of the State of Israel. Here too it is evident that they are aware of the repudiation that awaits them if they succumb to that fringe of so-called moralists who hate Jews. The Moral Majority are trying to say the right things about race relations, segregation, and the toleration of dissent among us. They should be taken at their word, thereby reinforcing among them the sentiments they have been obliged to endorse.

The question remains, then, of how it is best for liberals to deal with these people and their inevitable successors over the years, *to* deal with them even if these people may be in principle against "deals." Their moral concerns and calls for "moral sanity" should be respected and made use of; their naivete and errors should be anticipated and guarded against. There is, I repeat, something healthy in their old-fashioned appeal, however self-righteous and hence self-defeating it may all too often seem.

Certainly they should not be responded to in such a way as to make the cause of morality even more fragile than it is today. The more enlightened among us should not permit moral concerns to be left to the unenlightened, just as patriotism and the flag were left not too many years ago. It would also be salutary for the enlightened to remind the community that morality can be considerably more complicated than the Moral Majority makes it out to be. For one thing, morality should include a lively concern for social justice and for peace, about which too the Bible as well as sound politics has a good deal more to say than one would gather from the pronouncements of the curiously self-centered Moral Majority.

IX

Prudence, I have suggested, points to reasonable accommodation guided by those who do think and are calm and perceptive, something the new abolitionists, like the old abolitionists before them, have sometimes found it difficult to be.

How should *we* proceed?

1) We should recognize that our Country is so large and so complicated that a multitude of good and bad examples of just about anything can be found all around us. We should also recognize that it takes a lot to do much to such a large country, to do much either for better or for worse. A relaxed approach, not a strident tone, is called for; excitement and indignation should be held in check.

2) We should not permit superficial reporting to deceive us as to what is happening in the Country and as to what its leaders are like. The editorial-

page editor of the *Washington Post* observed during a discussion on the University of Chicago campus this past week that Mr. Reagan's performance in office thus far has shown a man "who is smart, who knows how to take over a government, and who knows a whole lot of things we thought he didn't," whereas the press had generally characterized him as a man who is too old, not smart enough, and the prisoner of "too narrow a band of the political spectrum." I recall that in many discussions with liberal friends in 1980, well before the election, I had to assure them, seeing that Mr. Carter was bound to lose, that Mr. Reagan as President would be nowhere near as bad as they sometimes seemed to enjoy expecting him to be.

3) In any event, we should remember that the people we view with alarm, whether they be the Moral Majority or Mr. Reagan, are after all fellow human beings. Consider, for example, the statement made by the President a few days ago about the man who shot him: he voiced the prayer that his assailant "can find an answer to his problem. He seems to be a very disturbed young man. . . . I hope he'll get well, too." (*New York Times*, April 23, 1981, p. B12) The compassion exhibited here is not unlike that which we have heard over the years from the social workers, the judges and psychiatrists that Mr. Reagan once excoriated as soft on crime.

Mr. Reagan's temperate language should be taken at face value as we commend it and hope that sensible things will now be done by his administration about international tensions and about the size, disposition, and possible use of nuclear weapons. At the very least, we are much in need of more moderate language than we have become accustomed to in our political discourse during the past two decades.

Temperance in discourse reflects the recognition that this is bound to be an imperfect world and that we must often choose between unattractive alternatives. We as citizens really have to trust our fellow Americans to be sensible most of the time, and to be patient as we wait for the pendulum to swing our way, when the time seems out of joint, as it no doubt does seem to be on occasion.

D.

Nature and Revelation

23

THE STATUS OF NATURE

23-A. The Challenge of Creationism

All men by nature desire to know.

I

Clarence Darrow is quoted as having said that it is "bigotry for public schools to teach only one theory of origins." (87 *Yale Law Journal* 561 [1978]) It may well turn out, then, that the best thing to have happened since Sputnik to the teaching of science in American public schools is the determined creationist challenge to what goes on there. This challenge has obliged us all to examine the presuppositions, methods and purposes of science. Such an examination can leave scientists on a firmer and more responsible basis among us, especially if it should confine an imperialistic science to its proper place.

Scientists do need to be pressed to examine what they take for granted and to explain themselves to others. We all need to have a sounder grasp of what *premises, hypotheses, evidence,* and *theories* mean, a sounder grasp of how such things contribute to the securing of truth, and of course a sounder grasp of what truth is, both for scientists and for others.

A proper examination of science, and indeed of all serious inquiry, leads us to an examination of nature itself—of what we mean by nature, of what

---

This talk was given at the Clarence Darrow Memorial Meeting, Jackson Park and The Museum of Science and Industry, Chicago, Illinois, March 13, 1985. It has been distributed for publication in newspapers by Public Research, Syndicated, Montclair, California.

The epigraph is taken from Aristotle, *Metaphysics* 980al.

the nature of nature is. The extent to which an explicit awareness of nature is special to Western civilization is not generally noticed. The creationist, perhaps without recognizing it, questions the very idea of nature insofar as he is grounded in an Old Testament that cannot acknowledge nature as such. But the creationist is also very much a modern man who takes nature for granted. Thus he is divided in his own soul.

The creationist challenge obliges us to reconsider (perhaps, for many of us, to consider seriously for the first time) the question of origins. This too bears upon the question of the nature of nature. The question of origins depends not only on considerations of chronology, but also on considerations of what is meant by cause and effect "then" as well as "now." Does not the modern scientific approach tend to depend on a philosophic materialism? May not this lead to a cultural relativism that can eventually undermine science itself?

These questions should remind us of the problems posed by the relations of religion, morality, and science to one another. Does there not remain, even for the most accomplished scientist, something of a mystery as to how the marvelous moves were made from the inanimate to the animate and from the pre-human to the human? Even if scientists discover a law which "explains" these developments, must there not remain for many people the question of why this law *is* a law? We are moved, then, to wonder about the nature of revelation and of the sacred, even as we recognize the perhaps inevitable tension between Reason and Revelation.

II

The most powerful revelation in the West with respect to the question of origins has been the story found in *Genesis*. Would we not have had to try to invent a story dealing with such matters if this one had not been given to us? Can anyone be regarded as truly educated among us today who does not have a thorough grasp of a book that is so much a part of our language, heritage, and art? Yet fewer and fewer youngsters know much about it. There is here an abysmal ignorance that can have profound consequences for serious education.

It should at once be added that a truly thorough reading of *Genesis*, and of *Exodus* also, poses a serious challenge to the conventional creationist position. The subtlety and complexity of such accounts are not generally appreciated; conventional notions about morality, politics, and prudence generally are challenged there, so much so that a simple-minded creationism is made vulnerable thereby. The thoughtful human being finds much to support, as well as to challenge, him in the great Biblical accounts.

Be that as it may, the community does have a legitimate concern to promote personal morality and public morale. Public morale may depend in large part on a sense of cosmic meaningfulness being shared by a people. The fact remains that it is far easier for most people to believe that the universe had a beginning—that something *somehow* came out of nothing—than that the universe, or at least its matter, has always been. We are hardly likely to develop for most people we know a more persuasive account of such things than that found in *Genesis*.

III

To suggest that there should be a serious study of *Genesis* in the public schools—a study in the form of conscientious "non-partisan" interpretation and explication—is *not* to suggest that modern biology, which *is* very much rooted in evolutionary theory, should not be taught. It is instructive to notice, sixty years after the Scopes Trial, that it is widely accepted that the theory of evolution should continue to be taught in our schools. Even most creationists concede this and with good reason. I also have the impression that State legislatures as well as church people generally have become much more sophisticated about these matters. This is evident in the Attorney General opinions that have been recently issued in various States, north and south, in response to creationist efforts to shape the curricula of public schools.

Several of the curricular problems we are facing today are related to misreadings by courts of the Religion Clauses of the First Amendment. It is a mistake to believe that the Religion Clauses pose any barrier to legislation for which there is a plausible secular purpose, including legislation which recognizes the considerable persuasive evidence in favor of evolution theory, especially as it bears upon and is useful for biological studies. We have here a legislative or political judgment, not a judicial one or even ultimately a question of family prerogatives. (Compare *Wisconsin* v. *Yoder*, 406 U.S. 205 [1972].) It is also a mistake to believe that the Religion Clauses pose any barrier to legislation aimed at developing genuine education, including the serious examination in public schools of the great sources, both religious and secular, of Western civilization. It should at once be added that if, in the judgment of a local school board, a particular subject cannot be pursued at the moment without provoking destructive partisanship around its school, then that subject can properly be set aside for the time being. (See Justice Black's concurring opinion in *Epperson* v. *Arkansas*, 393 U.S. 97 [1968].)

One of the consequences of recent judicial interpretations of the Religion Clauses has been the development by certain religious fundamentalists of something they call *creation science*. One can easily get the impression that there is something contrived about these efforts to dress up *Genesis* in scientific garb. They seem little more than a plausible way of getting a version of *Genesis* into the public schools, but a much watered-down version that does not give *Genesis* its due.

The arguments for creation science that I have seen strike me as sophistical. They may even represent a compromise with the morality, or sense of probity, one expects in truly pious people. I do not believe that the conscientious men and women who resort to creation science appreciate how much they undermine a serious respect for *Genesis* by trying to reconcile it *in the way* they do with geological, archaeological, and other such data. One consequence of this approach is tacitly to recognize science as sovereign, even as it exposes the creationists as "Ptolemaic" in their desperate efforts to make their "theory" fit the "facts." One sees such contortions again and again in education and elsewhere. Partly responsible for such shoddy contrivances have been the misreadings of the Religion Clauses to which I have referred.

If the *Genesis* account is tricked out in scientific garb rather than grappled with on its own terms, it not only loses much of its majestic appeal, but it also puts its underlying argument in grave jeopardy. This means that although the creationists may have been doing all of us a favor with their challenge to what is and is not being taught in the public schools, they may be doing this at great risk to the integrity of their own position. Good-naturedness and a sense of confidence are called for as we consider what we can do for them, thereby helping them help us even more than they have already.

23-B. On Speaking To and For Mankind

Years ago, in conclusion to a brief paper on the concept of work in a symposium entitled The Works of the Mind, *I suggested that it was up to the manual worker to keep alive among us a certain spirit of honesty and perfection which ought to be carried from level to level up to that supreme sphere of intellectual life where all work comes to an end and the image of eternal life appears. The good worker and the lover of truth, I wrote, have much in common, and the promotion of their understanding could do a great deal for the reformation of our concept of culture. Here, I wish to add a further suggestion. It is my feeling that our best immediate chances to begin to develop the culture with a contemplative ideal may lie in promoting collaboration between all kinds of technical work and the fine arts. Such a rapprochement has been enormously facilitated by the truly fantastic developments in modern technology, of which we should take utmost advantage.*

YVES R. SIMON

I

Perhaps the most significant aspect for us of Pope John Paul II's 1981 "reflections devoted to human work," *Laborem Exercens,* is that so massive a policy statement, of more than twenty thousand words, can be issued by this sovereign with the justified expectation that it will be studied by his subjects and others all over the world. (This is the third such statement, or encyclical letter, issued over the name of this pope. It was preceded by one on Christian redemption and by another on the mercy of God. In addition to these encyclicals there have been papal disquisitions on the family and on the Eucharist.) It is indeed remarkable that encyclicals should still be as important as they seem to be in the Roman Catholic Church,

---

This talk was given at a panel discussion on *Laborem Exercens,* Rosary College, River Forest, Illinois, March 23, 1982. It has been published in *Newsletter,* Politics Department, The University of Dallas, September 1983, pp. 9–13, and in *Catholicism in Crisis,* September 1983, pp. 6–7.

The encyclical text relied upon is in the translation published by *The Chicago Catholic,* September 18, 1981. See, also Claudia Carlen Ihm, ed., *The Papal Encyclicals 1958–1981* (Raleigh: McGrath Publishing Co., 1981), pp. 299–326; *Acta Apostolicae Sedis,* November 5, 1981, pp. 577–647.

The epigraph is taken from Yves R. Simon, *Work, Society and Culture* (New York: Fordham University Press, 1971), p. 187.

providing "authoritative," albeit not "infallible," guidance to the thinking of that institution on a series of timely subjects.

An encyclical is authoritative in large part because it draws—because it *obviously* draws—upon earlier encyclicals and, even more important, upon Scripture and the dictates of natural law, upon the most distinguished teachers of the Church, and upon great Church Councils. Even when earlier encyclicals are tacitly modified, as seems to be done in the 1981 *Laborem Exercens* of Pope John Paul II to the 1891 *Rerum Novarum* of Pope Leo XIII, it is evident that substantial continuity with a long and rich past is critical to the integrity and vitality of the Church. No doubt, this makes for steadiness and a kind of moderation if not at least a semblance of prudence in Church teachings and hence a refusal to conform easily to the fashions of the day. Such refusal, which is evident in this Pope's controversial reaffirmations on other occasions of established rules with respect to birth control, to the status of divorced people, and to the ordination of women, may be seen either as a dangerous rigidity or as a salutary reliability. In any event, the Church continues to conduct herself as a rare institution in which moral, political, and social adaptations must still be explicitly reconciled with long-accepted principles.

II

It is something very old that is drawn upon in one particularly telling observation in *Laborem Exercens* (Section 27, paragraph 125):

> There is yet another aspect of human work, an essential dimension of it, that is profoundly imbued with the spirituality based on the Gospel. All work, whether manual or intellectual, is inevitably linked with toil. The Book of Genesis expresses it in a truly penetrating manner: the original blessing of work contained in the very mystery of creation and connected with man's elevation as the image of God is contrasted with the curse that sin brought with it. "Cursed is the ground because of you; in toil you shall eat of it all the days of your life." This toil connected with work marks the way of human life on earth and constitutes an announcement of death . . . [*Hic labor dolorque viam designat humanae vitae in terris et continet mortis nuntiationem* . . .]

Still, someone speaking from the Classical perspective might well take issue with this emphasis upon the doleful consequences of mortality: for, when things are right, doing what one ought should be deeply pleasurable or, at least, not unduly painful; this should be so with meaningful work, as well as with virtuous action and perhaps even with various bodily gratifications. Of course, the sad response may be, "But, alas, things are not right—and have not been since the Fall of Man." This assessment is evident throughout this encyclical, despite its repeated insistence upon the human dignity of proper work.

Critical here, then, is the status of nature. When "the guiding thread of this document" is referred to in paragraph 54 of Section 12, nature is decisively subordinated (at least in its ultimate foundation) to the will of the Creator rather than being recognized as somehow autonomous and hence ultimately authoritative. (For example, *In omni gradu progredientis laboris homini donatio primaria occurrit, quam praestat natura et, ad summam, ipse Creator.* This sentence has been translated: "In every phase of the development of his work man, comes up against the leading role of the gift made by 'nature,' that is to say, in the final analysis, by the Creator.") The status for the Church of nature, and of that prudence which is rooted in a confident deference to nature, bears on the uses and significance of pleasure, and on the possibility of genuine happiness, in this life. We can do no more than thus notice on this occasion a fundamental critique one might make of certain deep-rooted Christian opinions about the necessarily blighted life of the human being on earth.

No doubt, a pope is able to influence to some degree the direction that the Church will move in his time. One sees in the current Pope a curious mixture of the Twentieth-Century intellectual and the Nineteenth-Century gentleman. The old-fashioned gentleman may be seen in how he says what he does, here and elsewhere, about the place in the home and in the Church of women (usually non-individuated persons, the vigilant feminist is likely to complain). Even so, the next generation of theologians who become influential in the Church is likely to ratify the considerable changes with respect to women made in recent decades by the faithful, who *do* have a good deal to say, over time, about what the Church is and will be.

It is, however, the sophisticated side of this intellectual Pope that is more intriguing: he is in some respects very much a modern, even with Marxist overtones in his vocabulary and in his mode of analysis, however concerned he may be in practice about Marxism, about atheistic Communism, and about any recourse to class struggle. Modernity may be seen in his reservations about the function of profit in the capitalist system, perhaps attempting to appeal thereby to chronically resentful intellectuals everywhere. He does not seem to want to recognize that workers who are supposedly being exploited by the capitalist's maximization of profits may also be beneficiaries of that economic efficiency (and hence of more and better goods at lower prices, or a reliably higher standard of living generally) which sustained competition tends to foster. If this *is* the way things are, the Pope's primary concern should not be with the status of labor *vis-á-vis* capital but rather with that subversion of the rule of law (especially in Marxist countries and throughout the Third World) which interferes with a genuinely free market and with that liberty, political as well as personal, which a free market both depends on and promotes. In this respect, *Rerum Novarum*, with its considerable emphasis upon the rights and the naturalness of private property, may provide despite its own shortcomings a sounder prescription than does *Laborem Exercens* for the economic ills of our collectivist-minded age. On the other hand, the social and moral, as distinguished from the strictly material, consequences of capitalism and its remarkable technology, of individualism, and even of liberty are continuing concerns of thoughtful men and women in the Church and out.

III

Whatever reservations one should have about *Laborem Exercens*, or about any other papal encyclical, the fact remains that mankind *is* being addressed by the Church in an apparently comprehensive way—in a way which recognizes, and hence teaches us all, that the human being does have a mind to be nourished and a moral sense to be invoked. All this means, at the least, that the Roman Catholic Church intends to be taken seriously and that she will be so taken, in large part because she does not habitually take the easy way out (however ambiguous her "universal" statements are sometimes obliged to be) in confronting the issues of the day.

24

WOMEN AND THE LAW

"Just like a sculptor, Socrates," he said, "you have produced ruling men who are wholly fair."

"And ruling women, too, Glaucon," I said. "Don't suppose that what I have said applies any more to men than to women, all those who are born among them with adequate natures."

"That's right," he said, "if they are to share everything in common equally with the men, as we described it."

SOCRATES

I

A burly truckdriver had just been served his hamburger sandwich, his french fries, and his coffee when three *macho* motorcyclists came into the truck-stop. One of them grabbed the driver's sandwich and began eating it, another did the same with his french fries, and the third took his coffee. He quietly got up, walked over to the cashier, paid his check and left. "He's not much of a man," one of the cyclists said to the attending waitress as he finished the french fries. "He's not much of a driver, either," she replied, looking out the window. "He flattened three motorcycles in the parking lot with his truck as he pulled out!"

What does it mean to be a man? What does it mean to be a woman? To what extent do the truckdriver and the waitress in this story suggest

This talk was given to the Law Alumni Association, The University of Chicago, Chicago, Illinois, April 29, 1980. (Original title: "Women and the Law: Fortescue and *The Merchant of Venice.*")

The Fortescue text quoted from in this essay is *De Laudibus Legum Anglie*, S. B. Chrimes translation (Cambridge: University Press, 1949).

The epigraph is taken from Plato, *Republic* 540B (Allan Bloom translation).

answers to these questions? And how do these answers, as well as these questions, bear on our subject today?

There is more than one sense to my title on this occasion. "Women and the Law" can refer to the status of women before the law. It can also refer to the status of women as practitioners of the law, whether as lawyers or as judges. These two senses are not necessarily related: thus, women may be as suitable for the practice of law as men without having to have the same status before the law as men; or women may have the same status before the law as men without being suitable, by and large, for the practice of law. Each of these two senses of my subject should be touched upon here. Also to be touched upon, in considering this subject, are works of the two authors mentioned in the announcement of this talk, Sir John Fortescue's *De Laudibus Legum Angliae,* a Fifteenth-Century legal classic, and Shakespeare's *The Merchant of Venice.*

Most people who devote themselves today to such subjects as women and the law are not serious. That is, they do not have a high enough opinion of their predecessors; consequently, they do not take seriously enough what others before them saw and knew. Perhaps fundamental to a prevailing lack of seriousness today is one consequence of the democratic movement which has swept the Western world: that movement means, among other things, that there is an emancipation of the low from subordination to the high.

I trust you will bear with me as I attempt to put in a usefully provocative form various sometimes-neglected questions of our day. But lest it be assumed that the question of the status of women is a modern one, permit me to report that my Roman Catholic colleagues at Rosary College are celebrating today "The Sixth Centenary of the Death of Saint Catherine of Siena." She is, I am told, one of the two women who have been proclaimed Doctors of the Church. She was, I am also told, critical to the successful effort in the Fourteenth Century to induce the Pope to return to Rome from Avignon.

II

Another introductory explanation is called for before I develop my argument proper. My concern today is *not* with the Equal Rights Amendment. I, for one, am not sure what difference that proposed amendment would make if ratified. It remains for me an open question whether such an amendment is needed for purposes of litigation or of legislation, whatever its symbolic importance. There *are* indications that existing constitutional and legal provisions, including the Fourteenth Amendment and various civil rights acts, can be and indeed are being used to achieve what the Equal Rights Amendment would achieve, both in legislatures and in courts. Only last week the Supreme Court ruled that workers' compensation laws that treat surviving widows and widowers differently are invalid. We learned the same day that United Airlines agreed to rehire some twenty-five stewardesses it had fired for being overweight because it did not also dismiss their fat male counterparts.

But, I hasten to add (and not only because my wife, who is vigorous in her support of the amendment, is here), there is a good deal to be said for ratifying the Equal Rights Amendment. For one thing, we could otherwise have a continuing controversy into the Twenty-first Century, and I do believe we have something better to do with our energy and attention. It does not seem to be appreciated that agitation for such an amendment might not stop if the present proposal should fail to be ratified by 1982. Efforts with a new proposal are likely to be renewed thereafter; it may be easier to secure ratification then, when it is recognized that the problem simply won't go away, unless judicial decisions should make the amendment obviously unnecessary, as eventually happened with the Child Labor Amendment proposed in 1924.

In any event, I hardly think that, in our circumstances, women will be denied what so many of them, including most of the politically active among them, are demanding as their right.

III

My primary concern on this occasion is to suggest how one might begin to think about the conventional opinions of our day regarding the appropriate relations between women and men, with or without constitutional amendments. If what I have to say today has merit, it will be because I confirm and reinforce what most of you have "always" known about these matters.

On the other hand, advanced opinion today (indeed, the opinion of most intellectuals, it seems, male and female alike) tends to hold that there are no significant differences between women and men which the law or the community should recognize, except for differences immediately related to the child-bearing functions of women. It is recognized, of course, that massive differences have long been reflected in the law, but these are seen as substantially the effects of unenlightened opinions rationalizing that male chauvinism which exploits the obvious male superiority in brute strength and which goes back to a time when birth control and pregnancy were quite different from what they are today.

This advanced opinion insists that women should be treated pretty much as men are. It is rooted for Americans in the historic dedication among us to equality. Our most venerable law school teacher, Malcolm Sharp, has recently provided testimony to the effect that he knows of no difference between women and men that is relevant to any determination by the law either as to the status of women or as to the capacity of women to practice law. His testimony is based on considerable experience, a sensitive judgment, and a deeply ingrained tolerance. His considerable experience includes early exposure to quite competent women in his own family; his sensitivity includes that remarkable intuition usually associated with the female temperament.

His testimony can be taken as a salutary caution with respect to some of the things I will be saying on this occasion. This is not to suggest, however, that he does not agree with whatever is sensible in what I am now about to say.

IV

One massive influence among us with respect to the proper relation between men and women has been the Old Testament. This may be seen in the Fortescue text I have mentioned. When one reads Fortescue, one has the sense of reading something *old*—less so when one reads Plato or Aristotle if only because they seem less dependent in what *they* say on chance, history and circumstances.

We are more concerned with how the issue addressed in the Fortescue text is approached by recourse to the Old Testament than we are with the particular issue itself. Under consideration by the author at one point are various "cases in which the rules of the laws of England and the civil laws [on the Continent] differ." (Chap. xxxviii; p. 93) One such case has to do with determining the status of a child when its father and mother are of different ranks in society (Chap. xlii; p. 101):

> The civil laws decree that *The issue always follows the mother;* so that, if a woman of servile condition marries a man of free condition, their offspring will be servile, and conversely, if a bondsman marries a free woman, he will beget none but free children. But the law of England adjudges the issue to follow, never the condition of the woman, but always that of the father. So that a free man engenders none but free children from a free woman, and also from a bondswoman; and a serf can beget in matrimony none but a serf. Which of these laws . . . is better in its rules? The law is cruel that condemns the guiltless children of a free man to servitude. Not less cruel, it is held, is the law that condemns the innocent children of a free woman to servitude.

Each of these responses—that of the civil laws on the Continent and that of the common law of England—is then considered. First, this is what is said about the civil laws, which held that "[t]he issue always follows the mother" (p. 103):

> The Civilians indeed say that the civil laws are superior in these rules of theirs. For they say that *A corrupt tree cannot bring forth good fruit, nor a good tree bring forth evil fruit.* And it is the rule of every law that every plant belongs to the soil where it is planted; also the issue is much more certain of the womb that brought him forth than of the father that begat him.

This argument on behalf of the civil laws does invoke a Biblical text ("A corrupt tree, etc."), but this is not one of the texts we *are* interested in today. The Biblical texts we are interested in are related to the creation of Adam and Eve. They are to be found, first, in the response by the English common law to the arguments of the Continental civil lawyers (*id.*):

> [T]he issue of a lawful bed knows its mother with no more certainty than it knows its begetter. For both laws now in contention say in unison that he is the father whom the nuptials indicate. Is it not, then, more convenient that the condition of the son should follow that of the father rather than that of the mother, when Adam says of married couples that *These two shall be one flesh,* which the Lord explaining in the Gospel said, *Now they are not twain, but one flesh.*

The common-law argument continues—and here, at last, we get to a Biblical text which purports to go to the root of the question of the proper relation between men and women (*id.*):

> And since the masculine comprises the feminine, the whole flesh thus made one ought to be referred to the masculine, which is more worthy. Wherefore the Lord called Adam and Eve, not Eve, but because they were one flesh, he called them both by the name of the man, namely, Adam, as appears in Genesis, chapter v.

The argument continues, in which still more Biblical texts are drawn upon, including the command to every wife, "Thou shalt be under the power of thy husband, and he shall rule over thee." (p. 105) It is what is assumed about the masculine inclusion of the feminine that we are particularly interested in here. This relation of the female to the male seems to be taken for granted throughout and may be seen in the closing lines of Fortescue's text where it is said that "all laws are in [a sovereign] potentially, as Eve was in Adam before she was formed." (chap. liv; p. 137)

Critical to the rationale for the effective subordination of women to men is the story that identifies Eve as having been made from Adam's rib. This Biblical story is taken seriously in determining how things are to be understood. The Bible is thereby taken as reflecting something vital about women in their relations with men. For example, it seems to be said that women need to be both protected and ruled. Such use of the Bible in the law raises questions about the legislation of morality, for it suggests to some that morality is usually little more than the establishment of a particular religious faith. Critics say that the law continues to incorporate Biblical teachings and attitudes with respect, for example, to abortion, divorce and inheritance. But that is a subject for another occasion.

Of course, there is the feminist response to all this. Woman, it is argued, "was not created from the side of man, but by the side of man." And just as the Old Testament supports one position on male-female relations, so the New Testament can be said to support another, however many traces of older views remain in it and may even be seen in the Fortescue passages I have drawn on. Thus one can read in *Galatians,* "There is neither Jew nor Greek, there is neither bond nor free, there is neither male nor female: for ye are all one in Christ Jesus." (3: 28. But see *Ephesians* 5: 24; *1 Corinthians* 11: 3, 7–9; *1 Timothy* 2: 8 –15. Compare *1 Corinthians* 11: 5; *Romans* 16: 1; *Philippians* 4: 2–3. Consider also the test in *Numbers* 5: 11–31.)

V

What are we to make, then, of these divergent Biblical responses: that in the Old Testament, which insists that "Eve was in Adam before she was formed" and that in the New Testament, which proclaims that "there is neither male nor female"?

Whatever may be said for the New Testament view, which does tend to look more to another world, is not the Old Testament account rooted in the life of this world, at least to the extent that it reflects traditional experience not only among the ancient Israelites but also around the world? Is that traditional experience based merely on the superior physical strength of males? Or does it reflect other fundamental differences between the sexes as well? It should be noticed, if only in passing, that a consistent difference in strength is not irrelevant for both psychic and social purposes. Thus, when Adam Smith considers the "causes of circumstances which naturally introduce subordination," the first in his list is "the superiority of personal qualifications," including physical strength. (See *The Wealth of Nations,* Bk. V, Chap. I, Pt. II.)

We did not have to wait upon the New Testament and the egalitarianism generated by it to see questioned the typical opinion about the appropriate relations between male and female. The "modern" position is anticipated in Plato's *Republic:* Socrates insists that the guardians of his "best city" should be chosen from qualified females and males alike. Even so, he and his male companions repeatedly relapse thereafter into talk that assumes the political superiority of the male. Socrates at times corrects this, reminding them of their principle of equality. (540 B. Compare 469D.) But are we not meant to see that these relapses are significant? And has not this pattern—a nominal insistence upon equality but a practical recognition of significant differences—been evident in every community which has thus far attempted to achieve a substantial similarity in the social treatment and functions of men and women?

What all this comes down to is, I suggest, the significance of *nature* in human affairs. What nature provides with respect to the woman's role in society may begin to be revealed anew by what will happen among us in the years immediately ahead. Clare Boothe Luce has recently observed (*Wall Street Journal*, March 26, 1980, p. 20):

> I think it is about time to leave the question of what is or is not woman's role in society up to Mother Nature—a difficult lady to fool.
>
> You have only to give women the same opportunities as men, and you will soon find what is or is not in their nature. What it is in women's nature to do, they will do, and you won't be able, in the end, to stop them.
>
> But you will also find, and so will they, that what is not in their nature, even if they are given every opportunity, they will not do, and you won't be able to make them do it.

Experience, however, is one thing, and perhaps what happens with women *will* be as decisive as Mrs. Luce anticipates, but understanding that experience is quite another thing. Understanding experience is critical to any effort to make sense of things and to chart our course, whether into new waters or back to familiar territory.

We are obliged, if only to protect ourselves from movements that may not really know where they are going, to consider such questions as the following: What is the nature of woman? What is the nature of man? What is the nature of their relations? What is the nature of society? Indeed, what is the nature of nature? Are the historic "disabilities" of woman truly disabilities? What, in fact, have they been primarily due to? Have they been due ultimately to superstition, to male selfishness, to chance? Or have they been due to nature?

I suspect that much of what we say about these matters today depends on a depreciation of nature. What *is* Mother Nature like and how are her dictates to be discerned? What status should be accorded to them, when they are discerned? The depreciation and even denial of nature suggest that sound reasoning about human affairs is limited and that enduring standards and hence prudential judgement are, in principle, ruled out. In fact, it may be that the question of male-female relations is the most critical issue bearing today upon the determination of what nature means to us, individually and socially. This issue can go to the heart of things, not only in the community but also in the family. How fundamental this issue can be is suggested by the response of a Rosary colleague of mine, Sister Kathleen Ashe, to an historian's "notion of an immutable and somewhat mysterious 'nature of women'." My colleague wrote, "This reveals a profoundly anti-historical attitude, since history deals with change over time, while talk about the nature of woman assumes that women are reassuringly static." What we see here, and this can be detected in much of what we hear and read on "the woman question" today, is the suggestion that there really is no such thing as a permanent nature of anything.

I venture now to make a few observations of my own on the subject of the nature of women and the appropriate relations between men and women before I turn to the question of women as practitioners of the law. We all know something about what men and women are like: after all, we have been associating with many women and men all our lives. It is hard for me to believe that the considerable and obvious differences between men and women, which have long been evident and which remain evident, do not have deep causes and profound implications. These differences bear upon contemporary efforts toward the sexual liberation of women. For example, I have long had the impression that the new sexual freedom amounts in the typical case to a thoughtless and sometimes cruel exploitation of women. For many reasons and in many ways women, who may be naturally more in need of modesty and more to be damaged by shameless activity, are more vulnerable than men in sexual relations. I see no prospect of change in this respect, but only more of the exploitation I have referred to. Substantial exploitation, in the name of liberation, may already be seen all around us.

It is also hard for me to believe that child-bearing and the hormonal and other physiological differences related to the child-bearing capacity of women do not have profound consequences for the female psyche. Here I return to what we have always sensed. I do not refer only to what happens in pregnancy, during which many women report subtle changes in their intellectual powers, but also to what may be generally true of women because of their remarkable capacity to be impregnated and to bear the fetus. *Is* it prudent to assume that the differences observed heretofore between women and men have always been culturally conditioned or that they can be limited to the reproductive functions narrowly understood? Do not the generality of men naturally tend to think differently from the generality of women on many things?

In many ways, women tend to be more practical, more sensible, less detached, than men. This may be in part due to their vulnerability and in part due to their more intimate connection with the generation of life. Indeed, life itself can be considered "female." (See Karl Reinhardt, 6 *Interpretation* 220 [1977].) Women can even be considered to have always "known better" than to sacrifice intimate associations by losing themselves, as men are more apt to do, in ascetic isolation or in philosophical pursuits. In fact, women can be said to be closer to nature than men, at least to nature in one of its aspects, and any depreciation of nature tends to cut the female loose from the moorings on which she instinctively depends. The city, which is man's "place," tends to be more concerned with conventions.

Nature, we have been taught by the ancients, makes nothing or almost nothing, in vain. Considerable differences between men and women have been evident over most of recorded history in all but the most primitive circumstances. Would it not be folly to suppose that these massive differences are *not* rooted in deep natural differences that have, are "intended" to have, and are bound to have, profound implications both for action and for an understanding of how things are? I urge you, whether male or female, not to disregard what you have long observed and perhaps have always known. I will return to these questions.

VI

I turn now to a less controversial subject, the role of women as lawyers. Perhaps we already have enough experience to permit us to recognize that women do well at the bar. It is fair that they be given in compensation and honors whatever men in like circumstances would receive. Two caveats are in order here: the child-bearing role of women is likely in most cases to affect their careers significantly; there is also the likelihood that women will have to do double-duty, carrying a full load in the law office and yet managing their households. Well-meaning husbands do promise to share the work at home, but that promise is hard to keep when it threatens to require the sacrifice of *his* full development in the career he has chosen. Does not the best among us require that *some* be fully developed professionally? But, it will be asked by the feminist, whose career in the world-at-large should be sacrificed? Why should it routinely be the woman's? Because, it can be answered in our circumstances, the woman who does bear and rear children will usually have chosen, whatever her intentions, to settle for less than the fullest development in her career in the world-at-large if the proper development of the children is not to be sacrificed to the professional ambitions of both parents.

Let us turn now to *The Merchant of Venice* for the light it can throw on our immediate concerns. All of you remember Portia: she may well be one of the most successful advocates in literature (even though, it should be noticed, she conceals her partisanship [because of her intimate association through her husband with Shylock's intended victim] even while she pretends to be an impartial judge). She takes charge in order to save the life of her husband's benefactor from Shylock's ferocity.

Is not Portia somewhat ruthless in the way she proceeds? This can be troublesome for the sensitive reader. It would be troublesome in a man also, but is it not even worse in a woman? Or is it unfair to deplore ruthlessness and combativeness more in a woman than in a man? We can again draw upon our opinions (our antiquated opinions, some would say) about the nature of women, but not without recognizing that Shylock does have to be stopped.

Portia's recourse to the conduct she exhibits in court points up the limitations of *her* man. Had he been the man he should have been (had he had the imagination of a Shakespeare, for example) he himself would have effected the rescue of his benefactor. Portia must conceal her gender (and not only because of the prejudices of her time, perhaps) in order to be able to do what she does. One wonders what the long-range consequences will be of her revelation to her husband, at the end of the play, of what she has done. What will their relationship be thereafter? Among the lessons perhaps taught to her somewhat immature husband is that a wife should mean more to him than a friend.

Portia is superior to her husband in almost every way that we can see. No doubt she is astute enough to recognize that the woman who parades her superiority to her husband is asking for trouble in her marriage, if only because of the "male ego," whether in her husband or in her husband's friends. Be that as it may, she is superior to him. But she somehow loves him and thereby is willing to subordinate herself to him in critical respects. She must be courted, and she must be protected until she is won. Her father does what he can to assure her a satisfactory marriage. Are most females in need of benevolent male protection in such circumstances? Still, Portia may control the determination of a spouse for herself, but perhaps no more than a wise father might anticipate. Be that too as it may, she is won; she then formally subordinates herself to a husband inferior to her in virtue, intelligence, and wealth. She gives herself to him as "her lord, her governor, her king." (III, ii, 165)

We are again driven to consider the nature of women and how that bears upon the relation between men and women. Does love usually mean more to a woman than to a man, and does this make her more vulnerable and more prone to that subordination which makes marriage possible? Does her greater openness to love, and perhaps a natural inclination toward compliance, narrow the range of her interests even while deepening them? Perhaps Portia did so well in her career at the bar because she had such a personal interest in the outcome of her case. Perhaps, indeed, women may be less inclined than men to throw themselves wholeheartedly into other people's quarrels. No doubt many a lawyer has at times felt that he was being used by his clients in quarrels that the world could very well do without. However that may be, this is likely to be the only case at law that the wily Portia will ever have, and she can break one rule after another in her successful effort to see justice done, or at least to prevent the worst injustice.

VII

Let us now set aside, if only for the moment, considerations of what individual women might prefer or be suited for with respect to the practice of law. Let us ask instead what, if anything, the community and the human race should prefer in the way of careers for women.

More women at the bar may be good for the bar. It may help to moderate certain passions that men are prone to. Mr. Sharp recently called to my attention an observation by an eminent scientist: "One of the reasons why, on the whole, women have had difficulty so far in making very good scientists is that they are not contrary enough. Happily time will cure all that. Time will produce belligerent, contrary, questioning, challenging women as it has produced belligerent, contrary, questioning, challenging men." (Jacob Bronowski, *The Origins of Knowledge and Imagination*, p. 120) "Happily," indeed! Would such a transformation of women—not of the occasional woman, but of women "on the whole"—really be good for the community? Is it good that the more talented women should become like men—that is, like men in their most combative, ambitious, and hence "productive" forms? Can we reasonably expect men to begin to supply routinely those gentler qualities we have come to expect from women? If we do not routinely get them from someone, are we not considerably poorer both as a community and as a species?

Still another concern for the community is where women come to the bar and to certain other professions *from*. My own law school class (the Class of 1951) had only a few women. Today one-third to one-half of a law school class is apt to be made up of women. This means that women are being drawn from teaching youngsters, which they may be naturally better able to do than men, into activities which they may not be able to do better than men, except perhaps as mediators. Also, it should be said, teaching, properly understood, may be intrinsically more rewarding than the practice of law. It pays far less, of course, but that is understandable: for one thing, teaching is apt to have much more compensation built right into the very activity.

A generation or so ago, high school and elementary school teachers, who tend to be mostly women, were in the upper third in academic qualifications on college campuses. Now, I am told, prospective teachers are in the lowest fifth of college classes in academic qualifications as measured by high school records and IQ tests. Is this good for the Country? Where *are* the brighter people needed, in education *or* in law and medicine and business? What should we, as a community, want? What changes in opinion are required to induce the better-qualified, men as well as women, once again to consider teaching youngsters? We should wonder, for example, whether the spiritual compensation for teachers has been lessened by the considerable use of schools to serve non-educational aims.

One cannot stress too strongly here the influence of opinion. Its influence can be seen as well in how women regard their role in the bearing and rearing of children. I suspect that that will always remain, nature being what she is, the most satisfying life for most women. But from time to time, ideology will conspire with faulty reasoning to mislead women as to what they should desire and be satisfied with. Still, nature can be depended on to reassert herself. Nature also depends on us to think about what she means and to use our reason both in making the best use of what she offers and in having the satisfaction of figuring out what is happening and why.

VIII

I have made various suggestions (some of them old-fashioned, some of them perhaps new to you, however truly old-fashioned they may be) about the question of the proper relations between female and male. I have suggested that it is not sufficient in these matters to rely on egalitarian doctrines or on legal resolutions. A massive recourse to law so as to reorder these relations is like our intermittent efforts to control prices by regulation. Such efforts can appear to succeed for awhile; but the more successful these efforts are in the short run, the higher their cost in the long run. Among other things, price controls usually conceal from us what is truly happening in the market.

Similarly, there may be decided limitations in "reforming" sexual relations by law. To the extent that the law "works" in these matters, it may be only with respect to secondary considerations; or it may simply distort vital relations and subvert much-needed standards. There may be profound differences between the sexes which law can somewhat control but whose implications it can never eliminate in a healthy and enduring way.

There are, of course, many similarities between male and female; otherwise, there could not be the powerful sexual attraction that is usually vital to human life. But there are also the profound differences which I have several times suggested; otherwise, sexual attraction would not be as troublesome as it sometimes is. We will all be poorer if the critical differences between the sexes are not recognized and made proper use of.

All this is still another way of saying that the question of natural differences and the question of the significance of natural differences are difficult questions at the root of this problem of the proper relations between female and male.

IX

Much of what we hear today about men and women depends on modern social science and on legislation and litigation grounded in the social sciences. All too often, however, social science seems to deny what is obvious to common sense. Of course, common sense is sometimes wrong, for example on the question whether it is the earth's movement or the sun's that accounts for the apparent daily motion of the sun across the sky. But generally, and especially with respect to human relations, common sense still has a lot to be said for it.

The limits of common sense are evident to us all. The vulnerability of the social sciences, on the other hand, tends to be concealed, at least from the sophisticated. But vulnerable they are because of their insistence that "values" cannot be truly known, but can only be arbitrarily accepted; because of their belief that only verifiable data and statistics can teach us anything; because of their "ideological" presuppositions; and because of their determined disregard of a common sense rooted in considerable observation, reflection, and experience. The modern social science often obscures facts that we are all somehow aware of, especially facts about nature and the nature of things.

Better guides to an understanding of human things are offered us by our greatest artists. The ancient Greek dramatists provide us impressive portraits of remarkable women—women such as Clytemnestra, Antigone, Alcestis, Hecuba, and Medea. Then there are other artists who have provided us insightful portraits of women in the ordinary walks of life— artists such as Sappho, perhaps the best lyric poet in antiquity, and Jane Austen, perhaps the best novelist in the English language.

Finally, there is Shakespeare. More than by any other artist available in English, it is by Shakespeare that we can be reminded of the distinctive contributions that male and female make, separately and together, to humanity. We are also reminded by Shakespeare that appearances of superiority, however they should be respected for the sake of "domestic tranquility," should not be confused by the thoughtful with true superiority, that superiority which depends on an informed concern with the enduring nature of things.

Permit me to end my talk with still another story. You will remember that I began with a story of the truckdriver, the motorcyclists, and the waitress. Who is the most noteworthy figure in *that* story? Some will say, the truckdriver. I myself am inclined to the waitress, the one who made sense, in her artistic way, of what had happened. But we need not decide between them: each contributed to the occasion what each could contribute best, in order that a rough justice might be done and in order that the meaning of things might be properly understood. (Other versions of this story present the truckdriver as a woman and the observer as a man. My talk on this occasion has in effect been addressed, at least in part, to the question, *Does* that rearrangement make as much sense?)

Art, too, may be seen in my concluding story, art in the hands of still another woman who recognized the distinctive contribution *she* could make to both her family and the common good. This story comes from the *Talmud* and should provide an additional commentary on the *Genesis* story about the creation of Eve, which my passages from Fortescue drew upon (*Theology Today*, October 1976, p. 268, citing *Sanhedrin*, 39a):

> A Gentile ruler said to Rabbi Gamaliel, "Your God is a thief, because he stole one of Adam's ribs." Thereupon the rabbi's daughter said to her father, "Leave him to me; I will answer him." Turning to the ruler she exclaimed, "Thieves broke into our house and stole a silver vessel, leaving a gold one in its place!" The ruler laughed and said, "I wish I could have burglars like that every day." "Well," she retorted, "that is what our God did: he took a mere rib from the first man but in exchange he gave him a wife."

Some would see in this story still another indication that the female was regarded by the Old Testament people as little more than the property of the male. But that would be to permit one's unexamined presuppositions to distort one's vision. Rather, one could well see here a most politic woman protecting her own in a manner worthy of a Portia at her best. When one notices that this *is* the *Talmud*, with its supposed male chauvinism, in which a woman distinguished herself thus, one is encouraged to question whether the lives of women in unenlightened times and places were always as oppressed and unrewarding as it is now fashionable to believe.

Does not nature assert herself on behalf of healthy relations between men and women in decent communities, no matter what the law may seem to say? I am prepared to believe that more often than not women have gotten their way in intimate associations of men with women, if only because most women may naturally have a more persistent and a more reliable sense than do most men both of what is good for them in family relations and of how best to secure that good.

E.

Sovereignty of the Law

25

GUN CONTROL, CITIZEN CONTROL

A well regulated Militia, being necessary to the security of a free State, the right of the people to keep and bear Arms, shall not be infringed.

THE SECOND AMENDMENT

I

Two recent experiences of mine have helped me think about the Law Week subject you have assigned me, "Law and Order". In these matters the experiences one happens to have help shape one's opinions, perhaps sometimes far more than they should.

A week ago yesterday at about 2:30 in the morning my wife and I left Interstate 55, on our way back to Chicago from St. Louis, for a look at Bloomington, Illinois, where we thought we might find a restaurant. But we saw nothing open at all; nor was anyone else on the streets, either on foot or in other automobiles. Our run through the town found us confronted at one point by a long stop-light. We stopped dead for what seemed several minutes. I wondered what the rationale was for our scrupulous obedience to a traffic signal which probably no one else in that town had any awareness of at that hour of the night. I could even imagine ourselves as the last people alive on earth, still moving about according to now superfluous rules. What does law-abidingness call for in such circumstances?

This talk was given to a Law Week Meeting, Optimist Club Luncheon, Oak Park, Illinois, May 5, 1984. (Original title: "Law and Order: Hope and Fears (On Handguns).")

The epigraph is taken from the amendments to the Constitution of the United States. See, for those amendments and for the amendments that have been proposed by Congress but not ratified by the States, Anastaplo, *The Constitution of 1787: A Commentary* (Baltimore: Johns Hopkins University Press, 1988), pp. 288–99. Discussion of these amendments is planned in Anastaplo, *The Amendments to the Constitution: A Commentary* (in course of preparation for initial publication in the Loyola law journal).

My second immediately relevant experience consisted of attendance this past weekend at a hearing on handgun violence conducted in my Hyde Park neighborhood in Chicago by two members of the Illinois General Assembly. This was in connection with a bill before the Assembly to curb the production and sale of handguns in this State. Familiar data and old arguments were presented, data and arguments that have been available for a very long time. It was said that there are in private hands in this Country some thirty million handguns. It has long been obvious to many students of this subject that the key question is not how these guns are distributed and regulated, but rather whether so many privately owned guns should exist among us. It has been said that we are the only advanced industrialized country in the world, with the exception of South Africa, to permit such a proliferation of handguns. It has also been said that the preponderance of informed opinion supports an effort to restrict severely the number of guns in this Country. It is evident from the hearing I attended that gun-control advocates believe themselves to have far the better arguments, including with respect to the limiting meaning of the "well regulated Militia" referred to in the Bill of Rights.

Yet it is also evident that the number of privately owned guns grows every year in the United States. What can one make of the steady escalation in deadly weapons among us? What should the law try to do, and why? So one can ask as with my Bloomington traffic light, What does law-abidingness call for here? I put both my Bloomington experience and the legislative hearing aside for the moment as I consider further our gun situation and what it suggests about the problem of law and order.

II

We do have an abundance of guns among us and, it seems, will long continue to have them. Is it merely a matter of "conditioning" that makes it so difficult for us to give up our guns as well as to induce others to give up theirs? Certainly it is in part that, a conditioning that draws upon the American frontier tradition and upon what it is believed that manhood demands.

But I suspect it is not only that. Gun possession has something to do as well with the desire many have to keep their fate somewhat within their control. It perhaps reflects in part a distrust of the willingness and ability of government to protect them. One articulate advocate of severe restrictions on gun possession suggested in an article written some ten years ago why it is that guns do have the appeal they have for so many (Franklin E. Zimring, *The Nation*, April 10, 1972, p. 458):

To some extent, the vicious circle of urban guns is the result of misinforma- tion about the risk of accidental death and the usefulness of guns in defense of the home. But it is foolish to think that millions of American families keep handguns merely because they have not read the statistics, or to suppose that shipping them the latest gun control article will change their minds. The risk of accidental or homicidal death from a gun in your home—though far greater than the chance that the gun will save life—is nevertheless small. In the great majority of gun-owning homes, the only real use of the gun is to make its owner feel less uneasy about the possibility that a hostile stranger will invade his home. This feeling of well-being is a statistical illusion, but an emotional reality. People will fight the statistics that show otherwise because, if their guns do not give them any real measure of protection, they have no other way to deal with their fears. In addition, everything that makes the handgun a spe- cial problem in America also makes it hard to understand that the handgun is not effective against the home-invading criminal. How can something so deadly be so ineffective? Trying to persuade someone that the gun in his house is not really protecting him is like trying to persuade a nervous friend that flying in a jet plane—7 miles above ground and going 600 miles an hour— is really safer than driving the family car to Florida.

It would seem, therefore, that the possession of guns offers some assur- ance with respect to the fears that many are subject to. On the other hand, the efforts to control these weapons among us testify to the confidence in the community that is expected when men govern themselves. Gun advo- cates respond to efforts to cut down the number of guns, "You should go after the criminals, those who make us fearful and who deliberately mis- use guns." To this the gun-control people reply, "It is far more effective in our circumstances to regulate the large body of the public who tend to be law-abiding and who pay for and thus make possible that abundance of guns in our country with which criminals threaten us all."

And so the argument goes back and forth. Perhaps one thing is agreed upon by the contending parties, and that is that guns are all too frequently made bad use of in this Country. But what should be done about that re- mains open to considerable debate, in which debate the National Rifle Association is given far more "credit" than it "deserves."

III

I suggest that the N.R.A. is regarded as much more influential than it really is. The underlying issues here are so critical for us that no single or- ganization is responsible for the presence of guns among us, however much credit or blame is assigned to it by partisans. (If the N.R.A. is as important as some believe it to be, gun-control advocates should consider joining it in large numbers in order to subject N.R.A. policies to a searching examination with a view to possible reforms.)

The underlying issues may be seen when we consider another American institution and the efforts that are made to regulate it. I refer to the automobile and the controversy we have about the speed at which it should be driven on the highway. Let us assume for our purpose what is generally believed, that speed does kill as well as waste energy. Still, difficulties arise when we attempt, especially over a long period and without the support of wartime dedication, to check our highway speed. It is apparent that these difficulties do not depend upon any organization comparable to the National Rifle Association.

There are two principal means that the community can use, in addition to public information campaigns and persuasion, to keep highway speed down. One is by so designing automobiles and highways that the speed cannot be much higher than 55 miles per hour. The other is by using sanctions, including fines and imprisonments, which are to be enforced by police, who are permitted to employ radar, helicopters, and other devices to help keep us "honest." How many of the sanctions we are prepared to pay for, as courts and prisons become overcrowded and police forces overworked, remains a question.

Which of these two means—the adjustment of designs or the dependence on sanctions—do we prefer and why? Automobiles can be so made as to keep most of them within the speed limit. Do we want such a restriction, aside from the risk we might run of being unable to accelerate above the speed limit in an emergency? Or do we want a choice left to us? Is it more dignified to be able to misbehave and yet not do it? Is there something demeaning in being kept from doing wrong? What does *free will* mean in these matters? Does a good life include a certain amount of risk-taking or at least the opportunity to take risks?

Besides, do we not always have some reservations about law itself, about the goodness of law? Furthermore, do we not often believe that we have a natural right to move around freely, that restrictions upon movement should be limited and always within our power to resist to some extent?

IV

Whether we are considering automobile control or gun control, we encounter an old issue that goes back before the very foundation of this Republic. It is because this issue is fundamental that it keeps cropping up, whether the concern is with the regulation of automobiles, guns, alcohol, drugs or sexual activity (including such matters as abortion). This issue was already a familiar one in the late 1780s, when ratification of the Constitution was being debated. On one side were the Federalists, who stood for a stronger central government; on the other side were the Anti-Federalists, who stood for more power in the States, if anywhere, either under the then-existing Articles of Confederation or under another constitution.

The Federalists made much of the need for *energy* (or what we would call efficiency) in the central government. The Anti-Federalists made much of their concern for *liberty,* so much so that Publius could criticize them in *Federalist* No. 26 for having "a zeal for liberty more ardent than enlightened."

This conflict between a desire for governmental energy and a desire for personal liberty is deep in the American character itself. It is not to be easily removed or even moderated, especially since most of us do want government to be effective with respect to some matters while respectful of personal liberty, or hands-offish, with respect to other matters.

It is, I suspect, a conflict that adds a certain vitality to the American way of life, just as the tension between Reason and Revelation adds a certain vitality to the life of Western Civilization. The question remains as to where the authoritative observer of such juxtapositions should be stationed.

Another way of putting the conflict between personal liberty and governmental energy is to say that one speaks to our fears and the other speaks to our hopes. That no simple distinction between them is possible, however, is evident from the fact that the advocates of liberty can say with some plausibility that free men are really more efficient, while the advocates of energy in government can say, also with some plausibility, that effective government is needed if liberty is to be enduring and, indeed, that true liberty may be seen primarily in genuine self-government by a people.

V

I have suggested that a desire for personal liberty may be seen in the opponents to gun control as well as in those who argue, as we have seen in some advertisements, that our right to drive is encroached upon by the current speed limits on our highways.

Perhaps a non-political liberty is made so much of in this way these days because we feel that we are now so limited in so many activities. Do we sense that we have less and less political control of our lives? We do feel that we should have some "responsibility" somewhere, that it is good for our character and for the tone of the community if we are left free to take chances and even to hurt ourselves.

When we are reminded of the sanctions we face if we misuse our liberty, it is argued, we become aware of our capacity as moral agents. On the other hand, when we have good done for us (by cutting down, say, either the supply of guns or the capacity of automobiles), we are treated as mere forces to be curbed, not as human beings to be reasoned with.

Besides, the advocates of liberty argue, there is danger of a police state that would curtail severely both personal and political liberty. They would rather have some violence among us than a pervasive repression. If our guns and our automobiles can be taken over, they ask, what would come next?

Still, it should be noticed that liberty does depend on the character of the free agent. Is not an effective regime needed, with its ability to train and teach citizens, if we are to have a people of the character required for a proper use of our considerable liberty?

At the very least, it can be agreed, a sensible government will take seriously the opinions the public holds. There is an intimate relation between the opinions that are generally held and the laws that are likely to be effective. What the law can do to shape public opinion, and how, is a delicate question. That the law can have a considerable influence may be seen in what the law has done in the quarter of a century since the 1954 Supreme Court opinion in *Brown* v. *Board of Education* to make out-and-out racial prejudice no longer respectable in this Country.

VI

If guns are to be virtually wiped out among us, public opinion will have to change about both the effectiveness and the respectability of gun ownership. That is for the long run, of course. What of the short run?

Talking to people is not enough in our circumstances, it seems. Should not the supply of guns simply be cut down, something that should be easier to do than was cutting down the supply of alcohol during Prohibition? It is easier to make liquor than it is to make guns *and ammunition,* and the supposed benefits of alcohol are more evident.

It should be obvious that guns are usually meant to be dangerous when they are used, whereas automobiles, for example, need not be dangerous most of the time. Besides, we can very well imagine our lives without guns, but hardly without automobiles, except in places such as New York City.

But even short-run corrections mandated by law sometimes seem unlikely. What then can one do? Unilateral disarmament is helpful to oneself here, as it is with television, no matter what one's neighbors do in most circumstances. It is said that "if handguns are outlawed, only outlaws will have handguns," to which one answer could be, "And it will serve them right!" Another answer, at least in this Country, is that the police would also have them.

It is also useful to try to persuade one's neighbor to give up his gun, just as it would be useful to discourage him from keeping rattlesnakes or pit bulls. This is the least that someone who is concerned to protect himself can do. As for the problem of home invaders, there are safer and more reliable measures that an imaginative householder can resort to in an effort to provide himself some measure of defense and tranquility, especially since he is on familiar ground. Thus an excitable dog is likely to provide more reliable protection than a gun, and not only because the dog is better able than a gun to distinguish between friend and foe. Inexpensive electric eye devices can also be useful.

It should go without saying that a general respect for law and order can help moderate the crime waves that are in part responsible for the massive recourse to the guns that threaten their respectable owners and that supply would-be criminals with many, perhaps even most, of the guns that do so much damage to everyone. A general law-abidingness is promoted, it seems to me, by doing what one can, even if ostentatiously at times, to obey whenever possible the laws one confronts. This could well include obeying stop-lights at deserted crossroads, and telling others about it. The salutary character of tales about deliberate law-abidingness becomes evident when one hears about nice college students who routinely bribe traffic policemen, both in Chicago and in its staid suburbs, upon being stopped for moving violations. The classic tale of deliberate law-abidingness is that told in Plato's *Crito* about a man who ranks high in the annals of liberty.

VII

I have suggested that there is among us an inevitable and perhaps healthy tension between the desire for personal liberty and the need for effective republican government, which can be understood as another form of liberty. Whether the emphasis is placed upon collective energy or upon individual liberty, law is needed. Thus law is needed both to regulate one's use of dangerous property and to identify and protect one's very possession of such and other property.

Where the emphasis is to be placed and precisely what action is to be taken depend on prudence—on a sense of what our regime is capable of and of what changing circumstances call for. No matter where the emphasis is placed from time to time, whether upon individual liberty or upon government action, we cannot help but rely upon one another. Or, as Publius put it in *Federalist* No. 29, "Where in the name of common sense are our fears to end if we may not trust our sons, our brothers, our neighbours, our fellow-citizens?"

26

HUMAN NATURE AND
THE CRIMINAL LAW

Socrates: *I think that you and all other men as well as myself hold it worse to do than to suffer wrong and worse to escape than to suffer punishment.*

Polus: *And I maintain that neither I nor any other man so believes. Why, would you rather suffer than do wrong?*

Socrates: *Yes, and so would you and everyone else.*

Polus: *Far from it! Neither I nor you nor anyone.*

Plato

I

Our old University of Chicago Law School teacher Malcolm Sharp did warn me that he would, in his introduction, propose that he has always recognized a greater role than do I for the irrational in human affairs. I must dissent, however, from this proposition, and not only because of the massive and even overriding fact which he did concede, the fact that there are so many more pets in my household than in his. I suspect I really make more of the irrational than even he does in that I make greater allowances than do most people for the vagaries of opinion in human affairs. Opinion very much depends on the irrational, even while it yearns for the sensible.

My case against Mr. Sharp in this respect is further supported by a

---

This talk was given to the Law Alumni Association, The University of Chicago, Chicago, Illinois, May 6, 1976. It has been published, with notes, in Anastaplo, "Human Nature and the First Amendment," 40 *University of Pittsburgh Law Review* 661, at 715–29 (1979).

The epigraph is taken from Plato, *Gorgias* 474B (W. D. Woodhead translation).

comparison of our markedly different abilities to deal with intermittently irrational bar admission committees. Consider the following facts: When Mr. Sharp retired for the second time as a law school teacher at the University of New Mexico, not long before we induced him to return to Chicago to take the post of chairman of the Political Science Department of Rosary College, he applied for admission to the New Mexico bar. This was done in order that he might become associated, down in Albuquerque, with the law firm established by several of his former students at the University of New Mexico Law School.

I first learned of Mr. Sharp's application for admission to the New Mexico bar when I received in the mail, here in Chicago, an official inquiry on behalf of a New Mexico Character and Fitness Committee considering his qualifications for admission to that bar. I responded to that inquiry in what I took to be the spirit which had prompted him to list *me* as a character reference. That is, I looked up the recommendation he had written on my behalf almost two decades before when I had reapplied, unsuccessfully and for the last time, for admission to the Illinois bar, and simply used in speaking about him almost word for word what he had said about me. It was pure plagiarism, of course, but it was evidently inspired plagiarism, for Mr. Sharp was thereupon admitted to the New Mexico bar without any difficulty. This, you will agree, must at least say something about our respective reputations as reliable judges of character. I trust you will keep all this in mind as you assess the kind things he has said about me on this and other occasions.

On the other hand, what I can say on my own about Mr. Sharp really does not need to be said, since it has long been known by all who have been his students over the years: you know as well as I his integrity, his desire and ability to be useful, and his old-fashioned charm, all matters I have touched upon in my tribute to him in the Summer 1975 issue of our *Law Alumni Journal*.

II

I turn now to the problem of crime. I begin by comparing certain attitudes I have noticed abroad with those to be found in this Country. Some years ago I used to conduct annual archaeological tours of the Greek mainland. One of the remarkable things I observed in the country of my forebears was how safe private property was there. For many years (I do not know whether this is still true) one could leave one's luggage unattended in the lobby of an Athens railroad station or hotel and expect to find it still there hours later. A sometimes fanatical respect for the property of another could be seen throughout much of Greece. It may be in its origin connected with the village mentality.

I was able to observe on one occasion something about how this mentality had taken root. During a steamship crossing from the Mediterranean to this Country, I happened to be seated with a table of quite lively young, Greek immigrants, ranging in age from twenty to thirty-five, on their way to a new life in Canada. A couple of days before the ship was due to make a stop in New York, one of the men announced to us at the table that a passenger had had something of value taken from her cabin. I forget now what it was that had been stolen, but I shall never forget the responses of my tablemates to the announcement. One of them said that of course no one would be permitted to disembark in New York City until the stolen property had been recovered. None of the others objected to this expectation on the grounds that it was either unlikely or unfair. When I observed these men's rather naive expectation that a shipload of passengers would be held in ransom until a theft had been righted, I began to understand better than I had why property was so safe in Greece. I could also see that one might well doubt whether a respect for property secured in this manner was worth the price exacted in official surveillance and in mutual accountability. Does not all this reflect the village mentality to which I have referred?

There is still another side to this part of the Greek character. Their respect for property is intimately related to the sense of shame. It would be shameful for both the culprit and his family for him to be exposed as a thief. The most troublesome consequence of this sense of shame—or, it can be said, this sense of honor—may be the difficulty Greeks have of making sensible political compromises except in the most extreme national emergencies. They are, among other things, easily offended. Exhibitions of passion, including fist fights in the streets, seem much more common there than here. One is not surprised to learn that their highway fatality rate, relative to the number of automobiles, is much higher than ours.

It should be evident from what I have said that the problem of crime is, in large part, the problem of the kind of community one wants to live in, the problem of the price one is willing to pay to get the assurances one may seek. Put another way, the problem may not be whether there are to be vices and crimes among us, but rather which kinds of misconduct and restrictions we prefer.

III

This is not to suggest that crime may not be a problem in itself or that it may not be perceived as a special problem. Certainly it has been a growing concern among us in this Country for some years now. No doubt, this concern is in part due to our heightened expectations or, put another way, to our lowered ability to absorb pain. As a more and more prosperous people, we have become somewhat soft, if not even somewhat decadent. Partly because of the communications industry, we have become more and more aware of the violence around us. We are also more apt to be intimidated by it than our predecessors would have been a century ago. Much more is made of the crime that there is around us. How distorted our perceptions can be is repeatedly brought home to me when I hear people from around the city and the supposedly safe suburbs speak in somber terms of what life in our inner-city neighborhood of Hyde Park must be like. It is hard to recognize from what they say the fairly safe life that we who live near the University of Chicago in Hyde Park have long been accustomed to. We, on the other hand, are apt to wonder how others can bear to live where so little seems to be going on in the way of cultural and intellectual stimulation.

But, surely, the growing concern with crime cannot be attributed only to a changed sensitivity. Statistics have to be taken into account, but the relevant statistics are difficult to interpret properly. For one thing, there is the effect of improved reporting of crime, due both to more sophisticated technology for this purpose and to our increased sensitivity with respect to such matters. Then, we are told, there is the relation of certain crimes, especially crimes of violence, to various age levels. When the violent crime-prone age group is particularly large in our society, the incidence of violent crimes can be expected to rise. This has evidently been true during the past decade or so due to the baby boom after the Second World War. We are told that crime rates can be expected to change as the age profile of the population changes, with violent crimes tapering off.

However this may be, the greater awareness of crime, partly because of the dramatization of it in the media, can drive people off the streets and thereby make those who have to be on the streets more vulnerable. Publicity does magnify trends and effects. Such dramatization may also so present crime as to attract to it various marginal types. Added to this are other contributions of technology, partly in the form of cheap lethal weapons, partly in the form of handy transportation (good roads and many, many automobiles), and partly in the form of more highly publicized goods to steal. All this means that crime becomes easier to fall into and "to get away with." This is especially so for a people which has always prized privacy and liberty, particularly the liberty of mobility and the contribution such mobility is supposed to make to the good life of the private man. (Compare traditional village life in this critical respect.) The American love of personal liberty may be at the core of our crime problem: we simply do not want to put up with the spiritual and social restrictions that would be necessary to reduce among us the incidence of crime to the level to be found in, say, Scotland or Saudi Arabia, two quite different countries I happen to know something about from personal experience.

The most we are willing to put up with in the way of restrictions is not with a view to fundamental reform of our way of life, which we seem to be fairly satisfied with, but with a view only to adjustments in the face of certain unfortunate derivations from that way of life. I believe it is significant, for instance, that our emphasis should be on "crime *control*," as in the "Omnibus Crime *Control* and Safe Streets Act of 1968," in the "Crime *Control* Act of 1973," or in the useful book by Norval Morris and Gordon Hawkins, *The Honest Politician's Guide to Crime Control.*

To put the emphasis on *control* is to concede that the causes of crime must remain largely untouched. In some respects, this is the least disruptive and the cheapest way to proceed. Related to this is the proposed remedy of getting rid of a good deal of criminality by decriminalizing various activities, the so-called victimless crimes. This reflects and reinforces the sense of liberty that Americans prize: people, it is said, should not be prevented from hurting themselves. The critical problem with the crime-control approach to crime, an approach that may be unavoidable in our circumstances, is that it can fail to recognize the role the law should have in shaping the character both of individuals and of communities. Rather, this approach to crime pretty much ignores underlying causes and the shaping of opinion and devotes itself instead primarily to intermittent containment of crime wherever it threatens to get completely out of hand.

The breakdown of this approach is rather charmingly illustrated by an official memorandum I found posted some months ago on a bulletin board in the Chicago Police Headquarters Building at Eleventh and State. This memorandum, of 13 May 1975, was addressed to the "Watch Comdrs., Tact. Lieut., Foot Patrol L.," with "Special Attention" to "Security Officers; Front and Rear Doors." I found particularly curious that the security officers at the front and rear entrances to police headquarters have to be alerted to the problem of crime getting out of control! The memorandum, issued in the name of the commanding officer of the Police Department, reads:

It has been brought to our attention by High Ranking Officers of our Department that we have a Major Problem existing IN & NEAR our Police Bldg.

The Problem is PROSTITUTES & PIMPS loitering in the Lobby and in front of the Police Building before going to Court and after leaving Branch 41 in this Bldg. . . .

Pimps are also loitering in the hallways on the 9th Floor soliciting the Prostitutes to work for them. This creates a situation whereby we can end up with a serious crime being committed inside our building immediately outside a Court Room. We are going to end up with a shooting or serious cutting where one Pimp will attack another. This same solicitation is taking place in our Lobby and in the Parking Lot across the street.

EFFECTIVE IMMEDIATELY: The Watch Commander and Fld. Lt. on the 2nd Watch will be held responsible for strict enforcement of Ch. 192–6 of the City Code . . .

This memorandum indicates the inevitable limits of our current emphasis upon crime control. It is an emphasis that depends too much on the police and courts. Indeed, it places an impossible burden upon them, ignoring as it does what has long been known about the relation of crime to human nature. There is something instructive in the desperate police official's pathetic prediction, "[W]e can end up with a serious crime being committed inside our building immediately outside a Court Room." This does bear thinking about.

IV

To say that this bears thinking about is not to say, however, that there are any ready solutions or easy programs. But there are a few question to be considered here, and perhaps a few tentative answers to these questions. These questions have to do, as I have indicated, with human nature as well as with what has long been known about it. To ask about human nature is to ask what man is like, what moves him, what shapes him. A prior question is whether there *is* such a thing as human nature, something that is somehow always there, independent of the culture or regime in which the human being happens to be found. Much of modern thought, with its relativistic biases, obscures what was once thought to be fairly obvious about human nature to all who looked at other human beings and into their own souls.

It is possible that certain early influences upon a child become so ingrained as to have for most practical purposes the effects of intrinsic or natural qualities. But is there not more than this? Is not intelligence, for instance, dependent on nature to a significant extent? If so, is not one's capacity for virtue thereby affected in that it does help, if one is to do the right thing, to be able to figure out what the right thing to do is and what the consequences of misconduct are likely to be? Such figuring out might well require intelligence.

A doctrinaire egalitarianism dominates those who should know better. Elementary school teachers, for example, often have such a faith in equality impressed upon them in schools of education that they cannot see and deal with what is before their eyes. That is, they cannot work with what they have, either to corral, to help, or to inspire. Particularly instructive in this respect are the occasional discussions by thoughtful observers about the natural inclination of some men to vice. Are not some people more receptive than others to certain passions, more easily moved by some things, less easily moved by other things? (See, e.g., *Ethical Writings of Maimonides*, pp. 15–16, 28–29, 61–64, 83–95, 124–35.)

Certainly everyone is born different, with a wide range of talents, intelligence, and appetites among people. Is there an intrinsic good-temperedness in some men? Are there vicious streaks in others? These inclinations, even if only differences in degree, cannot be ignored by sensitive people alert to human potentialities and concerned about human failings. Conditions and opportunities can suppress some features of the soul and give full rein to other features. We also know that tyrannical dispositions and bestial inclinations do find uglier expression in some times or places than in others.

By recognizing what is unchangeable in human nature, one can better deal with the changeable. It is useful to notice what human nature is like and the difference that differences among men make. To ask, then, about the natural basis for vice or crime, as well as for virtue, is to affirm the role of nature in human affairs—nature as seen both in the "stuff" she provides and in the standards or ends she holds out to us.

V

The failure of judges and lawyers to address themselves properly to the dictates of nature is the failure, in effect, of jurisprudence. Jurisprudence, or a serious study of what is sometimes called philosophy of law, has been practically non- existent in American law schools during the past generation, and perhaps since the First World War. Legal realism has taken its place and the moral relativism of something called "legal reasoning," which is all too often only a fancy name for sophistic rhetoric.

Some insist that the unprecedented monstrosities of the Twentieth Century call into serious question the old-fashioned reliance upon natural right or natural law. We are reminded of Hitler, of Stalin, and even of American atrocities. We are asked to be "realistic" about what man is really like and the terrible things of which he is capable. But even this evidence has not been properly thought about.

First, one must consider what it is in us which induces us, perhaps obliges us, to recognize certain acts of state as atrocities, as bestial, as simply indefensible. Merely to describe various of these acts clearly is to condemn them. We rightly suspect that the man who is not appalled by certain descriptions is a man who is himself defective in decisive respects. He is like the man who cannot, because of impairment in his sight, see what is before his eyes.

Second, one must consider, in assessing the evidence available to us, how even the perpetrators of the grossest atrocities conduct themselves. Take, for example, the Nazis. It is significant to notice what even they could *not* do, what even the regimented German people refused to countenance, such as the pre-war extermination program for the insane that had to be abandoned. It is also significant that the Nazis could not do publicly what they did do: they recognized that the German people would not have permitted a candid avowal of what all too many sensed was going on in the wartime extermination camps. There is in the decisive limitations encountered by even the Nazis something heartening about some perhaps residual impulses toward goodness in the human species. It can be salutary to be reminded of this again and again. It is significant as well that the Nazis could not do the most terrible things they did until under cover of a full-scale war: the war both permitted the loosening of civilized restraints and made it easier to conceal from both domestic and foreign view what was being done.

All this, I mention in passing, should bear upon our understanding today of what the Russian and Chinese governments can and cannot do. I suspect that those governments are much more obliged to take public opinion into account than we in this Country recognize. The Russian government, for example, must realize that any foreign risk it runs must reckon with the deep fear among the Russian people of another major war. It must also realize that there is in the Russian Communist Party, as well as among their people generally, a lively reluctance to return to the excesses of Stalinism. It would be folly, of course, to make too much of public opinion in a totalitarian regime. But it might be even greater folly not to reckon on it at all, which would be to cripple ourselves by failing to recognize what there is about human nature that is enduring and can be counted upon. Put another way, to ignore the significance of public opinion in a totalitarian regime or, for that matter, among ordinary criminals is to depreciate even more than current fashions incline us to do the very existence of such a thing as human nature.

To speak of human nature and of that natural right or natural law to which human nature is receptive is to recognize the decisive role of reason in the human being, despite all the irrationality of which he is capable and on which a healthy life to some extent depends. The authoritative statement for Americans of the claims upon us of natural right remains the Declaration of Independence with its affirmation of the right of revolution. That right reminds us of the role of reason in human affairs, of the ability and duty of human beings to judge by enduring standards the claims that their governments put forth from time to time.

VI

A proper understanding of human nature and hence of natural right is reflected in how one regards the law itself. It has been recognized since ancient times that one of the principal purposes of the law is to help make and keep men good. The legislation of morality has long been thought to be both possible and desirable. It is not fashionable to think so today. Some deny that the law can effectively legislate morality. Others insist that even if the law can do so, it should not. It is assumed by these people that men, if left to themselves, will somehow choose what they should want. Such an assumption fails to take into account what it is that leads men to want this rather than that. A sort of natural goodness is assumed, with civil society perceived only as a corrupting influence. Someone as gifted as Henry Thoreau can say in the opening pages of his celebrated essay on civil disobedience, "Law never made men a whit more just . . ." That such sentiments are generally applauded reminds us of how silly and hence irresponsible even intelligent men can become.

We are discussing, in effect, a very old question: How is virtue acquired? Once we recognize that this *is* an old question, we can usefully return to old discussions of this and like questions. A proper reading of authors such as Plato, Aristotle, Shakespeare, Augustine, and Hobbes can turn up helpful answers to the sometimes novel problems that confront us from time to time. Only someone who knows what has been thought by the best minds about the enduring questions is equipped to deal responsibly with the somewhat novel issues of the moment.

Let us return to the criminal law, which is, these days, much abused. Even though it can be poorly enforced and largely ineffective, does it not continue to provide a guide for most people as to what is right and wrong? We can speak of *the* criminal law. This law has developed or at least ratified a certain way of life among the British and the Americans for several centuries. Does it not reflect something natural in men, something uniform and enduring for at least a millennium now with respect to matters and standards both substantive and procedural? No doubt much has changed, but it is striking how much has remained the same. The problem remains, How are we to preserve and make best use of what is indeed worthwhile in the criminal law of the community? The simplest answer may well be that we must restore the place of the community in the life of man.

VII

To speak of a community is to speak of the opinions that men share about the most important things, including about what happiness consists of. Such opinions are sometimes illusory or cater to exaggerated sensibilities. The Illinois Privacy Commission, on which I served as a staff member, issued earlier this year a final report which includes in its concluding set of recommendations the suggestion that subsequent privacy commissions should "call public attention to coarsening 'cultural' developments threatening those human sensibilities upon which an abiding respect for privacy rests."

To stress the sensibilities and opinions of the community is not intended to discourage those who try to remedy the social and economic conditions which no doubt contribute to crime. Thus, one of our fellow alumni Ramsey Clark, when he was Attorney General of the United States, said something to this effect (Irving Wallace, *The R Document*, pp. 309–10):

> If we are to deal meaningfully with crime, what must be seen is the dehumanizing effect on the individual of slums, racism, ignorance, and violence, of corruption and impotence to fulfill rights, of poverty and unemployment and idleness, of generations of malnutrition, of congenital brain damage and prenatal neglect, of sickness and disease, of pollution, of decrepit, dirty, ugly, unsafe, overcrowded housing, of alcoholism and narcotics addiction, of avarice, anxiety, fear, hatred, hopelessness and injustice. These are the fountainheads of crime. They can be controlled.

One notices again the recourse to "control," but control of the conditions for crime rather than of crime itself. It would be foolhardy to deny that "the fountainheads of crime" are important, but we need not dwell upon them here, if only because most students of crime can be depended on to do so. Besides, it should be noticed, many, many peoples have long lived decently with many of the social and economic disabilities just listed. We can expect many of these disabilities to continue. What else can be done to deal with crime or with its underlying causes?

We cannot hope to *police* each other to the extent that would be necessary to secure a decent life: our communities are now far too large for that. Besides, efficient police power is too expensive and otherwise unattractive. Effective use of the police power we can afford must serve as a useful supplement to the largely internal self-regulation upon which we must rely. Self-regulation means that we must direct our efforts to certain of the opinions the community has. I catalogue a half dozen of these somewhat interrelated opinions:

1) The community should be taught that the criminal law is necessary; that it is in its formulation essentially fair; and that, by and large, it does work. It should be remembered, as complaints mount about the current "permissiveness of the criminal law system," that one important cost for many defendants, especially for those who are never imprisoned, is the psychic and financial cost of defending themselves, and there is something to be said for this, so long as the police, the prosecutors and the judges are fairly adept in selecting those who are to be put to the trouble of defending themselves.

2) The community should be taught what "to get away with it" really means. That is, it should be generally impressed upon people (and here religious instruction as well as family discipline can be useful) that there is about the undetected crime something like the undetected disease of the body, that crime *is* a disease of the soul which corrupts and destroys.

3) The community should be persuaded that much of the contemporary emphasis upon "success" is dubious. A significant part of organized or professional crime and gang conduct among us is a mirroring of what is taken to be successful business and sports activity in the community at large. Much more needs to be said on behalf of the noble and the self-sacrificing, as against the merely acquisitive or the successful.

4) The community should be taught that it is difficult for men to determine what they in fact want. Most men have to be shown that one gets what one truly wants only when one does or has what one should. It should be understood, at least by those who shape opinions, that opinions are decisive, even with respect to the things that we come to want most desperately. Nature, if given a chance, asserts herself in helping us determine what we should want.

5) The community should be persuaded that men are not free unless they act as they should. Our dedication to liberty has to be refined: if liberty is regarded as little more than activity in the service of mere willfulness, then we are truly prisoners of chance.

6) The community should be taught that an undue concern with self-preservation is self-defeating, if only in that it leads to a fearful, empty life.

7) Finally, the community should be taught that true happiness depends on a combination of virtue and moderate prosperity and that crime is an

acute, or socially harmful, manifestation of misery that results in an unhappiness that the criminal shares with his victims and the community at large.

Such are the opinions on which a healthy community depends, a community that is confident and humane enough to use the criminal law as it should be used.

VIII

Such opinions help establish and preserve the sense of community. These opinions contribute to the reinforcement of the old-fashioned understanding that "crime does not pay." Critical to the general revival of this salutary understanding is the repeated exhibition by police, prosecutors, defense counsel, judges, and prison officers of their own belief in law-abidingness and fair play. Criminals, suspected criminals, and potential criminals should be shown again and again that those in authority do consider rules to be good for themselves to follow, even when they themselves are not being watched. By and large, people *do* want what their "betters" cherish, what their betters choose for themselves when those betters can have anything they might want. It is difficult for many people to take law-abidingness seriously if they see, or if they are led by irresponsible publicity to believe, that those in authority really do not practice what is generally taught about the intrinsic goodness of law and order.

Who, one might ask, should do such teaching and persuading as I have suggested on this occasion? The simple answer is, Those who know. Among those who know something are lawyers imbued with the traditions and hence principles of their profession. A lawyer cannot help being influenced by the sense of community which the law inevitably reflects and respects. This is particularly true when the body of law one works with draws upon centuries of experience and argument. Lawyers tend to have a reliable sense of what justice is and of what good lawyering and good judging are. This should be brought to bear on the selection of judges and on the discipline of the legal profession. In addition, the lawyer's sense of his profession, and what a profession means, should help him recognize what contributes to and what detracts from a sense of community. He should recognize those elements in our community which make us strangers to one another, which weaken the bonds and undermine the standards that mean so much to a healthy community.

I return to an opinion which I have developed at length elsewhere, that a critical corrupting influence in the United States today is television. Television is, despite its occasional good program, a national disaster. The only sensible response to it, I have argued, is its complete abolition. I can think of no single action which would reduce crime as much, including crimes of violence and against property, as the abolition of television would—and, what may be even more important, reduce as well the national fear of crime. To abolish television, I should immediately add, is not to countenance an interference with our freedom to discuss the political issues of the day, including the question of whether we should abolish television. In fact, such abolition would probably improve the quality of public discourse in this Country and thereby help us govern ourselves better.

But whatever one may think about television, or about the half dozen opinions I have catalogued as desirable for the community to be taught, there is one opinion which is particularly vital in our circumstances, and that is the opinion we settle upon as to the legitimate role of the community in shaping the ideas and passions of its citizens. Ideas, it should be recognized, do have consequences. If we are not to be ruled substantially by chance, it is necessary that there be a sensible guidance of the opinions (the ideas and passions which combine into the opinions) we do hold. The role here of the arts is considerable. If, on the other hand, we insist that each of us is on his own, that the community cannot legitimately concern itself through education and otherwise with the opinions we hold, our sense of vulnerability is likely to be heightened and the asocial tendencies upon which crime draws will be reinforced.

I have been arguing that one of the principal purposes of civil society, and hence of any government serving that society, is to help citizens become and remain good. Precisely how this is to be done depends on circumstances. We must be sensible in how we proceed. For example, the follies of the Prohibition Era should never be forgotten, but neither should they be made too much of.

We cannot proceed at all, sensibly or otherwise, if we fail to recognize that civil society is the natural habitat of the human being. Following upon this is the further recognition that the just is more than the legal, critical though the legal may be, and that only if one has some awareness of the best can one be truly practical. This means, I repeat, an awareness of human nature, what it is, and what it is capable of.

These are indeed old, old questions, which means that we are not entirely on our own in thinking about who we are and what we should do.

IX

I remind you of *one* of the enduring questions that can throw light upon our contemporary preoccupation with the problem of crime: Which is ultimately more important, self-preservation or the good life? The good life can sometimes mean a dangerous life. I do not want to encourage reck-lessness, but I do want to suggest that a sense of proportion should be maintained in these matters, including the awareness that we are mortal and that we can make too much of mere life. Consider, in this respect, our sometimes excessive reliance upon medicine and upon "heroic measures" to prolong life.

A sense of proportion helps to curb both paralyzing fear and blinding indignation. After all, things are seldom as bad, or as good, as they seem. Bad as crime may be among us, life in this Country today is longer, more comfortable and in other ways better for more people, in relative as well as in absolute terms, than it has ever been.

It is also well to remember that however dangerous the streets of Chi-cago may be, life here on the shores of Lake Michigan today is much safer than it was, say, some two hundred years ago. It would be even safer if we should return to the intrepid firmness and the sense of purpose that the thoughtful men and women of those days, and the old teachers *they* relied upon, had with respect to the legitimate function of the community in making good men and in correcting bad men.

I return at the conclusion of these jurisprudential remarks to another story from Greece, a story which reminds us of the relation of public opin-ion to the sense in a community that justice *is* likely to be done. Some years ago my mother told of what happened once in her native village when a sheep was stolen. Some villagers went with the problem to a woman who was considered to be psychic, a woman with "second sight." This woman identified a man in the village as the thief, whereupon he was duly punished by his neighbors. When my mother was told that this was an irrational practice, that it was simply unfair and so forth, she in effect replied, "You don't understand. Everyone knew who was guilty, but someone had to say it." That is, she thereby indicated, it was necessary to make somehow "official" what everyone there "knew" before action could legitimately be taken by the community. (See Maimonides, *The Guide for the Perplexed*, II, 32–48.)

We are reminded by this story of the importance of the appropriate public opinion if the law is to work. We are reminded as well of the En-glish adage that not only must justice be done, it must also appear to be done. For the proper public opinion and hence a due respect for the opin-ions by which decent men and communities necessarily take their bear-ings, both compassion and self-confidence are needed, at least among a people's intellectual leaders. These qualities in turn depend on an informed awareness of human nature, its inherent inclinations, its limitations and, despite periodic lapses into barbarism, its enduring aspirations.

27

MEDICINE AND THE LAW

27-A. The Discipline of Medicine

Now, as there are many actions, arts, and sciences, their ends also are many; the end of the medical art is health, that of shipbuilding a vessel, that of strategy victory, that of economics wealth. . . . Politics appears to be most truly the master art, for it is this that ordains which of the sciences should be studied in a polis, and which each class of citizens should learn, and up to what point they should learn them.

ARISTOTLE

I

The rules by which hospitals, or at least their departments of surgery, conduct themselves may well be reflected in the fact that this is the earliest time òf day I have ever given a public lecture. I am sure there are good reasons for this sunrise service as well as fortuitous circumstances which have made such reasons compelling. The influence of both chance and rationality upon the laws, including the customs, by which we are governed can be considerable, with a sometimes unsettling variety as one result.

Variety may also be seen in the way that law and medicine come together. Doctors are licensed by the community and hospitals are established pursuant to community regulations; the allocations of medical resources are influenced in large part by community concerns. The im-

This talk, sponsored by Dr. Richard Shapiro, was given at Grand Rounds, Department of Surgery, Michael Reese Hospital and Medical Center, Chicago, Illinois, May 7, 1983. (Original title: "Who's Boss? Medicine & Law—An Ordering of Principles.")

The epigraph is taken from Aristotle, *Nicomachean Ethics* 1094a7–10, 1094a28–1094b2 (W. D. Ross translation).

munities as well as the liabilities of doctors are very much determined by
the community. There are things that doctors can do (for example, with a
knife) which others cannot; and there are things for which doctors are
more apt to be judged severely than are laymen. There are even modes of
treatment that the community may require or may forbid.

In these as well as in many other ways that I can do little more than
touch upon this morning, law and medicine come together, with the law,
as the authoritative voice of the community, claiming the right as well as
the duty to guide and to restrain medicine. Yet we are accustomed to hearing protests against governmental interference in the practice of medicine, protests which sometimes seem to assume that medicine should be
virtually autonomous.

How should one begin to think about these matters? Perhaps it would
be useful to reconsider at the outset, and at some length, the abortion controversy of which the tenth anniversary of the 1973 United States Supreme Court opinions in the Abortion Cases has recently reminded us.

II

I suspect that many, if not most, doctors favor arrangements by which
women and their physicians (but only physicians?) are left relatively free
to decide whether to resort to an abortion. If one does say of abortion that
the community ought to have a say about it, then that is likely in *our* circumstances (as compared, say, to Mainland China's circumstances) to be
seen as an argument against abortion itself. To recognize the sovereignty
of law here *is* to place a curb on personal desires which *are* inclined
among us toward freedom of choice.

I am not concerned on this occasion to examine the morality or social
propriety of abortion. Nor am I concerned to examine at length the merits
of the Supreme Court opinions on this subject, an examination which
could well include consideration both of State-Federal relations and of
Legislative-Judicial relations. Rather I will examine the merits of what is
suggested in those 1973 opinions about the proper relation of medicine
and law. The relation between law and medicine evidently preferred by
the Court on that occasion, whatever one thinks of the constitutional status claimed for that relation, no doubt has a considerable appeal. This
may be seen in the sticker that an aggressive feminist has pasted, along
with several other like-minded stickers, on the back of an automobile
parked for some weeks now in front of my house, KEEP YOUR LAWS
OFF MY BODY.

I find particularly instructive the fact that much of what the Supreme

Court says about the proper relation between medicine and law is questioned neither by dissenters on the Court nor by most critics of the Court. Yet I presume to suggest that what the Court has said and the presuppositions on the basis of which it is said are highly questionable. Much is made in the 1973 Abortion Cases of deference to "medical judgment" (410 U.S. 113, at 163, 165). One Opinion for the Court culminates in the following observation (410 U.S., at 165–66):

> [This] decision vindicates the right of the physician to administer medical treatment according to his professional judgment up to the points where important state interests provide compelling justifications for intervention. Up to those points, the abortion decision in all its aspects is inherently, and primarily, a medical decision, and basic responsibility for it must rest with the physician. If an individual practitioner abuses the privilege of exercising proper medical judgment, the usual remedies, judicial and intra-professional, are available.

Notice what is being said here: "Up to [certain points], the abortion decision in all its aspects is inherently, and primarily, a medical decision, and basic responsibility for it must rest with the physician." Up to what point *is* it "inherently and primarily a medical decision"? It seems to be assumed that it is *not* up to the community through its laws to say how much *is* to be left to doctors to decide. Rather, it seems to be assumed that the early months of a pregnancy are completely beyond the control of the community, at least so far as a physician's activity is involved. Compare those who argue that it is a violation of natural law for a statute to compel, or even to authorize, an abortion at *any* stage of a pregnancy.

We are told in a concurring opinion in the 1973 Abortion Cases that some doctors had filed an *amicus* brief complaining that certain State abortion laws interfere with their practice of their profession. (410 U.S., at 219) This complaint seems to have been prompted by the requirement that abortion decisions by physicians be ratified by other physicians. Much is made of the fact (if it is a fact) that the "imposition by the State of group controls over the physician-patient relationship is not made on any medical procedure apart from abortion, no matter how dangerous the medical step may be." (410 U.S., at 220. See, also, 410 U.S., at 219, 197–98, 199.) This point is related to emphases upon the right to privacy and upon the liberty of patients and of doctors. If only abortions are uniquely regulated thus, is this because only abortion operations, among the practices that doctors openly engage in routinely exterminate potentially human life? (See 410 U.S., at 222.)

What I am concerned to notice and thus to question here is the assumption by the Supreme Court and others that the judgment of the medical profession can be relied upon as authoritative, even in the face of a deliberate community attempt to regulate the activities of doctors. The abortion controversy and the recent "Baby Doe"-type controversy, of which I will speak later, are but illustrations of the general issue here.

Much is made of the privileged position of the medical profession. This claim of privilege is, I suggest, highly questionable, even aside from any considerations of the rights and wrongs of any controversial medical procedure.

III

It should be noticed that at the root of any immunity of the doctor may not be the privileged position of the medical profession itself, but rather the privileged position of the patient who chooses and directs the doctor. It is the patient who tells the physician what she wants. In a sense, then, the decision of the Supreme Court in the 1973 Abortion Cases reflects the considerable importance among us of the Self. The doctor can be seen, from this perspective, as little more than the servant of the desires if not even of the whims of the patient. Certain uses of cosmetic plastic surgery are dubious instances of such subservience. Extreme instances of such subservience would be the use of physicians for either executions or euthanasia.

Let us now consider the doctor with his own prerogatives (which seems to be the way the Supreme Court regarded him), however much those prerogatives may ultimately be in the service of patients. Much is made, if only implicitly in the 1973 opinions of the Supreme Court, of the license that the doctor has. (See, for example, 410 U.S., at 120, 122, 143.) This is seen as empowering the doctor and liberating him from improper or, as with respect to pregnancy-termination questions, premature interference by the State with the conduct of his profession.

But is not a critical implication of such licensing somehow lost sight of? How can it be said that a profession that depends on the State for its rights and perhaps even for its legitimacy should be able to operate in significant respects free of State regulation? Would doctors, without licensing and its attendant supervision, be as important or as successful as they are?

Consider what would happen to the medical profession (and perhaps to the caliber as well as the cost of medical care) in this State if anyone who wanted to, from anywhere in the world, could come here to offer unimpeded his services as a healer. Consider as well the difficulties doctors would have if various immunities and privileges provided them by law were to be withdrawn, such as the considerable control exercised by them over the uses of drugs. I am reminded of the defiant feminist's sticker enjoining us to keep our laws off her body. This may be found plastered next to the license plate on her automobile, the very license plate which testifies to her legal control of the vehicle and reflects the protection given her by law in the possession and operation of that vehicle, protection so extensive that she can safely deposit her rather unsightly automobile in front of my house for weeks at a time. That same law provides one considerable protection of one's body and of the property needed to minister to that body, including the houses we live in.

What, then, does the Court's emphasis upon the prerogatives of the medical profession, as against the efforts of the State to regulate that profession, come down to? Does it not substitute one body of principles and laws, those of the community, for another body of principles and laws, those of a medical association? How can an association licensed by the community take precedence over the community itself, except to the extent that the community provides? Underlying this deference to the doctor's prerogatives is the assumption that the self, or the individual, is really sovereign and that the medical profession is ultimately in the service of the individual.

IV

To make much of the status of individuality can be pleasing to modern tastes. A somewhat old-fashioned approach to such matters could perhaps grant the primacy of the individual, but the individual properly understood and directed to the right ends. It must then be added that only a relatively few can be depended on to identify and effectively pursue those ends. Most people are in need of law; this means in practice the sovereignty of the community over one and all, including the professions which are established or permitted by the community.

At the heart of the inquiry here is a determination as to which of various ends should be sovereign, among which are those which make much of life itself. Particularly concerned with life itself is the art of medicine, which has health as its primary end, an end ratified by nature. Consider Aristotle in his *Nicomachean Ethics:* "We deliberate not about ends but about means. For a doctor does not deliberate whether he shall heal . . . [He] assumes the end and considers by what means it is to be attained." (1112b12–17)

Even so, doctors are familiar with laws that determine how the end of medicine can be pursued and when. This can be seen in time of war when we keep our doctors from offering their services to the enemy. This can be seen in time of peace by determinations of what facilities will be developed (consider the perennial Cook County Hospital problem), what equipment will be purchased (consider the kidney dialysis problem), what medication will be used (consider the laetrile problem)—determinations by public bodies and quasi-public bodies (such as the governing boards of hospitals) representing the community.

In these matters chance and hence ignorance can no doubt play a critical role in shaping regulations and allocating resources. But that is unavoidable, I am afraid. Besides, as we shall see, ignorance may be seen as well in the elevation of one body of expertise at the expense of another. All of these observations should remind us that politics may well be the master art, an art which orders the art of the physician no less than it does the art of the shipbuilder. After all, are not all arts in the service of the good, with their relations (and the relations to one another of the aspects of the good each serves) being defined and supervised by the community?

Perhaps much if not all that I have said thus far about the sovereignty of the law is familiar to you as doctors. Not only have you been long aware of the rules of the profession which guide and discipline physicians (a set of rules that are somewhat derivative from and that depend on the law of the general community), but you have also been long aware of how the law of the community bears upon you directly. You need only to be reminded of malpractice suits, to say nothing of criminal charges levelled against physicians from time to time.

Much of what I have said this morning about the Justices' opinions in the Abortion Cases, which cases are instructive about how people do think today about the relation of medicine to law, can be restated thus: In the abortion opinions there is an undue reliance upon the expertise of the medical profession. A deference to expertise, to a kind of organized wisdom, is well and good. But why should deference be given here primarily to the expertise of the medical profession? Because, it will be answered, it is a medical decision that is critical to abortion situations. *Is* that so? May not these situations call as much, if not more, for religious decisions, ethical decisions, even social or political decisions? But, it will be answered, the patient decides which expert to rely upon. Still, one might wonder why the patient's choice of expert should be conclusive. It is not difficult to imagine circumstances in which widespread recourse to abortion or, for that matter, to procreation could have profound consequences for the community, consequences that would oblige a sensible community to curtail abortions or reproduction.

Nor should it be difficult to figure out why we must depend as a community on the law to make deliberate judgments about which experts should be relied upon, and to what extent, in regulating the place of abortion or of any other medical practice among us. This is but another way of saying with Aristotle that politics is truly the master art.

V

It should go without saying that doctors too are citizens and are entitled, sometimes even obliged, to make their opinions known to lawmakers. It should also go without saying that a sensible community will listen carefully to its medical experts and legislate accordingly. For example, the legislature considering abortion regulations should be told what can safely be done now with the patient as compared to, say, a century ago. (See 410 U.S., at 148f.) I notice in passing that a legislature, not a court, is usually the best forum in which to adjust contending positions in these fields and to do so in such a way as to make domestic tranquility more likely.

Some law must determine what techniques may be used by doctors on various occasions. Usually the law will determine that the techniques to be used are those that doctors want to use. In some instances, techniques and practices may have to be reinforced if not mandated by law (for example, how infants are to have their eyes treated upon delivery or what inoculations children are to receive and when). The law may also have to decide what risks we should run (for example, with respect to radiation in our factories or to chemicals in our food). Sensible laws will dictate that the techniques used by doctors usually be those generally accepted by the medical profession. (This tends to be reflected, for example, in how the law of negligence is apt to be applied in medical malpractice cases.)

In addition, sensible legislators will consider what can be controlled and what cannot. Here too experienced doctors can be helpful. For example, are not various sexual activities going to be found among us, no matter what the law says? Prudence has to be brought to bear upon a determination of how many and what kind of "hopeless causes" the law should permit itself to be identified with. In all these matters, the experience and advice of doctors can be useful.

I have recognized that doctors, too, are citizens. It should be recognized as well that doctors have ethical obligations (or, as it is said today, consciences). This means that they may be obliged from time to time (one hopes this is infrequent) to resist impositions that the community attempts to place upon them. But one's conscience cannot be decisive in all cases, and it certainly should not be decisive when one's conscience is uninformed or poorly constituted. One's conscience is more apt to be reliable—that is, a doctor is more apt to reason sensibly about ethical matters—if one has a sound awareness of the proper relation between medicine and the law, if one recognizes, as we have said, that even with respect to so-called medical decisions there are other experts besides those versed in medicine whose guidance is relevant.

VI

A sensible community, I have indicated, knows how to defer to its doctors, even as it remains aware of its ultimate authority over the art of medicine.

I have drawn thus far this morning upon the 1973 Abortion Cases for my principal illustration of the problems to be considered here. I could have used as well, but without the benefit of revealing Supreme Court opinions, the "Baby Doe" regulations which are now in the courts. These regulations attempt to keep doctors and parents from withholding food or medical care from severely handicapped newborn infants. There was, you will recall, a much-publicized episode in which a handicapped newborn was apparently allowed to die by its parents and an attending physician. This moved an agency of the federal government to issue regulations designed to discover and prevent such episodes. You will also recall that a federal judge has, in the words of an approving editorial by the *Wall Street Journal* of April 18, 1983, "told the federal government to keep its investigators out of the nation's baby hospitals and pediatric wards." (Are there not echoes here, however unlikely the source, of my feminist's defiant automobile sticker?)

The judge's order in the "Baby Doe" case did not, so far as I can tell from press accounts, get to the merits of the underlying controversy. That is to say, defects were found in the way the government went about preparing and issuing its regulations: if government is to make laws, it must do so in a lawful way. Presumably, relevant regulations about these infants could be developed in such a way as not to be vulnerable to procedural objections. What, then, should be the status of such regulations?

If our discussion of the abortion question has been sound, it would seem that *some* government should be able to determine what parents and doctors may do in caring for these infants. It does not make sense to insist that government should not be *able* to interfere with what doctors and families do in such circumstances, no more than it would make sense to say that government should not be able to interfere with what physicists or manufacturers do with the nuclear weapons they alone are able to produce. (In both the infant-care and nuclear-weapons cases, by the way, public funds are drawn upon.)

The principal medical illustrations I have used thus far have been concerned with governmental attempts to prevent termination of life, whether in the fetus or in the severely malformed infant. Similar problems can come up with respect to the terminally ill, especially those in great pain, and the hopelessly senile. I have argued that some government among us should be able to decide whether this or that life may or may not be *terminated* by the actions of others and, if so, how. But we need not stop here in applying the principle for which I have argued. Should it not also be recognized that similar problems arise with respect to whether massive efforts or great expenditures of resources should be devoted to *preserving* life in various circumstances?

Here too the self-centeredness of the people most intimately involved has to be called into question and, if necessary, restrained or redirected by law or by customs which have the effect of law. All too often, the people immediately involved and immediately affected may not be the best judges of what is called for, perhaps not even of what is truly in their own interest and in the interest of their families, to say nothing of the interest of the community. I would not be surprised to learn that decisions made every day by public and quasi-public authorities, including those responsible for the budgets of hospitals, place effective curbs on excessive efforts that might be made to preserve life in various circumstances.

VII

I have on this occasion called into question the autonomy that some doctors and many patients tend to believe they are entitled to. Autonomy means, literally, that one give a *law* to oneself.

Does it not make sense for government, or better still for the community for which government acts, to use its sovereign authority, including its taxing and spending powers, to regulate what may be done to terminate or to preserve life, restraining what doctors, patients, or the families of patients may be disposed to do in various circumstances?

Having said all this, it is prudent to add that a sensible community need not spell out in its laws things which are apt to be misleading or which are apt to be misused. Cannot a community have an understanding with its doctors and nurses about what should be done in a variety of circumstances? If a community is soundly constituted, such an approach can be safely relied upon, especially if the training and supervision of doctors and nurses are conducted with a view to producing and maintaining practitioners of both competence and integrity. I, for one, have been reassured in this respect by what I have been privileged to observe this morning of the morbidity and mortality conferences which preceded this talk. The sovereignty of the general community, I might add, is consistent with deliberately providing doctors considerable immunity with respect to discussions among them of their work and with respect to good-faith efforts on behalf of patients. In any event, it is not reasonable to expect that the community at large will be able to police intelligently and efficiently how doctors do conduct themselves from day to day. Much is necessarily left to doctors to decide.

The considerable and perhaps inevitable independence of the medical profession tends to reinforce doctors in their tendency to make much, perhaps too much, of life itself. There is much in the modern world that moves us in that direction. This can be devastating for nobility and for an enduring happiness. It remains to be seen what the community can do to correct this tendency.

The ultimate sovereignty of the community at large does remind us of the end to which that community and its laws are properly directed. This end, to which all the arts including the art of medicine should be subordinated, is that common good on which the happiness of human beings usually depends.

If one does not understand how and why the community should be sovereign, then one does not truly understand medicine itself, however skilled one may otherwise be in its practice. No art can be grasped for what it is if there is not among its practitioners some awareness of the whole of which that art is but a part. I have, thus far, done no more than touch upon how one should think about that whole, including about the nature and significance of life itself. I trust, however, that I have said enough to provide the basis for a useful discussion among us pursuant to the rule and customs of your distinguished community.

27-B. Abortion and Technology

These are the chief legal effects of marriage during the coverture; upon which we may observe, that even the disabilities, which the wife lies under, are for the most part intended for her protection and benefit. So great a favourite is the female sex of the laws of England.

WILLIAM BLACKSTONE

I

Ten years ago this month I had occasion to argue before an assembly of liberal lawyers in Chicago that "the virtually unlimited access to abortion now available in [the United States] is an unconscionable state of affairs." (See Section V of Essay No. 14, above.) I went on to say in that talk of October 12, 1979:

> The Roman Catholics among us are substantially correct in their deep opposition to what we now have, even though they (because of a misunderstanding of the dictates of natural law) have long been misled by their leaders with respect to birth control. Particularly serious here is the unwarranted reading of the Constitution by the United States Supreme Court, which has left local governments paralyzed in any attempt to deal compassionately but firmly with our dreadful abortion epidemic (which represents, among other things, a callous exploitation of women and an endorsement of mindless gratification).

Critical to the Supreme Court's 1973 landmark decision in *Roe* v. *Wade* was the assumption that medical judgment should be regarded as superior to legislative judgment, even though the doctor is licensed by the State and depends on the law of the community for his authority and immunities. The law in turn properly looks for *its* authority in such matters to moral and political, as well as to religious, guidance. Among the moral considerations that should be taken into account is the possible brutalizing effect of a widespread and casual recourse to abortion.

This talk was given at a Workshop on Fetal Rights, World Conference on Ethical Choices in an Age of Pervasive Technology, Guelph University, Guelph, Ontario, Canada, August 27, 1989. (Original title: "Ethics and Technology: The Problem of Abortion and the Law.")

The epigraph is taken from William Blackstone, *Commentaries on the Laws of England*, I, 433.

One year ago this month I had occasion to return to the abortion issue in another talk, this one on patriotism before a conservative Dallas audience in the closing weeks of the 1988 Presidential election campaign. I said then (Section XII of Essay No. 8, above),

> How do conservatives stand on abortion? I have long had the impression that neither Mr. Bush nor Mr. Reagan fully believes what he is saying about it. Certainly they could not permit the exceptions they do (such as for rape, incest, and a threat to the life of the mother) if they believed that abortion was murder. My own position is that there is no constitutional issue here for the judiciary to concern itself with, that these are matters for the political process to dispose of. I suspect that the political process, if left to itself by the courts, will have to rely more and more on the moral judgment of the pregnant woman, especially as safe abortion-inducing medication becomes readily available.

I believe I have been speaking from the same position over the past decade, with the obvious shift in my emphasis reflecting a shift in social circumstances that is due in part to technology. It still seems to me dubious to assume that the Fourteenth Amendment invalidates most State restrictions on abortions. Rather, it can be argued, the law can properly be used to encourage as well as to discourage births.

II

It is against the background of these opinions of mine that I now suggest both how technology bears upon the abortion issue and what if anything law, which is regarded with suspicion by many feminists today, can do about it.

Technological developments have helped dramatize the problems in this field. Technology has provided safe ways of performing abortions, at least in the early months of pregnancy, which is when most of them are performed. Indeed, an abortion operation is now evidently a safer activity than childbirth for the woman patient.

This does not mean, however, that abortion clinics, as well as hospitals where abortions are performed, should be immune from public-health regulation. Regulation is called for even if (perhaps, especially if) the abortion decision is designated by the law as strictly a medical matter. We must similarly assess the calls we now hear for reliance upon self-regulation by the experimenters in various kinds of medical and other research.

III

Technological developments have also helped make recourse to wide-spread abortion both "needed" and acceptable. Technology, as we know it, permits substantial anonymity, partly because of the mobility it fosters, partly because of the multitudes it can gather together without much mutual supervision. We are thus less likely than in simpler and more stable times to be guided and restrained by our neighbors.

In addition, technology tends to shield us somewhat from the consequences of our actions. It caters thereby to innovation and sensuality. Technology means, therefore, that the privatization of our lives is much easier to bring about, resulting in a breakdown of community, or at least of that community which is most apt to be concerned about and watchful of how we live every day.

It is possible, of course, that technology can be employed to supervise our daily lives much more intimately than was ever possible before by secular authorities. This becomes evident, for example, to those taxpayers who get inquiries from the government about unreported income of which even they may not be aware. An extreme instance of such supervision may be seen in George Orwell's *1984*.

Still, we are seeing in Eastern Europe these days the liberating effects of technology. The profound political changes now going on there have been prepared for in large part by worldwide communications and the interrelatedness of modern industrial economies. It has evidently become obvious even to the most dedicated Marxists not only that their system is inefficient but also that it is losing ground (and is known by their own people to be losing ground) when compared to the economic as well as the social progress in the advanced countries of the East as well as of the West.

Thus, the global communications and other manifestations of technology which have permitted, if not encouraged, the recent general weakening of abortion prohibitions have contributed as well to the subversion of another established way, the way of the Iron Curtain countries.

IV

The language we are hearing, both in Eastern Europe and in abortion clinics, is that of rights and liberty, which can be quite heady stuff. The passion of the young woman on this subject, with her emphasis upon wresting control of her body from the law, has to be reckoned with, however much the problem is aggravated in most such instances by an earlier passion that had led to an untimely surrender of her body. (That is, an insistence upon regarding woman as "equals" to men with respect to sexuality leads thereafter to an insistence in all too many cases upon recognizing women as so different that men and their laws should not be permitted any role in the regulation of abortions.) One encounters today a heightened sensitivity about the destruction of life by capital punishment at the same time that an often lethal pro-choice position is insisted upon. What is common to both of these positions seems to be passion itself.

Important to the future of abortion and its regulation is the considerable experience we have had with it. Have we not become habituated to a lack of restraint with respect to abortion and, perhaps even more influential, to that indulgence in sensuality that a routine abortion often caters to or at least provides a remedy for? This means, among other things, that even if there should be outright reversal of *Roe* v. *Wade* in the United States, we would be left with a radically different situation from that which we had before *Roe* v. *Wade*. The prevailing law since 1973 has, for the foreseeable future, shaped appreciably the opinions, desires, and expectations of many people in the United States, especially among the young. It may be due partly to chance, but still it is important to notice, that *Roe* v. *Wade* has had much more of an effect than any reversal of it is likely to have.

However much that a familiarity with abortion has changed our standards with respect to these matters and perhaps even made many wonder whether there are any "absolutes" here, this is not an issue that will simply fade away. Compare the 1954–55 Segregation Cases. Those cases appealed to fundamental principles in the American regime, principles that have always been more generally recognized in the United States than those appealed to by either side in the Abortion Cases. However dubious some of the arguments were in *Brown* v. *Board of Education*, there has been a widespread and steadily growing acceptance, even by determined States-Rightists, of the proposition that officially sanctioned racial segregation is ultimately indefensible. There does not seem to be a likelihood that the Pro-Life people will ever be similarly persuaded by the 1973 Abortion Cases. On the other hand, what are the Pro-Lifers' prospects, especially as they look to legislatures to further their cause?

V

The 1989 decision in *Webster* v. *Reproductive Health Services* seemed to provide the Pro-Life advocates the opening they needed in their efforts to deal with State legislatures. But, as a national columnist has aptly noticed in a discussion of the strengths and liabilities of "the Republican/

conservative coalition," one of the bonds of that coalition from 1980 through 1988 "was furnished by 'the social issues,' of which abortion was by far the most emotionally important. As long as Republicans could rail against abortion, while the Supreme Court protected abortion rights, the GOP could use the issue as a rallying point, without mobilizing those who were on the other side of the question. But that luxury disappeared with the *Webster* decision last spring. Increasingly, GOP strategists recognize they have to find some way to move off their strong anti-abortion position —or pay a high price." (David Broder, *Chicago Tribune*, October 25, 1989, sec. 1, p. 15)

The "consciousness" of women has been so "raised" that more and more of them consider themselves entitled to *choose*, something which technology evidently makes easier and easier to do. This dominant opinion among women, especially those of child-bearing age, is something that legislators are very sensitive to. For several years now I have been asking the Pro-Life advocates in my Constitutional Law classes to imagine what would happen if *Roe* v. *Wade* should be reversed. Did they expect State legislatures to enact readily the laws they wanted? "No." Did they expect prosecutors to indict and to try offending women and their doctors? "Well, perhaps some of their doctors, but rarely a woman." Did they expect juries to vote unanimously for conviction, as is still required in criminal proceedings, whenever trials did take place? "Not often." Is respect for law apt to be furthered if it should become evident, as I suspect it would soon be, that no anti-abortion criminal law of the old style is apt to be effective in most urban areas in the United States, even in those areas where the Roman Catholic Church is still strong?

Certainly, there is not likely to be a uniform anti-abortion law among the States in the United States. Nor can it be reasonably expected that any proposed constitutional amendment authorizing Congress to enact such a law would get very far. All this means that there will continue to be jurisdictions in which abortion may be readily and safely obtained in the early months of a pregnancy. Here, too, the effects of technological developments may be seen, in the form of the cheap travel now available. It is hardly likely that it can be effectively made illegal for a woman to leave her State in order to secure an abortion that is legally available elsewhere. This means, then, that local legislation prohibiting abortions will reach, if anyone at all, only the very poor.

VI

Pro-Lifers may be thankful that the poor are thus protected, perhaps even providentially, from corruption. But, it seems, not even the very poor are to be immune from the moral ravages of technology if anti-abortion laws should ever be restored to their former vigor. I return to the abortion-inducing medication referred to in the 1988 Presidential campaign remarks I have quoted.

How can such medication be effectively prohibited by law in our circumstances, especially if abortion pills become both safe for the typical woman to use and inexpensive for drug companies to manufacture? Legal prohibitions and the threatened boycotts of producers will not suffice here. If tons of cocaine can be routinely brought into the United States, it is hardly likely that inconspicuous abortion pills can be kept out of a State, especially since they are likely to be legally available in other Western countries if not in some of the other States in the Union. Making regulation even more difficult here is that the doctor—the party most vulnerable at this time to abortion regulations—may be gotten out of the picture by the abortion pills that will eventually be developed, if they do not already exist. I notice in passing that if the medication technology had developed earlier here, there would have been no occasion for *Roe* v. *Wade* and the resulting distortion of the judicial process and the related political turmoil. Or was it that the legitimation of abortion promoted the research? But that research did not depend only on legal and political conditions in the United States.

It should be evident from what I have said that it seems to me difficult for the law, in our circumstances, so to "accommodate" itself to the abortion problem as to significantly repress widespread recourse to abortion in the advanced industrial nations today. I do not believe that the "fetal rights" we are hearing about, however defined, are likely to matter much in the calculations and conduct of the various partisans engaged in this controversy.

VII

What does all this mean for the dedicated Pro-Lifer? So long as abortion *could* be effectively controlled by the criminal law, it seemed to me that the critical accommodation would have to be made by the Pro-Choicers, at least with respect to the multitude of conceptions that a proper chastity would have prevented. But once technology virtually immunizes those who seek abortions from legal sanctions, the critical accommodation may have to be made by the Pro-Lifers. That is, those opposed to abortions are probably going to have to recognize, along with their Pro-Choice opponents, that the decision about abortion is going to be more and more a personal decision, primarily by the woman involved. As the relevant technology develops, the legislatures that enact old-style anti-abortion laws will be doing little more than "grandstanding." Nor does it seem to me that the legal scholars currently discussing the abortion issue face up to the profound implications of the availability of the safe abortion-inducing medication that is being developed. One can be reminded, by such discussions, of generals who prepare to fight the last war.

Be all this as it may, we should not exaggerate the role of the criminal law in bringing about much, if not most, of the moral conduct that we need and expect from one another. Indeed, it may even become salutary for the Pro-Life people to forget about what the law says and devote themselves primarily to the moral argument, taking seriously the term *choice* in the Pro-Choice creed. One thing the Pro-Lifers will have to do, if they are to be effective, is to distinguish birth-control measures from abortion as ordinarily understood. Is it useful to argue, as some do, that any interference, however early, with a fertilized egg is to be condemned as an abortion? It is hardly likely that those women who employ anything like the diaphragm method of birth control will be persuaded that they routinely perform abortions by doing so. Yet some proponents of "fetal rights" seem to believe that this, too, is an abortion. One must wonder, however, whether it is either scientific or prudent to regard the immediately fertilized egg as a *person*.

Thus, the opponents of routine abortion must take the Pro-Choice position seriously: they must make efforts to persuade people, and especially young women, about the proper choice usually to be made. It will not hurt to remind people, Pro-Choicers and Pro-Lifers alike, that most of them probably were not planned or "wanted" by their parents and that most children, even when unexpected, are eventually regarded as net gains for and by their parents, at least in our part of the world. Permit me also to be so old-fashioned as to suggest that it is generally not good for people so to conduct themselves as to run a substantial risk of conceiving fetuses that they would be likely to abort if they could. The vital concern should now be with how women with the prospect of full practical control over both preventing and continuing pregnancies should think and how they should be addressed and counselled, not least with respect to ethical issues.

It may now be easier in our circumstances to promote temperance (which is likely to mean far fewer unwanted pregnancies) than it is to enact and enforce effective anti-abortion criminal laws. The effective promotion of temperance, whether with respect to sexual activity or with respect to drug indulgence, depends in part on addressing the emptiness, even desperation, that intemperance often attempts to minister to. Or, as Leo Strauss put it in 1959, in discussing "juvenile delinquency,"

People think about [juvenile delinquency] and try to do something about it, but it could very well be that all their thinking and all their devices are absolutely useless. It could be that juvenile delinquency is connected with the deep crisis of our society as a whole. It could be true that this phenomenon is due to a loss of hope in the younger generation, or to the absence of great public tasks which arouse public spirit. Now, if this is so, it is obvious that juvenile delinquency cannot be treated in isolation and a regeneration of society as a whole would be necessary.

Whether the palliative is gentle or tough is a secondary question compared to the question of society as a whole.

(See 11 *Nova Law Review* 295–96 [1987].) Most of the unwanted pregnancies for which abortions are sought are probably due to one form or another of "juvenile delinquency," a failing which is not limited to the young in years.

To doubt the effectiveness of the criminal law of abortion in our radically changing circumstances is not to suggest that the law should never be used in education, in moral training, and in the development of a responsible medical profession. Still, it is prudent to recognize both the limits of law and its reliance upon a sound moral sense in the people at large. In any event, we should notice that constitutional law questions often conceal vital ethical and political issues.

The abortion controversy of the past two decades has obliged us to consider the place of self-gratification, along with the law, in our way of life. We have been obliged to consider as well the circumstances that law depends on or must take account of. Abortion issues do raise questions about nature and about the relation of nature to morality, a morality which must, if it is to be sensible, pay due deference both to the sanctity of truly human life and to the sovereignty of the properly choosing will.

28

PSYCHIATRY AND THE LAW

It is evident that the polis *is among those things that are by nature, and that man is by nature a political animal. And he who is without a* polis *on account of nature, not on account of fortune, is either low or better than a human being. . . . He who is incapable of entering into community, or on account of self-sufficiency has need of nothing, is no part of a* polis; *so that he is either a beast or a god.*

ARISTOTLE

I

I consider first the "practical" side of my subject, then the "theoretical." The evident primacy here of practice is appropriate, since practical measures, drawing upon a general intuition of nature, usually precede theoretical discourse in these matters. Nature can soundly direct practice long before a community understands what it is doing. The epigraph taken from Aristotle's *Politics* anticipates the "theory" that I will draw upon here.

I am obliged, on this occasion, to treat psychiatry as monolithic. What I mean by it should be apparent from what I say. To the extent that I labor under a misapprehension of what psychiatry is or does, to that extent I am in need of your help. Since you as psychiatrists are professionally, to say

---

This talk was given at a Conference on Psychiatry and the Law, Department of Psychiatry, The University of Chicago, and the Institute of Social and Behavioral Pathology, Chicago, Illinois, October 12, 1979. (Original title: "Psychiatry and the Law: An Old-Fashioned Approach.") An edited version of this essay, with notes, was published in Lawrence Z. Freedman, ed., *By Reason of Insanity: Essays on Psychiatry and the Law* (Wilmington, Delaware: Scholarly Resources, Inc., 1983), pp. 167–77. See, also, Anastaplo, "Constitutional Comment," appended to Gera-Lind Kolarik (with Wayne Klatt), *Freed to Kill: The True Story of Larry Eyler* (Chicago: Chicago Review Press, 1990), pp. 367–79.

The epigraph is taken from Aristotle, *Politics* 1253a1–1253a29 (Laurence Berns translation).

nothing of your being temperamentally, helpful, I know I can count on you to offer me whatever correction I should need.

A man does something that should not have been done. What should we do about it? Should he be held responsible by the community, or at least treated as if responsible? Can psychiatry help us determine (1) whether this man knew right from wrong; (2) whether he knew this particular act was forbidden and hence wrong; and (3) whether, in short, he knew what he was doing?

I shall argue that an action cannot be truly seen unless one can also see whether it is good. In this sense, few if any know that they are doing something that is bad and hence wrong. But I shall also argue that the law, when it holds someone responsible, does not require in him the understanding of a philosopher. On the other hand, the law does require some recognition of what one is up to, if only the recognition that one's acts are forbidden.

Some argue that the community should have little to say about right and wrong once minimum standards of conduct have been established. There is something appealing about this approach, if only because of its simplicity, but it ignores one of the traditional functions of the law, that of reflecting and reinforcing pervasive opinions about good and bad in the community.

Certain kinds of people, badly disturbed though they may be, should be quickly and decisively dealt with by the law when it becomes known that they have done certain things. Something is wrong with the law (or with psychiatry, if an insanity defense is involved) when such people are not dealt with quickly and decisively. I am thinking of people such as, to use recent notorious instances, Berkowitz, Gacy, Manson, Oswald, Ruby, Sirhan, and Speck. All of us can be expected to be somewhat familiar with these people. My impression, based upon press reports alone, is that each of these men was competent enough for the purposes of the law: the purposes both of having guilt assigned to them and of being able to stand trial. (The latter consideration, it can be argued, is secondary. See 40 *University of Chicago Law Review* 66 [1973].)

There does not seem to be in any of the half-dozen cases that I have just mentioned any serious problem with the *facts*, in the ordinary sense of that term. Not much should be required in any of these cases by way of inquiry or trial, for the purpose of the law, whatever may be the complex scientific problems that the scholar may be intrigued by. I mention in passing that there should also be no serious problem in any of these cases with pretrial publicity. Much of our concern with respect to that seems to me rather silly in those cases where the magnitude of the crime and the identity of the offender are so notorious that only the village idiot could fail to be aware of what has happened. It is foolish to insist that we as a community cannot be permitted to know what every sensible person in the community knows.

Who would deny that there is something dreadfully wrong with each of the half-dozen people I have listed and with people like them whose bizarre conduct has happened to be limited to far less notorious acts? The magnitude of an offense should not automatically generate a comparable immunity. None of these people believed themselves to be killing anyone but another human being; none, it seemed, even had a paranoia that blinded them to what they were doing. The care taken, in almost every instance, to avoid prevention or apprehension is revealing.

To make it difficult or even impossible for the law to condemn such men promptly is to display a lack of confidence in the powers of observation and judgment in the community at large. It is doubtful that modern psychiatry, despite its relief of considerable suffering, has taught us anything about the human soul that should properly interfere with what the community would otherwise do in identifying and passing judgment upon such people.

II

What, then, should the relation be between psychiatry and the law? It depends, in part, on what is thought within the community about (1) the law, which concerns itself primarily with the common good; and (2) psychiatry, which concerns itself primarily with private interests. Critical here is how psychiatry sees human beings and why it is, as it often seems, more permissive than either the law or general community opinion.

To speak of the relation between psychiatry and the law is to speak to a considerable degree of the relation between the individual and the community, with psychiatry standing for one and with the law standing for the other. We moderns do invoke something called "personal autonomy." Is this not an attempt to blend individuality and legality, an attempt to have the individual lay down, or be guided by, a law to himself? In such a case is not the law subordinated to personal inclinations and is therefore not, strictly speaking, a law?

Psychiatry itself cannot do without law. Psychiatrists lay down the law for their patients, although it may not be called that. This law takes the form of rules about appointments, payments, and even therapy. In addition, the psychiatrist, in many more ways than he may be aware of, depends on the law of the land to legitimize (if not even to permit) his calling, to define (sometimes to enlarge) his powers, and to protect (as well as to restrain) him in various respects.

The individual to whom psychiatry can be said to be dedicated is also dependent on the law. The typical individual is who he is primarily because of opinions which come from his community. How productive and happy he will be depends, in large part, on the quality of the opinions his community supports. If that community is fragmented, institutions within the community, such as the family or the church to which he happens to belong, will be the primary source of the authoritative opinions that shape him. But even these institutions are themselves reflections of earlier communities.

It is not a question of the community *or* the individual, but rather the question of whether the supposedly liberated individual is aware of the community that has shaped him in an authoritative fashion. I will now say things about the community and the individual and about law and psychiatry that I depend on you to apply to your circumstances and problems.

III

Since it is common, upon thinking of the relation of psychiatry to the law, to consider the role of psychiatry in criminal proceedings, it would be useful to touch upon certain underpinnings of the criminal law.

The shaping of opinion, not the "control" of criminal behavior, is the most critical thing in any solution today of the formidable crime problem. When opinions and hence desires are sound, there is not much need for control. This was illustrated a week ago in Grant Park, where "one million" people who came to see the Pope were handled with ease by the Chicago police, even though the crowd had to wait for hours for a service that itself lasted a couple of hours. One police officer reported that the crowd at the Mass was "a piece of cake," adding, "We have more trouble with the Bears' football crowd." The Bears, it should be noticed, never draw one-tenth the crowd that was said to have been at Grant Park for the Pope.

Vital to the beliefs on which a law-abiding people depends is the opinion that insists upon the intrinsic goodness of justice. People have to be taught that "crime does not pay, really" and that they are harmed by the injustices they perpetrate, whether or not they are detected and apprehended. It is not necessary here to say anything more about the opinions rooted in human nature that promote law-abidingness. To approach these matters thus is to assume, contrary to what it is fashionable to advocate today, that the community should have a good deal to say and to do about what is right and wrong.

IV

To be a community means that all or almost all in the association are being "judgmental" in much the same way about the same things. If psychiatry should insist upon withholding judgment—if it should go so far as to insist that there is no such thing as right or wrong but that only "thinking," if not "feeling," makes it so—then psychiatry is to that extent alienated from the community, if not even antisocial.

The importance of the community is evident, I have suggested, in the reliance by the well-developed soul upon proper opinions, especially upon opinions that seem proper because they are in large part old opinions. But to speak of "the well-developed soul" is again to approach these matters differently from those who prefer to speak of the individual or of the self. Does not this latter approach appeal more to the psychiatrist?

What is the view of modern psychiatry with respect to the individual, the community, and the relation of the one to the other? Does not the psychiatrist tend to see each person as open to the truth, as well equipped as others to make a choice among "life styles"? Is not the psychiatrist often obliged to take issue with the inevitable demands of society?

To approach the human being thus is to pay homage to the presuppositions and aspirations of the Enlightenment. It is to assume, among other things, that there is naturally a self that yearns for expression independent of any community. (If one says with Nietzsche that man must *will* the self, that the self is not natural, there remains the question of the origins of that which does the willing.) Moderns tend to believe that the community, except perhaps at the most primitive level, is bound to confine or otherwise corrupt the would-be autonomous person.

In short, "man is born free but is everywhere in chains." This is usually taken to mean that there is not yet any truly good society, that there can be no enduring harmony between an individual and existing communities since it is such communities that suppress his full personal development.

V

The traditionalist would respond, however, that for most people the particular makes sense only in the context of the general: the typical individual can find solid fulfillment only as a social being, not in rebellion or in self-satisfaction. There must be an overall, prevailing standard by which he must take his bearings or he becomes a nobody, nowhere.

Psychiatry, the traditionalist would continue, is but one art among many, taking its place in and being subject to the general order of things. In this respect psychiatry is essentially like the ordinary medical art. A number of "medical" decisions—that is, decisions that doctors do make—depend on considerations that are not strictly medical. Doctors may be able to explain what this or that measure does, whether a preventive program, a routine remedy, or a "heroic" treatment, but they often cannot tell us, or we do not want to rely upon them to tell us, whether any particular measure should be employed. The decision to employ a measure often depends on an overall view of human life itself and of the good life. This is reflected, for example, in the decision as to what part or function of the body is to be sacrificed for the sake of preserving another part or function.

The dependence of ordinary medicine of the body on standards and objectives dictated or at least ratified by the community is evident to us. Why is it not also evident with respect to psychiatry, the medicine of the soul? That is, why is it not evident that community standards and objectives should govern with respect to mental-health determinations inasmuch as common opinion certainly affects one's sense of what is one's due, of what is good or bad, and of what is a grievance, all of which bear intimately upon one's mental health?

The critical question is not whether and how psychiatry is to be used in the law (for example, in the court system), but rather the extent to which psychiatry is to be guided by the law and by that community opinion of which the law itself is an instrument. Related to this are questions concerning both the extent to which psychiatry is to be respectful of common sense and the relative worth within the community of the strong as against the weak, of the good as against the bad.

VI

Although psychiatry can be considered to stand in the same relation to the law as ordinary medicine does, it is obvious that there are fewer problems raised by the relation of ordinary medicine to the law. Difficulties do arise from time to time, and especially in recent years, in the practice of ordinary medicine. For example, how should the terminally ill be dealt with, especially the permanently comatose? Such difficulties are made particularly acute because of remarkable technological developments. But by and large sound medical practice, including the proper relation between ordinary medicine and the law, is long established. This practice prescribes the standards of care that doctors should exercise in the light of available information, techniques, and equipment.

Why, then, should there be special problems for psychiatry in defining the proper relation between it and the law, problems that are not there for ordinary medicine? Is not this partly because the practice of ordinary medicine was well established at a time when an almost instinctive respect for nature still dominated the thinking of the Western world? Psychiatry, on the other hand, developed at a time when nature had gone under a cloud. Psychiatry has been deprived thereby of the moderating guidance of the old-fashioned attitude toward nature.

One might notice, however, that psychiatry as a modern intellectual movement has attacked repressive conventions, that is, traditions, regimes, religions, laws, and cultures, in the name of nature. Does not this reliance of modernity upon nature in its condemnation of various longstanding conventions suggest that it is a mistake to argue that psychiatry has been deprived of the influence upon it of nature?

Curiously enough, the modern attack (and not by psychiatry alone) upon conventions in the name of nature has had the effect of undermining the status of nature among us. It should be helpful to this inquiry about the relation of psychiatry to the law to review, if only briefly, how it is that the modern attack upon conventions in the name of nature has in effect undermined the authority of nature. This review should also say something about modernity and hence about that sense of individuality and of community that influences the relations between law and psychiatry among us. Here, then, are some suggestions about what the nature-based subversion of conventions has done to the authority among us of nature herself:

1) Conventions (including, of course, rather arbitrary and even silly conventions) are needed if men are to be properly trained and disciplined to take *some* standards seriously. Consider what is resorted to in basic training or in boot camp in the military services. Indeed, conventions seem to be necessary in order for human beings to learn anything, to understand nature herself, and to control themselves in accordance with the dictates of nature. This means that conventions can be truly seen for what they are and in the light of nature only by someone who has been subjected to the discipline of conventions and who has, in a sense, graduated from or risen above them. But if conventions are repudiated from the outset, the preliminary training that a conventions-minded community provides becomes deficient and a higher development becomes difficult if not impossible.

2) Related to the first way by which the modern attack on conventions

in the name of nature has undermined the authority of nature is this one: it is natural for men to have conventions. To rule out conventions completely, therefore, is to question the prompting of nature.

3) Furthermore, the modern attack on conventions in the name of nature was made on the basis of an inadequate view of nature. Nature was seen by many moderns primarily (if not only) as the desiring, not as the rational or moral or self-restraining, part of us. The aspect of nature seen in the persistent, instinctive physical desires of men was legitimated in the campaign against those restraining conventions which to some extent reflect the sobriety of nature. This campaign can be said to have gone too far in that it permitted one aspect of nature to overwhelm other aspects of nature in the human soul.

4) Perhaps critical to the development I am trying to account for here may have been an assumption made for some four or five centuries now by adventurous souls, that nature is to be harnessed. If this is how nature is to be approached, she is difficult to regard as a master or a guide. The conquest and exploitation of nature are to be accomplished, it should again be noticed, for the sake of our desires, including whatever peculiar desires happen to arise from time to time. Such "natural" desires begin to sound in their variability like conventions. Thus, the more enduring conventions are attacked in the name of nature, which comes to be understood to be itself in the service of quite changeable conventions.

5) A related consideration here is that nature is more apt to be set aside today because she is easily lost sight of. Manifestations of nature in growing things, whether woods and meadows or crops and flowers, to say nothing of all kinds of animals, are now largely concealed from view. But it goes deeper than this. Nature is also concealed from view in modern science. Ordinary experience and everyday observations can no longer be relied upon in the organized effort to understand the nature of things. In addition, the explanations constructed by modern science cannot be put in terms of ordinary experience, even as rough approximations or as crude analogies. Only mathematics can be used to "describe" what the scientists, especially the physicists, construct. These descriptions, however ratified they may be in common opinion by astonishing technological marvels, are simply incomprehensible to most of the community. It is not only in physics that nature is concealed from view. Ideological preferences have also tended to impede our ability to see nature. For example, the modern (and certainly defensible) emphasis upon equality can mean that what would once have been considered obvious distinctions, say between the sexes or between the bright and the dull, can be dismissed as merely conventional. In this way we lose sight of natural differences and hence of nature her-

self; in this way, too, we extend the domain (in our theories, at least) of the conventional, and hence of chance.

6) Furthermore, art is no longer seen as the imitation of nature but rather as the free expression of the unencumbered soul. Such free expression is extolled as natural, and not only by those oppressed by the boredom of modernity. We can again see that it is a less inhibiting aspect of nature that replaces the older understanding. This means that art no longer teaches or reassures us about nature.

7) Finally, the decline in the authority of nature can also be traced to the now prevalent opinion that constant change is good, that there always is something even better that lies ahead, that perpetual progress is necessary for the happiness of mankind. The emphasis here is on the process and not on the goal, which can be dismissed as "static." There is nothing fixed, no perfection set by or evident in nature by which we are to take our bearings.

Related to this eclipse of nature is what has happened to the status of the divine in the public discourse of intellectuals. At one time a useful way to talk about nature was to talk about the divine. The divine too provided standards, guidance, and goals; it provided a reliable context within which the arts, including medicine, could work. It was once considered natural, even among many skeptics, that the divine should be publicly respected. A general respect for the divine as manifested in various religious practices and commandments can very much affect conduct in most people. But such respect is considered by all too many intellectuals today as repressive, or self-deceptive, or as hypocritical, or as a kind of wish-fulfillment, or as mere fearfulness. Nevertheless, a respect for nature in the old-fashioned sense and a respect for religion do tend to go hand in hand today, whatever tension there may be evident between students of nature and students of the divine from time to time, and whatever ultimate divergence there always is between them.

VII

I have suggested a half-dozen causes of the decline of the authority of nature in modernity. No doubt there are others, necessarily so since nature is hard to "put down." After all, nature is always there, always powerful. Even when her status is depreciated, she continues *to be*, however distorted or even perverted she can come to seem because of the opinions people have about her.

Ordinary experience continually draws upon nature and communities instinctively rely upon her, whatever intellectuals may say. For example, an effort to invoke nature is routinely seen in the criminal law—in the misconduct that the criminal law anticipates, in the sanctions that it provides.

Critical to any consideration of nature's place in the life of a community is the awareness of the significance of the natural right teaching. Natural right is that body of principles and ends which invokes, independent of revelation, a law above the positive law of the land. Natural right points both to the best possible regime and to the best possible development of the human soul, between which two goals, too, there can be some tension.

Whenever natural right is not recognized, the community is ultimately subjected (in a skeptical age) to blind obedience in the name either of laws of history or of the fatherland, or it is ultimately reduced to mere permissiveness with each person allowed to gratify himself in "doing his own thing." Government under this latter dispensation is reduced to the minimal functions of a referee or umpire. Also, under this dispensation, the law is little more than a ritual or a formality.

VIII

The modern theory of nature is largely that of intellectuals. Various institutions, somehow grounded in nature, do endure. They impede that pursuit of personal gratification which has been liberated by modern doctrines. But, however much a neglected nature still guides us, it does matter whether she is thought about and how. Things do tend to go better when nature is cooperated with rather than left to have her effect without our knowledge or even against our resistance. This is especially evident when efforts are made to find the proper place in a community's life for salutary innovations such as psychiatry.

A depreciation of nature rooted in modern science and its marvelous accomplishments has had its effects on psychiatry just as it has on political science and law. The effects on law and politics of this depreciation of the authority of nature have been less than on psychiatry since the legal or political practitioner, as distinguished from the legal or political theoretician, must still appeal to unsophisticated multitudes in the forms of juries and electorates. The people at large are still attuned to common sense, at least in decent societies.

But, alas, the theoretician and the practitioner in psychiatry seem much closer together, at least to the layman, than they are in law or in politics. The depreciation of the authority of nature means, we shall see, that there is a tendency for psychiatry to see people as other than people and hence not truly to see them. Psychiatry shares here the failings of modern social science.

I have suggested that if one cannot see certain things as either good or bad, as either beautiful or ugly, then one cannot see them properly or in their entirety. In some respects the law, with its rituals and its precedents and with its other restrictions and even blind spots, comes closer to seeing people properly, or in their entirety, than does psychiatry. Perhaps the same can be said of long-established religions. Nature has had her effects there also.

Psychiatry, therefore, has much that is fundamental to learn from the law. The law is not merely old-fashioned in its venerability; rather, it draws upon centuries of experience of mankind with nature and with natural limits upon self-gratification and innovation.

Thus the familiar resistance of the law to some of the innovations of psychiatry may be well grounded, based at the least on a sound instinct.

IX

The tendency of psychiatry to see people as other than people can take two principal forms.

One misleading way that psychiatry sees people is primarily as products of causes of various kinds, just as do physiology, sociology, and economics. Recourse to such materialistic causation places an emphasis upon people as mere responses to outside stimuli. (These "outside stimuli" include, in effect, chemical processes within the human body. These too are outside the soul's consciousness.) This emphasis implies that our sense of freedom or of responsibility is an illusion.

Does not such an emphasis upon causation, which regards men as virtual automatons, make much of chance as the source of the critical stimuli? In any event, this approach to humanity is to see men as overinfluenced by the "outside." This is probably the more important stage of my analysis here, raising as it does questions about free will. But it is also a stage that is more difficult than, and not as immediately relevant to our concerns as, what is available in the second approach by psychiatry to man. (See, on the thoughtfulness of psychiatry in its insistence that even the most bizarre conduct is never simply meaningless, Section II of Essay No. 10, above.)

X

The second misleading approach for psychiatry, sometimes pursued concurrently with the first, is to see man as underinfluenced by the "outside."

Man is seen as an autonomous being, a self-generated self, with his own standards and goals. At the root of this approach may be an intense concern with the desire to avoid anxiety and pain. This approach can be quite subjective; in fact, it is hard to see how it can be anything but subjective and undisciplined and therefore ultimately unsatisfying.

This approach probably dominates psychiatric thought today, at least for the impressionable general practitioner who permits "theory" to overpower his native common sense. It is an approach that depends on particular views both of society and of the relation of the individual to the community.

The emphasis here is upon the prerogatives of the individual. There is little recognition of the causes of one's opinions and hence of even one's most intense desires.

This approach is nicely illustrated by the public response that the distinguished journalist Max Lerner made in Los Angeles last spring to a talk I had given on the unfashionable but nevertheless salutary moral concerns of Aleksandr Solzhenitsyn: "I don't want anybody telling me what to do." We are not surprised to learn, as a *People* magazine article about him testified, that Mr. Lerner is "into" hedonism these days.

XI

What is the truth about these matters? Which approach is the sounder, that which stresses outside stimuli or that which stresses the autonomy of man?

Is there not something to be said for each? It would be unnatural if either approach could be long adhered to with no basis in fact.

Certainly, one is shaped by stimuli that are to some extent beyond one's control. Chemistry matters, sometimes enough to impede clear thinking, perhaps even to make all thinking impossible. Furthermore, stimuli beyond our control seem to be critical to our instincts and desires, misleading and entangling us in many ways.

On the other hand, one can become somewhat independent, in a sense autonomous. One can be so shaped and instructed as to be able to rise above one's physiological and social origins, at least so long as one's health and bodily processes, including those in the brain, hold up.

A third approach is not merely a compromise between the two approaches just sketched. Rather, it combines parts of both and rises above them to a truly human level. When one is properly instructed, one is not only "liberated" and "autonomous": one is enlisted in and disciplined by a new regime.

Only when one has the right passions and can act upon them is one truly free. Only then is there the ability to know and to pursue what is truly desired. Of course, there remains the question, How does one come to have the proper passions?

For this, communities rely in part upon the law, which itself relies in part upon and is influenced by art. When one talks of public opinion or of proper passions, one looks to the law, to art, and to religion. Religion often combines in a mysterious way both law and art.

The artist reaches to the deepest level of our being, or at least appears to do so. What the artist does often reflects the prompting of nature properly conceived. This is best seen in the works of the greatest poets, who are influential, if not decisive, in shaping our opinions and hence our passions, and to some extent our thoughts.

Particularly critical for the English-speaking peoples has been Shakespeare. He does not repudiate or simply agitate against, but rather refines, community opinion and commonly held standards. His greatest characters reach up to that which the community yearns for from a greater distance. Shakespeare considers enduring community opinion to reflect nature. That opinion may be seen in the law, and certainly in the Common Law of England.

In Shakespeare the accountability of the human being for what he does is emphasized. "If your fellow men do not get you for your misdeeds, nature or God will," he seems to say. Social pressures and massive temptations provide at best partial justifications for misconduct. By and large, people do get what they deserve, and this includes doomed characters as attractive as Cordelia, Desdemona, and Ophelia.

In this respect Shakespeare continues to shape us, if only because he has helped shape the language in which we desire and think.

XII

Compare Ibsen, perhaps the most influential modern playwright. He is, despite his supposed realism, more sentimental than Shakespeare. He is generally critical of community opinion; he is not intent upon refining it. There is in Ibsen what Malcolm Sharp has called considerable "unnecessary woe." Does not nature tend to promote sensible conduct and reduce the amount of woe in well-established communities?

Again and again in Ibsen's work there are examples of how the community goes wrong and how the self-expressive individual is more apt to be right, especially if a female. (An implicit, though confused, reliance upon nature may be seen here.) Ibsen makes much of the repressiveness of the society of his day, that is, Norway before the First World War. Yet are we not entitled to look back upon that community as almost idyllic in many respects?

Has not Ibsen's rather than Shakespeare's attitude toward society, so-called repression, and personal fulfillment become in large part the attitude of modern intellectuals and hence of psychiatry? This is especially to be seen in Ibsen's emphasis upon the right and need of each person to express himself at almost all costs in order to realize what he has within himself.

Much can be learned from a comparison of these two playwrights and from a consideration of why the sentiments and attitudes of Ibsen hold out a greater attraction for moderns than does the inspired moderation of Shakespeare with its "instinctive" respect for law and order. Mr. Sharp's father observed at the turn of this century that "Shakespeare is nature." Does not nature tend to promote sensible conduct in well-established communities?

XIII

Perhaps only a little more needs to be said here, in the form of questions, about what follows from all this for anyone interested in the relation of psychiatry to the law.

A key question is, What is the competence of psychiatry in these matters? I offered a few observations on this point at the beginning of my remarks. Can psychiatry reliably know men for social purposes? Can it do so more than, or even as well as, thoughtful citizens? What are the presuppositions of psychiatry? Should it not have a limited role in the law, especially in trials? Perhaps its principal use, in the interest both of humanity and of justice, should be during the sentencing process and during pardon and parole deliberations.

I return to a few questions I have touched upon in this talk. What does psychiatry consider a good community? What does psychiatry consider a healthy or mature human being? What does psychiatry consider the proper relation between the community and the human being?

The answers to such questions along with the opinions they depend on and lead to, affect the extent and form of mental afflictions among us. They also affect decisions respecting humane treatment and standards of accountability in everyday life as well as in the courts.

I have argued that certain fundamental opinions not only affect how one responds to various kinds of human conduct, but also how one sees that conduct. The human being is most apt to see things properly and to act well when the fundamental opinions he has are sound, that is, when they are grounded in nature.

A healthy soul depends to a considerable extent on the doings and sayings of the community. In other words, psychiatry should be subordinated in many ways to a decent political order, to the politics which Aristotle spoke of as the master art and to which both medicine and the law are properly instrumental.

You as doctors of the soul are certainly much more familiar than I have been fated to become with the psychic afflictions of mankind. I trust that the old questions I have resurrected and the way I have suggested they should be thought about will be of service to you as the dedicated practitioners all of us very much rely upon.

29

ON CAPITAL PUNISHMENT

It is said that Aristotle was blamed for having been too merciful to a wicked man. "It is true," he said, "that I was merciful to the man, but not to his wickedness." The judgment of the ordinary man is provoked to exercise vengeance by the horror of the misdeed. That itself is enough to cool mine. Horror of the first killing makes me fear a second; and hatred of the first cruelty makes me hate any imitation of it.

MICHEL DE MONTAIGNE

I

The arguments *against* capital punishment in the United States today are in many respects rather dubious. But perhaps even more dubious has always been the case *for* capital punishment. Why is this so? There does seem to be something about this issue which makes it difficult for advocates to be completely persuasive one way or another. One consequence of this is that the issue is never really settled. Even in the days when the issue was hardly one for judicial consideration on constitutional grounds, there was considerable agitation of the issue, if only in the form of pleas for executive clemency in cases where the death sentence had been imposed.

The question of what should be done about capital punishment is one that simply will not remain answered in this Country today. It is complicated by the fact that those who argue for capital punishment as a public safety measure are inclined to be somewhat open to military adventures and even to the prospects of nuclear war, and by the fact that those who demand an end to capital punishment in the name of the sanctity of life

This talk was given at the Clarence Darrow Memorial Meeting, Jackson Park and the Museum of Science and Industry, Chicago, Illinois, March 13, 1984.

The epigraph is taken from Michel de Montaigne, "Of Physiognomy," *Essays*, III, 12 (E. J. Trechmann translation).

are inclined to be somewhat open to abortion on demand and perhaps even to euthanasia.

II

Neither those who call for the abolition of capital punishment nor those who call for its selective use seem able to come up with answers that can settle the question once and for all. This has been the state of affairs for some years now, and so we can hear talk about the considerable arbitrariness in meting out death sentences, about the mounting crime rate and the need for a plausible deterrence, about the disturbing risk of executing the innocent, and about the sanctity of life being manifested both in the principled refusal to execute and in the firm determination to exact a proper retribution. The abolitionists do seem to fare better among intellectuals, whereas those who urge the legitimacy of capital punishment do seem to appeal more to ordinary citizens.

There are certainly men among us whose crimes put them beyond any claim for gentle treatment by the community. Are such vile men entitled to a natural lifetime of attention and care by the community? Or is it that the proper concern should be not with what such men are entitled to, and at what cost, but rather with what the community does to itself by deliberately killing them?

Such are the questions we can hear debated on all sides today. There is here an underlying question that also needs to be addressed, but one which is seldom asked, let alone answered: Why or how is it that most great thinkers across the centuries simply have not had the reservations about capital punishment that are so widely held today among informed people?

Is it likely that the ancients missed something about human nature or about the nature of communities which makes capital punishment simply improper? What has been learned or what has been forgotten that permits if it does not even require the capital punishment debate to take the form it does today?

There can be said to be appreciated in modern times, perhaps as never before, the primacy of the individual soul. This can lead to an emphasis upon the preservation of life as the principal purpose of society. But has there been forgotten what may be needed to keep society itself going, that society which may be required for the effective nurture and protection of the individual? Is the individual too dependent on society to be able to stand alone? Is it sentimental to believe otherwise? Or is the critical change in modernity that we no longer consider it possible to ground public policy, in these and other matters, upon an understanding of a fairly constant human nature or upon enduring moral standards?

One element that has been constant, either in human nature or at least in the prejudices that human beings and communities are susceptible to, is the general opinion that a community worthy of the name will not allow itself to be imposed upon by certain kinds of criminals and hence that certain deeds are deserving of death. Is the general public, when it feels this way, deeply uninformed? Is it deluded, for example, as to what is likely to happen as a result of executions?

To what extent are the prejudices and limitations of the community to be catered to? Are the analyses and arguments of sociologists, statisticians, and criminologists, most of whom *are* opposed to capital punishment, really beside the point? Is something more fundamental, something naturally political and moral, being drawn upon by the public?

On the other hand, and this may be central to what can be said on this occasion, the advocates of capital punishment today defend only a very small part of the executions that were once believed necessary and proper, whether as retribution, or as requirement for the defense of society, or as affirmation of the worth of human life. The typical argument *for* capital punishment today is, in effect, a powerful argument *against* capital punishment both as it has long been practiced and as it is still being practiced in much of the modern world.

The more responsible advocates of capital punishment today repudiate many of the practices defended by the greatest thinkers of the past with respect to these matters. The typical argument for capital punishment today obviously would restrict considerably the crimes that the public, whose passions are often invoked in support of some capital punishment, would like to see punished with execution. Advocates of capital punishment over the centuries have been far more severe than can now be justified by any thoughtful student of the subject. Do the principles that have led to the general repudiation of at least nine-tenths of what were once capital offenses threaten as well the propriety of the remaining one-tenth? Consider, also, the implications of the concessions that the advocates of capital punishment are now willing to make to the demands of "due process" and to the requirements of "equal protection" in the allocation of capital punishment. (See, e.g., Walter Berns, *Encyclopedia of the American Constitution*, p. 207: "That the death penalty has historically been imposed, if not capriciously, then at least in a racially and socially discriminatory fashion seems to be borne out by the statistics.") It is difficult to escape the sobering conclusion that even the toughest advocate of capital punishment among us today would concede that ninety percent of the executions that have ever taken place around the world at the hands of one government or another have been simply unjust. There may be something remarkably presumptuous, then, about the opinion of any man who believes that he can define with tolerable precision the perhaps ten percent of traditional executions that can still be justified, and who also believes that he can thereafter persuade his fellow citizens to respect the definition he has provided them.

Does not all this tell us something about the passions involved in the resort to capital punishment? Are those passions too insistent to be restrained permanently, and yet too ugly to be permitted by a sensitive community whenever a people *has* been persuaded that they are indeed ugly and perhaps ineffective as well? Lest it be thought that modern man has become weak and hence paralyzed in his exercise of government power, it should be remembered that we do live in a century with unprecedented mass executions by governments whose excesses make those of harsh governments of earlier centuries appear models of restraint by comparison. What, then, has really made human life seem less sacred: the abolition of capital punishment here and there or the mass slaughter that governments have been responsible for or have permitted in times of peace as well as in times of war? Is it reasonable to suppose, as some advocates of the death penalty suggest, that the opinions upon which the abolition of capital punishment is based have been in some way responsible for the governments that do slaughter with abandon?

Much is heard from those advocates about the breakdown of morality that abolition of the death penalty is a symptom of and perhaps promotes. The efforts of abolitionists in this century, whether in the courts or in the legislatures of this Country, are sometimes looked to as responsible for this deterioration in moral purpose. Yet consider what Alexis de Tocqueville could say a century and a half ago on this subject (*Democracy in America*, Pt. III, Chap. 1; p. 564):

> There is no country in which criminal justice is administered with more kindness than in the United States. While the English seem bent on carefully preserving in their penal legislation the bloody traces of the Middle Ages, the Americans have almost eliminated capital punishment from their codes.

Is there any argument used for capital punishment today that could not have been used, in good faith, to support the English, as against the American practice in Tocqueville's time? Yet would not most of the advocates of capital punishment today prefer virtually total abolition, if not even total abolition, to what prevailed in the United States, let alone in Great Britain, at the beginning of the Nineteenth Century?

Tocqueville, in the passage from which I have quoted, adds the following observation: "North America is, I think, the only country on earth which has not taken the life of a single citizen for political offenses during the last fifty years."

What a blessing such restraint can be should be evident to anyone who considers how the death penalty was used by Hitler and by Stalin and how it is used today in Mainland China, in South Africa, and in the Soviet Union. When we recall the terrible Rosenberg espionage executions in this Country in 1953 (executions that were not *in their form* executions for political offenses) we can get a notion of what widespread recourse to executions for non-political as well as for political offenses can do to a community.

Most if not all executions are in effect political statements. What lessons do such statements teach? In what do people need training these days? In respect *both* for law and order and for the sanctity of life? How are they apt to get such training? By seeing a government deliberately kill and in circumstances where such killing is highly likely to be sensationalized, to appear bloodthirsty, and to be widely (although not generally) regarded as repugnant? Or by seeing a people and its government restrain themselves even under extreme provocation and in circumstances where the criminal has absolutely no claim upon our mercy? All too many of the better arguments for capital punishment today are little more than elaborate justifications for a recourse to anger, an anger which *can* be noble in its aspirations, but is all too often ugly in its implications and applications.

Questionable as capital punishment may be, it should be added, even more questionable may be its abolition, if abolition should be grounded on a repudiation of a community's moral sense or if abolition should make too much of the specter of death or if abolition should fail to recognize both the awfulness of certain crimes and the dependence of the community on a general opinion that certain deeds are indeed awful. Should the moral sense of the community be permanently subverted in one or more of these ways, far worse things can be expected among us than an occasional recourse to capital punishment.

Thus, the underlying argument today may not be about capital punishment, but rather about the nature of government and about the status both of morality and of mortality. (Here we return to the great thinkers who are neglected among us.) What the argument should *not* be about is whether capital punishment serves as a useful deterrent. This may require much more precision than is routinely available in such matters. After all, consider the problems that experienced politicians and astute political observers have during the current election season in predicting how normal people will vote or in figuring out what moves them to vote the way they do. How can we be reasonably certain about what the effects will be, good and bad, either of executions or of the suspension of executions?

What we can be certain about, at least for the foreseeable future, is that monstrous crimes will continue to be committed that will move many to want to execute the monsters responsible for them. Also certain, at least in modern communities, is that such executions will find both conscientious defense and a profound abhorrence, neither of which will simply be silenced.

III

It may well be, then, that the opponents of capital punishment will have the better case in the years immediately ahead, while the advocates of capital punishment will have the better arguments. The opponents may have the better case as reflected in the fact that even the advocates of capital punishment have conceded during the past two centuries that very few of the many offenses once regarded as capital should continue to be treated as such. The advocates of capital punishment may have the better arguments, as perhaps they always have had, in that they do continue to defend an old-fashioned morality, however mistaken they may be in the application of enduring moral principles to the present matter. The advocates of capital punishment tend to be more serious than the opponents of capital punishment about the very same moral principles that have been put to such good use during the past two centuries in staying the bloody hand of government. (However that may be, the efforts of the abolitionist have prompted even the determined advocates of capital punishment to think through their own case better. See, for discussions of two dozen noteworthy cases, my article, "On Trial: Explorations," prepared for the *Loyola University of Chicago Law Journal.*)

Thus, the contest *among us* today is between the ninety percent abolitionists and the one hundred percent abolitionists. That is, the most effective case *against* capital punishment among us today comes from considering carefully the arguments *for* capital punishment, especially when those arguments are compared with the arguments made to that end a century or two ago. In short, there is not such an abolitionist in the nation today as the more thoughtful advocate of capital punishment, after all.

F.

Politics
and Government

30

ON IMPEACHMENT

It is easy to praise Athens to Athenians.

SOCRATES

I

This is the first installment of an equivocating talk I am making this week on the problem of impeachment as faced today by the American people. The second installment is scheduled for the University of Dallas. That installment, which will take into account the markedly conservative sympathies of *that* community, should deal much more than my remarks today with the failings and liabilities of Mr. Nixon. (See Essay No. 8, above.) My remarks on this occasion, on the other hand, are directed to those of you who, in this Eastern intellectual setting just outside Washington, D.C., can be expected to be favorably inclined toward the current impeachment drive.

Thus I, like a prudent political man, deliberately tailor my remarks on controversial subjects to the prejudices of my audience. Since, however, I am *not* a political man but rather a student of politics, such tailoring consists of challenging rather than accommodating local predilections whenever I believe it useful to do so. My remarks will be of a more general character, designed to elicit, but not to limit the scope of, discussion. To make the few points that are useful for this occasion, I will repeat myself in various ways. (These remarks were anticipated by my February 24, 1974 talk in Chicago, "Impeachment and Statesmanship." That talk has been published as Essay No. 14 in *Human Being and Citizen*.)

This talk was given at St. John's College, Annapolis, Maryland, April 28, 1974. (Original title: "Some Reservations About the Impeachment of Mr. Nixon.")
The epigraph is adapted from Plato, *Menexenus* 235D.

II

"It has been frequently remarked," observes Publius in a passage in *Federalist* No. 1 familiar to many of you, "that it seems to have been reserved to the people of this country, by their conduct and example, to decide the important question, whether societies of men are really capable or not, of establishing good government from reflection and choice, or whether they are forever destined to depend, for their political constitutions, on accident and force." One is obliged to ask in the light of this observation whether we are necessarily trapped by the impeachment process. Can we neither pull out nor end it quickly? Do we have to ride out to the bitter end the excursion upon which we have embarked?

The inquiries of Congress and the maneuverings of the President are so complicated and so devious that it now seems that the current proceedings could stretch past the mid-point of Mr. Nixon's second term, with a consequent paralysis of the Administration and a deprivation of political leadership in this country. In the short run, the bureaucracy can run the Country, but this has bad features as well as good; in the long run, this can have serious effects, as could the flaring up of an emergency that the Government does not anticipate properly or respond to adequately because of the preoccupation in its several branches with impeachment. It is my opinion that a prolonged proceeding is irresponsible on all sides. I should also add that I urged in a talk published last fall in Chicago newspapers that all this should be brought to a close, one way or another, by February 1974. (See Section II of Essay No. 15, above.)

Such prescriptions as this reflect my opinion that impeachment is a political, not a judicial, proceeding and should be relatively free of the standards and procedures of judicial proceedings. The Constitution, in permitting the removal of a President, provides that the House of Representatives must "impeach" (that is, indict) him for bribery, treason, or other high crimes and misdemeanors and that the Senate must, in a proceeding chaired by the Chief Justice, convict him by a two-thirds vote. Impeachment of a President is a constitutional remedy for massive and palpable threats to the body politic, threats that cannot wait upon the ordinary political calendar and ordinary political and judicial processes. The impeachment remedy permits, and should permit, Congress to remove a President overnight.

An impeachment proceeding is, especially where a President is involved, an emergency measure. It is and should be a privileged proceeding that takes precedence over almost all others, once the Congress is constituted. It also is, again especially where a President is involved, too drastic to be used by a responsible people through their representatives in Congress except in the most critical circumstances. It seems to me absurd to assume, as all too many seem to do today, that if there *do* seem to be impeachable offenses against Mr. Nixon, we must by all means investigate and impeach him. It is a bad precedent to establish that the mere existence of genuinely impeachable offenses requires conscientious members of the House of Representatives to impeach. Such an approach regards this constitutional remedy as a judicial proceeding rather than as the exercise of political judgment of a high order.

Judicial proceedings, we should remember, depend on established ways of determining the truth designed to do justice between parties in circumstances where a particular law applies. On the other hand, political activity, of which an impeachment proceeding is one grim manifestation, is directed primarily to the service of the common good. This means that *prudence,* not *justice,* is preeminently the virtue to be taken into account here. Gerald Ford made a revealing comment when he said in the House of Representatives some years ago that an impeachable offense was whatever Congress said it was. Those who now quote that comment against the Administration do not appreciate how thoughtless such a formulation is in its implication that anything goes. The Framers preferred to reserve impeachment for circumstances where the gravest concerns are to be ministered to by Congress.

III

I have suggested that the common good, ministered to by prudence rather than by justice in the ordinary sense, is preeminently the standard to be taken into account here. (I should add that the common good *is* usually served by seeing justice done, but my use here of *usually* does recognize exceptions.) Consider the sort of thing that follows if the emphasis is placed upon the common good rather than upon justice in considering the proper use of impeachment. Such offenses as lying or even obstruction of justice should not ordinarily be the primary concern in the exercise by Congress of its Presidential-impeachment power. These offenses bear upon what we think of the Nixon Administration; they may bear as well upon how we vote with respect to men like Mr. Nixon. But deception is too much a part of the politician's stock-in-trade for us to make as much of it as is being made these days in the various indictments that affect the tone of the drive toward impeachment. Do we really want grand juries to be used systematically, as Mr. Nixon's Justice Department all too often tried to do, to put politicians in the "impossible" position of either telling the truth and suffering politically or lying and risking indictment when the temper of the times changes against them? Does not this push our politics to the brink of ruthlessness and desperation?

I emphasize that the issue should not be, for impeachment purposes, the truthfulness of Mr. Nixon and his subordinates. Truthfulness should not be the primary political concern here, but rather the common good. It is good, of course, to have truthful testimony presented to grand juries, before Congressional committees, in courts, and to the authorities generally. But how seriously we take perjury for impeachment purposes should depend in large part on how serious the problems are which the juries, committees, and courts consider. It does not make sense politically to allow such an ancillary offense as perjury to loom larger in significance than the matters being inquired into and with respect to which perjury might have been committed.

IV

I have argued, then, that not truth or justice but rather the common good is that with which political prudence should be primarily concerned. Such prudence should be expected of responsible men, whether in Congress or in the press. On the other hand, it may not be prudent to expect this distinction between the common good and truthfulness or justice to be appreciated or respected by the public at large. But the public can be assured by prudent men that it will get *its* chance to act on these matters in its capacity as the electorate, where the demands of truth and justice can be expected to be more significant. These assurances can include the explanation that restrained conduct by responsible men in Government will make it more likely that the conditions will be best for the public to express *itself* in a most useful way and, indeed, in the way the public can be understood to want to do.

When I emphasize as I do the virtue of prudence, I do not merely reformulate the common saying that governments are necessarily immoral or at least amoral. It is no doubt evident to all of you how it can happen that a community may, particularly in order to preserve itself from annihilation, countenance if not even require behavior in its public servants that would be highly improper in private life. But, as I have just indicated, this is not where I would prefer to put the emphasis on this occasion: a higher moral standard in the community and in those acting for the community is called for here than would be required in private persons. The community and its public servants should be careful not to use the impeachment proceeding simply to seek revenge or even to punish those who misbehave. Personalities should not be permitted to intrude; simple formulae should be avoided—that is, things must be thought through in the circumstances in which the Country happens to find itself. One must work much harder than in ordinary controversies, judicial or otherwise, to figure out what is called for. This requires sustained discipline, sacrifice of partisan political advantage, and judgment of a high order. All this can hardly be considered immoral. Rather, to fail to be this scrupulous may even raise questions about one's moral worth.

V

We should be particularly on guard against slogans and pat phrases which conceal from us the problems which should be faced up to. It can be misleading to place the emphasis upon how orderly the procedures of the relevant Congressional committees are these days, how the evidence is being carefully sifted, and so forth. These assurances, of which we now hear so much, depend on misconceptions about what our primary concern should be, even though such assurances of fairness may be important for public opinion in the event Mr. Nixon should be removed from office. I add another suggestion about the significance of the proceedings we are now witnessing: a prolonged inquiry is itself an argument against impeachment. The longer the proceedings stretch out, the more obvious it is that the Country can indeed live with Mr. Nixon and his shortcomings. Whether the government business, especially abroad, is being conducted as well as it can and should be remains to be seen.

If, as I have argued, the offenses critical to Presidential impeachment should be massive and palpable, then the leisurely pace at which all this is proceeding is a serious problem. Does it not become evident as the months go by that the Country is not immediately threatened by the current administration? Has not the publicity there has already been, to say nothing of the indictments and house-cleaning in government we have already witnessed, put a considerable restraint not only upon this President but also upon his successors? It should also be noticed that the offenses which have been made so much of in the press and Congress would not have really hurt the Country if they had never been exposed. For example, little if any damage has been done by the efforts to repress dissent in recent years, partly because of the incompetence of John Mitchell's Justice Department and partly because of the temper of the times. Since such offenses if unexposed would not have constituted a serious threat, should not those which chance to have been exposed be maturely lived with pending the next election? However that may be, nothing that Mr. Nixon has been charged with doing has been as intrinsically serious and as harmful as what was done by various of his Democratic predecessors since the Second World War: Mr. Truman with his uses of the Nagasaki atomic bomb abroad and of the government employees security programs at home; Mr. Kennedy with his brinkmanship in the Cuban Missile Crisis and his experimentations in Vietnam; Mr. Johnson with his promotion of a war that tore the Country apart and permitted, perhaps even required, someone of Mr. Nixon's temperament and genuine talents to succeed him.

VI

I have been arguing for self-restraint on the part of Mr. Nixon's critics who now find themselves vindicated in the eyes of the public with respect to the charges they have made against his character for years. On the other hand, the insistence we are witnessing in both the courts and the Congress upon pushing things to the limit may be grounded at bottom in a kind of civil hysteria. To be genuinely political is to be anything but hysterical. What explains this peculiarly excited state of mind? Or, if we cannot yet explain it, what triggered it?

1) There is the ungenerous character of Mr. Nixon himself and, by extension, the caliber of *some* of the men he attracted to him. Old animosities are being remembered on both sides. Mr. Nixon's peculiar isolation does not help, nor does his ultimate disregard of and even contempt for public opinion, whether in the Country at large or in Congress.

2) There is also the sleazy kind of misconduct that has been unearthed (even though by chance, even if not serious). This misconduct, especially in an Administration that had stressed common morality and "law and order," tends to demean the Presidency. But then, have we not made too much of the Presidency, or at least of Presidents?

3) Then there are the passions and circumstances of the Country that permit the President's personal character and the exposed misconduct to matter as much as they have. These passions and circumstances have been very much affected by the nature of the mass media, by the disturbing effects of the Kennedy assassination, and by the Vietnam War and its domestic ramifications.

Such are the elements that have gone into the civil hysteria to which I have referred. I am reminded by our current excursion into impeachment, although here on a minor and domestic scale, of the beginnings of the wars of 1914 and 1939. Things are somehow out of control, even though highly organized and well publicized, as if massive military forces have been set into motion and no one is in a position to countermand the fatal orders.

VII

All in all, it *is* interesting to watch, but one speaks thus as a student, not as a citizen. This points up not only the instruction motive, but the even more dubious entertainment motive, behind impeachment. We again notice the mass media and public tastes that have been developed independent of any political authority or public interests on the part of those who control the media. Technology has come so to shape tastes as to breed in us an insatiable curiosity, especially curiosity with respect to the violent, the low, and the private.

All these—entertainment, curiosity, and even a desire for revenge—are non-political, perhaps even anti-political, concerns. Yet one also hears today an emphasis upon duty. Is not this a peculiar view of duty, however, that one should insist upon doing something which may be harmful to the community? We are being told in effect that the prejudices and passions of the public at large now happen to be in such bad shape because of the machinations both of Mr. Nixon and his enemies that we have to have an impeachment proceeding to clear the air. I say *in effect* because intellectuals and the press do not yet recognize that *their* insistence upon impeachment has helped make the prejudices and passions of the public what they are. Are we obliged to concede that what has been done cannot now be undone? Is it true that the public cannot be maturely appealed to, by responsible leaders of all parties, to forego the extraordinary remedy of impeachment and to rely instead upon the Presidential election which we will be moving into some eighteen months from now?

VIII

In talking to a more conservative audience, one might be obliged to attempt to reconcile one's listeners to Mr. Nixon's fall and to suggest the things to be gained from such an experience. Perhaps we will come out all right, if not even strengthened by this experience. But I suspect that the salutary effects of this experience with respect to the rule of law and with respect to cutting the Presidency down to constitutional size have already been achieved. Anything more than this is to be gained at great risk, with far too much dependent on chance to constitute statesmanship. A different tone of political life, a ruthless tone which is somehow an extension of the fierce combative spirit long associated with Mr. Nixon, can well be left as a permanent part of our regime.

The statesman should be most reluctant to embark upon any course of action that threatens dire consequences unless he can control it or unless he has no reasonable alternative. The reaction against the impeachment drive, whether successful or not, can be as great as that against what we know as McCarthyism. It should be remembered that Joseph McCarthy was even more powerful and even less vulnerable in his heyday than those now identified with the drive for impeachment. The current drive may someday be condemned as an effort by a determined and highly articulate minority to "veto" a landslide that did reflect the concerns of the electorate. This can have serious long-run consequences in that it cuts to the heart of a republican regime.

Another risk of misuse of the impeachment remedy should be noticed: that remedy, and perhaps Congress with it, may be in effect repudiated once we get past this immediate crisis, thereby creating a vacuum into which the Presidency would eventually move. Furthermore, our vital impeachment remedy may be crippled by the precedent of extended proceedings. I repeat: any Presidential misconduct that invites impeachment should not require much argument or extensive documentation to establish. Something seems to me wrong when so much effort is required to bring Congressional Republicans into line. Really serious dangers for the Country should be quite apparent to most members of Congress, Republicans and Democrats alike. If they are not, recourse to impeachment, at least in circumstances such as the present, should be avoided.

However all this may be, we can see, in the way the case for impeachment is being made today, the limits of rationality in political life. Once passions have been allowed to build up, they do have to be reckoned with.

IX

The unseemliness of all this should put us on notice—the unseemliness both of the excessive fervor of many of the President's critics and of the shameless maneuvering of the President himself. Statesmanlike responses are needed to begin to minimize the effect of what has already happened to us. A Presidential resignation, couched in the most dignified terms, might be useful, but for us to rely upon that resolution is not to settle upon what *we* can do.

Prudence does seem to be called for. We can benefit from the purgation which would accompany deliberate, *explained* efforts at self-restraint on the part of Mr. Nixon's critics. We need, in short, a return to serious politics after having indulged ourselves for some years now in ruthless hostilities both at home and abroad. We liberals would do well to take to heart the lesson learned by another fervent warrior after a decade of war and rumors of war. Winston Churchill provided this moral for his history of the Second World War:

> In War: Resolution
> In Defeat: Defiance
> In Victory: Magnanimity
> In Peace: Good Will.

Does not Magnanimity in Victory contribute to a just and prosperous political regime, at peace abroad and with itself?

31

CITY LIFE

31-A. The Federal Idea and the City

No modern thinker has understood better than Rousseau the philosophic conception of the polis: *the* polis *is that complete association which corresponds to the natural range of man's power of knowing and loving.*

LEO STRAUSS

I

It is commonly observed that cities, unlike States, are not mentioned in the Constitution. Cities are creatures of the States in a way that States are *not* creatures of the United States. Thus, States have a free hand, so far as the United States Constitution is concerned, in forming, empowering and eliminating cities. Cities are not protected, say in Federal courts, from various State actions: in this respect they as public corporations are much more vulnerable than non-public corporations.

The silence in the Constitution of the United States with respect to cities is anticipated by a like silence in the Articles of Confederation. In the Declaration of Independence, moreover, there is only a passing reference to cities in one of the grievances against George III, "He has plundered our Seas, ravaged our Coasts, burnt our Towns, and destroyed the Lives of our People."

This talk was given at the Conference on the Constitution and the City, Community Renewal Society, Newberry Library, Chicago, Illinois, January 14, 1988. It was included, with some notes, in the collection of papers from the Conference issued by the Community Renewal Society.

The epigraph is taken from Leo Strauss, *Natural Right and History* (Chicago: University of Chicago Press, 1953), p. 254, n. 2.

The three kinds of entities that matter, then, for the United States Constitution are the Country, the States, and the people who appear in various capacities (and ultimately in the capacities of both rulers and ruled).

II

It is obvious to all of us, however, that despite the silence with respect to cities in our great national charters, cities have always played a vital part in the life of our people. Many cities today have the population and the importance in everyday life that the States of the Union had in 1787. In fact, many cities now are as large in population as any one of the States was then. Indeed, several cities in this Country are larger in population today than the entire United States was in 1787. (Census figures for the entire Country, not including Indians, were 3,929,214 in 1790 and 5,308,483 in 1800.)

For many people cities now have, more than the current States, the "feel" of the States of 1787. There is a growing proportion of our people who "identify" themselves more with their city than with their State. (Mayor Richard J. Daley, of Chicago, was particularly known, and respected, for such an allegiance.) It is in urban areas that more and more of the Country live, perhaps as many as three-fourths of the total population; and it has always been in cities that various governments in this Country (including National and State governments) operate. Even to have a government, staffed by personnel in legislative, executive, and judicial branches, is to have a city.

For these and other reasons, therefore, it is useful, in thinking about the city under the United States Constitution, to consider what we know about and expect from States, a subject to which I will turn after glancing at what the Constitution of 1787 does say about one city.

III

Even though cities are not mentioned in the Constitution of 1787, there may still be found there recognition of the importance of cities in the life of a people. This may be seen, for example, in the provision (in Section 8 of Article I) for what we now know as the District of Columbia. It is ordained that Congress shall have power to "exercise exclusive Legislation in all Cases whatsoever, over such District (not exceeding ten Miles square) as may, by Cession of particular States, and the Acceptance of Congress, become the Seat of the Government of the United States."

Negotiations for the development of the Federal City (as it was then designated) settled, during the early years under the Constitution, upon a tract of one hundred square miles acquired by the United States from Maryland and Virginia. (Since then, Alexandria has been retroceded to Virginia, leaving the District with less than seventy square miles.) The location of the national capital is said to have been agreed to by Northern Federalists in exchange for Southern acquiescence in the assumption of State revolutionary war debts by the General Government.

The First Congress, which got things going under the Constitution in March 1789, organized itself in New York City, where the Congress under the Articles of Confederation had been meeting at the time the Constitution was written in 1787. The First Congress, in its third (and final) session, moved to Philadelphia, where it remained for the decade during which the Federal City was being built. Congress assumed jurisdiction over the District of Columbia on February 27, 1801.

IV

It was evident to the Framers of the United States Constitution that the General Government would need a city of its own. Do we not all need cities of our own, and for some of the same reasons that the Government of the United States does? Much can and should be made, in our constitutional system, of the Union, the Nation, and the "sovereign States." But it is, after all, in cities that we live and in large part have our being. And it is city life which now dominates cultural activities among us, and not only through the mass media that are based in cities. The Framers believed in 1787 that the General Government had to be able to control fully what happened immediately around it, that it could be severely crippled otherwise. The General Government must be able to control a *place* of its own rather than reside in a district which is in effect a suburb to a large city controlled by some State. (See 1 *Debates and Proceedings; History of Congress* 925 [September 28, 1789].)

Is it not this "instinct" to be assured of one's own "turf" that we see today in the passions and efforts of city officials, neighborhood associations, block clubs, and even street gangs? This may be particularly so in Chicago, perhaps the most American and hence "natural" of our great cities in that it, unlike the great cities on our borders, does not look outward to other countries and peoples but is "home grown." To say, however, that one wants to be assured of one's own is *not* to suggest that "anything goes" in one's "neighborhood." Thus, precautions were taken in the First Congress, when the Federal City was being prepared for, to insure that the laws of the States of Maryland and Virginia would continue in force there until Congress could provide laws of its own. It is evident in all this that the legislature is considered to be ultimately in control among the three branches of government, whether State or National. It is also evident that the Framers believed in government: the initial complaints against Great Britain in the Declaration of Independence had been that the American people were systematically deprived of the legislative services they were entitled to.

It should also be noticed, however, that just as the General Government wants to be assured of its control of the area in which its principal officers operate, so do the people who live in the District of Columbia want to have more control over their everyday lives than is recognized by the Constitution with its grant to Congress of the power to "exercise exclusive Legislation in all Cases whatsoever" in the District of Columbia. There have been repeated efforts, and down to this day a continuing controversy, with respect to the complaints of residents in the District of Columbia who believe they are naturally entitled to more self-government, let alone seats in the national legislature, whatever the Constitution may happen to say.

The attraction of local self-determination, or "States' Rights," doctrines may be seen in the demands of cities for more and more control over what happens to them. Much can be learned about how to begin to think about cities in our circumstances today by reflecting upon the nature and place of the States in the constitutional system of 1787.

V

There has been from the beginning, and even before the beginning, a considerable interest among Americans in "States' Rights." That interest has been exploited both for good and for bad causes, the most notorious having to do with race relations in this Country.

The Anti-Federalists, who opposed in 1787–88 the Ratification of the Constitution, made much of the virtues of local government. They made even more of the dangers of a continental empire that would breed ruinous taxation, bloody adventures at home and abroad, and the arrogance of power. Limited republics were extolled as much sounder: local governments can more readily adapt to immediate circumstances; rulers and ruled are more likely to know each other and what is going on; kinship and friendship are much more important than distant impersonal relations.

In many ways, the Constitution of 1787 took account of such sentiments. There are various ways in which local governments are relied upon

by the General Government, including the dependence on State legislatures to provide for the selection of members of both Houses of Congress
and of Presidential electors. And, of course, the very establishment of the
Constitution and any amendments to it thereafter depend on the actions
of the American people organized State by State.

In a less formal sense, cities are very much relied upon to help shape the
General Government, as may be seen in the influence of urban blocs both
in Congress, especially in the House of Representatives, and in Presidential nominations and elections. A study of States' Rights, then, should be
instructive for anyone interested in the prerogatives and limitations of
cities.

VI

The history of States' Rights in this Country is particularly instructive in
assessing one remedy that the city's advocates are sometimes intrigued by
today, the remedy of secession from an oppressive or at least unresponsive State. Large metropolitan areas, it is sometimes said, need to form
separate States of their own.

Such a move would require the consent both of Congress and of the
State or States involved. The major examples of this we have had are the
separation of Maine from Massachusetts in the early years of the Republic
and the separation of West Virginia from Virginia during the Civil War.

The advantages of secession for large cities today may be seen, in a
tamer form, in the strengthening of "home rule" provisions in State constitutions. These advantages must be obvious to everyone interested in the
problems of the American city. The disadvantages, or at least some of
them, are also obvious: Would not the secession of our largest cities into
separate States usually mean the concentration of the poor of the Country
in urbanized States? Where would the prosperous suburbs choose to go?
That is, do the cities need the resources of non-urban areas to help them
deal with their problems, problems that are really due to the economy
and the social policies of the Country at large?

The resources needed by cities can be political and moral as well as
economic. Are not cities more apt than States to be adversely affected by
factions? That is, are not cities more severely divided and hence less
moderate than those more complicated State amalgamations in this Country that include rural, small-town, urban, and suburban elements? Consider, as well, the social implications of data recently collected in West
Germany (and perhaps applicable also to the United States): "There are
approximately 130 AIDS cases for every million people in urban areas in

West Germany to only 9 cases per million residents in rural regions." (*The Week in Germany*, January 8, 1988, p. 7)

It is prudent to recall that it was a misconceived effort at secession on the part of some States (in 1860–65) which led (in the Thirteenth, Fourteenth and Fifteenth Amendments, and thereafter) to a significant modification of the powers of all States under the Constitution.

VII

However appealing certain States' Rights sentiments may be to the champions of cities, cities in our time do tend to be more anti-States' Rightist in their doctrines. Federal funds, as well as other federal legislative aid of various kinds, are looked to by cities, whereas States' Rightists tend to be skeptical about direct dealings between the General Government and the cities or about the prospect of federal interference in relations between States and cities, to say nothing about any exercise of governmental power at all. Particularly threatening to States' Rightists is the growing movement to "constitutionalize" various welfare, education, and voting entitlements, so much so that Federal courts exercise more and more control over the operations of local governments. Legislative reapportionment, including for city council elections (as we here in Chicago have recently seen), is a particularly dramatic instance of this, following upon the even more dramatic desegregation campaign in this Country since the Second World War. We have yet to see, however, a proper consideration by the United States Supreme Court of those highly questionable arrangements that permit some public schools in a State to enjoy much more public funding than other public schools in the same State. (That is, *San Antonio Independent School District* v. *Rodriguez*, 411 U.S. 1 [1973], needs to be reconsidered.)

It remains to be determined what the long-term effects of various proposed constitutional and political changes would be. Consider, for example, what the effect would be upon the political power (or, to use a good Chicago term, the clout) of cities if we should ever have direct popular election of the President of the United States. I suspect that that would reduce significantly the power of concentrated minorities and of urban centers.

Be that as it may, cities do want more and more "home rule" even as they try to get more and more help from the General Government. In fact, home-rule powers are sought in part to enable cities to deal more efficiently with the General Government, thereby making cities less dependent on their States. On the other hand, astute citizens in cities should be able to take advantage of what properly led States have to offer. In any event, sensible city governments should be a blessing for all citizens in a State, especially when those governments are so organized as to be sensitive (as perhaps only enlightened local government can be) to the problems and talents found in neighborhoods.

Various developments, some of which we have noticed on this occasion, have contributed in recent decades to an empowerment of the city. Good government, certainly in modern republics, depends on healthy cities. This is reflected, I have suggested, in the provision in the Constitution of 1787 for a capital city which the United States government can make and keep healthy, however mixed its record there has been in practice for two centuries now. Perhaps most critical for the future of cities is that education of citizens which permits them better to appreciate the place and possibilities of cities in both the State and the Nation. Thus, our cities very much depend, as does the Country at large, on what happens to the schools and other institutions that must prepare citizens for genuine self-government.

31-B. Religion and the City

The Greeks rival the Jews in being [since ancient times] the most politically minded race in the world. . . . No other two races have set such a mark upon the world. . . . No two cities have counted more with mankind than Athens and Jerusalem. Their messages in religion, philosophy, and art have been the main guiding lights of modern faith and culture.

WINSTON S. CHURCHILL

This talk was given at the Conference on the Constitution and the City, Community Renewal Society, Newberry Library, Chicago, Illinois, January 21, 1988. It was included, with some notes, in the collection of papers from the Conference issued by the Community Renewal Society.

The epigraph is taken from Winston S. Churchill, *The Second World War* (Boston: Houghton Mifflin Co., 1951), V, 532–33.

I

An old-fashioned approach is naturally looked to whenever religion is taken seriously. A recent article in a Canadian newspaper about Sunday Closing laws and their enforcement in the Province of Ontario can remind us of how these matters were talked about in the United States once upon a time. (Here as elsewhere Canada tends to be a quarter century or so "behind" the United States.) Consider how the author, a chaplain at the University of Waterloo, puts it (John Rempel, *Kitchener-Waterloo Record*, December 12, 1987, p. A7):

> [The Ontario Solicitor-General] said on December 1 that the provincial government has given up on trying to rework the Retail Businesses Holiday Act and will allow municipalities to opt for Sunday shopping.
>
> This is cowardly. It is a victory for greed and consumerism. Big business will find it much easier to exercise its muscle against municipalities than against the province. If one municipality allows an open Sunday, adjacent towns will be under immense financial pressure to follow suit. . . .
>
> . . . The delusion that money, consumption and uninterrupted work provide meaning in life was not born in the twentieth century. In the eighth century BC the Hebrew prophet Amos denounced the traders at the city gate, "who trample upon the needy," impatient for the Sabbath to be over, "that [they] may offer wheat for sale . . . and deal deceitfully with false balances . . ." (*Amos* 8: 4-5)
>
> What the Sabbath symbolized was under siege. At the end of the weekly cycle all those who discriminate and oppress are stopped. Everyone is re-created each Sabbath as an equal.

This is the way that the origins of Sunday Closing can be understood. Immediately instructive for us is how an ancient religious heritage has been and still can be drawn upon for social purposes. I continue with the Canadian chaplain:

> Nineteenth-century trade unions were inspired by [the Sabbath] moral precept when they demanded a day of rest for workers. Of course, this does not end corruption and inequality in society, but we can reflect every seventh day on why we were created and who we really are. It revitalizes the class structure and the economic powers which rule us.
>
> The principle for which a day of rest stands—the equality of all human beings and a limit set to the tyranny of work—were fundamental influences on legislation developed in the North Atlantic world in the nineteenth century.

Its influence can be seen in the policies of traditional parties as well as in the trade union and socialist movements. In Europe . . . the symbolic and practical power of a day of rest receives almost universal acknowledgment, even if the original religious rationale is no longer believed.

One final principle, implicit in the traditions referred to above and in all faiths, merits mention: the celebration and nurture of community. Family is the primal form of belonging in most societies. On a day of rest family members let go of all their public roles and reaffirm their private, core identity.

Finally, we should notice how the chaplain, confronted by modern dilemmas, concludes his plea:

I freely acknowledge the anomalous situation created in a pluralistic society when the Christian day of rest is given legal sanction. It is urgent that religious, labor and business communities talk with each other about this matter.

I cry out, however, against the cynical misuse of this dilemma by big business. Since not all citizens are Christian, they argue, there should be no day of rest. But their materialistic logic also discriminates against Jews, Hindus, Moslems, Buddhists, Bahais and others.

Sunday as a day of rest stands as the symbol of a value system in which getting and selling have limits, in which rest, worship, and charity are seen as more central in meaning and purpose in life than its consumption.

Sunday nurtures an alternative to an individualized society in which the immediate gratification of the individual is preferred to the collective identity of a society which is sustained only by strong families, social groups and religious communities.

Sunday is one of the last chances our society has to assert community over unbridled, individualistic competitiveness, to assert a lifestyle guided by spiritual and moral reality rather than by self-indulgence.

A return to widespread Sunday closings is hardly likely to be seen in the foreseeable future in the United States. The only times we get a sense of what such a universal day of rest can mean is when a mammoth snowstorm shuts down everything and makes us depend on our own resources at home. Family intimacy, relaxed reflection, and an invigorating discipline are apt to be promoted on such occasions; the immediate community with its neighborhood activities is apt to be made much more of; it can be very peaceful. But, as I have indicated, the trend is in another direction, as may be seen in the anticipated emergence of a worldwide, round-the-clock stock market. (Consider, for echoes of the old way, César Franck's symphonic poem, *Le chausseur maudit*.)

Still, it is instructive to be reminded of how such matters as Sunday Closings were once discussed, especially the question of how people are to be shaped by the community to recognize and respect what is truly important. We are now left more on our own; much is made among us of individual decisions. But, as we should all know by now, the entire community can be profoundly affected by the independent decisions here and there of individuals concerned only to serve their own interests. This may be seen in the effects upon everyone of the public offerings of various films and publications and of other products and services of all kinds. Especially is this so in large urban areas where we can easily hide from each other. Thus, our entertainment can now be much more easily concealed from the scrutiny of our neighbors. Unfortunately, what is often beyond concealment is the cumulative public effects of the bad moral characters shaped by "private" activities.

II

We are now accustomed to the "principle" that the formation and preservation of the moral character of human beings and the moral tone of the community are not the government's business. Indeed, we seem to believe that a good-natured self will naturally emerge and develop if we are simply left alone by government. If pressed we might say that the family and religious institutions should of course train people. But it is not recognized that both religion and family very much depend on the general community for guidance and for much of their authority. They are in a critical sense agents of the community.

We are reminded by the Northwest Ordinance of 1787, the first constitution for the people here in the Midwest, of the intimate connection between community and religion. It is there commanded, "Religion, morality, and knowledge being necessary to good government and the happiness of mankind, schools and the means of education shall forever be encouraged." A decade earlier, in the Declaration of Independence, the public dependence on divine providence was clearly recognized.

In our own time, the collaboration of religion and community has been seen most dramatically in the Civil Rights Movement. The very name of the Southern Christian Leadership Conference reflects the critical role of churches in that movement. Local churches continued to provide, as they long had, spiritual support in the face of adversity; they also provided inspired language that appealed to the finest in everyone, friend and adversary alike. They provided as well buildings and equipment for meetings, money for programs, leadership and organizations for sustained efforts. It was particularly important then, and promises to remain so for the foreseeable future, that those churches, which are often the most (and sometimes the only) cohesive elements in their communities, are run by their congregations, able thereby to respond to local circumstances. We here in Chicago saw what this could mean in the election of Harold Washington as mayor.

III

Religious influences may be seen, furthermore, in other community organizations, such as civic-minded groups and labor unions, which often have their origins in religious sentiments and associations. (The Community Renewal Society, originally the City Missionary Society, comes to mind.) This may also be seen in various business leaders' associations.

We all obviously want people to do right by each other. But we are often reluctant to permit public support of the institutions that contribute to, sometimes are essential for, such right-mindedness. Religion-based organizations are accepted readily enough when they provide welfare services and the care of the most unfortunate among us. It is when these organizations are looked to by the community for more than charitable services that concerns about an "establishment of religion" can be heard.

Sometimes, we have noticed, the activities connected with the local church may be the only means available for any kind of constructive collective action within a community. The denominational ties between churches, from one neighborhood to another, may be virtually the only healthy way of connecting one part of a city to another.

True, such highly publicized enterprises as professional sports teams and rock concerts can often provide a sense of cohesiveness. But that sort of tie can be illusory. Besides, one does not see the truly poor at games and concerts or much caught up by them. Also illusory, and far from clearly constructive, is what television does. This, too, is a spectator sport that promotes both an unhealthy passivity and an incredible waste of time, even as it pretends to enlighten us and to bring us all together.

IV

Americans, like republicans elsewhere, used to be concerned about the risks of permitting one religion or another to become dominant in a state or even to exercise "sovereign" power within the community. But we no longer have these as problems, if we ever did in most American States. Rather, there is for us today the problem of whether religious institutions can retain the vitality necessary for them to supply the services and, even more important, the trained and dedicated personnel needed to supplement government services and to provide moral guidance for the community at large.

The vitality of a religious body probably depends ultimately on the doctrines at its core. Neither pragmatism nor good-heartedness is enough in the long run. The autonomy of congregations, which can be useful in that it permits tailoring church activities to local circumstances, can eventually prove destructive: the local church that is left pretty much on its own is not likely to remain coherent or disciplined in its articles of faith. (The extent to which pressing local necessities can lead to circumvention of the longstanding doctrines of a sect may be seen in how women and married men have had to be permitted to provide, in many Roman Catholic parishes in this Country and abroad, many of the services that have been traditionally supplied by priests.)

It remains to be seen how much disregard of theological doctrines there can be without striking at the heart of a religion. This is related to the question of whether, and if so how, ideas have consequences. This in turn is related to the question of the proper place of government, especially local government, in the education, including the moral training, of citizens.

V

One can, upon listening to any informed discussion today of such questions, hear echoes of the now antiquated Sunday Closing debates. It remains to be seen whether church-sponsored schools, a particularly lively subject of more recent decades, will go the way of Sunday Closing laws.

It is not generally appreciated how much church-sponsored schools will require, for their survival in a proper condition, more than the governmental toleration they have enjoyed thus far. Considerable financial help will be needed if these schools are to be able to continue to perform the services for the entire community that they do. Costs are going up, especially as expenditures for teachers' salaries and for equipment have to increase; tuition income can hardly be expected to keep up with these costs.

A common-sense approach would be to ask whether these schools supply services that the community either wants or benefits from. Consider, for instance, the Roman Catholic parochial schools in our inner cities, schools in which the student body can again and again be made up primarily of Southern Baptists. Poor minority students in inner-city parishes are subsidized by middle-class white parishes in the suburbs. How long can this be expected to continue? Are tax-exemption provisions the only proper way that the political community can help support these schools financially?

What may government properly do to help the considerable variety of sects that help make our lives civilized? An obstacle to a sensible approach here, I venture to suggest, is what the United States Supreme Court, misled by all too many intellectuals, has done in reading the Religion Clauses of the First Amendment. (See, for a variety of church-state issues, the essays collected in my *Loyola University of Chicago Law Journal* article, "Church and State: Explorations." See, also, Essay No. 16, above. The risks of religious controversies are evident in several of the cases discussed in my *Loyola University of Chicago Law Journal* article, "On Trial: Explorations.")

VI

There are, in discussions of church and state problems, a lot of dubious issues raised in our time. We act as if the Spanish Inquisition or at least the Salem witch-trials would be just around the corner if we ever let down our guard. So we make much of the danger of permitting *crèches* and *menorahs* to be displayed in public places.

At the same time, we consider ourselves powerless as a community to police obvious frauds and other deliberate misconduct perpetrated under the cloak of religion. This is hardly serious, especially as the allure of secularism grows and the influence of organized religion declines, whatever may happen to church membership from time to time.

It is shortsighted to try to provide for a community without being sensitive to the religious facets of most enduring enterprises. Aside from the usefulness of religion for social purposes, it is unnatural not to recognize the yearning of human beings for an elevated account of their relation to eternal things, an account whose plausibility is enhanced by the generality of its acceptance in a community. (See Plato, *Republic* 415D, 516A.)

Prudent leaders know that religious associations, especially in the larger cities, are vital to the soul of communities. These leaders need to be reassured that, no matter what judges, law professors, and other intellectuals do or say from time to time, it is perfectly respectable rather than a breach of our constitutional faith for "church and state" to collaborate in this Country. No better source of such reassurances can be found among us than the opinions and practices of the Founders of this Republic two centuries ago.

VII

The Religion Clauses of the First Amendment reflect the considered opinions on this subject of the Founders. A right to the free exercise of religion was generally taken for granted, as well as a national policy that recognized significant local differences with respect to religious activity. The considerable diversity of unregulated sects in this Country had long been an accomplished fact by the time the First Amendment was drafted in 1789. This made a national "establishment of religion" neither desirable nor likely.

Whatever the personal opinions of this or that Founder about Revelation, it was considered very much the duty of the statesman to accommodate himself to the dominant religious sentiments of the community. This may be seen in the uses made of the Biblical heritage by Abraham Lincoln in the Gettysburg Address and his Second Inaugural Address. It may be seen as well in the report of what happened on the occasion of George Washington's first inauguration as President. After the Inaugural Address, we are told by the *Connecticut Gazette* of May 8, 1789 (*Liberty's Legacy* [Ohio Historical Society, 1987], p. 114):

His Excellency, accompanied by the Vice- President, the Speaker of the House of Representatives, and both Houses of Congress, then went to [St.] Paul's chapel, where divine service was performed by the Right Rev. Dr. Provost, Bishop of the Episcopal church in this State [of New York] and Chaplain to Congress.

The spirit of these kinds of collaboration between "church and state" is something that prudent community leaders, in and out of government, should be encouraged to adapt to their own circumstances, and to do so in good conscience.

31-C. The Babylonian Captivity
of the Public Schools

Upon the subject of education, not presuming to dictate any plan or sys-
tem respecting it, I can only say that I view it as the most important sub-
ject which we as a people can be engaged in. That every man may
receive at least a moderate education, and thereby be enabled to read the
histories of his own and other countries, by which he may duly appre-
ciate the value of our free institutions, appears to be an object of vital
importance, even on this account alone, to say nothing of the advantages
and satisfaction to be derived from all being able to read the Scriptures
and other works, both of a religious and moral nature, for themselves.
For my part, I desire to see the time when education—and by its means,
morality, sobriety, enterprise, and industry—shall become much more
general than at present, and should be gratified to have it in my power to
contribute something to the advancement of any measure which might
have a tendency to accelerate the happy period.

ABRAHAM LINCOLN

I

There are many things which you as competent men and women of affairs know which I simply cannot know. There must be very few things I
know, and which may be of some use to you in your calling as educators,
which you do not already know. Perhaps all I can hope to do on this occasion is to take the little I may know, which you already know anyway, and
by drawing upon certain old books restate it in terms dramatic enough or
unfamiliar enough to be interesting and thereby instructive. I trust that
you, on the basis of your training and experience as public school principals, will select from the things I have to say whatever may happen to
serve your needs.

This talk was the Keynote Address for the Seventeenth Annual Education Conference,
Chicago Principals Association, Conrad Hilton Hotel, Chicago, Illinois, March 7, 1974. (The
meeting was chaired by Keith Weese, late principal of the Spry Elementary School, Chicago,
Illinois.) It has been published, with a few notes, in *Chicago Principals Reporter,* Spring
1975, pp. 7–17.
The epigraph is taken from *The Collected Works of Abraham Lincoln,* ed. Roy P. Basler
(New Brunswick, N.J.: Rutgers University Press, 1953), I, 8 (March 9, 1832).

A disciple of Confucius observed, some two thousand years ago, that if medicine does not raise a commotion in the patient, his disease will not be cured by it. (*Works of Mencius*, III, 1, 5) All kinds of disturbing remedies are being offered us today: such prescriptions as witchcraft and the occult, sensuality and the perverse, violence and the rebellious. These are all, in a sense, "medicines." What are they trying to deal with and to minister to? Are they not all efforts to come to terms with life? Are they not efforts either to understand what the world is like or to control what is going on? But are they not all mistaken efforts, however much commotion they raise?

To answer these questions, and to be able to speak with authority of mistakes, one must have some notion of what genuine medicine is. What is the medicine which you, as educators, are licensed to dispense? What helps you, what hinders you, in your efforts to do what is expected of you? With these questions, I address myself to your circumstances and to what I take to be my assignment.

II

The theme of your two-day principals' conference is "Humanizing and Individualizing the School." To humanize and individualize school life is, you all must appreciate, a difficult task. But, I suggest, it is even more difficult than many suspect, since that which may contribute to humanization is apt to undermine individualization, just as that which may contribute to individualization is apt to undermine humanization. That is to say, these two ends are often in conflict with one another. Serious humanization requires a community effort, whereas individualization (as it is generally understood) tends to cut us off from one another, to put each of us on his own, and in such a way as to diminish the sense of community. I will return to this problem, a problem that obliges us to consider further the meaning of such awkward terms as *humanizing* and *individualizing*.

Permit me to introduce still another term for your consideration, *Babylonian captivity*. I propose to show, or at least to suggest in such a way as to leave a few salutary questions with you, that there is at this time what I believe can usefully be identified as the Babylonian captivity of the Chicago Public School System. (I will defer my explanation of *Babylonian captivity*.) I say "Chicago Public School System" since we are in Chicago and I *am* addressing Chicago public school principals. I have investigated (by reading and by interviewing but not, I should warn you, by having children of my own in public schools) what is happening in Chicago. I suspect, however, that what is happening in Chicago is happening, to some degree, in most of the larger cities in this Country, especially in the North. Various elements of my analysis are in part derived from the mere. fact of size and hence are not limited to Chicago.

Chicago is, of course, a somewhat special case. It has, according to some, "one of the worst school systems in a nation of bad, big school systems." (*Chicago Guide,* February 1974, p. 105) Whatever the truth may be about the badness of the Chicago school system, there certainly can be no question about its bigness. It was recently announced that the next budget for the Chicago public schools could for the first time exceed one billion dollars, less than a year after the city government budget reached that sum.

We are obliged to wonder whether we get from the school system the services and advantages we believe we get from the city system. Our city government does have, whether or not deserved, a better reputation nationally than does our school system. The school system amounts to a second local government, of at least the significance of the city government, but perhaps with less serious citizen interest in and less reliable information generally available about it. Yet much depends on what does happen in the schools of a city. It is there that future citizens are given their decisive shaping and guidance.

Our schools are beginning to assume immediate political significance. We are told, for instance, that our mayor is now convinced that his principal opponent in the coming election, an independent alderman, intends to make schools a top issue, perhaps the major issue, in his campaign. It is unlikely that such a challenge would be anticipated if Chicago schools were generally considered to be in good shape.

Some go so far as to see the administration of the school system and that of the city government as being engaged in a conspiracy to keep education from most Chicago students. For, it is argued, serious education would eliminate the ignorance and prejudice on which the local political "machine" depends for its hold upon the levers of patronage and power. But, I should immediately add, I have long been dubious about charges of conspiracy in political affairs. Such charges tend to oversimplify the complexities of life and thereby conceal from us what is really happening. Charges of conspiracy make two assumptions which are usually questionable: (1) that the alleged conspirators know what is really going on, and (2) that the alleged conspirators can effectively control what is going on. I do not believe that it would be useful to dwell here on the nature and shortcomings of conspiracy charges. Suffice it to say, I hardly think it useful to consider either you principals or your administrative superiors as conspirators.

It is too bad, though, that you are *not* conspirators, for then the correction of Chicago's school problems would be relatively simple. Our salvation would then lie in reforming or replacing many of you and your superiors and some people in City Hall as well. But the Babylonian captivity I have spoken of goes much deeper than anything that ordinary reforms and replacements, to say nothing of indictments and condemnations, can do much about. There need not be, it should be emphasized, any villains in the story I am telling.

I return to the term, *humanizing.* In order to be humanized, to become and to remain human, one must know or at least be aware of what it means to be truly human. Once one is aware of what it means to be fully human, one then has standards by which practical action, of a humanizing character, can be guided.

One is therefore obliged to consider human nature, whether there is such a thing and, if so, what it is. A proper respect for human nature, and for the role of nature in developing any good thing, leads to several practical suggestions. It can help us determine how long or which students should be compelled or permitted to remain in school. It can help us determine what should be done, and to which students, in school. It can help us induce students to learn and to enjoy learning what they are capable of learning. Perhaps most important for political purposes, it can help relieve some educated men of their bad consciences and other educated men of their callousness. Underlying all of these problems is a question that is fundamental to any democratic regime: How seriously, or in what sense, should we take the "self-evident" truth that "all Men are created equal"?

III

That radical democrat, Thomas Jefferson, wrote in 1813 to John Adams, his longtime conservative opponent and yet old friend, "For I agree with you that there is a natural aristocracy among men. The grounds of this aristocracy are virtue and talent." (See Section IV of Essay No. 7, above.)

How can such a natural aristocracy be reconciled with our democratic faith? In what sense, that is, are all men created equal? Perhaps a tentative answer will suffice for this occasion. The natural aristocrats, the men of virtue and talent, found among us should be listened to by the rest of us. Such men can be expected to know and say best what should be done on behalf of us all. What better lead can we follow? Who would better qualify as "opinion leaders"? Of course, natural aristocrats are not always in agreement with one another. This is what gives the rest of us both an opportunity and the duty to decide—to choose if only on the basis of apparent character—among the better men who contend for our support and allegiance. But in so doing, we should not deny that there are superior men among us, men equipped by nature and by the proper training to conduct the affairs of the community.

It is at this point that we should recall the second term with which we began, *individualizing*. Does it not mean, at least among us, such things as creativity, originality, and non-conformity? If it does mean something like that, it also means resistance to, or rebellion against, any standard of excellence to which the truly human must be dedicated. If a man is determined to "be himself," to indulge himself in self-expression, then he is apt to resent any effort to discipline him, to shape him in accordance with certain standards or with a view to certain ends. In addition, if the truly human depends on an informed and healthy community, then an emphasis upon individuality is apt to lead to determined, even "principled," opposition to the demands of that community and hence to any movement toward humanization.

I should add, however, that a sensible regard for humanization can and should take proper account of what particular students need. Individual attention may be needed and is appropriate. But sentimentality should be avoided, lest we make too much of individuality and thereby reduce humanization to mere individualization. An informed tough-mindedness should insist upon the recognition of standards which are hard to live up to but which are nevertheless genuinely valuable as aspirations and hence as enduring guides to and reassurances of worthwhile endeavors.

To be truly human, then, is to act as human beings should act; it is to know what human beings should know. What, one might well ask, should human beings know? They should know (1) how human beings should act; (2) what human beings have done; (3) what human beings wonder about; (4) what human beings have believed and perhaps even know about the things they have wondered about; and (5) what it means *to know*. Thus, emphasis should be placed upon human beings as moral agents and as knowers.

We need not concern ourselves here as to which has ultimate priority, knowledge or morality. For most of our purposes as educators, these two go hand in hand. The means by which school children are made better, both as moral agents and as knowers, include what they are shown and what they are taught. What they are shown includes the examples of both caring and inquiring that their principals and teachers place before them. What they are taught comes to them for the most part out of books. For this purpose, the best books are the best teachers, those few books from every century which constitute both the seed and the flowering of our civilization.

It is only when we look at the best that has been said about the perpetual questions and the enduring problems, questions and problems of which thoughtful human beings have always been aware, that we can begin to understand ourselves and thereby to become truly human. In order to see what and where we are, we need to examine what others have said. We can thereby notice things about ourselves that might otherwise escape our attention. Perhaps we can even be instructed both about what can be changed to good effect and what had better be left pretty much as we happen to find it.

IV

When I speak of the Babylonian captivity of the Chicago Public School System, I draw upon the two great sources of our civilization, Judaism and the Classical World. As I have indicated, one important purpose of our schools is to permit and equip students who are so minded to learn and thereafter to use the best of what has gone before.

I am sure that you are familiar with the Biblical version of the Babylonian captivity to which I have alluded. Thus, the Old Testament describes the forced removal from the Holy Land, first, of the leaders of the Israelites and, subsequently, of thousands of others to a subjugated status in mighty Babylon. (See, e.g., *Jeremiah*, chaps. 25, 50–52.)

My reference to the Babylonian captivity has another source as well, Aristotle's *Politics*. It is there that Aristotle discusses the appropriate size of the *polis*, the city. By way of comparison, he refers to the metropolis of Babylon, a place so large (he reports almost in disbelief) that a part of it had once been captured for three days before some of its inhabitants became aware of the fact. (See Aristotle, *Politics* 1276a28–31.)

The Babylonian captivity to which I refer means, then, both *to be taken over by Babylon*, in the Biblical sense, and *to become like Babylon*, in the Aristotelian sense. Let us consider both of these senses for the help they can provide us in thinking about Chicago schools. (If we can do this properly, we may even reassure ourselves that the ancient writers, whether Biblical or pagan, whether scientific or literary, still have something to teach us in our effort to understand ourselves.)

Consider, first, what the Babylonian captivity of Israel meant. It meant, primarily, that the Israelites could not decisively control their own lives. The proper development of one's own life, or of the good one is capable of achieving, seems to require independence and integrity. One's sense of purpose is very difficult, if not almost impossible, to establish and maintain if one is subordinated to alien rule. That was evidently the case of the Israelites under Babylonian rule. I suspect this is often the case as well for Chicago schools today.

Of what does Babylonian rule consist for you? Is it not reflected in the fact that so much of your efforts and energy as public school administrators must be devoted to the custodial care of students assigned, if not even sentenced, to your jurisdiction? Are not the schools being used, in large part, for purposes foreign to those appropriate to them? In this way, their integrity is undermined and their vitality is sapped. This may be partly due to the failure of other institutions that would normally insure elementary moral training and social discipline in youngsters. Religious teaching has lost much of its traditional impact; the family no longer has the control it had. The family itself is no longer what it was: neither children nor teachers are guided by parents who both know and care sufficiently about what should happen in the schools. This means, in effect, that alien ways (those of Babylon, not those of the ancestral faith) come to dominate the life of the school community. This leads, in turn, to the demoralization of both students and teachers, making them all feel like prisoners of "the system." One wonders what a new Jeremiah should say in his effort to instruct his people about the proper response to such a Babylonian captivity.

Consider, also, what Aristotle's Babylon means. We find ourselves once again returning to what nature teaches us. How big can an association be and still be one's own? How big can it be and still be good? A village is far too small: there is not enough variety, not enough opportunity, to permit a reasonable development of human potentialities. On the other hand, Aristotle argued, Babylon is far too big: what kind of a city is it which *can* be subjugated without having that subjugation felt at once all over the city? That is as unnatural as an animal having a body which is so disconnected that a crippling affliction in one part is unknown to the rest.

How many of your chronic problems as administrators stem from the mere fact of size? Is not our school system simply too large? Is that unavoidable? Does it merely reflect what is happening in the Country at large? Is this the price we must pay for the industrialization that makes possible our remarkable standard of living? Does not such productive industrialization depend not only on the efficiency of size but also on a general mobility which undermines the sense of community even more than size does? When associations, whether a country or a metropolitan school system, grow as large as ours have, it becomes more and more difficult for us to remain in intimate contact with one another. Mechanical means of communication, such as television and a flood of memoranda, are resorted to; bureaucratic methods and relations have to be relied upon. Under such circumstances, no one really knows anyone else: stereotypes replace personal awareness; it becomes difficult for parents, teachers, or administrators to take themselves or one another seriously; there is no *whole* about which anyone knows enough either to care for or to be able to govern. The primary concern becomes that of "keeping the lid from blowing off." The resulting emphasis upon the custodial purpose of the school system only makes matters worse because it depreciates or at least conceals from view those other purposes, moral as well as intellectual, that traditionally made academic life not only bearable but attractive. The greater the emphasis upon the custodial, the greater the need there will be for it.

Thus, the urban public school system has both been taken over by Babylon, by alien concerns, and become like Babylon, a clumsy leviathan unable to get a grip on itself. This has led, in some quarters, to demand for greater community control of education, whether in the form of neighborhood school councils or in the form of the use of vouchers which would permit parents to purchase schooling of their choice for their children. But what defines, in either case, the decisive community? Geographical propinquity? A market? Before there can be effective community control of schools, must there not first be a genuine community, something the typical school, even as it is constituted today, may be closer to than either the neighborhoods from which the children come or the impersonal market place? The critical problem with public education today may be not only that there is no education as the primary goal of schools but also that there is no sovereign public, a community with generally shared opinions about the most important matters, whatever the full truth of such opinions may be. Do we wish to recreate a public? Can we? Or have we gone too far toward self-expression and self-gratification, or at least self-preservation, to be able to dedicate ourselves to constructive common purposes?

One need not assume, by the way, that to identify a problem is to permit one to do much about it. The patriotic Israelites who first listened to Jeremiah, as well as the thoughtful Babylonian who might have read Aristotle, probably recognized that very little could be done immediately to improve the circumstances of either Israel or Babylon. There are times when little can be done, when one can do little more than try to understand how bad things may be. One result of a serious study of the great authors is to instruct us in the limits of our powers: moderation is promoted by a due appreciation of what can be reasonably expected. At the same time, one is constantly reminded of the standards by which one should personally live and according to which the little that can be done should be guided in due time.

V

What *can* be done about the Babylonian captivity of the Chicago Public School System? One should recognize, first, how much the problems of our urban school systems are due to "forces" beyond the control of any educator and, perhaps, beyond the control of any local politician. One should also recognize that as education declines in a country, educational standards also decline. It thus becomes steadily more difficult to reform whatever goes wrong. Finally, it should be recognized that the public resources likely to be available on a reliable basis for our public schools are not apt to be much more than what we are accustomed to having allocated to those schools. But then, money may not be the critical problem for these schools. People have done much better with far less money than we spend on education today. Put another way, money usually becomes the critical issue when failures of vision, of principle, or of nerve lead to difficulties which one is tempted, if only in desperation, to try to buy oneself out of. (The best high school I have ever been associated with—the school run by Elbert Fulkerson in Carterville, Illinois during the Depression and the Second World War—had very little money.)

What then can be done? What is available to us under the circumstances we happen to find ourselves? Permit me to be rash. It seems to me, from my observations of the public schools, from my own experience in education, and from what I have learned about the nature of community and of self-government, that it is almost impossible for conscientious educators to do what *can* be done today if they do not have a reasonable amount of control over what happens in their settings, whether that setting be a school or a classroom. This means that a principal should be able to determine far more than he now can who teaches in his school and what goes on there. He should be able to have a budget for which he is primarily responsible. He should not have to spend much time trying to obtain information and supplies from inefficient bureaucrats that are commercially available.

But does not such liberation of the principal also mean that the faculty of a school should have a role in determining who their principal is and how he conducts himself? Just as principals now feel helpless when dealing with and depending on the central administration of the system, so teachers feel helpless when dealing with and depending on their principals. As things now stand, no one is able to do his best—neither the central administration, principals, or teachers, to say nothing of the students to whose welfare all of these public servants should be dedicated. An effort should be made to determine what can be done best at each level: at the levels of the Board of Education, the Office of the Superintendent of Schools, the Area and District Superintendents, the Principals, and the Classroom Teachers.

Without such reconsideration of functions and such decentralization, there cannot be the most effective use of the considerable intellectual, spiritual, and material resources which are available for education. It is indeed difficult for anyone to run efficiently the everyday lives of others, especially the lives of a multitude of others. It is difficult to know who is hurting and where. Babylon, in its massiveness, comes to mind. It is difficult to care for what is not perceived as really one's own. Again, Babylon, this time in its role as a colonial power, comes to mind. Thus, principals should be liberated, but liberated in a way that leaves them truly responsible for what happens in their schools. Only then can they begin to consider seriously enough their duties as guardians of the educational trust which they are privileged to exercise.

Principals should insist that they are educators who know what they are doing. They should be able to say, for example, how many students they can deal with responsibly, what kind of help they need for the work they must do, and what the functions are that schools can properly be expected to discharge. What is the appropriate school size? Should not the criteria include this limiting condition, that the principal be able to recognize, not necessarily know the names of, all of his students and that he be able to know well all his teachers? The ages and sensibilities of the students also bear on this formula. In fact, it can be argued, elementary schools could well be limited to some two hundred students, high schools to some five hundred students. Instead, we have become accustomed to elementary schools of more than a thousand students and high schools of almost five thousand students.

Excessive size is bound to make most of the problems of urban schools even worse than they would otherwise be. An inevitable depersonalization becomes evident in discipline problems, in teacher passivity (with the consequent recourse to unionization as a form of self-assertion), and in a general malaise. One all too often hears complaints about a pervasive "don't care" attitude in the schools, an attitude exhibited by students and teachers alike. The remarkable thing is not that there is such demoralization, but that there is not much more, considering the effects of excessive size on personal relations.

In short, should not a school, just like a class, be small enough to permit it to be suited to the students in it and thereby to have a personality of its own? And, pending the building of smaller school buildings in this city, cannot the buildings we now have be divided into manageable, autonomous units, each with its own principal, teachers, and students? Impractical as this may seem, is it not much more practical than what principals are obliged to wrestle with now?

VI

But even without such decentralization as I have suggested, something can still be done. The temptation to blame everyone but oneself for one's frustrations and troubles must be resisted. I have counselled that suspicions about conspiracy should be avoided and an emphasis upon money should be played down. It is demoralizing constantly to look elsewhere for the causes of one's troubles, whether to the school administration "Downtown," City Hall, the Governor, the teachers' unions, the State Legislature, Congress, or the President of the United States. Each self-respecting educator must look much more to himself and must do what he can. That is to say, one must cultivate one's own garden and thereby earn the right and the opportunity to extend that garden more and more, keeping in mind however the risks run by extending one's domain too far.

Thus, even if a principal must adjust to various decisions originating elsewhere in the system, he can at least maintain control over what he himself does and what happens in his immediate vicinity. He can conduct himself, and thereby help influence both his teachers and his students to conduct themselves, in a civilized manner. There should be provided every day, and all day, models of grace and good taste in the corridors, assembly halls, classrooms, and playing fields of the school: everyone should sit, talk, and move like human beings who appreciate what it is to be civilized; everyone should be taught by example what it means to deal quietly yet firmly with one another; everyone should be shown that human beings are being dealt with, not animals or convicts. Things are not as bad as they could be when the principal, who knows who he is and what he is doing, conducts himself with assurance and dignity. Others will notice, learn, and imitate.

A principal should stand for something: for first-rate books, for authority in the classroom, for intellectual skills that can and should be mastered by the serious student, and for a standard of conduct that can and should be respected by everyone in his school. He can, in his awareness of his station, avoid that cheapening and vulgarization of his calling that poses even more of a threat to respectable education than does the hostility of students and the disillusionment of teachers.

A show of camaraderie by a principal may be mistaken for worthwhile educational relations, whereas hostility and disillusion cannot. Both disillusion and hostility are symptoms of a disorder and hence can be instructive. Disillusion reflects a vision that has been disappointed; hostility reminds us of expectations that have not been realized. Even youth gangs may be seen as a groping for community, a groping that can be as hopeful as it is destructive.

The principal who insists upon being a "buddy" to either his teachers or his students may merely be concealing from view the serious problems that would otherwise be evident. These problems will eventually catch up with his successor, if not with him. Need I add that the proper alternative to the buddy is not the petty tyrant?

Certainly it should be added, in this review of where we stand and what our prospects are in Chicago, that things are not always as bad (or, perhaps, ever as good) as they may seem from time to time. Indeed, things may even be looking up among us, notwithstanding the recent murder by a student of a conscientious and gentle elementary school principal. In some ways, this city, which remains curiously vital despite all its problems, is becoming safer and more "livable" than it was a decade ago. I myself expect to see a gradual return to the city of people who have fled to the suburbs, especially when it becomes evident that the suburbs are not what or where they are expected to be.

Race relations among us seem somewhat more relaxed; employment, as well as education, opportunities for minorities seem somewhat more hopeful in spite of our current economic difficulties; the decisive steps may well have been taken to open up all kinds of jobs and assignments to qualified aspirants. Put another way, hard work, reinforced by a little bit of luck, does seem to hold out hope for men and women of various local minorities, or at least more so than a generation ago. Insofar as there is such a general improvement, evident in what one can see among shoppers in the Loop, some of the current disruptive social pressure on the schools should be relieved.

It would be inappropriate for me to digress any further than I have into a sociological assessment of what is happening to life in this city. It suffices merely to add that there are hopeful signs and that those signs may be detected in the schools as well. I do want to stress the duty of everyone in an exposed academic position to serve as a model for impressionable students. It was Confucius himself who observed, "The grass must bend when the wind blows upon it." (*Works of Mencius*, III, 2, 4) *What do students feel now?* How does the wind strike *them?* It should be emphasized that students cannot be expected to take seriously what their elders in the schools do not take seriously.

Critical, then, to all I have said this morning is a need to restore among upright educators a lively interest in the works of the mind. I say "restore" because it is both essential and encouraging to recognize what it is which probably attracts most educators to their professions in the first place.

VII

There is no better way to restore a lively interest in works of the mind, and thereby to encourage students to develop such an interest, than to have faculty engage among themselves in periodic, organized discussions of important books, the kind of discussion that, unfortunately, is quite unusual in most schools and colleges today. Intellectual interests should be the common concern of every intellectual community. What I am saying could be seen on my way here this morning from Hyde Park. One of my neighbors, a distinguished chemist at the University of Chicago, stopped to show me a blown-up picture he had of an egg cell. Its regularity and detail were stunning. He obviously wanted to share what he had learned; I could not help but be enlightened and even elevated by his effort to improve my understanding. It is such sharing which characterizes genuine intellectual communities.

Students, too, should be encouraged, partly by the examples of their teachers, to form special-interest groups of an intellectual character. Highly publicized and expensive athletic matches should be played down (not altogether eliminated) and widespread participation in intramural sports encouraged. School-wide endeavors in theatre and art work should also be encouraged, including such activities as community efforts to paint wall murals, not only on school property but also throughout the neighborhood.

The proper organization of all such activities does depend on an awareness of the best. They all presuppose both a manageable size for the school and legitimate educational governance. I have returned, that is, to the problems of the Babylonian captivity of a school system—to the problem of cumbersomeness and the problem of rule by alien creeds. Permit me to return as well, as I prepare to close, explicitly to the problem of humanization and individualization.

Humanization requires, I have argued, that our institutions should be cut down to a human scale wherever possible. Only then can the better standards be applied with some hope of success; only then can one become the individual one should really want to be. For this to happen, an awareness of the best which has already been thought and done is essential.

Thus, on the highest level, the humane and the individual can be the same. To reach that level, or to help others reach for and in a few cases attain it does require that understanding which only the greatest teachers across the ages provide us. If we ignore such teachers and strike out on our own, whether out of despair, provincialism, or arrogance, we are not likely to make an intelligent use of the resources we do have available in the difficult circumstances we may find ourselves from time to time.

But difficult as present circumstances may be, they have been far worse. Things are looking up: there are, I have indicated, signs of hope. Besides it is well to remember, as we gather here this morning just a mile or so south of old Fort Dearborn, that difficult as things are these days in Chicago, they were far worse here, in almost every way, a couple of hundred years ago. They have probably been far worse as well, in those days and perhaps to this day, in those countries from which your forebears came to these shores. If it is any comfort to you, it can safely be predicted that things will eventually be far worse than they are now in this place. That is, after all, the way of human existence. Happiness depends on making the best of whatever confronts us. This requires a tolerable understanding of what has been known and done by those who have preceded us. It also requires that we not take ourselves too seriously even as we embark upon challenging adventures.

I close by reminding you that today's date, March 7, was once a memorable one for Americans. It was this day in 1850 that Senator Daniel Webster delivered his famous speech, "For the Constitution and the Union." It was made in a period of great crisis, a far more serious crisis than anything we face today. For many years that famous address was widely known as "The Speech of the Seventh of March." I believe it noteworthy that modern audiences have to be reminded of the significance of this date, for it further instructs us that that which may be considered vitally important by one generation can be forgotten by the next. Such forgetfulness can be good as well as bad. No doubt, generations after us will ignore problems by which we are consumed and will fervently devote themselves to problems which we have not bothered to notice. Things do manage to work their way out among a sensible people just as things do manage to get messed up from time to time no matter how sensible a people may be. That is to say, it is instructive to be reminded of the importance of chance in human affairs.

It is useful as well as instructive, if not even entertaining, to be able to step back now and then and to contemplate our troubles in a detached way. Is not creative detachment the privilege, the duty, and the salvation of the humane individual? Should not such detachment contribute something precious to the productive, decent, and interesting careers to which you as educators have been so fortunate as to have dedicated yourselves?

31-D. Chicago Politics After Daley

Moreover, he hath left you all his walks, His private arbors, and new-planted orchards On this side Tiber; he hath left them you And to your heirs for ever—common pleasures To walk abroad and recreate yourselves. Here was a Caesar! When comes such another?

MARK ANTONY

I

Two questions have been put to us in this conference, questions of a kind that naturally come to view in any community where longstanding political relations are shaken up: (1) Is the Chicago Democratic political organization, as we have known it, going to survive the death last year of Richard J. Daley? (2) Should it survive?

The second question, it seems to me, is likely to be decisive with respect to the first: survival of the organization is likely to depend, barring chance developments, on whether it should survive. To put the matter thus sug-

---

This talk was given at the "Richard J. Daley's Chicago" Conference, Department of History, The University of Illinois at Chicago, and the Chicago Historical Society, Chicago, Illinois, October 14, 1977.

The epigraph is taken from William Shakespeare, *Julius Caesar*, III, ii, 247–52.

There is appended to this talk a statement by George Anastaplo in support of the candidacy of Harold Washington against Bernard Epton, April 6, 1983, prepared in the closing week of the Chicago mayoral contest won by Mr. Washington. This statement was requested for, but was not used by, a prominent Chicago Democrat who finally decided not to add anything to his earlier formal endorsement of Mr. Washington as the mayoral candidate of his party. The long-run success of the Irish-American politician for whom this statement was prepared will depend in part on whether he can ever win the support of reluctant African-American voters who now outnumber whites in the City of Chicago. See *Chicago Sun-Times*, March 17, 1990, p. 1; *New York Times*, National Edition, November 12, 1989, p. 18.

gests that we are really talking about the soul of this city and about who can most plausibly minister to it.

II

One conference paper we have had emphasizes the role of certain wards in this city in the perpetuation of the Democratic Organization. That paper, in developing its argument, works from the hypothesis that the jobs and other economic prizes at the disposal of that organization are critical for insuring the votes in the wards referred to.

Seven wards are identified as particularly important for the organization. These wards, alone, we are told, gave Mayor Daley 88,000 votes of his 432,000-vote primary win in 1975. But consider what these figures suggest: seven wards out of a total of fifty wards (which are roughly equal in population), a little less than one-seventh of the wards, provided Mr. Daley a little less than one-fifth of his vote. When put this way, the role of these wards is not as great as it is often said to be. Consider also the fact that one of these wards went strongly for Democrats Richard Daley and Michael Bilandic in 1975 and 1977, respectively, and yet could go for Republican Gerald Ford in 1976.

Does not this sort of thing call into question the hypothesis of one conference paper, that "machines use selective incentives and tangible ones—jobs, gain, even payoffs—rather than ideologies or programs to attract voters"? Does not all this suggest that the appeal of the Democratic organization may be substantial all over this city? Whatever may be said about political machines usually or elsewhere, must we not wonder about the basis of the strength in Chicago of the Democratic Organization in recent decades?

What *was* Mr. Daley's appeal? What is it likely that Mr. Bilandic will be obliged to do if he is to retain his predecessor's appeal? Critical to Mayor Daley's appeal was the assurance he gave to various ethnic and racial groups here that someone *was* in control of the life of the city. This is an assurance that is particularly important in turbulent times and especially in large cities, where people can easily come to believe that things are out of control and that their very gathering together on such a large scale in such intimate anonymity is somehow unnatural. That there are jobs available to be distributed is, of course, testimony *to* such control, even more than that such distribution is the source *of* control. To be *able* to provide jobs shows that one must really be running things: the assurance that someone *is* running things may be more important than the jobs themselves. Perhaps even the most modest of these jobs are attractive because the jobholders feel that they are contributing to control of the life of the city. One of my most sophisticated teachers, Malcolm Sharp, has observed that a modern city is so complex that it must be the Holy Ghost who really runs it. It is no wonder, then, that ordinary people seek reassurance that someone is indeed in control of the life of the city.

III

It does not suffice, of course, that someone be in control. If the required reassurance is to be deeply-felt and enduring, it is also important that it be generally believed that those in control are trustworthy, that they are truly in control, and that they are disposed to do or to permit to be done what is desired by the people of the city. This means that for a leader to be durable he must be perceived to be sound on certain critical issues about which the public truly cares.

The ethnicity referred to in one of our papers may itself be a way of organizing issues for various segments of the public. To be an "ethnic" is to take certain issues seriously, to be sensitive to them. I am suggesting that that which has been called "ideologies or programs" may be considerably more important than that which has been called "jobs, gain, even payoffs" in explaining the remarkable success of the Democratic Organization in this city in recent decades.

If a leader is to be perceived as sound on certain issues, in a community as complex as Chicago, he must often keep these issues muted, especially if the most popular position is not intellectually or morally fashionable. Many of the people of the city may believe in or want things which cannot be acknowledged publicly and which the most respectable organs of opinion do not recognize as plausible or sound. In these circumstances, leaders can be attractive because they permit prejudice and respectability to coexist. Or, put another way, Mr. Daley was perceived as thinking and feeling much as people generally thought and felt.

I suggest, therefore, that it would be unrealistic to consider the appeal of the Democratic Organization to be primarily to the kind of selfishness which can be served by jobs and other forms of patronage. The issues I have referred to may reflect a certain selfishness as well—but of a different order, having to do with the preservation of a familiar way of life, with the preservation of family life and old neighborhoods, even with physical self-preservation. Such concerns point to something higher than mere economic interest and they have to be taken seriously by any politician who is serious about his calling.

IV

The life of the politician very much depends on fellow-feeling, on appeals to loyalty, and on a shared sense of common purpose, all of which are critical to a viable community. It is easy here in Chicago, the city which evidently gave *clout* its modern meaning, to make much of the corruption and shenanigans likely to be found in any long-established political organization. But we must take care not to lose sight of what is ultimately responsible for the vitality of any sustained common effort. Something of what I have been saying about the shared moral and political concerns of the Chicago public and its most successful politicians is reflected in a statement made not too long ago by a prominent local Democrat (a professional politician himself) upon the death of one of his colleagues of years past (*Chicago Tribune*, August 22, 1977, sec. 1, p. 14):

> This man was for many years a public official and political leader, and he never made a constructive contribution to either field. He had a beautiful son . . . , a thoroughly decent man, who must have taken after his mother. And when his son died, [he] had an opportunity to help his grandchildren and daughter-in-law and he just walked away from them. You can't be worth much when you walk away from your own flesh and blood.

> The first and only person I ever knew him to take care of was [himself]. I suppose you shouldn't say anything bad about the dead, but you asked me a question. They'll probably have to hire Andy Frain ushers to be his pallbearers.

Very few people *did* turn up for this once-prominent politician's funeral, unlike the turnouts for the funerals of Jacob Arvey and Richard Daley. I do not know, by the way, whether the frank criticism I have just quoted is fair. (There was a report after the death of the politician criticized here that he finally did provide for his grandchildren in his will.) Important for our purpose here, however, are the standards sincerely invoked in the criticism I have quoted.

Perhaps it should also be added that one of the criticisms which began to develop among local politicians against Mr. Daley himself in his last years, and this may have been due to the "natural" effects on him of old age itself, was the tendency to look out a little too much for himself. However that may have been, Mr. Daley enjoyed and very much relied upon the reputation of being a man who cared to a remarkable degree for the welfare of Chicago. Even his most serious lapses, in early 1968 with his "shoot-to-kill" order during the riots after the death of Martin Luther King and in August 1968 with his self-destructive response to the demonstrators at the Democratic National Convention in this city, no doubt reflected his love for Chicago. This conduct by him probably reflected as well, it must be said, the opinions of many throughout the city for whom he instinctively spoke.

V

To speak of lapses *is* to suggest that although ideology or issues and ideas may be more important than jobs and patronage, it is not to say that the Democratic Organization in this city has always been right on the most critical issues. It was noticed in one of our conference papers that "there is one overriding issue in Chicago politics, and that is race."

Race *is* a critical concern of the people of this city. This concern has several facets, having to do with the various forms of self-preservation reflected in responses to difference and to deep-rooted prejudice. Projected changes in population are critical, if only because one is obliged to wonder about the adequacy of preparation of non-whites for assuming a larger and larger share in the governance of this city. The quality of our public schools is particularly important, made even more important by the distorted constitutional doctrines that make it difficult to supply much-needed public funds to support valuable inner-city schools that happen to be church-sponsored. That there *is* a serious problem with our schools is confirmed by the fact that the first substantial division among City Council regulars since Mr. Daley's death, aside from the succession issue itself, has been provoked by school issues which are to a considerable degree race-related.

VI

The critical question in the years ahead may be how the people of the city generally are to respond to the problem of race relations. What is it that Chicagoans will require of their leaders? In such matters, the Democratic political organization is indeed the servant of the public. That organization may not itself be decisive in *shaping* the opinions of its constituents, opinions shaped partly by constitutional teachings and political traditions, partly by chance and other events, and (one can hope) partly by sensible discussion of what is happening and of what could happen.

Sensible discussions of race-related issues today depend on the realization that most people in a decent community want to be both safe and fair. It is the duty of prudent politicians and of their advisors to show by precept and example that no people can reasonably expect enduring safety if it is not by and large fair. It can be pointed out that things are not quite right when one sees in a city that is one-half non-white, almost nothing but white faces in museums, the more prestigious concert halls, legitimate theatres, graduate school classrooms and lecture audiences such as this one, as well as even among the spectators at professional baseball and football games and in the front offices of businesses that *are* now color-blind on the playing field and at the sales counter. One can detect in these kinds of segregation the continuing effects of longstanding cultural and economic deprivations. The half-dozen illustrations I have just given are particularly appropriate to notice this week, a week during which the United States Supreme Court has heard oral argument in a case having to do with so-called reverse discrimination.

VII

The local Democratic political organization, however astute it may be, can govern at best one city, not two cities, especially when the second is a grossly underprivileged city that is partially concealed within the other, hidden enough from view as to become a constant source of fears, animosities, and unpredictable eruptions. Even so, the Democratic Organization is one of the few prominent associations in this city to be racially integrated to a substantial degree from the bottom almost to the top, and in a sustained manner. Both its critics and its defenders can agree that at least that aspect of the organization should survive if this city is to preserve its remarkable vitality.

APPENDIX TO ESSAY NO. 31–D

A Statement Requested For, But Not Used By, A Prominent Chicago Democrat (April 6, 1983)

As a lifelong Chicago Democrat who is very much concerned both for the welfare and reputation of our city and for the integrity and continued effectiveness of the Democratic Party, I once again call upon my fellow citizens to vote for Harold Washington for mayor on April 12th.

Mr. Washington, who has had a long and honorable career in public service, won the nomination of our party in an open and honest primary. Nothing new about his private life which would call into question his capacity to serve as mayor has been revealed since his nomination in February. There is nothing about the way he lives to suggest that he has ever made improper financial gains from his career as a public servant.

It has been known for some years, of course, that Mr. Washington did not file income-tax returns for the years 1964 through 1969. In those years almost all of the taxes he owed were in fact regularly paid by him through the withholding process to which most of us are subject.

It has also been known for some years that Mr. Washington has repeatedly expressed remorse for his neglect in these matters—and that he paid fully the penalties required of him by the judicial system. Just this week, a prominent group of responsible lawyers investigating his record has reminded us that when a man has made mistakes, and has paid for them, he should be permitted to redeem himself by whatever public service his fellow citizens find him worthy of. Is not this what all of us believe? Is not this how we would want ourselves, and those dear to us, to be treated? Is not this the way a fair-minded community does treat those who, after regrettable lapses in conduct, pull themselves together and make something useful of their lives?

No one can deny that racial considerations are affecting how Mr. Washington's misconduct in the 1960s, his subsequent rehabilitation, and his present candidacy are being regarded on all sides. Nor can it be denied that no matter how the election comes out next Tuesday, there will be major parts of this city that will be disturbed. But significant differences in reactions, and in how those reactions may be dealt with, should be noticed.

If Mr. Epton is elected, it will not be by voters who genuinely support him or his policies but it will be primarily by voters who were determined to vote *against* someone else, all too many on the basis of unfortunate racial stereotypes. Because of this, a major part of the city electorate, people who are themselves decent and law-abiding, will, rightly or wrongly, feel cheated for years to come. The difficulty Mr. Epton would have governing effectively in such circumstances should be apparent to all, including to those who make much of Mr. Epton's virtues.

On the other hand, if Mr. Washington should be elected, he will have solidly behind him and his program a significant part of the city, whereas those who are disturbed and fearful because of *his* election surely can be reassured thereafter by sincere efforts on Mr. Washington's part to provide moderate leadership, something which it certainly would be in his interest to attempt to do and which the Democratic Party, of which he has long been a member in good standing, will want to help him do.

Some of you, my fellow citizens, remember the deep concern in this Country not too many years ago at the prospect of a Roman Catholic being elected President of the United States. But once John Kennedy was actually elected, that kind of concern vanished as a divisive public issue.

Cannot we hope that, with the election of Mr. Washington, we here in Chicago will similarly put behind us racial considerations as an overriding factor in city-wide political campaigns?

Chicago has long been known as the city that works, and of this all of us can be proud. But Chicago can continue to work only if it is, and if it is generally believed to be, a city in which every citizen, regardless of race, color, or creed, gets a fair crack at the opportunities that we, the voters, control. Certainly, we do not want to do anything next Tuesday that we and our children will be ashamed of in the days and years ahead. Therefore, I once again call upon my fellow citizens to elect as mayor of this city Harold Washington, the duly nominated candidate of the Democratic Party.

32

HEROES AND HOSTAGES

A Spartan woman sent forth her five sons to war and, standing in the out-
skirts of the city, she waited anxiously the outcome of the battle. When
someone arrived and, in answer to her inquiry, reported that all her sons
had met death, she said, "I did not inquire about that, you scoundrel, but
about how our country fares." When he reported that it was victorious,
she said, "Then I accept gladly also the death of my sons."

PLUTARCH

I

Congratulations are, of course, in order for those among you who, having
distinguished yourselves as students of political science, are to be initiated
into an honor society of your profession. Such initiation is, it should go
without saying, both a privilege and a duty: you have distinguished yourselves, for which you are honored, and you have thereby joined the ranks
of those from whom even more is expected.

The very existence of an honor society testifies to the opinion that there
is among us the possibility of excellence with respect to things that matter.
This meeting, then, celebrates achievement, not ordinary conduct and
work, however important these may be. Since those chosen by the honor
society are told publicly of their election to membership, it must be assumed that one is encouraged to take pride in one's accomplishments. To
put all this in old-fashioned terms, one is encouraged thereby so to pursue
ambition as to win the esteem of sensible people and to be worthy of such
esteem.

This talk was given to the Theta Lamba Chapter of Pi Sigma Alpha, Political Science
Honorary Society, Northeastern Illinois University, Chicago, Illinois, March 4, 1981.

The epigraph is taken from Plutarch, *Sayings of Spartan Women.* See Plutarch, *Moralia*
(Cambridge: Loeb Classical Library, Harvard University Press, 1931), III, 461.

It would not be amiss, therefore, to consider further on this occasion the status among us of that special kind of excellence in social relations known as the heroic. And since old-fashioned terms have been invoked, it is only natural for us political scientists to recall that in the old days this would have been the date of the Presidential Inauguration. We are reminded thereby of what was once a more leisurely pace of life, one which could permit some four months to pass between election day and inauguration day. Things move much faster and more often now, and perhaps this affects our notions about the good and the bad, and consequently about the heroic, its possibility and its worth.

II

Let us consider, if only briefly, what we can gather about our subject tonight from the inauguration day of this year, that of January 20 in Washington, D.C. As political scientists, we should be alert to activities all around us which are either political or which are shaped by and in turn shape the political.

There were this past Inauguration Day, as you all remember, not one but two major "events." There was, of course, the public celebration of the transfer of the powers of the Presidency from one man to another, an orderly transfer which all sense not only in this Country but abroad to be remarkable testimony to constitutional government and the rule of law.

There was also on that occasion the release of fifty-two American diplomatic hostages who had been held in Iran for more than a year. Their fate, it had come to be felt, was related to the political fate of the incumbent in the White House. He had made use (sometimes, it seemed, improper use) of the hostages in beating back a formidable challenger in his own party; but he was to suffer in the election itself because of the continued plight of the hostages. Much had been made of the hostages by the White House (far less had been made, for instance, of a comparable number of men (albeit military men) held for a comparable period of time when the *Pueblo* was seized by the North Koreans a dozen years before), and much continued to be made of them to the last minutes of the incumbent's Presidency. The President, who was asked questions by the press even as he travelled from the White House to the Capitol for his successor's inauguration, had hoped to be able to announce the hostages' release while he was still in office. Perhaps it can be said that the President himself had become a hostage to an issue of which far too much was made. Perhaps it can be said as well that both the attractions and the limitations of that President were evident in the way he handled this issue. His patience was considerable and he very much cared for the lives of his fellow-citizens. But one must wonder whether he cared too much. Did he take it too personally, not only diverting himself from other duties in which perhaps even many more lives were at stake, but also jeopardizing the hostages themselves and others similarly vulnerable by showing that attention could be gotten from the United States by strong-arm methods?

III

There was something questionable about the way the media, and particularly the television networks, "played" the hostages story on Inauguration Day. We were switched back and forth from the site where a President was to be inaugurated to news centers for the latest reports from Teheran.

Did we really have to have those reports? What need was there to learn immediately what was happening halfway around the world? What would have been lost if we had had to wait a few hours, if not even another day, for this news? No doubt, network executives felt that audiences would be lost to their competitors if their stations did not appear to be "up-to-the-minute."

We can see here how the purveyors of news respond to a volatile public demand which they have themselves in large part shaped or, if you will, misshaped. It was all in all rather silly business and perhaps not worth much comment, except that it is a symptom of a deteriorating political sense in the American people. Deterioration may be seen in the expectation of immediate self-gratification, in the transformation of civic activities into theatrical productions, and (consequently on that occasion) in the much-publicized identification of ourselves with the hostages and their families in their trials and tribulations.

Perhaps the most critical effect of developments which see us making so much of the accidentally afflicted is that we tend to have our judgment as well as our sensibilities blunted with respect to the truly heroic. Many more men exhibited truly heroic conduct in the course of the Vietnam War, both among those who fought and suffered there and among those here who opposed vigorously American participation in that war. To make as much as was made of the hostages in Iran was to make too much of victimization, of passivity, and of mere endurance. It was, in effect, to make it appear that all of us (or, at least, tens of millions among us) are also capable of heroism.

IV

To say all this is to suggest that our sense of the heroic has been diminished. A trend toward such diminution was anticipated by our artists. Thus, it has been noticed, James Joyce's *Ulysses* "shifts the Greek epic and its heroes toward ironic modernity." (*New Yorker,* February 9, 1981, p. 115)

How far we have gone in accommodating old-fashioned notions of the heroic to the century of the common man may be seen, curiously enough, in the Inaugural Address of last January. We could hear statements made during that solemn hour which fit all too well with the rather sentimental interest in the hostages that the networks were catering to even as the constitutional ceremony was being presented to the Country.

The new President asked his countrymen to begin "an era of national renewal," assuring them, "We have every right to dream heroic dreams." He then added,

> Those who say we are in a time when there are no heroes just don't know where to look. You can see heroes every day going in and out of factory gates. Others, a handful in number, produce food enough to feed all of us and much of the world beyond.
>
> You meet heroes across the counter—on both sides of that counter. There are entrepreneurs with faith in themselves and an idea who create new jobs, new wealth, and opportunity.
>
> They are individuals and families whose taxes support the government and whose voluntary gifts support church, charity, culture, art, and education. Their patriotism is quiet but deep. Their values sustain our national life.
>
> I have used the words "they" and "their" in speaking of these heroes. I could say "you" and "your" because I am addressing the heroes of whom I speak— you, the citizens of this blessed land.

Thus everyone is a hero who does his job. The President of the United States, whatever he himself really believed about this, ratified in this part of his speech the tendency now several decades, if not centuries, in process, to make the heroic prosaic, to convert it into sobriety and industry and reliability.

V

But it was suggested by a nobleman in one of the Gilbert and Sullivan operettas a century ago, *The Gondoliers,*

> In short, whoever you may be,
> To this conclusion you'll agree
> When every one is somebodee,
> Then no one's anybody!

One might wonder whether it truly matters if "no one's anybody"? After all, what else does equality mean, the very equality to which we are dedicated by the Declaration of Independence?

Whatever equality meant to Jefferson, and later to the Lincoln who grounded his own political career upon the "created equal" language of the Declaration, it must be something consistent with the liberty that is also made much of in the Declaration of Independence and in the Constitution of the United States, that liberty which can more easily be seen to open the way, if only for a few, to heroic deeds.

No doubt, one's circumstances may determine whether one has the opportunity to act heroically. We, as students of political things, always have the opportunity to study what is around us and to try to understand ourselves as well as our fellow citizens. Not the least of the things we can grasp are the ways in which the few differ from the many. If one was not caught up as so many of one's countrymen seem to have been by the drama of the hostages' return, one was again reminded and indeed warned how much one can be isolated from the prevailing sentiments of one's day, even as one can share the Country's relief that needless bloodshed was avoided.

Such isolation can be threatening. After all, man *is* a social animal: many of his pleasures come from wholehearted association with his fellows. But detachment can also be a privilege, and it can remind one of a duty. The privilege of being able to understand what others do not understand can lead to the duty to observe the tendency of public opinion and to make suggestions about how that opinion might be corrected when it has been led astray.

VI

What happens to the ordinary man when his model of the heroic is mass-produced? Is the common man made tamer thereby? Life may thus become more orderly: security and prosperity may thereby be served. But at what price? Do men all become hostages to their comforts? Are they encouraged to invent "needs"? Do phony dramas take the place of genuine tragedy? Does life thereby make less sense?

In such circumstances the glow is off human existence, since we do know how mundane most of our lives are. Men may live more fully when they can bask in reflected glory, when they can believe that they contribute and are somehow related to those who are truly heroic.

Furthermore, if the heroic is not appreciated for what it is or seems to be, problems can arise in the defense of the community. Patriotism and genuine sacrifice tend to be depreciated, and the shirking of one's duty becomes fashionable. At the least, the morale of those who are prepared to do their duty is subverted.

Even more dangerous to the community, however, may be a pervasive sense of boredom (all too common in modernity) when the unheroic has really taken over. In such circumstances, men (perhaps out of desperation) may become peculiarly susceptible to foolish adventures. Truly to live, all too many can come to believe, is to live recklessly and to experiment. Novelty and risk (and not only in the arts) can then become the order of the day and this can have cataclysmic consequences, especially when small men happen to find themselves with opportunities to look and act like big men.

VII

Even so, it should be recognized that there *are* problems with that nobility to which the heroic is dedicated. Nobility, rooted in a kind of liberty, can all too often ignore justice. It can also be unproductive and even destructive. The dedication to equality *is* rooted in a kind of justice. It may have been repeated abuses of the trust vested in aristocrats that contributed to skepticism about old-fashioned heroism in the West.

Nobility is not served well by a pervasive skepticism. Far more constructive in controlling the heroic without destroying it are the responsible artist and the somewhat disinterested political scientist. Old-fashioned tragedy can remind the noble, or the would-be-noble, of the pitfalls not just of their weaknesses, but also of their strengths.

VIII

It is up to the political scientist to insist upon the possible usefulness as well as the intrinsic attractiveness of the noble. In order to be able to do this, especially as circumstances change, he must be alert to the limitations of the noble. He must notice, for instance, how troublesome and even dangerous the heroic can be when it magnifies challenge unduly. This means that the political scientist should stand for prudence, but a prudence that is not an excuse for opportunism or for mere passivity.

If we return for a few more minutes to the President's Inaugural Address of last January, we can notice toward the end of his remarks an effort to resurrect something of genuine heroism. He must have sensed that the earlier comments which I have quoted suffice for everyday affairs; they may even flatter one's audience. But if grave risks are to be run and the greatest sacrifices are to be called for, if war itself is to remain available as an instrument of national policy, then something of old-fashioned heroism must be available. Thus the President could say,

> At the end of this open mall are those shrines to the giants on whose shoulders we stand. [He then spoke of the Washington Monument, the Jefferson Memorial, and the Lincoln Memorial.]
>
> Beyond these monuments to heroism is the Potomac River, and on the far shore the sleeping hills of Arlington National Cemetery with its row upon row of simple white markers with crosses and Stars of David adding up to only a tiny fraction of the price that has been paid for our freedom. Each one of those markers is a monument to the kind of hero I spoke of earlier.

However this may be (for there *is* a problem about what can be expected in time of war from the "kind of hero [he] spoke of earlier"), the President then singled out one of the markers under which lies a young man "who left his job in a small town barber shop in 1917 to go to France with the famed Rainbow Division." He was evidently killed while "trying to carry a message between battalions under heavy artillery." What particularly distinguishes this man, it turned out, was the "pledge" he had written in the diary found on his body:

> America must win this war. Therefore I will work, I will save, I will sacrifice, I will endure, I will fight cheerfully and do my utmost, as if the struggle depended on me alone.

The President, by drawing as he did upon these sentiments, reminded us of the singleminded dedication of which the heroic is capable. (See Section VII of Essay No. 17, above.) But he also reminded us of the limitations to which the heroic can be subject. What did the young man mean, that "America must win this war"? After all, was not that war one that the United States had no business even being in? Was it not one that our allies should not have fought or, at least, should have negotiated an early settlement of? It is hard to say now what that war was all about. Yet it called for sacrifices on so grand a scale as virtually to wreck European civilization and expose it in the coming decades to the rampages of those "heroes" of Satanic proportions, Hitler and Stalin.

It should be evident, therefore, that individual heroism and community sacrifice must be guided by statesmanship. This is well to keep in mind, and for political scientists to speak clearly about, at a time when the call for adventure is again being heard in the land.

IX

In another speech to the nation (on February 5) the President spoke of a determination to "restore the freedom of all men and women to excel and to create." This invocation of excellence, too, is a reminder of old-fashioned aspirations.

Still, there is the problem, again for political thinkers to ponder, of what true excellence is. What is fundamental to our institutions? What kind of citizenry do we need? What opinions among us are salutary and what opinions are corrupting? What challenges truly face us and how should they be faced? I have touched on this occasion upon answers to these questions. But I have merely touched upon them. Perhaps it is enough to remind political scientists such as you of such questions, questions that need to be addressed by informed men and women who are prudent enough to sense what they need to know in order to be able to advise responsibly those entrusted with the conduct of our affairs.

I need hardly add that true excellence is not limited to practical affairs. There is as well that full development of the reason, and not only with respect to political matters, which can usefully be regarded as the highest accomplishment of the entire human race, an accomplishment shared both by the few in whom it is manifested and by the many who help sustain the community that provides the opportunity for those few to become what they should be.

I congratulate, therefore, not only those who are honored on this occasion but also others who have made their achievements possible: their families, their teachers over the years, and the many unheroic but nevertheless productive citizens of this State who support this university. All of us are grateful, in turn, for the reminder provided by this honor society and those whom it honors, the reminder that excellence is indeed to be treasured as something we are all privileged and perhaps entitled to have among us.

33

OF COUNSEL—AND THE LIMITS OF POLITICS

As they prepared to break up, de Gaulle paused, charmingly cited the prerogatives of age and ventured to suggest that [Kennedy] not pay too much attention to his advisers or give too much respect to the policies he had inherited. In the last analysis, the General said, what counted for every man was himself and his own judgment. He was expounding, of course, the Gaullist philosophy of leadership. His counsel, after the Bay of the Pigs, fell on receptive ears.

ARTHUR M. SCHLESINGER, JR.

I

The political scientist cannot reasonably expect to hold public office. That is, the accomplished political scientist cannot expect to become a practicing politician. He may not, perhaps he should not, want to become active in the pursuit of office if he has learned well the old lessons of political philosophy. But if a political scientist is truly accomplished, he should expect to be called upon occasionally to counsel men and women both in public life and in private: to counsel both those who are fated to seek public office and those who content themselves with a private station. (See, for example, the Statement appended to Essay No. 31–D, above.)

At the heart of sound counsel are (1) an ability to see what there is to be seen, and (2) an aptitude for judging what has been seen in the circumstances which prevail. Observation and interpretation go together,

---

This talk was given at the Pi Sigma Alpha Political Science Honor Society Banquet, Memphis State University, Memphis, Tennessee, December 1, 1978. See, for counsel given to a king who probably would have done far better by heeding it, Anastaplo, *Human Being and Citizen* (Chicago: Swallow Press, 1975), p. 228. See, on prudence, the Preface to this book, *The American Moralist.*

The epigraph is taken from Arthur M. Schlesinger, Jr., *A Thousand Days: John F. Kennedy in the White House* (Boston: Houghton Mifflin Co., 1965), p. 352.

integrated by an awareness that can reliably determine when there are sufficient observations to be interpreted for the purpose at hand. Such determination remains, in most cases, aware of its tentativeness. It is often difficult and sometimes impossible "to be absolutely certain," but one can be sure enough for an occasion if and only if one is aware of how difficult it is ever to be certain.

The dependence on one another of observation and interpretation is nicely illustrated by an ancient Chinese story about Confucius:

> Confucius and those traveling with him were in distress between Ch'en and Ts'ai. They had not even vegetable soup to drink, and had not tasted grain for seven days. While Confucius was sleeping in the daytime, Yen Hui [who is known as Confucius's favorite disciple] sought for rice. He obtained some and cooked it. When it was almost done, Confucius saw Yen Hui grasp some rice from within the pot and eat it. After a short time the food was cooked. Yen Hui went to Confucius and offered him the food. Confucius pretended that he had not seen Yen Hui reach into the pot. Confucius rose and said, "Just now I dreamed that I saw my deceased father. Since the food is pure, I will offer some of it to him as a sacrifice."

A modern editor explains that Confucius was seeking thereby to make Yen Hui confess that he had greedily reached into the pot, making the food ritually impure for a sacrifice. The story continues:

> Yen Hui replied, "It cannot be used in sacrifice. A little while ago some soot fell into the pot. To discard food is an act of ill omen. I therefore reached into the pot, withdrew the soiled rice, and ate it." Upon hearing this, Confucius sighed and said, "That which one believes is the testimony of the eyes, and yet the eyes can still not be believed. That which one relies on is the mind, and yet the mind is still not adequate to rely on. My children, remember it. To understand men is indeed not easy."

(See H. G. Creel, *Shen Pu-Hai*, pp. 184, 378–79. See, also, *Analects of Confucius*, IV, 9, XV, 1; *Works of Mencius*, IV, 2, 29. See, as well, "An Introduction to Confucian Thought," *Great Ideas Today*, vol. 1984, p. 124.) It should be noticed that Confucius must have told this story on himself, which reveals his attempt to use a pious deception in an effort to test and "counsel" his disciple.

II

The best counsel depends on that understanding of which Confucius spoke. One has to have a reliable opinion both about what is going on and about what is called for if one is to be a responsible adviser. The most responsible counselling in many circumstances may consist primarily in asking sensible questions, thereby bringing to the attention of the party being advised that which is relevant to the situation in which he finds himself— questions about matters that the man advised, and perhaps only he, knows the answers to.

To say that questioning is important, perhaps even decisive in many instances, is to recognize that there are standards that are being brought to bear upon the situation: standards of right and wrong, of the prudent and the imprudent, of good and bad. Questioning or mere talking is not carried on for its own sake on such occasions. The adviser should have a sense of what should be desired and an ear for relevant information. Sigmund Freud, in defending the need of the psychoanalyst to *interpret* the material presented by the patient (be that material "memories, ideas, or dreams"), observed, "A certain fine ear' is required, in discovering what is unconscious and repressed, and not everyone possesses it to the same degree." (*The Question of Lay Analysis*, pp. 73–74)

To invoke, as I have, enduring standards is to distinguish *counsel* from the *counselling* of which one hears so much today. Counselling is all around us. A recent cartoon shows a roadside building marked, "Last counselling center before turnpike." (*New Yorker*, November 13, 1978, p. 223) Thus, also, a recent Federal Trade Commission staff report says, "In many instances, funeral 'counselling' is really thinly disguised salesmanship designed to persuade consumers to purchase additional and costlier funeral merchandise and services." (*Chicago Tribune*, November 7, 1978, sec. 3, p. 10) Thus, as well, we in Chicago have been reading about what "counselling" means for the unfortunate women who consider themselves obliged to resort to abortion clinics. Counselling was included by Illinois lawmakers in the list of services such clinics must provide, but this has meant to all too many abortion-clinic proprietors that prospective customers should be ruthlessly counselled in, not out.

Counselling, even when conducted in good faith, may make far too much of process, not enough of goals that are informed by sensible standards. There may be something seriously wrong when there is considerable formal counselling in a community: it suggests that there are not enough informal rules that are generally accepted nor enough authoritative training by the community. Is there apt to be a greater need for such counselling wherever tradition is played down and innovation and novelty are made much of?

Something which is predominantly process can become merely *pro forma*, when it is not simply manipulated to serve the ends of the "counsellor." This kind of manipulation can be seen in much that is said today about legal reasoning: the activity itself—the arguing that lawyers and judges do—takes precedence over ends such as justice and the common good that arguments, laws, and the Constitution should be developed to serve. Process takes precedence over purpose, becoming virtually an end in itself. This leads to both a ratification of selfishness and a "value-free" political science.

III

The counsel provided by old-fashioned (and hence "value-laden") political science tends to be conservative in its inclinations. It reflects an awareness of the difficulty of knowing what has happened and what is needed, the difficulty of preferring the common good to one's own advancement. Francis Bacon counselled in his essay on innovations, "It is good . . . not to try experiments in states, except the necessity be urgent, or the utility evident, and well to beware that it be the reformation that draweth on the change, and not the desire of change that pretendeth the reformation."

Change for its own sake, which an emphasis upon process may encourage, is dubious. Even when change is not for its own sake, but rather for grand purposes, it can be "unrealistic." The following story, relayed to me by Malcolm Sharp, is one that a distinguished University of Wisconsin political scientist, John Gaus, used to tell on himself. He was confidently rearranging the map of Europe in a 1939 seminar on European affairs: a new confederation here, boundaries fixed up there, populations and territories redistributed—all with a view to heading off the great war which was threatening. A graduate student who had come to this Country from the Baltics, having listened quietly to the Gaus Plan, finally observed, "Professor, all that you say is fine, but there is one thing you don't understand: we hate each other." Nothing more needed to be said.

We know that longstanding national opinions and problems place limits in establishing public policy. We should also learn that public affairs are often so complicated that it is hard to predict what is going to happen, as we can see today in our efforts to develop a sound economic policy in the United States. Even so, what it is important to know, at least as bearing upon the broad sweep of policy (as distinguished from day-to-day operations), *can* be learned by the intelligent citizen who is determined to be informed on the issues of the day. One need not be in government to be able to learn what can be known about what to expect in the months and years ahead.

In fact, for a variety of reasons, someone not at the moment in government service may be better equipped to see the whole than public servants hampered by partisan dictates and by daily routines. This was evident to me during the American involvement in Vietnam. It was also evident during the decade I followed the Colonels' tyranny in Greece. In both instances, informed American citizens knew better than their State Department what was going on and what was needed. To become and to remain informed do require considerable effort, and the responsible citizen who presumes to speak on such subjects (this can be seen with respect to South Africa today) senses what he needs to learn in order to know enough.

My concern on this occasion, however, is *not* to argue for freedom of speech, for the right, duty, and ability of citizens to inform themselves adequately in order to be able to comment responsibly on the issues of the day. The usefulness of such freedom of speech and the full discussion by citizens of political matters should be apparent, hedged in as it should be by the cautions I have indicated to be appropriate. Our awareness of these cautions is usually such as to make it apparent also that most of what we say as citizens is not primarily counsel, but rather constitutes an effort to share with one another inquiries into and information about what is going on.

Bad habits do develop, however, which induce us to pass judgment on what we have not troubled to study and to prescribe for what we are not in a position to diagnose. These are habits which are all too often nurtured by what we do or permit to be done in our private affairs. What we do there, especially as counsellors, may affect how we deal with public affairs. (See, on the intermingling of public and private affairs, Plato, *Gorgias* 481D.)

IV

Private affairs are, it should at once be noticed, easier to predict the consequences of. Thus, for example, if a man indulges his appetites a great deal, it can be expected he will damage his body; if a woman is undisciplined, it can be expected she will not be able to develop her talents; if students are devious, it can be expected they will neither be trusted nor be obliged to learn what they should. These consequences are far easier to predict than the effects of raising the interest rate or the effects of switching from one weapons system to another or the effects of clandestine intelligence operations abroad.

Private consequences, then, are far easier to predict, once the facts are known, but it may be more difficult than in the public situations I have just mentioned to know what the facts are. That is, *does* this man over-indulge? *Are* our students devious? *Is* this woman undisciplined? My illustration from Confucius' life is particularly apt here. In some ways, therefore, public affairs in this Country may be considerably easier to speak responsibly about than private affairs.

Everything that is relevant with respect to public affairs, at least with respect to domestic public affairs and with respect to at least the broad outlines of foreign policy, should usually be available to the citizen determined to be informed. But private affairs are by nature limited in this respect: they are not called *private* for nothing. Are Americans so used to passing judgment upon public affairs that they easily misapprehend private affairs, not noticing the critical differences in information available? Do uninformed pronouncements upon private affairs contribute to bad habits and undisciplined passions that in turn are all too often brought to bear on public affairs?

Is it not usually better to wait to be asked before advising about private affairs outside one's own family and the most intimate circle of friendship—to be asked by someone who provides the information that is relevant? Failing such requests, which can of course be implicit, is it not usually better to speak more generally, rather than to attempt to pass judgment on a particular case, and thus allow private parties to apply what is said to the particular circumstances that only they may know? On the other hand, when one has been *offered* advice which is quite beside the point, because the adviser is either inadequately informed or not thoughtful enough, may it not be better (especially when one cannot be sure what moves the adviser or how he may be affected by an explicit rebuff) to limit one's response, when the opportunity presents itself, to general observations on the nature and limitations of counsel?

In private affairs, especially in another's family affairs, I have suggested, it is difficult to advise sensibly. It is especially difficult to do this in the United States: there is so great a variety here of family "ways" of doing things, ways that reflect the divergent foreign origins of our people, ways that are, to some extent, self-consistent in themselves for a person or for a family, but that are difficult for an outsider to grasp or to be sensible about. Of course, it may also be difficult to know what is going on in one's own family, especially when one's parents bring together two or more ways of life but *there* one parent may be obliged to determine, explain and insist upon the protocols of family relations, present and future, if there *is* to be a family.

The natural divergence among families is suggested by the modern Greek proverb, "In another's house, one is a blind man." This divergence is accentuated, with the institution of the family thereby undermined, in a community such as ours: a community that promotes various sentimental opinions about "equality," about "personal liberty," and hence about "love."

V

Further complicating any counsel about private affairs is the fact that people more often than not will simply do or permit to have happen to them what they "want" to do or to have happen to them. This is not to say that the observer should not try to be helpful and compassionate; it *is* to say that the friendly intervenor is apt to be misdirected and ineffectual, even when he is not exploited or turned into a scapegoat.

The realization that people will all too often do what they want to do inclines me, as a "teacher," *not* to try to serve as a policeman for students. I try to offer them more than they bargained for; and I suggest why I believe in the importance of the questions I raise, partly by showing that *I* consider such questions important for myself as the student I still am. Although I suggest the importance of certain questions and of questioning, it is up to students to take advantage of what is made available to them. Unless they should truly want to do so, no genuine learning is likely—at least not at the age students come to my classes.

How difficult it is to move people responsibly is indicated by what happens to people of talent. I have known several people with artistic genius who have failed to use their talents fully. In a sense, they do not want to do so; they are afraid of the consequences of a full dedication to their art. One should be reluctant, as an adviser, to try to induce such people to act otherwise: the consequences are unpredictable; the psychic compulsions that have paralyzed them artistically may be beyond a layman's prudent ministrations. Unless one is remarkably talented as a counsellor, one should probably allow them to continue to do what they want to do, wasteful as it may seem.

Why it is that people "want" what they do is, of course, a major question in itself. No doubt we should as a community address ourselves much more than we do to assessing and reshaping the influences among us that largely determine what it is we happen to want. But that is a problem of public policy and, as such, can be an easier problem than that which confronts us in dealing with the individual who does happen to want what he does.

That one thing is wanted rather than another may even be seen in who is approached for advice and how one is approached. When critical facts are omitted in the account one is given on which one is to advise, the alert adviser suspects that there is in the person seeking advice an awareness both of what is wanted and of how the suppressed facts can prove troublesome in justifying or securing what is wanted. Freud makes much of such concealments (as well as of so-called mistakes), but the significance of such selectivity has always been known. Something like this may be seen in 2 *Chronicles* 10 where it is noticed that Solomon's son Rehoboam, upon considering how he should conduct himself as king, preferred the counsel of the young men to that of the old men.

The public policy I have referred to, with respect to influences among us that shape our wants, can determine how the whole is regarded, and thus can help us make sense of and guide the private conduct we observe. Consider, as suggestive both of what we have always known about the complexity of a man's character and of the overall view of things on which that character can depend, the following story from 2 *Samuel* 12:

And David said unto Nathan [the prophet], "I have sinned against the Lord [by taking Uriah's wife, Bathsheba]." And Nathan said unto David, "The Lord also hath put away thy sin; thou shalt not die. Howbeit, because by this deed thou hast given great occasion to the enemies of the Lord to blaspheme, the child also that is born unto thee shall surely die." And Nathan departed unto his house.

And the Lord struck the child that Uriah's wife bare unto David, and it was very sick. David therefore besought God for the child; and David fasted, and as often as he went in, he lay all night upon the earth. And the elders of his house arose, and stood beside him, to raise him up from the earth; but he would not, neither did he eat bread with them.

And it came to pass on the seventh day, that the child died. And the servants of David feared to tell him that the child was dead; for they said, "Behold, while the child was yet alive, we spoke unto him, and he hearkened not unto our voice; how then shall we tell him that the child is dead, so that he do himself some harm?"

But when David saw that his servants whispered together, David perceived that the child was dead; and David said unto his servants, "Is the child dead?" And they said, "He is dead." Then David arose from the earth, and washed, and anointed himself, and changed his apparel, and he came into the house of the Lord, and worshipped; then he came to his own house; and when he required, they set bread before him, and he did eat.

Then said his servants unto him, "What thing is this that thou hast done? Thou didst fast and weep for the child, while it was yet alive; but when the child was dead, thou didst rise and eat bread." And he said, "While the child was yet alive, I fasted and wept; for I said, Who knoweth whether the Lord will not be gracious to me, that the child may live?' But now he is dead, wherefore should I fast? Can I bring him back again? I shall go to him, but he will not return to me."

And David comforted Bathsheba his wife, and went in unto her, and lay with her; and she bare a son, and he called his name Solomon. And the Lord loved him.

David, unlike the servants counselling him, seems to have had a lively awareness of what it was that he wanted, of what the limits were of what he could do about what he wanted, and (as is seen in his recourse to Bathsheba, who is now called *his* wife) a lively awareness of what it was *he* could do and have. The best counsel, whether it emanates from within one or appears from without, can do no more, perhaps, than help one know oneself, which may be what the better psychiatrist encourages his patient to try to do. (See, e.g., the end of Section II of Essay No. 10, above.) I will return, in my concluding remarks, to "the overall view of things" on which such self-knowledge depends.

To speak as I have of the critical influence in these matters of "want" may suggest that I consider the psychiatrist the best possible counsellor one could have. That is hardly so. Consider the insoluble problems that psychiatrists, among others, have in giving counsel: they do not, and in most troublesome instances cannot, find out what has truly happened, except perhaps with respect to what may be of immediate practical interest, the "state of mind" of the patient. In short, they may not be able to learn *what is*. (See, on whether *true* and *being* are convertible terms, Thomas Aquinas, *On Truth and Falsity*, Pt. I, Q. 16, A. 3.)

The accounts, recollections, and even records of psychiatrists cannot help but be full of misinformation, not least because the troubled people who consult them are often the least able to observe either what is happening to them or what the associates they describe and perhaps complain of are doing. It is difficult to get all the relevant facts from one side of a passionate encounter, whether the person complained of is the parent, sibling, child, spouse, or superior of the complainant.

This is not to suggest that the psychiatrist cannot be helpful. At times, he may be the only one who *can* help, especially if the patient has confidence in him. It is not unimportant that the psychiatrist has legitimate access to useful drugs. In addition, he may be familiar with patterns of deviant conduct and hence with the kind of pathological behavior that his particular patient exhibits. He can treat the patient, or at least the symptoms of the patient, thereby allowing nature an opportunity to exert her own healing powers as well.

Even so, the psychiatrist as counsellor does tend to minister to the wants that his patient happens to have. Or, rather, he addresses the problems caused for the patient by conflicting wants. The temptation among partisans of psychiatry, if not among psychiatrists themselves, is to take a low view of human nature in order to resolve whatever conflict there may be. But that is a long story, better left to another occasion. Our story of David and his servants bears thinking upon here: it is difficult, if not impossible, for inferiors to understand and counsel someone truly superior.

It suffices here to add to what I have said about human nature and the nature of wants what one woman said to another in still another recent cartoon, "I got what I wanted, but it wasn't what I expected." (*New Yorker*, October 23, 1978, p. 51)

VI

Let us return to everyday counsel, putting the psychiatrist and his troubled patients to one side. I continue to marvel at the counsel people volunteer to give others, especially when there is no family duty to do so. It is difficult to escape presumptuousness, or an attempt at self-elevation and undeserved intimacy, in such matters.

I shudder when I recall the counsel I myself have at times presumed to give. I recall, for example, what I once told the wealthy parent of a fellow graduate student, a quite serious student who *has* remained a serious student to this day. You would do well, I suggested a quarter of a century ago, to give your son *now* a good deal of the money you eventually plan to leave him; he is a dedicated scholar, and can be expected to remain that; your money can do him far more good and help him more with his studies and his life now than it is likely to do later. This kind of consideration is probably something for every wealthy parent to take into account. Whether it was sound advice in that particular case, however, I still do not know. Should I not have known much more about that family's finances and about relations within that family than I did before I presumed to speak?

It is difficult to counsel effectively anyone at a distance, whether a good friend or even a family member, and when one is not well informed, one *is* at a distance. (Aristotle noticed that intimate friendship, a truly helpful friendship, is difficult to maintain when people live apart.) One does not and indeed cannot know, in such circumstances, the details that are essential in providing reliable guidance. For example, to appeal to another's prudence in support of one's uninformed advice may only reveal how little one appreciates the need for that grasp of particulars on which prudence depends. To cite a parade of venerable authorities or to invoke all kinds of classical models in support of advice that is misdirected may only reveal that one does not take those authorities and models seriously, using them rather than learning from them. One can wonder about the common sense and sentimentality of those who insist upon passing judgment upon another's personal affairs when they should know that they cannot know the facts.

In short, one should make an effort, especially in serious matters, to find out what one is talking about. Otherwise, proper counsel is impossible. Bearing on all this, it seems to me, is the sadness of Saint Augustine upon recognizing that some of his friends thought him better than he was: "I take no pleasure in being thought by my dearest friends to be such as I am not. Obviously they do not love me, but another in my name, if they love, not what I am, but what I am not." Similarly, an uninformed counsellor is not advising me, "but another in my name." (See Sister M. A. McNamara, *Friends and Friendship for Saint Augustine*, p. 225.)

Need it be added that the prudence in counselling I speak of should not be taken to justify neglect, self-centeredness, or cowardice? But neither should prudence be abandoned lest one be thought to be neglectful, callous, or otherwise at fault. Perhaps the most effective counsel usually follows upon the timely inquiry, "Is there anything I can do to help?" One may often be most helpful simply by indicating one's willingness to be helpful: that can serve to encourage a troubled man about the kind of world he lives in.

The troubled man may also need to be reminded, and thereby assured, that there *are* enduring standards of right and wrong, of the prudent and the imprudent, of good and bad, and that, therefore, he should not do or even continue to desire whatever happens to appeal to him. It is one thing to recognize that one may not be able to counsel another properly in the circumstances one finds oneself. It is quite another thing, and even more irresponsible than uninformed counselling, to suggest to another that "it does not really matter" what he wants, thinks, or does.

Prudence induces us to consider now, however briefly, whether the counsel one gets is only as good as the conduct of the one giving the counsel. It can be hard to take seriously the counsel of those whose lives are hardly models of sensibleness. "Physician, heal thyself," is an appealing retort to the insistent counsellor. But, alas, there *are* physicians who can heal others and yet can do little for themselves.

It would be simple if we *could* count upon an inevitable or at least a likely reciprocity between prudent conduct and good counsel, between imprudent conduct and poor counsel. It might be helpful if we *were* able to judge in advance the advice people give by considering the kinds of lives they themselves have led. But I am far from sure that it would be helpful to be saved from considering the advice given us by people whose lives we know to be questionable. Might we not still have something to learn from what they say and how they say it? May they not have a hold on something worth considering? May not something sound or at least fortunate in them have enabled them to touch upon considerations that should be taken seriously by us?

There does not seem to be an invariable relation between good counsel and prudent conduct. Why is there not? What, that is, *is* the relation between knowledge and virtue? That too must be left for another occasion. It suffices here to observe that passions and reason, including what one learns from experience, can diverge. Would they diverge if one fully understood the passions, if one truly knew oneself?

Short of such full understanding, divergences between passion and reason can be expected. We are obliged to think about the counsel we get, if only to put it in its proper place, even as we take care to provide responsible counsel ourselves both in public and in private.

VII

I reserved for this afternoon the final preparation of my concluding remarks tonight, anticipating that I might be better able thereby to exploit that element of topicality, that awareness of circumstances, to which counsel should pay its respects.

My approach has been rewarded, for I *am* able to draw upon my experiences as I waited out a snowstorm at Chicago's O'Hare Field this morning. Permit me, then, to conclude with three "words of counsel" which take advantage of what I have happened upon today. One word is "private," one is "public," and one touches upon both the public and the private.

My first word of counsel takes its point of departure from a financial magazine which I do not ordinarily have recourse to, but which was among the journals I glanced through on our snowbound airplane. A noted and now quite wealthy investor, upon being asked for advice to young people starting out, said (*Forbes*, November 27, 1978, p. 52),

> Save as much as possible. Every person gets some luck in his life and the only reason most never fulfill their business potential is they don't have the savings to take advantage of the luck when it comes along.

This advice can be taken in its literal sense and is no doubt useful on that basis alone. Even more important for students, and not just for students of political science, is that sense of this advice which recognizes that the most precious savings one can have come from the wisest teachers, both the few who are alive in one's time and the others found in the books of old. ("It was truly said," Francis Bacon observed in his essay on counsel, "*Optimi consiliarii mortui;* books will speak plain when counsellors blanch.")

My second word of counsel follows upon my extended observation this morning of the activities of many men working on the airplanes which managed to get to our gate at the airport. Each man had his job; all was efficiently coordinated. I was reminded of the activities of ants I observed one hot afternoon at the Agora in Athens, activities that, for a couple of hours, were of considerably more interest to me than the classical ruins I had come to inspect.

The design of a truck used for spraying de-icer fluid on snowladen planes was particularly instructive. It had on the top of the cab a horizontal window with its own windshield wiper, so that the driver could look *up* for the wings of the planes to be driven under and serviced. The truck was, as were many other tools and vehicles and people I watched, specially adapted to its task. I was reminded here too of the ants and of what we have been taught about both Evolution and the Creator. There was in what I saw all around me at the airport a wonderful adaptation of form to function.

The desire for gain has no doubt provided much of the incentive for the organization and equipment of the airport team I observed this morning. Also influential, one senses, is a simple delight in gadgets, reinforced as it is in this case by the cost-saving desire to reduce reliance upon skilled manpower. But is there not as well here, as in the Creative-Evolutionary impulse itself, the expression of a striving for the best—that is, for the good of which life is inherently capable?

My second word of counsel, stimulated by what I have just described, has been summed up by a comedian of our time: "You only live once, but if you work it right, once is enough." (See *Chicago Tribune*, November 22, 1978, sec. 5, p. 1.) What does it mean to "work it right"? It means, among other things, that one knows what one is doing or, at least, that one relies for counsel upon someone who does know. Among the things to be known (we are reminded by the parallels between the ants and the airport crews) may be the interconnectedness of things, perhaps indeed the wholeness of what we observe. One thing can lead to another, and thence to all, if properly pursued. (See Plato, *Meno* 81C–E; Maimonides, *The Guide of the Perplexed*, II, 38 (83b).)

My third word of counsel draws upon a conversation I had on the plane with my seat partner, a former member of the Tennessee legislature. It is fitting that I virtually conclude with a recollection which can serve to reassure those of you interested in active politics that political scientists *can* be useful, if only in that they can recognize and relay to others the practical advice they have happened upon.

The retired legislator observed about his fellow Tennesseeans, "You can bus their children or take their money, but *don't mess in any way* with their horses, dogs, or guns." No doubt the budding politicians among you already sense the soundness of this counsel. It is important, however, not to leave it at this. For the true politician—that is, the statesman—should think about what the attachment to horses, dogs, and guns means. What does such attachment mean as an assurance of security? What does it mean as a striving for nobility? It is prudent to recognize what it is that people do happen to be attached to, what those attachments mean, and what, if anything, can and should be done about them. Only if one does recognize such things can one both provide effective counsel and learn what there is to learn about things enduring as well as transitory.

Still, it is well, lest one take oneself too seriously either as mature counsellor or as youthful counselled, to keep in mind, for human life, both the immediate appeal of certain urges and the transcendent significance of the erotic. Consider, here, the counsel implied by William Butler Yeats's *Politics* (published just before the Second World War):

> How can I, that girl standing there,
> My attention fix
> On Roman or on Russian
> Or on Spanish politics?
> Yet here's a travelled man that knows
> What he talks about,
> And there's a politician
> That has read and thought,
> And maybe what they say is true
> Of war and war's alarms,
> But O that I were young again
> And held her in my arms!

G.

Lessons
from Abroad

34

THE GREEK CASE

34-A. Politics versus Ideology

Hating this world they never made, after its debauchery of centuries, the modern Communists—revolutionaries and logicians—move toward intellectual rigor. In their decision lies the sharpest reproach yet to the desertion of intellect by Renaissance man and his successors. Nothing is more disturbing to modern men of the West than the logical clarity with which the Communists face all problems. Who shall say that this feeling is not born of a deep apprehension that here are the first true realists in hundreds of years and that no dodging about in the excluded middle will save Western liberalism?

RICHARD M. WEAVER

I

I suspect, upon reviewing the radical program of your organization, there are critical differences between us as to how to think about contemporary Greek affairs. But I also suspect there can be some agreement between us about how the United States should respond to the government in Athens these days.

This talk was given at the Militant Forum, Chicago, Illinois, January 11, 1974. (Original title: "Politics versus Ideology: The Greek Case.") It was published in the *Journal of the Hellenic Diaspora*, October 1974, pp. 28–34, and reprinted in part in 121 *Congressional Record* 10321–23 (April 15, 1975). Most of my publications in this Country on Greek affairs during the time of the Colonels (1967–74) may be found by consulting the Index of the Congressional Record where they were reprinted between 1969 and 1975.

The epigraph is taken from Richard M. Weaver, *Ideas Have Consequences* (Chicago: University of Chicago Press, 1948), p. 9. See, also, *ibid.*, pp. 99, 124.

Let me begin by making some general remarks about what I think is a serious difference between us, a difference which goes far beyond our respective opinions about Greek affairs. My own inclination is to try to think about the issues of the day more politically than economically or ideologically. I believe, for instance, that there is something seriously deficient in the mode of understanding that one finds in the typical radical analysis of these issues. I am dubious, in other words, about the usefulness of doctrinaire analyses of such problems. Such analyses, whether "radical" or "reactionary," tend to give people the impression that they understand things when in fact they are merely imposing upon them a predetermined form.

Another problem is that the language this sort of supposed understanding is usually couched in tends to be more violent or combative than is consistent with my taste as an old-fashioned liberal. I put it as merely "taste" for the moment, although I believe it goes much deeper than that. I mention this violent language, which is evident in the literature your organization has been good enough to supply me, as one serious problem with the ideological approach to political matters. Among the things it leads to is lack of generosity toward one's opponents. It does not seem to be appreciated by the dogmatic that honest differences of opinion must be expected in politics, no matter what one tries to do.

Your particular approach tends to describe things very much in terms of "history" and of "forces," economically based forces primarily. It is difficult for me to see that this is really the way things work. I believe the truth is much harder to come by than is suggested by reliance upon "laws of history."

It makes a difference in considering the issues of the day whether one thinks that there *are* laws of history. It makes a difference in the kind of approach one takes to those issues on any particular occasion and in the kind of remedies one advocates. To put it a different way, I believe that what I call a doctrinaire approach does not pay due respect to the role of chance in human affairs. It can lead, in arrogance or in desperation if for no other reason, to ruthlessness. This seems to me a serious problem, to say nothing of what happens to freedom and human dignity in the process.

Permit me to put what I have been saying in still another way. I do not believe one can properly think about these matters in terms of such concepts as "the masses." "The masses" is a quite modern term which seems to come to us from physics. Consider what "the masses" implies. It implies a public that no longer has a rational component to be addressed. Such a public is not something to be reasoned with to some extent but merely something to be moved: to be moved by forces, by propaganda, by slogans. Ideas, as Leon Trotsky put it somewhere, are the small change of objective interests. He evidently did not consider them something to be thought about on their own terms.

All this points to the underlying problem with the ideological approach I have been sketching, and that is the problem of what the nature of human understanding is. To what extent can one rise above one's class, to what extent can one so stand aside from one's particular interest as to be able to see the full range of the interests of the human being? The perennial problems one has to deal with here are the problems of nature: what is human nature, and what are the highest activities called for by human nature?

I would point, as a contribution to the solution of the problem of nature, to the ancient opinion that the highest human activity is somehow involved in understanding, not in action. Is not sound understanding ultimately dependent on the proposition that ideas are not merely the emanations of "objective interests"?

II

I hope I can now show that what I have said thus far may have something to do with how one looks at "the Greek situation" today. For one thing, I believe it very easy to underestimate the role of chance in what has happened in Greece the past ten years. It is also very easy to underestimate the role of bad judgment on the part of all the men who were in responsible positions during this period—men who were liberals, men who were of what is called the Left, and men who were of what is called the Right.

The Colonels' coup of April, 1967 took place in large part because of the serious mistakes made by virtually every major group in Greece that had had a part to play in the constitutional crisis leading up to that coup. Conditions had been allowed to deteriorate in such a way as to seriously disturb the stability of the country and to frighten people badly, thereby permitting self-seeking and ruthless Army officers to make the move that they had long wanted to make and were always looking for an opportunity to make. I believe that when one puts one's analysis this way, one *is* talking about political developments: one is emphasizing leaders who did this rather than that; one is talking about the role of mistakes and of moral failings. One is not talking primarily about broad movements in history.

Now, one *can* think about Greece in terms of broad historical movements. I assure you that such movements are far more profound than those which one talks about when the stock radical analyses are relied upon. One problem in Greece is to decide where to begin in trying to understand that country and its people. It is plausible to suggest that one

should begin in the Fifteenth Century with the occupation of Greek-
speaking lands by the Turks. The results of four centuries of occupation
remain with Greece to this day. This is not an irrelevant consideration and
has something to do with what is known as the Greek temperament. It has
something to do as well with certain contemporary Greek problems.

One can, to show you how unrealistic I can be about this, go back much
further: one can even say that "the Greek problem" began in the Fifth
Century B.C. when Alcibiades failed to lead Athens to the conquest of Sicily, a conquest that would have seen Greece assuming the role Rome later
took in the Mediterranean. Although Syracuse had to become like Athens
in order to defend herself against Athens, she could not, because of her
circumstances, lead the Greeks the way a triumphant Athens might have
done or even as much as a defeated Athens has done. Have not Greeks
"always" suffered from having been denied the political preeminence to
which they are "entitled"?

These speculations are, I must say, more interesting in some ways than
modern notions about "the masses" and "laws of history," seeming to me
to go deeper into what human endeavors are all about. They bring in not
only economic, but also political and religious considerations.

III

As one comes to modern times there is, of course, the Greek Revolution of
1821. That revolution continued for a hundred years, in the sense that
there were lands still being added to an independent Greece. In fact, that
revolution can be thought of by some Greeks as continuing down to our
time with certain Greek-speaking lands yet to be added. Things have not
really been settled yet and the problem is when, if ever, they will be
settled. What will cause them to be settled?

Now if one looks at the situation today, one also has to say that it is hard
to know whether or how things have been settled, even on a day-to-day
basis. It is hard to know what is going on at this very moment in Greece.
Who is really in charge? There have been, I gather from what one can
hear outside that country, two principal contenders for control of Greece
since the November 25 revolution or *coup d'état* or whatever one calls
that uprising of six weeks ago.

There is a general who is a more or less straightforward Army man,
more conventional, less flamboyant, less ideological (I take it) than the
Colonels. He is the President of the country and hence at least the nominal
leader of Greece today. Then there is in the background a colonel—in referring to these people as "colonels," I refer to the rank they had at the time

the last legitimate government in Greece gave them a rank. This colonel is evidently not a man to be trifled with. He is, from reports I have had and which I have reason to believe, an Army officer who has been very much involved in the recourse to torture that Greeks have been subjected to since 1967. He is something of a tyrant. Which of these two men will control Greece in the immediate future remains to be seen. If anyone here knows, he can do us a service by telling us.

IV

My own position as to how the United States should conduct itself toward Greece may be found in a letter of mine, which has been recently published in several newspapers in this Country. An earlier, shorter form of it was published in the *New York Times* of December 7, 1973. I will now read the expanded version of that letter (which was reprinted in the December 22, 1973 issue of the *Congressional Record*) as the best statement of my current understanding with a view to immediate action (vol. 119, p. 43505):

> The crisis which has toppled the bloody Papadopoulos dictatorship in Athens cannot be resolved, or even smothered, by recourse to still another military strong man, especially one with so much recent experience in torture of his fellow citizens. This crisis is rooted in the incompetence and arrogance of colonels who cannot be expected to handle intelligently the complex social and economic problems of Greece. Such usurpers cannot enlist the necessary services and good will of the better professionals, politicians and military officers of that country for the great work of reconciliation and austerity which Greece so desperately needs.

> The shortsighted role played by our government since the Colonels first took over in 1967 has already (and perhaps even permanently) compromised, in the eyes of the resentful Greek people, our legitimate interests in that country and hence in the Middle East. Among our mistakes of the past six years has been that of publicly backing the wrong men in Greece. I have found, in my visits at the State Department and the Pentagon during this period, that our policy-makers have been remarkably unequipped to consider seriously the long-range consequences of the policies they were pursuing.

> We should, before still another dictator becomes consolidated in Athens, try to redeem somewhat our good name by using our remaining influence in Greece and NATO to help the Greek people recover control of their own affairs. This can best be done, it seems to me, by vigorously encouraging the Colonels to step aside for Constantine Karamanlis, the man whose prestige as

a former conservative prime minister still recommends him to the Greek people as the best way to avoid the even bloodier crises which now threaten their country.

Greece may be the only country in the world today where the genuine popular alternative to domestic tyranny is so moderate and so experienced a politician as Mr. Karamanlis. What more can the Greeks or the United States hope for? Dare we or they risk further deterioration in Greece and in American-Greek relations? Everyone should realize by now that phony constitutions and fake elections cannot work in Greece today.

(See *Human Being and Citizen*, p. 230. See, also, *The Artist as Thinker*, pp. 331–53.)

V

Let me make two observations about what I say in this letter. One has to do with what I have referred to as the "legitimate interests" of the United States in Greece and in the Mediterranean. I take it that you and I would probably have some difference of opinion as to what are in fact legitimate American interests in various parts of the world. I can suggest what may be at the root of this difference between us by making one simple comment, which has to do with the proper role of the United States with respect to such a country as Israel. That is to say, the position which many of your group take toward Israel is, fundamentally, what I would call "ungenerous."

The other observation I have to make about what I say in my December, 1973 letter is that the causes of the November troubles in Greece were quite deep. The Colonels *are* incompetent. They had shown themselves incompetent prior to the troubles with the students in November, 1973. Students were, for the most part, expressing resentments that were not limited to just the student population of the country. One had begun to hear even from returning Greek-Americans, who had up to a year ago been more or less favorably inclined to the regime in Athens, serious complaints about the Colonels' regime. One complaint was that "they have stayed too long." Whatever plausibility there had been in the Colonels' restoring a certain kind of order had begun to vanish. In addition, Greek-Americans returning to this Country complained that inflation has become very serious in Greece.

Both of the developments complained about were, I believe, intrinsic to the Greek situation from the beginning of military rule in April, 1967. Anybody who saw the Colonels in 1967 should have recognized that they intended to stay as long as they could and would stay there the rest of their lives if they could manage that. The inflation of which everyone speaks now is directly related to the demagogic course the Colonels have pursued all along. It was quite evident from various economists one talked with over the years (conservative economists, liberal economists, it didn't matter) that the Colonels were callously mortgaging the future in order to have an immediate popular effect, and the future has already caught up with them.

VI

The need today, among friends of the Greek people, is to advance a common cause built around the agreement that the crowd now in Athens should not be permitted to stay, that the support given that crowd by the United States is improper, that that support is harmful to both Greeks and Americans, and that there should be serious efforts to make this clear to those in Washington who may be in a position to do something about it.

But I want to emphasize that the principal consideration here is a prudential one, the kind of prudence that is invoked in the Declaration of Independence where it is held up as a limiting consideration in deciding upon revolutions against illegitimate regimes. I do not believe it prudent to think in terms of revolutionary "mass movements" in Greece, for such an approach would, in effect, sacrifice Greek lives to our delusions and our theatrical inclinations. We must take care lest we stir up trouble that the Greeks will have to live with for a very long time.

One reason the Colonels have been able to stay in power so long with as little support as they have had is that most Greeks do not want civil war to break out again. They simply are not going to go back, if they can possibly help it, to what happened to them between 1945 and 1949. We should be careful not to push them in that direction. One has to keep all this in mind when thinking about what the Greeks may do and what we should expect them to do.

One hears arguments *pro* and *con* about American intervention in the affairs of other countries. I *am* willing to see American intervention in Greece, if by "intervention" one means making certain things "perfectly clear." We should make it clear that the United States will not continue to support the government in Athens; we should make it clear what we consider our legitimate interests and duties in that part of the world to be; and we should make it clear that we intend that the Greek people should resume control of their own affairs.

VII

But we should have no illusion that once the Greek people do resume control of their own affairs they will do much better than they have done before or, for that matter, even as well as we do in this troubled country. That is to say, we should have no illusion that there *is* a final solution to the problems of any people.

This takes us back to my opening remarks of this evening. I believe the nature of politics to be such that it is dangerous, reckless and, in some ways, ruthless to proceed in the faith that there is indeed a final solution or an utopian state of affairs which a people will surely reach by resolutely following a particular program. One does try to make things better. Even so, one recognizes that whatever one does will almost certainly require further improvements, that there will be falling back as well as moving forward. This is, I have observed, the nature of human affairs, and no ideology can permanently change that, however long it may conceal the truth.

34-B. The Colonels and the Press

There is about Greece a vitality, all too often undisciplined, that makes many other European countries seem tame, even dull, by comparison. This is evident immediately upon sailing into a Greek port or upon crossing a Greek border: sounds, smells, movements, colours—the very tempo of things—conspire to heighten sensibilities and intensify expectations. But alongside all this is the serene coolness, even aloofness, of what remains in Greece from classical antiquity, the visible monuments of which

---

This essay was published, in a slightly abridged form, in 3 *Journal of Modern Greek Studies* 105–10 (May 1985).

The citations in the text, unless otherwise indicated, are to Robert McDonald, *Pillar and Tinderbox: The Greek Press and the Dictatorship* (New York: Marion Boyars, 1983).

I am grateful to William H. McNeill for the opportunity to review this book as well as for opportunities to prepare, upon his recommendation, various things for the *Encyclopedia Britannica* (such as its current article on Censorship). I am also grateful to Robert and Donna McDonald for the counsel and protection they provided me during those summers in Athens (1967–70) that I was out of favor with the Greek Colonels because of what I was saying about them in the United States. See Anastaplo, *Human Being and Citizen* (Chicago: Swallow Press, 1975), pp. 3–7; Anastaplo, *The Artist as Thinker* (Athens, Ohio: Ohio University Press, 1983), pp. 331–53. See, also, the headnote for Essay No. 33, above.

The epigraph is taken from my contribution to the article on Modern Greece in the Fifteenth Edition of the *Encyclopedia Britannica*.

constantly stand as a challenge to (if not even a rebuke of) contemporary endeavours. . . .

There have been many tyrannies in Greece, tyrannies that are as much a part of the much-discussed "Greek experience" as (if not even the most frequent result of) their volatile democracies. Perhaps, it might even be said, memories of intermittent tyrannies remind Greeks of the unpredictability of human things, of the disaster that can follow upon prosperity, of the trials that even the most successful people encounter from time to time. Life can be expected to be as hard, as unyielding, and as toughening as the soil and the sea from which Greeks have for centuries wrested their livelihood. But it can also be as enriching and as exciting as the landscape and the light for which Greece has always been celebrated and that can be seen, if not at this moment or place, then surely in a little while or down the road a few kilometers.

ENCYCLOPEDIA BRITANNICA

I

Robert McDonald's account of Greek press censorship during the Colonels' 1967–74 dictatorship, *Pillar and Tinderbox*, provides as instructive an introduction in English to the political history of that troubled period as may be available anywhere in such short compass. The efforts of the Colonels to deal with the press are particularly revealing, displaying as they do both the aspirations and the shortcomings of their somewhat old-fashioned and yet curiously cynical regime. Mr. McDonald explains (p. 9):

A regime's relations with the press . . . are an excellent symptom of its essential nature and, in the case of the Colonels, the evolution of their attitudes closely mirrored their approach to society at large. In the beginning they were absolute, rigorously stifling all dissent and dictating the news. Later they tried to present a semblance of legality while maintaining control through covert, coercive means. Always, the aim of the Revolution was to create a guided political life, never to restore full democracy as was perpetually promised.

How the military regime saw the press, not without some justification, is suggested by the following observation by Mr. McDonald (p. 30):

The Colonels mistrusted the press and were afraid of it. They had an image of publishers as ruthless, unscrupulous press barons prepared to do or say anything to turn a profit and they believed newspapers to be manipulative instruments irresponsibly influencing public life from behind the scenes.

Mr. McDonald takes the title for his book from a comment on the press by the Colonels' most gifted "professional propagandist" (p. 36):

> The problem of the press is one of the most acute problems facing the free world. Press freedom is a great blessing and the pillar of the democratic way of life, but it can become a tinderbox threatening its own foundations if and when it degenerates into license or becomes a means to serve obscure interests.

This comment (at p. 2) is offset by Mr. McDonald with a line attributed to Aesop, "A liar will not be believed even when he speaks the truth."

II

The first part (pp. 13–91) of Mr. McDonald's book describes the relations of regime and press primarily in terms of personalities and episodes. The second part (pp. 93–176) describes various technical features of Greek press law and of the economics of Greek publishing; this part is supplemented by censorship regulations collected in the appendices (pp. 209–26). The third part (pp. 177–208) indicates the circumstances of the press since the fall of the Colonels, circumstances which include the development of television and a shift of the press from personal to corporate ownership, hence something of a shift from journalistic adventurism to more staid management. Always important for the standing and operations of the Greek press have been distortions due to the constant awareness on the part of barely solvent publishers that "State advertising contributes [in Greece] up to a quarter of newspapers' advertising revenues." (See pp. 129, 131, 142–43, 179, 192f, 207.)

All this is presented from the perspective of a working journalist. Mr. McDonald served, during the years of the Colonels, as a correspondent in Athens of the B.B.C. I know of no one who worked as a journalist in Greece during those years more qualified than is Mr. McDonald to tell this story. Few foreign correspondents have had the experience he has had in Greece, and Greek journalists are not likely to be temperamentally suited to provide the objectivity needed.

III

Journalism among the Greeks has long been very much a partisan activity, so much so that the press contributed significantly to the excitation of the passions which led to the 1961–1967 crisis culminating in the coup of April 21, 1967. One came to expect from Greek journalists an odd combination of the most lofty (even overblown) sentiments and the most crass (however understandable) self-interest. (See, e.g., pp. 74–75, 123, 144f, 148–49, 157–59.)

This combination was to be seen as well in the Colonels' efforts to deal with the press. But the Colonels could speak effectively neither to the higher nor to the lower elements in the press: their patriotic appeals were considered by journalists to be provincial and outdated, as well as paranoid; their financial enticements were insignificant, especially since newspapers produced pursuant to the Colonels' directives became dull and anything but profitable. Along with the effects of a sustained inflation, it was the self-righteous dullness of the Colonels' regime that helped undermine it. Then the Colonels, out of desperation and consistent with their longstanding posturing, attempted to salvage their steadily deteriorating power by exploiting the "sacred" Greek desire for *enosis* with Cyprus. The debacle that resulted both toppled the Colonels and messed up relations among Turkey, Greece and the United States for a generation. (See, e.g., pp. 90–91, 185–86. Such adventurism was predictable. See, e.g., 120 *Congressional Record* 14371, 15597, and 26618 [May 31, May 20, and August 2, 1974].)

IV

The Colonels were simply incompetent. The only thing they could do halfway well was to mount a conspiracy, and even that required extraordinary foolishness on the part of the Greek "establishment." The Colonels' ruinous inflation was prepared by the largesse they recklessly distributed in their early years to army officers, farmers, and others in an effort to make up by appeals to greed what they could not win by political skill. The Colonels' management of the press was no more competent than anything else they did, as is again and again evident from Mr. McDonald's account. Particularly revealing in this respect were the late afternoon informal press conferences for the foreign press that Stylianos Pattakos, then Minister of the Interior, conducted almost daily during the first few months after the 1967 coup. The unpredictability of all this was pointed up for me, as a participant in those bizarre affairs, when a reporter asked about a rumor that Andreas Papandreou was seriously ill in the prison where he was being held. The Minister at once picked up the telephone, demanded that he be connected with the prison, whereupon he ordered

Mr. Papandreou to be brought to the telephone. We correspondents then heard, in the course of our press conference, one side of a conversation in which Mr. Papandreou was asked whether he was well, what complaints he might have, and whether he needed anything in addition to the food being brought him from home. (I was later to confirm with Margaret Papandreou her husband's side of that surprising conversation.) This episode illustrates the direct action of which the Colonels were capable, often with considerably more disruptive effects than on this occasion. (See, e.g., pp. 25, 41, 62–63, 73, 75–78, 88–90, 173–74.)

Two summers later, I was myself surprised to see published nationwide in Greece certain embarrassing questions I had put to Prime Minister George Papadopoulos during a nationally-broadcast press conference. Newspaper publication of the complete transcripts of Mr. Papadopoulos's formal press conferences was evidently mandatory. This reflected, as much as anything did, the extent to which the Colonels' self-confidence and rigidity contributed to their failure to appreciate what was likely to hurt them. I had pressed the question whether army officers, who were troubled as many then were by developments in Greece, were as entitled to resort to the right of revolution as the Colonels believed themselves to have been in 1967. The Colonels eventually came to recognize their blunder in permitting foreign correspondents the latitude they sometimes had. This recognition was reflected in the decision to declare me *persona non grata* a second time. (I had been admitted to Greece that summer after an earlier *persona non grata* declaration had been rescinded upon the urging of an officer of the Foreign Correspondents Association in Athens. See Section I of Essay No. 40–A, below.)

V

The Colonels' press conferences, which served to expose the vulnerability of their rule, exhibited the sensitivity of virtually any Greek regime to Western, and especially American, opinion. It is evident throughout Mr. McDonald's account that the Colonels were inhibited in much that they could do or say by their concern about what foreigners would say and do. Both the military and the economic resources of the country were, as always, very much dependent on Americans and Western Europeans. (See, e.g., Helen Vlachou, "The Colonels and the Press," in Richard Clogg and George Yannopoulos, eds., *Greece Under Military Rule* [1972]. See, also, her *Kathimerini* column, November 10, 1983.) This is a dependence that may now be reinforced by Common Market arrangements, perhaps moderating thereby the disruptive effects of the often engaging Greek individuality. Also likely to have a considerable effect on Greek life is television (p. 170):

> Nightly television programming began [in 1968–69]. Set ownership soared from 10% of the population in 1970 to 83% in 1977 . . . The innovation wrought a dramatic change in Greek lifestyle. A once gregarious society, living in cafes, restaurants and cardrooms, became introverted, focussing on the domestic environment.

(See, also, pp. 166–67, 173, 206–07.) It remains to be seen what effect all this will have upon, among other things, the Greek appetite for conspiracy theories, an appetite which has contributed to the plausible complaint that the Greek press has been "'the most yellow' in the western world." (See p. 186. See, also, pp. 22, 86–87, 185–87.)

VI

Perhaps the most instructive part of Mr. McDonald's book for the Western reader is its detailed account of how press censorship did work under the Colonels. (See, e.g., pp. 40f, 107, 210f, 214f.) One can get a sense from this account of how censorship must also work, albeit much more "efficiently" and hence even worse, in countries such as the Soviet Union, where government resources are considerably greater and the ruling ideology [seems to be] more firmly established. (See, e.g., *The Soviet Censorship*, Martin Dewhirst and Robert Farrell, eds. [1983]; Harold Swayze, *Political Control of Literature in the USSR* [1962]. I should note here for the record that I have also been declared *persona non grata* by the Russians, having been expelled from the Soviet Union in the Summer of 1960. See *Human Being and Citizen*, pp. 226–28.)

One can see, as well, in Mr. McDonald's book how much more difficult it is for journalists to circumvent a prior restraint, or censorship, system than it is for them to deal with the prospect of post-publication prosecution. This was a distinction I touched upon in a memorandum I prepared for a beleaguered publisher, Helen Vlachou, while visiting her in Athens in the summer of 1967 (*The Constitutionalist*, p. 680):

> Anyone familiar with the Anglo-American tradition of "liberty of the press" appreciates the importance for friends of liberty of an insistence upon "no previous restraints." That is, the effort in the 18th and 19th Centuries to establish and secure the liberty of the press was, in large part, an effort to protect the right of anyone to publish whatever he chose without any prior control by government of the contents of such publication. It was accepted that there

could be, when something was published contrary to the law of the time or disliked by the government of the day, prosecution of the offending publisher. But it was nevertheless thought that such prosecution was not as destructive of the common good or as offensive to personal dignity as a prior review by the government of the contents of publication. Indeed, some publishers have always preferred the safety of censorship to the risk of undertaking the obligation of deciding in each case what could be responsibly and safely published.

What is or should be prosecuted after publication depends on particular circumstances, both social and personal. It should be remembered that the censor's prior restraint may be completely arbitrary and without any challenge, while the punishment for publication has at least the safeguard (except in the most oppressive regimes) of some judicial process in open court. It should be remembered as well that self-regulation recognizes the dignity and sense of responsibility of the publisher.

In the best of all worlds, there would be neither censorship (previous restraint) nor any punishment for honest publication. But it is certainly important that there at least be no censorship, leaving the publisher free to run the risks of honest publication.

VII

It will not do, after having noticed the irresponsibility of the Greek press in the 1960s, to leave this subject without acknowledging that Greek intellectuals, including journalists, did refuse by and large to cooperate with the Colonels in power. In fact, their response was generally far better than that exhibited by all too many influential Greek-Americans, including those in the Greek-American press, who proved remarkably respectful of the Colonels, thereby encouraging the American State Department to rely upon the disastrous policy that it pursued with respect to the Greek dictatorship. It should be noticed as well that the Greeks have been able, under the Conservative leadership of Constantine Karamanlis, to pursue a "policy of reconciliation" since the fall of the Colonels. Mr. McDonald reports (p. 185):

> The military had handed back power to Karamanlis on the tacit understanding that punishment would be limited to those who had committed crimes such as treason, torture and corruption and that there would be no purge of collaborators. Karamanlis concurred because he believed such leniency would alienate the least number of people and limit the breeding ground for future revolt. The *quid pro quo* was the legalization of the Communist Party and free access to public life for left-wing citizens.

The extent of reconciliation is reflected in the fact that Mr. Papandreou could, as a Socialist prime minister, endorse Mr. Karamanlis's reelection to the Greek presidency in 1985. This policy of national reconciliation has yet to be extended, however, to King Constantine, who did try to conduct himself gallantly in the face of the Colonels, atoning thereby for the serious mistakes that he as a new, young, and badly advised monarch had made in 1965–66. That is, it remains to be seen whether the Greek people can some day, after the Karamanlis presidency, make proper use of King Constantine's informed and sobered good will. (See pp. 19, 22, 34, 40, 50–51, 108, 165–66.)

It is useful, then, to have Mr. McDonald's account both of what the Colonels were like and what censorship, whether in Greece or elsewhere, can look like. What is not properly appreciated in such accounts, and this does suggest the general limitations of modern intellectuals, is the legitimate power of the community through its governments and otherwise to shape the citizen-body. That the Colonels misconceived and misused that power does not mean that the community as preceptor should never be taken seriously. (See pp. 36–37.) Thus just as Marxists can respond to and often exploit any chronic sense of social injustice among a people, so can militarists exploit any apparent disregard by politicians and intellectuals of old-fashioned moral and patriotic concerns.

To put all this another way, readers should be reminded that Mr. McDonald himself was so competent and trustworthy a journalist in large part because he himself had been shaped both by the Canadian community from which he came and by the British community for which he prepared his reliable reports from Athens.

35

POLITICS, GLORY, AND RELIGION

*Now we not only proceed from the assumption that no one should inter-
fere in matters of the individual's conscience. We also say that the moral
values that religion generated and embodied for centuries can help in the
work of renewal in our country, too.*

MIKHAIL GORBACHEV

I

Of all the memorials here in Santa Croce which is, as the guides say, the
Florentine equivalent of Westminster Abbey, the inscription for Niccolò
Machiavelli is one of the simplest and perhaps most ambiguous: TANTO
NOMINI NVLLVM PAR ELOGIVM. "For such a name, no eulogy." This
can be taken to mean, "For one of such a name, no praise suffices." Or,
"For one of such a name, no praise is possible." Or, both, if not something
else also.

This sort of recognition does reflect the ambiguous status of Machiavelli, suggesting that whoever composed the epitaph knew what he was
doing. Machiavelli's status was evidently such that it took three centuries
to get "him" into this church. Even so, his memorial got into this church
before his books got off the Index. In fact, I believe his books remained
on the Index until that institution was itself abolished a few years ago.

Similar comments could be made about the recognition of Galileo Gali-
lei in this church. He did get in considerably before Machiavelli did; but,
then, Galileo did not deal directly with the Church, religion, and moral

---

This talk was given to the Rome Program, The School of Law, Loyola University of Chicago, at Santa Croce Church, Florence, Italy, June 6, 1984. (Original title: "Niccolò Machiavelli and Florence.")

The epigraph is taken from the *Christian Science Monitor*, December 11, 1989, p. 12 (reporting a statement made by Mikhail Gorbachev in Rome, Italy, December 1, 1989).

issues. After all, Machiavelli is remembered by many as a teacher of evil. An exchange I overheard here this morning between an American college student and his mother sums up our problem nicely: "He wrote the *Prince*. It justifies anything." "And he is buried *here*?"

Consider by way of comparison Dante Alighieri, who has here both a memorial within the church (he is buried in Ravenna, where he died an exile) and *the* monument in front of the church ("L'Italia"). Dante is remembered not only as a great Italian patriot, but even more as the founder of the modern Italian language, especially in his great poem describing the Inferno, Purgatorio, and Paradiso in terms which appear more or less compatible with orthodox religious belief.

There was, it seems, considerable resistance to bringing Machiavelli into this church, honoring him here as he now is. Was not that an understandable resistance by pious men of some discernment? What is interesting, however, is that the partisans of Machiavelli should have wanted him brought in.

II

Why was Machiavelli brought into this church? There is, of course, a prior question which we need only touch upon on this occasion: Why bring anyone here at all? That is, why recognize anyone, here or anywhere else? Is not this related to the existence of a desire for continuity and the development of a sense of community? Consider, for example, the significance of the D-Day celebrations this past week. (One recalls where one was when the news came exactly forty years ago; one may even recall one's regret then of not having the opportunity to be in France on that great day.) Do not such recollections make things appear more meaningful? All this is related to the appeal, and perhaps the limitations, of that glory of which Machiavelli seems to make so much, and to which I will return.

Perhaps Machiavelli himself was brought into this church not so much to legitimate him, although there may be some of that, but primarily because he *is* eminent. (To what degree, or in what way, is one's name related to one's *self*?) He is especially eminent as an advocate of a united Italy, and the Nineteenth Century did see the attainment of that goal. Machiavelli, after all, had said in the final (the twenty-sixth) chapter of his *Prince* that the barbarian domination of Italy stank.

Machiavelli was seen as a great son of Florence, just as had been Michelangelo, whose body was secretly taken from its Roman burial place for return to his city. He too may be found in this church. The recognition here of Machiavelli points up not only the importance of his accomplishments and reputation; it also reflects the special place for Italians of *their* Church. It is not simply a religious institution; it is also social and political. There is a dimension to the Church here that we Americans are not apt to appreciate, with our casual talk of "the separation of church and state," which may be related to the fact that there is no single obviously dominant church in our Country. Westminster Abbey is another instance of the sort of thing found in Italy: the religious orthodoxy of those buried or otherwise commemorated in the Abbey is *not* guaranteed—everyone understands this—but their eminence certainly is.

III

So, midway along the right-hand wall in Santa Croce, which is the lefthand wall as one looks to the entrance from the altar, is to be found Machiavelli's monument. Similarly, in the Piazza degli Uffizi the statue of Machiavelli is (with that of his intimate associate, Francesco Guicciardini) midway in the array of the statues of the great men of Florence. The Florentine Renaissance was a remarkable flowering, like Fifth Century Athens. Also remarkable is how many of those people still matter. The accomplishments of the men gathered in that piazza are reflected in and related to the visible signs of Florence's onetime greatness, which may be seen all around them: in the Signoria next door; in the nearby statues of David, Perseus, and others; in the Uffizi Gallery itself; and in the Duomo and the Baptistry, just down the way.

There are twenty-two statues in the Piazza degli Uffizi array, with Machiavelli's the eleventh and Guicciardini's the twelfth. If one adds the two Medici statues, just behind the first ones, at what is now the entrance to the Uffizi Gallery, there are twenty-four statues in this collection facing the Piazza, with Machiavelli's still one of the central ones as the thirteenth, along with Giovanni Boccaccio's at Machiavelli's right as the twelfth. Reminders of these men may be found all around us: thus we are told that the Rosary College establishment in which my wife and I are staying this weekend (the Villa Schifanoia) was where Boccaccio wrote some of the *Decameron*.

The position in the Piazza degli Uffizi array of the Medicis is another nice touch. The two Medici statues are set back, which properly reflects the way the Medicis ruled Florence: not openly, but nonetheless firmly. One wonders just who did plan all this with the considerable insight evident here. The first of the statues thus set back is that of Cosimo de

Medici, "the Old One," who held power for thirty-one years; he is shown looking down, quite serious. He is here acclaimed as "the Father of his Country." (Cosimo de Medici, although perhaps something of a free thinker, is buried most prominently in the Church of St. Lorenzo, right before the altar; he is recognized there as well as "the Father of his Country.") Lorenzo de Medici's face in his Piazza de Uffizi statue here resembles his rather startling portrait in the Uffizi Gallery, the portrait of a quite intelligent, perhaps somewhat crafty, and certainly tough man.

IV

Our observations about the Uffizi arcade, the corridor of fame, also point up the social-political character of the Church, especially as an institution which is very much the Italians'. The Italians can especially appreciate a joke now making the rounds in Rome: A very pious priest is granted by God the opportunity to ask Him three questions. He begins, "Will women ever be ordained?" To which God answers, "Not in your lifetime, my son." "Will priests be permitted to marry?" "Not in your lifetime, my son." "Will there be another Polish pope?" "Not in my lifetime, my son."

I am reminded of the time, described by Machiavelli in his *History of Florence,* when the Pope placed Florence under a ban. Machiavelli matter-of-factly reports, however, that the Florentines forced their priests to provide services. Although the authority of the Pope was not fully or even simply denied, it was assumed it could be circumvented and that the services thus conducted (under compulsion) would "work." (Would Americans think so in like circumstances? Would they not be "obliged" to deny either the authority of the law-giver or the validity of the compelled service? This raises the questions, as much else we have been discussing in our seminars does, of what *law* means, what it depends on, and what it does.)

It is remarkable that the Pope should for so long have been openly involved in politics and in war without losing altogether his spiritual authority or his personal physical immunity, however careful they had to be about being captured. (We notice that the attempted assassination of a Pope in our own time was at the immediate hands of someone who came from a non-Christian background.) Even so, it may be true that what the Florentines did in forcing their priests to provide services anticipates the Reformation. In addition, the willingness of popes to fight others, as earthly princes, may well have gotten communities into the habit of opposing them in such a way as to open the way to the Reformation.

V

What would Machiavelli himself have thought of his memorial here? No doubt this elevation would have at least appealed to his sense of humor. But what he would have fully thought of his recognition here depends, in part, on what he truly thought of the Church as well as of glory.

One massive fact would have been apparent to Machiavelli: the Church must have been doing something right to be able to endure and to prosper as it has, maintaining as it has its dominion for almost two millennia. Also, the Church provides means down to our day for Italy to have a world-wide influence quite out of proportion to its numbers, just as Russia has had a worldwide influence throughout much of the Twentieth Century because of Communist Parties in various countries. The Church can be recognized as a significant political institution, one to be studied by the student and to be reckoned with by the political man.

It seems to me likely, considering what Machiavelli says about the nature of public opinion, that an institution ministering to and shaping people with a view to morality and mortality is inevitable in every community. But did he not consider pre-Christian Roman religious opinions more useful for serious political endeavors? Consider here what he says in *The Prince* about Moses as one of the greatest Founders and what the relation is between Moses and Christianity. A papal mass, especially in St. Peter's, permits one to see how theatrical, and even spectacular, religious ceremony can be. Has the Church continued and perhaps refined Roman traditions and practices with respect to such matters? It *is* difficult to see in such manifestations, however, the primitive religious sensibility associated with Jesus and his immediate followers in the Holy Land. One can appreciate upon first coming to Rome what Luther was put off by. He evidently did not stay there long enough to allow the place to "grow" on him, as it obviously can.

VI

A useful comparison can be made between the regime of Florence and that of the Church. Machiavelli indicates in his *History of Florence* that his city was really governed by princes, but from behind the forms of a republic. (Consider how the Roman emperors continued to use the Senate, the title of Consul, and other institutions of republican Rome. Was this not a tribute to and a dependence on the greatness of their predecessors? Consider, also, what Thucydides says about Pericles' standing in Athens.) The princely family, the Medicis, were, it is evident, quite cultured: this is obvious in the Uffizi Gallery, which is in large part *their* collection; this may be seen, also, in the library at the Church of St. Lorenzo. Some deterioration in family taste had set in, to be sure, by the time the Medici chapel was built at St. Lorenzo.

At the same time, was not (is not?) the Church substantially republican, even though it exhibits the form of an absolute monarchy? This may be seen in how its leader is chosen, especially since there is clearly no hereditary succession. A man of ability, without any family connections, can rise to the very top of the hierarchy. Does not this reflect the underlying opinion that all souls are equal in the sight of God? One of the most interesting features for me of the papal audience we attended last Wednesday at St. Peter's was the way the Pope conducted himself after the formal proceedings, not only with the people who surged up to him, but even more with his colleagues on the stage: he was "pressing the flesh," embracing and being embraced like a Chicago "politico." (One wonders who was permitted and by whom to go up on the stage at the end. Also instructive was to see one of the red-capped leaders of the Church coolly and smilingly beat out two women for a taxicab on a nearby street a half-hour or so after he had been on stage with the Pope.)

How effective a monarch a pope can be may depend in large part on how he does get on with the princes of his church, the very men who have chosen him. Among the things he must do to secure their support—the help of the bureaucracy and the respect of the many—seems to be his willingness at least in appearance to submit to the forms required of him in public manifestations. Thus, except for the homily he may deliver, a pope during a service such as a papal mass is dressed, undressed, and in various ways moved around and used like an instrument of the Church. (It is in this respect surprisingly like what is done to St. Peter's statue in the basilica on the Feast Day of Saints Peter and Paul, which is dressed up magnificently, crown and all.)

Such are the considerations that Machiavelli could well have taken note of in assessing the Church as a political institution, even as he retained his reservations about what this particular religion does to the ability of a people and its leaders to act with the toughness and astuteness required by serious politics and hence war.

VII

All this is not to deny that Machiavelli had deep differences with the Church. But he did seem to recognize its merits and its uses, including its political usefulness. It is, after all, an institution which can assimilate even

a Machiavelli to a considerable extent. I understand that Machiavelli himself recognized the power of the Church as it bore not only upon his family, but perhaps also upon his reputation and long-run influence, in that he
exhibited a proper deathbed relation to the Church.

Machiavelli, it can be said, recognized in the Church a worthy opponent, not only with respect to temporal political, moral, and educational
matters, but also with respect to what it offered of enduring worth. Is not
the power of the Church rooted in what it can plausibly say about immortality? But, Machiavelli complains, the Church-inspired concern with
immortality can lead to a harmful disregard for the things of this world.

Machiavelli is also aware of the attractions of immortality. Does he not
offer a kind of immortality in what he says about glory? He argues that
the man who knows what he is doing can control the relevant evidence
and his enduring reputation far more than people, including the ancient
thinkers, generally recognize.

Yet reputation and hence glory can be most unreliable. Does it not depend to a considerable extent on the doings and the opinions of others?
Cannot the same be said, in a way, about the Church's offer with respect
to immortality, in that one does depend on others if one is to be exposed
to the decisive Message and to be properly instructed to take advantage
of it? One's dependence on others, including as to whether one's writings
and hence one's teaching can do what one intends, may be seen in how we
ourselves respond to the many plaques we see here in Florence as in
Rome celebrating a great life or a great deed: such memorials may be
barely noticed or, if read, hardly understood.

It can be said, therefore, that one who is moved by glory *is* at the mercy
of others. Compare an approach that says, "The good is worth pursuing,
or contemplating, for its own sake." But this latter approach does presuppose a reliable or permanent and knowable good. This in turn reminds us
of the problem of nature for Machiavelli.

To speak of nature is to ask whether the good may be secured independent both of political success and of one's recognition by others. Machiavelli seems to have thought not. Yet he seems to have believed that the
political activity he directed and made so much of did minister to a natural desire, the only serious natural desire men are sometimes capable of
satisfying. He seems to have thought that men are far more capable of
controlling fortune and hence political life than the ancient thinkers believed, and that men are far less capable of possessing and contemplating
unchanging truths than the ancients believed. He evidently saw one form
of acquisition as illusory, the other as more reliable.

This is not to deny that he recognized that even the political success of
the greatest founders was limited to a few millennia, however long there-

after the memory of such success might linger in some form or other. Must Machiavelli settle, then, for a "manufactured" good which can have only the appearance of the enduring?

VIII

The problem of glory is reflected in how varied the stories are that the guides tell before the memorial to Machiavelli here in Santa Croce. The dates that are given seem to be correct; also correct are his name and the facts that he wrote a famous (or infamous) book and that he is identified with the unity of Italy. Beyond that, what the guides are moved to say is quite a chancy business.

But it is not only the slippery Machiavelli who is hard to be clear about. A bored young man who was in our train compartment on our way up here to Florence last Thursday had spent most of his time sleeping, when he was not working out line-drawing games in a popular magazine. But he brightened up when we pulled into his Florence, as he pointed out to us the landmarks: "the Duomo of Michelangelo, the Campanile of Giotto." Of course, he was no more than half right, if that: it is not the Duomo of Michelangelo, but rather of Brunelleschi (at least the dome is Brunelleschi's); as for the Campanile, it was begun by Giotto.

There are better and worse ways of remembering someone's accomplishments. Indeed, *how* one is remembered may testify to the effect one truly has on others. Brunelleschi, who seems to be buried in the Duomo, is provided a rather modest epitaph there, as if to recognize that he needs no memorial other than the Duomo itself. The same, it can be said, is done with Machiavelli's eulogy here in Santa Croce: *his* work is the modern world, even more than Italy herself.

Still, it can be argued that Michelangelo *is* properly associated with the Duomo not only because of what he did in "retroactively" making the Duomo (and Florence itself) his work (he is said to have been influenced by Florence when he turned to designing or, rather, redesigning St. Peter's in Rome), but also because of what he is reputed to have said about the attempt to provide the Duomo the marble facing it obviously needs around its middle. The bare brick work we see makes it appear that something has fallen off, except for the one section that *was* done and to which Michelangelo is supposed to have reacted so unfavorably ("It looks like a cricket cage.").

It is a perverse tribute to Michelangelo that the Duomo's exterior should remain unfinished to this day. Certainly, the rest of the proposed "cricket cage" would be better than what we now have.

IX

Do not modern recollections of Machiavelli also tend to be "no more than half right"? This may be partly because of the limitations of those who recall him and partly because of his own efforts and limitations.

Even so, what our fellow traveller on the train said about the Duomo and the Campanile is significant. For it *was* said with a joyful pride, which exhibited the considerable pleasure it can give one to claim such things as somehow one's own.

Such pride often does rest, perhaps even necessarily, on not altogether reliable information. But it *can* provide satisfaction, sustenance and guidance. Joyful pride—the pride of the patriot who senses in his bones what is his own—may be seen in the way the Florentines to this day respond to their lovely, vital city (the product, in part, of chance circumstances, immunities, and developments). Last night, for example, one could see up on the Piazzale Michelangelo a remarkable crowd, including many young people, visiting with each other and obviously enjoying their city, especially the view they have from there of the Duomo, the Signoria, and the Campanile. Something of this may also be seen in Rome at the Observatory site overlooking the city, not far from our quarters at Loyola's Rome Center, and up at the Pincio, among other places.

Contributing to the effect of Florence upon its citizens must be the fact that it *is* a city of human proportions. This is reflected in the fact that we have repeatedly run into each other here the past few days, something that has not been happening to us in Rome. This is even more so, I have been told, when one lives here a while: one begins to recognize Florentine residents and to be recognized by them. (I have also been told that one can come to appreciate the cynical wit of the Florentines one encounters.)

X

The pride of citizens in their men of distinction may be seen in happenings very much in the news since we have been here in Florence. Perhaps you have noticed the newspaper headlines, since yesterday morning, about the grave illness of Enrico Berlinguer. He is, some of you know, the Secretary-General of the Italian Communist Party; he suffered a massive cerebral hemorrhage Thursday night in Padua, which he is not expected to survive.

The Berlinguer role both in Eurocommunist discussions and in Italian politics, where he has been for some time now a figure much respected as a humane and honest politician who is first an Italian and then a Communist, makes him a man of considerable distinction in Italy. A similar respect, it seems, was accorded to his most illustrious predecessor as Secretary-General of the Italian Communist Party, Palmiro Togliatti.

To go back even further, there is Girolamo Savonarola, a friar who did much of his work, and was executed, here in Florence: he also can be recognized as someone of distinction, even though he too was ultimately denied the power he sought. There is in this city a Piazza Savonarola, and his cell at the Church of San Marco is on display despite the fact that he was finally repudiated as a demagogue. (One notices that there are relatively few clergy in evidence here, compared to Rome. Florence may not be a fully congenial place for them.)

Stature can be recognized in one's opponents, especially if that opponent should be, in a sense, one's own. Even a memorial by and to Benito Mussolini remains in Rome. The Romans explain its presence by complaining that the Americans once kept them from destroying that shaft, but what keeps them from doing so now? Machiavelli recognized that deeds of imagination and breadth, even when shocking, can engage the interest of one's people.

XI

We return now to our opening inquiry into the relation of Machiavelli to the Church.

I suspect Machiavelli saw much of Italy and of himself, and even of the ancient Romans he praised, in the Church. He would have preferred to have the Church more "manly," more "Mosaic," than he believed it to be in his day. (It is odd that he should be recognized in this church of the Franciscans, a quite peaceable order; it is, as you can see, a large but simple church, certainly when compared to many others you have seen by now.)

In any event, Machiavelli's influence *is* seen in the manly delicacy of the inscription on his memorial here. As for the possible manliness of religion: consider the role of the Church in Poland today, the role of piety in the Roman Republic, and the role of the Greek Church during the Turkish occupation, to say nothing of the Crusades and of the Inquisition.

I also suspect that the Church, however grudgingly, has seen much of itself and of the Italian patriot in Machiavelli despite what Leo Strauss called his "anti-theological ire." After all, one can notice in Rome's Piazza San Pietro that although St. Peter has the keys, St. Paul has the sword. One is reminded of Machiavelli's warnings about the limitations of an "unarmed prophet" such as Savonarola. A picture showing the burning of

Savonarola was on exhibit, when I was last there some twenty years ago, in the house where Machiavelli lived in exile a few miles outside of Florence. It would be instructive to learn whether it or its equivalent was there during Machiavelli's stay in that house.

XII

Is this passion on Machiavelli's part—his "anti-theological ire"—itself somewhat "theological" in character? It is hard to imagine a Socrates, for instance, moved by such a passion, even though Socrates was more apt than perhaps Machiavelli so to conduct himself as to run risks of trouble with religious authorities. Consider, also, what Socrates would have said about the importance for Machiavelli of political success.

We are raising the question now of what Machiavelli did say and whether he truly understood himself. He is not simply a revived ancient. For one thing, much of what he thinks, feels and does is in relation, albeit somewhat in opposition, to the Church. One way or another, he has been to a considerable extent shaped by the Church.

XIII

One senses not only that there has been in Christendom, partly because of (and partly in opposition to, or in spite of?) the Church, not only a remarkable disciplining of human energy, but also an even more remarkable generation of energy over many centuries, something by which the unbeliever as well as the believer can be impressed. Perhaps the non-believer should be impressed even more than the believer, since the believer can more easily account for all this outpouring of spirit as manifestations of the divine will. But then, one might ask, are the great idolatrous monuments of Egypt and of India to be similarly understood?

It can be said that for the Italian to take pride in and show allegiance to both *his* established Church and *his* iconoclastic political thinker may depend not only on making much of one's own, but also on a failure to understand either fully. Perhaps another way of putting all this is to recognize that we are challenged by these manifestations, including the great movements of the spirit which, for example, permitted bringing Machiavelli into this church upon the promptings of partisans who wanted him thus accepted. We are challenged to try to understand what the relation is between the earthly and the spiritual, between the eternal and the temporal.

36

IN GOD WE TRUST?

Professor Goldwin Smith, with whom [the Earl of Rosebery] was on terms of intimate acquaintance and correspondence, said of him to me in Toronto in 1900, "Rosebery feels about Democracy as if he were holding a wolf by the ears." This was a harsh judgment and probably beyond the truth; but it was not opposed to the truth. As the franchise broadened and the elegant, glittering, imposing trappings faded from British Parliamentary and public life, Lord Rosebery was conscious of an ever-widening gap between himself and the Radical electorate. The great principles "for which Hampden died in the field and Sidney on the scaffold," the economics and philosophy of Mill, the venerable inspiration of Gladstonian memories, were no longer enough. One had to face the caucus, the wire-puller and the soap-box; one had to stand on platforms built of planks of all descriptions. He did not like it. He could not do it. He would not try. He knew what was wise and fair and true. He would not go through the laborious, vexatious and at times humiliating processes necessary under modern conditions to bring about these great ends. He would not stoop; he did not conquer.

Winston S. Churchill

I

My primary concern on this occasion is to reconsider and refine a few questions about American constitutional law, especially with respect to

This talk was given at the Annual Convention, American Political Science Association, Washington, D.C., September 1, 1984. (Sponsor: The Center for the Study of the Constitution. Original title: "Machaivelli, Veronese and Lincoln on Political Religion' and 'The Separation of Church and State.' ") Reproductions of the two paintings commented on were made available on that occasion.

The epigraph is taken from Winston S. Churchill, *Great Contemporaries* (London: Thornton Butterworth, 1937), pp. 18–19.

the Religion Clauses of the First Amendment. Although the questions themselves should be familiar, the materials used in addressing them here (materials from Sixteenth-Century Italy, for the most part) are not of the kind usually considered by American constitutional scholars. It is hoped that the novelty of such materials in this context can help enliven and even illuminate discussions of a subject that is all too often limited to parochial issues.

There is in Venice a marvelous painting by Paolo Caliari Veronese, *The Battle of Lepanto*. It depicts the great naval battle of October 7, 1571, in which the outnumbered ships of Europe beat back the Turkish navy in the Corinthian Gulf, thereby marking the beginning of the end of the ascendancy of the Ottoman Empire in Southern Europe and the Western Mediterranean. The Battle of Lepanto was for Sixteenth-Century Europe what the Battle of Salamis had been for Fifth-Century Greece, a vindication of the integrity of the West as against the East.

The principal European allies at Lepanto (also known as Naupactus) were Venice, Spain, and the Papal States. Veronese's canvas, which may be seen in Venice's Gallerie dell'Accademia, is divided virtually in half by a heavy bank of clouds. In its upper part, fervent pleas are being made to the Virgin, pleas that obviously refer to the momentous naval battle in the crowded sea depicted in the lower part of the painting. Rays of light and flaming shafts are directed through the cloud bank into the embattled fleets below.

The pleas to the Virgin (at whose side St. Peter stands, holding his keys) come primarily from a kneeling woman, wearing a diadem and holding a dagger (pointing down) in her right hand. This is said to be St. Giustina, on whose feast day the battle was fought. She seems to be sponsored by St. Mark, with his lion by his side. To her left is another kneeling figure in Dominican garb, St. Rocco. St. Mark and he serve as the patron saints of Venice. Immediately to St. Giustina's right, also kneeling, is a figure of whom nothing can be seen but its white garb and one hand. The rest of the heavenly host seems to be made up of angels, including one who is quite actively dispatching burning arrows into the Turkish fleet.

The anti-Ottoman alliance, or Sacred League, at Lepanto was Christian as well as European. Rather, one could say that it was European (or anti-Ottoman) in that it was Christian. The appeal to the Virgin depicted by Veronese suggests the historic dependence of Europe, as such, on divine providence. It is taken for granted that Europe could not be the Europe we know without Christian sanction in heaven as well as on earth.

It can also be said to be taken for granted by Veronese that the well-being, or at least the survival, of Europe is in the interest of heaven. Both

St. Peter and St. Mark seem to be interested parties, and the Virgin herself, it was assumed, could be moved to intervene. The heavenly powers
care for what happens on earth: is it not there and only there that things go
on which permanently affect dispositions of human souls after death?
One is reminded of comparable scenes on Homer's Olympus where the
gods are again and again entreated to intervene in human battles (as Zeus
is by Thetis on behalf of her son Achilles) but where earthly doings provide important diversions, if not even the decisive sense of purpose, for
divinities.

There is celebrated in Veronese's painting an alliance between Heaven
and Earth, between the Eternal and the Temporal. Neither the religious
(or spiritual) nor the civic (or political) stands alone. The dependence of
the city on the beneficence of the divine is evident. Also evident, although
not as noticeable at first glance, is how important the city considers itself
to be, so important that it can indeed secure divine aid: what happens on
earth is not so inconsequential that it would be presumptuous to invoke
the divine. It remains a nice question as to which trait is primary here, the
humility of the city or its pride.

Such depictions as Veronese's remind us that the distinctions we conveniently make between "church" and "state" can be to some extent arbitrary if not even contrived. The typical Sixteenth-Century European would
have regarded the political and the spiritual as inextricably interwoven,
just as an ancient Greek would have considered meaningless the advocacy
of any attempted "separation" of "temple" (or "cult") and "*polis*."

It should at once be added, however, that the Greeks would not have
assumed, as pious men would be apt to do today, that "religious" considerations should be sovereign in the conduct of one's life. Rather, they
could as easily have understood even ritual and worship to be within the
legitimate power of the *polis* to prescribe and regulate, however much
they could sympathize with the plight of an Antigone. To what extent or
in what sense was this true in Sixteenth-Century Christendom as well, especially in those places where religious leaders exercised temporal power?
Be that as it may have been, is not the governance of any religious institution likely to be itself the expression of temporal concerns and hence an
exercise of *political* power?

The Western way of life, which was believed to have been at stake at
Lepanto, is then very much influenced by Christianity. In this sense Christianity has long been vital to the West. But is not the converse also true,
that Christianity (or, a transformed Judaism for the Gentiles) is very much
dependent on the pagan West, especially on Greek thought and Roman
law? In this sense too the spiritual is keyed to the political.

This may be glimpsed in still another painting to be found in the Accademia of Venice, the *Apparition of Eternity* by Bonifacio de' Pitati. That work, painted two to three decades before Veronese's canvas, is about the same size as *The Battle of Lepanto*. Like Veronese's, it is divided by a heavy cloud bank between a heavenly domain, where a bearded divinity (the Eternal Father) and several angels may be seen, and an earthly domain, where there may be seen in considerably dimmer tones a vision of eternity that takes the form of a neatly portrayed Piazza of St. Mark in Venice. The Campanile, on the right-hand side of the picture, thrusts up into the cloud bank. Thus Venice at its finest can provide a model for eternity. We can again see that our distinction between "church" and "state" depends on modern presuppositions which, however salutary they may be in our circumstances, are all too often unexamined.

A traditional American concern is that religion, if not scrupulously kept in its proper place, is apt to intrude into and inflame political matters. But pious men before the Nineteenth Century were sometimes more concerned, as they can still be today, lest political considerations be permitted to control and exploit religious life, however more elevated the latter may seem. Consider the view one gets from the top of the Campanile in Venice: it is only when one stands well above it all that one can see that St. Mark's Church, which dominates the Piazza for the pedestrian below, is little more than an appendage to the adjoining Ducal Palace. Parallels have been seen in British life, as should be evident from the following passage in a 1927 English account of Veronese's career (Percy H. Osmond, *Paolo Veronese*, p. 1):

> He has rightly been called "the painter of the glory of Venice." That glory was a matter, not of intellectual pre-eminence, but of material prosperity and wealth. It was a type of greatness which should have a special interest for the average Englishman, since it was based on sea-power and trade. Lepanto, twice celebrated by Veronese's brush, was the Venetian Trafalgar, and Venezia, who so often figures on his canvases as the personification of the Republic, becomes by degrees almost identical in build and aspect with the wave-ruling Britannia. In both States a buxom matron becomes, to all intents and purposes, the object of popular worship. Even the prescriptive religion of Venice bore a distant resemblance to Anglicanism in its subjection to the State and its independent attitude towards the papacy.

Both of the paintings glanced at here, *Apparition of Eternity* and *The Battle of Lepanto*, were executed within a half-century after Niccolò Machiavelli's death. How would he have regarded their presuppositions and teachings?

II

Machiavelli, when he begins to discuss "the most excellent" men "who have become princes by their own virtues and not by fortune," takes Moses as his point of departure. His Hall of Fame includes "Moses, Cyrus, Romulus, Theseus and the like."

This array is to be found in the first of the passages in *The Prince* where Machiavelli clearly draws upon the Bible. All of the Biblical texts drawn upon are taken from the Old Testament. (They are in Chapters VI, XIII, and XXVI of *The Prince*.)

Christianity (or the New Testament) is again and again dealt with in its contemporary temporal manifestations such as the doings of popes, in its effects on civic duties and on the character and capacities of citizens, and in its seeming dependence on unarmed prophets who are bound to fail in this world. Insofar as Machiavelli deals with the distinctive teachings of Christianity, he can be said to criticize their political consequences. Insofar as he deals with the Church as a political "force" to be reckoned with, he can be said to have somewhat anticipated that assessment by what he says about (the superior?) Old Testament leaders and institutions.

The first of the three invocations of the Old Testament by Machiavelli in *The Prince*, upon which we have already drawn, can now be set forth in its entirety as it is found in Chapter VI:

> But in order to come to those who have become princes by their own virtue and not by fortune, I say that the most excellent are Moses, Cyrus, Romulus, Theseus, and the like. And although one ought not to reason of Moses, he having been a mere executor of the things that were ordained by God, he ought yet to be admired, if only for the grace which made him worthy to speak with God. But let us consider Cyrus and the others who have acquired or founded kingdoms: you will find them all wonderful; and if their particular actions and orders are considered, they seem not discrepant from those of Moses, who had so great a preceptor. And in examining their actions and life, one sees that fortune provided them with nothing other than the occasion which gave them the matter into which they could introduce whatever form they pleased; without that occasion the virtue of their mind would have been extinguished, and without that virtue the occasion would have come in vain.

> It was necessary, then, for Moses to find the people of Israel in Egypt, enslaved and oppressed by the Egyptians, so that they, in order to escape their servitude, would be disposed to follow him. It was fitting that Romulus not remain in Alba, that he be exposed at birth, so that he might want to become king of Rome and founder of that fatherland. It was needful that Cyrus find the Persians malcontented with the imperium of the Medes, and the Medes

soft and effeminate from long peace. Theseus would have been unable to demonstrate his virtue if he had not found the Athenians scattered [in the countryside]. These occasions, therefore, made these men happy, and their excellent virtue made the occasion known; whence their fatherland was ennobled and became most happy.

Is it not evident here that all of "the most excellent" political leaders, or founders, do much the same things that God did through Moses? Put another way, even God is a "Machiavellian" in that He recognizes and applies the political principles that Machiavelli has rediscovered. Therefore, to speak of "the separation of church and state" does not make much sense in this setting either. (That Romulus and Theseus, as well as Moses, put "religion" to thorough use politically is generally known. Perhaps this can also be said of Cyrus, especially if this should be taken to be Xenophon's Cyrus.)

It should be noticed not only that these God-like leaders were made "happy" by the exercise of "their excellent virtue," but also that such exercise permitted their respective fatherlands to be "ennobled" and to become "most happy." It seems that it need not matter for the effective promotion of a people's nobility and happiness whether the established and utilized religion be pagan or Biblical, whatever reservations Machiavelli may have had about contemporary teachings and practices grounded in the New Testament.

The second of the three invocations by Machiavelli of the Old Testament in *The Prince* may be found in Chapter XIII (all of our passages from *The Prince* are taken from the pioneering translation by Leo Paul S. de Alvarez):

A wise prince, therefore, has always avoided [the arms of others] and turned to his own. He has wished rather to lose with his own than to win with those of others, judging that it is not a true victory which with alien arms has been acquired. I shall never doubt of citing Cesare Borgia and his actions. This Duke entered the Romagna with auxiliary arms, conducting only French troops, and with them he took Imola and Forli. But when such arms no longer appeared to him safe, he turned to mercenaries, judging that these were less dangerous, and he hired the Orsini and Vitelli. Finding them uncertain and unfaithful and dangerous to manage, he then extinguished them, and turned to his own. One can easily see the difference between the one and other of these arms, if one considers the difference in the reputation of the Duke when he first had only the French, then when he had the Orsini and Vitelli, and finally, when he was left with his own soldiers and himself to depend on; and one will find it always growing—never was he so esteemed than when everyone saw that he was entirely the possessor of his own arms.

I did not want to depart from Italian and fresh examples, yet I do not want to omit Hiero of Syracuse, who was one of those named above by me. That man, as I said, was made the head of the armies by the Syracusans. He immediately came to know that the mercenary militia was not useful, because it was like our Italian *condottieri;* and since it seemed to him that he could neither keep them nor let them go, he had them all cut into pieces: and from then on he waged war with his own arms and not alien ones. I wish also to recall to memory a figure of the Old Testament, made for this point. When David offered himself to Saul to fight Goliath the Philistine challenger, Saul, in order to give him courage, armed him with his own arms, which, as soon as David had them on, he rejected, saying that he could not be of as good worth with them as by himself, and that he therefore wished to find the enemy with his sling and with his knife. In fine, the arms of others either fall off your back, weigh you down, or constrict you.

It is taken for granted here that David, however he may have been chosen and inspired by God, conducted himself as other knowledgeable leaders have done, including somewhat questionable characters such as Cesare Borgia and Hiero of Syracuse. "Machiavellian" wisdom thus manifests itself in still another agent of the divine.

How much David *is* the divine agent is made abundantly clear by the long passage in *1 Samuel* in which his encounter with Goliath is described, a story that Machiavelli knows well. He does not trouble in Chapter XIII of *The Prince* to consider the question about David which he had considered about Moses in Chapter VI, where he had said, "And although one ought not to reason of Moses, he having been a mere executor of the things that were ordained by God, he ought yet to be admired, if only for the grace which made him worthy to speak with God." Are we not to understand that this question had been decisively disposed of with respect to David as well by what Machiavelli had said about Moses?

Moses is returned to, first explicitly and then implicitly, in the last of the three invocations of the Old Testament by Machiavelli in *The Prince,* which invocation may be found in Chapter XXVI (the final chapter of this short treatise):

Having considered, then, all the things discussed above, and thinking over within myself if presently in Italy the times were ready to honor a new prince, and if there was matter which could give occasion for one prudent and virtuous to introduce the form which would give honor to him and good to the general body of her men, it seems to me that so many things are concurring to benefit a new prince, that I do not know whether there ever was a time more proper than this. And if, as I have said, one wished to see the virtue of Moses it was necessary that the people of Israel be enslaved in Egypt, and to know the greatness of the mind of Cyrus that the Persians be oppressed by the Medes, and [to know] the excellence of Theseus that the Athenians be dispersed—so, at present, if one wishes to know the virtue of an Italian spirit, it was necessary that Italy be reduced to her present terms, and that she be more enslaved than the Hebrews, more servile than the Persians, more dispersed than the Athenians, without head, without order, beaten, despoiled, torn asunder, overrun, and having borne every sort of ruin.

And although before this a gleam of light showed itself in a certain man [note 2: Cesare Borgia or perhaps Machiavelli himself?], whereby one might have judged that he was ordained by God for her redemption, yet afterwards one has seen how he was reprobated by fortune at the highest course of his actions. Thus, left as if without life, in such a mode [Italy] awaits whoever will be able to heal her wounds, put an end to the plunderings of Lombardy and to the taxation of the Kingdom [of Naples] and Tuscany, curing these her sores which have already been long festering. Look how she prays God, that He send someone who might redeem her from these barbarous cruelties and insults; see also how she is ready and wholly disposed to follow a banner, provided there be one who takes it.

Nor is there anyone to be seen at present in whom she can hope more than in your illustrious House [of the Medicis], which, with its fortune and virtue, favored by God and the Church (of which it is now the prince) could make itself the head of this redemption. This will not be very difficult, if you call up before you the actions and the lives of those named above. And although these men are rare and marvelous, nonetheless they were men, and each of them had less occasion than that of the present; for their enterprise was not more just than this, nor easier, nor was God more a friend to them than to you. Here is great justice: "For just is the war for those for whom it is necessary, and pious the arms where there is no hope but in arms." Here is the greatest of dispositions; nor can there be great difficulty where there is a great disposition, provided that one takes, as a target, those orders which I have proposed. Besides this, here are to be seen extraordinary things without example conducted by God: the sea has opened; a cloud has escorted you on the road; the rock has poured out water; here it has rained manna; everything is concurring for your greatness. The rest ought to be done by you. God does not want to do everything, in order not to take away free will from us and that part of the glory which falls to us.

It is not enough, it would seem, for God to prepare the way, even when he provides remarkable signs of the kind which appeared to Moses. The true leader of Italy must seize his opportunity and rise to the occasion available to a second Moses. Almost incidental to this return by Machiavelli to Moses is the suggestion, quite unlike what is said in Chapter VI, that God was really no more a friend to Moses than he would be to a proper Italian prince at this time. What seems to be critical is not that one be graced by God, but rather that "one takes, as a target, those orders which I [Machiavelli] have proposed."

Is it not evident that the prince who employs the "Machiavellian" order prudently makes use of both the divine and the human? He can even discern and exploit signs, such as those Moses encountered. *Were* there such remarkable manifestations in Machiavelli's time as well? Does he magnify and dramatize what there may have been, in order to serve his immediate purpose? For that matter, Machiavelli might have asked, were there such clear manifestations in Moses' own times or did he or his reporter also make the most of what happened to have been provided? We once again see how a Machiavellian could bring "church" and "state" together in the service of "the most excellent."

III

All this is not to suggest, however, that the traditional American insistence upon "the separation of church and state" would have no meaning or appeal for Machiavelli. Certainly, he would try to weaken any religion that tended, because of *its* teachings, to disarm political men and that encouraged citizens to be more concerned with their eternal salvation than with their earthly happiness and hence civic duties. If religious toleration and "no established church" should lead to a diversity of sects, and this in turn to the political impotence of otherworldly religion, he would probably settle for that as second-best. Would not "first-best," or at least "better," be what an inspired Moses or Romulus could do as a guide to a political-religious order?

Even so, the Machiavellian might well be dubious about any constitutional argument which left anything as significant as the religious life of a people completely outside the control of government. He might argue that "the separation of church and state" is acceptable only so long as its result is to reduce the power of any religion such as Christianity in the political or public life of the community. But if the result of such "separation" is to immunize religious activity from political control, and if that religious activity should be considerable and influential, then it could make the influence of Christianity even worse than it was evidently considered by Machiavelli to have been in his day.

If a still-powerful Christianity should be exempt from political control, the Machiavellian might continue, everyone would tend to become personally immunized the way popes and bishops once were. But popes and bishops had usually to be political men in order to get where they were. They could usually be depended on, if properly instructed, to become somewhat sensible in exercising temporal influence and power. The man of conscience, on the other hand, may be beyond effective political instruction and calculations. Hence the body politic suffers from the irresponsibility of gifted men "of character" who are more concerned about the salvation of individual souls than they are about the political good of the community (or, what amounts to virtually the same thing for Machiavelli, the temporal well-being of the prince).

The Machiavellian is not likely to be concerned to advance any "separation of church and state" doctrine that would completely liberate the faithful from temporal concerns and from political controls. He is likely to prefer to see religion properly subordinated to the political order, recognizing both that there may be a natural appetite in a people for ritual and worship and that the greatest founders dare not neglect such matters. In short, Moses the prophet-prince is to remain what he is by nature, the superior of his priestly brother, Aaron.

It should be evident that "the separation of church and state" can lead to political consequences that Machiavelli would consider dubious. To what extent is the prideful Machiavelli responsible for this development? That is, to what extent or in what way do modern notions about "the separation of church and state" depend not only on Machiavelli's reservations about the political paralysis induced by Christianity, but also on his notions about "the state"?

Does not "the state" in the sense decisively established by Machiavelli depend in turn on something of a "separation" of things once naturally combined? May not one have, in Machiavelli's scheme of things a "state" (or "imperium") both in civil government and in religious authority? If so, may there not "legitimately" be two or more powerful "states" in one country? Is this not an unnatural state of affairs leading to difficulties and dangers, ranging from ineffectual government to civil war, if accommodation is not resorted to?

Such accommodation may be seen, for example, in how a masterly Abraham Lincoln makes use, especially in the Gettysburg Address and the Second Inaugural Address, of the religious heritage of his people in fashioning, or refashioning, "the political religion of the nation." By so doing, he both submits and rules.

We are thus reminded of the confident pleas made in and responded to by heaven for the sake of Venice and her allies in Veronese's *The Battle of Lepanto*. We are reminded, that is, that the truly political man, as one "worthy to speak with God," must know when and how to stoop (if not even to kneel) in order to be able to conquer.

37

CIVIL DISOBEDIENCE
AND STATESMANSHIP

The argument [in the Crito] *of the Laws—with a capital L—suffers from generality. The problem of obedience to the laws cannot be simply decided. On the other hand, and that is why Plato wrote the dialogue as he did, as a crude rule of thumb it is sound teaching. People should really be law-abiding, by all means. There are cases where it is not possible to be law-abiding, but [one should not] teach people that [which] is true [only] in extreme cases, because that has a bad effect. That makes them extremists themselves and that's not good for any society. But there are extreme cases. I think any of you can find extreme examples—I hope fictitious examples—where he would not obey the law. Mr. Anastaplo—I don't know if some of you know him—has not been admitted to the bar because he stated this principle. He stated it, I think very soberly; it is, of course, an undeniable principle. But it is also a principle which—how should I say it?—which one shouldn't teach in the first grade of elementary school, because it is also a disconcerting point.*

LEO STRAUSS

I

My mandate this evening is to speak to you about something called *civil disobedience*. I am glad to have this opportunity to return to Germany, the first time in a somewhat formal capacity since my service here as a fly-

This talk was given at the Max Planck Institute for International Law, Heidelberg, West Germany, May 29, 1984. (Sponsors: The Max Planck Institute and the German-American Institute in Heidelberg.) The Hitler Bunker escape-party story which I told on that occasion was confirmed by several members of the audience.

The epigraph is taken from a 1960 University of Chicago, seminar by Leo Strauss on The Problem of Socrates. See 10 *Interpretation* 334 (1982). See, also, Anastaplo, *The Artist as Thinker* (Athens, Ohio: Ohio University Press, 1983), pp. 474–75, n. 282.

ing officer at the end of the Second World War, at which time one could not help but notice the terrible things that human beings can do to one another. Since I will speak for only an hour or so, I cannot pretend to comprehensiveness in the remarks I have prepared for this occasion. I do hope that what I have to say will provide a useful basis for discussion among us after my talk.

The questions we encounter about civil disobedience turn upon a much older, indeed enduring, question: How far is one obliged to go in compliance with established authority? Civil disobedience, as usually talked about, presupposes an acceptance of the overall and ordinary authority of the particular government being dealt with.

Civil disobedience is that deliberate defiance of the law which lies somewhere between mere law-breaking or criminality on the one hand, and an exercise of the right of revolution on the other hand. Criminality may be seen in murder, theft, and fraud, as these are ordinarily understood. Such crimes are characterized by selfishness or self-aggrandizement on the part of the culprit. The right of revolution, on the other hand, purports to be directed to the common good or in behalf of the rights of citizens. Probably the most notable expression of the right of revolution, at least in modern times, may be found in the American Declaration of Independence of 1776, where it is said,

> We hold these Truths to be self-evident, that all Men are created equal, that they are endowed by their Creator with certain inalienable Rights, that among these are Life, Liberty, and the Pursuit of Happiness—That to secure these Rights, Governments are instituted among Men, deriving their just Powers from the Consent of the Governed, that whenever any Form of Government becomes destructive of these Ends, it is the Right of the People to alter or to abolish it, and to institute new Government, laying its Foundation on such Principles, and organizing its Powers in such Form, as to them shall seem most likely to effect their Safety and Happiness.

Immediately critical to our concerns this evening are these words, "whenever any Form of Government becomes destructive of these Ends [that is, the ends for which governments are instituted among men], it is the Right of the People to alter or to abolish it . . ." It is recognized that the most radical refashioning of government is sometimes not only justified, but even required.

Civil disobedience, I have suggested, is seen as something between mere criminality (which is generally to be condemned) and a legitimate invocation of the right of revolution (which is generally to be permitted, even though it *can* degenerate into mere terrorism). No doubt it can be difficult to judge what is a proper act of civil disobedience: it can be difficult to determine whether any particular act is closer in spirit to an improper criminal action or closer in spirit to the legitimate exercise of the right of revolution. This determination is sometimes affected by another complication: acts which are ordinarily criminal may sometimes be justified as proper, as in times of war or in moments of desperation; on the other hand, the right of revolution is sometimes, perhaps even often, invoked without adequate justification. It is not sufficient in such matters to be sincere, to believe oneself entitled to act as one does.

It is evident that any proper assessment of acts of this character (whether improper criminal acts, privileged acts of civil disobedience, or the natural right of revolution) depends on considerable information and a sensible moral and political judgment. It is, I will argue, difficult or even impossible to attempt to deal with these matters in a doctrinaire manner: general rules are not likely to be helpful; they can even be misleading; much depends on examining case by case each instance as it arises. One is obliged to dwell upon particulars; and it is this I now propose to do, in order to suggest how one might begin to think about civil-disobedience problems.

I propose to lay before you a half-dozen cases upon which I will comment as I go along. Thereafter I will offer a few additional general observations about civil disobedience. I hope that I will have in our discussion the benefit of your experience and reflections with respect to various of the matters I touch upon. The perspective I will be speaking from is that of traditional liberalism, but a liberalism informed, I hope, by classical political philosophy.

II

Permit me to begin my half-dozen cases with two German instances. These are not contemporary examples, but rather examples that draw upon German experiences during the Second World War.

The first situation I offer for your consideration comes out of the Occupation of Denmark. A Danish professor, who lived as a young man in Denmark in those days and who now teaches in the United States, suggested to me just the other day why the heroic efforts by the Danes on behalf of the Jews during the Occupation were as successful as they apparently were. He modestly said nothing about the character of the Danish people itself, which of course was a precondition for what did happen. Rather, he stressed three other elements, two that are probably generally known and a third that is far less generally known.

What is generally known is the proximity of Denmark to Sweden, with the Swedes receptive to the Danish effort to rescue the Jews of Denmark. Also generally known is that there were relatively few Jews in Denmark at the outbreak of the war, and so a rescue effort could more easily be mounted when the crisis came. Similarly, I imagine, although my informant did not say this, the Jews were probably more thoroughly assimilated in Denmark than they were in some other parts of Europe, thereby making it easier for them to be hidden and moved about by a people that was determined to save them. This seems to have been an important consideration in Greece, for example: the Jews in Thessaloniki, who *were* not assimilated into the general Greek population, were almost completely destroyed, whereas the Jews in Athens, who *were* a much smaller community and had been substantially assimilated, were almost all saved by their Gentile friends among the Greeks.

These facts and facts like these, I have said, are generally known and help account for the success of efforts on behalf of the Jews wherever an occupied people wanted to help them. But, I should at once add, such efforts by an occupied people would not usually be regarded as acts of civil disobedience. Rather, they are more usefully considered acts of resistance or, in effect, partial exercises of the right of revolution.

On the other hand, acts of civil disobedience in Denmark in those years may be seen in the third element testified to by my Danish professor as critical to the successful Danish effort on behalf of the Jews. As perhaps some of you know (even though it is not generally known), this third element, without which many if not most of those Jews could not have been saved, was that the ordinary German soldier (as distinguished from the S.S. and the Gestapo) simply refused to do what his government expected of him in rounding up Jews. Instead, my Dane insisted that the ordinary German soldier preferred to allow the Jews quietly to escape. I gather that the Danes may even have relied upon such a preference.

What these German soldiers did in the interest of humanity (including their own sense of well-being) can, it seems to me, be considered commendable acts of civil disobedience. I am sure that all of you here know of someone in your family or among the friends of your family who likewise simply disobeyed the Government when it made its demands for cooperation in the performance of dreadful deeds. The considerable efforts made by the Nazis to keep their worst crimes secret testified to their fear, a justified fear, I suspect, that the support of the German people would have been denied them if it had become publicly known what was really going on. Civil disobedience would have been even greater than it was and in Germany itself, if the truth had had to be faced up to openly by the German people.

But notice: if the conduct of, say, the ordinary German soldier stationed in Denmark should be considered proper civil disobedience or conscientious insubordination, then a question is thereby raised about the validity of one of the conditions (Kantian in its character?) sometimes identified by theorists as necessary for a legitimate act of civil disobedience. This is that the citizen who acts thus should do so publicly and should be prepared to suffer the stated punishment for his act. Yet it should be obvious that what the ordinary German soldier routinely did in Denmark required for its effectiveness that the soldier act quietly and without publicity, preferably without the slightest suspicion by his superior officers. To regard this kind of conduct as civil disobedience is therefore to see civil disobedience not simply as a form of political expression, which it certainly can be, but also as a useful and surely ethical means of serving humanity, justice, and the common good.

III

My second particular, also a German one, is concerned with a failure on the part of German soldiers to engage in civil disobedience when it was obviously sensible for them to do so. Or, at least, I believe so, and it should be interesting to learn from you whether you agree and whether the story I am now about to tell could be true. If it is true, what can be said to account for what happened on that occasion?

The scene is Berlin in May, 1945. Russian soldiers were steadily occupying the city, street by street, and the soldiers and civilian employees, men and women alike, who were assigned to the Hitler Bunker were frantic to get out of Berlin and to permit themselves to be captured by the Americans or the British somewhat to the West rather than by the Russians. One group of men and women, under the leadership of a battle-experienced general, decided to try to make its way to "freedom" (that is, to American or British internment) by avoiding the streets where the Russians were to be encountered—and this they would do by using the by-then inactive Berlin subway system. This would permit them to remain underground until they had moved westward beyond the Russian lines, at which point they would come to the surface and keep moving West. I will now read you the way the general officer commanding this escape-party described what happened (James P. O'Donnell, *The Berlin Bunker* [1979], p. 225):

It was now around 1 a.m. and we were going down on the tracks leading out of the Friedrichstrasse [subway] station. We were dog-weary but still tensed up, for we feared that we might meet with Russians at any turn in the winding

track. We were coming ever closer to where I assumed their lines must be.
The one organization we were not braced for was the BVG. That's the Berlin
Municipal Transport Company.

Less than a hundred yards after we had passed the Friedrichstrasse station
platform we came on a huge steel bulkhead. Waterproof, it was designed to
seal this tunnel at the point where the subway tube starts to run under the
Spree river.

Here—and I could not believe my own eyes—we encountered two stalwart,
uniformed BVG guards. Both, like nightwatchmen, were carrying lanterns.
They were surrounded by angry civilians imploring them to swing open the
bulkhead. They kept refusing. One clutched a giant key. When I saw this ridiculous situation, I ordered them to open the bulkhead forthwith, both for
my group and for the civilians. The guards categorically refused. They cited
regulation this and paragraph that of the BVG Standing Orders.

Not only were these stubborn fellows going by the book; each had a copy of
the book and began reading from it. The regulation, dating from 1923, *did*
clearly state that the bulkhead was to be closed every evening after the passage of the last train. It had been their job for years to see that just this happened. I was flabbergasted. No trains had been running here for at least a full
week, but these two dutiful characters had their orders, and that was that.

We were armed, of course, and they weren't, and I feel that we just might
have made our escape had we been able to follow my original plan to the letter. I sat for long years in Soviet captivity quietly cursing myself for my
strange hesitancy at this critical moment.

It is evident from the general's account that this escape party, finding its
route blocked by the two stubborn old men with their regulation books,
returned to the streets of Berlin where they were soon captured by the
Russians.

Cannot we say that while the ordinary German soldier in Denmark
acted as he should have, in defiance of his government's policy with respect to the Jews, the general and his escape party in the subway of Berlin
did not act as they should have? Perhaps we should also say that the natural humanity of German soldiers was appealed to, in effect, by the Danish
spirit. Such civil disobedience, we can now see, was in the interest of
everyone involved, including the German government itself, which was
thereby kept from doing even more of the evil that it was attempting to
do.

The subway-escape party, on the other hand, acted foolishly, if not
wrongly, in their refusal to defy the law. Was their response typically
German in such circumstances? Certainly it is impossible to imagine

Americans, Frenchmen, or even law-abiding Englishmen acting like this in similar circumstances. Should this difference in how people respond to the demands of the law affect what should be said among them about law-abidingness and about civil disobedience? This does remind us that critical to any consideration of civil disobedience and of its approval or disapproval is the likely effect that any recourse to civil disobedience, especially by prominent and influential people, may have on the character and habits of a people. This may well differ from people to people, which means that one may be obliged to say different things to different audiences on this delicate subject.

I return for a few minutes to the general who languished for years in Soviet captivity, "quietly cursing [him]self for [his] strange hesitancy at [that] critical moment" in the Berlin subway. (p. 225) The general then went on to speculate (pp. 225–26):

> Perhaps there is no rational explanation. As German officers, we had been raised in the strictest Prussian tradition. Orders are there to be obeyed, even if, as in this case, the order was no more than a BVG regulation, not even a military command. Even today, though I admit the situation was ludicrous, I harbour a lingering respect for this eccentric devotion to duty of those two stubborn, Cerberus-like guardians of the bulkhead. I suppose it was my own ingrained sense of duty that led me to respect theirs.

It *is* difficult not to respect such devotion to duty as is described here, especially when one sees it manifested to this day all over Germany in routine efficiency and welcomed reliability in all walks of life. One can wish for more of such an attitude elsewhere, perhaps even in one's own country. The Kantian influence can be salutary as well as dubious in its applications.

Still, cannot one see upon considering such an account as this (which does seem to be true as poetry, whatever may be its status as history) the attitude which stood in the way of a proper resort by German officers during the Second World War to the right, indeed to the duty, of resistance and even of revolution in defiance of their oaths of allegiance to their Leader? Is not a sensible judgment needed as to what laws or rules should be respected, when, and for how long? Perhaps it can even be said that occasional exhibitions of civil disobedience by respectable citizens and in obviously good causes can help nurture among *certain* people a respect for the right of revolution, thereby encouraging their government to be humane and cautious in what it demands of its people.

There may be seen in our second German example another problem often raised in civil disobedience discussions: may a relatively minor rule or law be violated for the sake of a quite important interest? In the subway, it was a BVG regulation. Today, it is often a trespass, noise or traffic regulation that is being violated in order to publicize opposition to a major government policy. How people should conduct themselves—what rules or orders should on occasion be violated by citizens and what misconduct should on occasion be countenanced by government—does depend on a sense of proportion, something which is difficult or even impossible to reduce to rules, doctrines, and formulae. Certainly, one should not permit oneself to be trapped by either one's highest aspirations or one's lowest passions.

IV

The third and fourth examples in our investigation of how to begin to think about civil disobedience are contemporary examples, but examples that reflect not simply questions of the moment, but rather enduring concerns among many peoples around the world.

My third example draws on South African experiences. What should Europeans and Native Africans living in South Africa today do in response to the restrictions and demands of Apartheid?

Certain facts should be taken into account, even though they cannot be decisive. One fact is that life in South Africa today is in many ways preferable for Native Africans to life in virtually all other Sub-Saharan African countries. It does seem that Native Africans willingly go there to work, even under the harsh terms laid down by the South African government. Another fact is that economic pressures, not from abroad but rather within the country, are forcing a considerable relaxation of restrictions upon what Native Africans may do in the productive life of the country—either that, or allow the economy of the country to stagnate and to deteriorate. Things may be getting better in South Africa, which is not to suggest that there are not still numerous injustices there.

What is to be expected as things do get better in South Africa? One thing to be expected may be something not in the interest of any of the peoples of that troubled country: a serious attempt at violent revolution. Either a failed revolution or a successful revolution is, in the circumstances of South Africa today, likely to be disastrous for everyone concerned. But things getting better can often have the effect of making oppressed peoples less patient than they have been.

How, then, should one think about civil disobedience in South Africa today? My own impression is that the government should be pressed to take what may be its last good opportunity in the years immediately ahead to institute the reforms which would assure everyone of a secure and not unjust place in the system. But, one must wonder, pressed how and by whom? How? I would answer, By the use of boycotts, disruptive trespasses, and recourse to activity that leads to publicized arrests. By whom? I would answer, By members of the European part of the population, which would thereby help redeem the unfortunate acquiescence by all too many Europeans for some forty years now in the policies of the government.

That is to say, civil disobedience by a sufficient number (albeit a minority) of concerned Europeans is less apt to escalate out of everybody's control than would civil disobedience by Native Africans. I leave it to you to consider why this may be so. I am not myself concerned to demonstrate this, but only to suggest a mode of analysis which recognizes that whether civil disobedience is resorted to should take account of, among other things, *who* is going to do it. I am reminded here of the Sabine women who, after having been unwillingly carried off by the Romans in search of wives, threw themselves (with babes in arms) between the Sabines and the Romans when their parents and brothers came in arms to reclaim their daughters and sisters from their new husbands. Certain kinds of civil disobedience are most effective when the party exposing itself to the struggle does seem to care for and is cared for by both sides in the conflict.

V

My fourth example, also an enduring contemporary concern, draws upon what we know about the Soviet Union. There may not be any major country in the world today that routinely finds its government subject to more civil disobedience than that of the Soviet Union. This may be seen in responses to its measures both abroad and at home.

The considerable civil disobedience at home is made possible in large part because there seem to be relatively few Russians who continue really to believe in Marxism, even among the ruling class. Much of the corruption to be found in the Soviet Union today, as in much of Eastern Europe, reflects the fact that all kinds of adjustments are required to make the system work, at least in its civilian economy. The government evidently acquiesces in much of this avoidance of the official way by the people (including many bureaucrats). We see here, and have seen for years, a kind of defensive civil disobedience.

Much more spectacular, of course, is the offensive civil disobedience evident in the Soviet Union today, as may be seen in such deliberately dramatic actions as those by the Sakharov family. This is something the whole world knows about and about which the Soviet government seems to be able to do nothing constructive. Rather, the government is trapped by its rigidity and hence allows matters to get out of control, as can be seen even in the fact that a member of the Sakharov family could be publicly received, just this past week, at the Vatican.

This is the sort of thing happening inside the Soviet Union. But there is also what is happening *to* the Soviet Union abroad, where things are even more out of its control. The most spectacular instance here is what has been happening for several years now in Poland. The Solidarity Movement can be understood as a massive and highly disciplined effort at civil disobedience, conducted with a view to bringing the governments of Poland and of the Soviet Union to their senses. Here again the response by outsiders is significant, such as the obvious sympathy manifested by the Pope himself. How deeply felt the opposition to the Soviet-imposed regime is may be gathered from the story this past week about the participation in recent years of a number of Polish families in the hiding of a Russian deserter in Poland. (One is reminded of the Underground Railroad in the United States, with its protection of fugitive slaves, more than a century ago.)

There is one feature about both the Sakharov-type effort and the Polish Solidarity Movement that points up something else which is often associated with civil disobedience efforts. That is the stress placed by the "disobedient" on legality, on appealing to the official doctrines and constitution of the regime. We do not appreciate sufficiently why even such a regime as that of the Soviet Union must acknowledge more or less liberal principles in its constitution, nor how such expressions can be taken advantage of. An appeal is thereby made to the highest aspirations of the regime, something which may be seen in the successful invocation by the Solidarity Movement of official doctrines rooted in socialism and the rights of workers. (See, e.g., Section V of Essay No. 26, above.)

The question remains, How far should civil disobedience be pressed in and around the Soviet Union? Obviously a third world war makes no sense. The enduring hope of mankind lies in an eventual reform of the Soviet Union itself. Not that there are no deficiencies in the West, but it is hard for me to avoid the conclusion that the faults of the Soviet Union go deeper and are much more difficult to deal with. Put another way, the most critical deficiencies of the West, rooted as they are in the very nature of modernity, are also to be seen in the Soviet Union, which has in addition special deficiencies of its own.

The question is how an appeal can be made to the best in the Soviet Union, or at least to its sense of realism. The nature of the problem is suggested by the disturbing fact that the Soviet Union does not seem to be making serious efforts, while it can still somewhat control the solution, to reach agreements with the West about the eventual unification of Germany, about a properly constituted European community, and about the permanent status of the still-subjugated countries in Eastern Europe. The chronic anti-Communist civil disobedience encountered both at home and abroad, and especially in Poland, should make it apparent that there *can* come a day, should things suddenly become difficult for the Soviet Union in other parts of the world, when the continuing division of Germany and the continuing occupation of Eastern Europe after almost half a century will lead to simply unpredictable developments that can be dangerous to everybody on earth. The question for us all is how the Russians can be helped to act sensibly at a time when calm negotiation and a genuinely safe settlement may still be possible. I shall say more about all this later, but first we must devote a few minutes to what we can learn about civil disobedience from American experiences.

VI

When one thinks of American experiences, two sets of problems are most likely to come to mind: those related to the status of the American Negro and those related to the war in Vietnam.

It was in connection with resistance to slavery that the term "civil disobedience" was probably first used, since this was the title given, a few years after Henry Thoreau's death, to the famous essay he wrote in 1848. Thoreau's refusal to pay certain taxes, the abolitionists' defiance of the law in their efforts to undermine slavery, and the cooperation of citizens with fugitive slaves were instances in the 1840s and 1850s of civil disobedience. Here too the efforts were both defensive and offensive: defensive, in that many people simply would not do what the law required in aid of slavery; offensive, in that some people used their defiance of the law to dramatize and organize their opposition to slavery.

The abolitionists' position, which can be seen in Thoreau's essay, eventually led to the insistence that decent citizens should not have anything to do with any regime or constitution that permitted slavery. This meant, in effect, that the abolitionists were willing to permit and even to require the Northern Free States to separate themselves from the Southern Slave States. This also meant that the Slave States would thereby have been left free of whatever restraints were imposed upon them by the National Union. How the slaves themselves would have been better off by such Northern purification is hard to see.

It is evident upon examining Thoreau's argument that it is easy for the advocate of civil disobedience to slip into the position of disparaging, if not altogether denying, the legitimacy of government itself. Thus the approach to these matters of the abolitionists can usefully be compared to the approach of an Abraham Lincoln. His approach is much more political and statesmanlike.

President Lincoln recognized that he had to keep together diverse elements in the American community, especially those which were most law-abiding. The abolitionists could be useful to Lincoln so long as he could control them, rather than be controlled by them. For one thing, the threats of the abolitionists could be used by the statesman to induce the law-abiding to permit anti-slavery changes in the laws themselves.

The statesman is obliged to exhibit greater respect for the law, and especially for a constitution, than the civil-disobedience practitioner is apt to do. But this also means that the statesman can build more firmly for the future, as may be seen in Lincoln's Emancipation Proclamation and in the "new birth of freedom" for which Lincoln was in part responsible. It is difficult for those who resort to civil disobedience, especially if the emphasis should be placed on their own sense of purification and righteousness, to exhibit the concerns and approach of the statesman, the leader who must take seriously the demands of political "necessities," of national survival, and of justice and the common good.

Something of a statesmanlike approach to civil disobedience can be seen in the civil rights efforts in Montgomery and Birmingham (in 1956 and 1963), which efforts were said to have been modeled in turn upon the efforts of Mohandas Gandhi in South Africa and India. Martin Luther King drew effectively on two elements in American life: a deep religious faith and an abiding respect for the Constitution. How indigenous he was may be seen even in the title of his most famous statement on the subject of civil disobedience, his *Letter from Birmingham Jail,* for this echoes a well-known folk song in which the forlorn narrator speaks from Birmingham jail.

Critical to the King *Letter* is his insistence that he is in principle law-abiding, that the laws his movement is violating are not truly laws. In this he draws upon such authorities as Saint Augustine and Saint Thomas Aquinas. He could very much rely upon the interpretations of the law of the land that had by then been developed by the United States Supreme Court, especially its salutary 1954 decision in the School Segregation Cases. In short, Martin Luther King and his colleagues could insist that *they* were the ones who were truly law-abiding, not the men who were throwing them into jail. By and large, the courts and the Country came to agree with them.

Vital to the success of the King movement in the United States was its determination to remain non-violent no matter what the provocation. But the decisive non-violence here may not have been that of Negroes but rather that of the whites. The whites did have, at all times and to this day, the power to crush the Negro protesters. The non-violence of the protestors made it more difficult for whites to persist in violence, especially since the Negroes appealed to the best in the American people at large. This campaign of civil disobedience was as effective as it was because it was both highly disciplined and quite articulate: it required and permitted the American people to face up to an obviously unjust state of affairs and to put things in the course of an eventual just and humane resolution. People have wondered, of course, how Mohandas Gandhi and Martin Luther King would have fared in Hitler's Germany or Stalin's Russia. (See, e.g., Section III of Essay No. 13, above.)

Fears have been expressed from time to time that campaigns of civil disobedience, such as the King campaign, undermine respect for the law. No doubt there is that risk. But even more importantly, it seems to me, such campaigns have helped promote a deeper respect for the law. This is certainly true among American Negroes who for a long time had regarded "the Law" as something the white man used to exploit and oppress them. But whites also have been liberated and ennobled in that they have been able, after decades if not centuries of partial self-deception, to live up to the principles that mean so much to all Americans. In this way, then, Martin Luther King was closer to the Lincoln than to the Thoreau approach to civil disobedience, regarding it as something to be subordinated to the demands of statesmanship.

VII

The American experience with civil disobedience in connection with the war in Vietnam is not as significant or as instructive as that which was connected with the civil rights movement. Indeed, much of the Vietnam War civil disobedience campaign seemed at times a mere imitation of what had been so dramatic a decade or more before in the civil rights arena.

Looking back at the Vietnam War period, one does not get the impression that civil disobedience, as distinguished from legal demonstrations, was decisive to what happened then. The Vietnam War civil disobedience was most dramatically expressed by American university students, but even there most if not all of the significant protest was legal, however provocative and bad-mannered it could sometimes be. (See, e.g., Essay No. 17, above.)

What is easily lost sight of in considering the significance of civil disobedience with respect to the Vietnam War is that it was always possible throughout that war for Americans to speak freely against it, and many respectable citizens did so from the very start. Perhaps no war in American history faced from its beginning such solid criticism as that one did. This is partly because we moved gradually into it and partly because there were eminent people, including the incumbent President himself in his 1964 election campaign, who had been critical of any American military involvement in Vietnam.

Questions did come to be raised whether laws that were ordinarily justifiable, even necessary, could properly be violated in order to make a point against the war. But all too often such violations were more indicative of desires to express oneself than they were serious contributions to the massive criticism of the war that could be heard all over the Country. Certain acts of civil disobedience tended to divert attention from the folly of the war to the foolishness of various critics of the war. There was even at times the danger that the reactions against certain highly publicized law-breakers would be used to undermine the effectiveness of the criticisms of the war that were being made legally. But, as it turned out, there was not throughout the Vietnam War period anyone in America who was imprisoned only for something he *said* against the war. Among those who said things, and said them effectively, *were* students on American campuses. But they, as impatient students, did not appreciate how effective what they were saying was, and so they sometimes had recourse to dubious conduct which was as likely, depending on the circumstances, to hurt as to help their cause. This is not to deny, of course, that certain acts of civil disobedience did serve to accentuate what was being said so well and so widely on the campuses of the Country.

This reminds us of one of the critical risks of any civil disobedience that is not governed by statesmanship: it is apt to be at the mercy of chance developments.

VIII

My last case-study of civil disobedience has to do with matters that require the maximum of statesmanship and the minimum of chance in their governance. I refer to the problem of nuclear war and how nuclear weapons should be dealt with. That considerable informed discussion is needed should be obvious. Less obvious, it seems to me, is the obligation to move with great care, not only in the distribution and use of nuclear weapons, but also in what one does in opposition to the manufacture, deployment, and use of such weapons. I sometimes have the impression that campaigns of civil disobedience are not apt to be sensitive and restrained enough to deal properly with these matters.

It should be remembered that the prevailing set of arrangements has somehow kept the nuclear peace for forty years. Political leaders do tend to be more sensible here than they may be elsewhere. Consider, for example, how calmly the Reagan Administration has recently responded to the threat of an increase in Soviet submarines armed with nuclear weapons just off the American coast and compare this with the somewhat irresponsible response by the Kennedy Administration to the reports twenty years ago about nuclear weapons in Cuba.

It is also important to remember that stability is important in these matters, and that it often requires considerable technical information to be able to determine what is indeed destabilizing. The long-term solution of the nuclear problem depends, I have indicated, on the Soviet Union, what happens to it and how it conducts itself. This is not to suggest that the United States is not without deficiencies, but it is certainly not a tyranny. One necessity, therefore, is that we in the West must continue to do for the Soviet Union, and particularly for its leaders, the thinking that their institutions and their traditions make it difficult for them to do for themselves.

One problem with the Soviet Union is that it does tend to keep itself from proper appreciation of basic principles and of fundamental questions. A regime which has such a comprehensive system of censorship that the very word *censorship* cannot be officially used to describe what it does is not likely to be a regime which thinks things through to their foundations. It is apt to be a fear-ridden regime that is both woefully uninformed and consistently callous, whatever its ultimate aspirations. But, some will explain, the Soviet censorship does not keep the leadership itself from being realistic, sensible, etc. One must wonder even about this, however, since the principles assumed by the regime may well keep its leaders from appreciating all of the relevant facts. After all, as we can see in Poland, not only may a government come to believe its propaganda, but it can so cripple political discourse within its country as to make it difficult even for the government itself to find out what is really going on.

I have suggested from time to time that we in the West must do for the Soviet Union much of the thinking necessary for the true self-interest of humanity, including the Russian people, to be protected. For the American people to conduct itself as it should, as the principal guardian today against universal tyranny, an informed self-confidence is needed. There is no practical way to keep the American people and its government sensible about these matters if there is not a substantial American faith in the adequacy of the military strength of the free world. The greatest danger

in the years immediately ahead is not that the United States should arm itself too much, or that nuclear weapons should be too easily available, or
that a nuclear war might start by accident, however grave all these dangers
may be. The greatest danger for all mankind would follow from a sustained American fear of its inability to defend itself and its principles.
This opinion could have a disastrous political effect in the United States
and hence abroad. On the other hand, the United States, as a young and
relatively inexperienced nation, is always in need of suggestions, encouragement, and rebukes from vigorous allies and vigilant adversaries alike
about the way it conducts its affairs. Neither ignorant self-assertion nor
sophisticated isolation is in our interest.

We should, therefore, approach with considerable caution any acts of
civil disobedience that tend to substitute the immediate personal satisfaction of "direct action," including misled and hence misleading public
opinion polls and plebiscites, for the more statesmanlike course of steady
and informed discussion of the alternatives that a people, acting through
its duly constituted government, faces. Far too much is apt to be made
these days by highminded citizens of the demands of "the individual conscience" and not enough of the requirements of politics and the advantages of a predictable order.

IX

Although I have already made considerable demands upon your patience,
I ask your indulgence for a few more minutes as I try to pull together
some of the things I have referred to.

You will have noticed that it has not been possible for me to discuss civil
disobedience without recourse to political assessments of the various kinds
of situations that do arise. This reflects my opinion that civil disobedience,
including determinations both of its propriety and of the appropriate
government response to it, *is* primarily a political question, not a legal, a
constitutional, or even a simply moral question.

You will also have noticed that I have not attempted a precise definition
of *civil disobedience*. I have indicated that it does tend to make use of deliberate, but not always open, defiance of established authority over civilians. How one can begin to think about civil disobedience should be
evident from the half-dozen cases I have commented upon.

Perhaps it is also evident that I do not consider civil disobedience *capable* of genuine definition, despite the fact that practitioners and scholars
often refer to it as if it were something distinctive. I believe it instructive
to wonder how the actions we sometimes call "civil disobedience" would

have been referred to by the ancient Greeks and Romans or by that remarkable Eighteenth-Century generation who framed the American Constitution. Would not they have spoken simply of law-breaking, even as they considered the circumstances and character both of the law-breaker and of the community in determining whether this or that act was somehow justified or what responseit was useful and proper for the government to make?

Modern discussions of civil disobedience do tend to draw upon the terms in Thoreau's original title for his innovative civil disobedience essay, "On the Relation of the Individual to the State." But all such terms—*the individual, the state,* and *civil disobedience* itself—may well depend upon modern "state of nature" theories about the origin and purposes of social order, theories which usually reflect a more doctrinaire view of the law and of politics than the ancients had.

This means that prudence, in the service of both justice and the common good, is lost sight of, that very prudence which is vital to the Declaration of Independence. It is prudence to which political philosophy, unlike doctrinaire ideologies, looks in its effort to promote a thoughtful account of and response to political things.

Modern doctrines tend to make much of self-expression and of sincerity, thereby placing greater emphasis upon the means rather than upon the ends. This can be seen in many civil disobedience discussions, which consequently make much (in the Kantian manner) of modern subjectivity, of personal integrity, and of the private will (which can be somewhat tyrannical in its exercise). Traditional political philosophy, on the other hand, looks more to public and objective standards which do not preclude a man's deliberate recognition that certain acts demanded by his government simply should not be done or that certain conduct would be salutary to engage in, however illegal it may be. Also salutary is the insistence that tyranny be resisted in the name of a higher law, or natural right. Lawabidingness is thereby still respected, since the community is asked to honor its own principles and laws, even as it is cautioned against fanaticism, public or private. One can effectively violate the law from time to time only if there is a general respect for the law in the community. (See, on the limitations of consciencious objection to military conscription, "Church and State: Explorations," Part V.)

I have suggested that the perspective from which so-called civil disobedience should ultimately be viewed is that of the statesman. It is the citizen with the perspective of the statesman who must assess various acts of civil disobedience in order to determine what should be done about them, and to determine as well which of them point to problems that should be dealt with, whatever may have to be done to the law-breakers involved (who can include ordinary criminals, rioters, and terrorists, as well as harmless visionaries and concerned human beings). Certainly, many acts of disobedience and law-breaking have to be anticipated. A few of them do have to be responded to in a special way. This calls for a largely political judgment on the part of the prudent statesman, the compassionate judge, and the sensible community.

I trust it is evident, from what I have said, that it is critical for citizens and rulers alike to have and to believe themselves to have sufficient information on the basis of which they may themselves act and on the basis of which they may properly judge the actions of others.

Citizens' conduct and a government's response should depend to a considerable extent on circumstances, including such factors as I have indicated: the temperament of a people, the history of a country, and the powers, level of decency and stability of a government. Perhaps even more important is that at least the teachers of citizens in a community be informed about what the permanent political questions are which should always be kept in mind and what the enduring standards are to which the community and its citizens should dedicate themselves.

Permit me to emphasize in closing that I have assumed throughout my remarks this evening that there can be no serious political action or discourse with respect to civil disobedience problems without due recognition of the obvious but nevertheless profound differences between tyranny and the rule of law. I consider it a privilege to have been given an opportunity to offer my opinions, however tentative some of them may be, before this distinguished audience and in an enlightened country that must be among the leaders of the free world today.

38

EASTERN EUROPEAN PROSPECTS
AND THE UNITED STATES

Muscovy has tried to leave its despotism; it cannot. The establishment of commerce requires the establishment of the exchange, and the operations of the exchange contradict all Muscovy's laws.

In 1745, the Czarina Elizabeth made an ordinance driving the Jews out because they had sent to foreign countries the silver of those who had been exiled to Siberia and that of the foreigners who were in her service. The subjects of the empire, like slaves, were unable to leave or to send out their goods without permission. The exchange, which gives the means of transfering silver from one country to another, contradicts, therefore, the laws of Muscovy.

Commerce itself is in contradiction to these laws.

MONTESQUIEU

INTRODUCTION

A member of the Soviet Parliament observed this week, "We must create presidential power to get rid of Politburo power, which is arbitrary. Yes, it is dangerous. Today, we introduce presidential rule, tomorrow he may become a dictator. But freedom in this country will remain in danger for the next hundred years or so." (*New York Times*, February 21, 1990, p. A9)

To expect one hundred years of testing for Russian "freedom" is probably prudent. After all, seventy years of Marxist effort have proved largely

---

This talk was given at Duke University, Durham, North Carolina, February 22, 1990. (Sponsor: The Institute of Policy Sciences and Public Affairs.)

The epigraph is taken from Montesquieu, *The Spirit of the Laws*, IV, xiv (Anne M. Cohler and Basia C. Miller translation).

unsuccessful in the Soviet Union, even though some of those efforts were, in critical respects, in conformity with the character and heritage of the Russian people.

Consider what has been required to make the American constitutional system work as well as it has. I prefaced my 1989 Commentary on the United States Constitution with a survey of the dozen "constitutions of the Americans" that have been available in this Country for more than two centuries:

    I. The Language of the English-Speaking Peoples
    II. The British Constitution
    III. The Declaration of Independence
    IV. The Common Law
    V. The Law of Public Bodies
    VI. The State Constitution(s)
    VII. The Best Regime (Temporal)
    VIII. The Best Regime(s) (Spiritual)
    IX. The Character of the People
    X. The Law of Nations
    XI. The Articles of Confederation
    XII. The Constitution of 1787
    XIII. The System of the World.

It should be useful to look, however briefly, at each of these "constitutions" in turn as a guide to our effort to assess Eastern European constitutional prospects. The opening pages of my *Commentary* provide an examination of the "constitutions of the Americans," suggesting thereby how deep-rooted the Spirit of '76 was.

The primary concern these days seems to be Germany or, if not that, the immediate consequences of any breakup of the Soviet Union. Behind the scenes are the relations among the smaller countries of Eastern Europe, relations that can be so explosive as to engage and trap the great powers in unexpected ways. (See Section III of Essay No. 33, above.)

My emphasis on this occasion will be upon the opinions, principles, or doctrines that affect constitutional government and a democratic regime. Material conditions, and especially economic "forces," can no doubt help shape opinions, just as the opinions that a people hold can guide economic developments. One must wonder, however, whether the seeming collapse of Marxism in Eastern Europe extends to a repudiation of certain fashionable assumptions (and not only among Marxists) about the influence of material conditions upon thought.

To place as I do here an emphasis upon ideas is not, however, to deny that circumstances can very much matter. The growing economic gap between East and West, which threatens to become even greater after the 1992 Western European economic amalgamation, has contributed to the crises in confidence among supporters of Marxist regimes in Eastern Europe.

The importance of circumstances can be noticed in still another way: the considerable exposure to television which has been so harmful to us in the West has perhaps been good, at least for awhile, for the Eastern Europeans in that it has helped undermine a long-established tyranny.

I

The Language of the English-Speaking Peoples. I wonder, in my *Commentary,* whether it is "possible to have a sustained constitutionalism on a large scale in the modern world wherever the political and human sensibilities of a people have not been shaped by the language (that is, the thought) of a Shakespeare."

Everyone recognizes the necessity of language for rationality and humanity. (Consider the persuasive depiction of Caliban in Shakespeare's *The Tempest.*) But are there not different political inclinations and possibilities to be found in different languages? The language, or thought, of a people suggests what should be attempted by that people. This seems evident to me, for example, with respect to the modern Greeks, who have a hard time with Western-style democratic government.

What or who provides the critical guidance in Eastern Europe? I had the impression, while visiting the Soviet Union in 1960, that Dostoyevsky provides us to this day the best instruction about the Russians. Did authors such as Dostoyevsky and Tolstoy, however, come so late in the life of their people as to serve more to describe than to shape the Russians? What about in Eastern Europe generally? Is there among those peoples anyone who has had the stature and influence of Shakespeare? In Germany, Goethe and Schiller have been vital: what kind of people, and expectations, have they helped produce? What form of government would be best for that people in the long-run?

Such are the questions to which an inquiry into language, or thought, can lead. Consider what that Europe must have been like, and what its possibilities as well as its limitations were, which had Latin as a common language. What has been the influences of the Russian language in Eastern Europe over the centuries?

II

The British Constitution. The Framers of the Constitution of 1787 built upon the traditions of the British regime. Various delegates in the Constitutional Convention could refer to the British Constitution as the best in the world at that time, however difficult it would have been for Americans simply to adopt it. Even to speak of, let alone to use, political constitutions as is done today is to look to something rooted in the English-speaking tradition.

Is there anything comparable to the British constitutional tradition available in Eastern Europe? Such a tradition does take time, as well as sound thinking, to develop. The history of most of Eastern Europe, for a century or more, has been that of scrapping one political system after another. That is hardly good training either in freedom or in self-government.

It is not generally appreciated that the American Constitution, including the Bill of Rights, has worked as well as it has from the beginning because much of it was already being used when it was formally adopted. What do the Russians, for example, have to work with now? They have the heritage of a large empire, with its quite diverse populations, and perhaps high expectations as to the possibilities of a national "family." A centuries-old appetite for social justice nurtured by Christianity may have been intensified by certain Marxist teachings about the dubiousness of economic "exploitation." This has bad, as well as good, aspects—and suggests that Western-style constitutionalism may be a problem in Eastern Europe, where there is not found that well-developed sense of enlightened self-interest relied upon among the peoples of the West.

III

The Declaration of Independence. The Declaration invokes British constitutional standards in announcing a regime which we date formally from July 4, 1776.

That instrument includes an inventory of the grievances that justify a declaration of independence. But the instrument is also a statement of principles grounded in a political order. These principles are not created by the Declaration but rather restated there.

Is there anything comparable in Eastern Europe today? It is not the "style" to talk thus these days; nor is there the general awareness of enduring standards which can supply depth for such a statement. What is provided by the Charter 77 manifesto and related documents in Czechoslovakia or by the United Nations Universal Declaration of Human Rights? Are not these proclamations too general, and too sophisticated, in their approach, making much more of "freedom of expression" than of constitutional government?

Perhaps certain influential literary works by dissidents in Eastern Europe can provide guidance. But are not these apt to appeal more to the passions than to the reason, while the Declaration of Independence appeals more to the reason in invoking both natural right and British constitutional principles? Eastern European statements have tended to be transitory political manifestos and maneuvers.

We have seen what the lack of an equivalent to the "created equal" language has meant in South Africa, where it is hard to find common ground for the various factions there. It is hard enough in the United States with that principle, or self-evident truth, in the background.

In a way, then, the Declaration of Independence is a tribute to Great Britain, just as Christianity is a tribute to the Judaism from which it separated itself. Britain had provided invaluable training in self-government and constitutional principles to the Colonists. Has the Soviet Union done anything like that in Eastern Europe? Fear and hate are hardly to be recommended as the principal bases for proper political development.

IV

The Common Law. The common law, in evidence throughout the Constitution and relied upon from the beginning of the American Republic, may be understood as the systematic application of human reason, working from generally accepted standards of justice, to the circumstances of the day. The standards relied upon can be apprehended naturally.

Is there anything comparable to build upon in Eastern Europe? The old civil law? Some of the more respectable Marxist teachings about social justice? Residual Christian teachings, if only as incorporated in laws and customs? Is there, that is, a prevailing system of morality and law, no matter what political form the regime takes from time to time?

The Anglo-American common law reflects deep-rooted opinions about private property and personal responsibility, about financial relations, and about how economic activities should be conducted. The common law also looks to a general opinion about justice and a respect for common sense. Underlying the system is a respect for the rule of law. Again we must ask, what is there that is comparable to all this in Eastern Europe? It is *that* which must be built upon by any regime which is to be reasonably hopeful of success. We notice in passing that the recent dramatic breakdown of economic life in Eastern Europe has been in large part due to the absence for decades of the rule of law in the conduct of what is now called a "command economy."

V

The Law of Public Bodies. The rule of law extends to a general understanding of how government should be established and regulated. The Framers had a "common law" with respect to governance that they could rely upon.

In Eastern Europe today the prevailing "law of public bodies" is likely to lead, when democracy is aimed at, to one-house parliamentary government. Whether this provides a sufficient check on power can be questioned. (It is, for example, easy to underestimate the continuing power and usefulness of the British House of Lords.)

Also likely to be found in Eastern Europe today is a reliance upon proportional representation in legislatures. Whether this permits strong and responsible government can also be questioned, but it *is* the constitutional fashion of the day.

No doubt, it is difficult to export American constitutional arrangements. We hear these days of American constitutional-law experts being consulted in Eastern Europe. Something is apt to be, and to remain, seriously wrong when outsiders have to be called upon to any significant extent for such purposes. One must wonder if such recourse to strangers is likely to lead to the development of any system that is appropriate to a people and its circumstances.

VI

The State Constitution(s). These constitutions reflect the fact that in the United States the States somehow exist independently of the national government established in 1787–89. They also mean that federalism can be vital in the United States; the States are not administrative units or simply agents or subordinates of the national government.

State constitutions permitted considerable experimentation that the Framers of 1787 could draw upon. On the other hand, do not the Marxist experiments of the past seventy years in Eastern Europe serve primarily as warnings or indications of what should *not* be done?

Are there any constitutional instruments in Eastern European countries which can be put to good use by their would-be Framers? I do not know enough to be able to say—but I suspect that there is not much that can be relied upon in any country over there with the expectation that the people at large will readily take to it.

Germany, which is in some ways the key to the problem of Eastern Europe, is special here also: Eastern Germany can pretty much attempt to accommodate itself to the West German constitutional system, a system which has a few decades behind it. This is not very long as serious constitutions go, but still it *is* something. It remains to be seen whether the Germans understand what really went wrong with the Weimar Republic—and what the democratic dogmas were that contributed to the post-Weimar debacle.

VII

The Best Regime (Temporal). The most thoughtful human beings should eventually be able to reach substantial agreement as to what the best regime is, however rare its actual establishment. The reason, having discovered what the simply best would be, makes sensible adjustments in applying the best to a variety of circumstances in order to develop decent regimes.

The objectives of a decent regime include a respect for justice and liberty. These are served by, and in turn serve, personal and collective security without making too much of mere self-preservation. Also important, especially in modern settings, is a comfortable standard of living, especially when the people at large are in a position to compare what they have to what is available elsewhere. To make much of the standard of living, however, does open the way to corruption and decadence. This can be seen not only in the West but also in Eastern Europe, where the ruling classes have shamelessly indulged themselves for years now.

A decent regime must also make provision for some exercise in, or at least exposure to, nobility. This can take the form of a respect for extraordinary virtue both public and private. In a few cases, this can also mean a life devoted to philosophy. Unless life can thus be made to seem significant, we can expect to see more and more recourse to adventurism and drugs, including the reliance upon various kinds of diverting music and other arts.

Marxist regimes have, of course, drawn from time to time upon intimations of the best regime. Perhaps they were naturally bound to do so. But they made the critical mistake of cavalierly overriding popular judgments that take immediate consequences seriously. In the process they unnaturally disregarded such considerations as ordinary self-interest and personal happiness, to say nothing of the consent (as distinguished from the compelled acquiescence) of the governed.

The intense nationalism that threatens to flare up in Eastern Europe can interfere with a properly informed judgment in another way: people can be provoked to disregard, if not even to deny, justice in the name of an overriding concern for one's own. People do have to be reminded again and again of what a good human being looks like and what a decent community should be and do. However important patriotism is, it is not enough.

The American Framers of 1787 could work with a salutary natural-right tradition. Patriots today are not apt to be similarly guided and restrained, even though opinions drawing ultimately upon natural right provided (along with religious teachings) the bases for much of the serious criticism of Marxist regimes since the Second World War, even by those who "don't believe in" natural right.

The lack of an informed and confident natural-right understanding among his people poses one of the most serious limitations for the would-be constitutional statesman today. The duty and opportunities here for educators should be evident. It can be instructive and even reassuring to notice how even the most oppressive regimes in Eastern Europe as elsewhere have had to *espouse* justice and the common good.

VIII

The Best Regime(s) (Spiritual). My emphasis thus far has been on the significance of the best regime in the temporal realm. Things become more complicated when we move beyond the temporal, especially when faith in one or another spiritual dispensation can affect how one conducts oneself here on earth. The Framers of 1787 knew that there is a place for religion in the life of communities. They knew as well that care must be taken to respect the prerogatives of both religion and politics, not mistaking one for the other.

A universal natural-right teaching can recognize a need for particular sets of religious opinions and practices appropriate to time and place. Such beliefs can help make life seem significant, partly by providing moral guidance day in and day out. The American Framers in the late Eighteenth Century had at hand various, and generally useful, religious associations in the several States.

The thoughtful statesman recognizes the need to rely on some religion for his people. An old religion is to be preferred, partly because nature has had an opportunity to shape it to the circumstances of that people. (See Socrates' deliberate recourse to the Delphic oracle in Plato's *Republic*.)

Are there usable and useful religions in Eastern Europe today? Or have the Marxists done enough to discredit religious institutions, however limited they have been in establishing respected institutions of their own? Discrediting religion does cater to the modern temperament, both East and West.

An obvious exception to effective discrediting of religion may be seen in Poland. (The Pope's role here seems to have been important. Was the choice of him by the College of Cardinals in 1978 due to Providence, to politics, or to chance? The effect here may be independent of the original cause.) Roman Catholicism provided for the Poles a focus of resistance to Russian rule, just as Eastern Orthodoxy had done centuries earlier for the Greeks against Turkish rule. Have the major religious organizations in the other countries in Eastern Europe, except perhaps for the Judaic, been compromised by decades of accommodation to Marxist regimes?

The Framers of 1787 knew that care has to be taken not to liberate religious organizations, as distinguished from religious faith, from the proper constraints of civil society. Is there any sound reason to believe that the guidance provided by revelation, properly understood, should ever conflict with the guidance provided to the statesman by nature? Even so, modern European statesmen, both East and West, find it difficult to be relaxed about the place of religion in the commonwealth.

IX

The Character of the People. The character of a people shapes institutions and is in turn shaped and reinforced by those institutions. A critical problem with respect to Eastern Europe is what the people of that part of the world are like.

Diverse as Americans were in 1787, their differences from region to region now seem far less than the differences found today in Eastern Europe, not only between countries but also within countries. Even so, we must wonder what forty to seventy years of Marxist governments have done to those peoples.

Their suffering seems to have had in some cases an ennobling effect; certainly, it has made many individuals much more serious than they might otherwise have been. But we should be careful not to suggest that a half-century of oppression can be depended on to be good for anyone. Oppression *can* have a corrupting effect, in that it tends to make a victimized people self-seeking as well as distrustful of government and the community.

Generally, tyranny is not likely to be good for human beings. Furthermore, is there not something seriously defective in that community which can put up with tyranny for decades at a time and which produces a steady supply of tyrants from among themselves? Outbursts of enthusiasm, such as we have been witnessing around the world the past year, are not sufficient to insure sustained republican effort, however useful they may be in toppling a tyranny.

Outbursts of enthusiasm, long suppressed, may also be seen in the manifestation these days of nationalistic passions, of which a revived anti-Semitism in Eastern Europe is one example. Liberty, we are apt to be reminded in the years ahead, serves a people best when a community is well-grounded in mutual trust and self-discipline.

The considerable recourse of Eastern European movements to artists and other intellectuals for leadership indicates how badly crippled those peoples have been by tyranny: mature and reliable political men do not seem to be readily available to take charge. Intellectuals, however attractive they may be, are not apt to be as prudent as an enduring political life requires.

One cannot consider the character of the peoples of Eastern Europe without at least wondering what has become of the character of the American people since 1787. Have the American people been disciplined in critical respects in recent decades by the Marxist threat? Once that threat is perceived to be gone, what will be the reaction here? Are hedonism, moral relativism, and a sense of purposelessness likely to become even stronger than they already are? Cannot that lead to desperate experiments in the United States as well?

In short, we Americans should take care that we do not become victims of our successes both at home and abroad.

X

The Law of Nations. The law of nations, or at least what is considered the proper relation between nations, now seems to be more ideological, and hence less principled, than it was taken to be in 1787.

The longstanding problems of the relations between the countries of Eastern Europe have been muted since the Second World War by the overbearing Russian presence. Serious boundary problems remain, as does the divisiveness arising from the longstanding mistreatment of ethnic minorities in one country after another.

Is a voluntary Eastern European federation likely to emerge? Should it be encouraged, and on what terms? Do we see there some of the intractable problems that face the eventual world government that some look to? Are we apt to see in the next half-century, with the continuing effects of mass communications, enough of a world community to subvert natural attachments, as well as national discipline and satisfactions, but not enough to provide firm and responsible world governance?

American statesmen in the late Eighteenth Century recognized that they had an obligation to exhibit a "decent Respect to the Opinions of Mankind." The enduring opinions of mankind—those opinions to be taken most seriously—were rooted in reason and natural right. Those opinions provided principled guidance as to how nations should treat one another. If those opinions should be discredited, then force and war are likely to mean more than reason and justice in the conduct of foreign policy.

XI

The Articles of Confederation. The Framers of 1787 built on their national constitutional experience. Are the predecessor systems in Eastern Europe, Marxist or pre-Marxist, to be built upon today—or are they to be thoroughly dismantled and discarded?

East Germany is, again, a special case. There is a working constitution in West Germany that can be extended to the entire country. Serious difficulties in accommodation will remain, including various kinds of complicated economic adjustments and property reallocations, but these difficulties may seem minor compared to those that will become evident elsewhere in Eastern Europe.

Are the recent military and economic associations in Eastern Europe of any further use? The United States had an effective union in critical respects well before 1776. Is there anything comparable in Eastern Europe? And what is in the long-run interest of the various peoples within the Soviet Union? Can they now trust the dominant Russians enough to remain in voluntary federation with them? Should they? It is hardly for us to say.

Nor are we in a position to determine what the role will be of the somewhat independent military organizations found here and there in Eastern Europe.One can imagine developments in one country after another that would leave the army as the only apparent guardian of stability and responsible government. Consider, for example, what happened in Greece between 1963 and 1967: excesses in liberty were followed by seven years of harsh rule by incompetent Colonels. Poland, on the other hand, has seemed to be more fortunate in its military intervenors during the past decade.

The Russian generals, perhaps sobered if not disillusioned by their "Vietnam" in Afghanistan, remain a mystery. Ultimately, however, they too depend for their decisive opinions on the community at large. It is in the short-run that they are likely to be dangerous at home, especially if a sense of betrayal by political leaders should pervade their ranks.

Perhaps the Russian generals' professionalism and sense of restraint, as well as their awareness of their limitations as political men, can be nurtured and appealed to by their counterparts in the West. Here, as elsewhere, we must depend on the sense of duty, as well as on the good sense, of our own generals.

XII

The Constitution of 1787. Is anything comparable to the 1787 Constitution—comparable either in effectiveness or in potential longevity—apt to be developed during the next decade or so in Eastern Europe?

To be confident about this is to fail to appreciate what was required in America, after and perhaps before the revolution began in 1776, for the Constitution of 1787 to emerge. It also fails to appreciate what that Constitution is like, how well-crafted and solidly grounded it is, even with the original accommodations to slavery in it that have taken two centuries to begin to work out of the system.

Perhaps the best hope for constitutional developments in Eastern Europe (aside from the Soviet Union) lies in what is happening in Western Europe, where political as well as economic union is deepening. What kinds of association are feasible between Western Europe and the Eastern European countries, especially as a free market develops in the East in the coming decades? The Western Europeans do speak of their union as "Europe"—and the Eastern Europeans can be encouraged by this.

What about the Russians? So great a people, with so rich (however troubled) a heritage, will find its own way into the modern world. The United States should stand ready to help, however difficult it may be to determine what is truly helpful. It remains to be seen how we will deal in the Twenty-first Century with a Russia that could eventually be much more powerful than it is now once it has liberated itself from most of its Bolshevik shackles.

XIII

The System of the World. One's overall view of things is reflected in how these diverse matters are discussed and dealt with. Is the overall view changing? Is there any opportunity to get back to the Eighteenth Century as we move into the Twenty-first Century? That is, can an old-fashioned respect for a reasoned natural-right approach be restored? Or are we moving back only to 1914, with various deep-rooted antipathies yearning to be played out? We have seen in the decade-long war between Iran and Iraq that the senseless slaughter of the First World War can be revived in our time. We still may not sufficiently appreciate how such "medium-sized" wars can get out of hand.

I have already referred to the excesses of liberty and what they can lead to. One form of such excesses may be seen in more and more reliance upon "market-driven" economies, which can lead to national if not international "communities" made up primarily of consumers. Such a displacement of civic-minded relations can eventually lead to political and religious cataclysms as desperate efforts are made by one people after another to restore a sense of humanity and of enduring purpose to their everyday lives.

CONCLUSION

What, then, is to be expected? For one thing, we should not expect the restoration, or in some cases the inauguration, of "democracy" automatically to take care of old problems in Eastern Europe. What is already happening in Yugoslavia is instructive. We see there a development that is a generation ahead of what is now happening in various Eastern European countries: old passions and old ways are reasserting themselves, threatening a dissolution of what had seemed to be for decades a useful union.

What should the United States do about all this? We should face up to the facts, including such facts as I have noticed about what it took to develop a thriving, however flawed, constitutionalism in the United States two centuries ago. We should also recognize how certain supposed threats against even so powerful a nation as the United States have been exaggerated in recent decades and what this has cost us and others. We should now be cautious about accepting predictions of too hopeful a character.

Certainly, we should not overestimate what we can know or do, and not only because of the frustrations, fear, and cynicism that that can lead to. For example, it can be instructive to consider whether much of what our anti-Communist crusaders did at home as well as abroad in recent decades might not have postponed rather than hastened the collapse we are evidently seeing of one Marxist tyranny after another.

The surprise generally exhibited at what is now happening should remind us that we may not, in our collective capacity, have appreciated what was really going on in Eastern Europe, a place where life has long been both remarkably grim and comically inefficient. At the very least, we should not overestimate what we can do now, even as we remain receptive to reasonable demands upon our generosity and good will. Certainly, it is not prudent to believe that the United States will determine what will happen in the Soviet Union and Eastern Europe in the decades ahead.

I return to the Russian legislator who predicted that freedom in his country "will remain in danger for the next hundred years or so." This assumes, of course, that freedom will be established, in some form, in the near future. Even so, there is something reassuring in this long view: it suggests that what takes a long time to secure may also take a long time to subvert. I have suggested, by considering what went into the making of the Constitution of 1787, that ours is a sturdier regime than it may sometimes seem. Such a recognition should help steady us as we confront longstanding issues at home that may now become more apparent and more pressing.

The most serious problem for us—or the problem *we* can address with some hope of understanding and controlling developments—is not what is likely to happen in Eastern Europe but what should happen to us. Our primary concern should at last be with the American character and a just appreciation of the institutions tailored to that character.

We should be reluctant, in any event, to promote the opinion that any particular form of government is best for all mankind at this time. A more salutary teaching from us for Eastern Europeans is that they should, by and large, let bygones be bygones rather than succumb to the "natural" temptation to settle old scores, something that can delay healing for a generation.

The most important contribution the United States can make to struggling peoples elsewhere is to offer a properly explained illustration of a healthy constitutionalism that permits on this continent a decent life for citizens of diverse origins. Our defects and limitations should be noticed, but they should not be exaggerated, certainly not in the terms that congenitally imprudent intellectuals are apt to employ. (Consider, for example, observations I had occasion to make at a Defense Intelligence College conference in 1986: "We should be on guard against that cleverness which can be easily mistaken for prudence, thereby lulling us into a general thoughtlessness, whether in the academy or in the councils of state and of war. . . . The world depends upon us to conduct the informed debate that is needed over the next decade for a sensible guidance of mankind into the Twenty-first Century. Not the least of the beneficiaries of our virtues should be the Russians themselves, whom it would be prudent *not* to regard always or simply as adversaries." See "What Is Still Wrong with George Anastaplo?," pp. 551–52, n. 41; 16 *Teaching Political Science* 81 [1989].)

It is important for everyone on earth to be reassured, or at least to have the opportunity to be reassured, that the rule of law is both possible and productive—and that it is a source of, as well as a salutary restraint upon, great power.

EPILOGUE

39

LESSONS FROM LIFE

*[Mark Twain was in 1907] very old and snow-white, and combined with
a noble air a most delightful style of conversation. Of course we argued
about the [Boer] war. After some interchanges I found myself beaten
back to the citadel "My country right or wrong." "Ah," said the old gentleman. "When the poor country is fighting for its life, I agree. But this
was not your case." I think however I did not displease him; for he was
good enough at my request to sign every one of the thirty volumes of his
works for my benefit; and in the first volume he inscribed the following
maxim intended, I daresay, to convey a gentle admonition: "To do good
is noble; to teach others to do good is nobler, and no trouble."*

WINSTON S. CHURCHILL

I

I have been invited to share with you lessons that can be gathered from
life, perhaps even from my own life. It is hard to be both interesting and
responsible in offering up such lessons. It is well in these circumstances to
recall the injunction long ago laid down by Hippocrates for doctors, "Do
no harm." That is to say, if you do not know what you are doing, do
nothing.

Of course, I may be unduly concerned here, since there does tend to be
something ineffectual about advice-giving. The "realistic" purpose of such
a talk as this may not be to convert a crowd but rather to reassure those
two or three people in the audience who are predisposed to go along with
the speaker anyway. Certainly, one cannot hope to make much difference
to anyone. But then, even that most influential of teachers, Confucius,

This talk was given at the Law School, The University of Chicago, Chicago, Illinois, May
13, 1986. (Sponsor: The Chicago Law Foundation.)

The epigraph is taken from Winston S. Churchill, *My Early Life: A Roving Commission*
(London: Thornton Butterworth, 1930), pp. 375–76.

could be recognized in his day as the man who "knows it's no use, but keeps on doing it." (*Analects*, XIV, 41)

My first lesson, then, has emerged almost on its own: *Be careful about the lessons you dispense.* Certainly, circumstances must be taken into account in applying any lesson. One form this lesson takes may be seen in what I consider a cardinal rule of draftsmanship: There are times when there is nothing to say, and then you don't say anything.

Perhaps the surest way to be careful about the lessons one dispenses is to tell people only what they want to hear. This seems to me proper enough, provided that it is appreciated that what people truly want to hear is what they *need* to hear, which of course may not be at once recognized by them. In fact, all too many people have but the faintest idea of what they are thinking and doing, and so are very much in need of informed and good-natured instruction.

II

I continue to play it safe in my lesson-giving by beginning with the most prosaic matters. Lawyers like the support of authority—so I go to a venerable one, Malcolm Sharp, an old teacher of mine here in this law school (but in the old, and better, building on the main campus of the University across the Midway). It was almost forty years ago, I believe, that I first heard from him the sage advice, which is our second lesson on this occasion: *Never take an elevator for less than five floors.* Mr. Sharp lived some eighty years, quite vigorous almost to the very end, a sturdy advertisement for his recommendation.

A reasonable application of such a rule is taken for granted. After all, you may be carrying things, or you may have a delicate heart condition, or you may have already gone up and down the stairs many times that day, or you may be unusually tired, or you may be with someone with whom you want to continue talking. If I did not expect you to be sensible, I would not dare offer the lessons I am providing you.

The elevator rule can be extended by analogy, something else that lawyers like to do. And so I suggest that you should not use automobiles for less than a couple of miles. On the other hand, I am rather dubious about jogging and running and, indeed, about most exercise as such, much of which seems, and may well be, unnatural.

But, it is also prudent to notice, whether or not you take the elevator lesson to heart, you are and will remain mortal.

III

Still, there are better and worse ways of using the time one does have on earth. I come now to a lesson that I worked out for myself. Indeed, I urged it upon Mr. Sharp from time to time in recent decades, but to no avail, and that is: *Take a nap every afternoon.*

Now, it need not be a long nap. Indeed, it should be no longer than an hour. Often, half an hour will do; sometimes, five or ten minutes make a difference. This means that one should have a cot in one's office, or at least a reclining chair.

You cannot nap? Rubbish! Simply lie back, close your eyes, and relax. It will do you a world of good, even if you do not doze off. A proper nap can affect the tempo of the day and make one's nights much more productive.

In fact, it can be a useful test, when law firms come around interviewing, to ask them what provision they make for napping. Such a question can help establish the proper tone for negotiations.

IV

You have heard, no doubt, that things are made for man, not man for things. For law students this axiom takes the form of this lesson: *Cut up your casebooks.* I give this advice all the time to law students. Since the young are very conventional, however, most of them continue to lug around those mammoth collections.

But does not cutting up a book affect its resale value? I should hope so! Anyone who appreciates what I am saying should be willing to pay you more for a casebook which has already been cut up for him, so that it can be comfortably used as needed.

You will again and again confront the casebook problem, not only in how you should handle volumes of law reports (photo-copying is handy there), but also in determining where doors and windows should be or what you should wear or where you should live. That is, we should be repeatedly reminded, things are made for man, not man for things.

V

Particularly vital things are food and drink. The lesson here is remarkably simple: *Keep your tastes simple.* The presumption—something else beloved of lawyers—the presumption should be in favor of bread, cheese, fruit, vegetables, water, and the like, all adjusted to one's own constitution, of course.

This moderation should be extended to the more romantic gratifications as well. But that is less of a problem, since moderation does tend to develop there as one gets older. But it can be different with food and drink, since as one gets older, one usually has more money—and besides, food and drink come to be used more and more as means to divert oneself.

Neither the poor nor the rich eat well (that is to say, properly) in this country. I am reminded of the problems of the rich whenever I am bumped into First Class on an airliner. It is evident that one's travel companions of the moment believe they have to do a lot of fancy eating and drinking even to begin to feel it is all worthwhile. It is much the same in their homes, especially if they have gone to considerable expense for cooks and the like.

VI

Keeping your food simple can be good practice for keeping your life, and especially your career, properly simple as well.

Law faculties, especially in the best schools, have been somewhat remiss in the advice they give (and don't give) about the careers their students follow. Absurd models are all too often held up for "the best and the brightest" to emulate. It *is* an absurd state of affairs when senior partners in the "best" law firms can routinely make half a million dollars a year and when youngsters fresh out of school can make up to $65,000 a year. ($40,000 a year is bad enough, and that is all too frequent.)

An elementary fact should be noticed before I get to my next lesson: making a living is not likely to be a problem for you as graduates of this law school. You will be able to afford the luxury of living up to my next rule: *Do not devote your career as a lawyer to anything you would not do if you were not being paid for it.* Of course, there *are* things you would do for free which you should not do, but that is another matter.

Of course, also, there are jobs you can, perhaps should, take upon leaving school only for the purpose of training yourself further. But you should be warned that it can be hard to abandon such jobs, and the steady (and steadily increasing) income they provide, once the "training" period is over.

VII

The great advantage of the law school credentials you will have earned is that you, unlike those less fortunate, are in a position to take some control of your lives, to conquer chance to some extent. And yet it is all too frequent that "the best and the brightest" are being captured by the larger (and supposedly better) law firms, where there is much talk of "billable hours" and much evidence of burnout and family disruption and just plain misery, however exciting it may sometimes seem and indeed be.

All too often there is, about the legal careers of "the brightest and the best," a gilded slavery in which partners as well as associates are trapped, and not only in the larger firms. Against this backdrop the "naive" advice given by Periander some two thousand years ago begins to sound most realistic: "Never do anything for money; leave gain to trades pursued for gain." (Diogenes Laertius, *Lives of Greek Philosophers* [Loeb Classical Library], I, 101)

This leads to, if it is not summed up in, our next lesson: *The middle way is likely to be best.* This touches upon a problem many of you will have: how are you going to spend the fairly substantial income you are likely to earn? It is likely that you will, sooner than you may realize, be locked into a high-earning, high-spending and hence high-wasting life.

But, it should be recognized, there is very little of real use that lots of money buys you in this country that people in the middle class do not have available to them also, except perhaps for extensive travel. Whether such travel is an advantage depends, however, on what you take with you—that is, on what you are. By and large, the rich people I know share the opinions of the community at large—and why not? They accept unexamined opinions from the same sources as everyone else. It is hard to see that the ready travel that the rich *can* afford makes much difference.

Besides, the best travel is by those who can do it at leisure—and for weeks, if not even months, at a time. I always advise students not to take summer jobs in law firms while they are in law schools, unless they really need the money. Those will be the last summers they are ever likely to have free again—until they become decrepit senior partners. Rather, they should take a friend and go backpacking across Scotland or some other such place.

I believe it unfortunate that law school faculties, perhaps under pressure from law firms, should encourage law students to waste their summers by working—and thereafter to waste their lives by the wrong kind of work.

VIII

It is now a commonplace that the practice of law has become, much more than ever, a business. The size of firms, the horrendous overhead, the competitiveness for clients, and even double shifts in some firms—all these point up the commercialization, if not even the industrialization, of the practice of law.

But it is an inferior business in one critical respect—in that it does not have, at least in the corporate-law practice, the same kind of risk-taking that the business entrepreneur confronts every day. All too often such law practice falls in between an honest business and a noble profession. Even the fanciest lawyers, who have to become more and more specialized, permit themselves to be regarded as the servants of their masters.

Our next lesson then, is an obvious one: *One should, as a lawyer, make a determined effort to practice law.* And this means, in the typical case today, a general practice, with no more than a dozen partners and with a substantial participation in the criminal-courts work of the community. This also means that one is more likely to be engaged in meaningful public service and to live a more humane life in the process.

IX

If it is indeed the practice of law that one is going to engage in, then one must take more seriously both the end and the mode of the profession. The end is, of course, justice; the mode is honor. The lawyer's honor is his primary credential: judges and lawyers simply know who can be trusted; even in so large a city as Chicago, word gets around. One's reliability is vital to one's ability to do good by bringing out the best in others; and it affects what is expected of one by one's clients.

Thus our next lesson is an old-fashioned one: *One should so conduct oneself as to be worthy of trust.* This means, ultimately, that one cannot be guided merely by the opinions of others. Rather, one must have a lively awareness of the standards of justice and of right that are at the root of one's activities as a lawyer. With that awareness as a guide, one will so conduct oneself as to be, as well as to seem, worthy of trust. Otherwise, one's practice of law becomes meaningless, so much so that money and the things money can buy have to be looked to as solace. (See my essay, "Natural Right and the American Lawyer," in *Human Being and Citizen*, and my essay, "A Primer on the Good, the True, and the Beautiful," in *The Artist as Thinker*.)

X

Of course, it is not enough to be honorable, however important that may be. Before I go to my next lesson, I must inform you that most of your classmates will never again be as interesting as they will be on the day they graduate from law school. This figures: most of them have just finished four years at a good college, and now three years in a fine law school. Their minds have been nourished and stretched for almost a decade in a way they are not likely ever to be again—unless my next lesson is taken to heart: *One should try to be a student all one's life.*

This means that one should keep studying things, but not as lawyers tend to do in "mastering" a field for a particular case or client, only to forget it when the next assignment develops. Nor does it mean that one should be a legal specialist, in the way that usually comes about. Rather, one should investigate the roots, including the history and purposes, of the law that one may have to be a specialist in.

There is a tendency on the part of lawyers to feel superior. They should, therefore, systematically subject themselves to a course of study which obliges them to recognize their limitations, even as it instructs them in what superiority truly means. One's course of study should include, then, a thorough inquiry into some non-legal subject of significance. Someone working in the Loop, for example, could well investigate the development, character and influence of Chicago architecture. Care should be taken, however, not to mistake a hobby for serious study.

XI

My next lesson is a related one: *One should read.* This may be somewhat more passive than the systematic studying I have just been speaking of. One should so arrange one's life as to be properly stimulated by the best that is available. Thus, you should subscribe, even while in law school, to a concert series at Orchestra Hall, where there is, after all, one of the best orchestras in the world and where the cheapest seats may well be the best. And you should make regular visits to the Art Institute in such a way that you become quite familiar with its holdings. Other such things will occur to you when you begin to think about them, including the theatres and zoos of this area.

But the lesson about reading depends ultimately on books. This means, among other things, that television should be gotten rid of, or at least watched for the most part only in public places. This should go without saying but, alas, it does need to be said. Television is not only grossly inefficient (a terrible waste of time) but it is also profoundly corrupting (not least in what it does to our passions, promoting as it does both fear and envy).

I used to say that one should be most reluctant to read anything written since 1900, especially if one wants to understand what is going on around one. But I find that this may seem impractical—and I do want, above all, to seem as well as to be practical. (Besides, some might point out, that was before I began publishing books of my own.) And so I offer this compromise in the implementation of the reading lesson: for every Twentieth-Century book you read, you should read at least one written before 1900.

In any event, you cannot become a first-rate lawyer in the Anglo-American tradition if you do not know well the plays of Shakespeare. It would help, as reminders of what it is to be human, to add to your daily prayers the working out with your breakfast (or on your way to work) one of the propositions of Euclid and the thinking through on your way home (or before retiring) a poem. (Here we should be reminded of my fourth rule: good anthologies of poetry as well as a copy of Euclid, and later Galileo's *Dialogue* and then Newton's *Principia*, should be kept in your office where you can photocopy your allotments for each week.)

Particularly helpful, in promoting your own reading, I should add, is the systematic reading of good books to your children, books you yourself want to go through. Besides, if *you* don't read to your children, who will?

XII

A proper profession, proper study, and proper reading all depend on and contribute to my next lesson, which is, *One should remain open to greatness*. We touch here upon the problem of piety, of course.

There is much around us, and especially among lawyers, that discourages such openness: competitiveness, egotism, celebrity-worship, novelties, and "progress." It becomes hard in such circumstances to respect one's betters, especially when one cannot recognize them as betters. I find it sad, for example, to hear—as one does from time to time even around this law school—the dismissal as merely eccentric or obtuse of someone such as William Crosskey, perhaps the greatest scholar ever associated with this institution.

To be capable of greatness oneself, one must be open to it and one must want to see it respected in a proper way. To disparage one's better is, ultimately, to blind or to paralyze oneself as to the good. Unless there is an openness to greatness, one is not able to recognize certain challenges and adversities as opportunities.

There are, of course, few marvelous opportunities in one's life, and so one must take full advantage of them when they do happen to appear. It is impossible to advise another about the genuine opportunity that will confront him, for it is likely to be unique and unexpected. This means that one's soul should be in such condition that one can recognize a proper challenge when it does appear and respond to it in an appropriate manner.

XIII

I have, on this occasion, been talking about things of both the body and soul which may equip one to do and to be the best. One's passions and one's mind need to be so shaped that one can step back and see things for what they are. This brings us to our final lesson: *One should ask the obvious questions.*

Here I can turn for authority to one of the great men of the century, Winston Churchill. Consider what he had to say about the fall of Singapore to the Japanese in 1942 (*The Second World War*, IV, 49):

> I do not write this in any way to excuse myself. I ought to have known. My advisers ought to have known and I ought to have been told, and I ought to have asked. The reason I had not asked about this matter, amid the thousands of questions I put, was that the possibility of Singapore having no landward defenses no more entered into my mind than that of a battleship being launched without a bottom.

One should wonder what the obvious questions of one's own day are. Particularly to be searched out are one's own failings, especially when one finds oneself unduly troubled by the more obvious failings of others. Still, one should also be aware, if not even proud, of one's own merits.

One has to make an effort to see, and to ask, obvious questions, especially when the received opinions in one's circle are so firm. I hope that one or more of the lessons I have presumed to share with you today encourage, if only in a few of you, a sound independence and contribute to a reasonably long and a properly happy life, both as lawyers and as human beings.

40

SUMMING UP

40-A. Body and Soul

Amadeo in his mountain kingdom far from war was constantly being chosen as arbiter by one party or the other and he was considered the only one of them all who knew how to give good counsel to himself and others. The folly of others made him seem wise.

POPE PIUS II

I

Festive occasions, when everyone else is more or less obliged by the proprieties to magnify one's accomplishments, do tempt one to believe that there is something to be said for the observation by Samuel Johnson that he "never knew a man of merit neglected; it was generally his own fault

---

The talk was given on the occasion of a celebration of my fiftieth birthday, which was on November 7, 1975. (Original Title: "Body and Soul: Thoughts at Fifty.") The gathering, which included Malcolm P. Sharp, was made up principally of University of Chicago graduate students in political science. At that time, the expected retirement age in academic life was sixty-five. On Mr. Sharp, see Anastaplo, "Malcolm P. Sharp and the Spirit of '76," *University of Chicago Law Alumni Journal*, Summer 1975, p. 18 (reprinted in 18 *Congressional Record* 40241, December 12, 1975). On Leo Strauss, see "The Thinker as Artist," in Anastaplo, *The Thinker as Artist* (Athens, Ohio: Ohio University Press, 1983), pp. 250–71. Mr. Strauss and Mr. Sharp are drawn upon (as are Laurence Berns and Harry V. Jaffa) in the Epigraphs and Preface for this book, *The American Moralist*.

This talk has recently been supplemented by a talk given at a celebration in San Francisco, California, during the American Political Science Association Annual Convention, September 1, 1990: "What Is Going on Here Anyway? Thoughts at Sixty-Five." (That talk is not included here.)

The epigraph is taken from Pope Pius II, *Memoirs of a Renaissance Pope*, Florence A. Gragg translation (New York: G. P. Putnam's Sons, 1959), p. 221.

that he failed of success." (*Chicago Tribune, Magazine of Books*, September 13, 1959)

Be that as it may, your remarks and my response may be little more than an extended version of an exchange I once heard on Studs Terkel's radio show, after the illustrious entertainer Bricktop had been regaling him with tales about her quite colorful life (WFMT, Chicago, Illinois, May 7, 1975):

"Bricktop," he said, "you are *sui generis.*"
"Oh, no darling," she replied, "I'm just myself."

Be that also as it may, there *is* something about the half-century mark which naturally stimulates among men the desire to celebrate. An old friend has written me, upon noticing the calendar, "Are congratulations in order? You certainly have made the course more interesting for quite a few people, surely for me." Well, the course has been rather interesting for me too—and I interpret this dinner, to say nothing of what has been suggested to me about making a response to your kind remarks, to be an invitation to say something about what I have learned since I came into the world at St. Louis, Missouri on November 7, 1925.

I put you on notice, however, that my record on after-dinner talks is not a very happy one. One such talk I made in Athens a few years ago when the Colonels were trying to run things, with the help of an American State Department that did not know what it was doing either, got me declared *persona non grata*. And a talk I made a few weeks ago after a quite fancy meal provided by the American Civil Liberties Union was received in a somewhat skeptical manner, since it too followed my rule for such occasions, which is that one should tell one's listeners what they need to hear, not what they believe they want to hear. The A.C.L.U. was told, upon giving me its Harry Kalven Freedom of Expression award, it should consider what needed to be done to insure in the community at large the character that would permit Americans to make proper use of the freedom that organization has so gallantly worked for. That is, I argued for an exhibition by them of a greater measure of concern about corrupting influences among us. (See *Human Being and Citizen*, pp. 3–7; Section IV of Essay No. 34–13, above. See, also, 50 *Southern California Law Review* 370–72 [1977].)

II

I gather that fifty appears much older to you than it does *now* to me. The signs of deference exhibited by some of you toward me from time to time, as well as what has been said on this occasion, indicate what fifty-ness must look like to you. Your attitude, as political science graduate students of a somewhat conservative bent, is not unnatural and licenses me to take myself seriously, if only for a few minutes.

I felt the same way about fiftyness when I was your age, for it was when I was your age that I first met Malcolm Sharp and Leo Strauss, two teachers who have been very important for me and who were then about the age I am now. They did seem to be quite mature, not ancient, mind you, but mature, and consequently men of experience and sagacity. I mention in passing that you can see, in the printed Supreme Court record relating to my "unsuccessful" bar admission appeal, a photograph of me at your present age. (p. 384) I look as serious as some of you must now feel. If, then, my present impressions are of any use to you, you should take to heart my observation that I seem much older, much much older, to you now than you will seem to yourselves when you attain my age.

But perhaps I do not realize what has happened to me, what I have lost in resiliency and acuteness and all the other things we associate with youth, even though I can still read without glasses and my hearing remains good. One can see such loss more easily in others than in oneself, as was evident the other evening at the Field House when my youngest child and I (she is twelve) watched the University of Chicago varsity basketball team in the annual varsity-alumni game run rings around the team of top-flight varsity players of other years. My daughter was saddened to see some of the stars of her youth—some three or four years ago, that is—unable to shine as they once had. The old campaigners were being harried by frisky, young puppies; the good-humored self-restraint of the puppies only accentuated the debility that had set in among the alumni because of spiritual fatigue, lack of practice, and gain of weight.

Fifty was once the threshold to old age. It does not seem to be so at this time. But it *is* the threshold to the old age of the typical academic career. That is, one's academic career usually runs, from the time of entering college to the time of retirement, some forty-five years. The youth of that career is between twenty and thirty-five (a period which included for me, in addition to academic training and some teaching, both military service and the considerable bar admission litigation described in *The Constitutionalist*). The middle age of that career is between thirty-five and fifty (much of which has been devoted on my part to the Basic Program of Liberal Education of Adults here at the University of Chicago and to the political science and philosophy departments out at Rosary College). Heaven only knows what will happen for me between fifty and (if it is fated) sixty-five, the old age of that career. I have in some twenty years of teaching yet to lose a day to illness, but one should not expect such a record to be extended much longer. [Fifteen years later, at age 65, this record continues to thrive, less so the abundant hair that is evident in my Supreme Court record photograph.]

To turn fifty in 1975 is particularly instructive, I should add. For to be fifty now means that one has been alive for one-fourth of the two-hundred year history of one's Country. This shows either how old I really am or how young this country is—or perhaps both. Let's say "both," with the qualification that this country is both young and old, for it drew at its birth in 1776 upon an English heritage already five hundred years in the making. To say "both" invests me with the trappings of age and hence with the standing, if only for this occasion, of someone with something sage to convey to you as a result of his years; it also leaves me young enough to be able to speak your language.

The best of what I may have learned has presumably been incorporated in my writings. But perhaps a few of the things I have learned can be refashioned for this occasion, an occasion, as all birthdays are, when the soul can pay appropriate homage to its dependence on the body.

III

What, then, do I know which may be of some use to you? Three things come to mind. The first is that this is not really a threatening world, certainly not as threatening as various talented, but yet timid, people take it to be.

One of you has observed to me, "You walk around Hyde Park at night as if it were an art museum." That is something of an exaggeration, but it is certainly true that I am not intimidated by this place the way some people are. This does not mean, however, that I do not take precautions, nor does it mean that I have not been careful about what I have permitted my wife and children to do and not do in this neighborhood at night. But I have never thought it useful to regard Hyde Park as a jungle. Perhaps I would feel differently if someone were to assault me. I *have* had a gun drawn on me, by a chap who had been chased out of a neighbor's house and whom I had helped follow to the end of the block. I said to him, as he waved his gun at us, something to the effect that he could do neither of us any good with that thing, at which he turned and ran into the hands of the police.

There is in most of us still something of the child which can be very much intimidated by the world around him and which is susceptible to an apocalyptic view of things. When one becomes feeble, or imagines oneself to be quite vulnerable, that childish timidity and a seeming dependence on chance can begin to reassert themselves. The child *is* often obliged to seek reassurance.

The most trivial things can intimidate him, even, for example, information innocently conveyed to him at the breakfast table. Consider the "Nutrition Information" available on a milk carton these days (I recall similar information on cereal boxes in my youth). Nutrition Information "per serving" is listed in some detail. One is told that there is in one cup of milk 6% of one's "U.S. Recommended Daily Allowance" (U.S. RDA) of Vitamin C, 8% of one's U.S. RDA of Thiamine, 6% of one's U.S. RDA of Zinc and of Vitamin B6. This kind of information was somewhat disconcerting for me as a child: *only* 6% of this or that in one serving! How could one possibly consume enough to supply oneself that magic (perhaps even patriotic) "U.S. Recommended Daily Allowance"? What happens if one does not get enough? When one comes to Niacin and to Iron, the situation becomes truly desperate: for a cup of milk contains, one is told, "less than 2% of the U.S. RDA of these nutrients."

No doubt all this information was provided to point up the goodness of the product; but for me, as for anyone else who could calculate and who also knew the limits of what he could consume in milk or cereal, this information was a repeated source of concern. The same kind of distorted concern, I suspect, came to be seen in those eminent prosecutors and judges in the 1950s who could somehow regard the minuscule (and much-infiltrated) Communist Party of the United States as a threat to the security, if not even to the very existence, of this Country—a concern which had disastrous effects in both our domestic and our foreign policy for at least a decade. An informed clearsightedness, I am suggesting, is necessary for a sensible assessment of things, for prudent action, and for peace of mind.

One has to leave behind the concerns and grievances of one's childhood, lest one join the legion of those still very much concerned about what did and did not happen to them thirty or forty or fifty years ago. Decisive for me with respect to these matters, I sometimes think, was my youthful service in the Air Corps during the Second World War, service which saw me hold my own with men older and physically stronger than I was and in the course of which I earned my wings and commission and found myself on more than one occasion staring sudden death in the face and finding it all rather interesting, as I find life itself. Or as one of our Southern Illinois "heroes" (Charles Birger) said, looking around as he was about to be hanged, "It *is* a beautiful world."

It is an interesting world as well; and it is good that human life be preserved, made useful, and spared from gratuitous pain. I was intrigued a few months ago upon visiting the illustrious Panda bears at a Washington zoo to notice the common sparrows and field mice drawn, along with a multitude of tourists, to those cages to cadge what they could. Or consider the plant life that somehow emerges out of rock crevices wherever the thinnest film of soil may be found. Vital living things do keep trying to preserve and hence to perfect themselves, and from that constant effort much can be expected, perhaps even intelligent life.

But, we are told, the universe is running down, energy is steadily being dissipated, and dark, cold matter is all there is destined to be some day. Yet others say that when a large quantity of that matter collects and presses in upon itself, as it must also some day do if it *is* to be scattered in a completely fortuitous manner, heat and eventually life may then be generated once again. Put another way, has not all this perhaps happened before?

To say that this is not a threatening world is not to deny that there is in it a considerable amount of folly and even needless cruelty. One learns, however, to expect such failings and to do what one can in one's own precinct to suggest corrections. But one should take care not to permit oneself to be intimidated by what one learns about the disagreeable things that are done to others or even to oneself. In short, congenital timidity has to be overcome. One should grow up and not take oneself too seriously.

IV

The second thing I have learned that may be of special use to you is related to what I have said, in speaking of the limits of timidity, about how interesting life can be, how interesting it is to learn things both practical and theoretical. Only the unimaginative or very tired man need ever be bored with his life. There *is* so much which is worth knowing.

Unless one is singularly gifted, however, one cannot learn much without working hard. The importance here of energy and discipline is hard to overestimate: one must simply sit down *and work*, preferably at a desk, with pencil in hand. When one cannot be at one's desk, one can at least mull over the questions one is currently examining. These should be questions one is interested in oneself, not merely questions assigned by others. After all, there is more to learn than one can ever learn, so why not pursue matters of genuine interest? This also means that one should not permit career or publication considerations to be primary in the determination of what one works on.

But however one goes about learning, there is one caution particularly appropriate for people who are interested in the things you are interested in and who have been influenced by the people you have been influenced by, especially when much is made among them of guarded writing. You must beware of overinterpretation of the texts you address yourselves to. It is very difficult to simplify, to be simpleminded enough, so as really to *see* what one is looking at.

V

The third thing I have learned which may be of some use to you draws upon what I believe I have noticed about the limits of what one can reasonably expect to accomplish in the world of affairs. You appreciate, I am sure, the dangers of rising and hence often disappointed expectations, and the related inability to recognize and hence to preserve what is good and is not likely to be much improved upon without serious costs.

The first lesson I sketched this evening with respect to the folly of timidity encourages one to recognize that one is not helpless. Now I am addressing myself to the other extreme: one should recognize that one is not omnipotent, either in one's ability to discern the good or in one's power to act on what one has discerned. It is particularly important for political scientists attracted as you are to old-fashioned natural right, and who want to see the good prevail in this wicked old world of ours, to take care lest they be either swept along by floods of indignation or sucked under in a whirlpool of disillusionment.

One should try, that is, to assume the best in others without becoming either sentimental or suicidal. I have myself found upon examination that there is usually more to "the other side" of an issue than was evident at first glance. Classical political thought, it seems to me, is particularly useful as a moderating influence upon people likely to be caught up by the passions of the day.

One model I can hold up to you of a useful curbing of indignation without sacrificing one's dedication to virtue and the common good may be seen in Mr. Sharp's book, published in 1956 on the *Rosenberg-Sobell* case, *Was Justice Done?* Because of its disciplined examination of the complicated passions of others, it remains the best book written on that disgraceful episode in our history. Great harm was done because of the indignation which blinded our government at that time. But great harm can be done as well because of indignation evoked among the unwary upon learning of the callous deeds generated by the indignation of others.

Indignation, like timidity, should be left to children and to the trainers of children of all ages.

VI

The three things upon which I have presumed to preach on this occasion have to do with excesses: excesses in self-preservation, in scholarship, and in righteousness. They are excesses not unrelated to the kinds of lives the best of you consider yourselves preparing for. Timidity can naturally follow from a complete dedication of oneself to things of the mind as one's vulnerable body is left to fend for itself, so to speak. Pedantry, albeit an inspired pedantry, can naturally follow for one who wants to delve to the very foundations of things, as the surface or common sense of things is left to more prosaic minds. Indignation can naturally follow as one result of a highminded enlistment in the ranks of those in pursuit of virtue, as chance, crossed purposes and the limits of one's information, to say nothing of ordinary human compassion or of a noble generosity, are lost sight of.

I have thought it useful on this occasion to report upon these matters partly because several of the most gifted of our contemporaries in the line of work you happen to be interested in have exhibited in quite interesting forms one or another of these failings. The first and third of these classic failings come from taking oneself too seriously; such failings make true happiness difficult. The second failing, due perhaps to a kind of *mania*, comes from not taking selfness (and hence ordinary experience, if not mortality itself) seriously enough; this may ultimately impede a full understanding of things. Thus the first failing in the catalogue assembled for this occasion has the body exerting an undue influence on the mind; the second has the mind disregarding the body completely; the third has the mind exerting an undue influence on the body.

These are, I suggest, the failings that you too are most likely to be prone to and that you should religiously guard against. There is still another failing, but one that may be unavoidable. It has to do with what more and more serious work will do to the personal relations you will have formed in your less serious days. There *is* an inevitable tension between the human being and the citizen, between the human being, who is fully dedicated to the life of reason, and the citizen, whether his primary associational allegiance be to a family or to a city or to a faculty.

Why is this? I have already spoken of the discipline necessary if one is to learn. Between those who make themselves work and those who do not, a divergence is quite likely. The one who has been able to work is no longer the person he was. People grow up, or at least grow apart, and their relations change, if only because the one who is working seriously will, if he is any good, come to regard the work he is doing as more important than any conventional or "historical" relations. In addition, the opinions upon which associations depend are apt to be reconsidered by him.

Of course, such a man does recognize certain duties, including duties relating to his very existence and its sources. Even so, the truly gifted should take care not to permit the best in himself to be subverted in deference to the conventional, to the sentimental, or to the allegiances he happens to have.

You will be surprised someday to learn how far you have moved, if you continue with what you are doing, even from those of your fellow students (now as talented and lively and learned as you are) who go into more practical pursuits, whether in academic life or in "the real world." If these ties matter to you—if your temperament is such as to depend on intimacies with the irreplaceable companions of your youth—you should reconsider the kind of life you are pointed toward. But perhaps this advice is superfluous, since such a temperament may be quite able to take care of itself by diverting the threatened student into more congenial pursuits.

Please do not understand me to suggest that you make a deliberate effort to cut off ordinary human contact, but only to anticipate what is likely to happen to certain associations you will have made in your formative years. People truly interested in political philosophy should appreciate what human contact is: it does matter, in the communities that political philosophy studies, whether one's neighbor is a cat or a man and whether one knows which it happens to be.

Certainly, I should be the last to discourage you from exhibiting respect toward those whom you leave behind, but a decent regard for the conventional attachments of mankind may be more likely if one anticipates what often happens to the man seriously interested in a life of inquiry. I have put you on notice.

In any event, I urge upon you a continued respect for the proprieties, and even kindness.

VII

Your kindness toward me may be seen in the meal we have enjoyed together this evening and, in a more enduring form, in the formidable briefcase you have entrusted me with, to say nothing of the challenging things you have said about me.

The last briefcase I was given came from the Air Corps when I got my wings as a nineteen-year-old, and it accompanied me on many instructive flights all over the world. Thus the auspices are favorable, and I am entitled to hope that the briefcase you have so kindly provided me tonight will prove, for a long time to come, similarly useful in furthering my education.

An even more enduring form of kindness, I presume to suggest as I bring this festive occasion to a close, is that which is traditionally exhibited by one-time students to a would-be teacher. If he is mistaken, they quietly ignore him or, if he is not incorrigible, they correct him (if possible, gently). If he should happen to be correct, they someday do for *their* students what he was privileged to do for them.

40-B. The Teacher As Learner

Charicles, one of the Thirty Tyrants in Athens, said, "The fact is, Socrates, you are in the habit of asking questions to which you know the answers. That is what you are not to do."

XENOPHON

I

Discussion is made much of today: Much is made of discussion techniques, the function of the discussion leader, and that sort of thing.

There *are* some things one can do to make discussion more effective—things to be learned from instruction and things to be picked up from experience. But it is important to keep in mind that discussion is not something to be pursued for its own sake. In fact, an undue concern for discussion can bring out the worst in students. This should be kept in mind as one hears much made today of "participation" and of discussion leaders.

This talk was given at the Teacher Training Conference, Paideia Program, Kilmer Elementary School, Chicago, Illinois, November 30, 1984. (Original title: "The Teacher as Learner: On Discussion.") It has been published in the *Claremont Review of Books*, Summer 1985, pp. 22–23.

The Paideia Program has been developed under the leadership of Mortimer J. Adler. I have served since 1984 as a consultant for the Paideia Program in the Chicago Public Schools and elsewhere.

The epigraph is taken from Xenophon, *Memorabilia*, I, ii, 36 (E. C. Marchant translation). See, on what Socrates did know, Anastaplo, "Freedom of Speech and the First Amendment: Explorations," 21 *Texas Tech Law Review* 1941, at 1945–58 (1990).

II

The ultimate leaders of the best seminar discussions are the authors of the best books. It is only in the best books that one is likely to encounter the finest examples of minds at work—and it is vital to the development of the best in students that they become aware of how the very best do think. Is there any reliable way to develop such an awareness except by helping students begin to grasp what the best minds—that is, minds truly thinking—say?

There is a need, then, to figure out what the particular author being discussed on any occasion has argued: What does he stand for? How does he put what he says and why? What position is he speaking against?

Critical to a full understanding of any argument is an informed opinion as to whether it is sound. Still, we should not make too much in our circumstances of having students pass judgment on the best minds, especially when it is easy to come to believe in an egalitarian age that one man's opinion is just as good as another's. Rather, students should be helped to appreciate that one is always obliged to *reach* in order to grasp what the very best minds have thought.

It should be evident, then, that I am talking about how one learns to read. Of course, various technical skills are needed. Often they follow from, or are enhanced by, mastery of the subject. Of course, also, the opinions of students—opinions grounded in whatever experience they happen to have had—should be drawn upon if discussion is to be vital.

But all this is, I repeat, subordinate to the inquiry: What does this author say here?

III

This means, among other things, that students should be disciplined to examine and to understand their text, not to talk about it as if they were preparing a new text of their own. Only when they understand properly the guides available to them can they usefully apply what they learn to issues of the day.

On the other hand, a text is treated differently, and all too often inadequately, when it provides little more than an occasion, or the point of departure, for discussing matters of current interest.

This means, in turn, that the discussion leader must have a confident sense of what is relevant, what contributes to an understanding of whatever is being said by the text, and what is (however "interesting") no more than a digression, if not even mere self-indulgence. The better the leader knows the book at hand, the better he knows what questions should be pressed, what lines of discussion should be pursued, and what more remains to be explored.

To know a book means, among other things, that one is aware of its presuppositions, principles, and ends. One is hardly likely to be an "expert" with respect to each text one leads a discussion of; but a tentative grasp of each such text is useful, especially if one is aware of one's own limitations.

IV

To say that the leader is limited is not to say that he cannot do good things. In fact, just the opposite may be true. The best discussions often depend on the fact that the leader himself has a genuine inquiry which he is personally pursuing with his class. Much is to be said for not doing the same things each time one discusses a particular book, for not going over the same parts each time one returns to that book. One must be careful not to make too much of the teacher as actor.

The most effective way to proceed may be to settle upon a particular passage, preferably an unfamiliar one, using it as the occasion for studying the whole work. In order to do this, one should have a reliable sense of the overall organization and argument of the work. (Students should be permitted, as much as possible, to do all the reading aloud that is done in class. This not only helps accustom them to using the best language available to them, but it also helps their teacher resist the temptation to put on a show.)

One advantage of an approach which has the class settle upon a particular passage is that it helps remedy the short attention span evident in students, especially those steeped in television. They need to be encouraged to make sustained intellectual efforts. (Working through poems, as well as through Euclid's demonstrations, should also contribute to this end.) Another advantage of settling upon a particular passage is that it helps compensate for any lack of preparation among the students present.

V

The discussion "method" I have been sketching is one which is much richer for everyone concerned than what usually goes on in class. This way the teacher is constantly learning and hence is more likely to remain vital himself. The alert "teacher" should expect to learn more than anyone else. (See "What is a Clasic?" in *The Artist as Thinker*.)

Students surely do want the best for themselves, but they need repeated testimonials as to what is truly good. Not the least of the ways in which young students are helped is by their observing and imitating adults who are obviously, and with considerable effort and satisfaction, constantly learning themselves.

VI

It is important, then, when considering books of the highest stature, to suggest by precept and example that there *is* an argument to work out, that such an argument depends on certain presuppositions and objectives, that there are better and worse points to be made in such arguments, that we do have the ability to understand such things, that we also have the ability (as well as the duty) to judge what is often said about such things, that some people who talk a lot (even quite intelligent people) simply do not know what they are talking about much of the time, and that others (also quite intelligent people) can actually believe that such talkers know what they are talking about. It is important, I say, that students come to appreciate these things.

VII

Thus, in this way, students should get a better idea than they would otherwise have of a first-rate text, of how to talk about it, and of how to assess others who talk about it.

They should develop, over time, an awareness of the fundamental and enduring questions that the best books define and try to answer. When they do have this awareness, they can better notice, and do something with, the facts all around them.

Until the enduring questions are grasped, one cannot truly notice (that is, even see) what is immediately around one. Nor does one know what to ask about or what to do with the things that one does happen to notice.

VIII

Perhaps the most important thing for many students, especially for the more intelligent and articulate among them, is that they develop a proper sense of their own limitations.

They should also have developed in themselves both a confidence in their abilities and an assurance that there are standards to be applied to what they do. But first and foremost, they should be led to sense what one needs to know in order to know enough for the matter at hand.

All this, it should be impressed upon contemporary students, is not just for the sake of utility. Too much around us already stresses utility—and this can encourage mere hedonism, which tends to be shortsighted and fragmented, and ultimately frustrating and destructive. Rather, students today should be encouraged to recognize that much is to be said for "understanding for its own sake," including that understanding provided us by things of beauty.

IX

Among the many consequences of an emphasis upon utility can be the notion that discussion should be made much of. But however useful discussion may be for providing students practice in thinking things through, it bears repeating that students should be taught that they should not want merely to talk. Rather, they should be thoughtful—and this depends on, among other things, an awareness of what one needs to know in order to become thoughtful.

Properly trained students should come to recognize and to defer to genuine thoughtfulness in others. Put another way, students should be so trained that they come to discourage facile talk wherever they are likely to encounter it, thereby promoting serious public discourse all around them.

In short, then, a proper respect should be developed in our students for the art of reading and for the ability to think—that ability to think which serious reading, as well as fruitful discussion, promotes, depends on, and cherishes.

40-C. On Giving Thanks
in Dark Times

She did no more but die; if after her
Any shall live, which dare true good prefer,
Every such person is her delegate,
T'accomplish that which should have been her fate.

JOHN DONNE

I

It is no accident that we have Thanksgiving as a national holiday. Can any enduring holiday be accidental, one might well ask, however much its particular date (for example, the Fourth of July) may have been determined by chance? Every civilized community wants to have much made of certain occasions, both public and private, and so there are commemorations for the new year, for the resurrection of spring, for one's birthday, name day, wedding or other anniversary, for the founding and founders of the country, for the memory of those who have gone before, for a bountiful harvest, and for the end of the year, which can also be seen as preparing the way for a new, if not miraculous, birth.

There are in the cycle of the year enough regularities to be noticed. There should be in the community enough art to be able to identify and to distinguish in an appropriate fashion such regularities.

So it is with Thanksgiving, which it is obviously fitting to have follow upon the harvest season of the year.

II

What is there, generally, to be thankful for? Official proclamations, which go back to the earliest days of the Pilgrims, which were revived by the Continental Congress, and which have been issued on an annual basis since the Civil War, indicate what is usually noticed at Thanksgiving time. The bounty of the Lord is acknowledged, seen most immediately in plen-

---

This sermon was given at the Lake Shore Unitarian Universalist Society, Winnetka, Illinois, November 28, 1982.

The epigraph is taken from John Donne, *A Funeral Elegy.*

tiful food. That bounty is seen also in the preservation of the community from dangers both at home and abroad.There is thus a recognition of the goodness of God.

There is furthermore on such occasions a recognition of a people's limitations and shortcomings, if not sinfulness, as well as its general rededication to the vision which has made the community what it is.

We are reminded on such occasions of what parents, family, unknown benefactors, friends, and the community, all somehow agents of the divine purpose, have done for us. Thanksgiving inspires us to join in our thoughts and in our prayers the particular to the universal, the whole to the part.

III

The community is urged at Thanksgiving to count its blessings. This is called for even though it should be obvious that there are likely to be at any particular time some in the community who will be in troubled straits and hence in anything but a thankful mood. Besides, one can come to learn that the very things sought and welcomed as blessings may turn out to be causes of tribulation.

Thus, no doubt, this Thanksgiving finds some of us here today who are anything but content, anything but inclined to consider life at this time to be good. Some of us may even go so far as to wonder whether life can, on net, ever be really good. For such people, men live always in dark times. As one modern composer put it, "I could never have a symphony pour out into jubilant fanfare as a tremendous *yea* to life. Because man *doesn't* win the struggle." (*Program*, Chicago Symphony Orchestra, November 26–27, 1982, p. W9)

IV

Indeed, so radically uncertain can human life be that its very desirability may be seriously questioned. "There is an ancient story that King Midas hunted in the forest a long time for the wise Silenus, the companion of Dionysus, without capturing him. When Silenus at last fell into his hands, the king asked what was the best and most desirable of all things for man. Fixed and immovable, the demigod said not a word; till at last, urged by the king, he gave a shrill laugh and broke out into these words, Oh wretched ephemeral race, children of chance and misery, why do you compel me to tell you what it would be most expedient for you not to hear? What is best of all is beyond your reach forever: not to *be* born, not to be, to be *nothing*. But the second best for you—is quickly to die.'" (See Friedrich Nietzsche, *The Birth of Tragedy*, sec. 3. Compare secs. 4, 7, and 24.)

Stories such as this one are plausible, even when not persuasive, because they do exploit typical responses to all-too-frequent human afflictions. We can be reminded by these discouraged responses of critical elements in the assessment of the human condition made by the perhaps compassionate Silenus, a demigod who is himself not subject to death. For, you will remember, he opened his reluctant reply to King Midas with these words, "Oh, wretched ephemeral race, children of chance and misery." The mortality of mankind, it is evident, is critical to its unenviable condition. One of the consequences of that mortality is that man is decisively subject to chance and hence to misery.

Silenus' assessment of mankind obliges one to ask what the meaning of "all this" is. What sense does the universe make, and man in it? Is not this for most men a question about the status of the divine? Does not a communal thanksgiving itself imply or take for granted some view of the divine? To whom, for example, is thanks to be given, and why? Perhaps a few people of a philosophic inclination can approach these problems dispassionately or "abstractly," but most people, it seems, need graphic accounts about how things are ordered; so revelation becomes important, something which intellectuals are apt to ignore. Revelation teaches, to quote a preacher of note, "We come from God, we live by God, we belong to God: we are His, inalienably His. God loves with a divine love every human soul and every human soul lives in that love. How could it be otherwise? Every breath that we draw, every thought of our brain, every instant of life proceed from God's inexhaustible goodness." (See James Joyce, *A Portrait of the Artist as a Young Man*, chap. 3, p. 128.)

V

Revelation does suggest a response that calls into question a decisive premise of Silenus' grim prescription: revelation can insist that man is not truly a member of an ephemeral race, but rather that he as an individual has an immortal soul. But if one is not moved to adopt this approach, at least as it is usually affirmed, what further responses can one make to the Silenus challenge? There seem to be three of them, two of which we notice immediately.

One response to Silenus takes the form of "abandonment" or letting oneself go: mere hedonism (in its variety of manifestations, with its yearning for novelty) is resorted to. If for men all is here and now, why not simply indulge oneself with one physical pleasure after another? After all, there is something immediately satisfying and hence alluring about the common gratifications of the flesh.

Another response to Silenus takes the form of "desperation": this too appears in a variety of manifestations, ranging from all-engrossing social and political activities (which may depend on a considerable amount of self-delusion) to personal suicide (which can be seen as an extreme form of the attempt to control matters by one's own act).

Both of these responses—the response of abandonment and the response of desperation—can be understood as routine reactions to an awareness of human mortality. Contemporary existentialism combines in a curiously willful way these two responses to the modern awareness of mortality, an awareness that is somehow surprised and resentful. The same should be said, perhaps, of the resort to addiction, whether to drugs or modern art.

VI

Death does pose a problem for us. How *is* one to understand and to come to terms with the deterioration and the ultimate cessation of earthly activity which await us all, some sooner, some later?

There may be a sense in which it can be said that immortal beings such as Silenus do not truly live. Or at least it is difficult, if not impossible, for mortals to imagine how they live. Certainly they do not face the challenges—they do not have the vitality—that self-conscious mortals do. It has been observed that death is the salt that gives to life its tasty sting. (See Nikos Kazantzakis, *Odyssey*, XVIII, 912.)

Consider also how one should regard the trials one personally faces. Of course, as we have noticed, many of one's supposed trials are not truly burdens, but rather opportunities. That is, "wanting" is not the same as "needing": it is sometimes hard to know whether to congratulate or to comfort a friend who does not get what he sought or who does get what he tried to avoid. Most obviously in need of compassion, on the other hand, are those who have lost a youngster of promise.

In any event, the worthwhileness of a thing does not depend only on its duration. Various things can be treasured as good in themselves no matter how ephemeral their appearance before us, whether a sunset, a song, or the short life of a courageous man who dies serving his country in a just cause. To be thankful for life—for its inception, its sustenance, and its regeneration—is ultimately to be thankful for the best of life. Hence one can say again with Plato and Aristotle that the greatest pleasures come from doing what is good.

In opposition, then, to the ancient Silenus' grim dismissal of human life there is another ancient teaching, that left by the philosopher who observed that existence can be sweet. (See Aristotle, *Politics* 1278b25–29.)

VII

What is human existence? It is not exhibited merely in what animals have, a desire for immediate physical gratification and the attendant desire to preserve the ability to pleasure oneself. These are important, partly for themselves (or so it can seem) and partly for what they permit, including a serviceable body to house the soul on earth, whether that soul be considered mortal or immortal.

What existence means for mankind may be seen not only in man's happiness, but also (perhaps even more, since happiness is less likely to induce us to think) in man's misery, that self-centered misery which takes the form of anxiety, bitterness, depression, paranoia, or alienation.

Such responses *can* make one feel that life is simply not worth having. What do they reflect? Do not they usually draw upon noble aspirations and elevated standards? Do not they testify to a state of things finer and better than what one now has? Do not such responses usually depend on tacit opinions about the good? If so, one salutary way of limiting the effects of misery is to recognize that the sense of misery itself presupposes that there *are* goods very much worth having.

These are not goods that are always or even usually fully realized in everyday life. They may indeed be quite rare. But there is one good that thinking beings do have with them always, no matter how desperate the times become. That is the good (available, it seems, only to human beings among all the mortal creatures we know), the inestimable good, of recognizing that there are better and worse, higher and lower. It is this informed awareness that makes human existence meaningful, even in the worst of circumstances. For example, the most depressed woman could not despair as she does if she did not retain a sense of something better or finer than what then seems available to her. Perhaps critical to the condition of chronically unhappy people is that they emphasize the good things they do not happen to have or the bad things they do happen to have; they make much of these things rather than of the one wonderful thing they always do have access to, an awareness of what goodness is. This is keyed to an awareness of what wholeness is, and hence can be an awareness of the limitations of any one part. This awareness of goodness is worth much pain, including the pain of facing up to the fact—the terribly painful fact, for many people—that one cannot secure perfectly or permanently whatever good things may be available to mankind on earth.

In any event, things good in themselves, whether thoughts or deeds, whether a momentary insight or a lifetime of proper activity, have a beauty that seems to need no further justification. It is easy to lose sight of this through the influence of desire, ambition or resignation, diversions which can be misleading and even destructive, however useful each of these may be in some respects. When we understand things properly, we appreciate how independent we can and perhaps should be of accomplishments and disappointments that either encumber or cripple us.

Things good in themselves are what they are, however transitory they may be. Particularly to be singled out, as the ground for all good things, is the innately human awareness that there are things good in themselves. Recognition of this permits us, if only now and then, a conquest of chance. In being what they are, things good in themselves are a reflection of the natural, of the eternal, of (if you will) the divine. When we reach for and treasure things good in themselves, we participate for the time being in that which always is, as others have participated before us and as others will after us, on this earth and elsewhere. For this fortunate privilege—whatever, whenever and wherever our circumstances—should we not be profoundly thankful?

INDEX